Autodesk Inventor 2027

A Tutorial Introduction

L. Scott Hansen, Ph.D.

SDC PUBLICATIONS

SDC Publications
P.O. Box 1334
Mission, KS 66222
913-262-2664
www.SDCpublications.com
Publisher: Stephen Schroff

ISBN-13: 978-1-63057-799-5
ISBN-10: 1-63057-799-5

Printed and bound in the United States of America.

Table of Contents

CHAPTER 1

Getting Started

Objectives:

1. Create a simple sketch using the Sketch Panel
2. Dimension a sketch using the Dimension command
3. Extrude a sketch in the 3D Model Panel using the Extrude command
4. Create a hole in the 3D Model Panel using the Extrude command
5. Create a Fillet in the 3D Model Panel using the Fillet command
6. Create a counter bore in the 3D Model Panel using the Hole command

Chapter 1 includes instruction on how to design the part shown.

Start Autodesk Inventor 2027 by moving the cursor over the Start button and left click once.

1. A pop-up menu of the programs that are installed on the computer will appear. You may have to select "All Apps". Scroll through the list of programs until you find Autodesk Inventor Professional 2027.

2. Move the cursor over **Autodesk Inventor Professional 2027** and left click once.

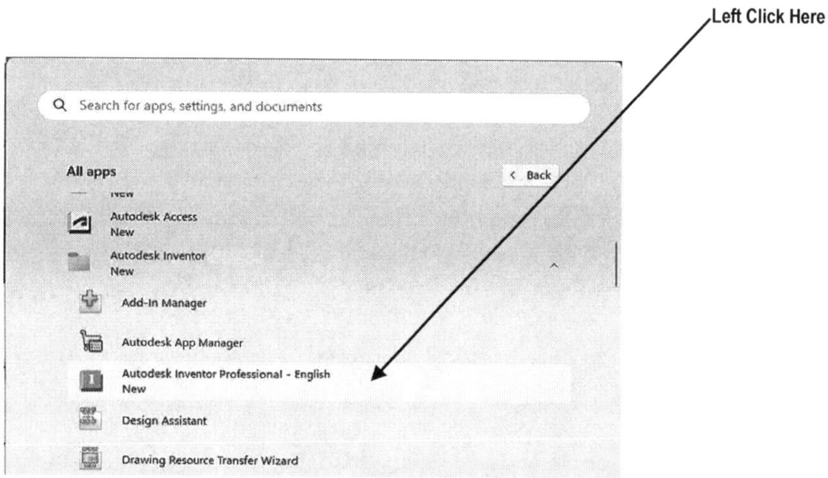

Figure 1

3. Autodesk Inventor Professional 2027 will open (load up and begin running).

4. The Autodesk Inventor 2027 banner will appear as shown in Figure 2.

Figure 2

5. Left click on **File**. A drop-down menu will appear. Move the cursor over **New** in the drop down menu. Left click on **New** as shown in Figure 3.

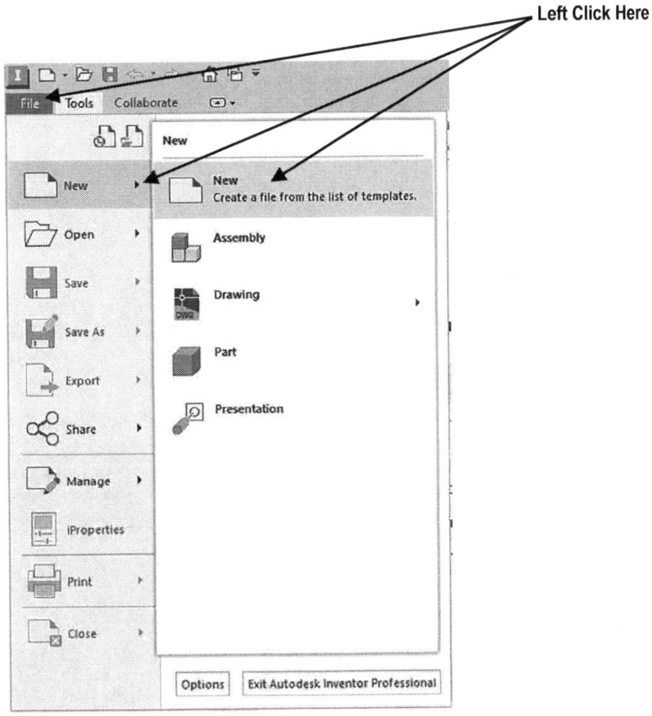

Figure 3

6. The Create New File dialog box will appear. Left click on **Standard.ipt**. Left click on **Create** shown in Figure 4.

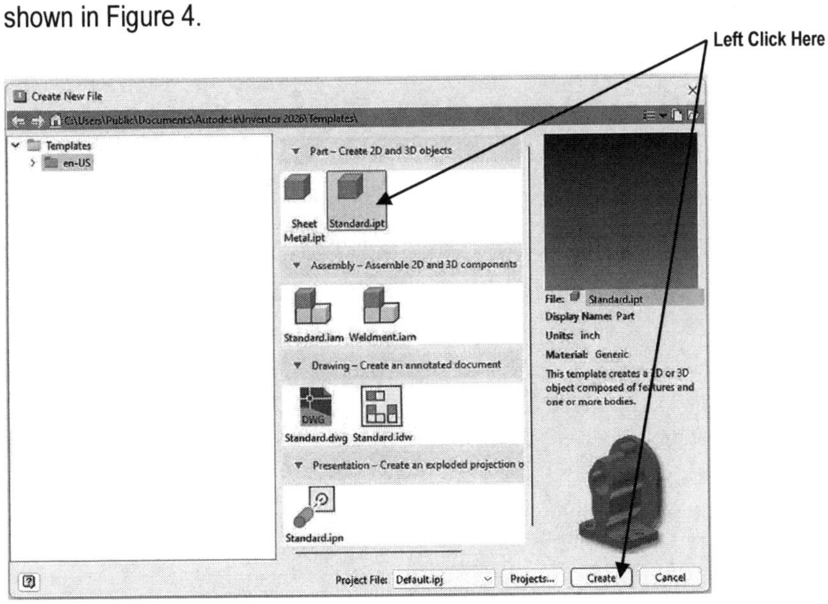

Figure 4

7. Inventor is now ready for use.

8. Your screen should look similar to Figure 5.

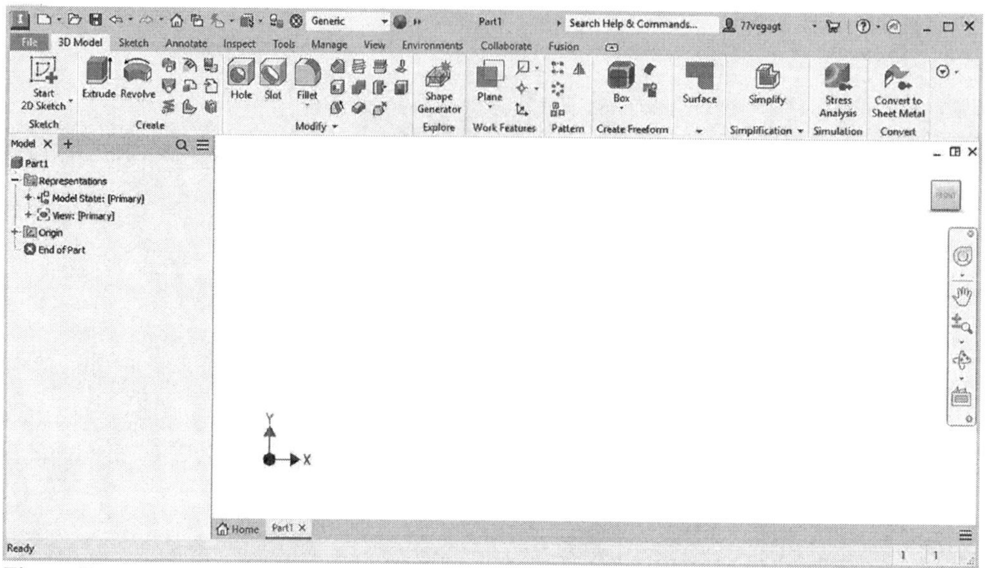

Figure 5

Create a simple sketch using the Sketch Panel

9. Begin a drawing by first constructing a “sketch.” Move the cursor to the upper left portion of the screen and left click on the **3D Model** tab (if not already selected). Left click on **Start 2D Sketch**. Select the **XY Plane** as shown. To know what any icon or command will do, move the cursor over the icon or command and wait a few seconds. A yellow banner will appear describing the icons or commands function.

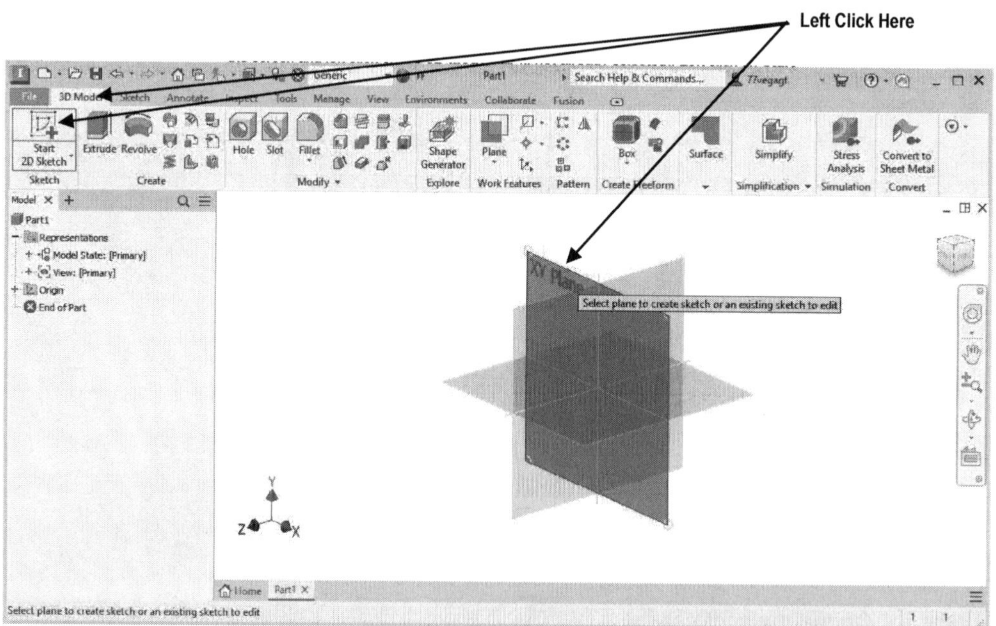

Figure 6

10. Move your cursor to the upper left portion of the screen and left click on the **Sketch** tab (if not already selected). Move the cursor to the upper left portion of the screen and left click on **Line** as shown in Figure 7.

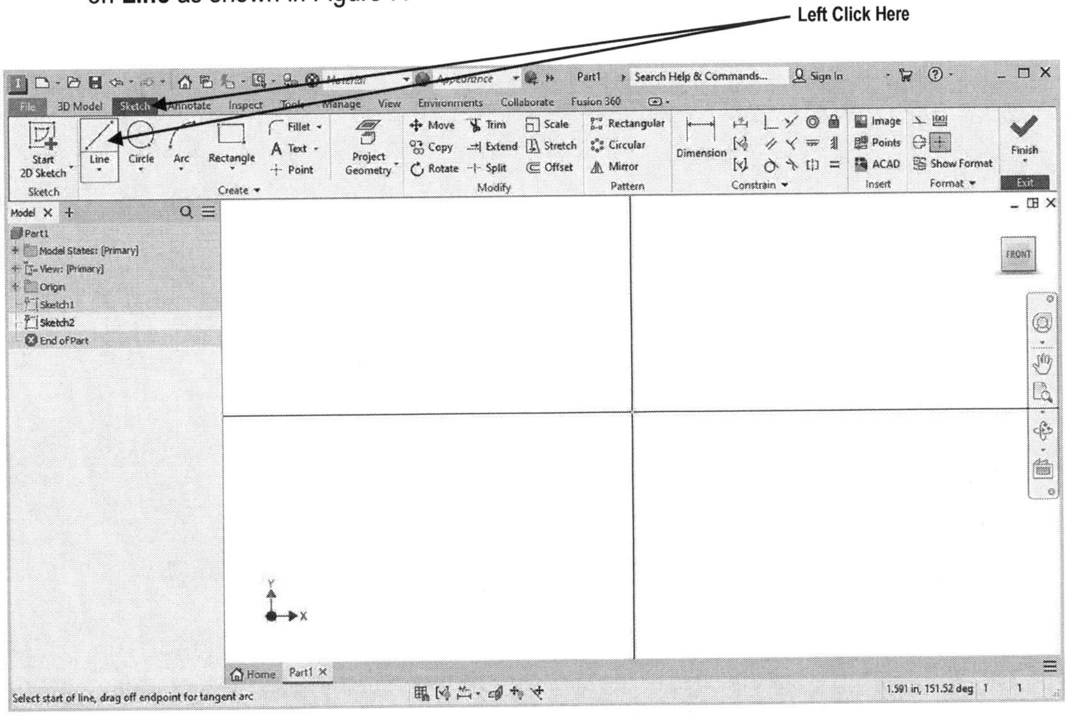

Figure 7

11. Move the cursor somewhere in the lower left portion of the screen and left click once. This will be the beginning end point of a line as shown in Figure 8.

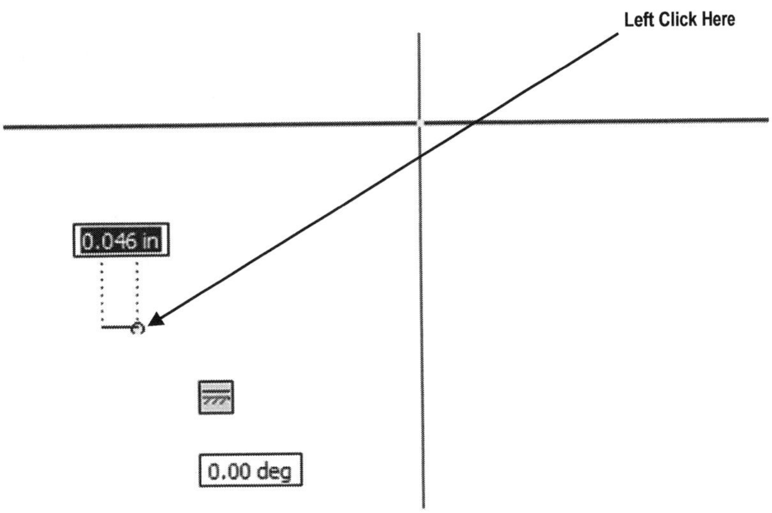

Figure 8

12. Move the cursor towards the lower right portion of the screen and left click once as shown in Figure 9.

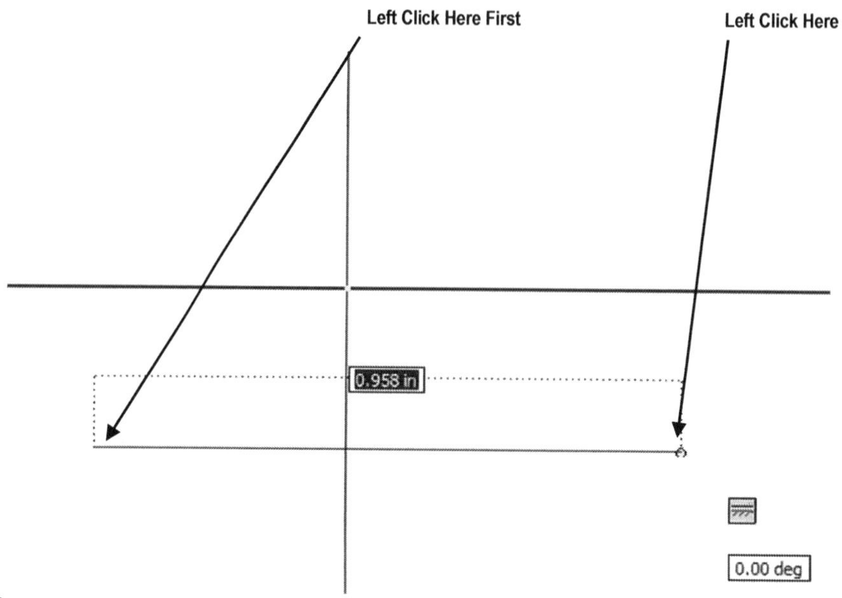

Figure 9

13. While the line is still attached to the cursor, move the cursor towards the top of the screen and left click once as shown in Figure 10.

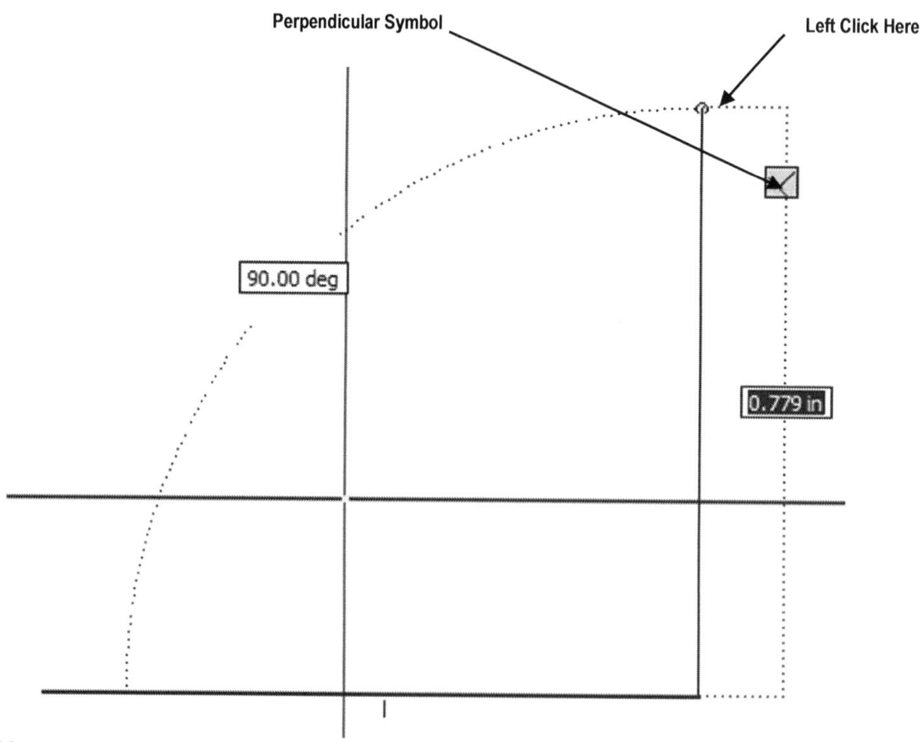

Figure 10

14. This signifies that the vertical line is exactly 90 degrees (perpendicular) to the horizontal line.

15. With the line still attached to the cursor, move the cursor towards the left side of the screen as shown in Figure 11.

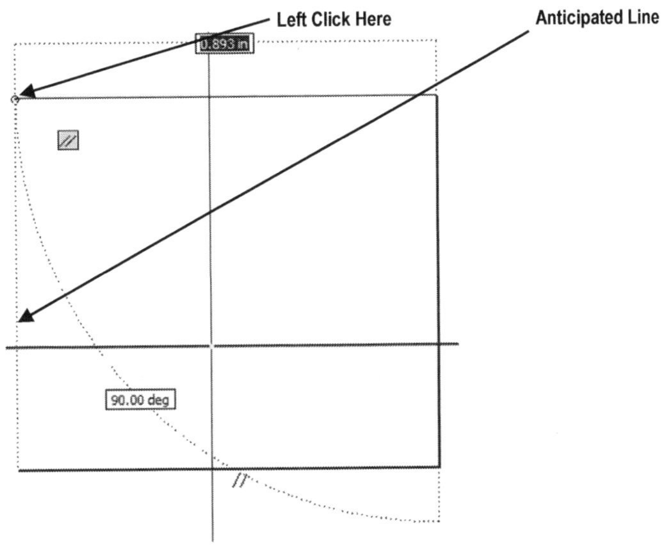

Figure 11

16. Notice the line of small dots connecting the first and last points together. Left click once when the small dots appear as shown in Figure 11.

17. This will form a 90 degree box. Move the cursor down towards the original starting point. Ensure that a green dot appears (as shown in Figure 12) at the intersection of the two lines. This indicates that Inventor has "snapped" to the intersection of the lines. After the green dot appears, left click once as shown in Figure 12.

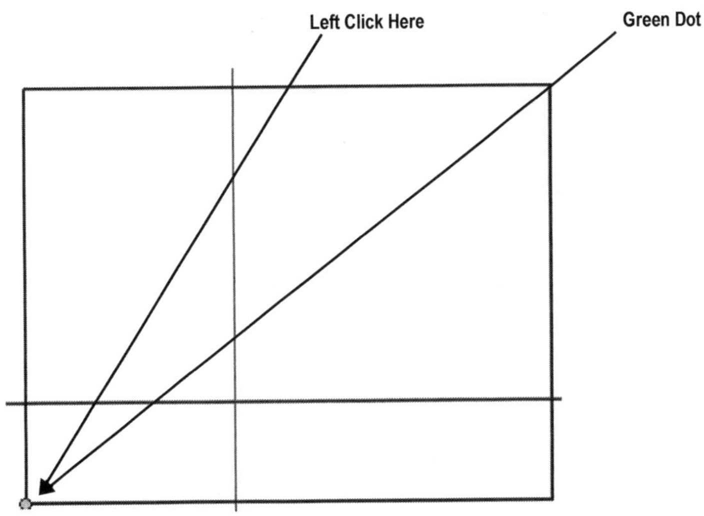

Figure 12

18. Your screen should look similar to Figure 13.

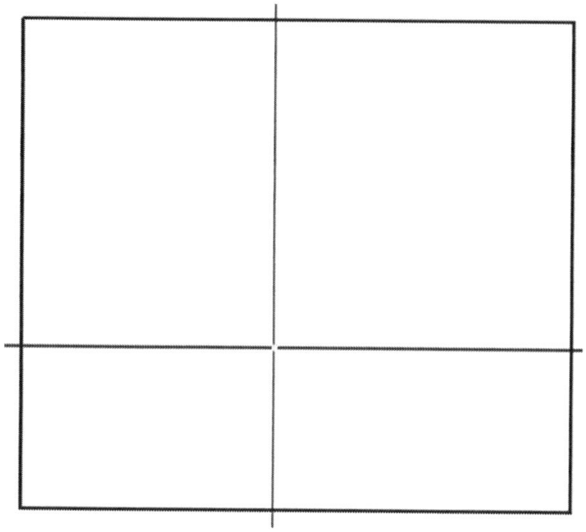

Figure 13

Dimension a sketch using the General Dimension command

19. Right click anywhere around the sketch. A pop-up menu will appear. Left click on **OK** as shown in Figure 14. Hitting the **Esc** key will also "get out" of the Line command.

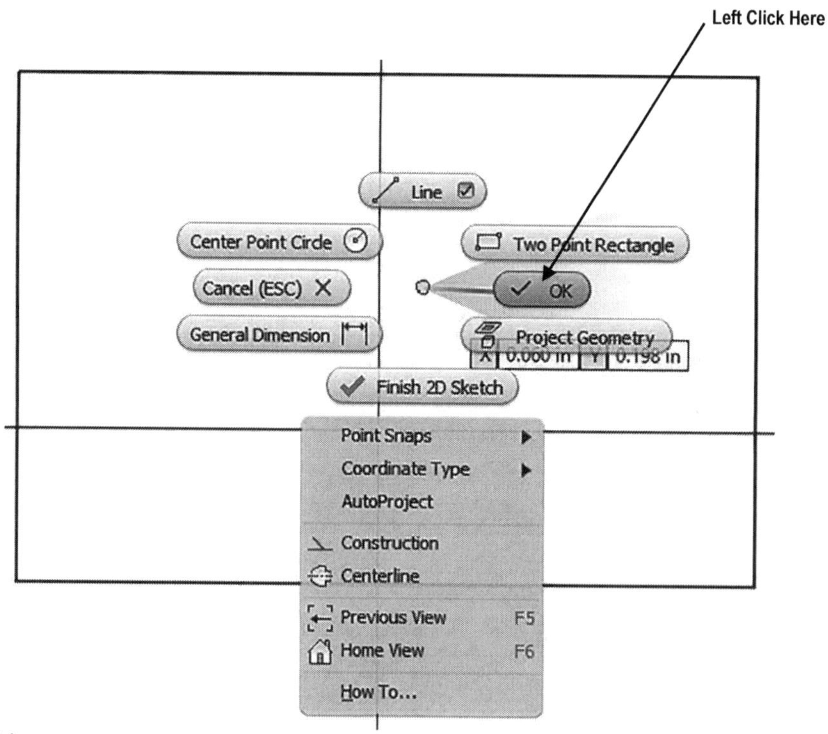

Figure 14

20. Move the cursor to the upper middle portion of the screen and left click on **Dimension** as shown in Figure 15.

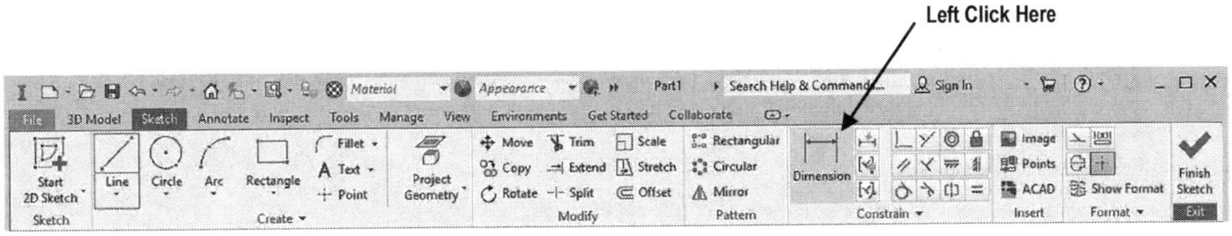

Figure 15

21. After selecting **Dimension** move the cursor over the bottom horizontal line. The line will become highlighted as shown in Figure 16. Select the line by left clicking anywhere on the line **<u>or</u>** on each of the end points. To use the end points of the line, move the cursor over one of the end points. A small red square will appear. Left click once and move the cursor to the other end point. Another red square will appear. Left click once. The dimension will now be attached to the cursor. Move the cursor up and down to verify it is attached.

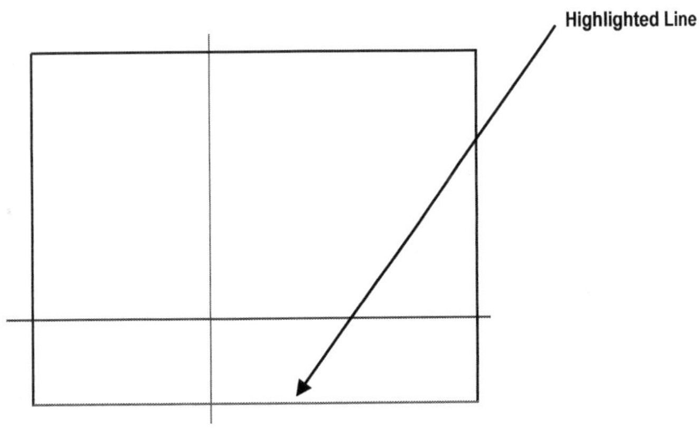

Figure 16

22. Move the cursor down. The actual dimension of the line will appear as shown in Figure 17.

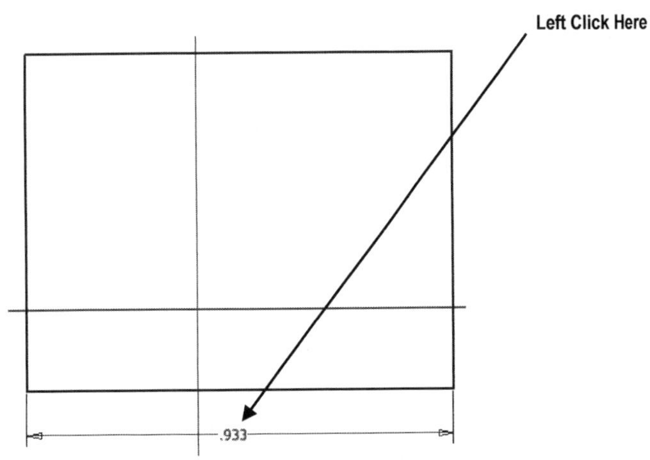

Figure 17

23. Move the cursor to where the dimension will be placed and left click once. While the dimension is still highlighted, left click once. The Edit Dimension dialog box will appear as shown in Figure 18.

24. To edit the dimension, enter **2.00** in the Edit Dimension dialog box (while the current dimension is highlighted) and press **Enter** on the keyboard.

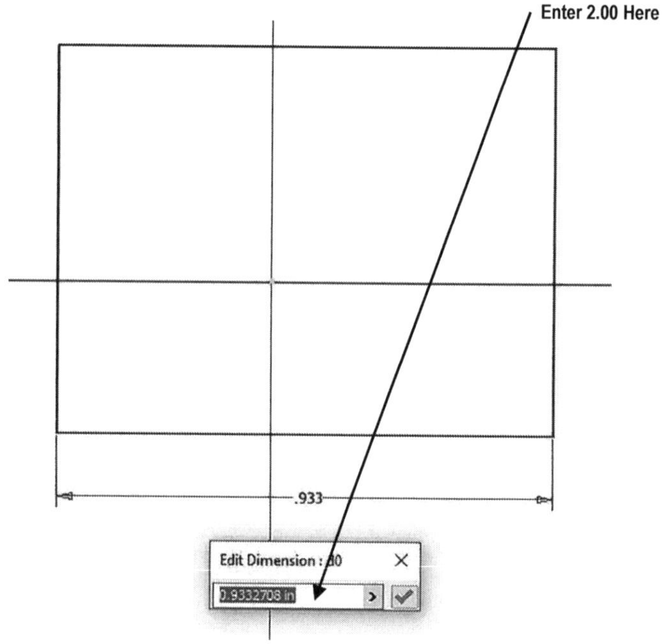

Figure 18

25. The dimension of the line will become 2.000 inches as shown in Figure 19.

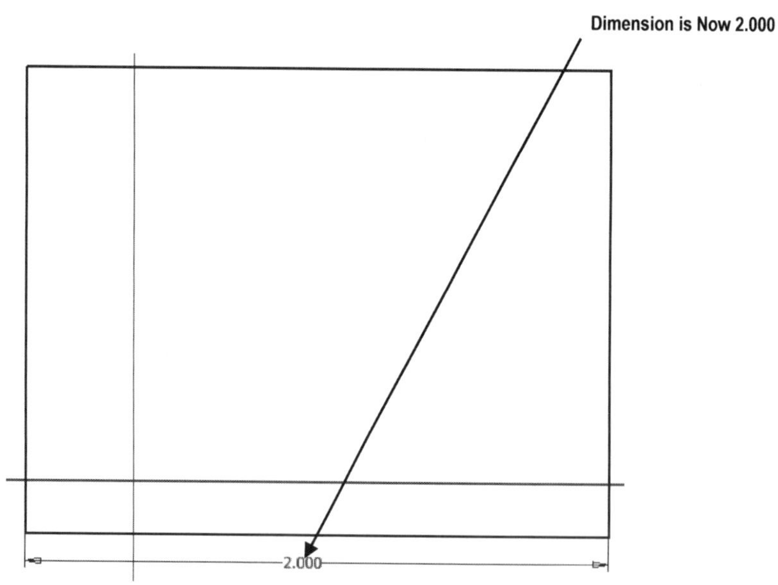

Figure 19

26. Move the cursor to the upper middle portion of the screen and left click on **Dimension** as shown in Figure 20.

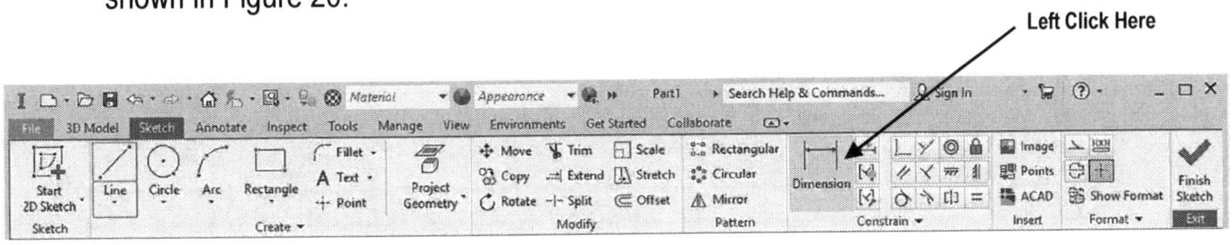

Figure 20

27. After selecting **Dimension** move the cursor over the right side vertical line. The line will become highlighted. Left click once on the line as shown in Figure 21.

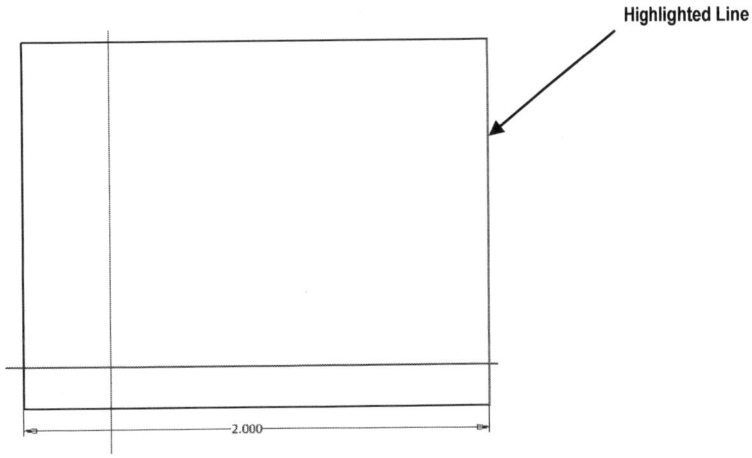

Figure 21

28. The dimension will be attached to the cursor. Move the cursor up and down to verify it is attached. Move the cursor to the right of the line where the dimension will be placed and left click once. While the dimension is still highlighted, left click once. The Edit Dimension dialog box will appear as shown in Figure 22.

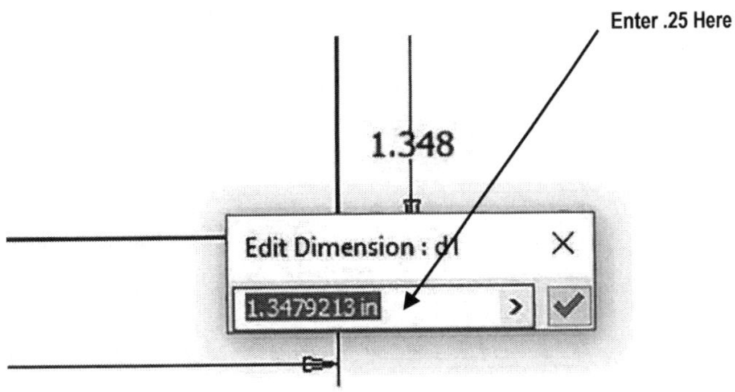

Figure 22

29. To edit the dimension, enter **.25** in the Edit Dimension dialog box (while the current dimension is highlighted) and press **Enter** on the keyboard.

30. The screen should look similar to Figure 23.

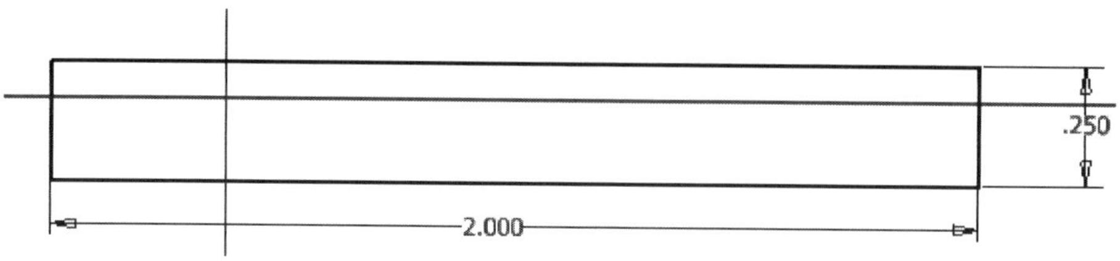

Figure 23

31. Complete the remainder of the sketch as shown in Figure 24.

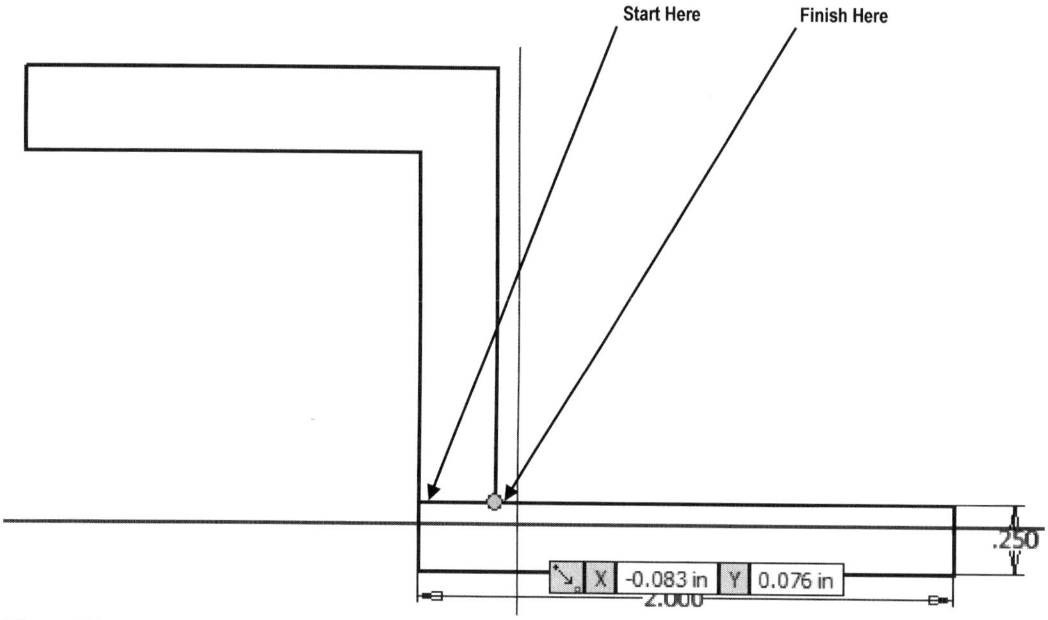

Figure 24

32. Move the cursor to the upper middle portion of the screen and left click on **Trim** as shown in Figure 25.

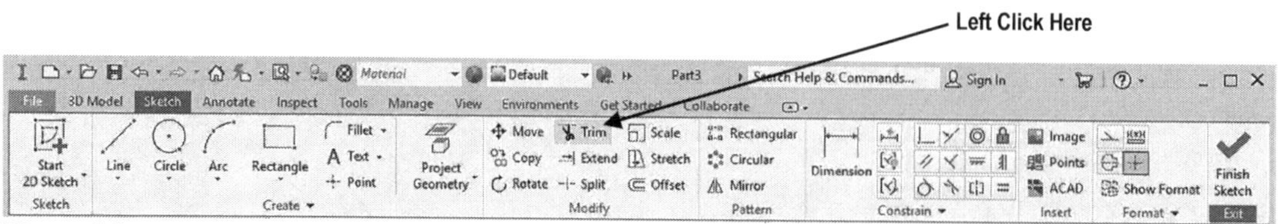

Figure 25

33. Move the cursor over the portion of the line that is shown in Figure 26. The line will become dashed. Inventor is guessing that this line is what needs to be trimmed.

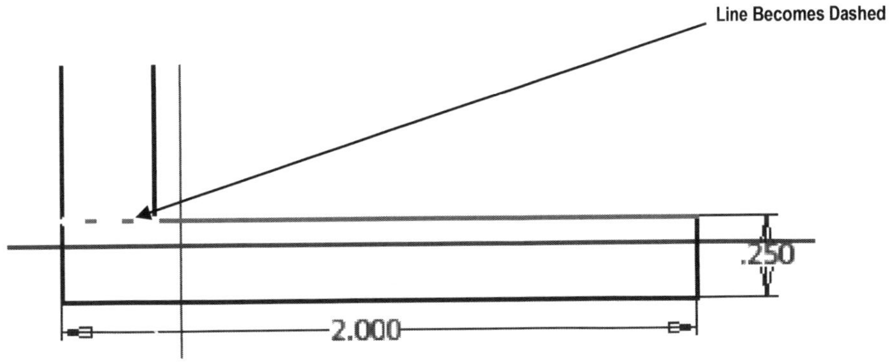

Figure 26

34. While the line is dashed, left click on the dashed portion. The line will be trimmed as shown in Figure 27.

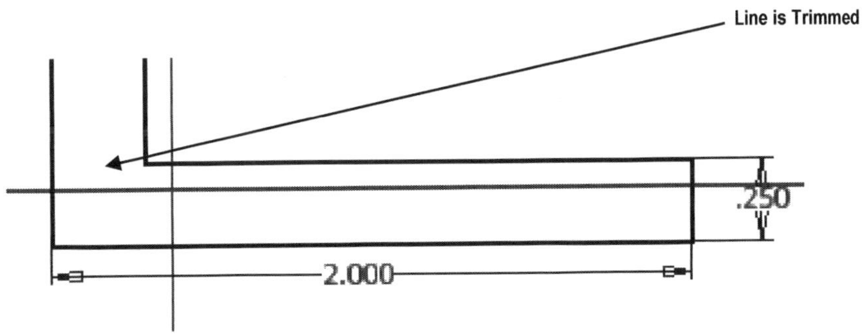

Figure 27

35. Move the cursor over the line in the lower left corner of the drawing as shown in Figure 28. The line will become highlighted. This particular line will have to be deleted so that the line above can be extended the full length.

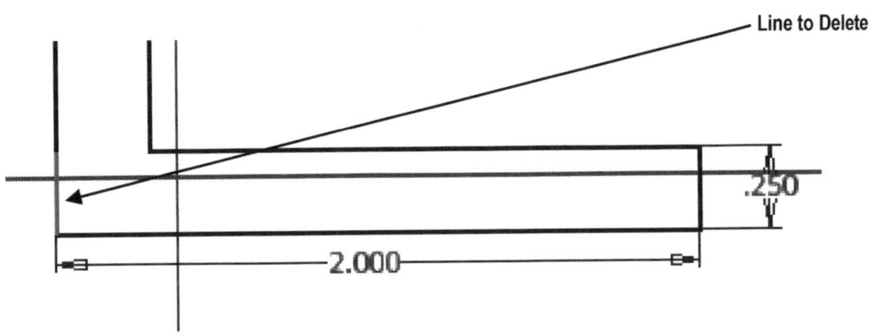

Figure 28

36. After the line becomes highlighted, right click once. A pop-up menu will appear. Left click on **Delete** as shown in Figure 29.

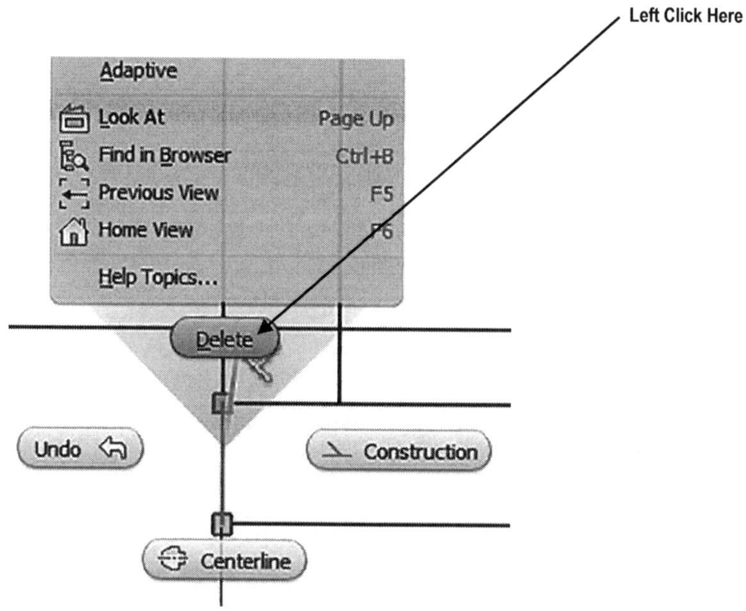

Figure 29

37. The line will be deleted as shown in Figure 30.

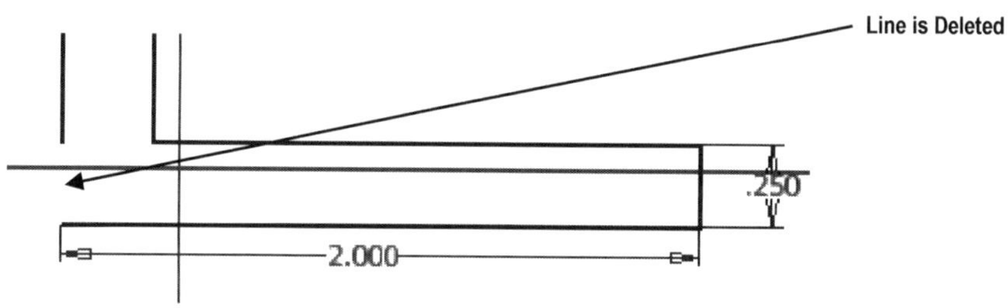

Figure 30

38. Move the cursor to the upper middle portion of the screen and left click on **Extend** as shown in Figure 31.

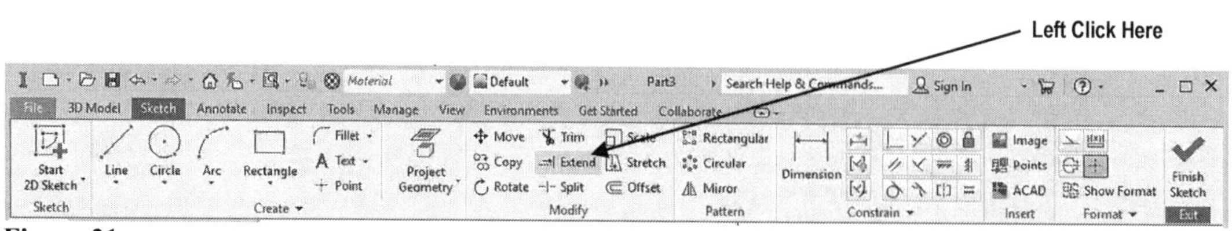

Figure 31

39. Move the cursor to the line above the recently deleted line. This is the line that will be extended. After the cursor is over the line, it will become highlighted and extend a line downward, as shown in Figure 32.

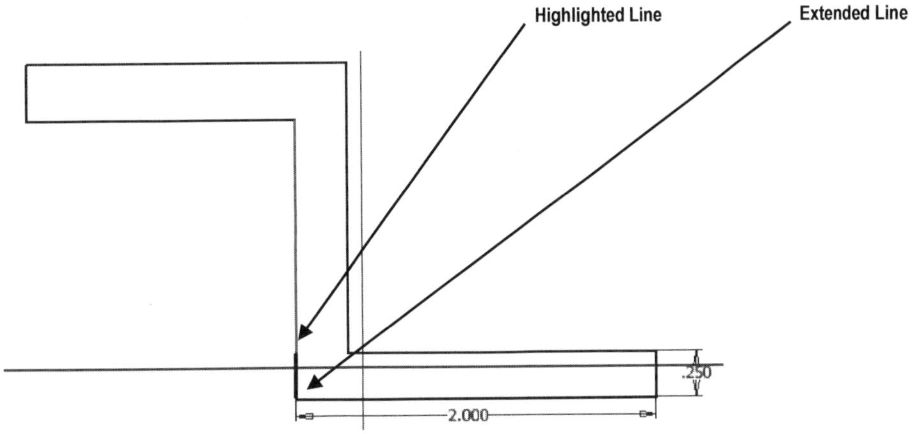

Figure 32

40. After the extended line appears, left click the mouse once. The line will extend, creating one continuous line as shown in Figure 33. This is crucial in creating a sketch that can be extruded into a solid model.

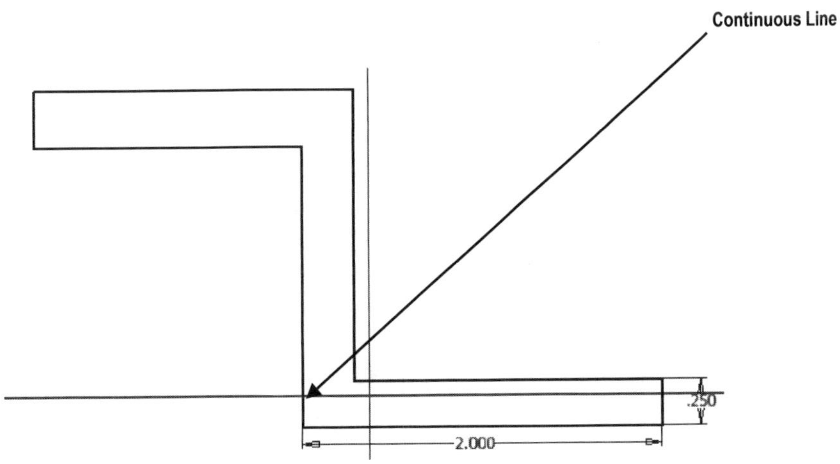

Figure 33

41. Move the cursor to the upper middle portion of the screen and left click on **Dimension** as shown in Figure 34.

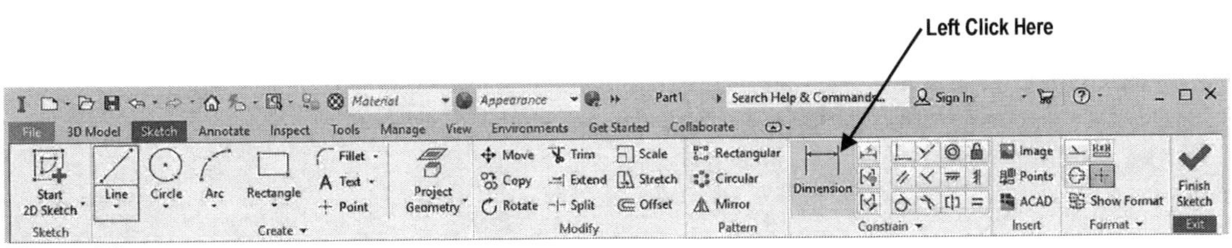

Figure 34

42. After selecting **Dimension**, move the cursor over the left vertical line. The line will become highlighted as shown in Figure 35. Left click once on the line.

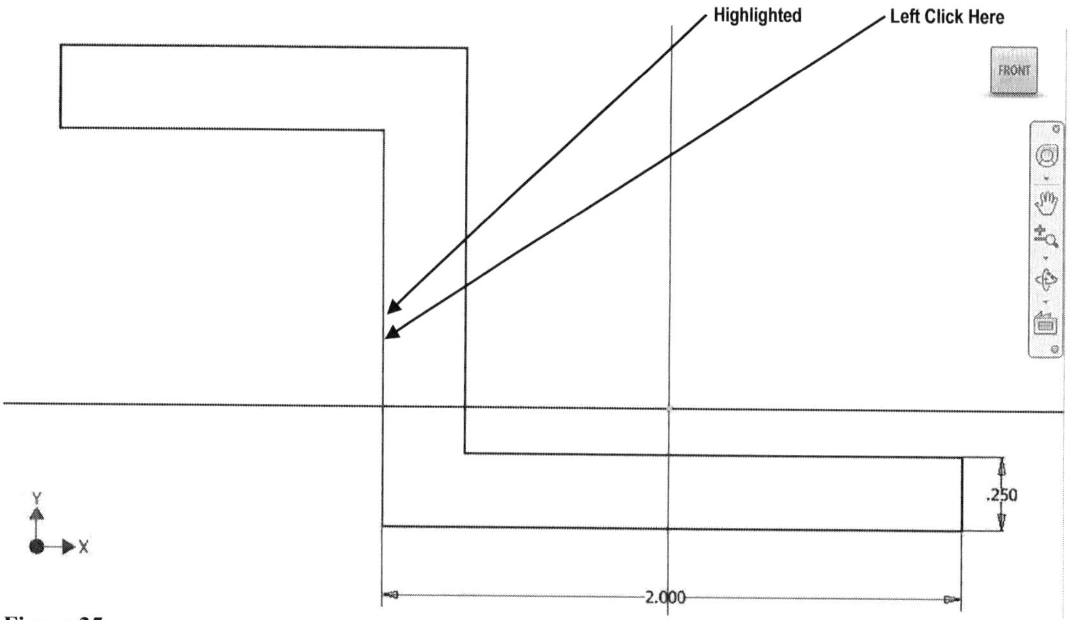

Figure 35

43. Even though a dimension will be attached to the cursor, simply ignore it and move the cursor to the right vertical line and left click on it after it becomes highlighted as shown in Figure 36.

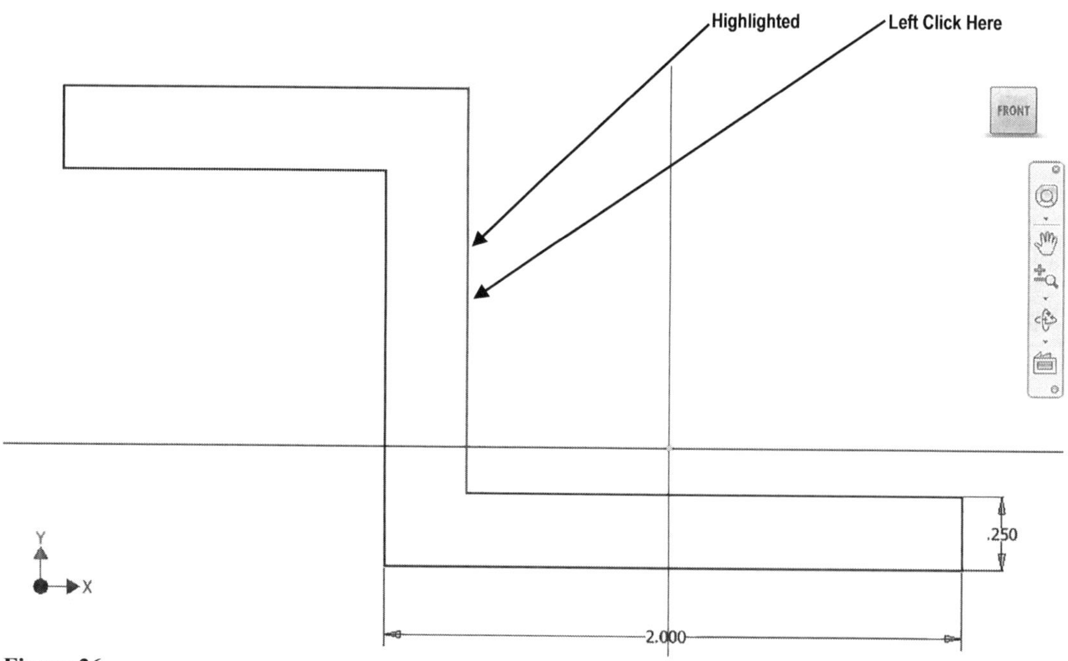

Figure 36

44. Enter **.25** in the Edit Dimension dialog box (while the current dimension is highlighted) and press **Enter** on the keyboard.

45. Complete the remainder of the sketch as shown in Figure 37.

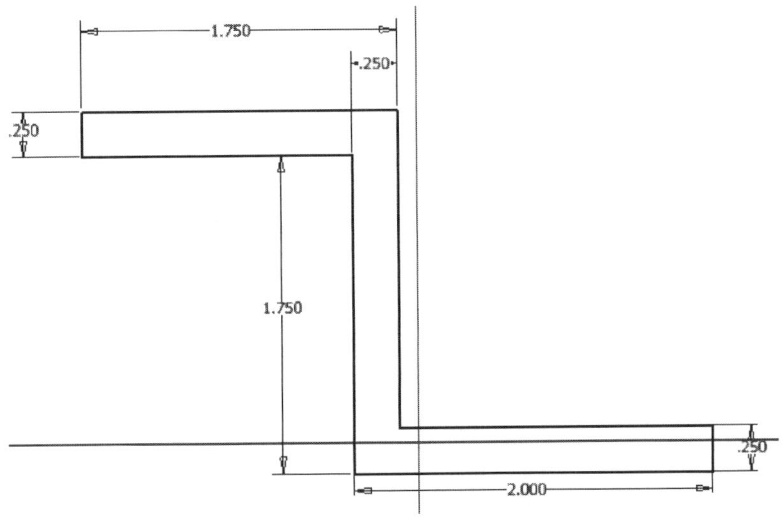

Figure 37

46. Once the sketch is complete, it is time to extrude it into a solid. Right click anywhere around the sketch. A pop-up menu will appear. Left click on **OK.** This will "get out" of the Dimensions command. Hitting the **Esc** key will also "get out" of the Dimension command as shown in Figure 38.

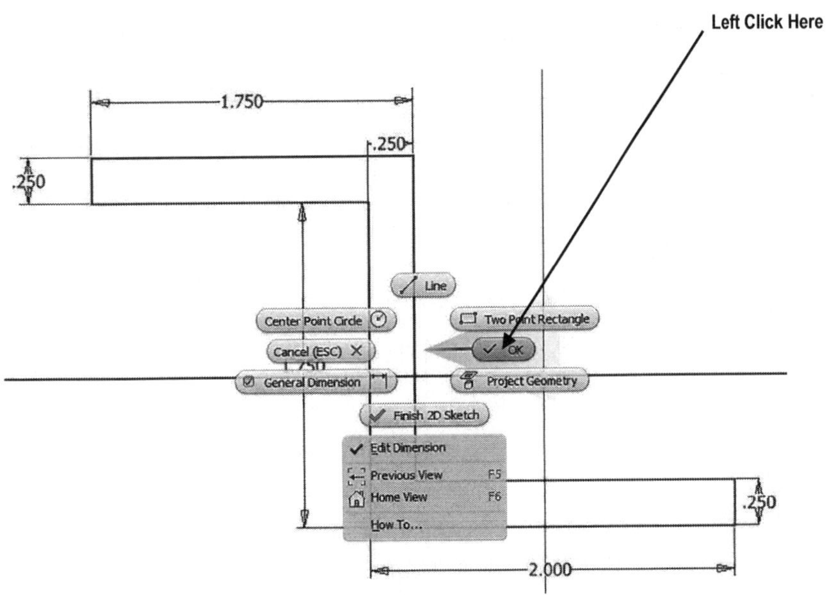

Figure 38

47. After you have verified that no commands are active, right click anywhere on the sketch. A pop-up menu will appear. Left click on **Finish 2D Sketch**. Right click again. Left click **Home View** as shown in Figure 39.

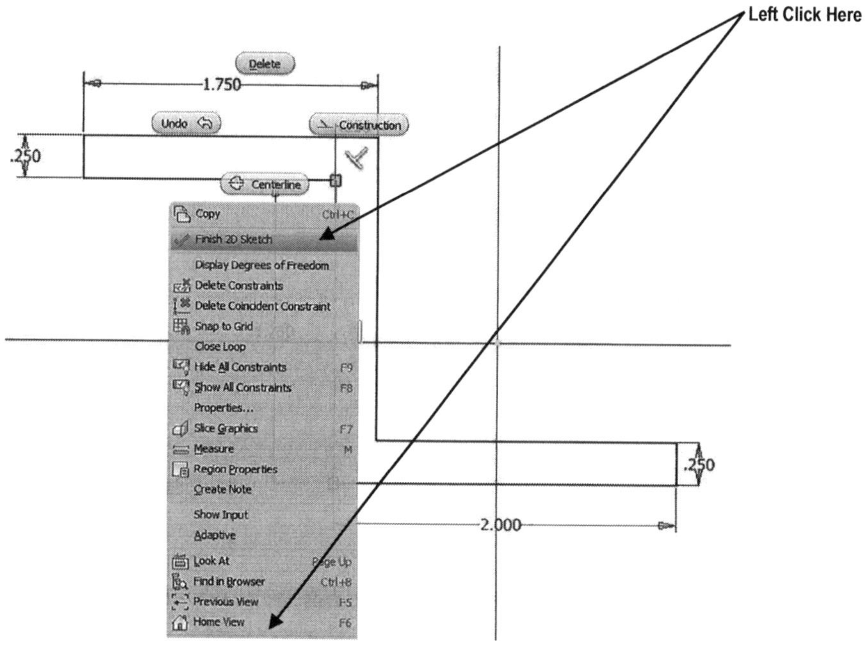

Figure 39

48. Inventor is now out of the Sketch Panel and into the 3D Model Panel. Notice that the commands at the top of the screen are now different. To work in the 3D Model Panel a sketch must be present and have no opens (non-connected lines). If there are any opens in the sketch an error message will appear. The view shown below is an Isometric/Home view. Your screen should look similar to Figure 40.

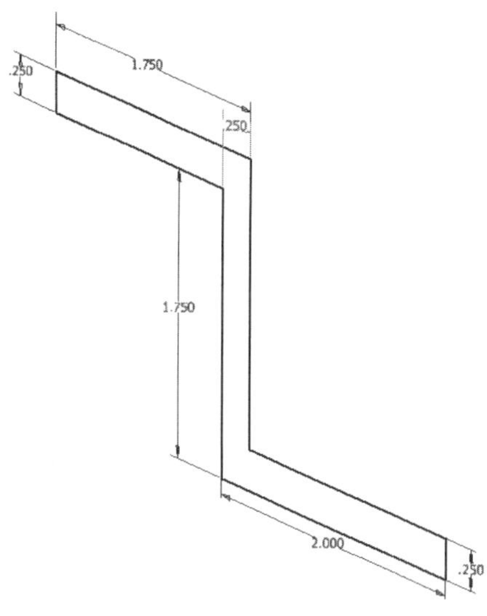

Figure 40

Extrude a sketch in the 3D Model Panel using the Extrude command

49. Move the cursor to the upper left portion of the screen and left click on the 3D Model tab (if needed). Left click on the **Extrude** icon. Inventor also provides a preview of the Extrusion. If Inventor gave you an error message, there are opens (non-connected lines) somewhere on the sketch. There could also be multiple lines where one single line should be used. There could also be a line over an existing line. Check each intersection for opens by using the **Extend** and **Trim** commands. Also ensure that there are no lines over or under existing lines. Your screen should look similar to Figure 41.

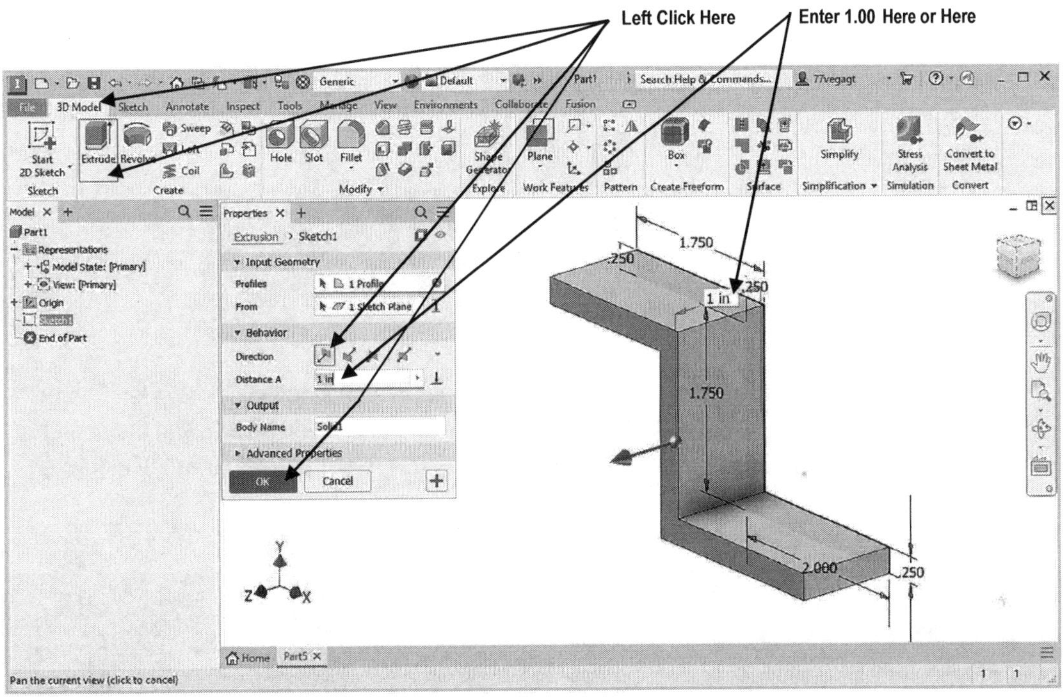

Figure 41

50. Enter **1.00** as shown and left click on **OK**. Inventor will create a 3D solid from the sketch as shown in Figure 41.

Create a fillet in the 3D Model Panel using the Fillet command

51. Your screen should look similar to Figure 42.

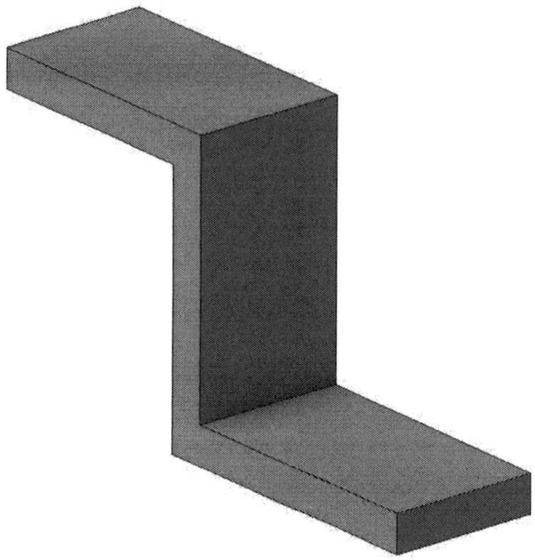

Figure 42

52. Move the cursor to the upper middle portion of the screen and left click on **Fillet**. The Fillet dialog box will appear in collapsed form. Left click on the drop-down arrow in the center of the collapsed dialog box. This will cause the dialog box to expand as shown in Figure 43.

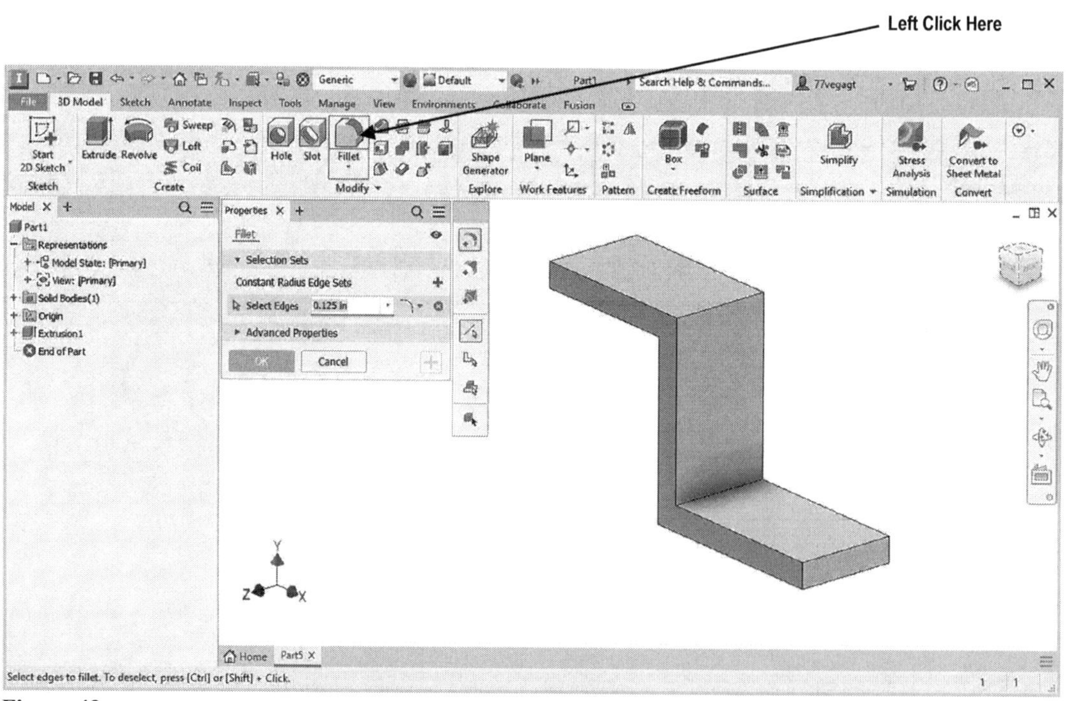

Figure 43

53. Move the cursor to the lower left edge of the part. After the edge turns red, left click once as shown in Figure 44.

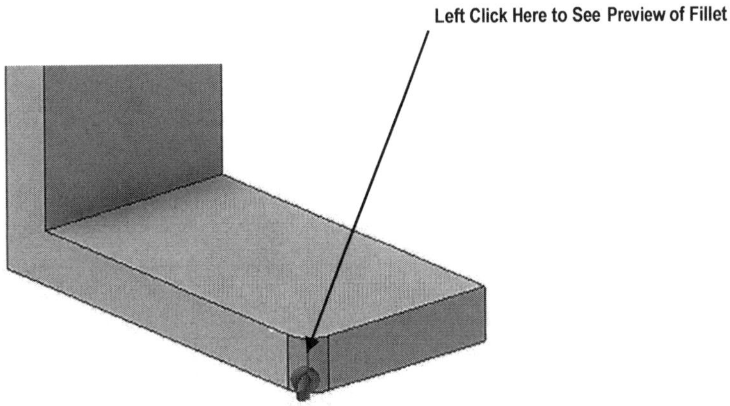

Figure 44

54. Notice the blue mesh illustrating a preview of the fillet. Left click on the opposite edge as shown in Figure 45.

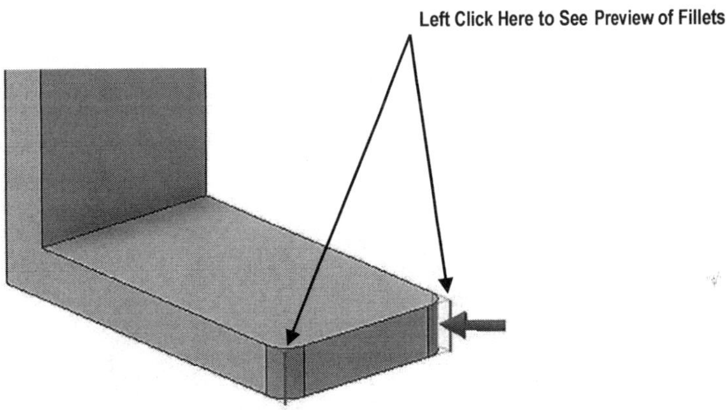

Figure 45

55. Left click on the two upper remaining edges. Even though the far upper edge is not visible, move the cursor to the location of the edge and Inventor will find it as shown in Figure 46.

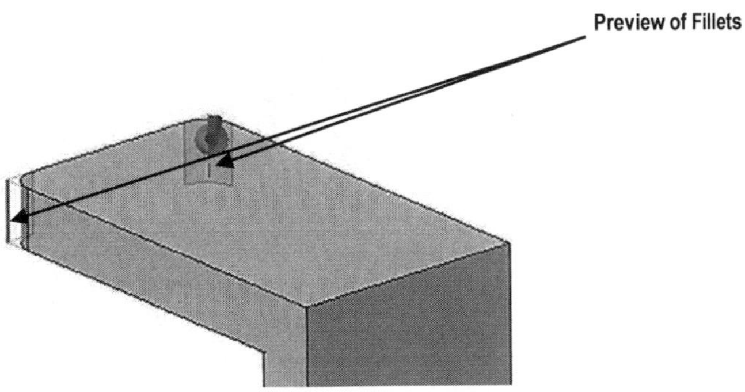

Figure 46

56. Move the cursor to the dimension located in the dimension box and left click once. Enter **0.5** and press **Enter** on the keyboard as shown in Figure 47.

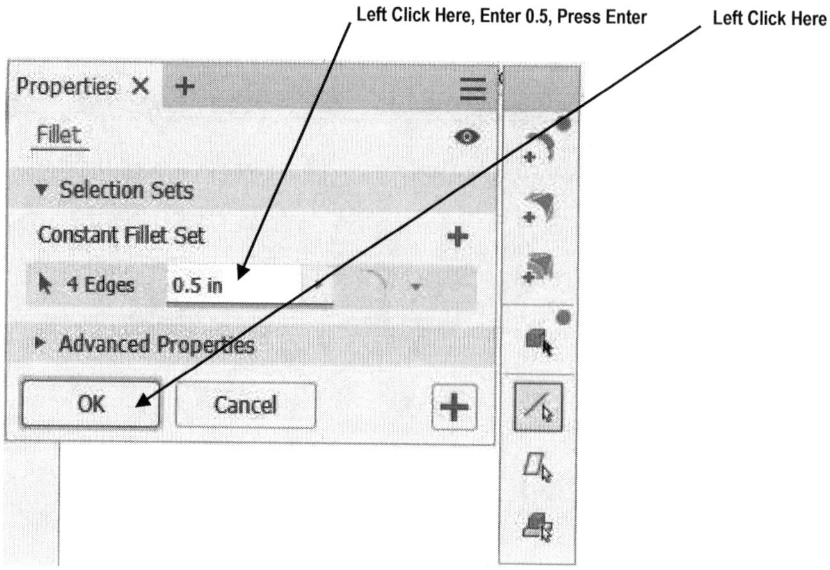

Figure 47

57. Your screen should look similar to Figure 48.

Figure 48

58. The next task will include cutting a hole in each of the ends. To accomplish this, a sketch will need to be constructed on this surface. Move the cursor to the surface that will have the new sketch. Notice the edges of the surface have become highlighted as shown in Figure 49.

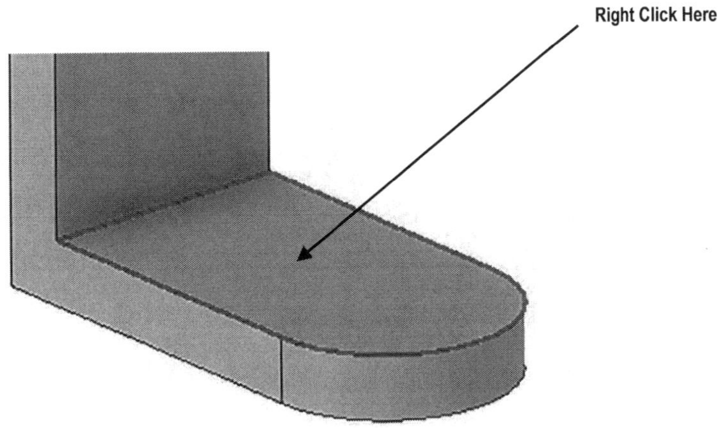

Figure 49

59. After the edges of the surface become highlighted, right click on the surface. The surface will change color. A pop-up menu will also appear. Left click on **New Sketch** as shown in Figure 50.

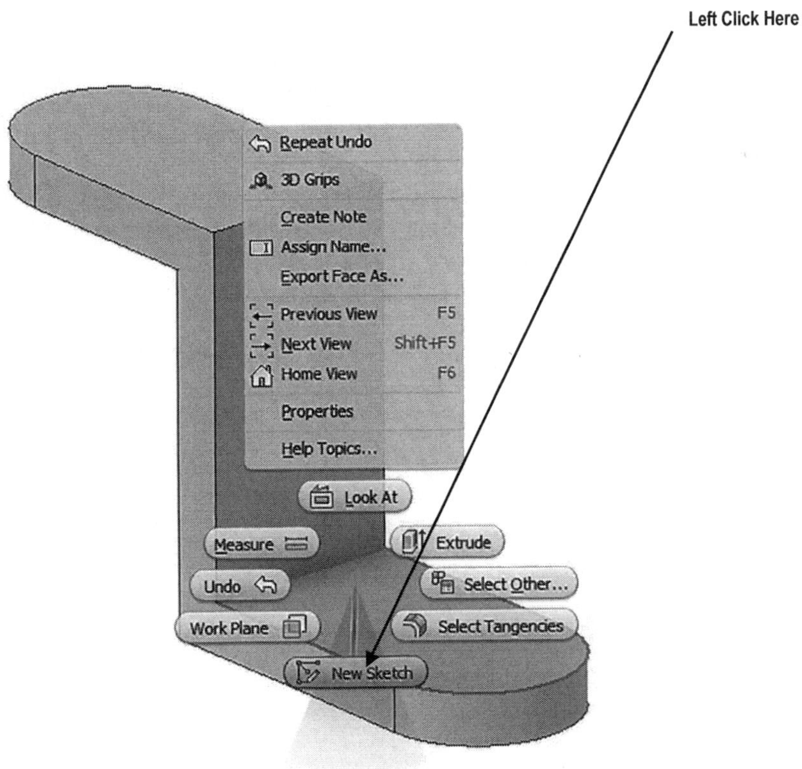

Figure 50

60. Inventor will create a "sketch" on that particular surface. Notice the menu at the top of the screen has changed back to the options available in the Sketch Panel. Inventor has now returned to the sketch panel.

61. Your screen should look similar to Figure 51.

Figure 51

62. Move the cursor to the upper left portion of the screen and left click on **Circle** as shown in Figure 52.

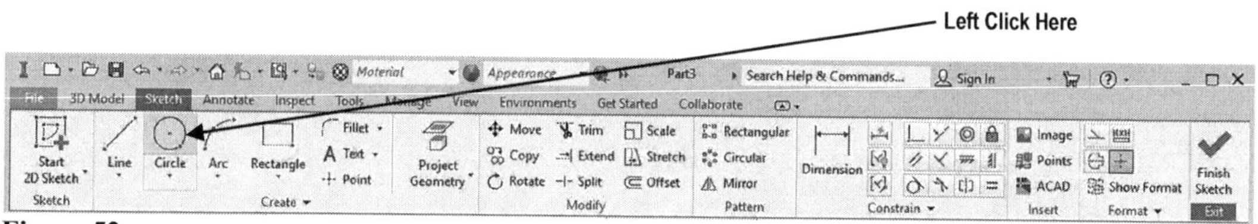

Figure 52

63. Move the cursor to the edge of the newly created Fillet radius. Right click once. A pop-up menu will appear. Left click on **AutoProject** (ensure a check appears) as shown in Figure 53.

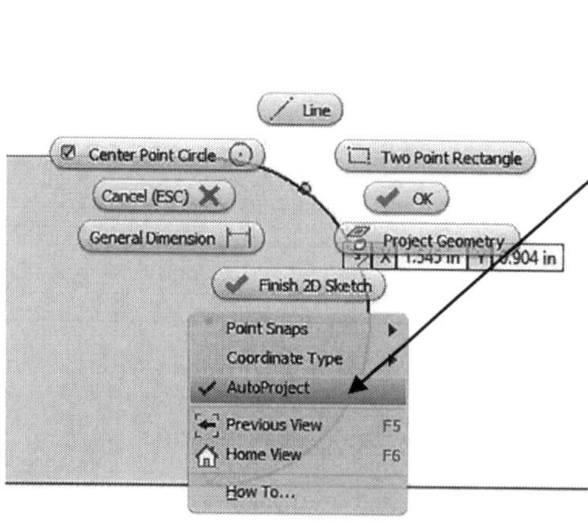

Figure 53

Create a hole in the 3D Model Part Panel using the Extrude cut command

64. Move the cursor to the outside edge of the Fillet. Eventually, a black dot will appear in the center of the Fillet radius. After the black dot appears, move the cursor to the black dot and left click once. This will be the center of a circle, which will later become a thru hole. Drag the cursor to the side causing the circle to become larger and left click once. Right click once. Left click on **OK**. Inventor projects the outside edge of the fillet on to the sketch. To delete the line, right click on the outside edge of the Fillet. A pop-up menu will appear. Left click on **Delete** (if necessary) as shown in Figure 54.

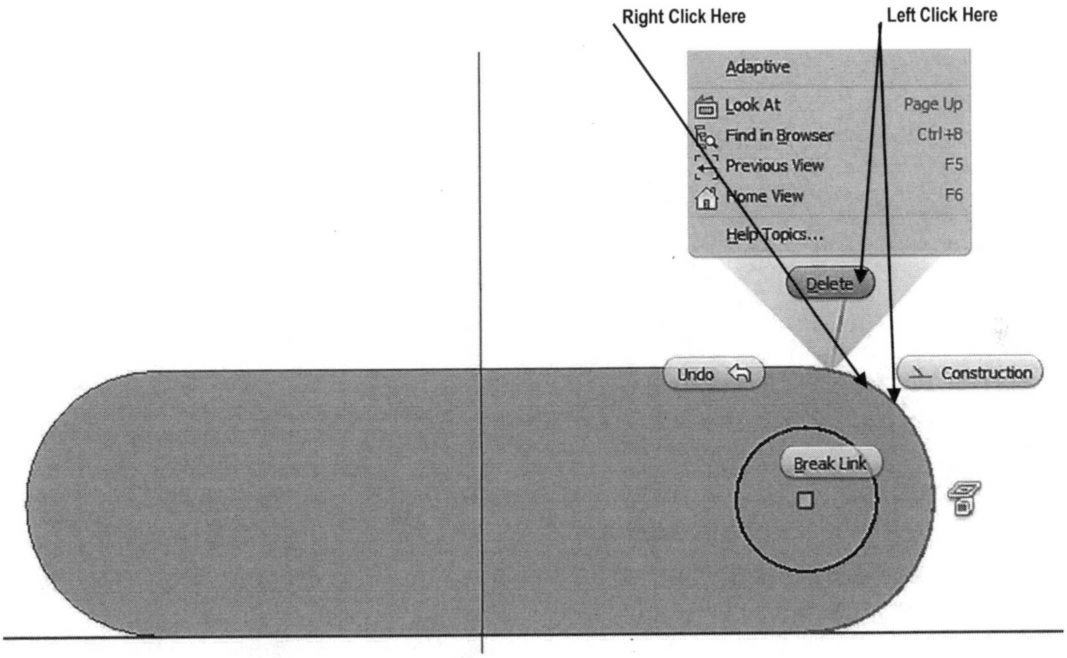

Figure 54

65. After the hole size looks similar to Figure 54, left click once.

66. Using the **Dimension** command, enter **.50** in the Edit Dimension dialog box and press **Enter** on the keyboard. The diameter of the hole will become .50 inches. Press the **Esc** key to ensure that no commands are active.

67. Right click anywhere on the drawing. A pop-up menu will appear. Left click on **Finish 2D Sketch** or left click on **Finish Sketch/Exit** at the upper right portion of the screen. Left click on **Home View** as shown in Figure 55.

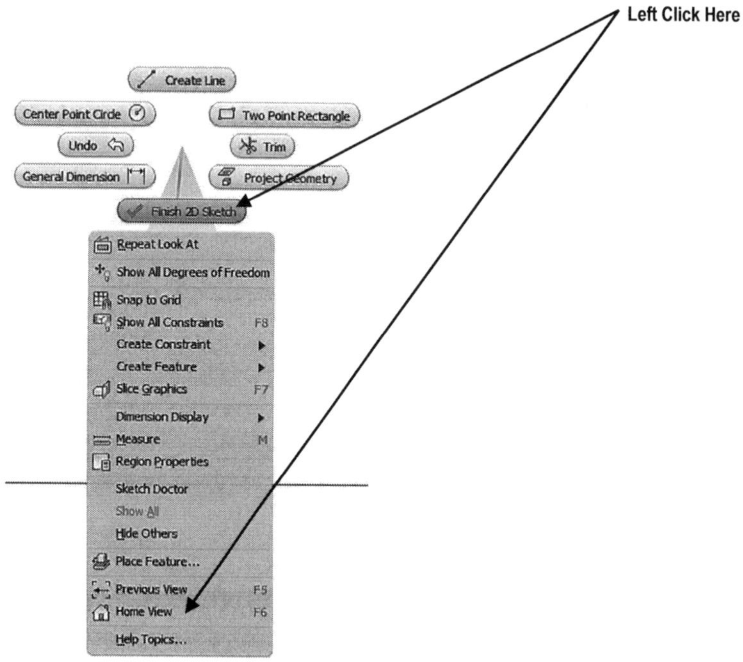

Figure 55

68. Inventor is now out of the Sketch Panel and into the 3D Model Panel. Your screen should look similar to Figure 56.

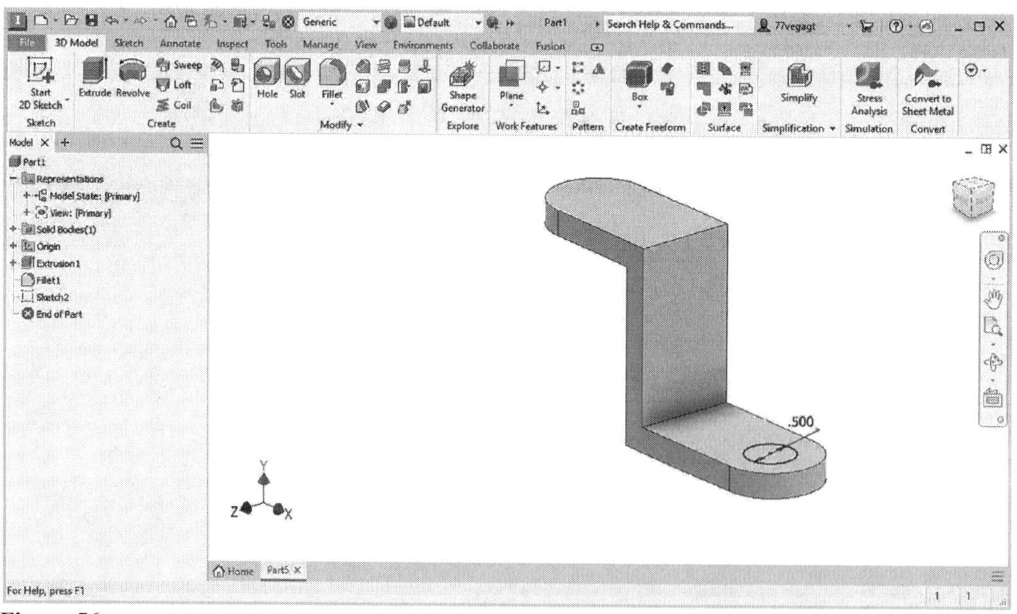

Figure 56

69. Move the cursor to the upper left portion of the screen and left click on **Extrude**. Now move the cursor over the edge of circle. Once the circle turns red, left click once. Enter **.25** for the depth. Left click on the directional arrow to define the direction of extrusion. Left click on the **Cut** icon (the right of Boolean) to define the type of extrusion. Left click on **OK** as shown in Figure 57.

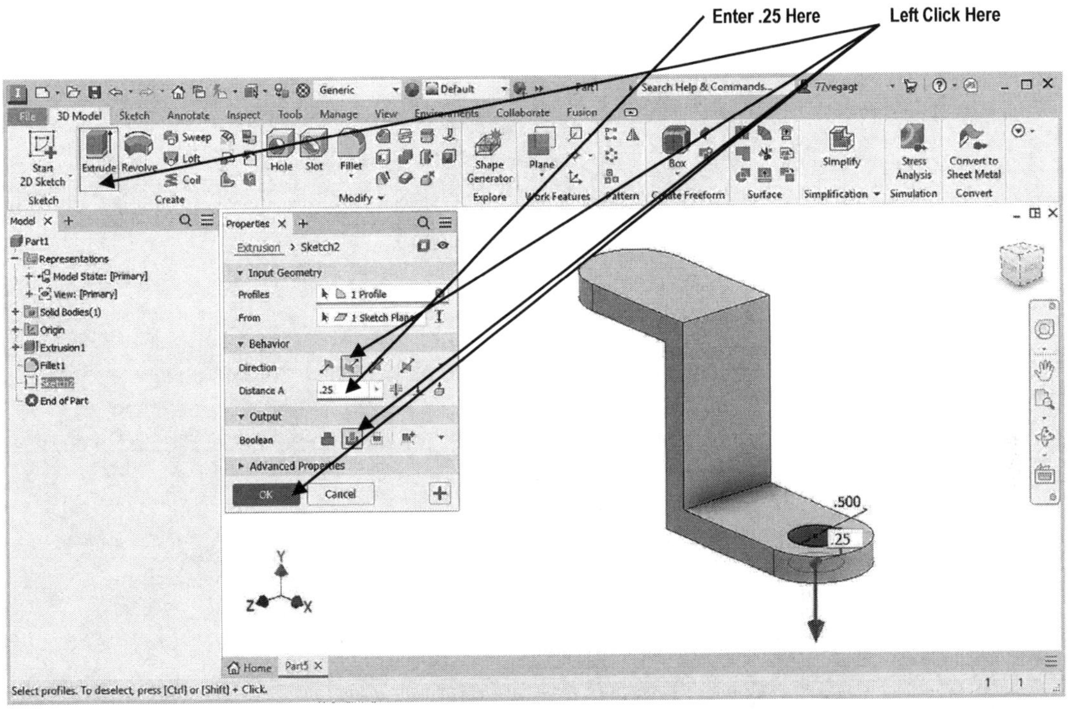

Figure 57

Create a counter bore in the 3D Model Panel using the Hole command

70. Your screen should look similar to Figure 58.

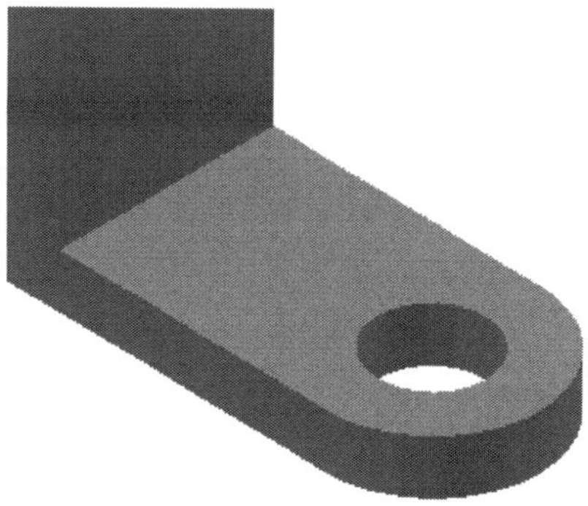

Figure 58

71. Another method of creating a hole is to use the Point, Center Point command.

72. To use the Point, Center Point command, Inventor will need to be in the Sketch Panel. Right click on the surface as shown in Figure 59.

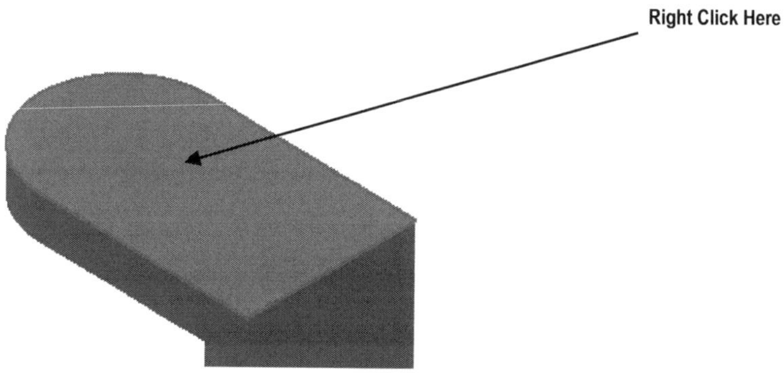

Figure 59

73. The surface will change color. A pop-up menu will also appear. Left click on **New Sketch** as shown in Figure 60.

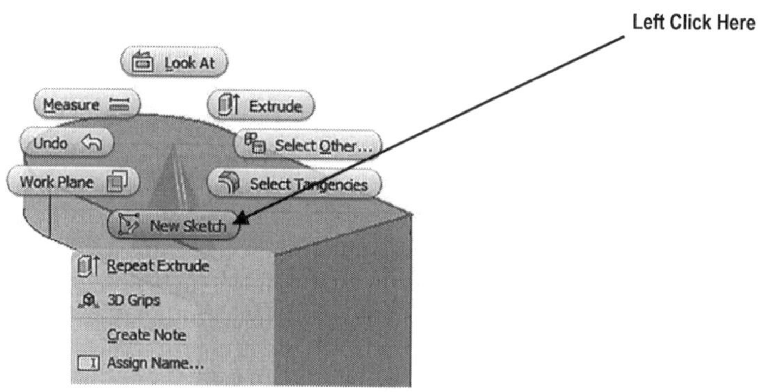

Figure 60

74. Inventor will return to the Sketch Panel as shown in Figure 61.

Figure 61

75. Move the cursor to the middle left portion of the screen and left click on **Point** as shown in Figure 62.

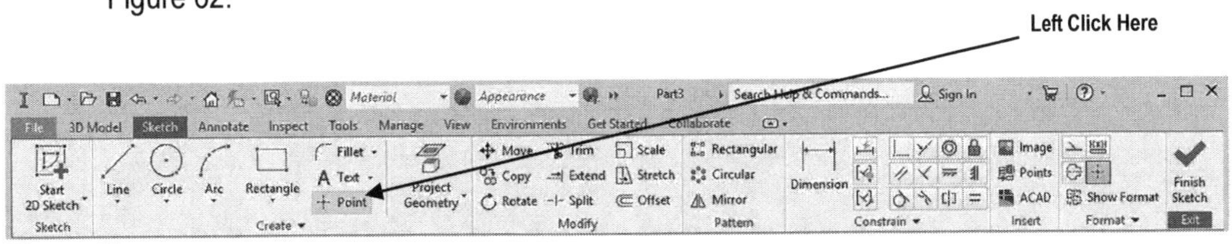

Figure 62

76. A green dot will appear at the center of the Fillet radius. Left click on the dot as shown in Figure 63.

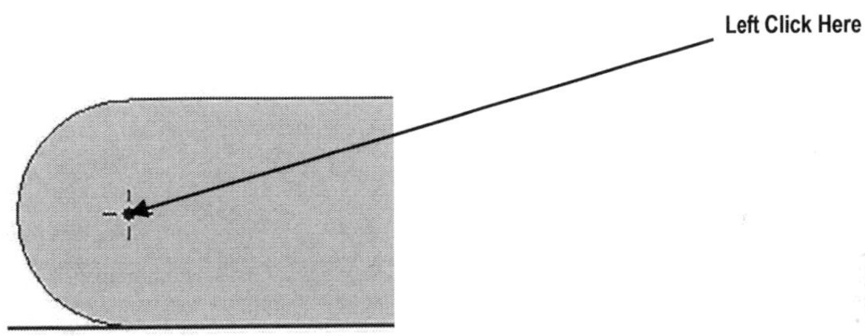

Figure 63

77. After left clicking on the center point, Inventor will place a small center marker on the center of the fillet radius. You will also need to delete the projected line on the outside edge of the fillet radius as shown in Figure 64 and described in step 64. Press the **Esc** key once.

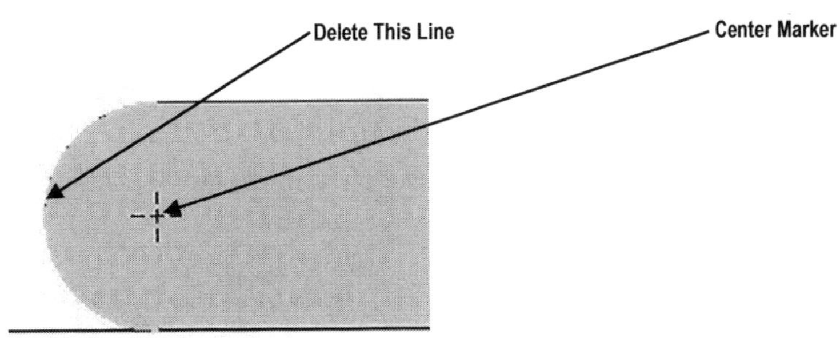

Figure 64

78. Right click anywhere on the drawing. A pop-up menu will appear. Left click on **Finish 2D Sketch** as shown in Figure 65.

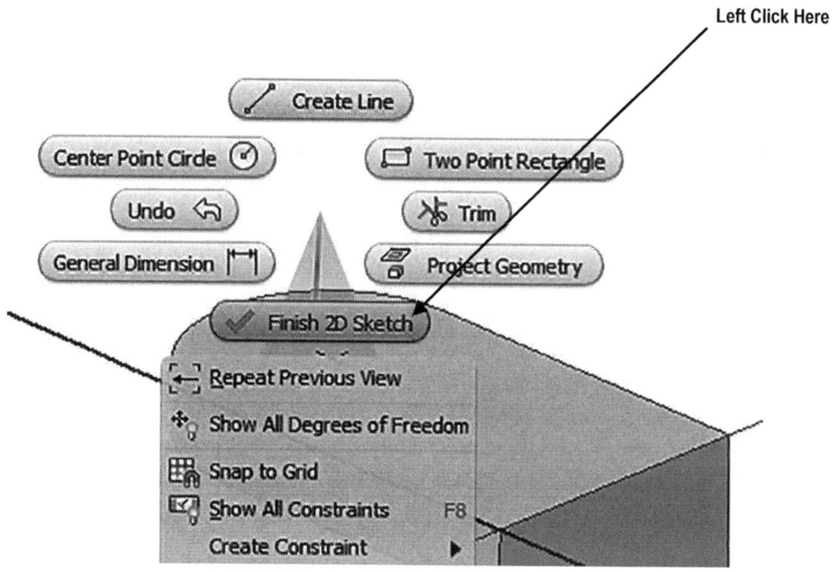

Figure 65

79. Inventor is now out of the Sketch Panel and into the 3D Model Panel. Your screen should look similar to Figure 66.

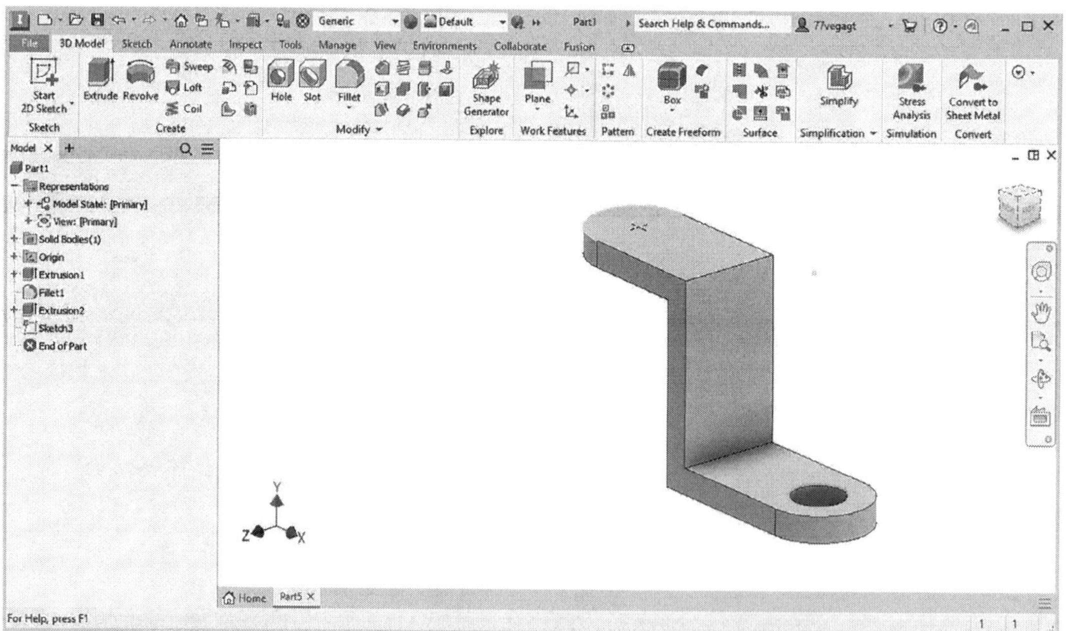

Figure 66

80. Move the cursor to the upper middle portion of the screen and left click on **Hole**. The Hole dialog box will appear as shown in Figure 67.

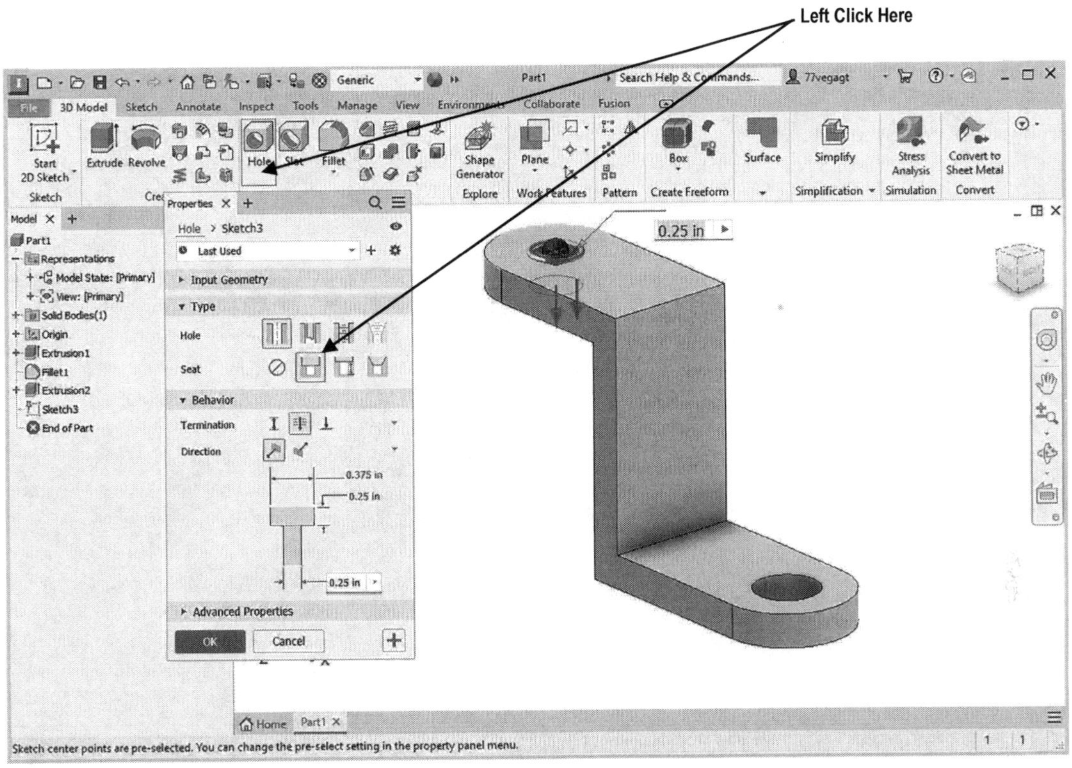

Figure 67

81. Left click on the Counterbore icon as shown in Figure 67.

82. To edit the dimensions of the Counterbore hole, use the cursor to left click on the desired dimension as shown in Figure 68.

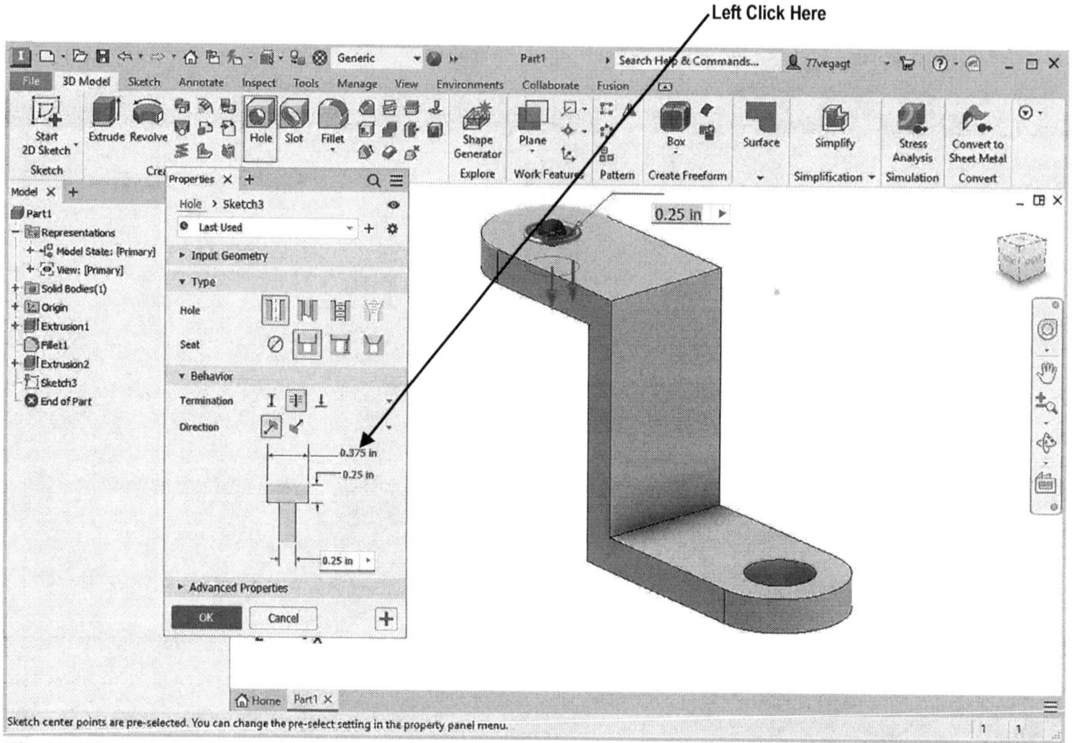

Figure 68

83. Your screen should look like what is shown in Figure 68.

84. Enter .**50** for the Counterbore diameter. Enter in **.125** for the counter bore depth and **.25** for the hole diameter. Left click on **OK** as shown in Figure 69.

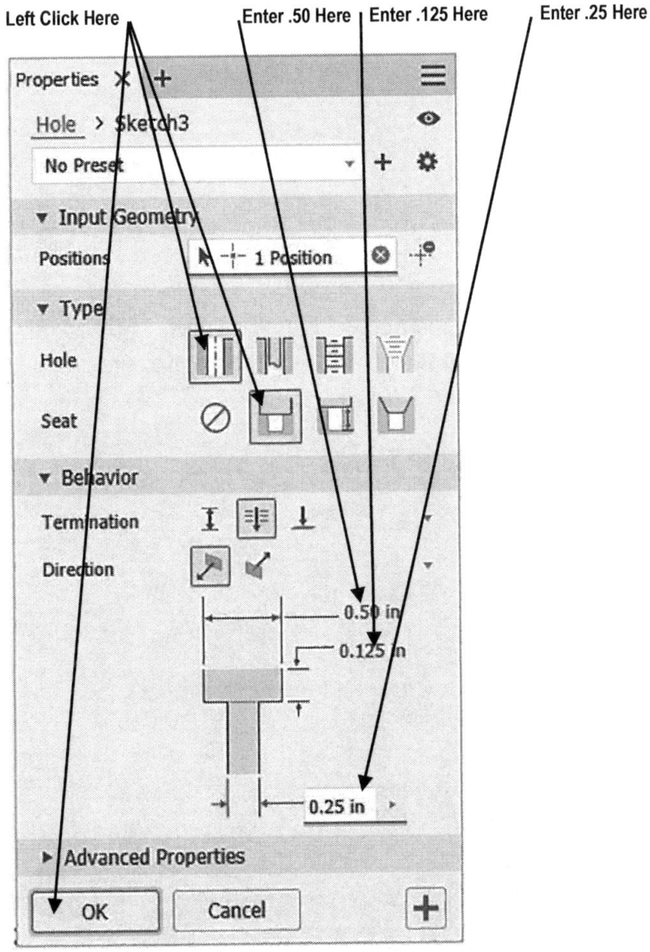

Figure 69

85. Your screen should look similar to Figure 70.

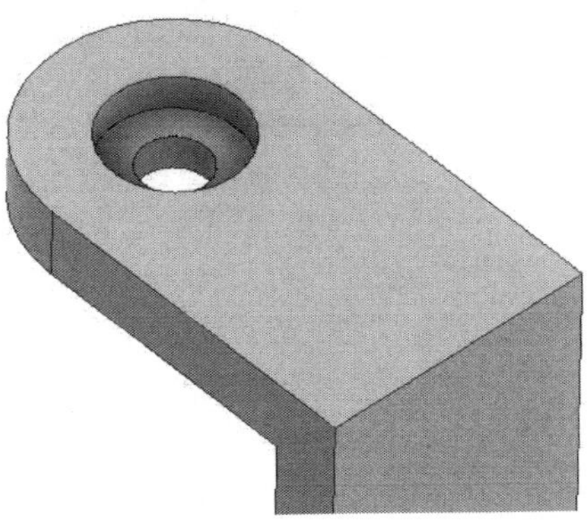

Figure 70

86. To ensure that the hole is correct, move the cursor to the upper left portion of the screen and left click on the **View** tab. Left click on the "Free Orbit/Orbit/Rotate" icon (previous versions of Inventor display "Orbit or Rotate") as shown in Figure 71.

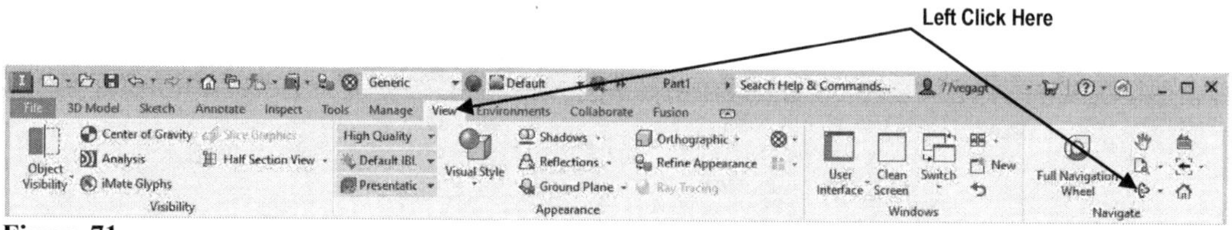

Figure 71

87. The Free Orbit/Rotate command will become active. Left click anywhere <u>inside</u> the white circle, hold the left mouse button down, and drag the cursor upward. The part will rotate upward as shown in Figure 72.

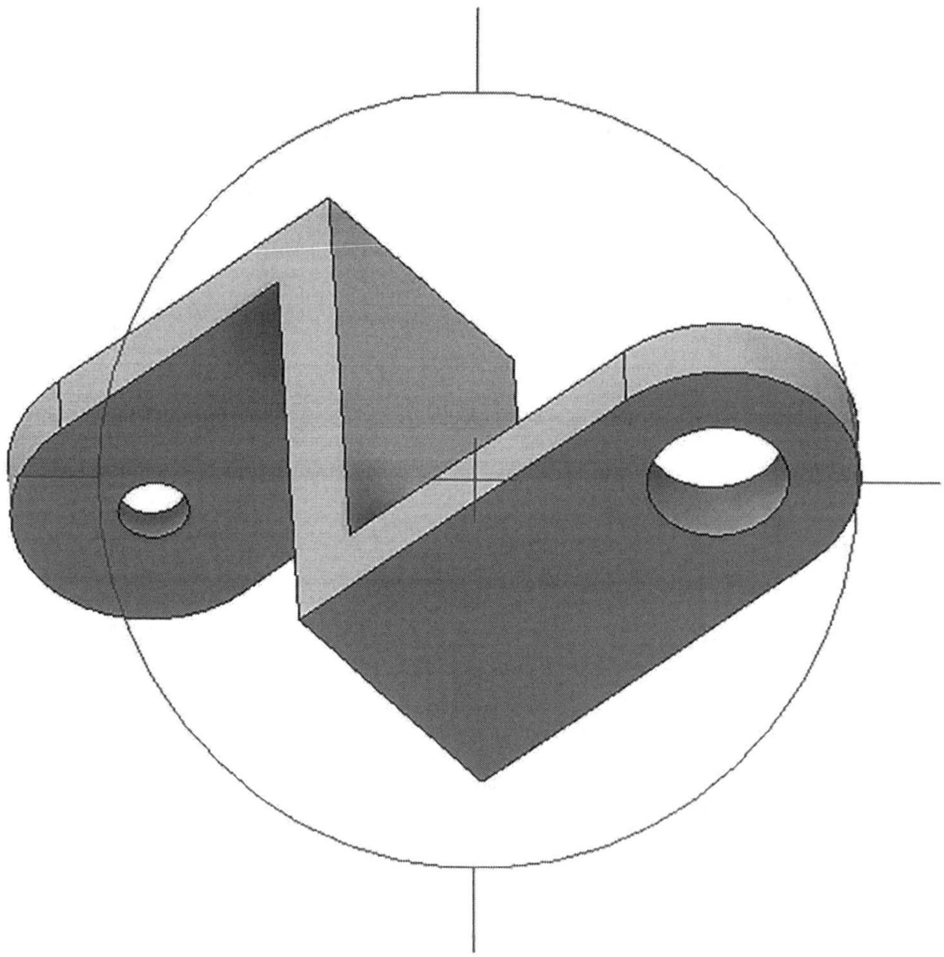

Figure 72

88. Holding the left mouse button down keeps the part attached to the cursor. To view the part in Isometric, right click anywhere on the screen and left click on **Home View** from the pop-up menu as shown in Figure 73.

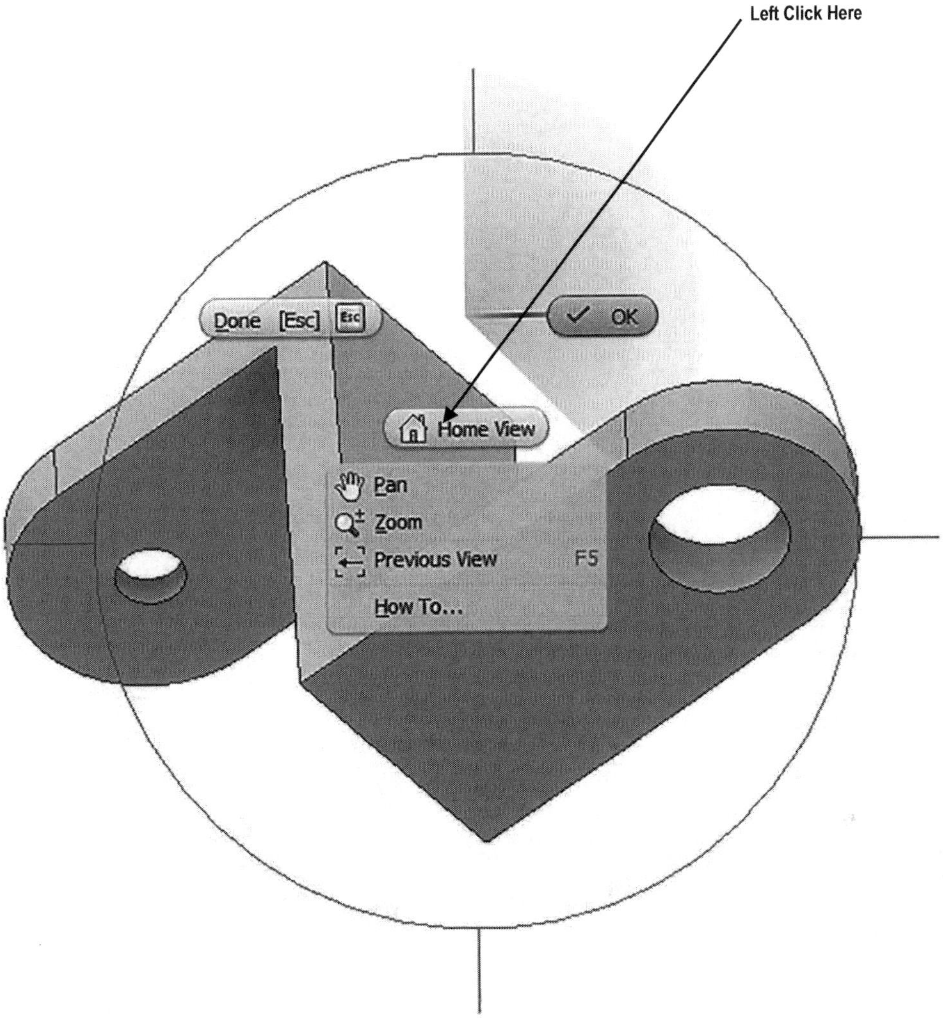

Figure 73

89. As long as the white circle is present, the Free Orbit/Rotate command is still active. To get out of the Orbit/Rotate command either use the keyboard and press **Esc** once or twice, or right click anywhere on the screen. A pop-up menu will appear. Left click on **OK** from the pop-up menu shown in Figure 74.

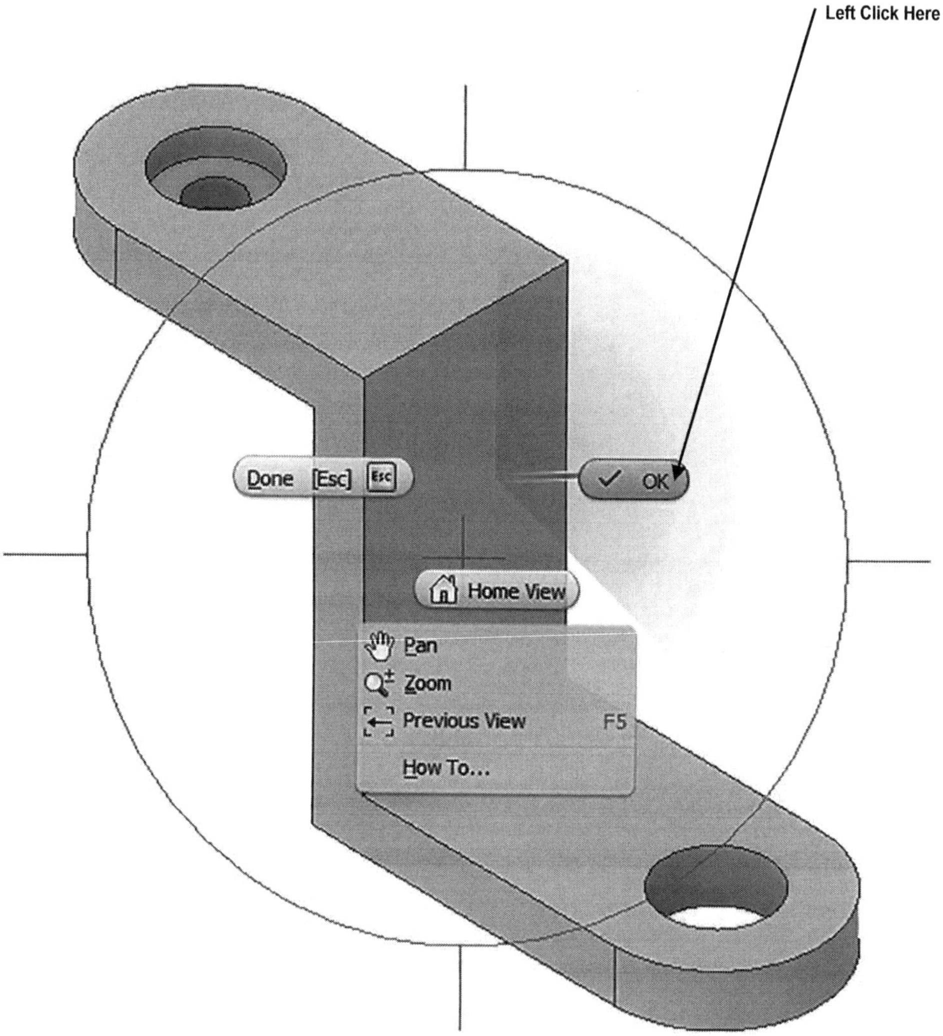

Figure 74

90. Other commands for viewing are at the upper right portion of the screen. Left click on the **View** tab to access each command. You can also use the icons located at the far right. Each icon has a drop-down arrow to locate more viewing options. Left click on the drop-down arrow under each command to become more familiar with what options are available as shown in Figure 75. Probably the most convenient tool for Zooming in and out is the mouse wheel. Simply roll the wheel forward to move the view away. To bring the view closer, simply roll the wheel towards you. You can also use the view cube. Left click on Front on the view cube and the model will rotate to show a perpendicular view of the front of the model.

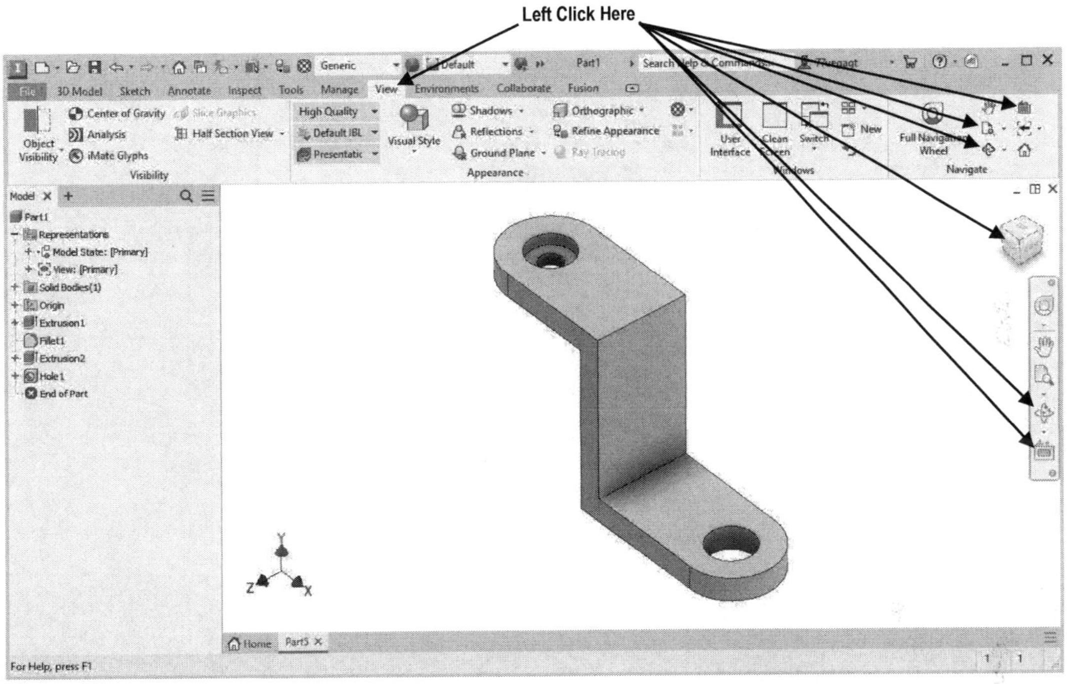

Figure 75

91. To save the model, move the cursor to the upper left portion of the screen and left click on the "I" at the far upper left. A drop-down menu will appear as shown in Figure 76. Save the file where it can be retrieved later.

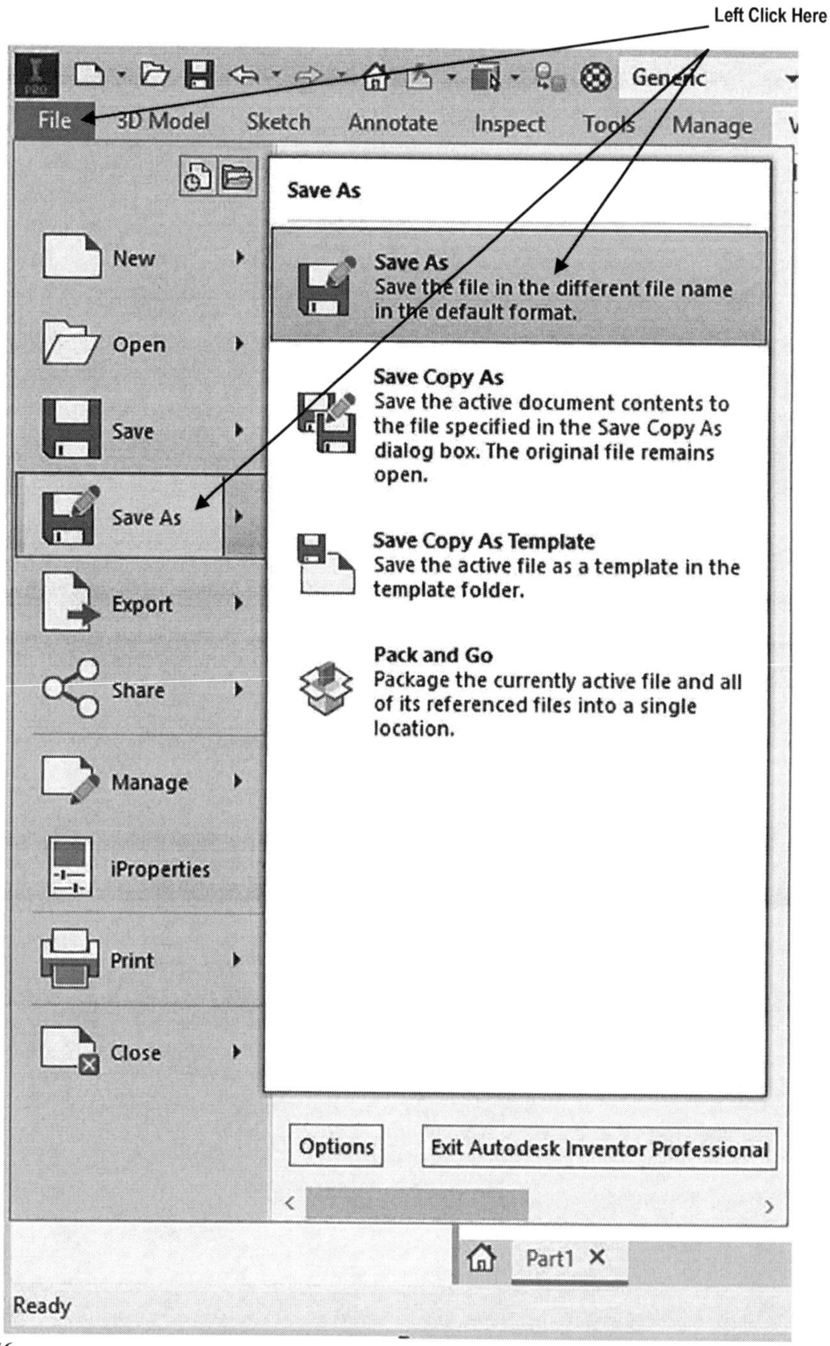

Figure 76

Chapter Problems

Use the Extrude and Extrude-Cut commands to complete the following.

Problem 1-1

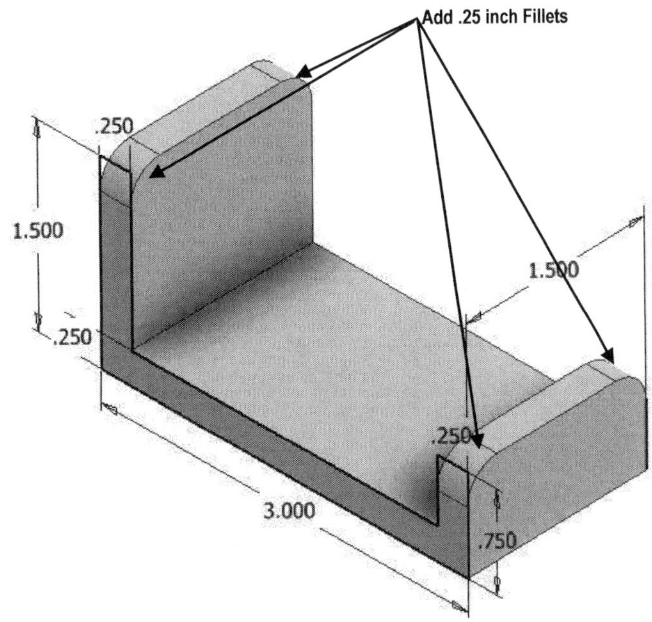

Problem 1-2

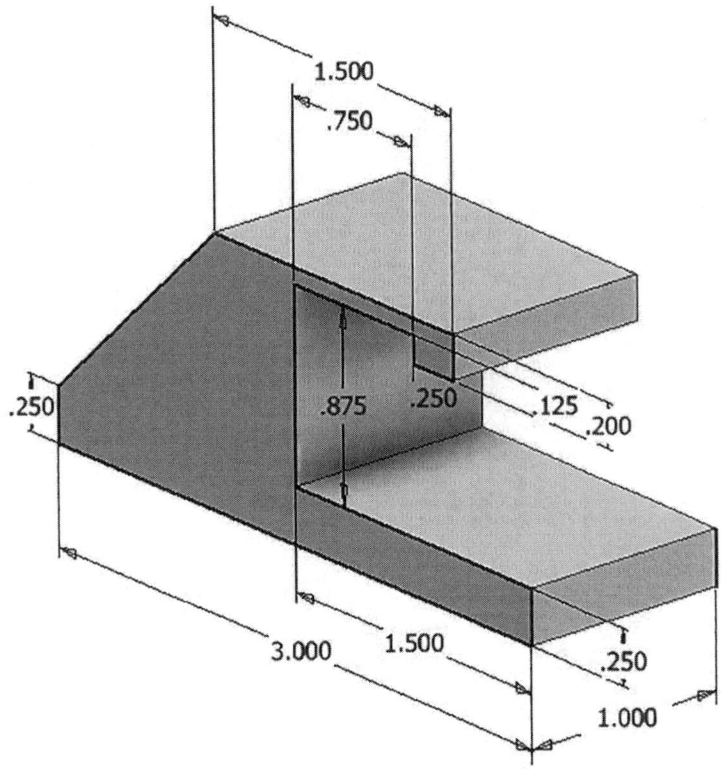

Problem 1-3

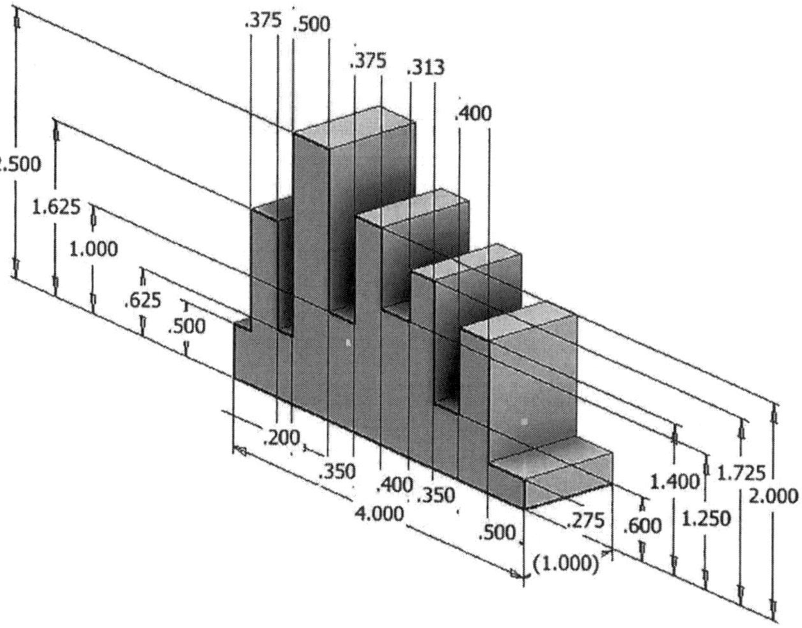

Problem 1-4

Hint: Use Extrusions to "Cut" features into the Part as shown.
L-Shaped Extrusion with Two (2) Extrude Cuts

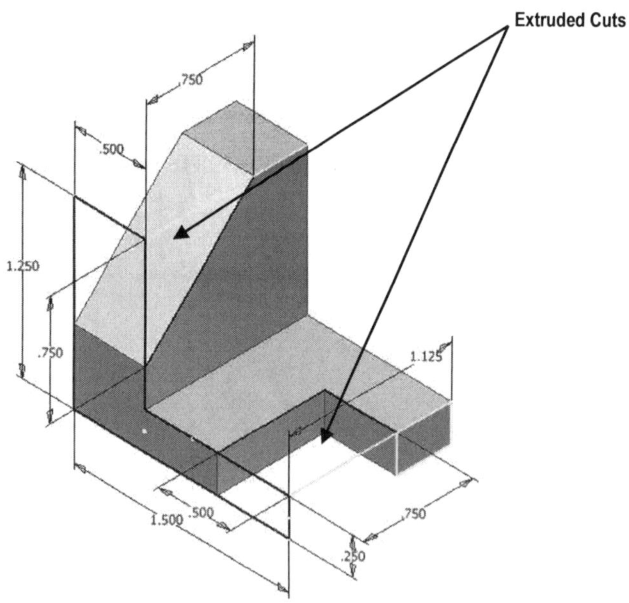

Problem 1-5

Hint: Use Extrusions to "Cut" features into the Part as shown.
H-Shaped Extrusion with One (1) Extrude Cut

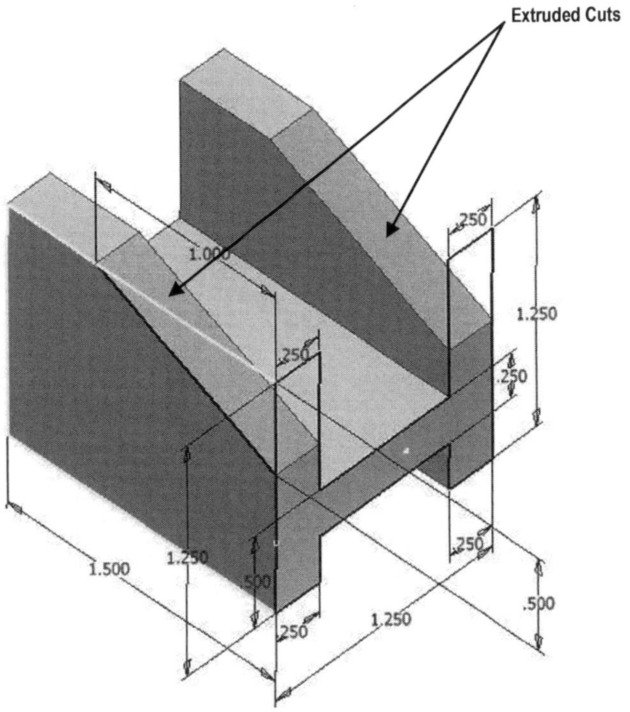

Problem 1-6

Hint: Use Extrusions to "Cut" features into the Part as shown.
Z-Shaped Extrusion with One (1) Extrude Cut

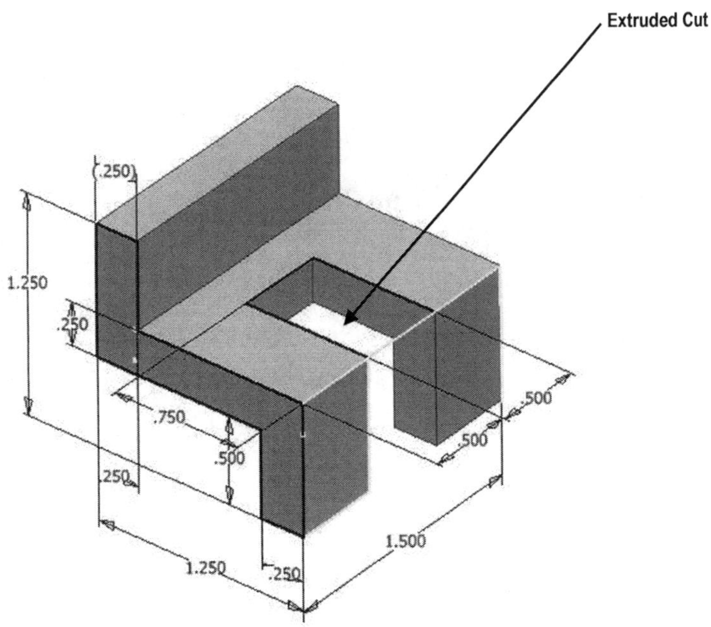

Problem 1-7

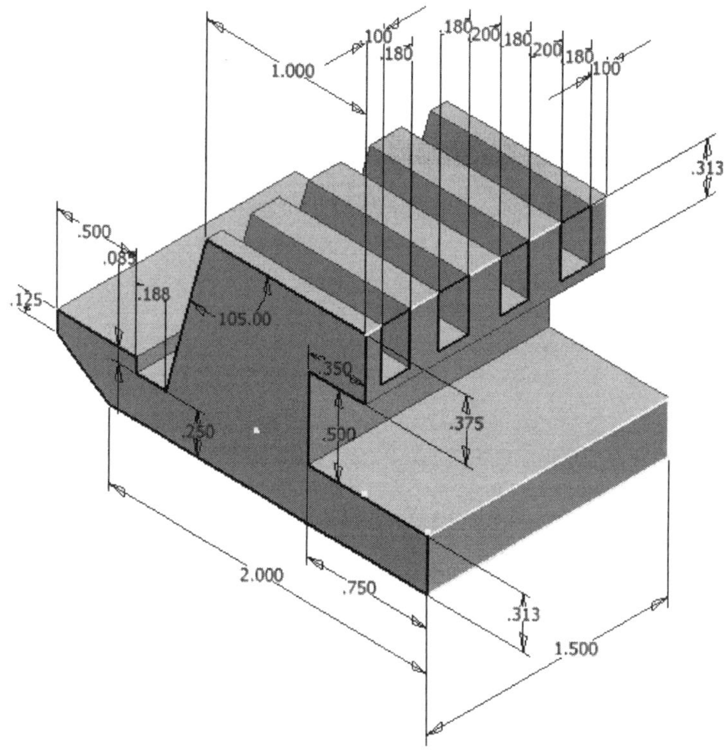

Problem 1-8

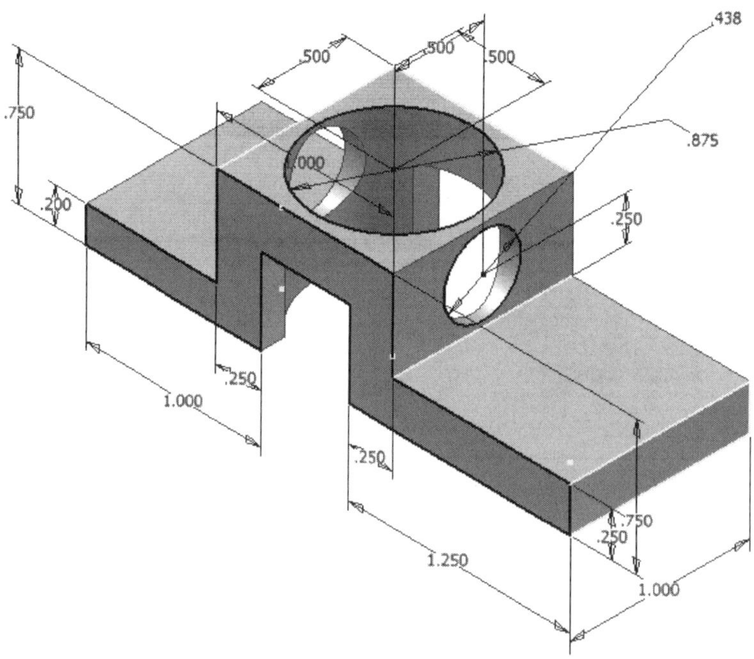

Problem 1-9

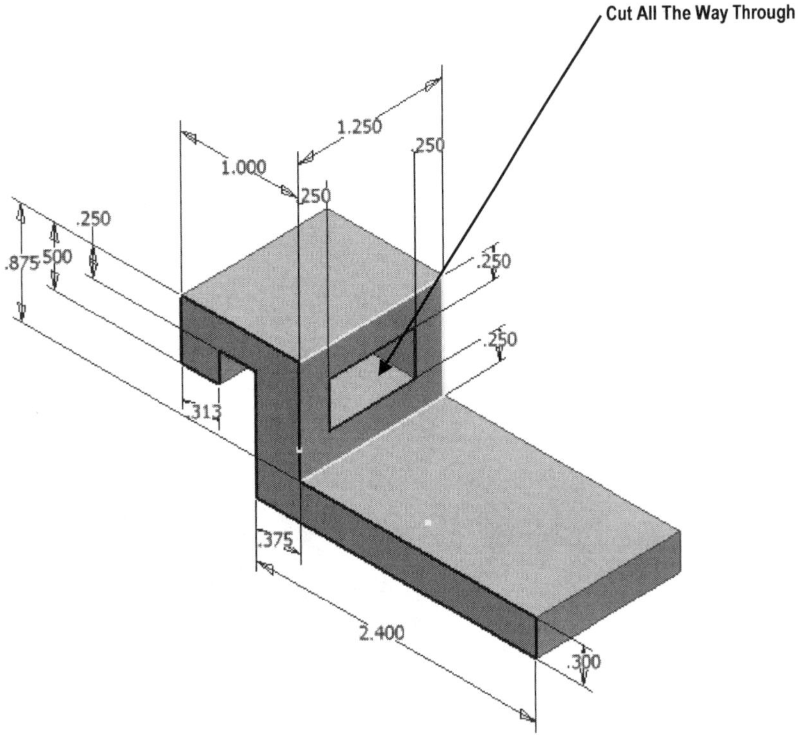

Problem 1-10

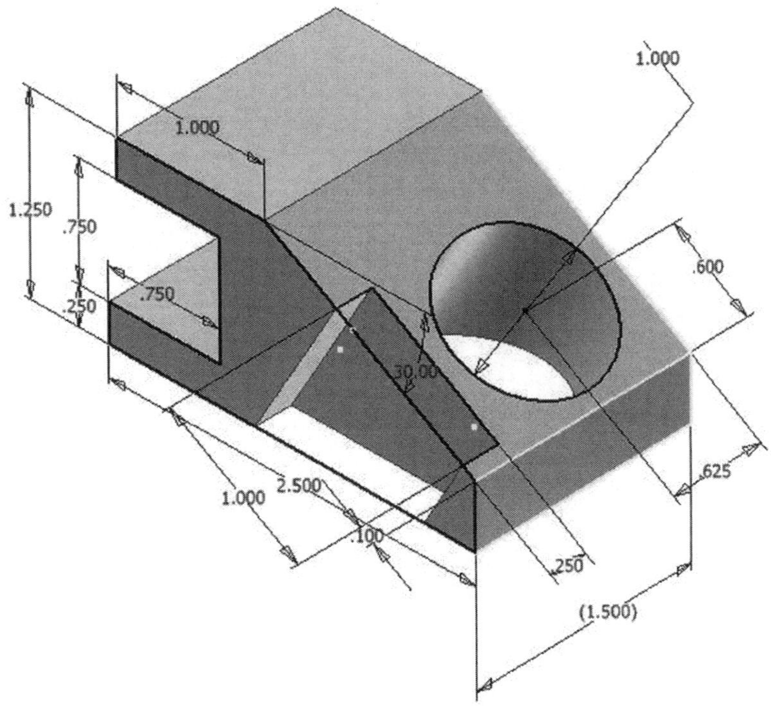

Problem 1-11

Hint: Create a Point while in the Sketch Panel to use the Hole Wizard
Counterbore Diameter .50 x .125 Deep
Thru Hole Diameter .25

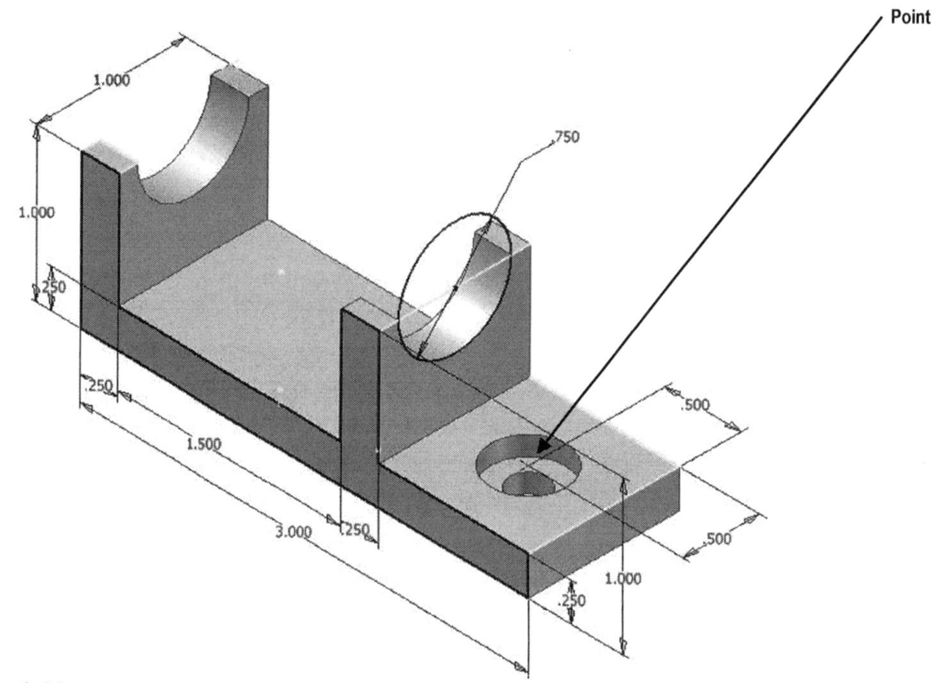

Problem 1-12

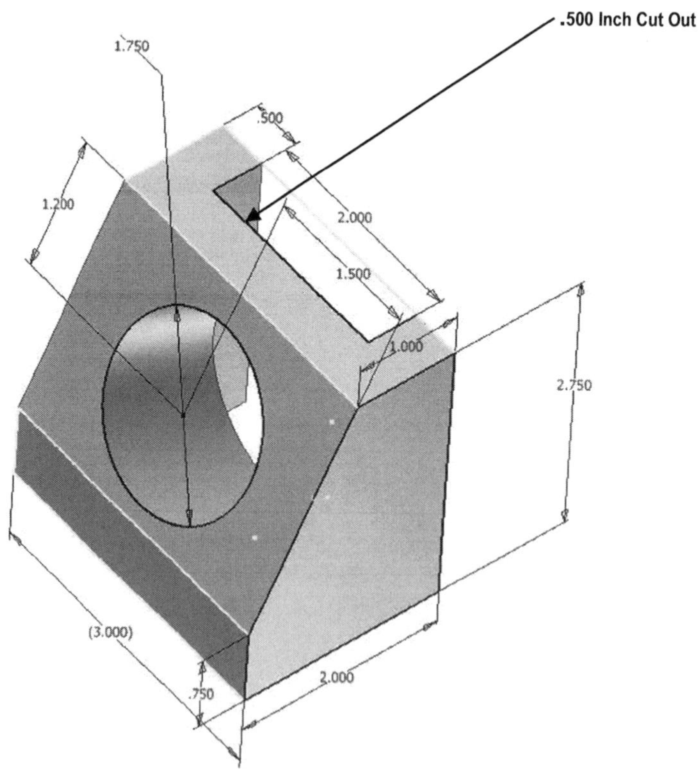

Problem 1-13

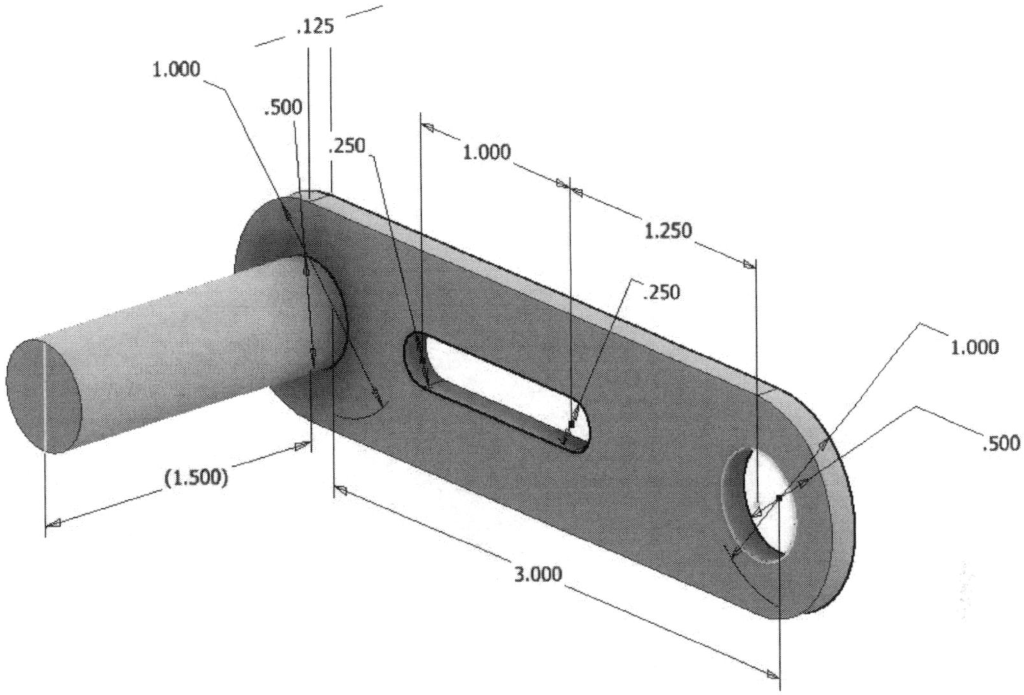

Problem 1-14

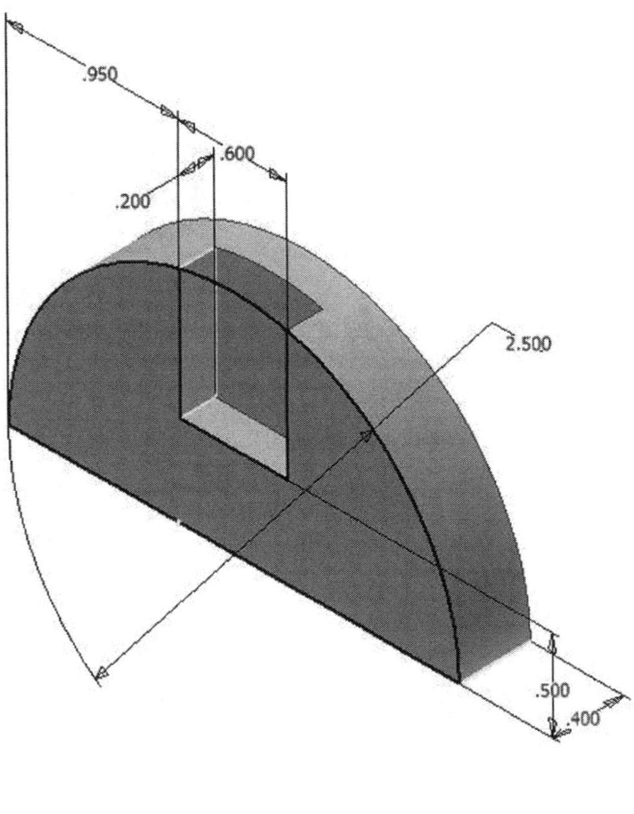

Problem 1-15

Hint: (2) Counterbored Holes
.75 Diameter x .375 Deep, Thru Hole Diameter = .375
Fillet Radius .375

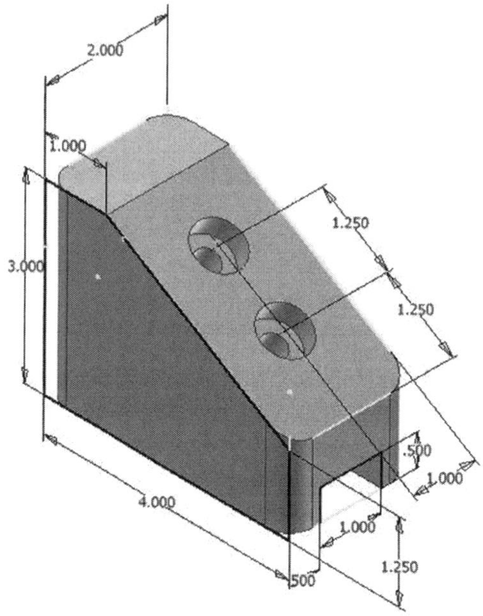

Problem 1-16

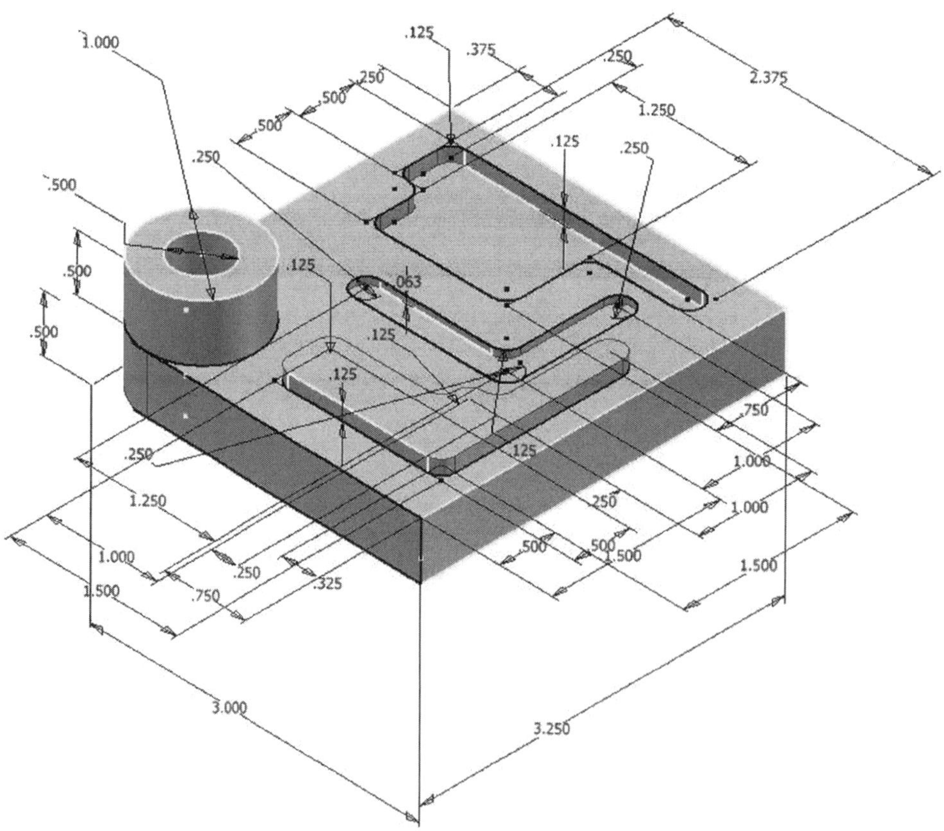

CHAPTER 2

Learning More Basics

Objectives:

1. Create a simple sketch using the Sketch Panel
2. Dimension a sketch using the Dimension command
3. Revolve a sketch in the 3D Model Panel using the Revolve command
4. Create a groove using the Revolve Cut command
5. Create a hole in the 3D Model Panel using the Extrude cut command
6. Create a series of holes in the 3D Model Panel using the Circular Pattern and command

Chapter 2 includes instruction on how to design the part shown.

1. Start Autodesk Inventor 2027 by referring to "Chapter 1 Getting Started."

2. After Autodesk Inventor 2027 is running, begin a new sketch.

3. Complete the sketch (including dimensions) as shown on the **XY Plane** including the line above the sketch. This line will be used to revolve the sketch around (known as the Revolve Line) as shown in Figure 1.

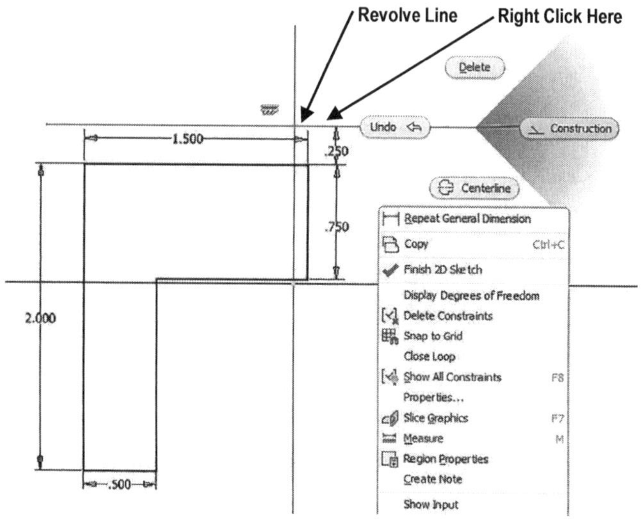

Figure 1

4. Right click around the sketch. A pop-up menu will appear. Left click on **Home View**, then left click on **Finish 2D Sketch** as shown in Figure 2.

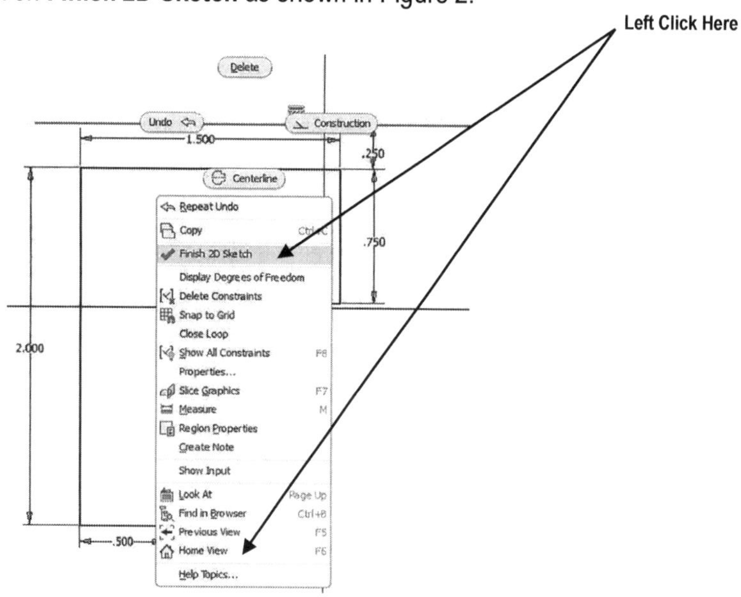

Figure 2

5. The view will become isometric as shown in Figure 3.

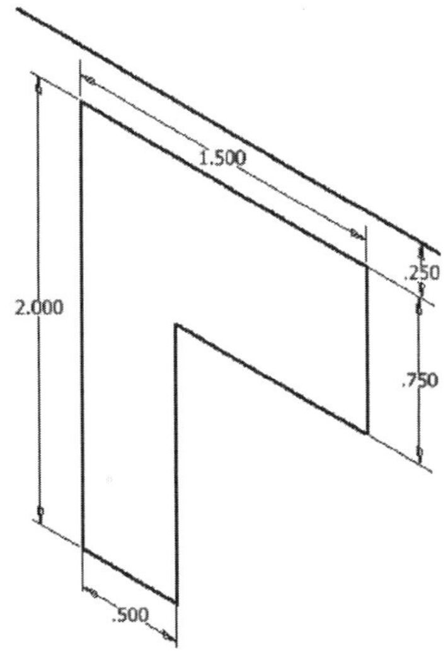

Figure 3

Revolve a sketch in the 3D Model Panel using the Revolve command

6. Move the cursor to the upper left portion of the screen and left click on **Revolve**. Left click inside the profile causing it to become highlighted if it is not already highlighted. Your screen should look similar to Figure 4.

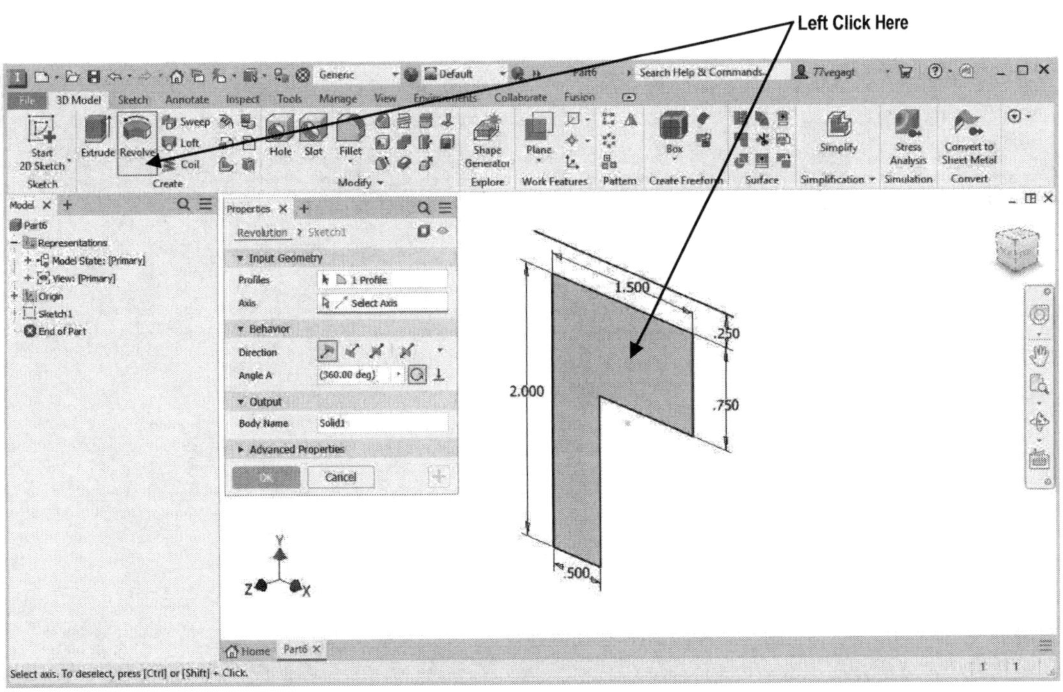

Figure 4

7. Notice that the sketch has already been selected. Because there is only one sketch present, Inventor assumes that particular sketch will be selected. If the drawing contained more than one sketch, you would have to first select the sketch icon in the revolve dialog box then use the cursor to select the desired sketch.

8. Move the cursor over the axis line causing it to become highlighted and left click once as shown in Figure 5.

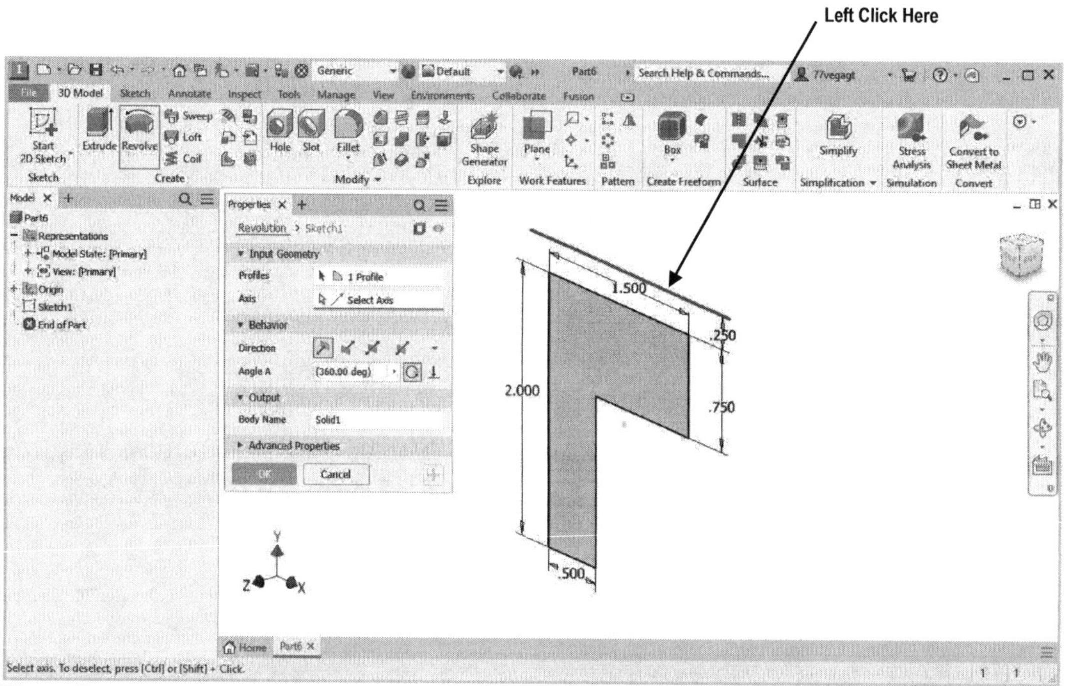

Figure 5

9. A preview of the revolve will appear as shown in Figure 6.

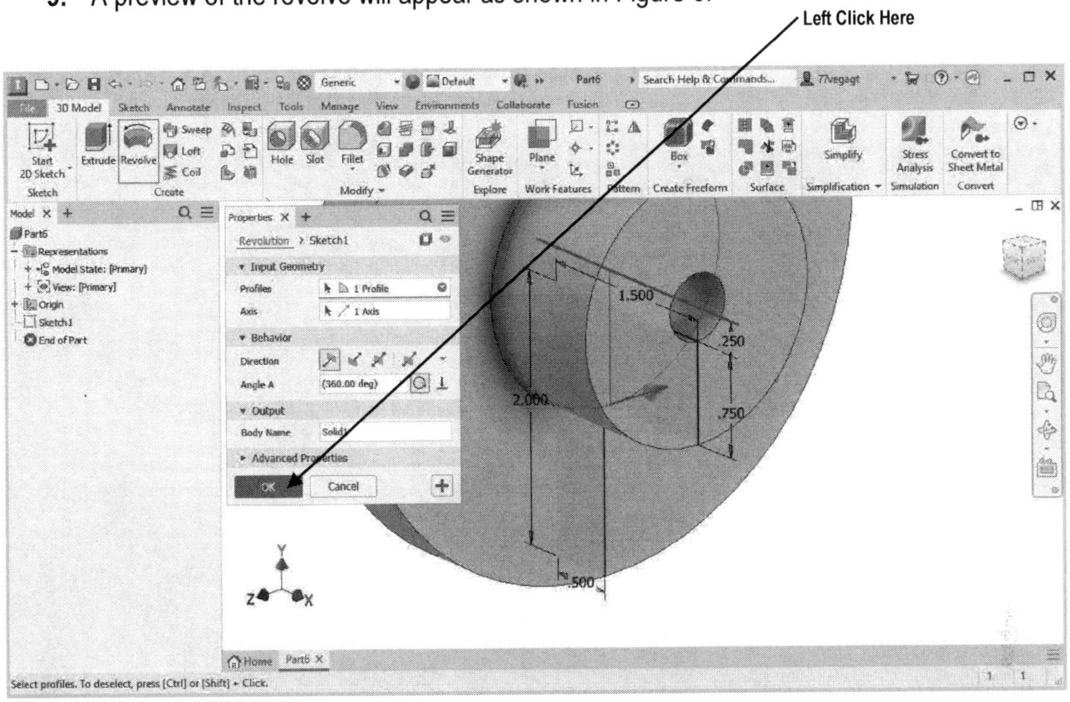

Figure 6

10. Left click on **OK**.

11. Your screen should look similar to Figure 7. You may have to zoom out to view the entire part.

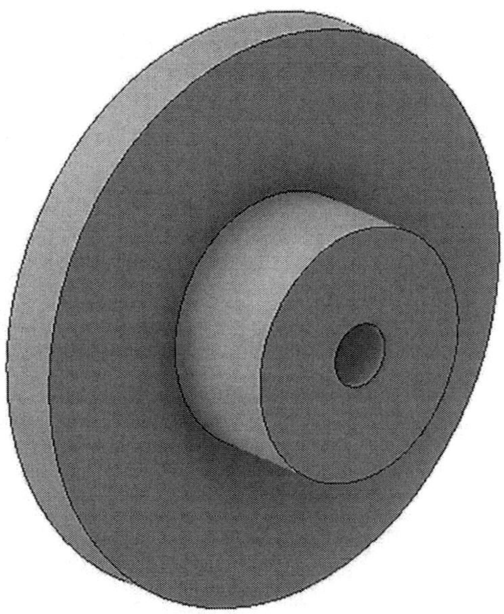

Figure 7

12. Move the cursor to the middle left portion of the screen and left click on the "+" sign to the left of the Origin folder. This will cause the default work planes to appear. Move the cursor over "XY Plane" and right click once. A pop-up menu will appear. Left click on **New Sketch** as shown in Figure 8.

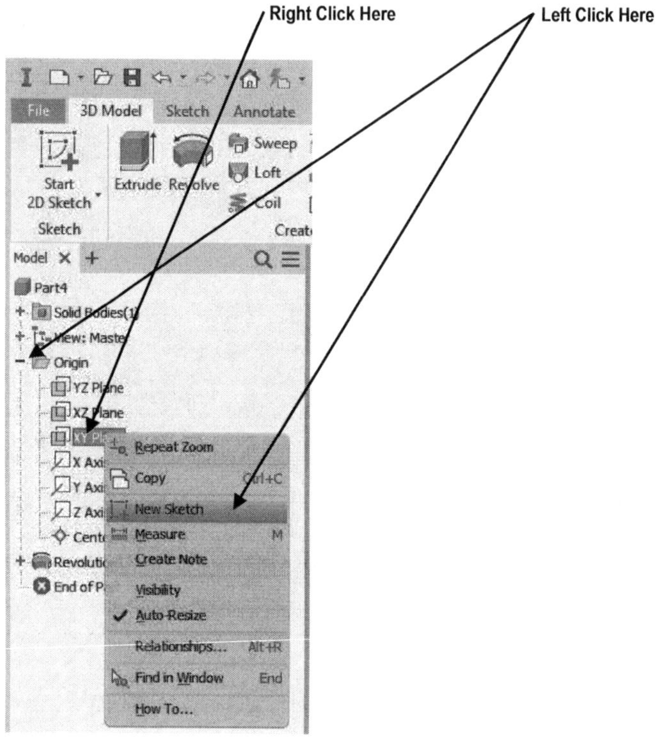

Figure 8

13. Inventor will create a work plane in the center of the part. You may have to select **Home View** to see the plane as shown in Figure 9.

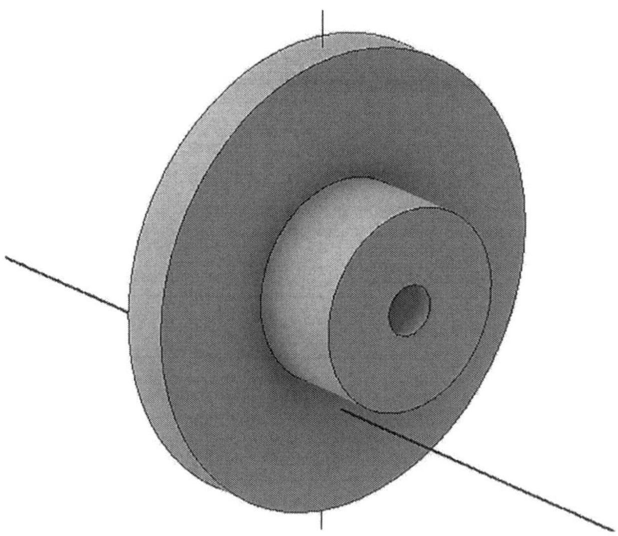

Figure 9

14. Move the cursor to the upper middle portion of the screen and left click on the **View** tab. Left click on the arrow under "Visual Style." A drop-down menu will appear. Left click on **Wireframe Model edges only** as shown in Figure 10.

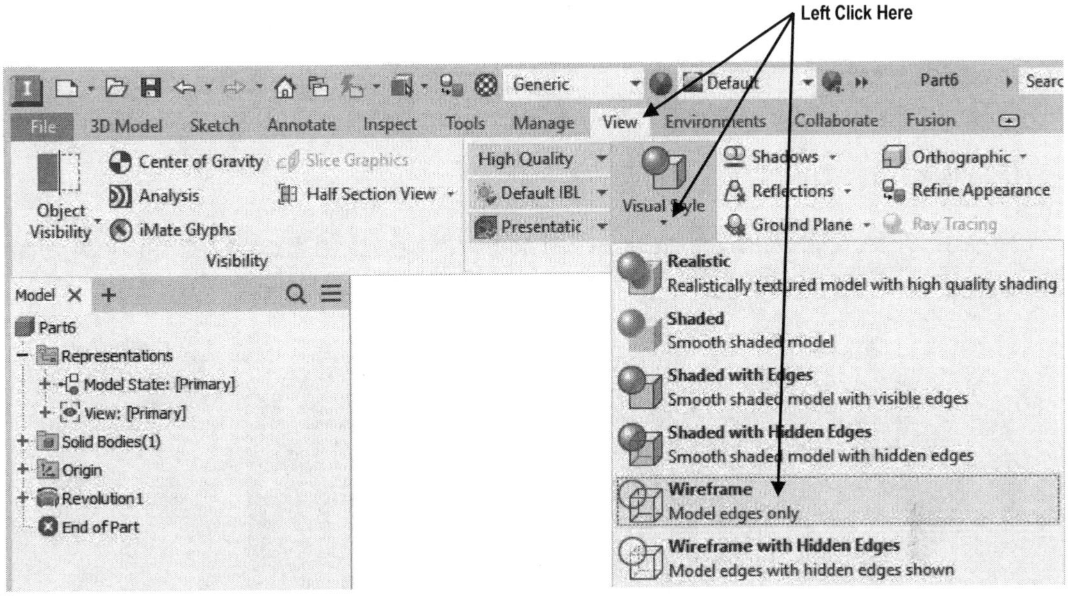

Figure 10

15. Inventor will change the display of the model to wire frame as shown in Figure 11.

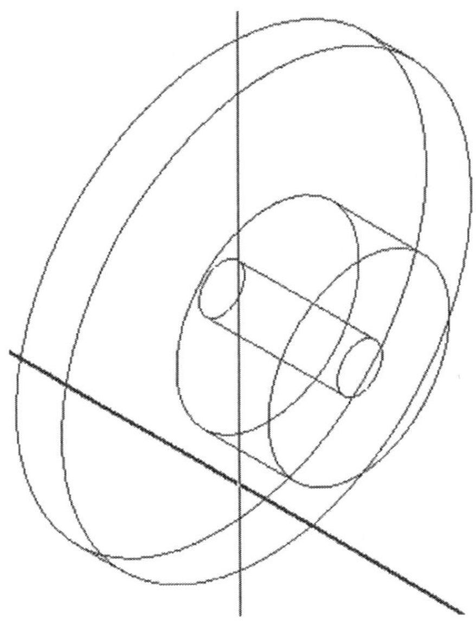

Figure 11

16. Move the cursor to the upper middle portion of the screen and left click on the **View** tab. Left click on the "Look At" icon as shown in Figure 12.

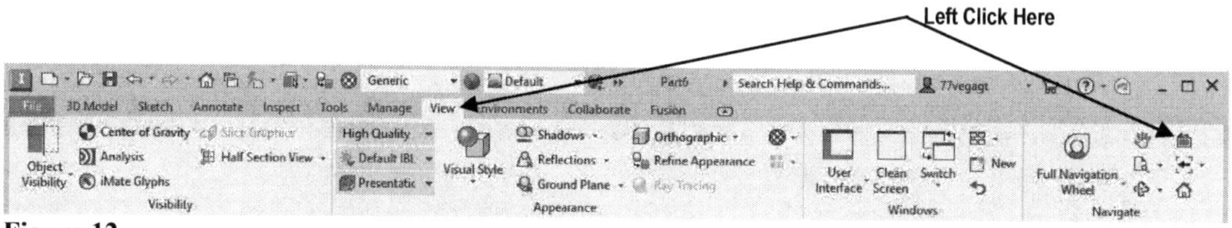

Figure 12

17. Move the cursor to the upper left portion of the screen and left click on the XY Plane as shown in Figure 13.

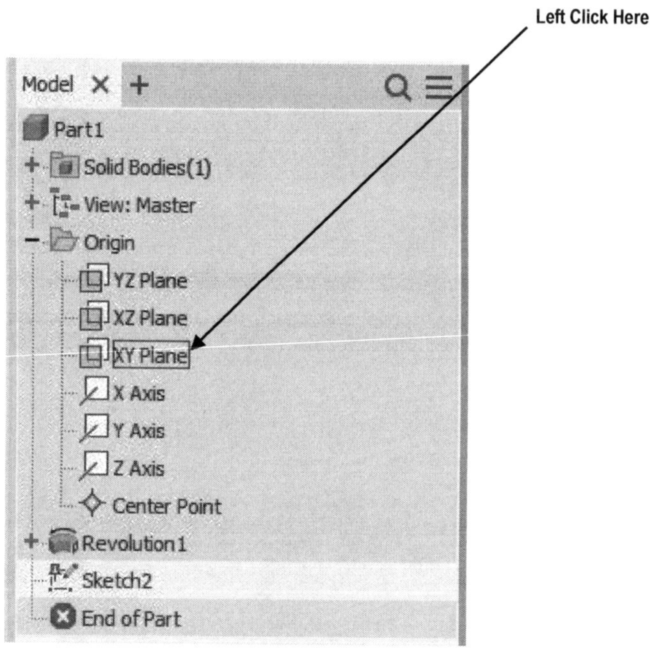

Figure 13

18. Inventor will rotate the model around providing a perpendicular view of the XY plane as shown in Figure 14.

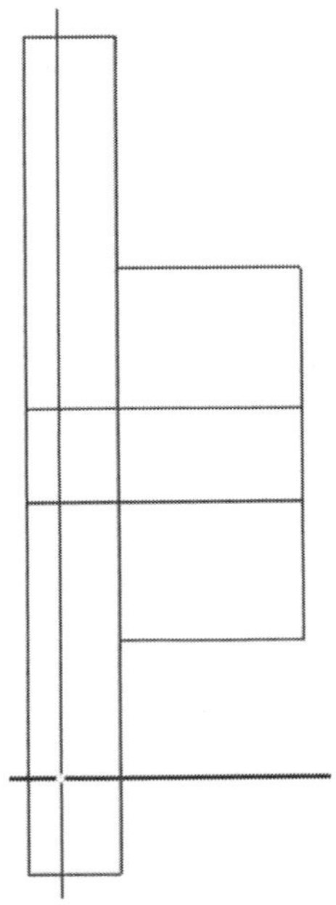

Figure 14

19. Use the Free Orbit/Rotate command to rotate the part slightly from perpendicular as shown in Figure 15.

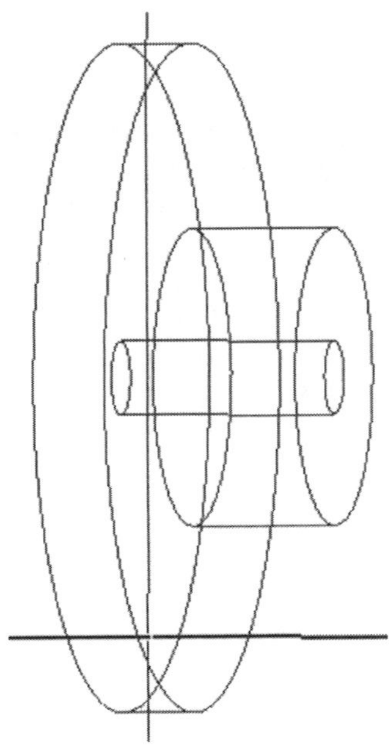

Figure 15

Use the Revolve Cut command to create a groove

20. Left click on the **Sketch** tab. Move the cursor to the upper middle portion of the screen and left click on **Project Geometry** as shown in Figure 16.

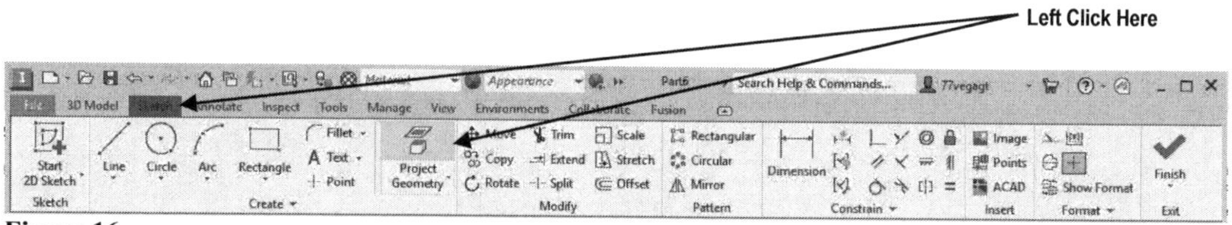

Figure 16

21. Move the cursor to the left side line. When it becomes highlighted left click on it once as shown in Figure 17.

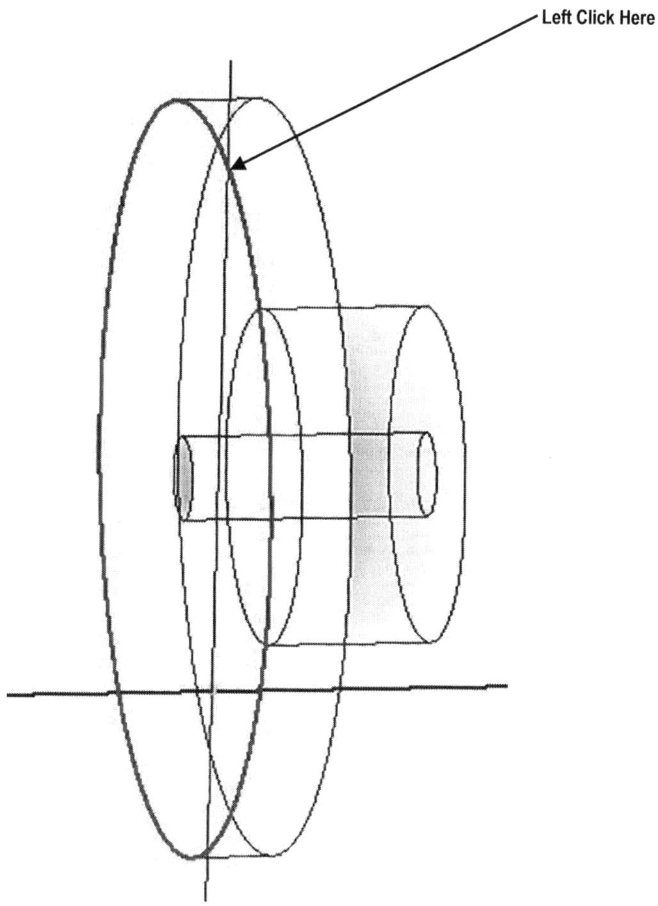

Figure 17

22. Inventor will project this line onto the New Sketch as shown in Figure 18.

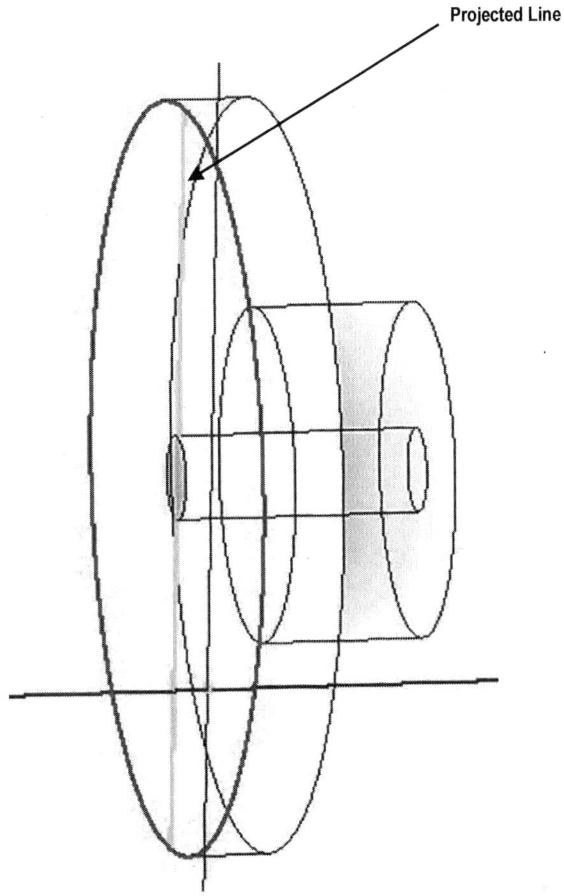

Figure 18

23. Left click on **Project Geometry** as shown in Figure 19.

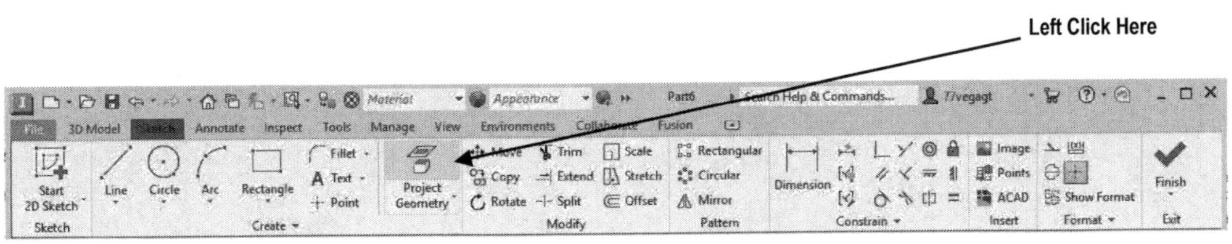

Figure 19

24. Move the cursor on the right-side line. When it becomes highlighted left click on it once as shown in Figure 20.

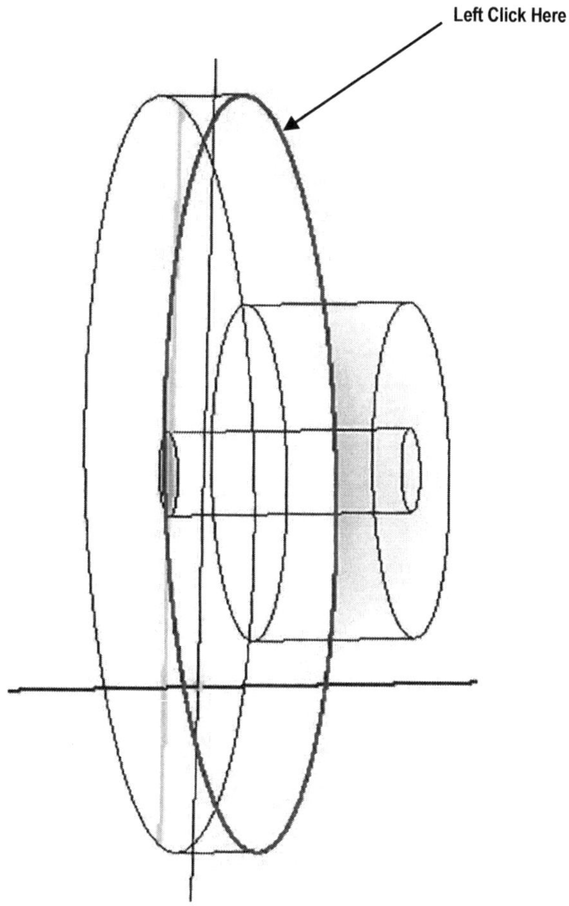

Figure 20

25. Inventor will project this line onto the New Sketch as shown in Figure 21.

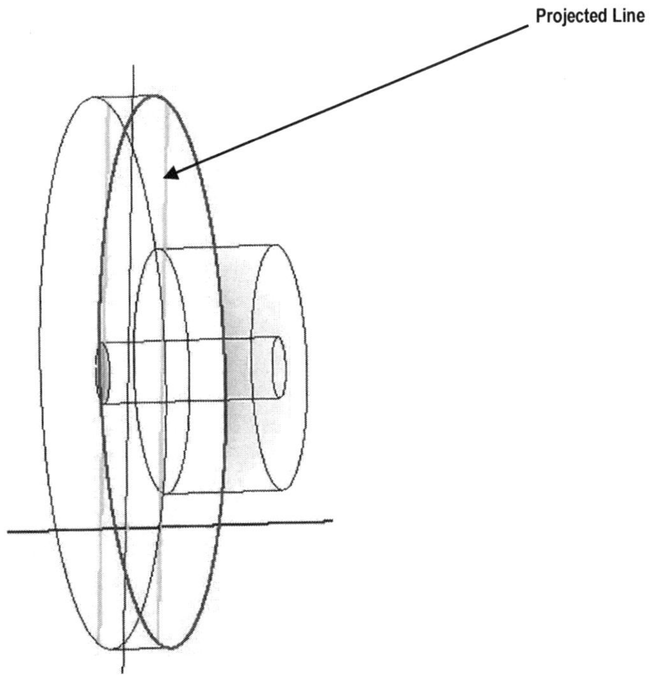

Figure 21

26. Move the cursor to the outside edge of the part and left click. Move the cursor to the bottom portion of the part and left click as shown in Figure 22.

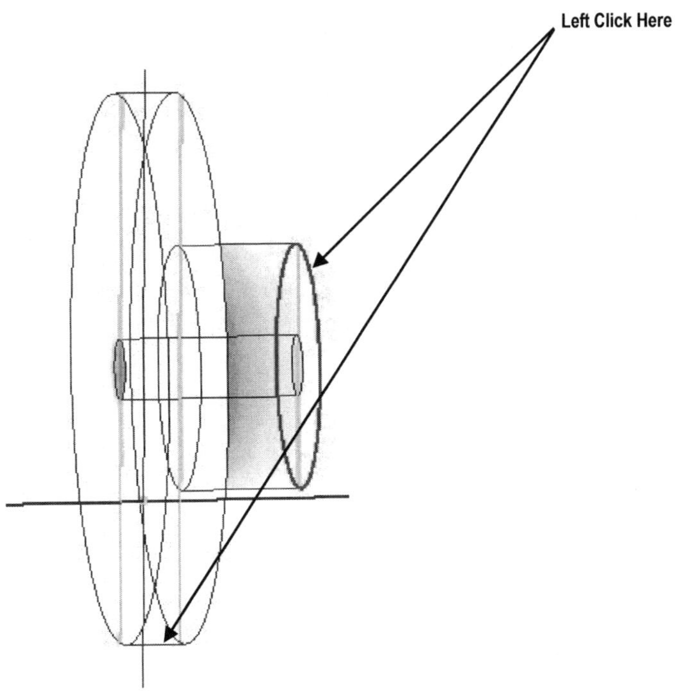

Figure 22

27. Your screen should look similar to what is shown in Figure 23.

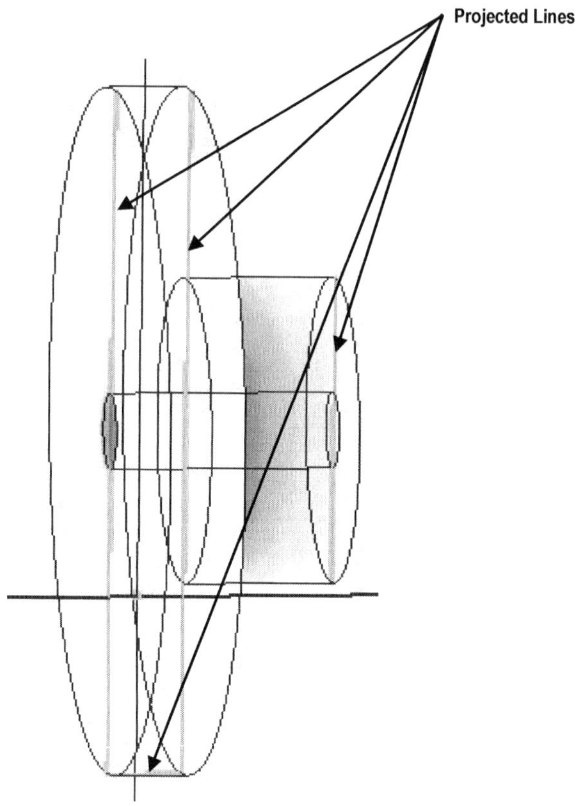

Figure 23

28. Move the cursor to the upper middle portion of the screen and left click on the **View** tab. Left click on **Look At** as shown in Figure 24.

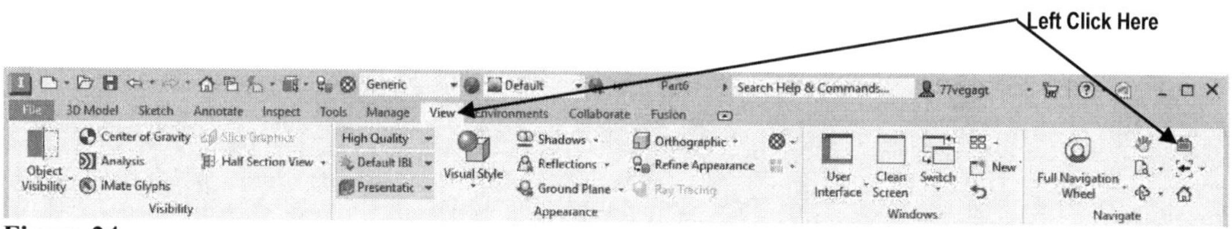

Figure 24

29. Inventor will provide a perpendicular view of the lines that were just projected onto the sketch as shown in Figure 25.

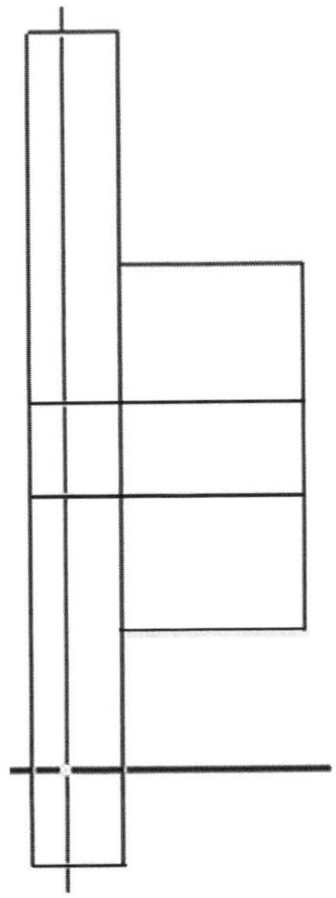

Figure 25

30. Complete the sketch as shown (draw a triangle) at the bottom of the part. Once the triangle is complete, delete all Projected lines as shown in Figure 26.

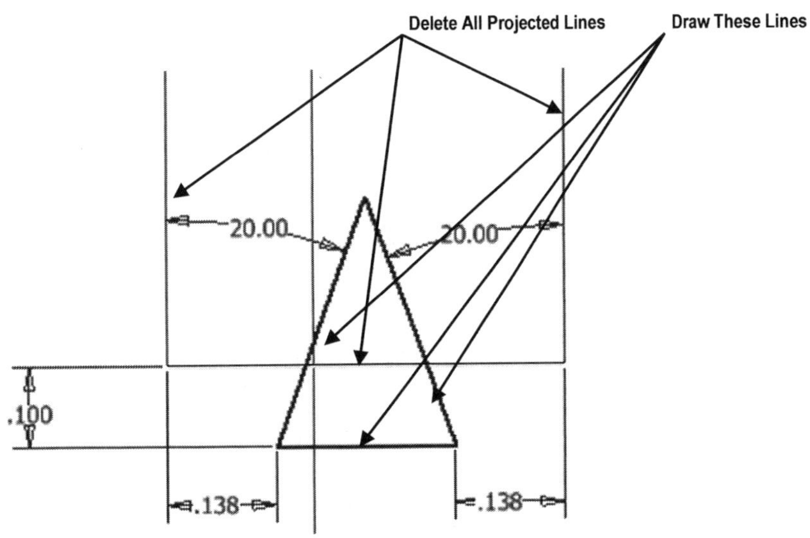

Figure 26

31. Draw an axis line/revolve line in the center of the part. Finish deleting all projected lines. Once deleted, projected lines may still appear in yellow. This is not a problem as shown in Figure 27.

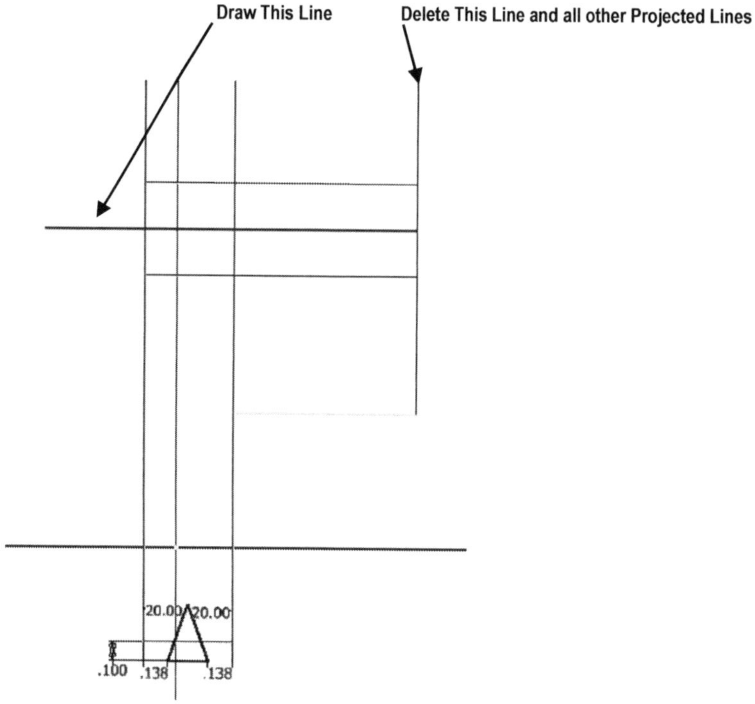

Figure 27

32. When deleting projected lines, if the option to delete a projected line does not appear in the pop-up menu, then the projected line is already deleted even though it still appears in yellow as shown in Figure 28.

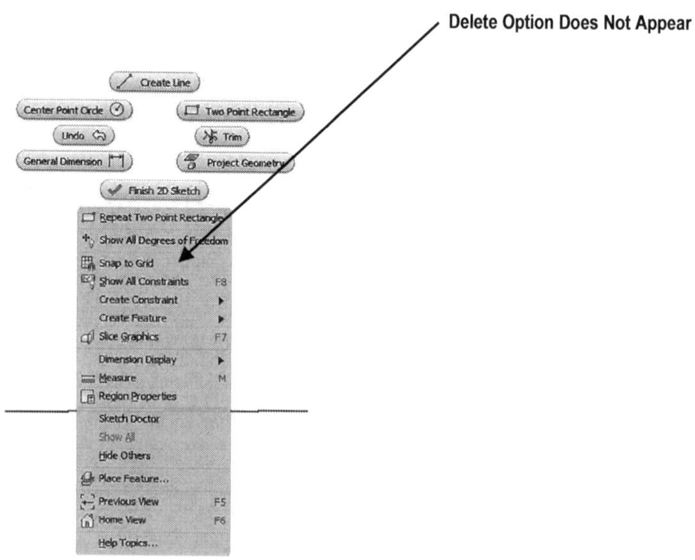

Figure 28

33. Exit out of the Sketch Panel using the Finish 2D Sketch command. Use the Orbit/Rotate command to rotate the part off to the side. Your screen should look similar to Figure 29.

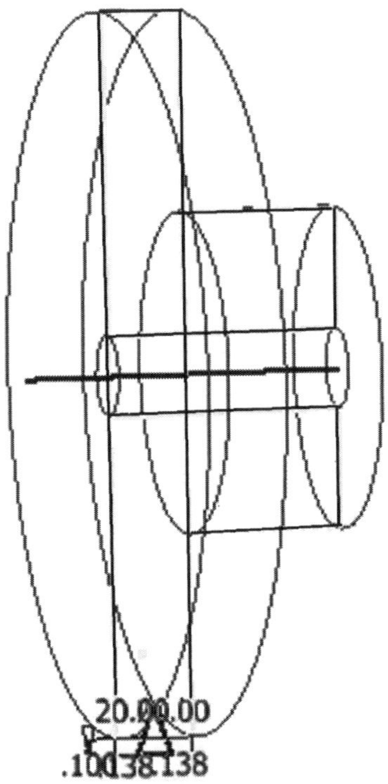

Figure 29

34. Move the cursor to the upper left portion of the screen and left click on the **3D Model** tab. Left click on **Revolve** as shown in Figure 30.

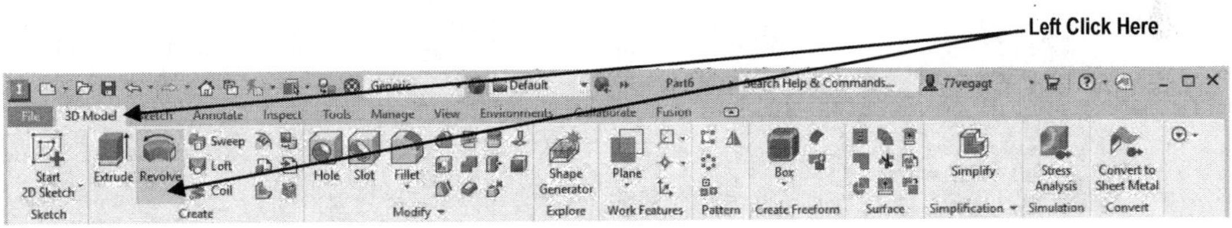

Figure 30

35. The Revolve dialog box will appear. Left click on the **Select Profiles** window. Left click on the triangle created in the Sketch Panel as shown in Figure 31.

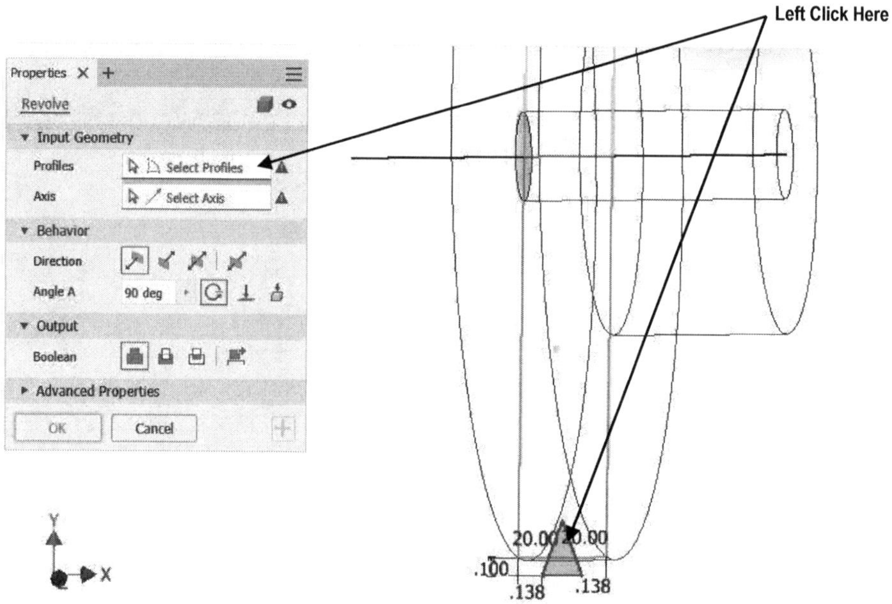

Figure 31

36. Left click on the **Axis** window. Left click on the axis you created. Left click on the "Cut" icon. Left click on **OK** as shown in Figure 32.

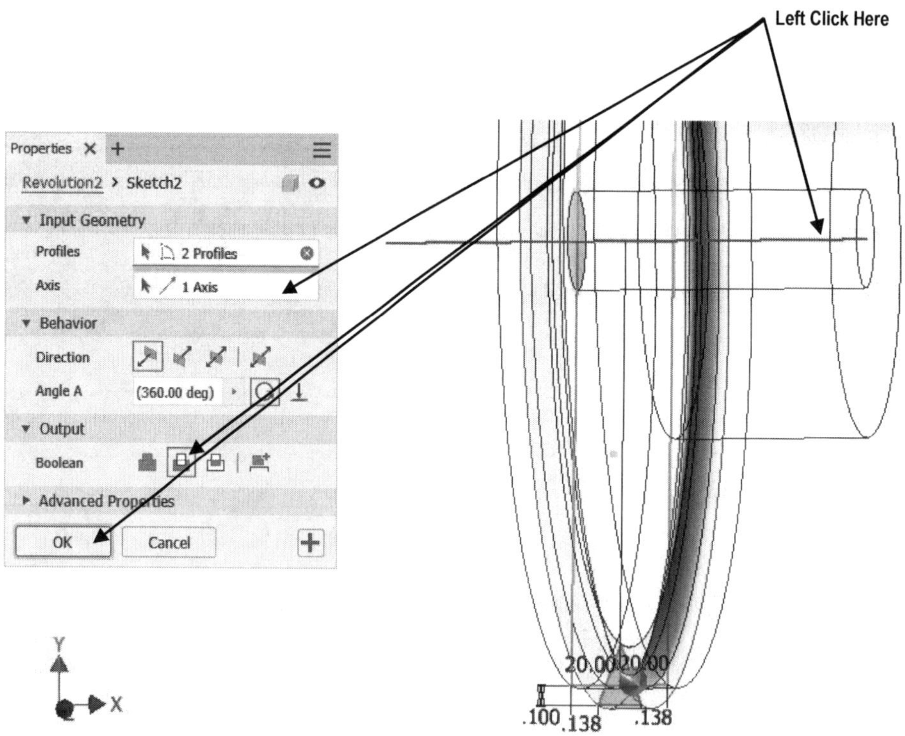

Figure 32

37. Your screen should look similar to Figure 33.

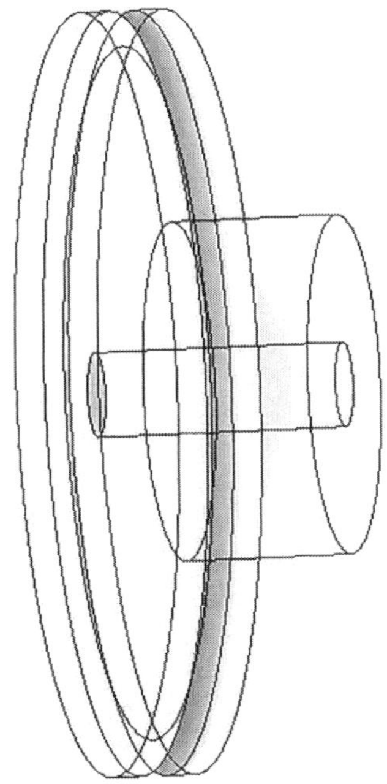

Figure 33

38. Move the cursor to the upper middle portion of the screen and left click on the **View** tab. Left click on the arrow under "Visual Style." A drop-down menu will appear. Left click on **Shaded with Edges** as shown in Figure 34.

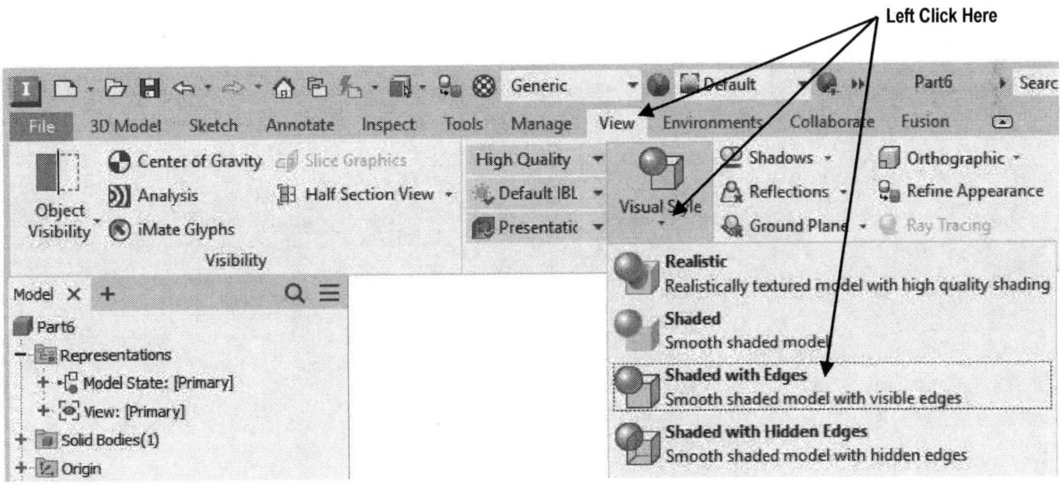

Figure 34

39. Your screen should look similar to Figure 35.

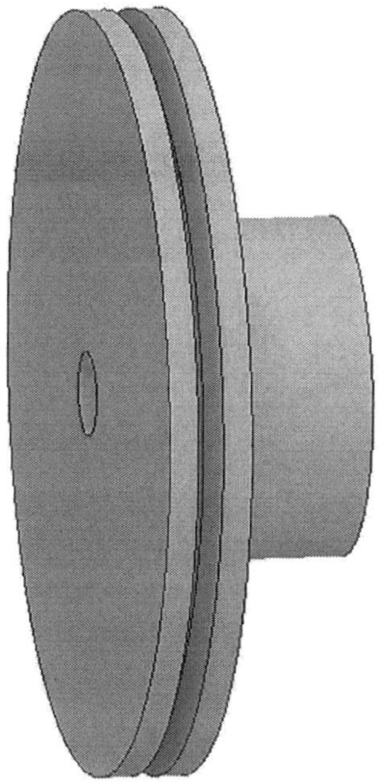

Figure 35

Create a hole in the 3D Model Panel using the Extrude command

40. Rotate the part around using the **Home View** command. Move the cursor to the surface of the part causing the edge to become highlighted. After the edge becomes highlighted, right click on the surface as shown in Figure 36.

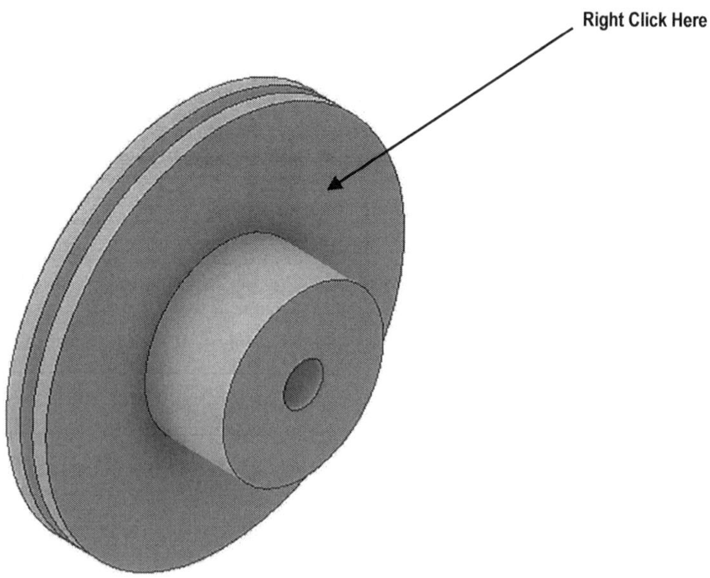

Figure 36

41. The surface will become highlighted and a pop-up menu will appear. Left click on **New Sketch** as shown in Figure 37.

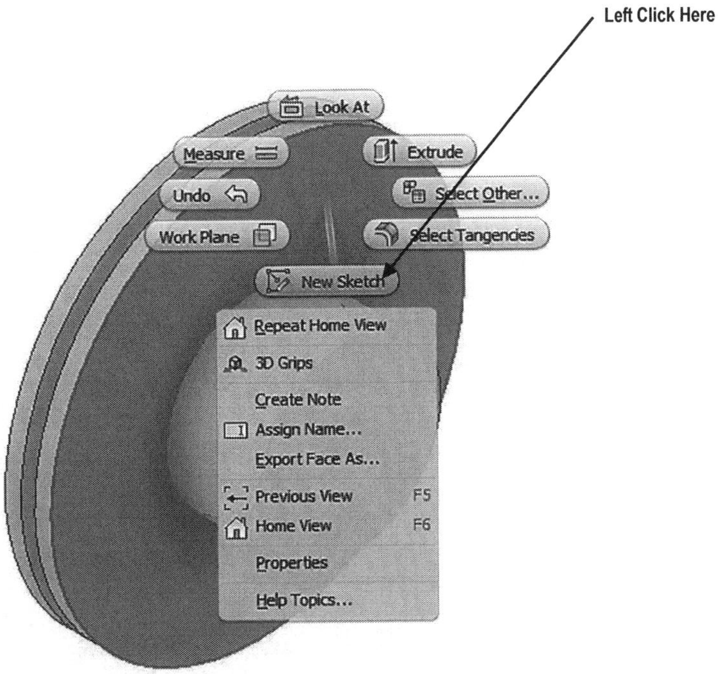

Figure 37

42. Inventor will begin a new sketch on the selected surface. Inventor will turn the view to the Front. You will need to use the **Home View** command to provide an isometric view. Your screen should look similar to Figure 38.

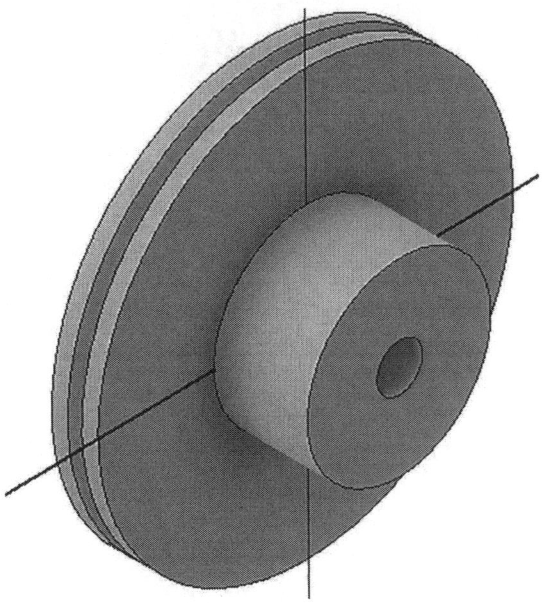

Figure 38

43. To gain a better look at the selected surface, move the cursor to the top center portion of the screen and left click on the **View** tab. Left click on the **Face View/Look At** icon. You can also left click on the “Orbit” command.

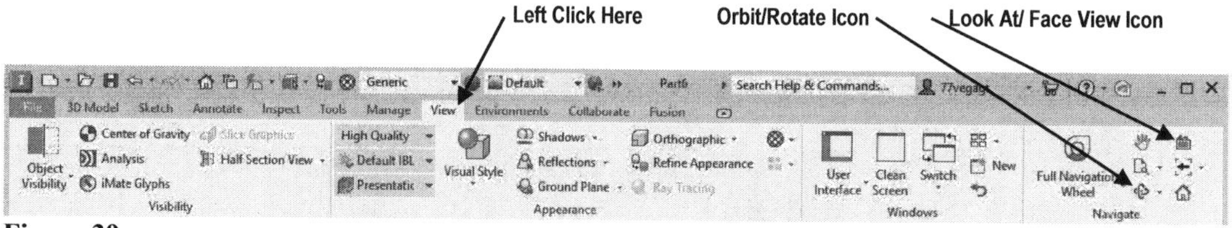

Figure 39

44. Left click on the surface; the new sketch will be constructed as shown in Figure 40.

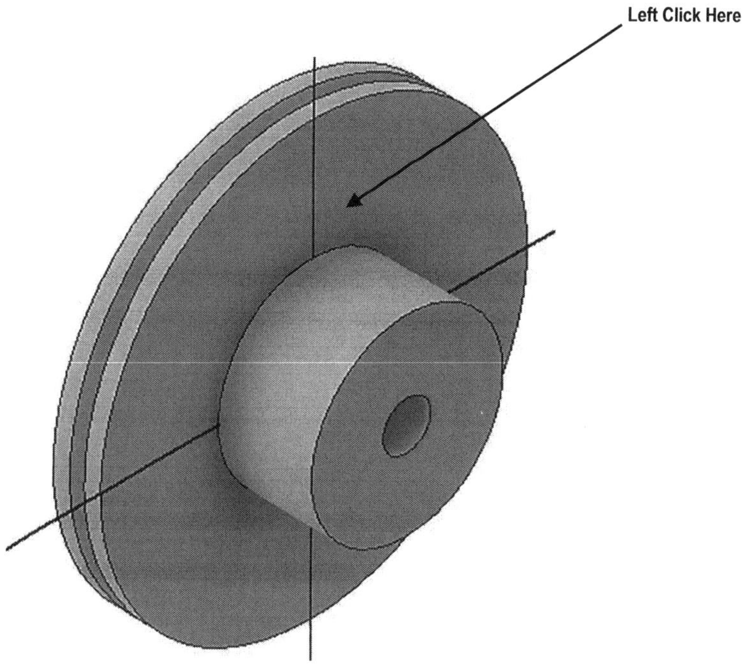

Figure 40

45. Inventor will rotate the part to provide a perpendicular view of the selected surface as shown in Figure 41.

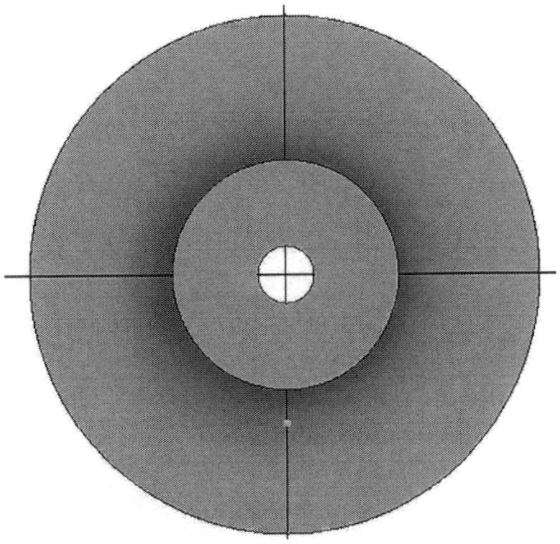

Figure 41

46. Move the cursor to the upper left portion of the screen and left click on the **Sketch** tab. Left click on **Line** as shown in Figure 42.

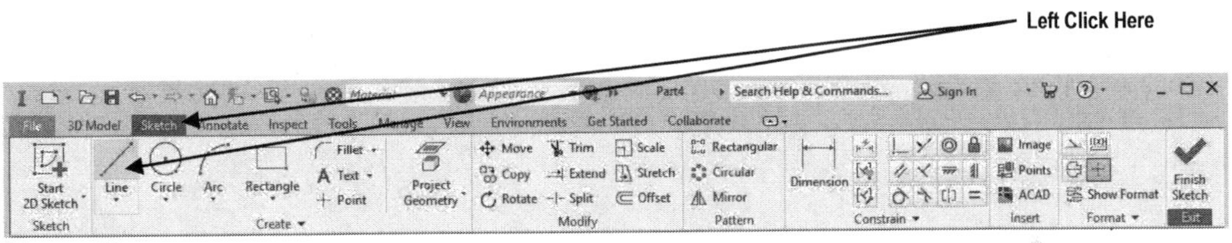

Figure 42

47. Left click on the center of the hole. Ensure that a green dot appears as shown in Figure 43.

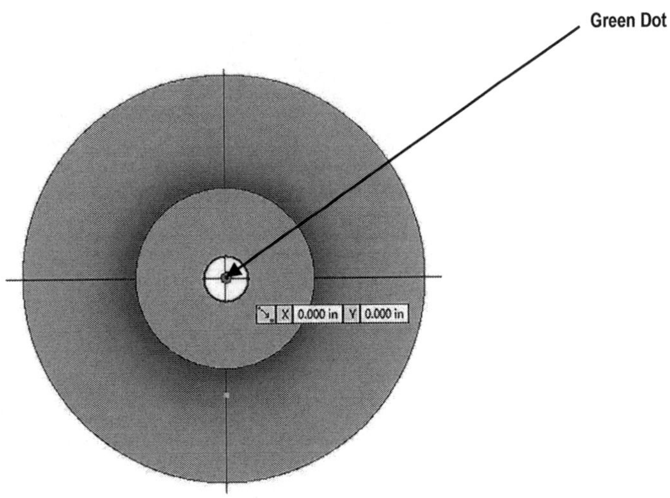

Figure 43

48. Move the cursor straight up and left click as shown in Figure 44.

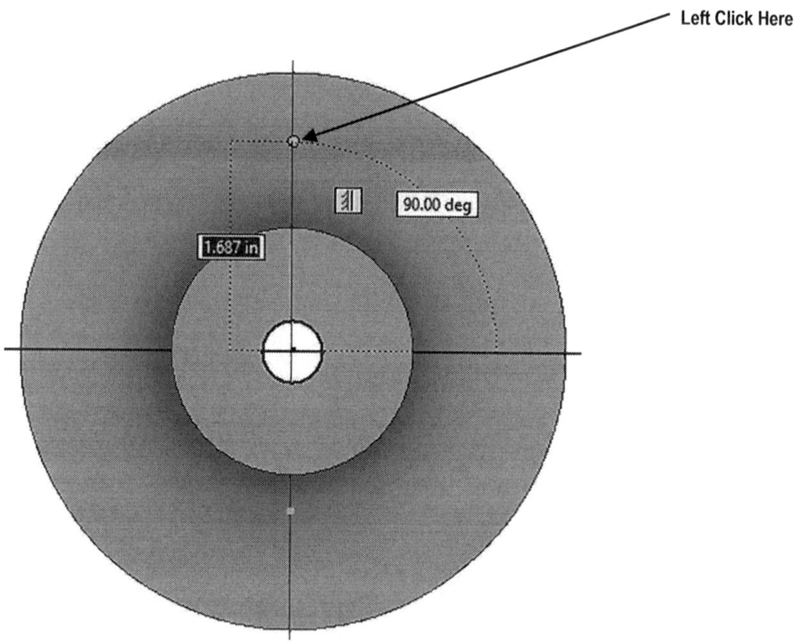

Figure 44

49. Right click. A pop-up menu will appear. Left click on **OK** as shown in Figure 45.

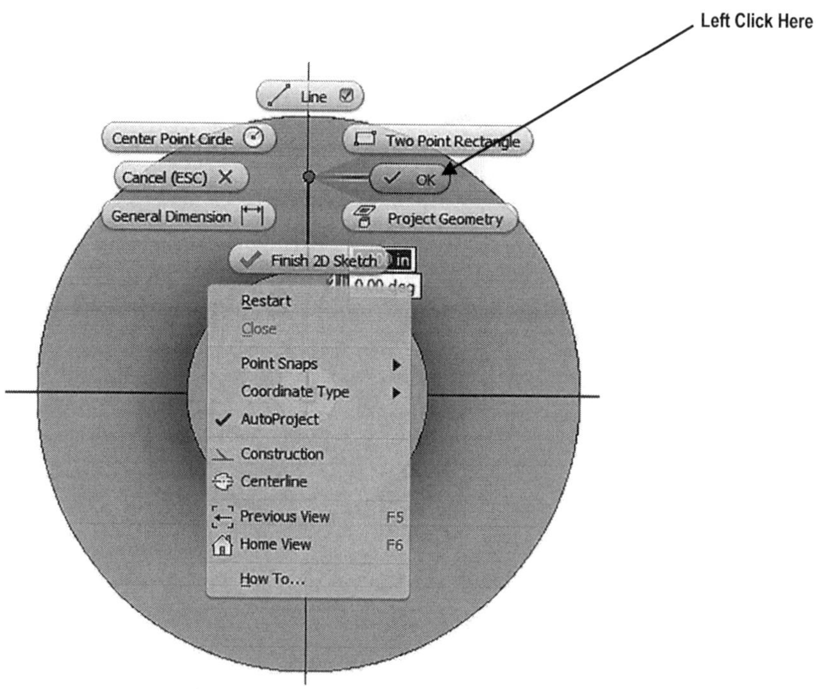

Figure 45

50. Move the cursor to the upper middle portion of the screen and left click on **Dimension** as shown in Figure 46.

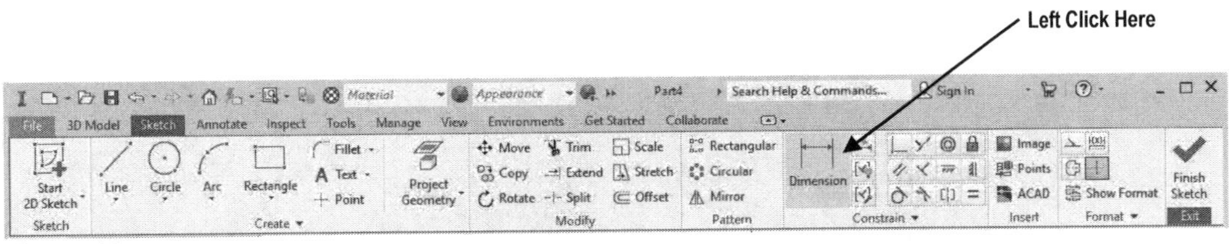

Figure 46

51. After selecting **Dimension** move the cursor to the line that was just drawn. The line will turn red as shown in Figure 47. Select the line by left clicking anywhere on the line **<u>or</u>** on each of the end points. To use the end points of the line, move the cursor over one of the end points. A small red square will appear. Left click once and move the cursor to the other end point. After the red square appears, left click once. The dimension will be attached to the cursor.

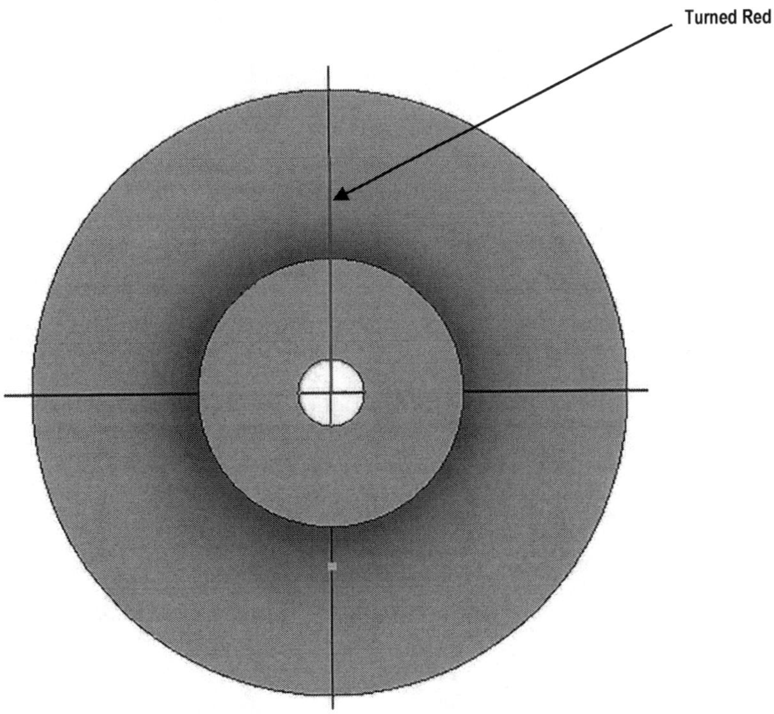

Figure 47

52. Move the cursor to the side. The actual dimension of the line will appear as shown in Figure 48.

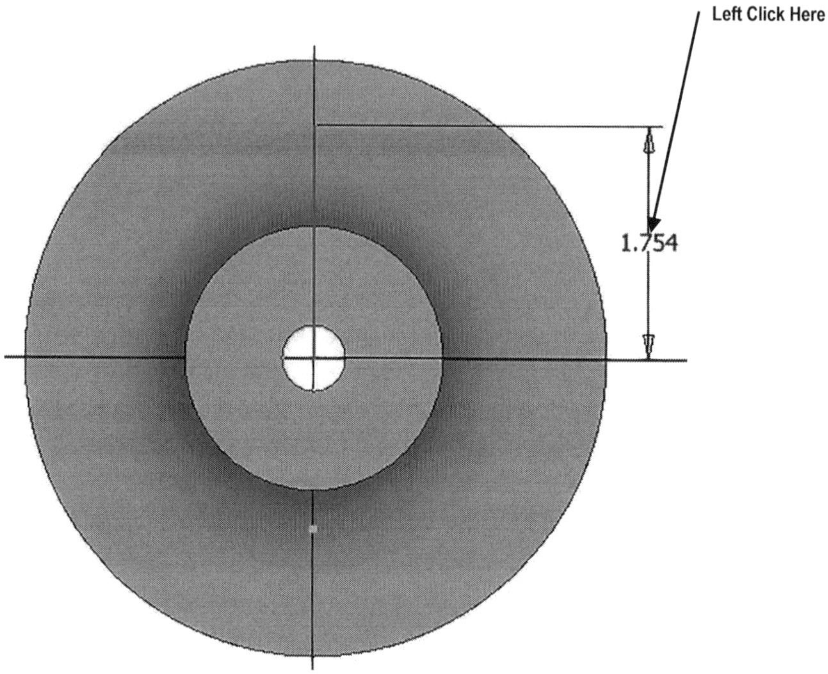

Figure 48

53. Move the cursor to where the dimension will be placed and left click once. While the dimension is still in highlight, left click once. The Edit Dimension dialog box will appear as shown in Figure 49.

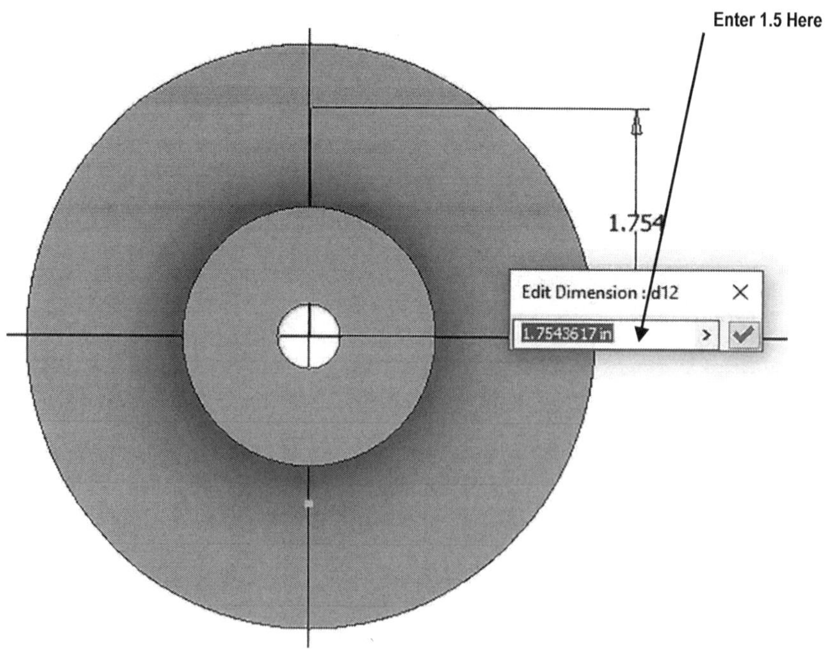

Figure 49

54. To edit the dimension, enter **1.5** in the Edit Dimension dialog box (while the current dimension is highlighted) and press **Enter** on the keyboard.

55. The dimension of the line will become 1.5 inches as shown in Figure 50. Use the Zoom icons to zoom out if necessary.

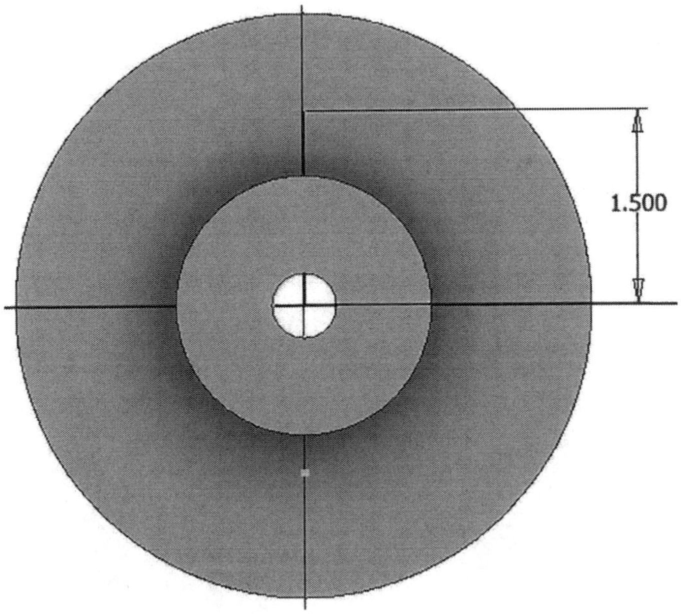

Figure 50

56. Move the cursor to the upper left portion of the screen and left click on **Circle** as shown in Figure 51.

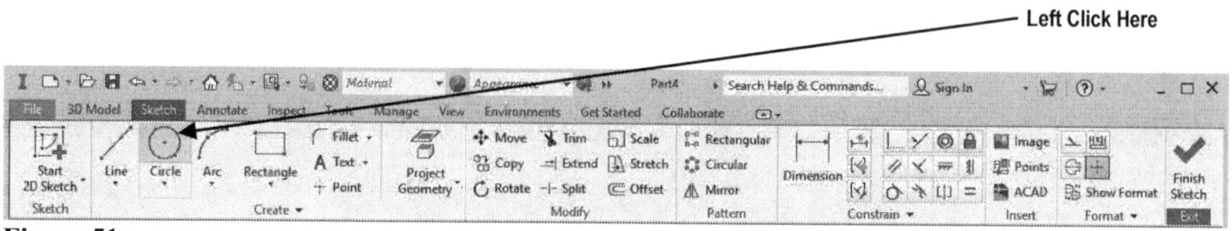

Figure 51

57. Left click on the end point of the line as shown in Figure 52.

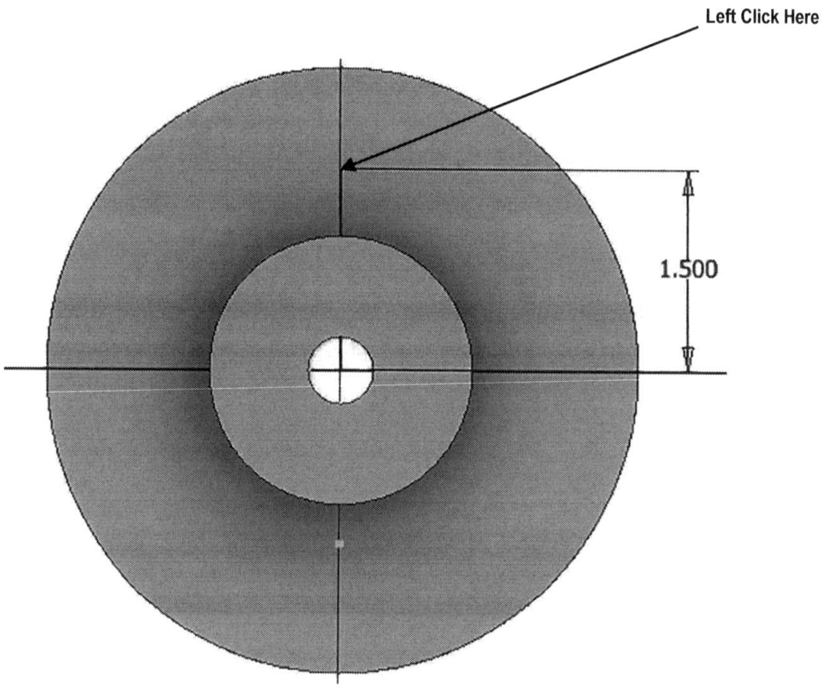

Figure 52

58. Move the cursor out to the right to create a circle as shown in Figure 53.

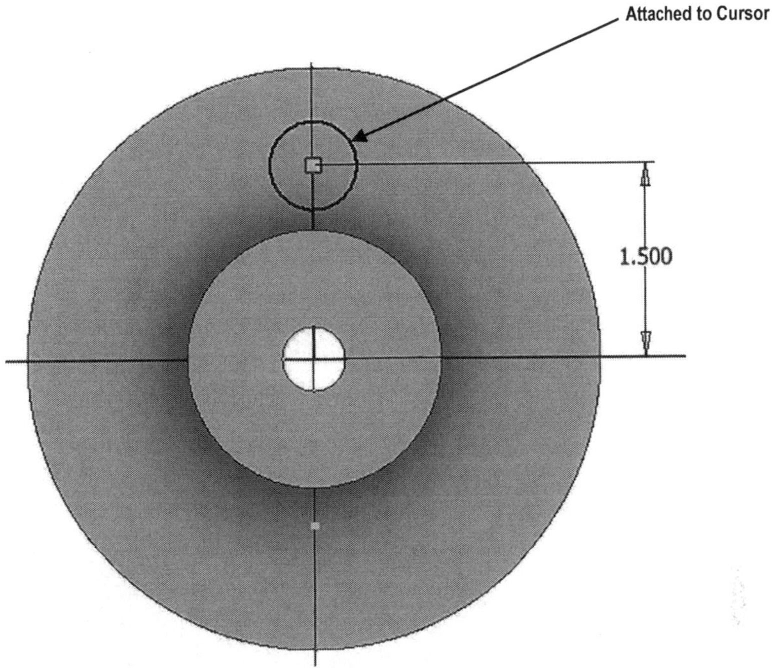

Figure 53

59. Left click as shown in Figure 54. Press the **Esc** key once.

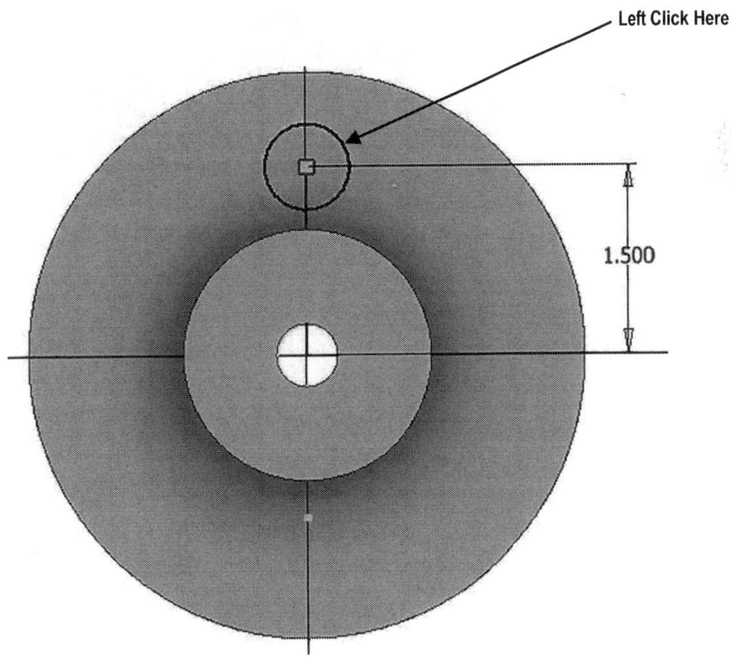

Figure 54

60. Move the cursor to the upper middle portion of the screen and left click on **Dimension** as shown in Figure 55.

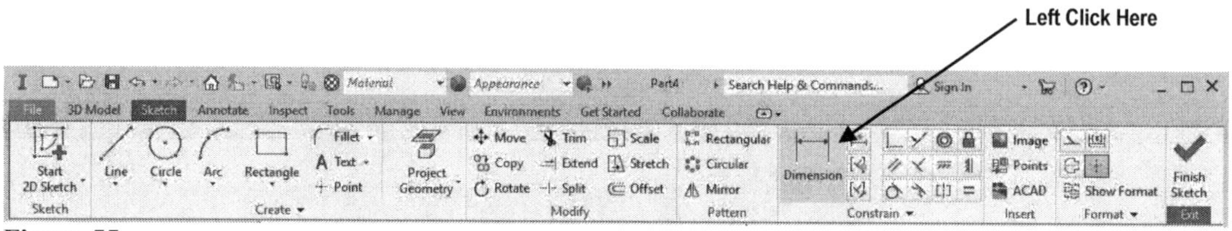

Figure 55

61. After selecting **Dimension** move the cursor to the edge of the circle that was just drawn. The circle will become highlighted. Select the circle by left clicking anywhere on the circle (not the center) as shown in Figure 56. The dimension will be attached to the cursor.

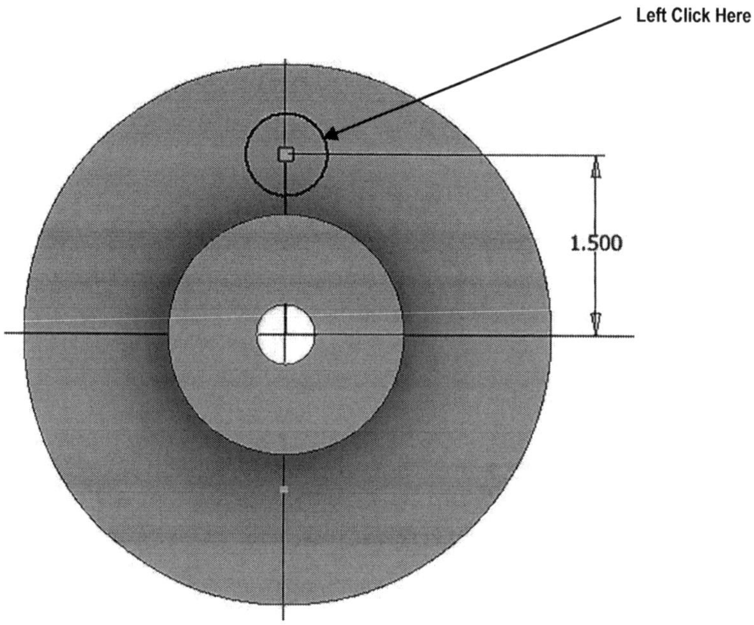

Figure 56

62. Move the cursor to the side. The actual diameter of the circle will appear as shown in Figure 57.

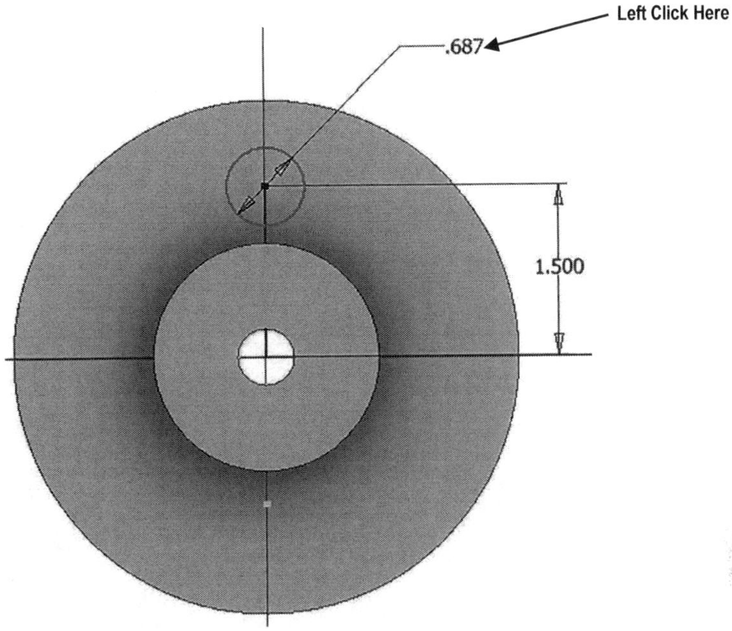

Figure 57

63. Move the cursor to where the dimension will be placed and left click once. While the dimension is still attached to the cursor, left click once. The Edit Dimension dialog box will appear as shown in Figure 58.

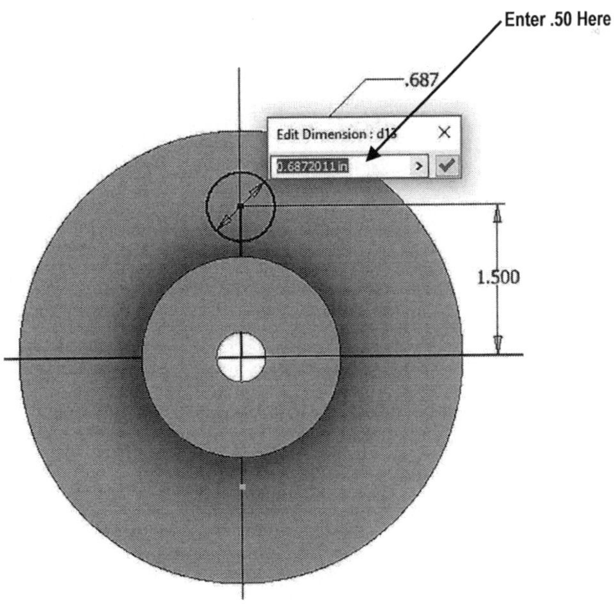

Figure 58

64. To edit the dimension, enter **.50** in the Edit Dimension dialog box (while the current dimension is highlighted) and press **Enter** on the keyboard. Press the **Esc** key once or twice.

65. The diameter of the circle will become .50 inches as shown in Figure 59. Use the Zoom icons to zoom out if necessary.

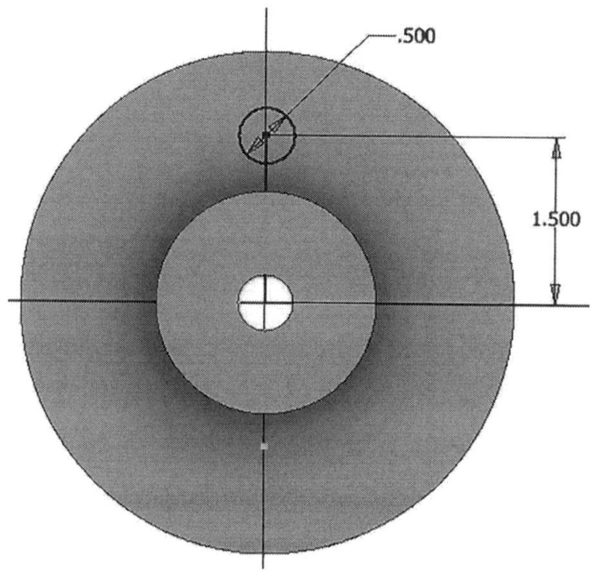

Figure 59

66. Move the cursor to the line that was used to locate the center of the circle. The line will become highlighted as shown in Figure 60.

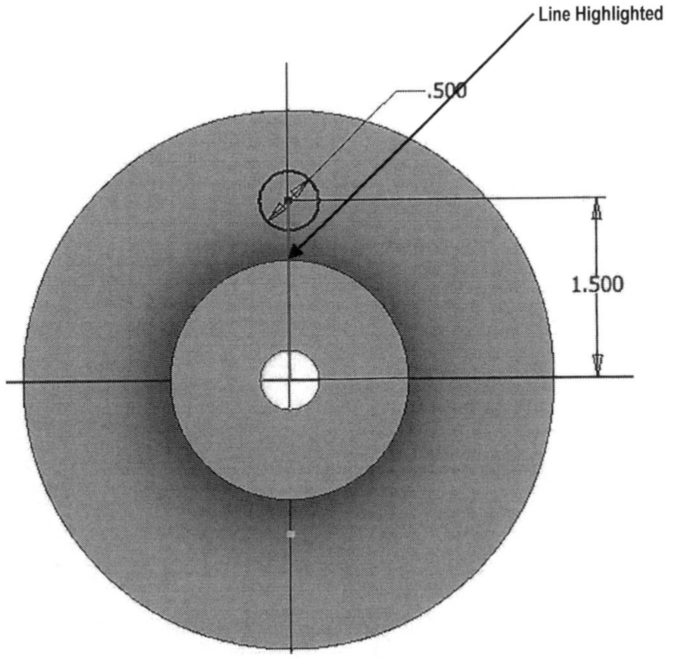

Figure 60

67. Right click on the line once it becomes highlighted. A pop-up menu will appear. Left click on **Delete** as shown in Figure 61.

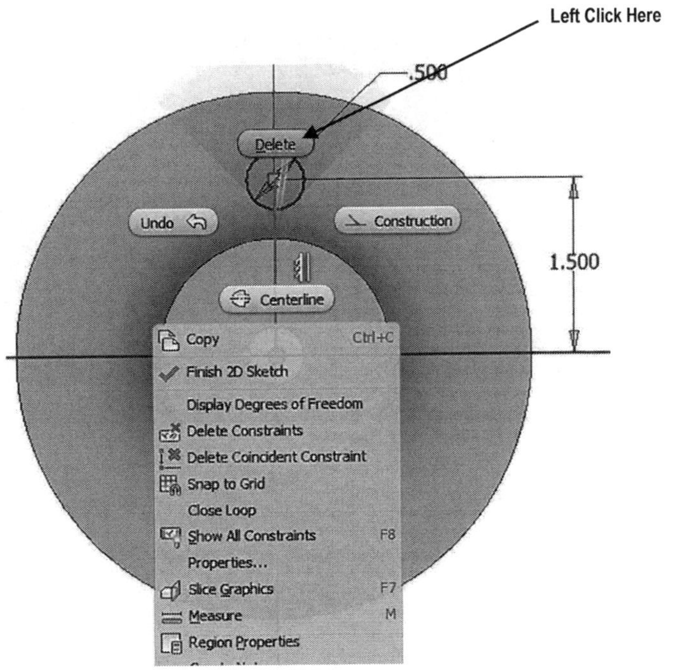

Figure 61

68. If needed, press **Esc** once or twice, or right click around the drawing. A pop-up menu will appear. Left click on **OK** or **Cancel (Esc)** as shown in Figure 62.

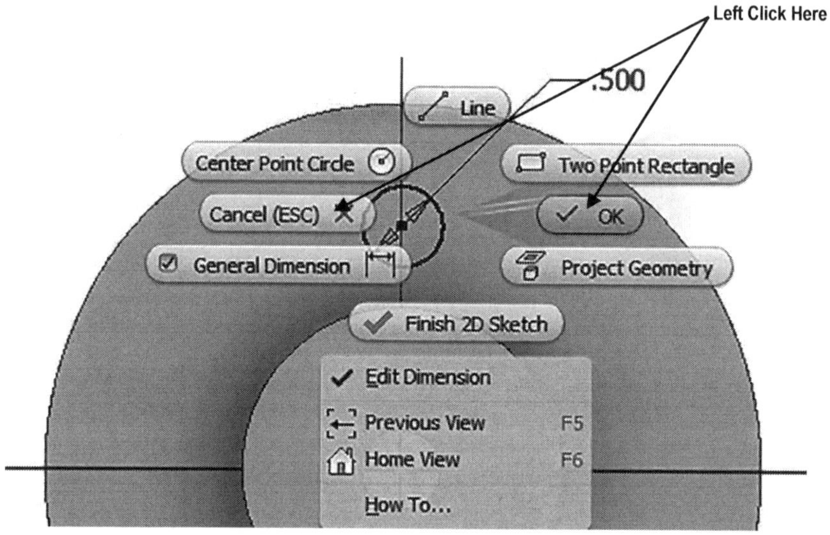

Figure 62

69. After you have verified that no commands are active, right click anywhere on the sketch. A pop-up menu will appear. Left click on **Finish 2D Sketch** as shown in Figure 63.

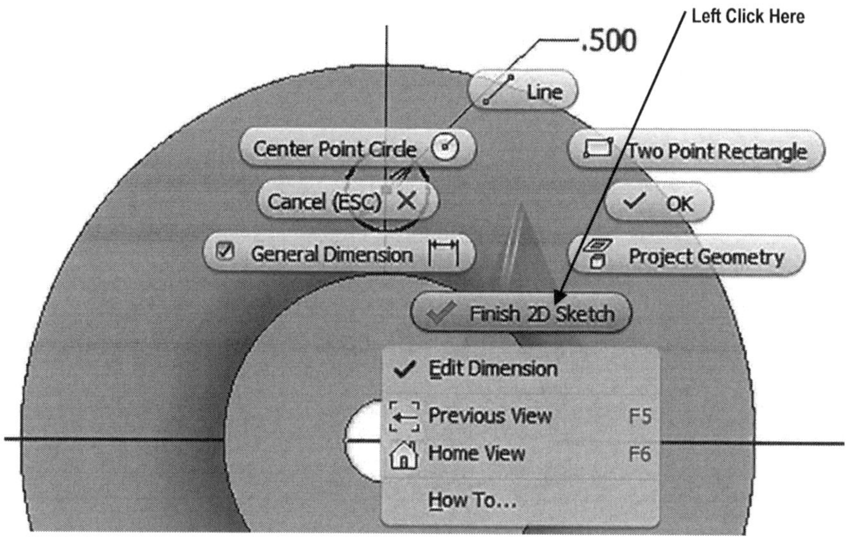

Figure 63

70. Inventor is now out of the Sketch Panel and into the 3D Model Panel. Notice that the commands at the top of the screen are now different. Your screen should look similar to Figure 64.

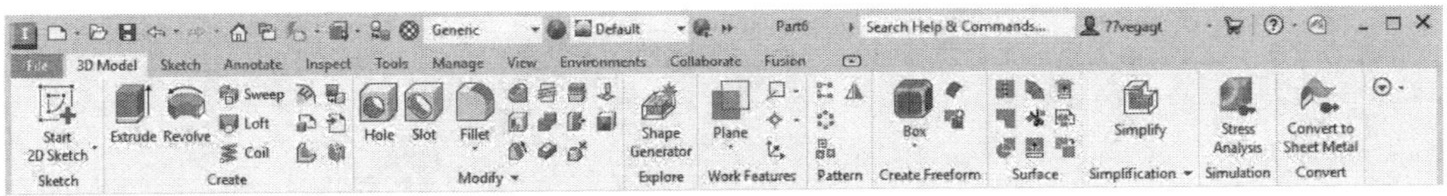

Figure 64

71. If needed, right click around the part. A pop-up menu will appear. Left click on **Home View** as shown in Figure 65.

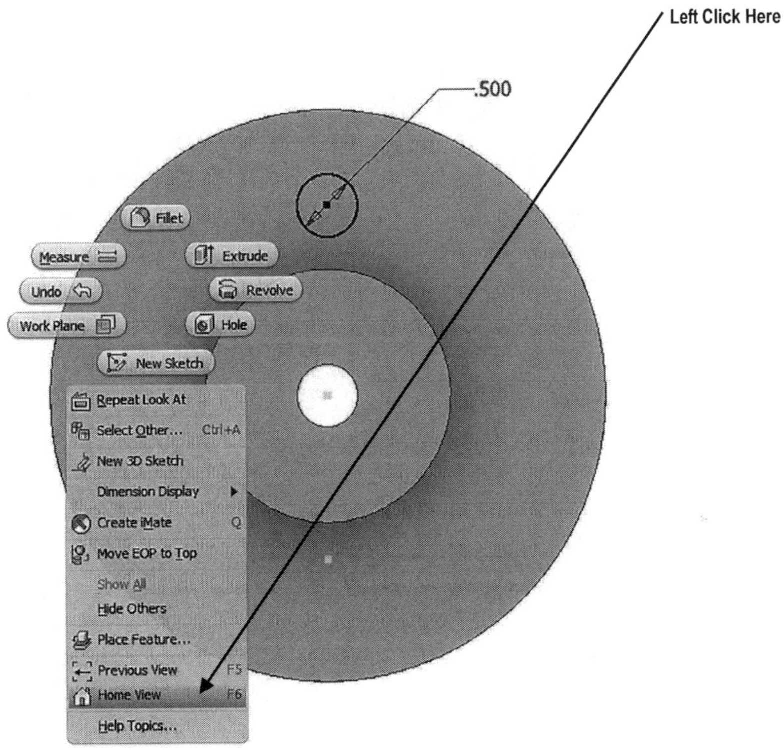

Figure 65

72. The view will become Isometric as shown in Figure 66.

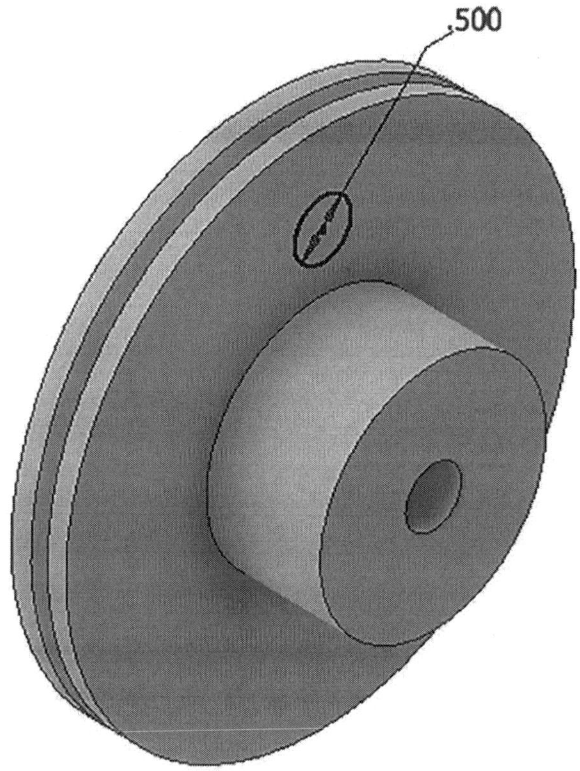

Figure 66

73. Move the cursor to the upper left portion of the screen and left click on **Extrude**. The Extrude dialog box will appear as shown in Figure 67.

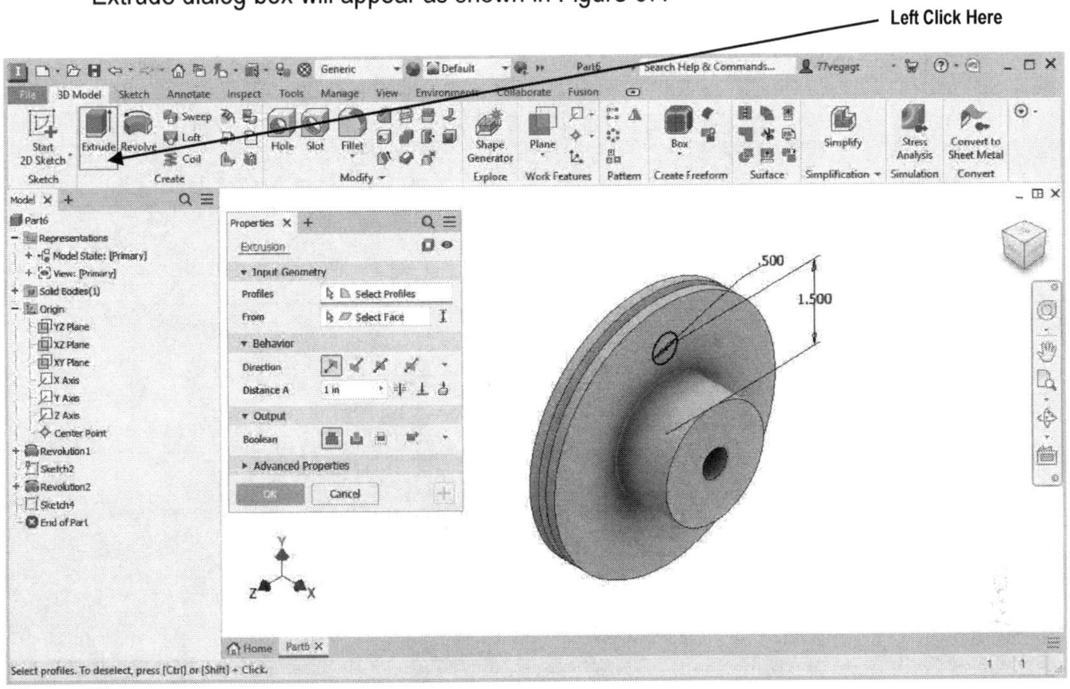

Figure 67

74. Enter **.75** for the Distance. Move the cursor to the inside of the circle causing it to turn red as shown in Figure 68.

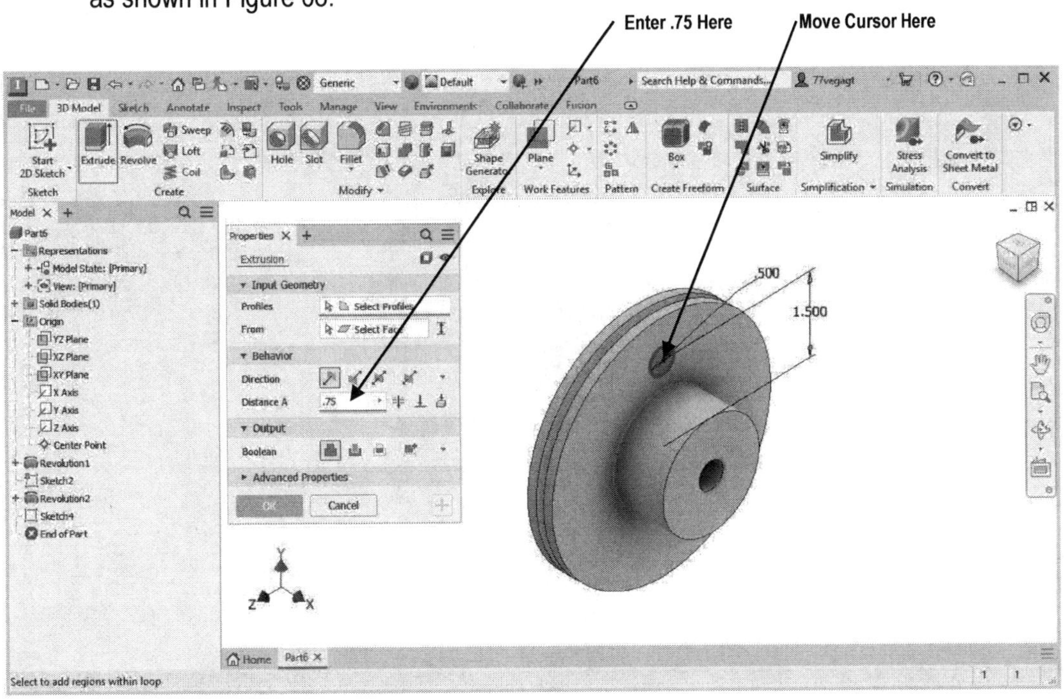

Figure 68

75. After the hole turns red, left click once. Select the "Cut" icon in the Extrude dialog box. Select the "Direction" icon to ensure the extrusion occurs in the right direction and left click on **OK** as shown in Figure 69.

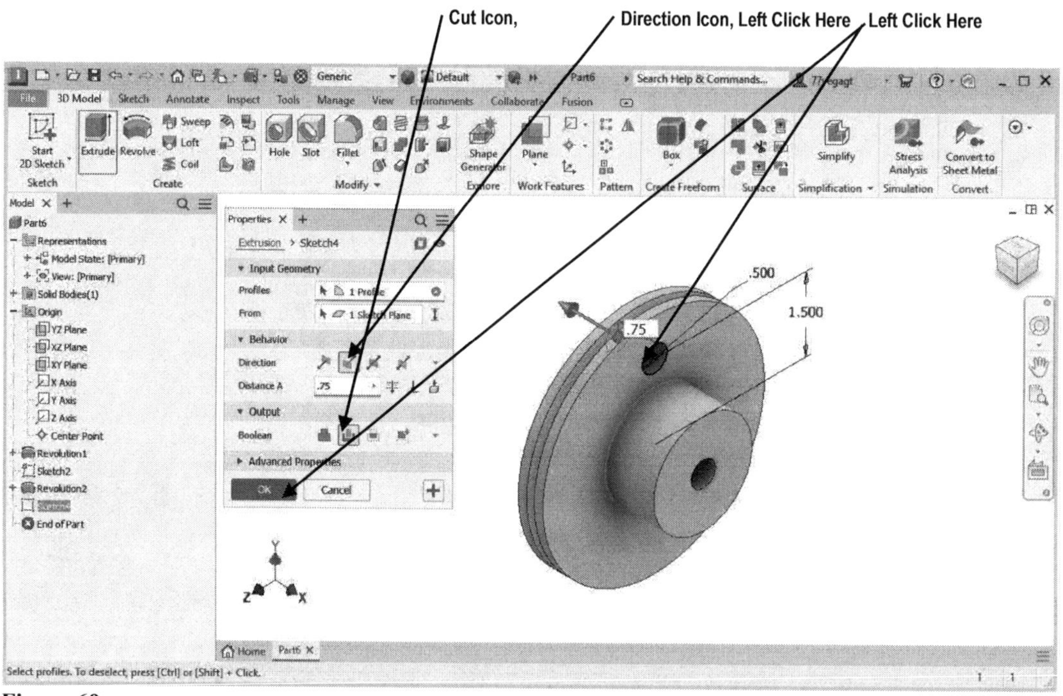

Figure 69

76. Your screen should look similar to Figure 70.

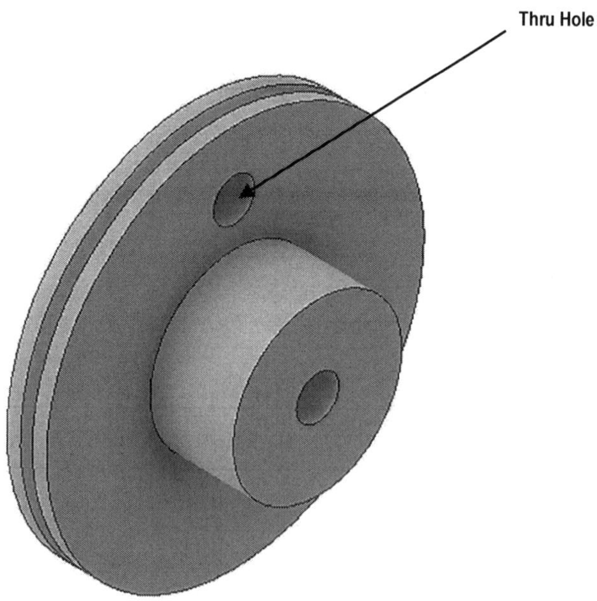

Figure 70

Create a series of holes using the Circular Pattern command

77. Move the cursor to the upper right portion of the screen and left click on the **Circular Pattern** icon. The Circular Pattern dialog box will appear as shown in Figure 71.

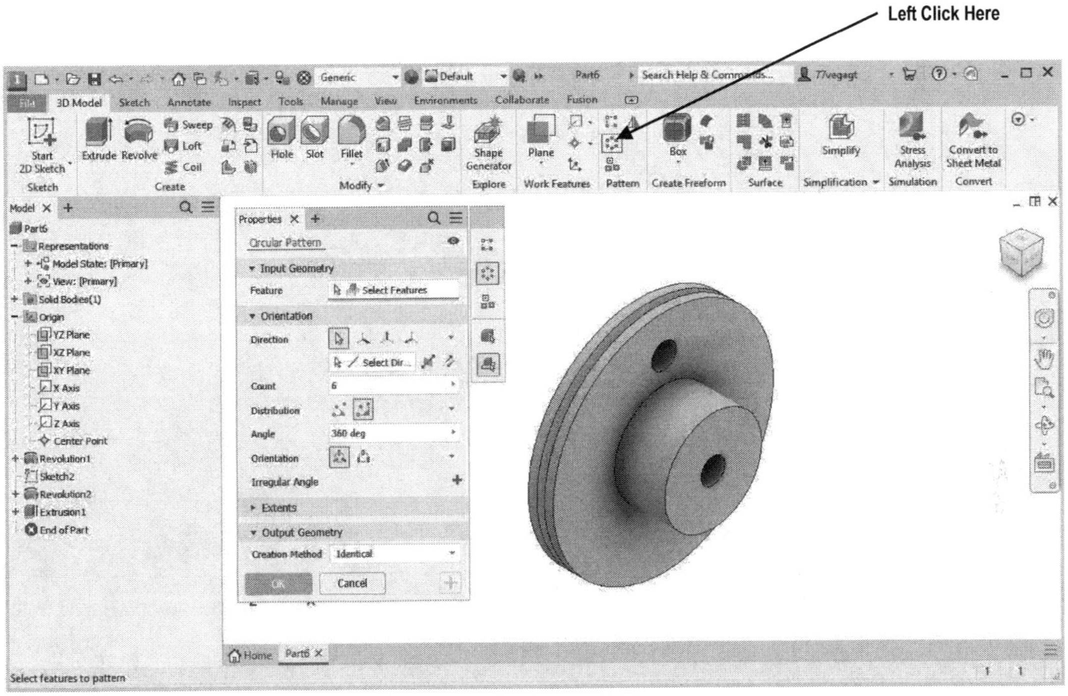

Figure 71

78. Move the cursor to the center of the hole causing red dashed lines to appear, and left click once. *The part must be displayed in Home/Isometric view for Inventor to find the hole as shown in Figure 72.*

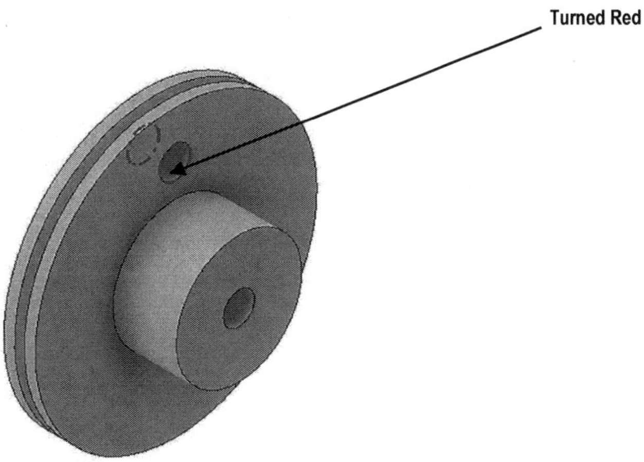

Figure 72

79. Left click on the **Rotation Axis** icon as shown in Figure 73.

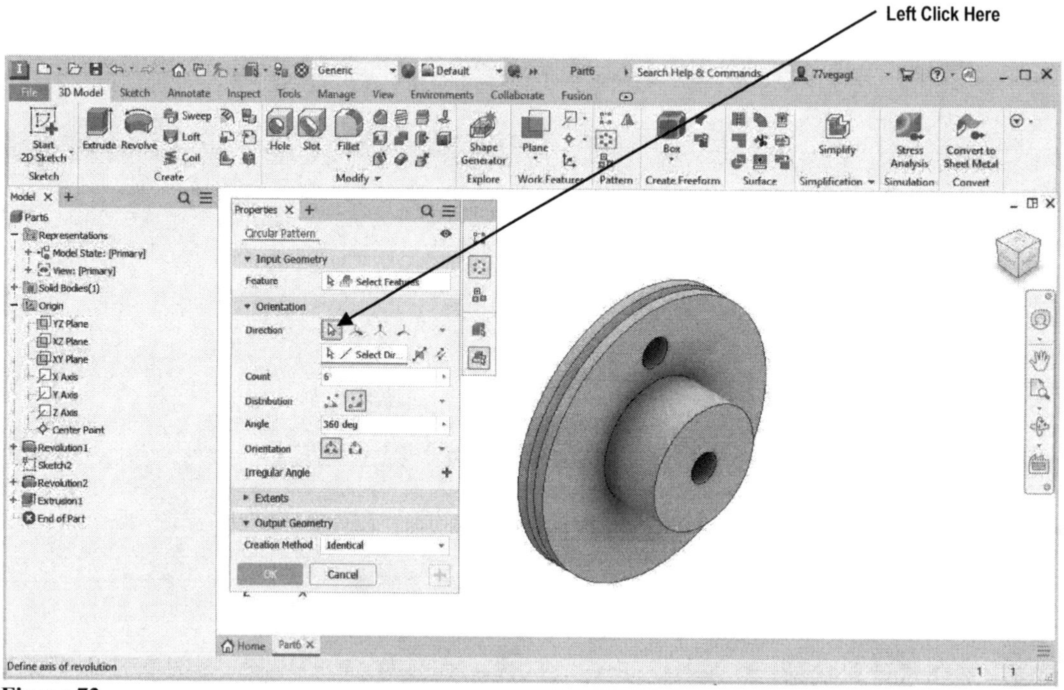

Figure 73

80. Move the cursor to the edge of the part. The edges will turn red as shown in Figure 74.

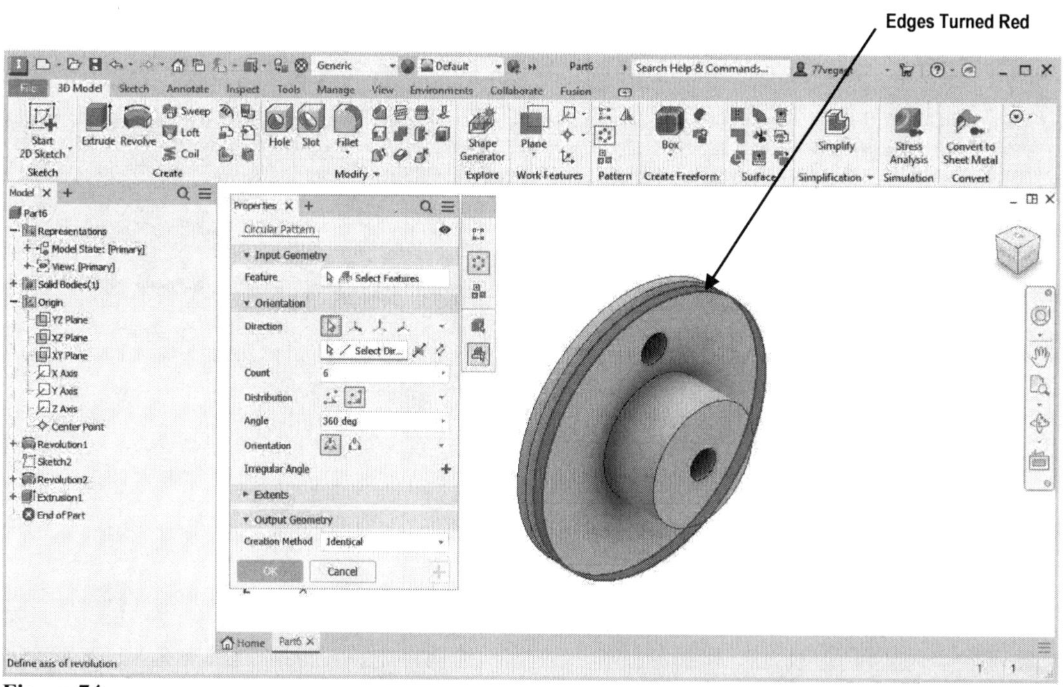

Figure 74

81. After the edge turns red, left click once. Inventor will provide a preview of the hole pattern as shown in Figure 75.

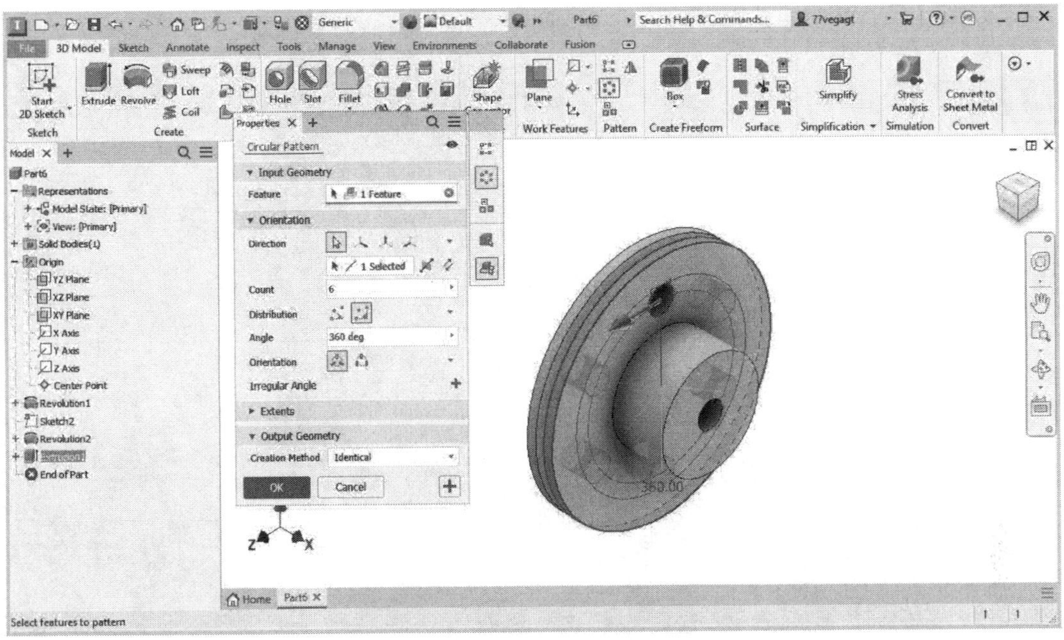

Figure 75

82. There are options in the Circular Pattern dialog box that are used for dictating the number of holes to be produced and the number of degrees between the holes. Verify that **6** is displayed for the number of holes. Verify that **360 deg** is displayed for the number of degrees. Left click on **OK** as shown in Figure 76.

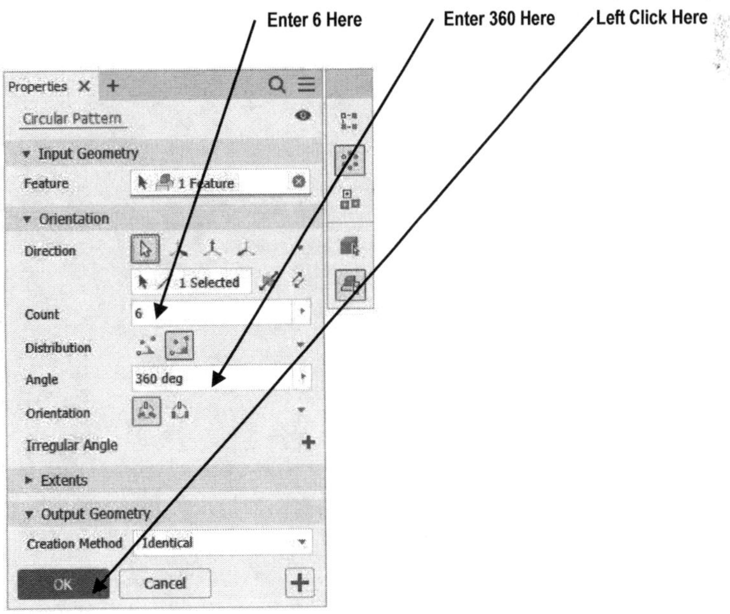

Figure 76

83. Your screen should look similar to Figure 77.

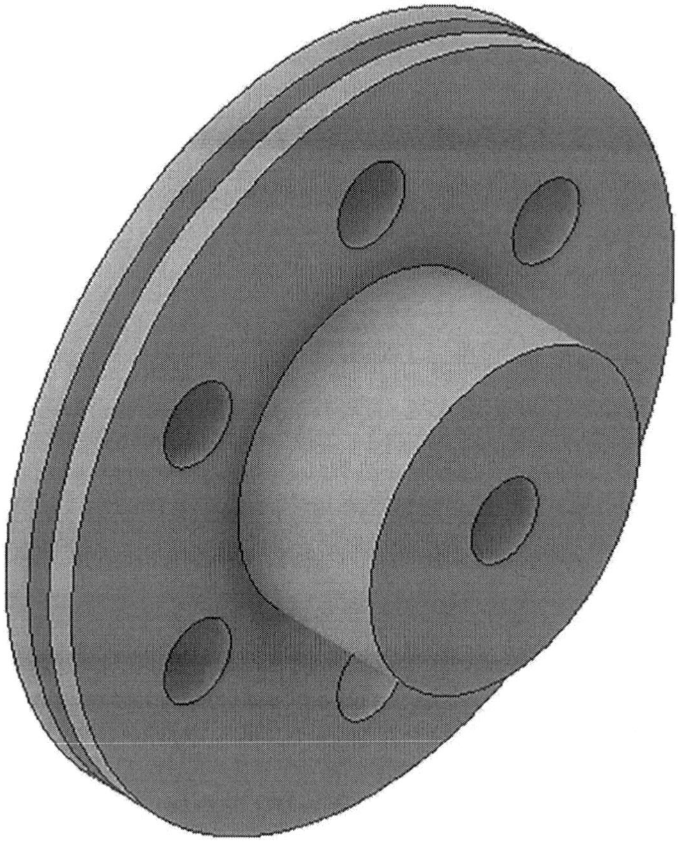

Figure 77

Chapter Problems

Use the Revolve and Revolve Cut Commands to complete the following.

Problem 2-1

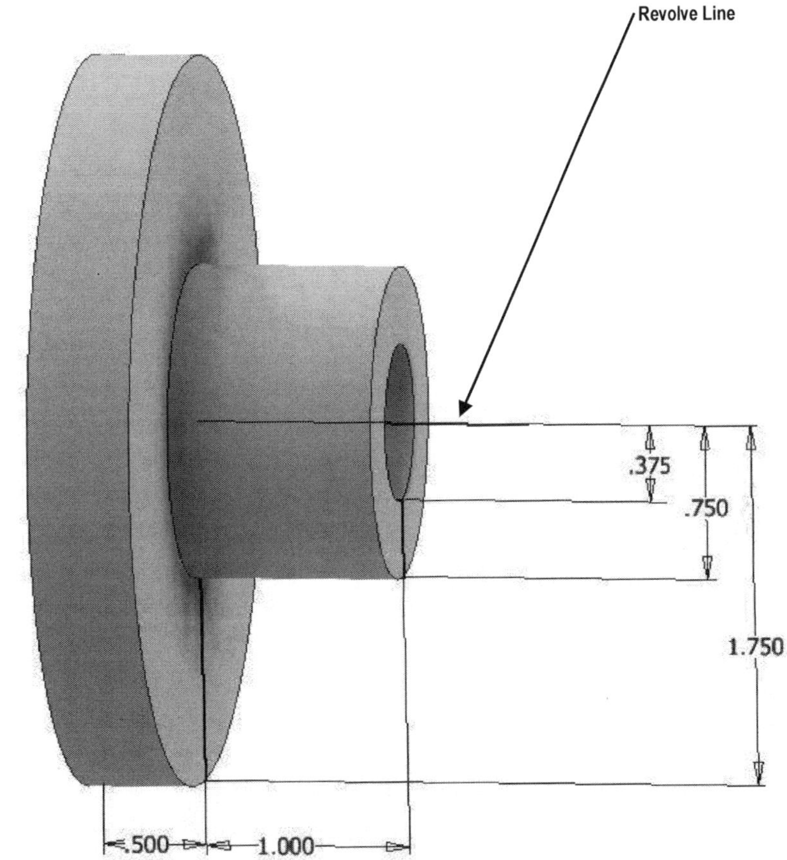

Problem 2-2

Hint: Create the solid revolve and then use the Revolve Cut command to create the groove

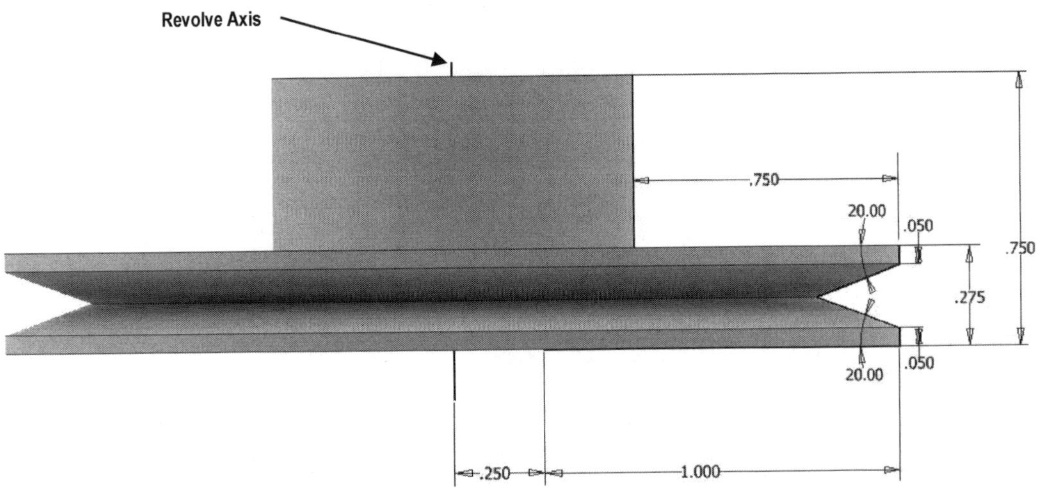

Problem 2-3

Hint: Create the solid revolve and then use the Revolve Cut command to create the groove with 8 .125 Holes Equally Spaced on 1 inch diameter center circle.

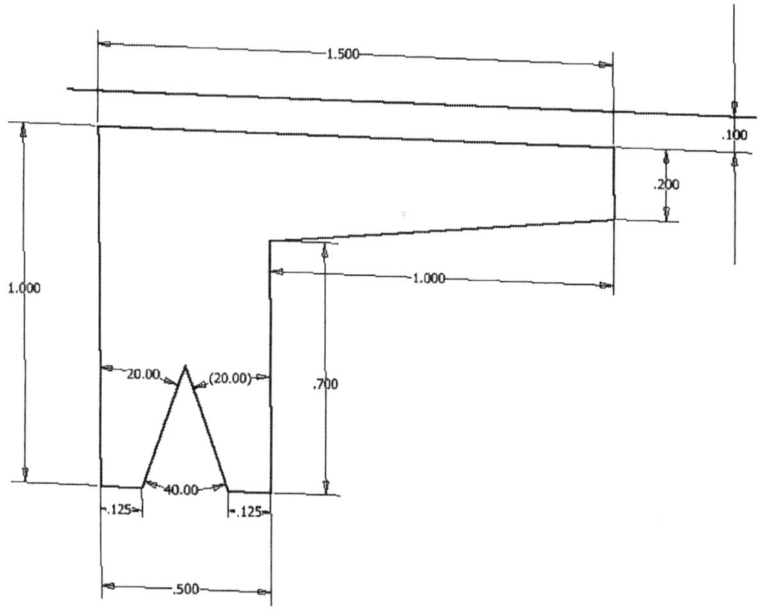

Problem 2-4

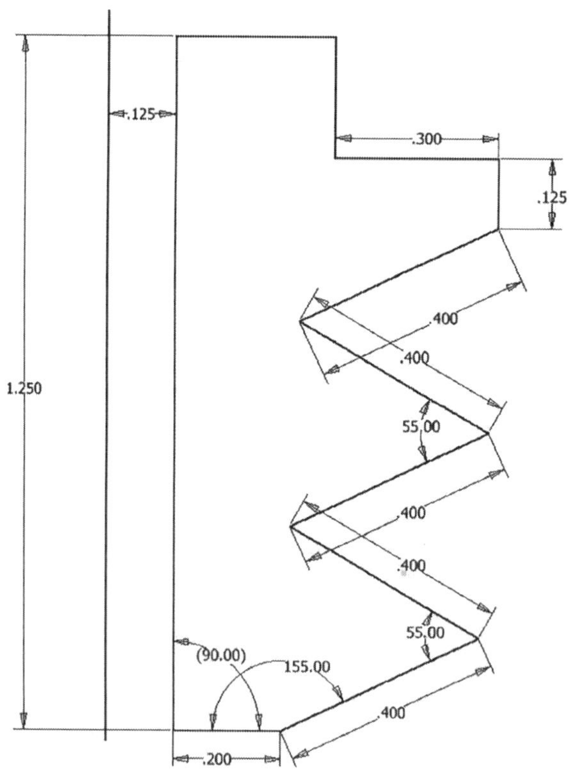

Problem 2-5

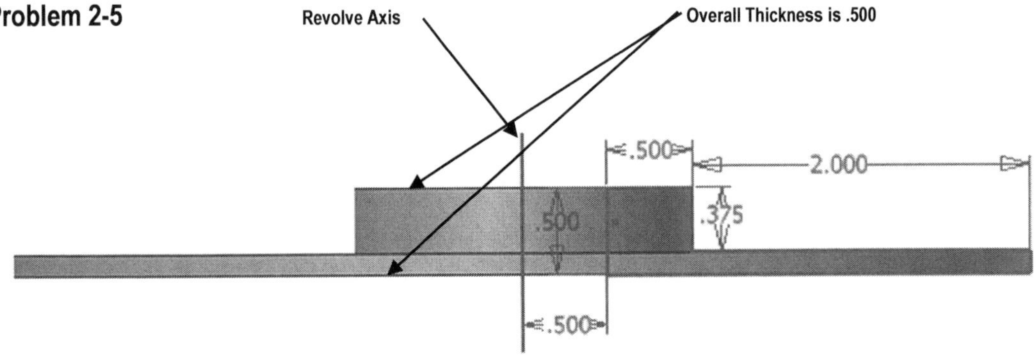

Problem 2-6

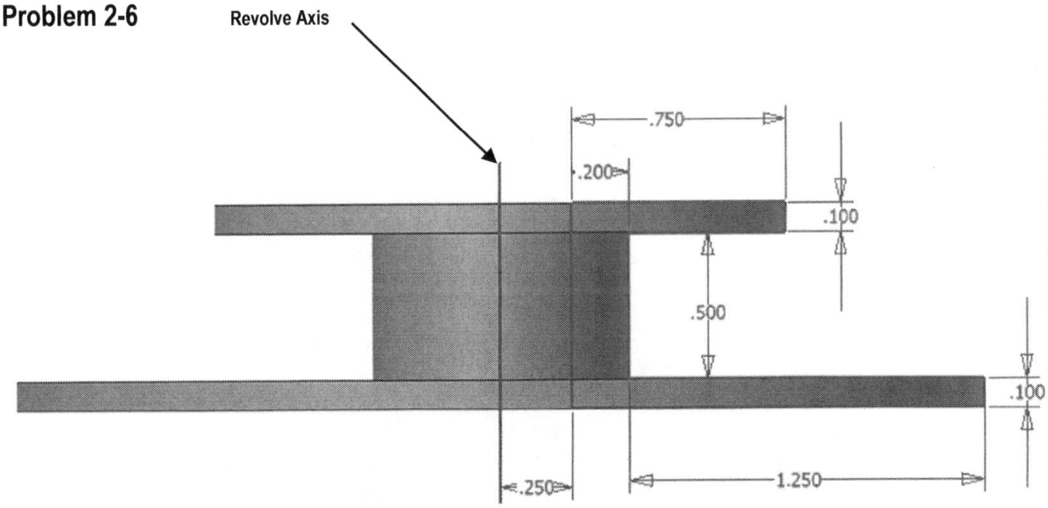

Problem 2-7

Hint Sketch

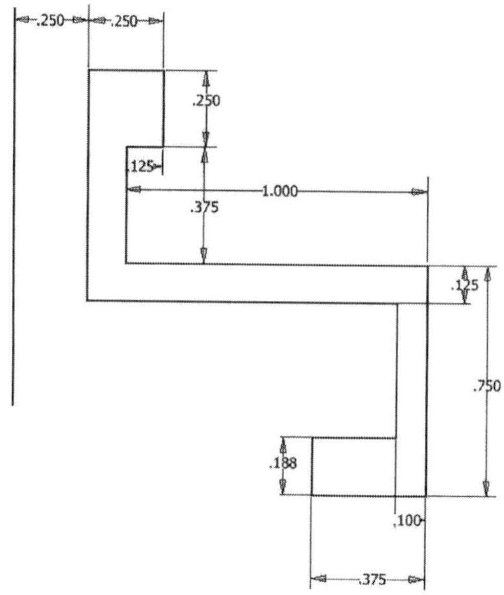

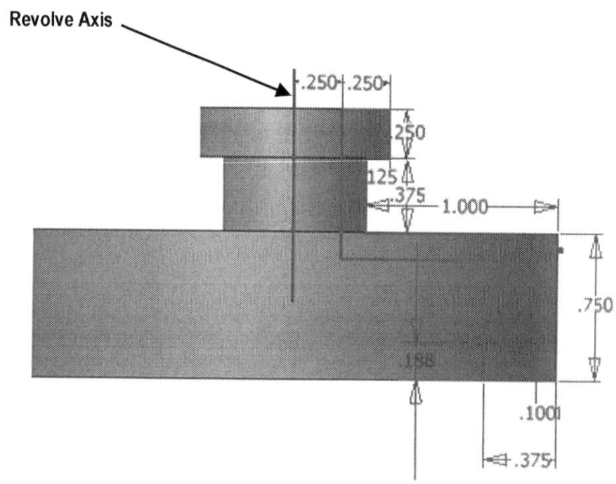

Problem 2-8

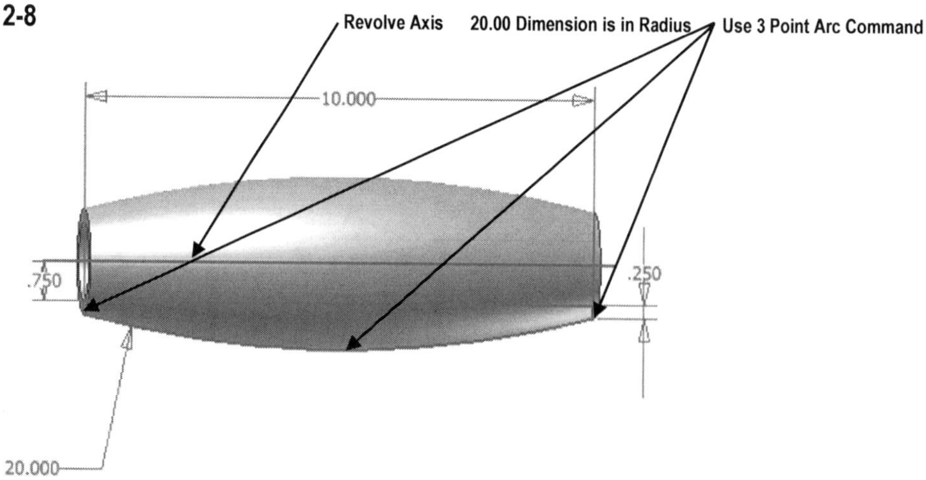

Problem 2-9

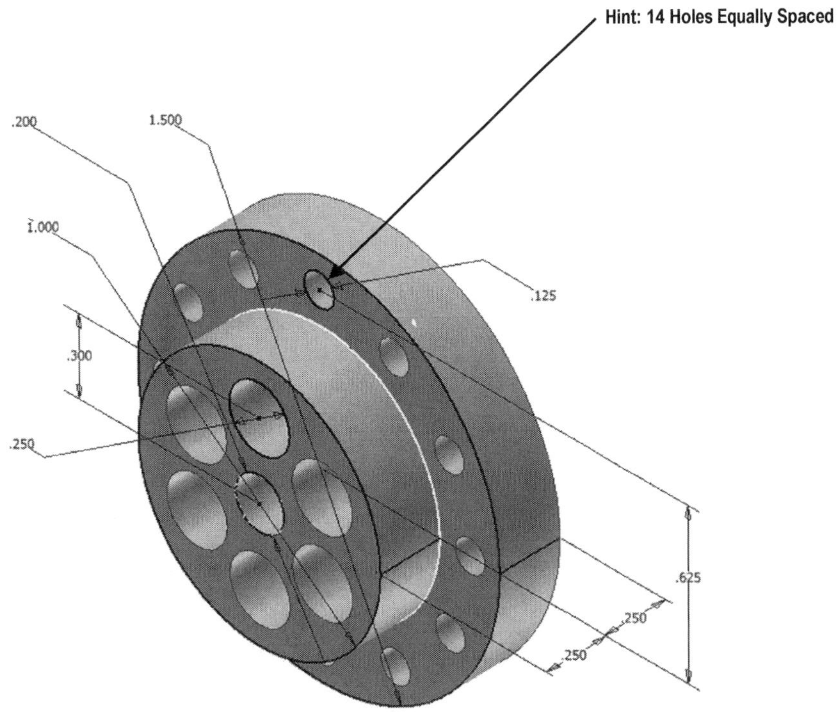

Problem 2-10

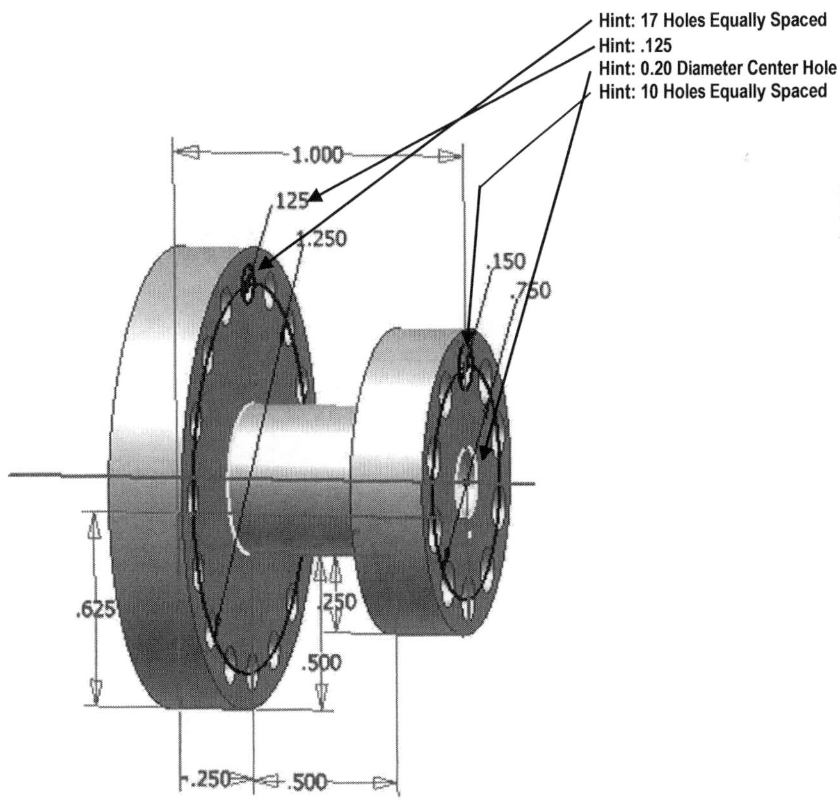

Problem 2-11

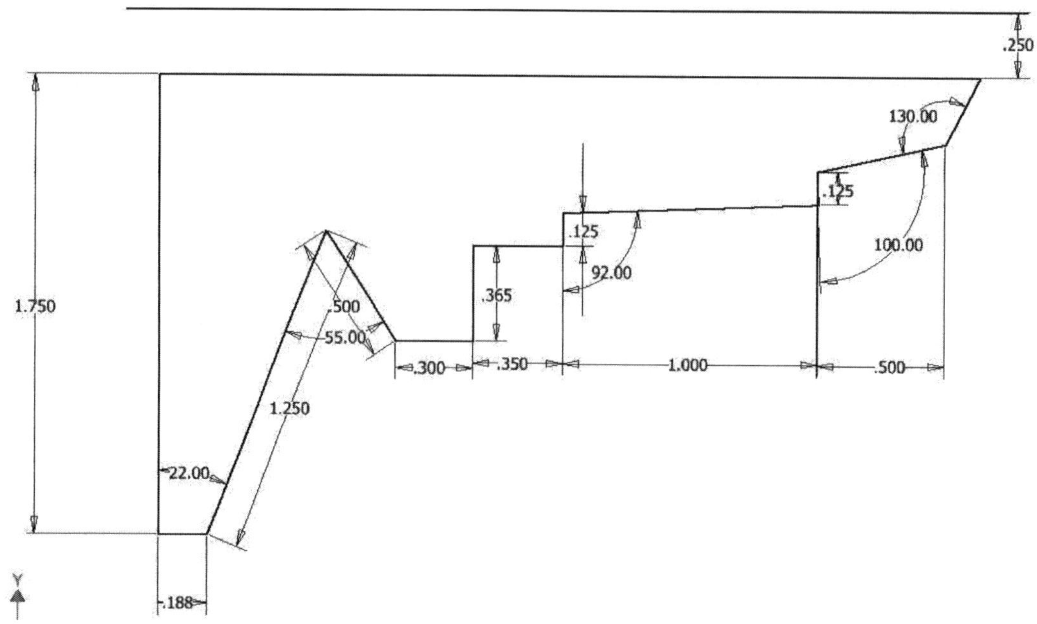
.250
130.00
.125
.125
100.00
92.00
.365
.500
55.00
1.750
.300
.350
1.000
.500
1.250
22.00
.188
Y

Problem 2-12

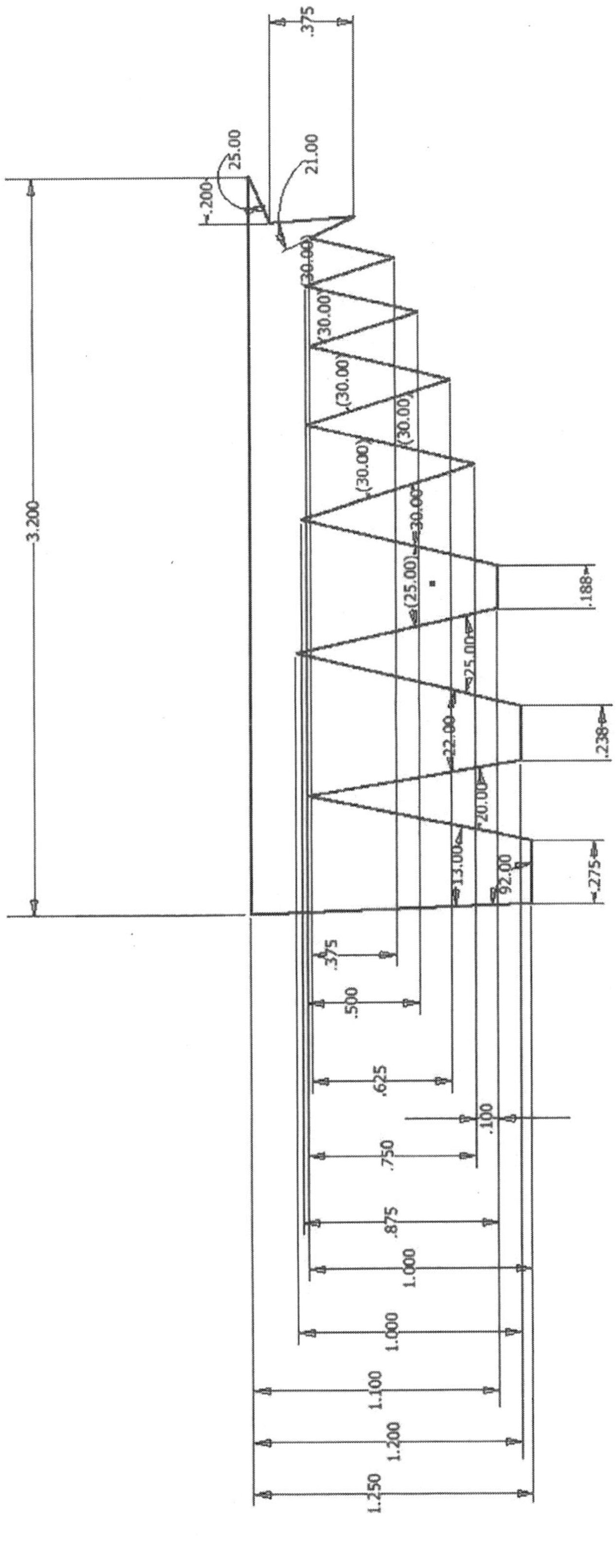
.375
25.00
21.00
.200
3.200
(30.00)
(30.00)
(30.00)
(30.00)
(30.00)
(30.00)
30.00
(25.00)
25.00
22.00
20.00
13.00
92.00
.188
.238
.275
.375
.500
.625
.100
.750
.875
1.000
1.000
1.100
1.200
1.250

CHAPTER 3

Learning to Create a Detail Drawing

Objectives:

1. Create a simple sketch using the Sketch Panel
2. Extrude a sketch into a solid using the 3D Model Panel
3. Create an Orthographic view using the Place Views/Drawing Views Panel
4. Extrude a sketch in the 3D Model Panel
5. Edit the appearance of a Solid Model using the Edit Views command

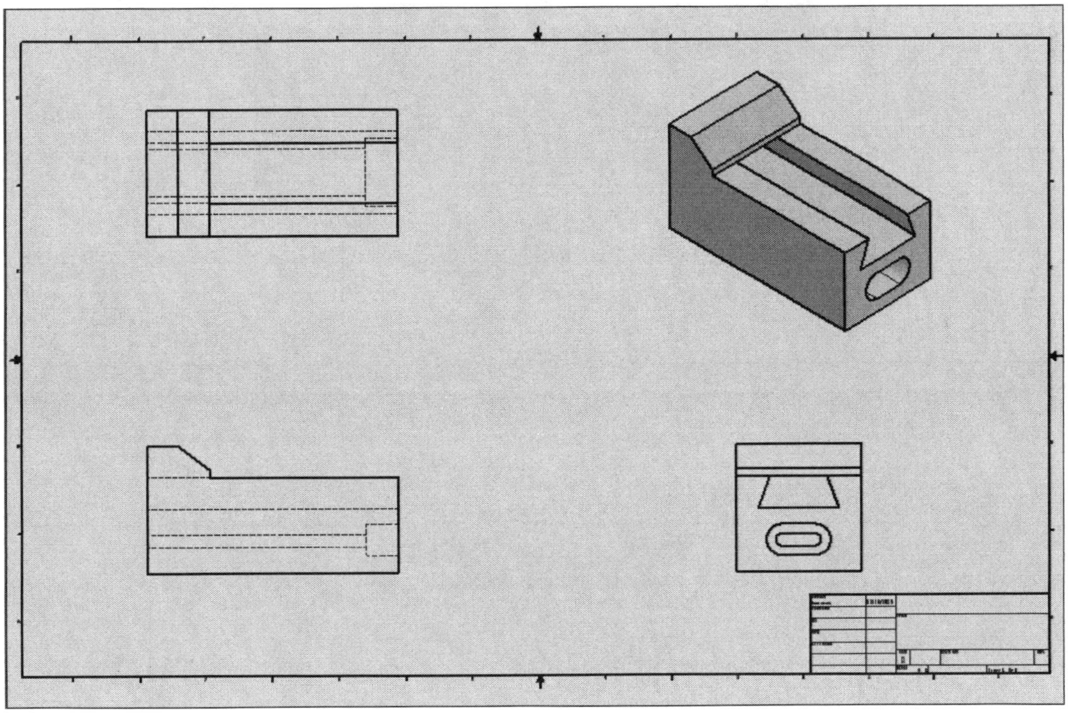

Chapter 3 includes instruction on how to design the part shown.

1. Start Autodesk Inventor 2027 by referring to "Chapter 1 Getting Started."

2. After Autodesk Inventor 2027 is running, begin a new sketch.

3. Complete the drawing on the **XY Plane** including the Point on the lower right face of the part shown in Figure 1.

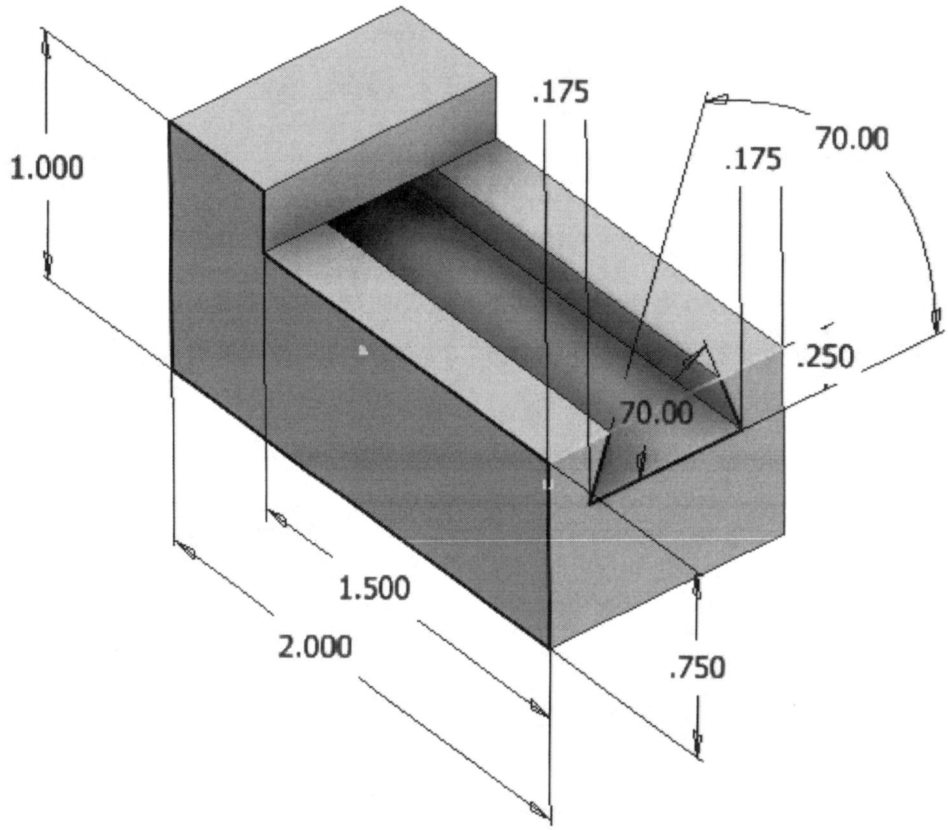

Figure 1

4. Move the cursor to the right portion of the screen and left click on the 3D Model tab. Left click on the **Chamfer** icon as shown in Figure 2.

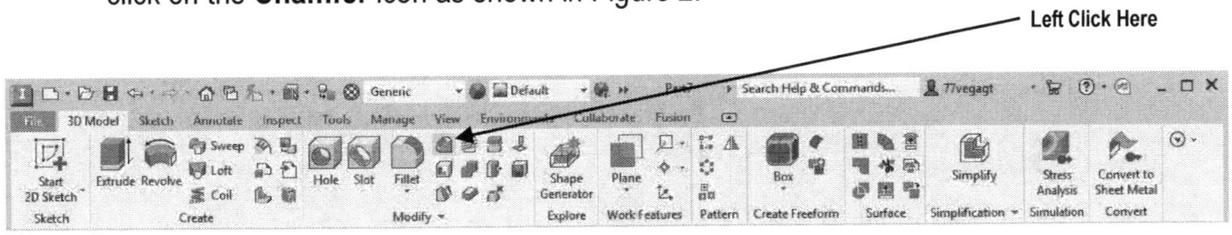

Figure 2

5. After selecting **Chamfer**, the Chamfer dialog box will appear. Left click on the anticipated chamfer edge shown below. Left click on the **Edges** icon. Left click on the "Two Distance Chamfer" icon. Enter **.25** for Distance 1 and **.1875** for Distance 2. Left click on the "Flip" icon to reverse the direction of the Chamfer if necessary. Left click on **OK** as shown in Figure 3.

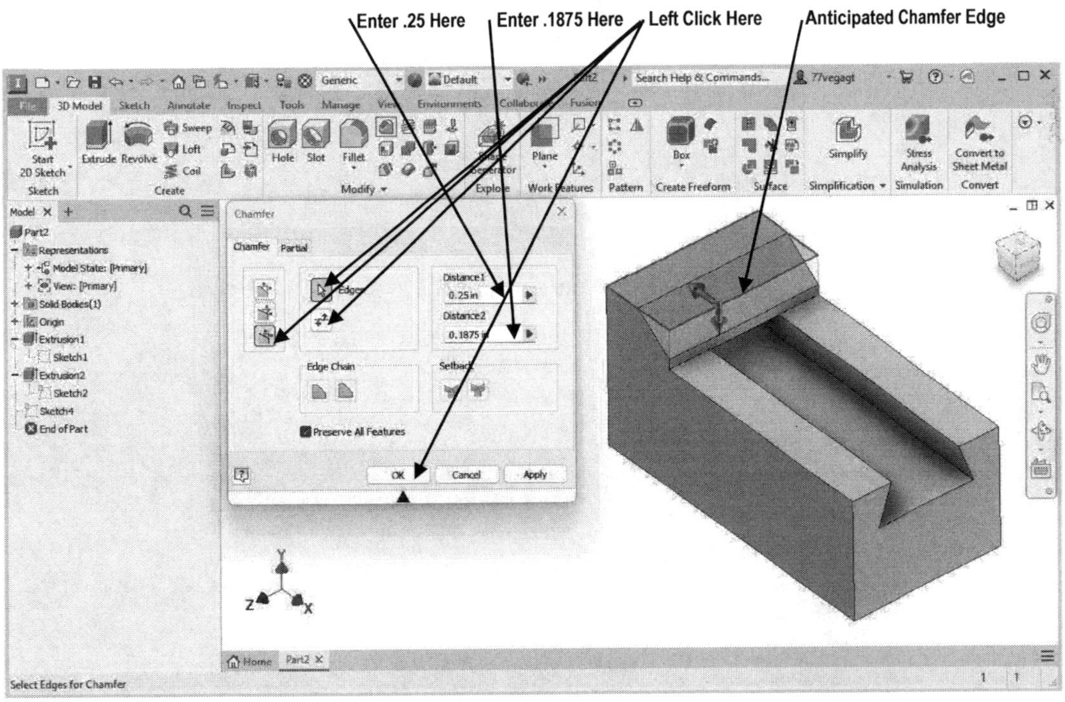

Figure 3

6. Your screen should look similar to Figure 4.

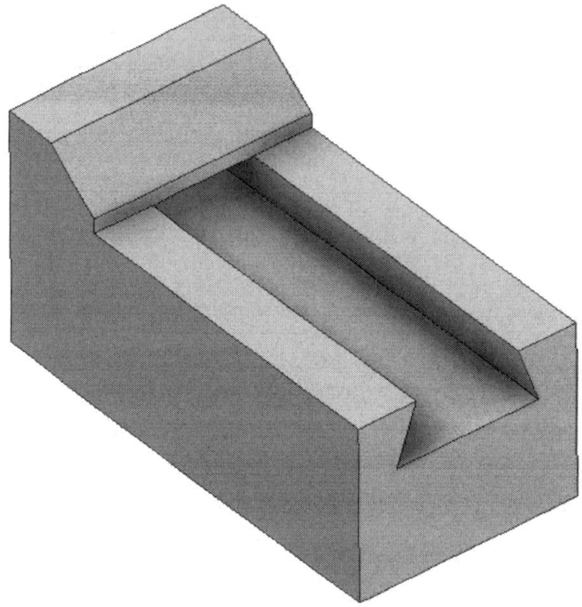

Figure 4

7. Begin a New Sketch and create a **Point** on the surface shown in Figure 5.

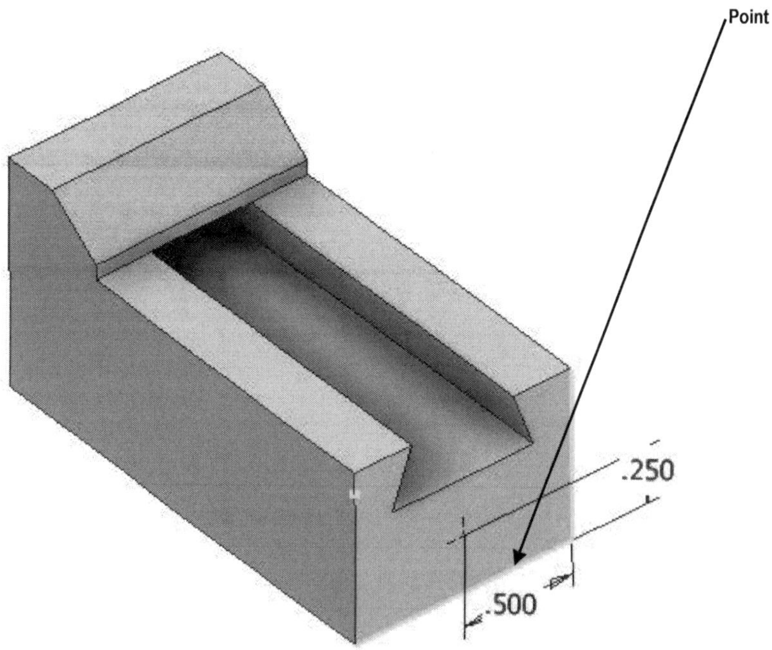

Figure 5

8. Left Click on the **Slot** icon. The Slot dialog box will appear. Enter **.375** for the bore width, enter **.25** for the counterbore height as shown in Figure 6,

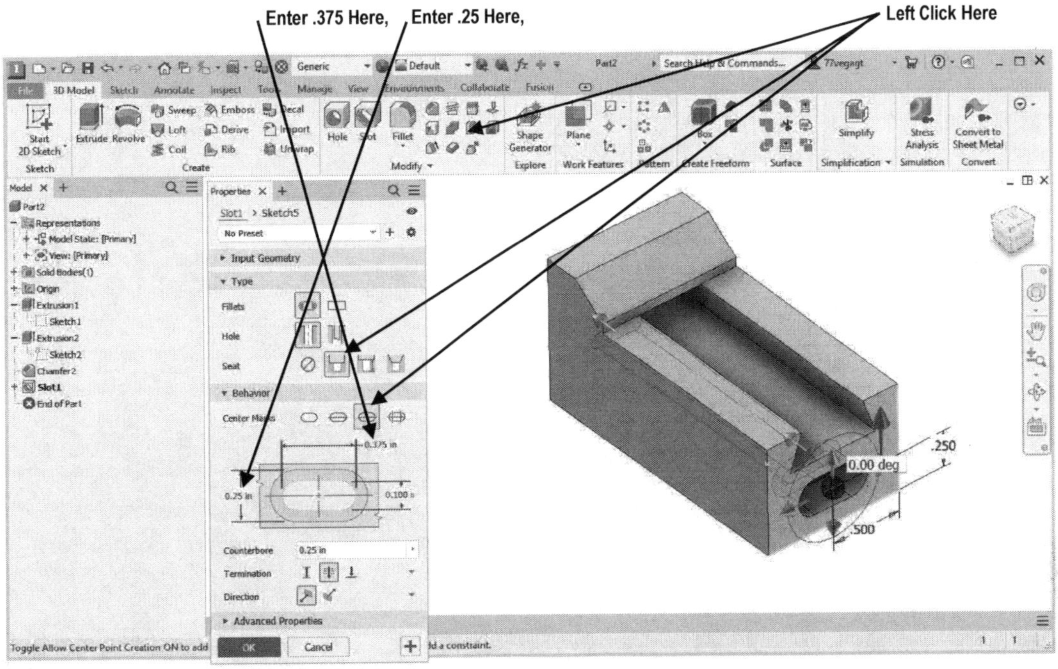

Figure 6

9. Enter **.100** for the bore height, enter **.25** for the counterbore depth, left click on **OK** as shown in Figure 7.

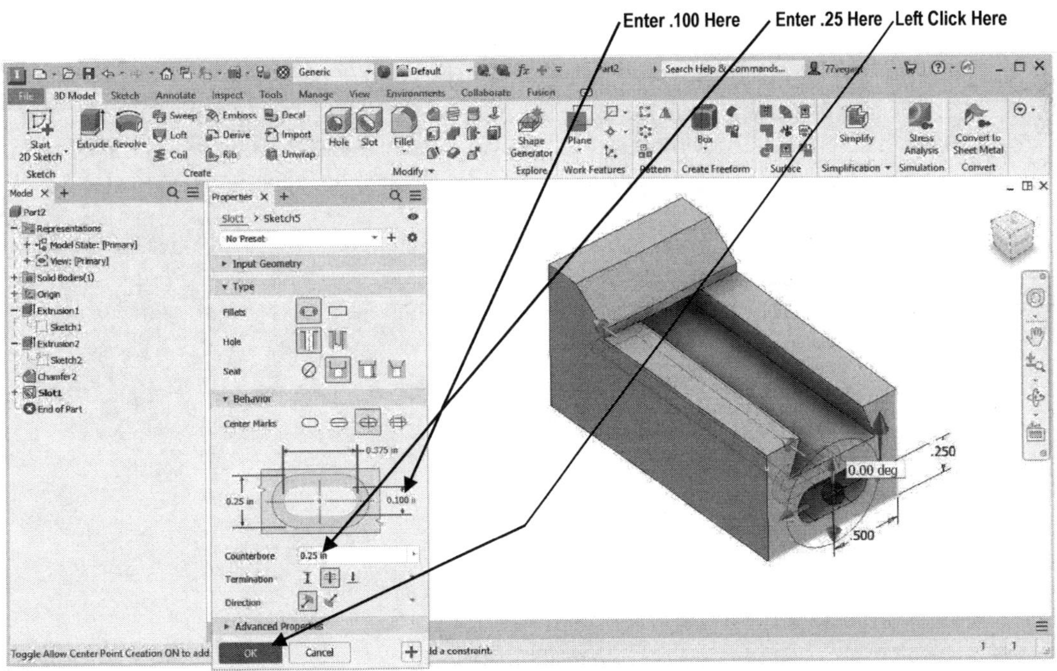

Figure 7

10. Your screen should look similar to Figure 8.

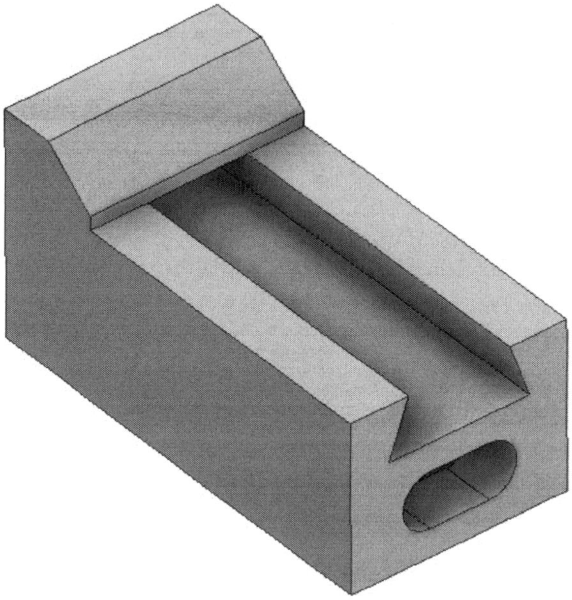

Figure 8

11. Save the part file for easy retrieval to be used in the following section. Do not close the part file.

Create an Orthographic view using the Drawing Views Panel

12. After the part file has been saved, move the cursor to the upper left portion of the screen and left click on the drop-down arrow to the right of the "New" icon. A drop-down menu will appear. Left click on **Drawing** as shown in Figure 9. Once the Drawing Views Panel appears, skip to step 14. If the Drawing Views Panel does not appear, move to step 13.

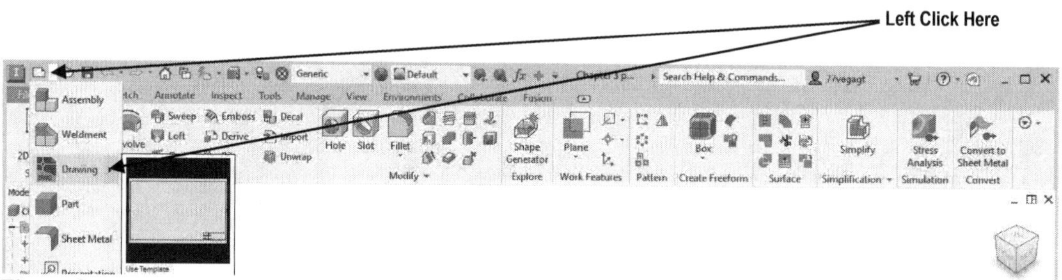

Figure 9

13. The Create New File dialog box is shown below. Left click on the drop-down arrow next to en-US. Left click on the **English** folder. Left click on the **ANSI (in).idw.** Left click on **Create** as shown in Figure 10.

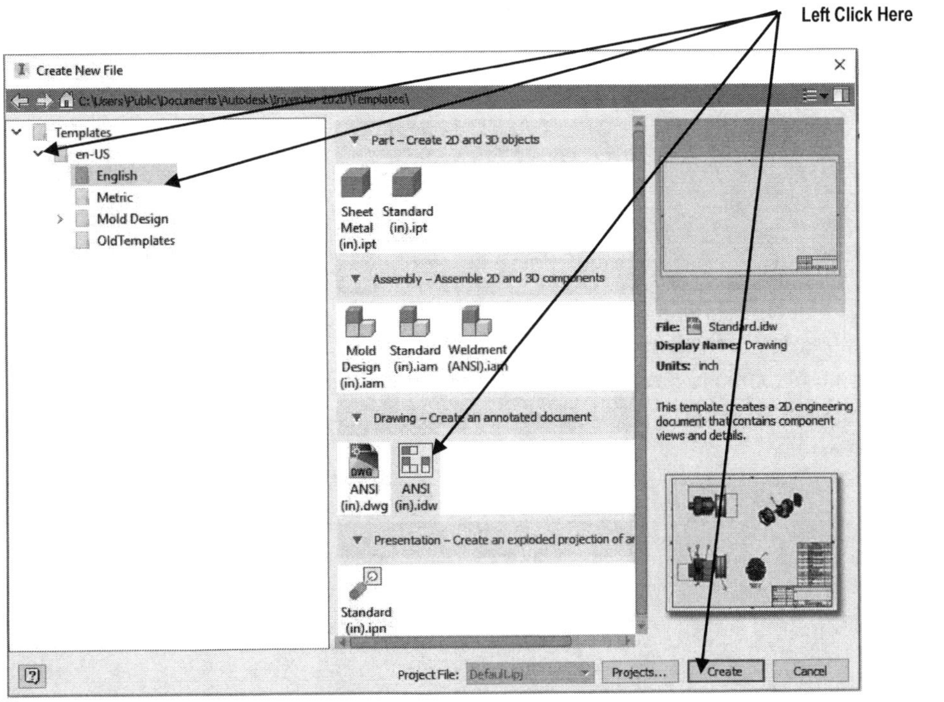

Figure 10

14. Your screen should look similar to Figure 11.

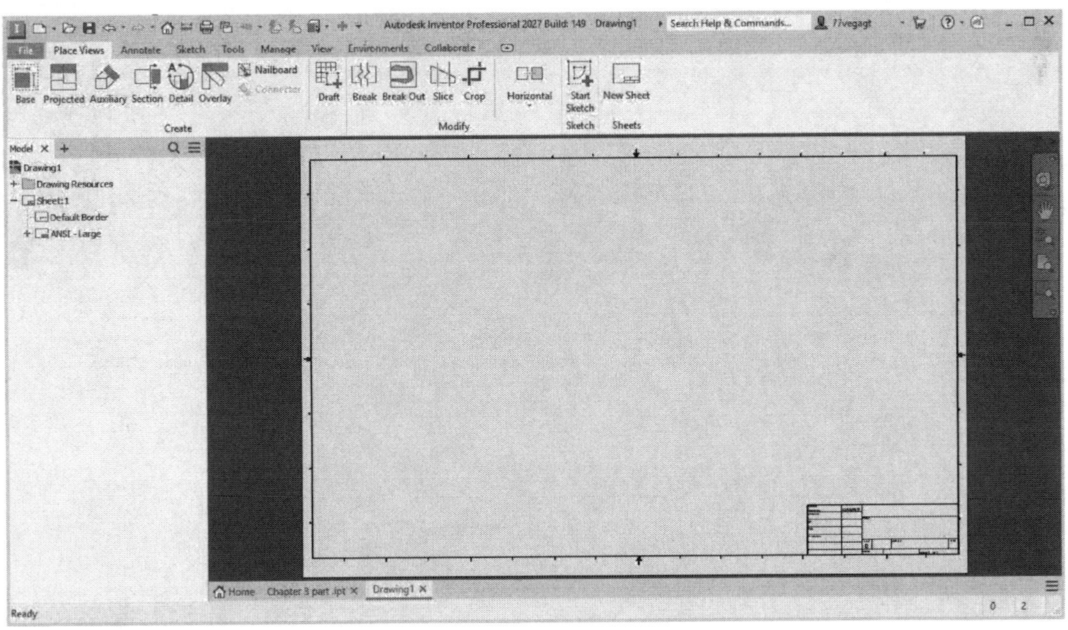

Figure 11

15. Inventor is now in the Drawing Views Panel. Notice the commands at the top of the screen are now different.

16. Move the cursor to the upper left portion of the screen and left click on **Base** as shown in Figure 12.

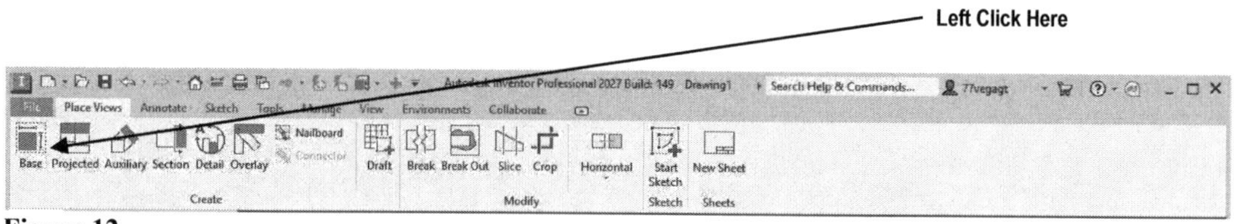

Figure 12

17. The drawing of the wedge block should appear attached to the cursor. If the part does not appear attached to the cursor, use the "Explore" icon to locate the part file as shown in Figure 13.

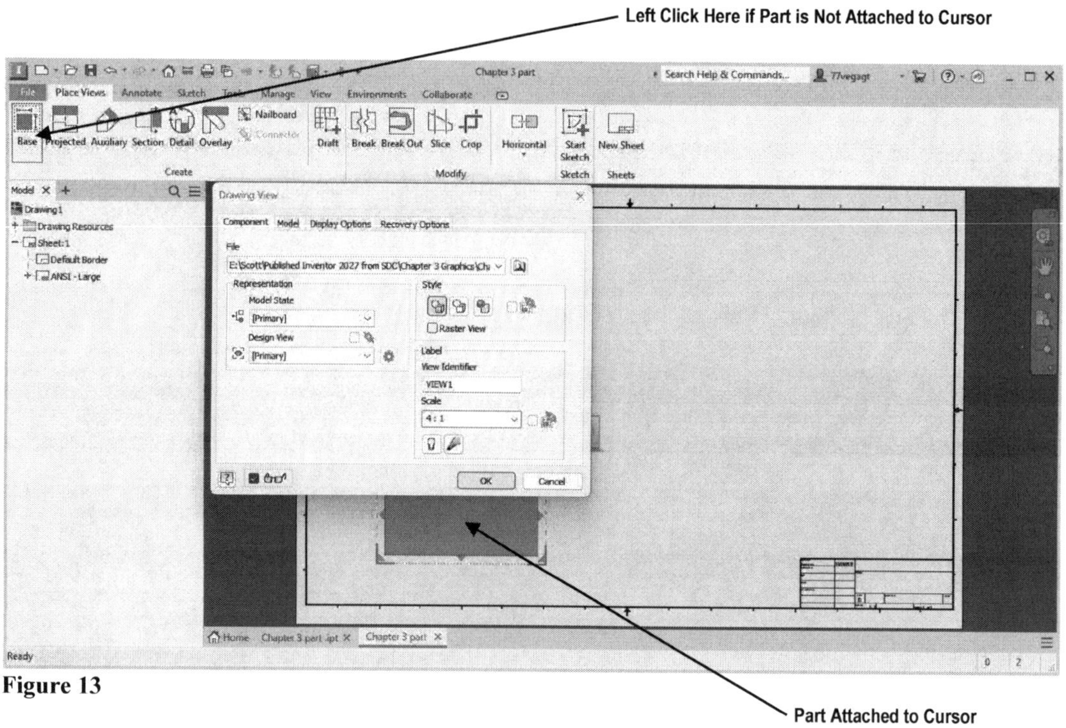

Figure 13

18. Different views can be selected for the front, top, and side views. Select the desired view from the view orientation cube as shown in Figure 14. To understand how the view orientation cube works, left click on the arrows that signify **Top, Left or Right** to have the top view, left view or right view as the front (base) view. Select the **Front** view for the base view as shown in Figure 14.

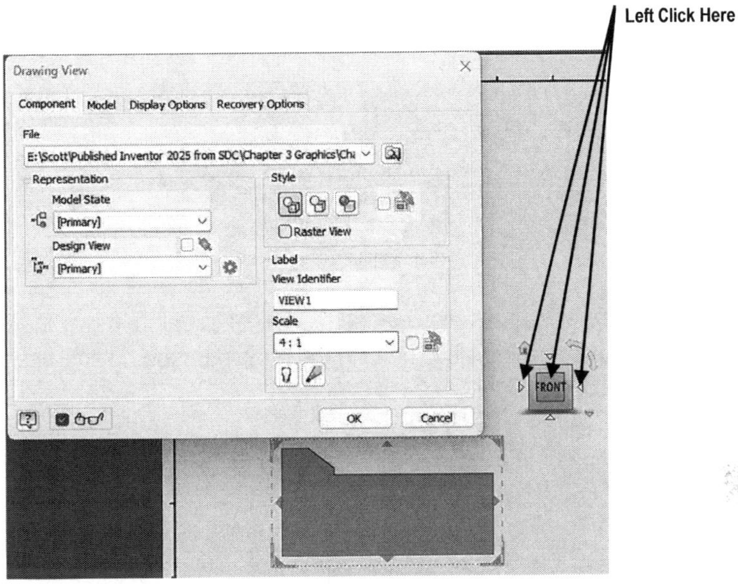

Figure 14

19. Left click on the **Scale** drop-down box and set the drawing scale to **4:1** (if it is not already set to 4:1). The size of the wedge block will become larger as shown in Figure 15. Left click on **OK**.

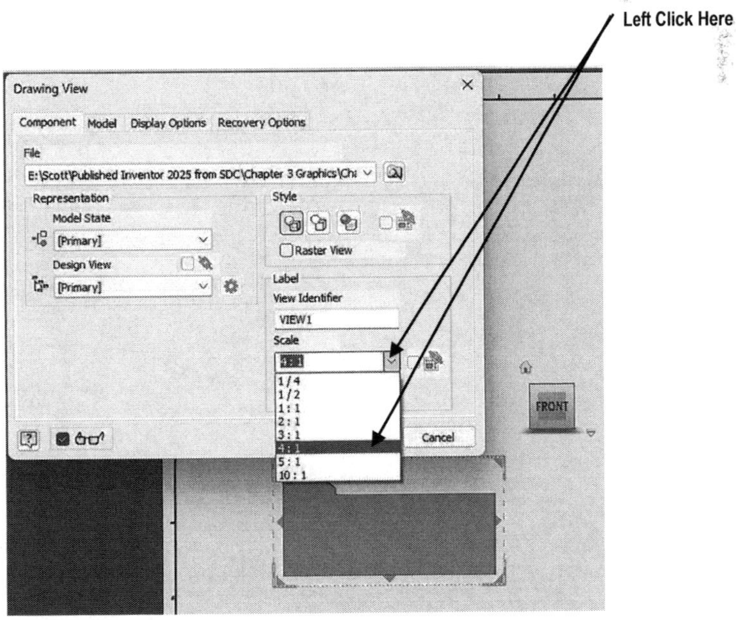

Figure 15

20. Place the part just above the title block that is in the lower right corner of the screen and left click once. This will place the part as shown in Figure 16.

Left Click Here

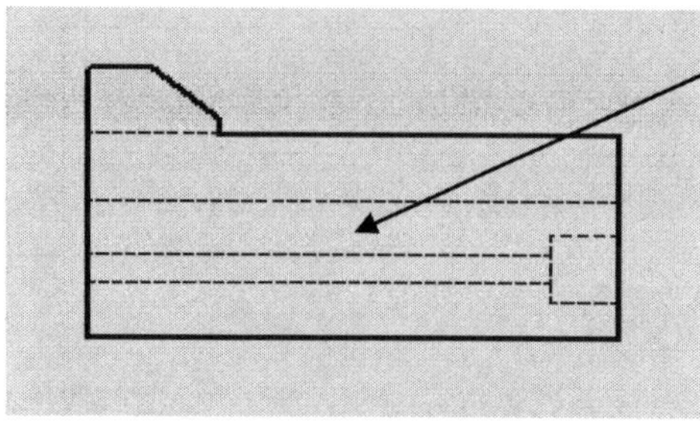

Figure 16

21. If the part was inadvertently placed too low or too high, move the cursor over the dots that surround the part, left click (holding the mouse button down), and drag the part to the desired location.

22. Move the cursor to the upper left portion of the screen and left click on **Projected** as shown in Figure 17.

Left Click Here

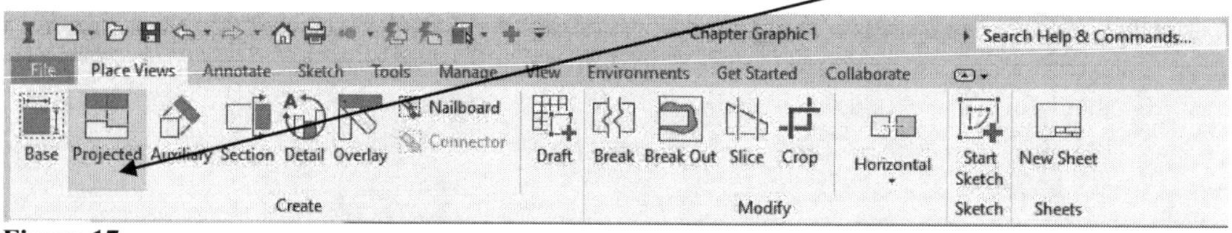

Figure 17

23. The part will be attached to the cursor. Move the cursor upward and left click as shown in Figure 18.

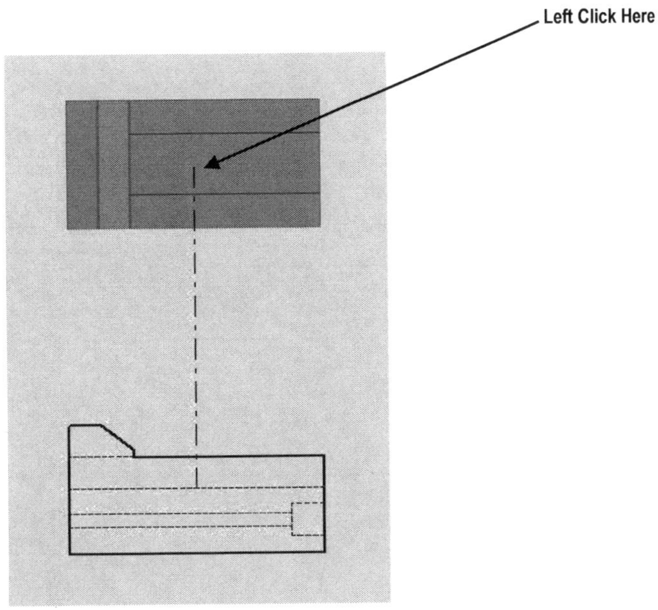

Figure 18

24. Notice the dashed lines outlining the top view as shown in Figure 19. This indicates that the view has been placed.

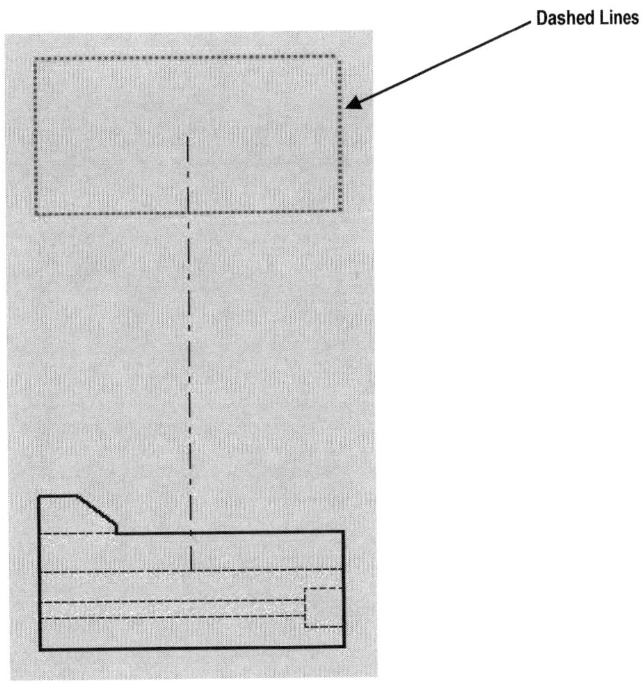

Figure 19

25. Move the cursor over to the upper right corner of the page and left click once as shown in Figure 20.

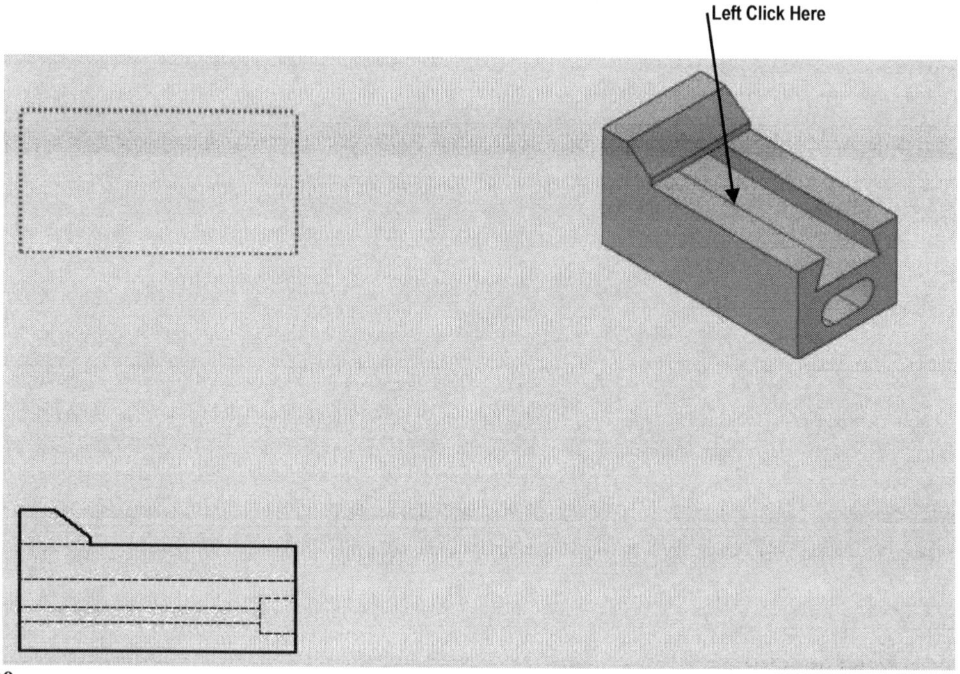

Figure 20

26. Move the cursor down to where the side view will be located and left click once as shown in Figure 21.

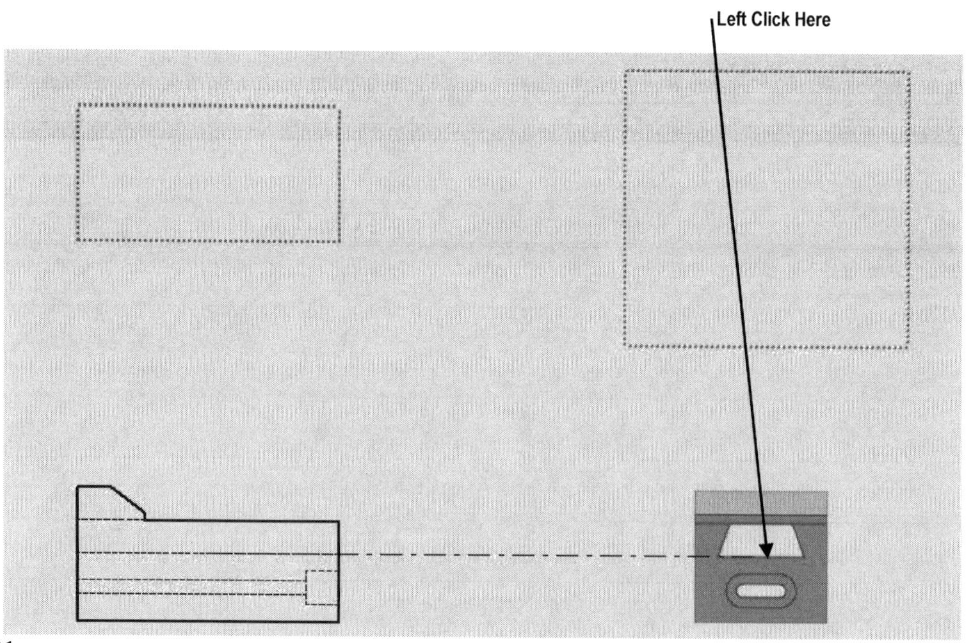

Figure 21

27. Left click to place the Side view. Then, right click on the side view. A pop-up menu will appear. Left click on **Create** as shown in Figure 22.

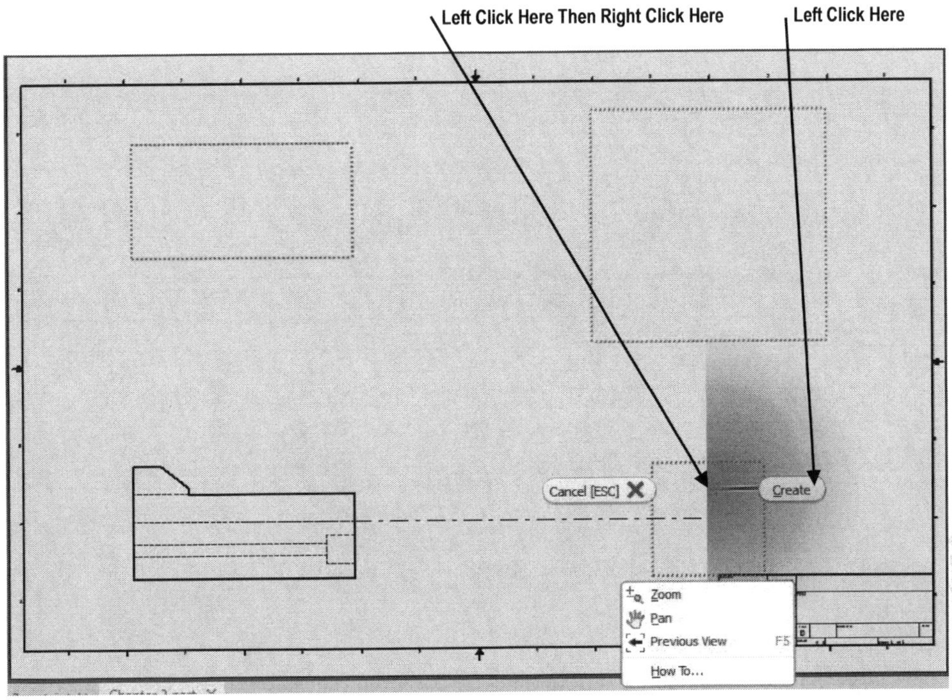

Figure 22

28. Your screen should look similar to Figure 23.

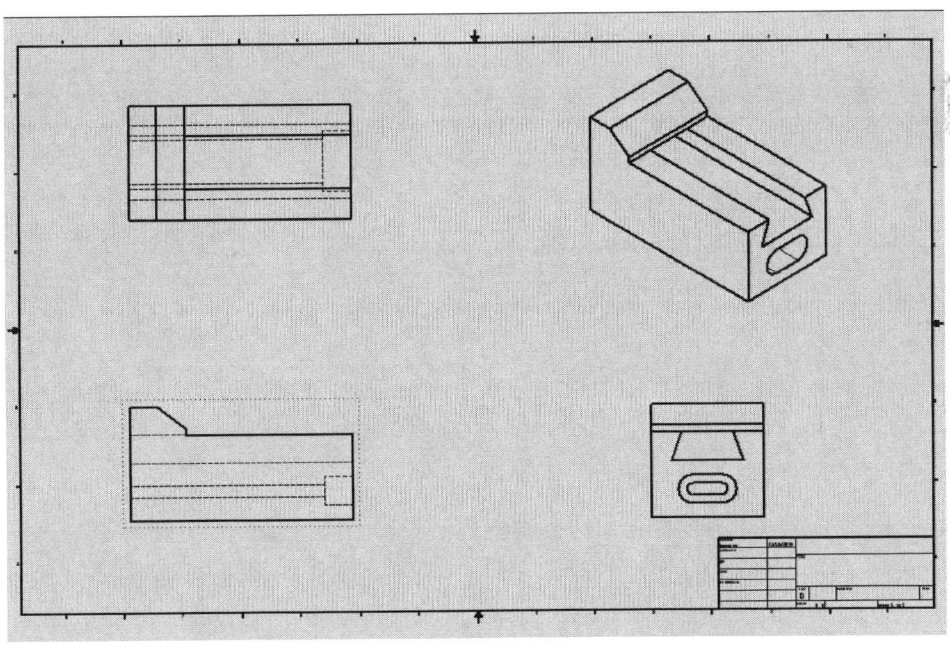

Figure 23

Create a Solid Model using the Edit Views command

29. Move the cursor over the isometric view in the upper right corner of the drawing. Dots will appear as shown in Figure 24.

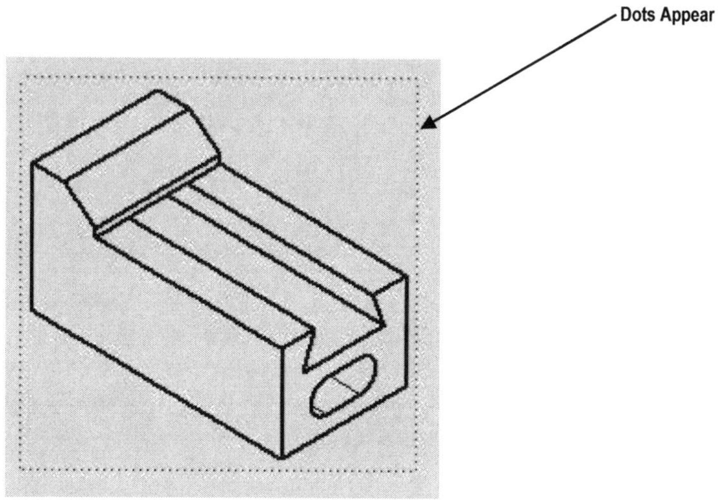

Figure 24

30. After the dots appear, right click once. A pop-up menu will appear. Left click on **Edit View** as shown in Figure 25.

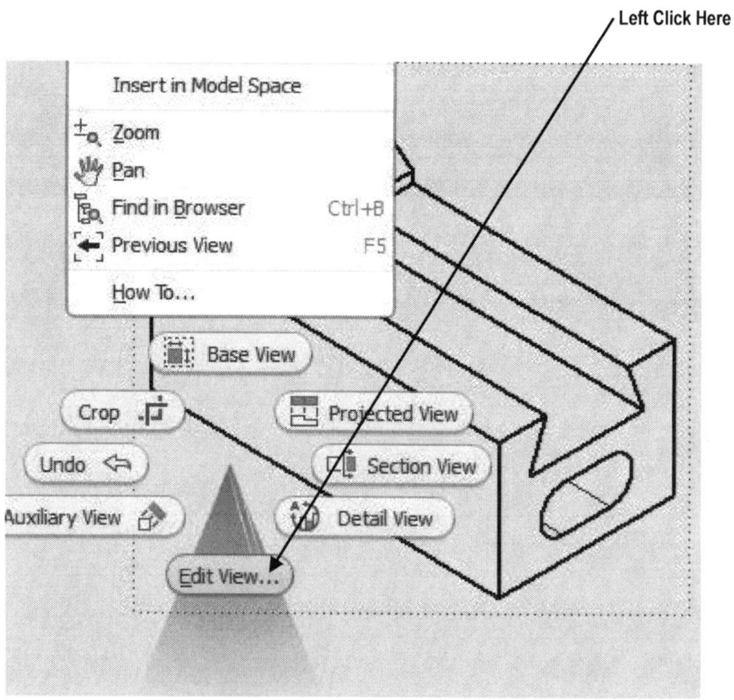

Figure 25

31. The Drawing View dialog box will appear. Left click on the "blue sphere." Remove checkmark as shown. Left click on **OK** as shown in Figure 26.

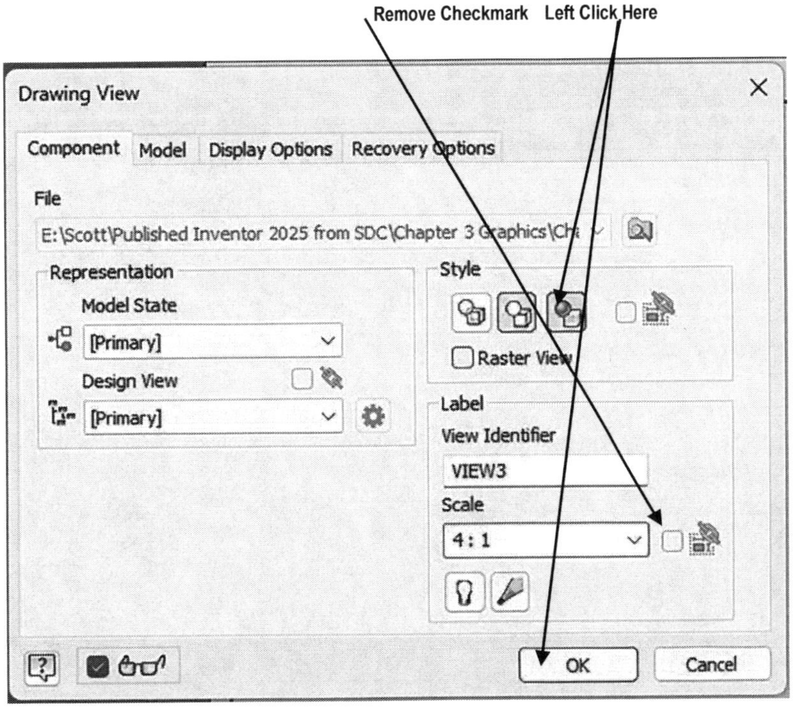

Figure 26

32. The isometric view will become a miniature 3D solid model as shown in Figure 27.

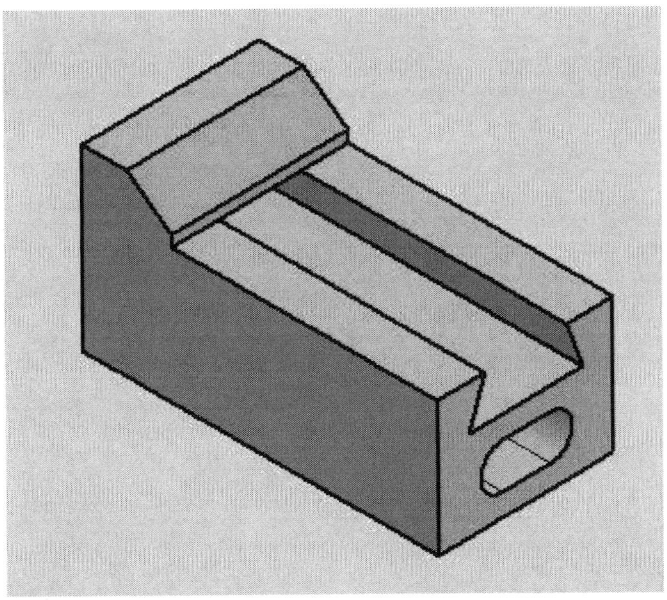

Figure 27

33. Your screen should look similar to Figure 28.

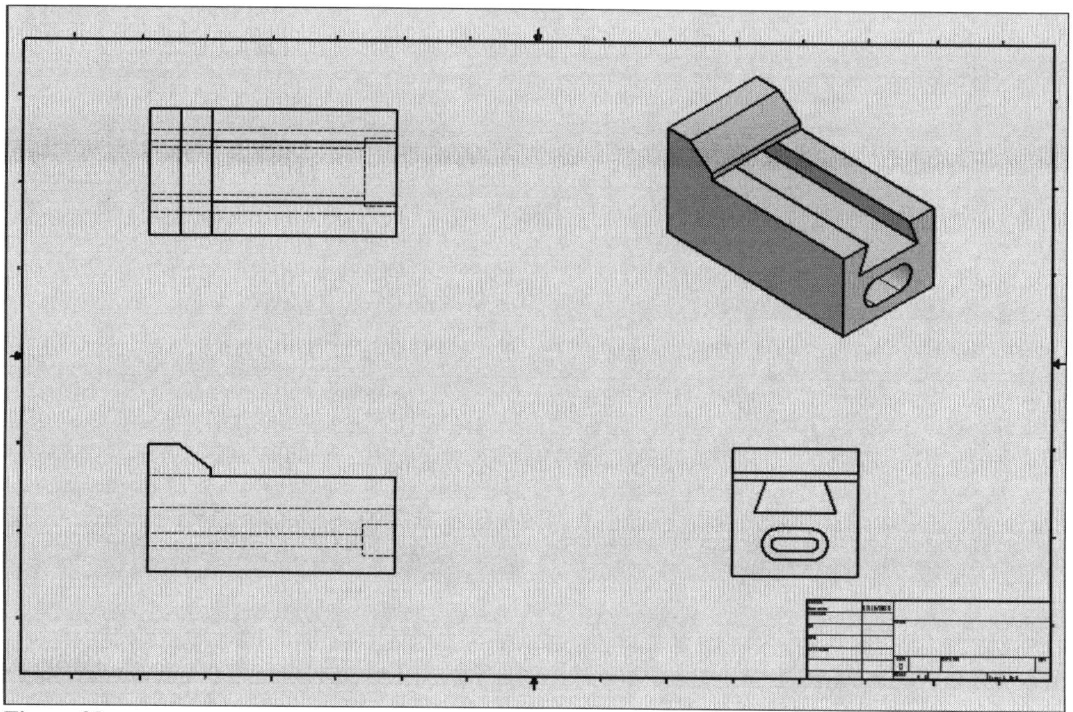

Figure 28

Chapter Problems

Create 3 view/multi view drawings of the following parts.

Problem 3-1

Hint: Dimension the angle between the lower and upper section to 105 degrees.

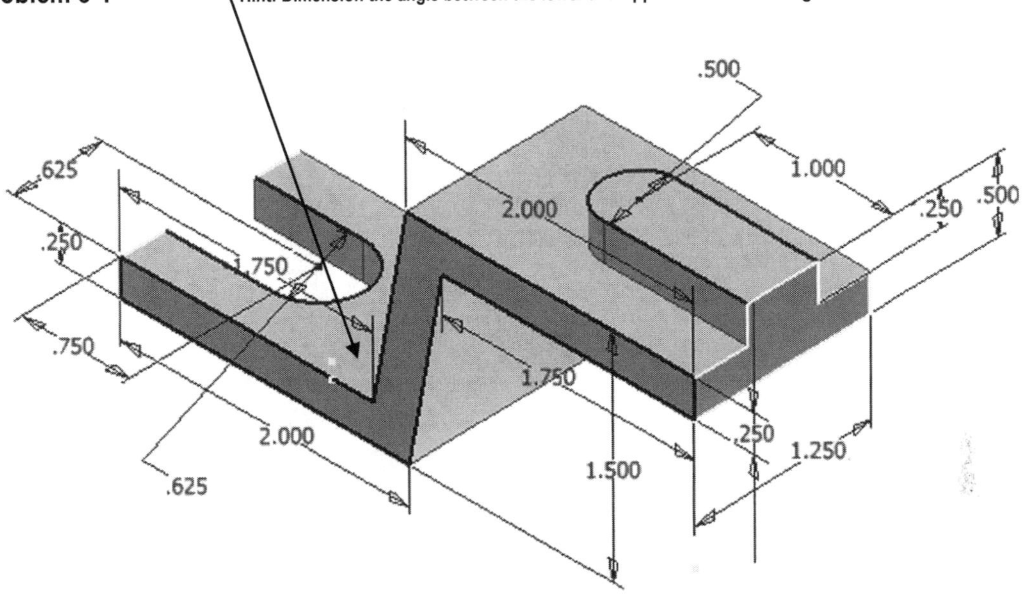

Problem 3-2

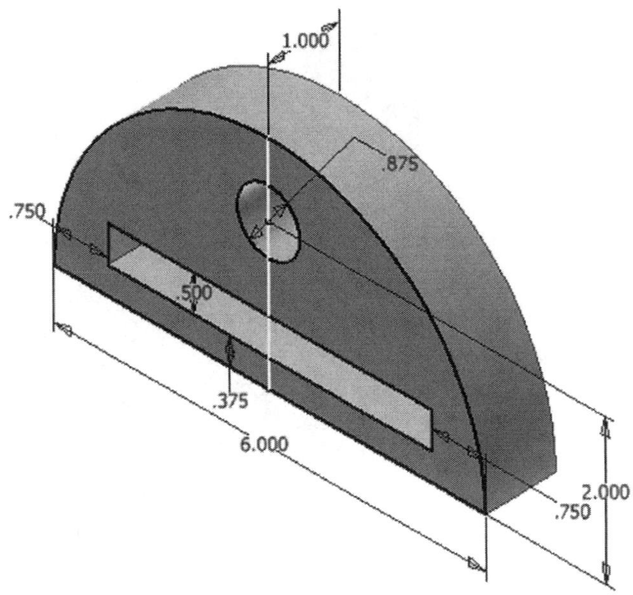

Problem 3-3

Hint: Extrude to .25 inches

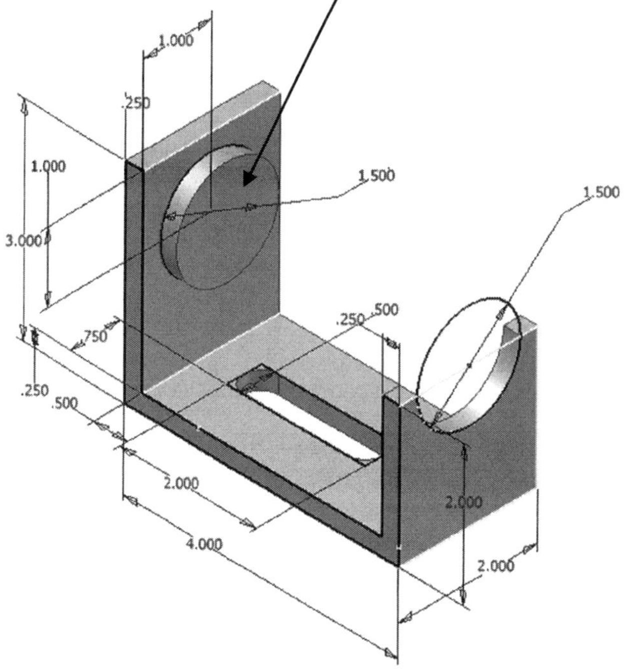

Problem 3-4

Hint: Use the 2 directional Extrude-Cut command to create the 1.625 Diameter Hole

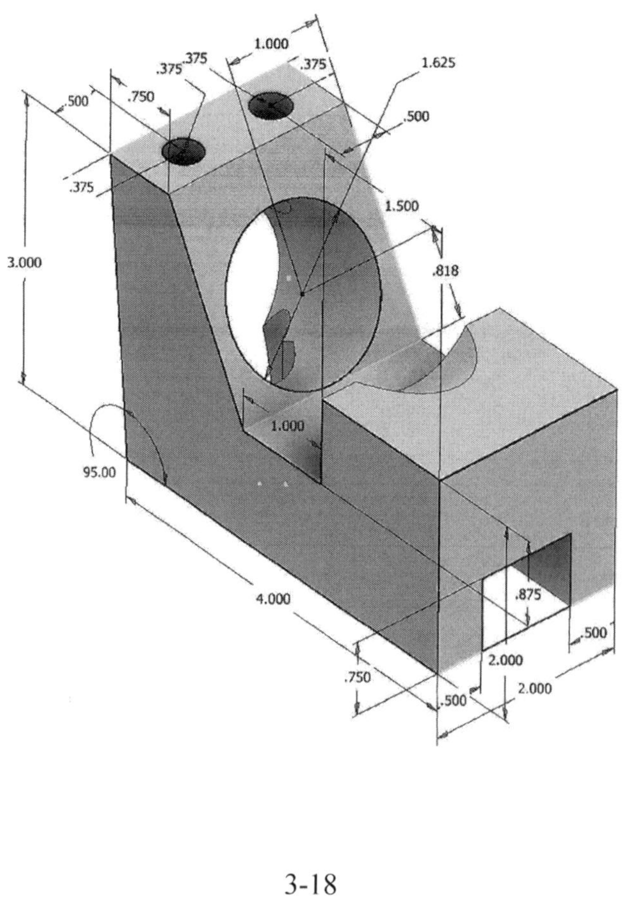

Problem 3-5

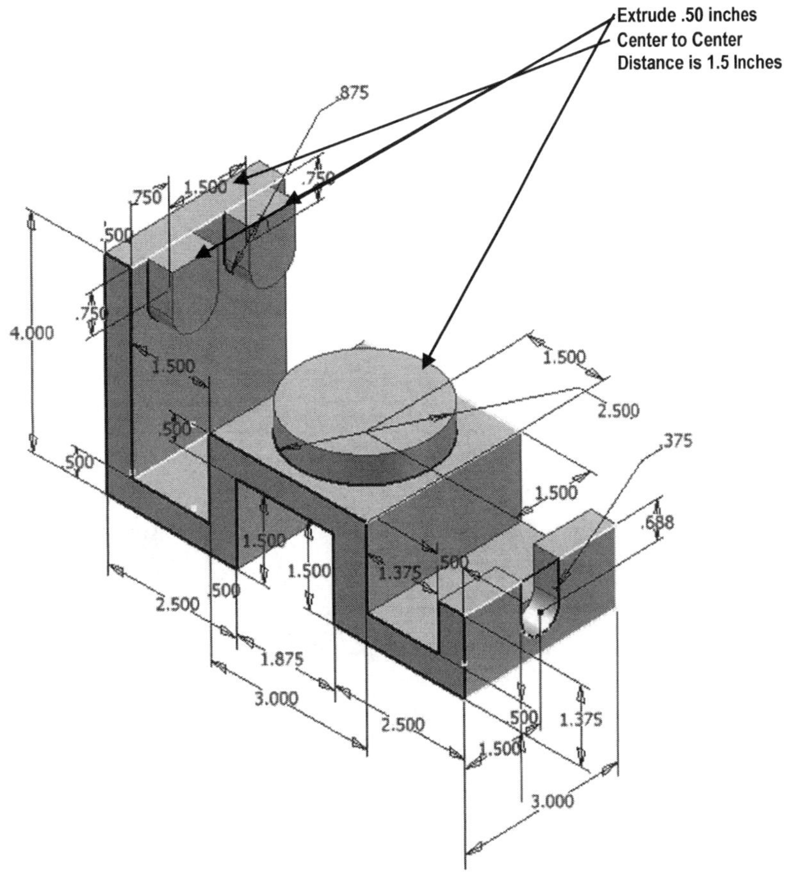

Problem 3-6

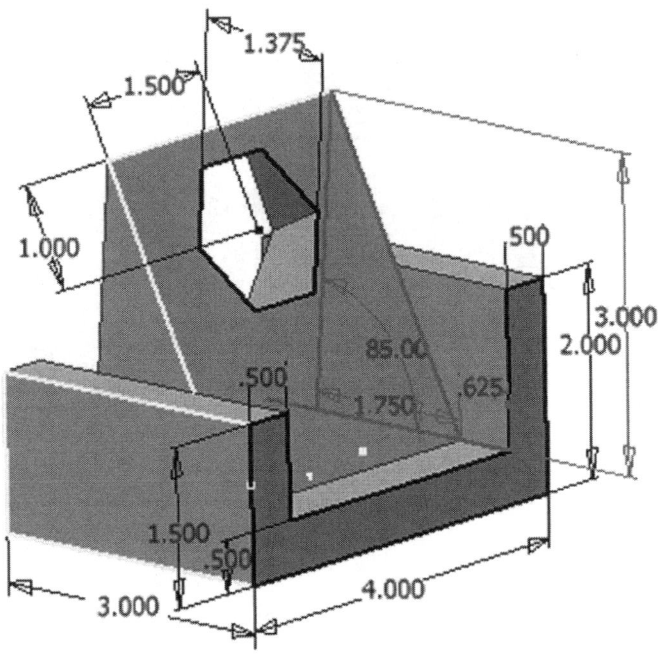

Problem 3-7

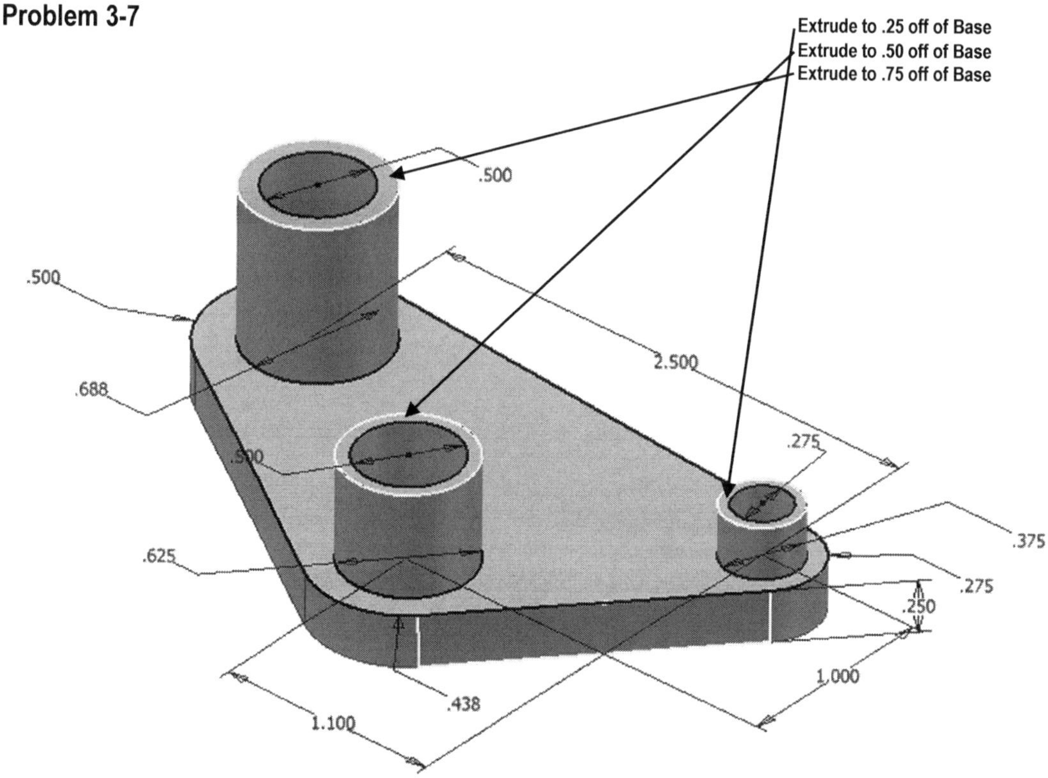

Problem 3-8

1 inch Fillets

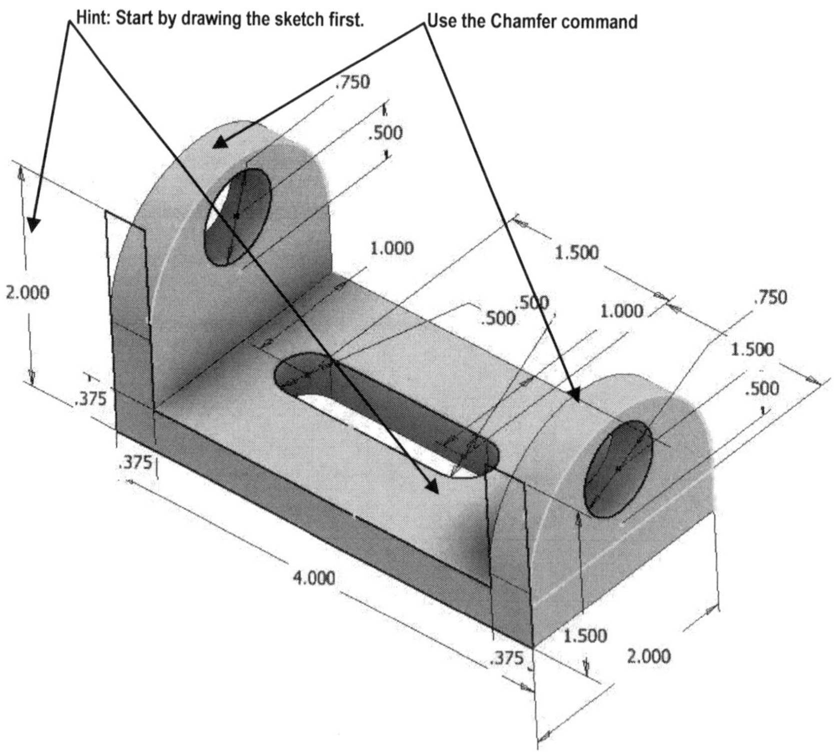

CHAPTER 4

Advanced Detail Drawing Procedures

Objectives:

1. Create an Auxiliary View using the Place Views/Drawing Views Panel
2. Create a Section View using the Place Views/Drawing Views Panel
3. Dimension views using the Annotation/Drawing Annotation Panel
4. Create Text using the Annotation/Drawing Annotation Panel

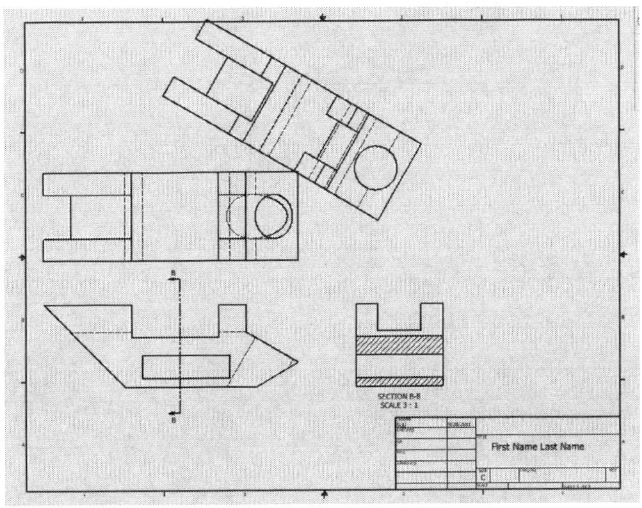

Chapter 4 includes instruction on how to create the drawings shown.

1. Start Autodesk Inventor 2027 by referring to "Chapter 1 Getting Started."

2. After Autodesk Inventor 2027 is running, complete the following part. The numbers 135, 150 and 60 are all in degrees as shown in Figure 1.

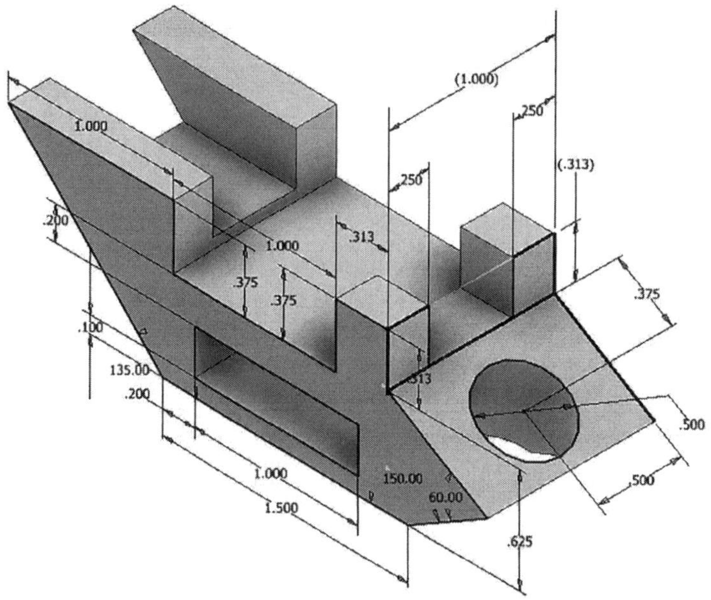

Figure 1

3. Once the part is complete, project the part into a 3 view drawing as discussed in Chapter 3 using a 4:1 scale as shown in Figure 2.

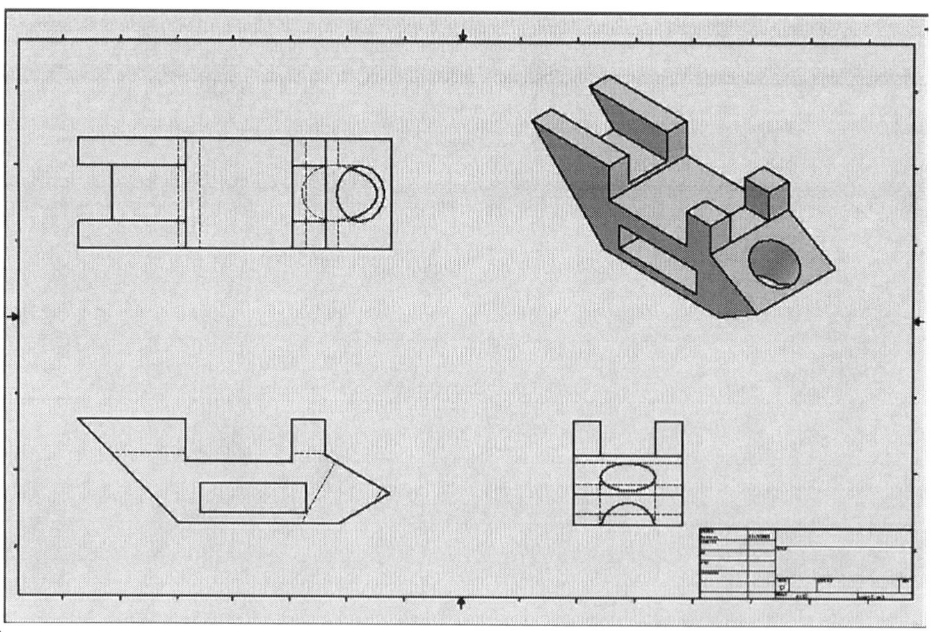

Figure 2

4. Start by moving the views closer together to provide additional room on the drawing. Move the cursor over the top view causing dots to appear around the view. After the dots appear, left click on the dots (holding the left mouse button down) and drag the view down closer to the front (base) view as shown in Figure 3.

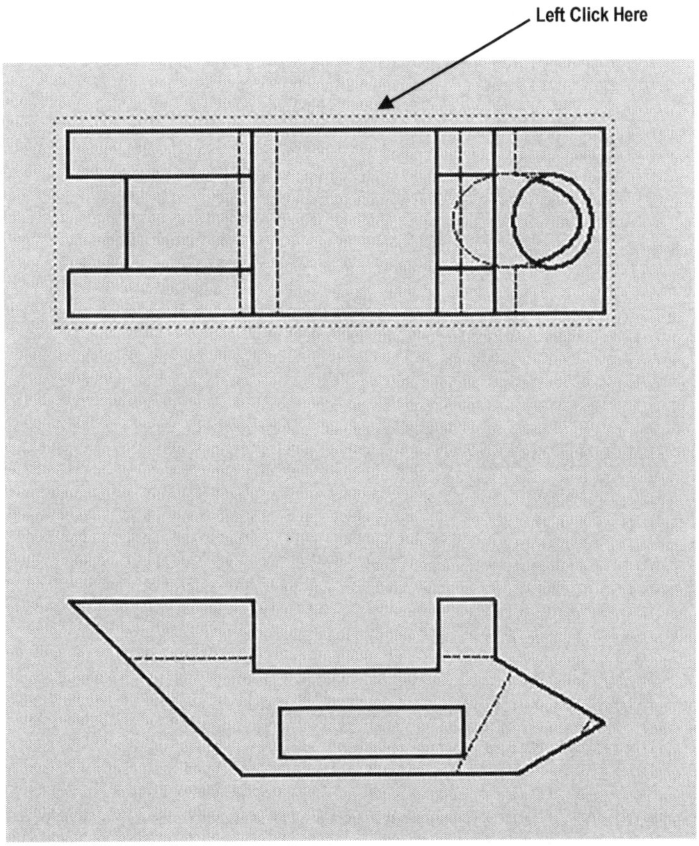

Figure 3

5. Move the side view closer to the front (base) view. Start by moving the cursor over the side view causing dots to appear around the view. After the dots appear, left click on the dots (hold the left mouse button down) and drag the view closer to the front (base) view as shown in Figure 4.

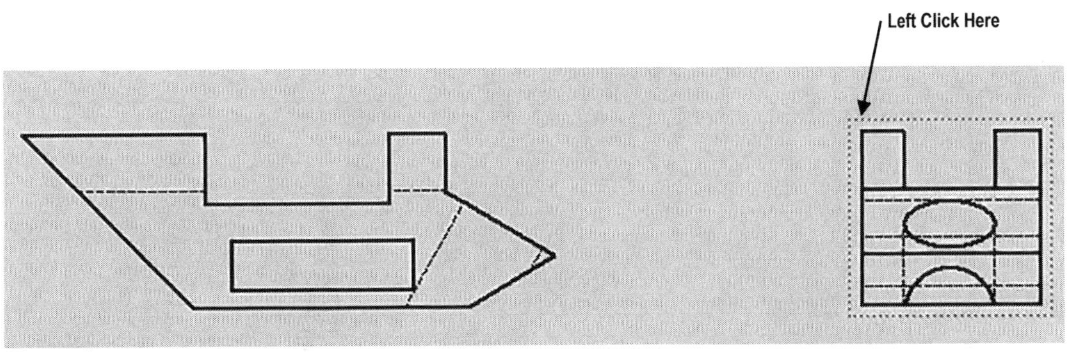

Figure 4

6. You will need to delete the isometric view that was created in Chapter 3. Move the cursor near the isometric view causing red dots to appear. Right click. A pop-up menu will appear. Left click on **Delete** as shown in Figure 5.

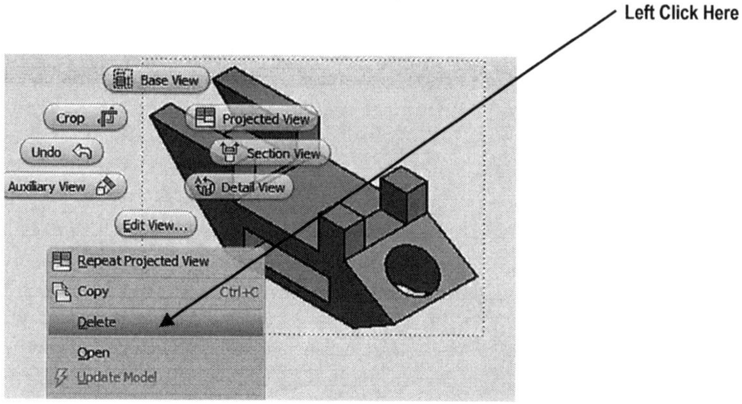

Figure 5

7. The Delete dialog box will appear. Left click on **OK** as shown in Figure 6.

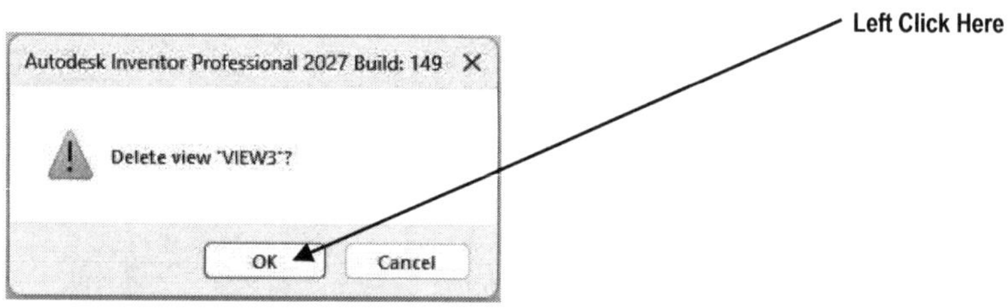

Figure 6

8. There will now be more room to work. Your screen should look similar to Figure 7.

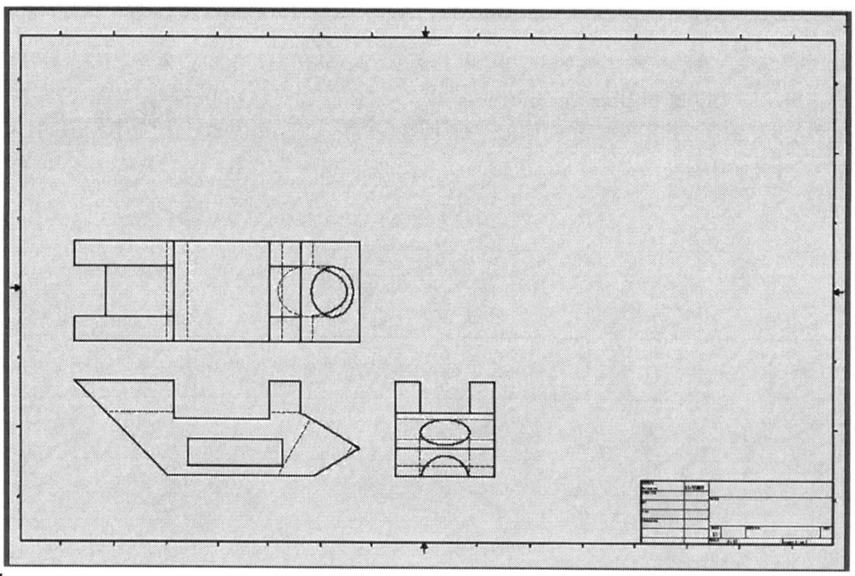

Figure 7

9. To provide more space on the drawing, the drawing view scale will have to be reduced. Right click on the front (base) view. A pop-up menu will appear. Left click on **Edit View**. Left click on the drop-down arrow under Scale. Reduce the scale of the drawing to 3:1 as shown in Figure 8.

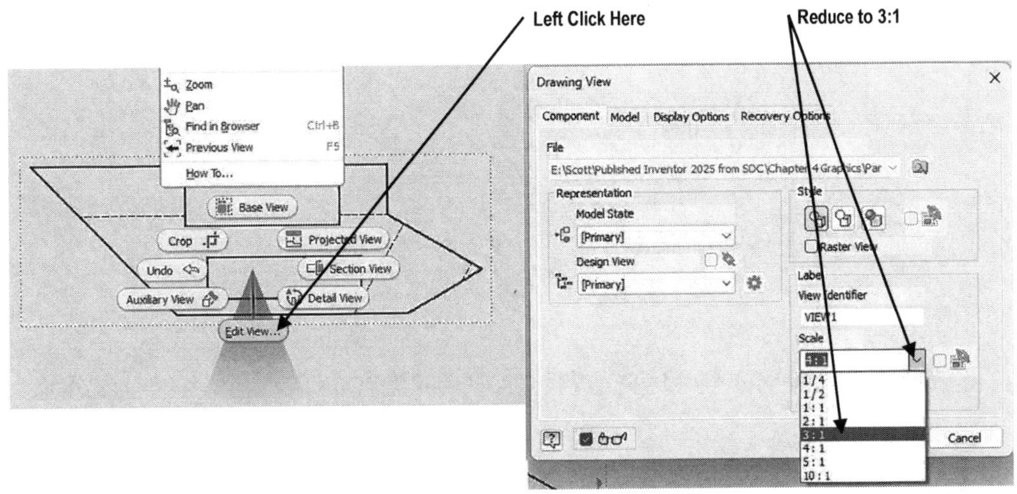

Figure 8

Create an Auxiliary View using the Drawing Views Panel

10. Move the cursor to the upper left portion of the screen and left click on **Auxiliary View** as shown in Figure 9.

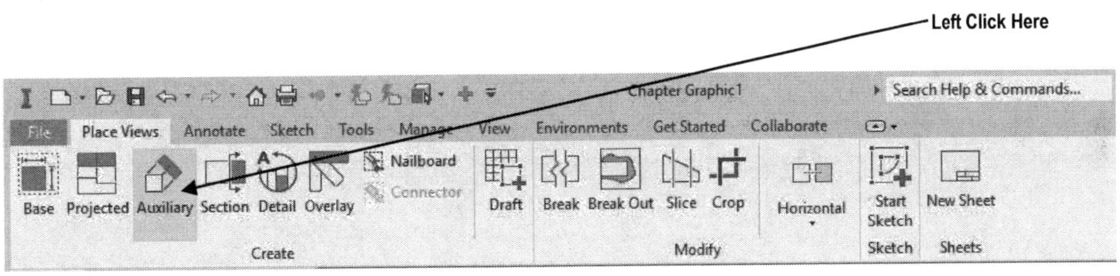

Figure 9

11. Move the cursor to the front (base) view causing red dashed lines to appear around the view. Left click once as shown in Figure 10.

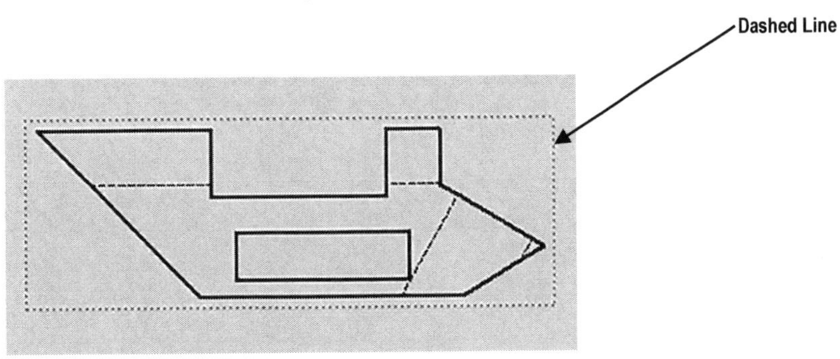

Figure 10

12. The Auxiliary View dialog box will appear as shown in Figure 11.

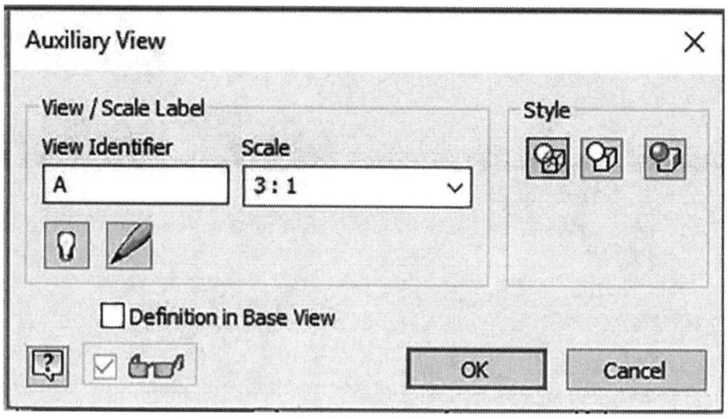

Figure 11

13. Move the cursor over the wedge line causing it to turn red. Left click as shown in Figure 12.

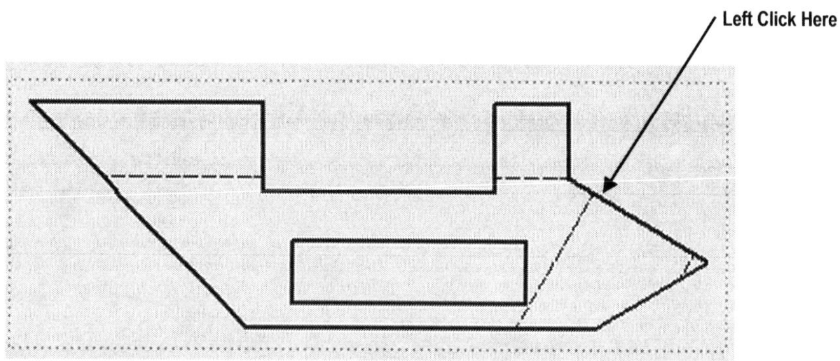

Figure 12

14. Inventor will create an auxiliary view from the selected surface. The view will be attached to the cursor as shown in Figure 13.

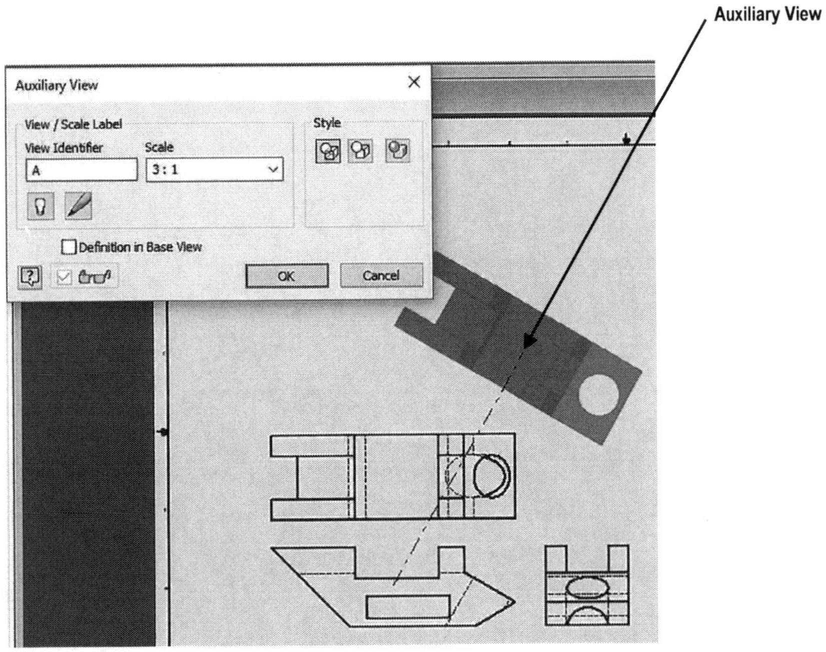

Figure 13

15. Move the cursor towards the upper right and left click. The Auxiliary View dialog box will close as shown in Figure 14.

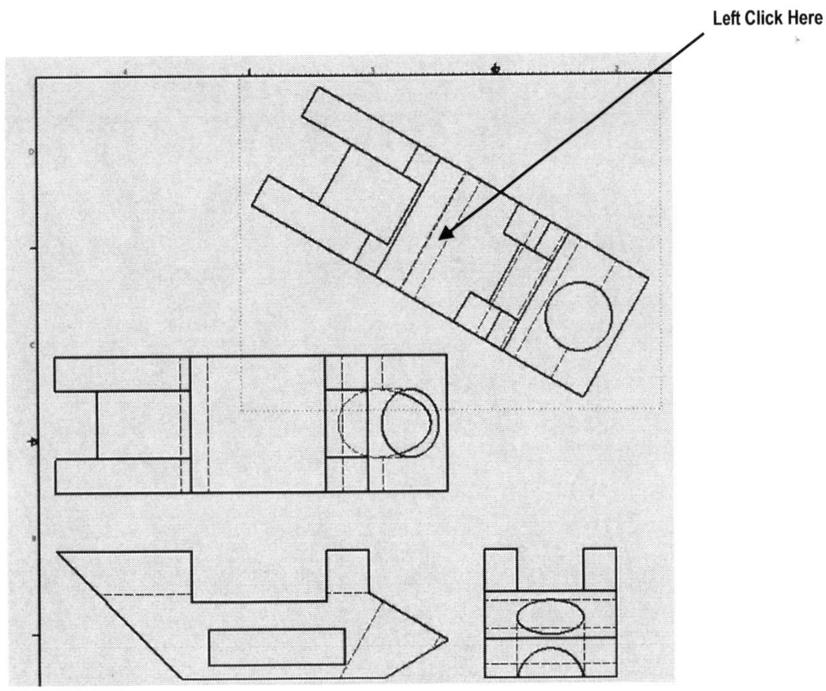

Figure 14

16. Your screen should look similar to Figure 15.

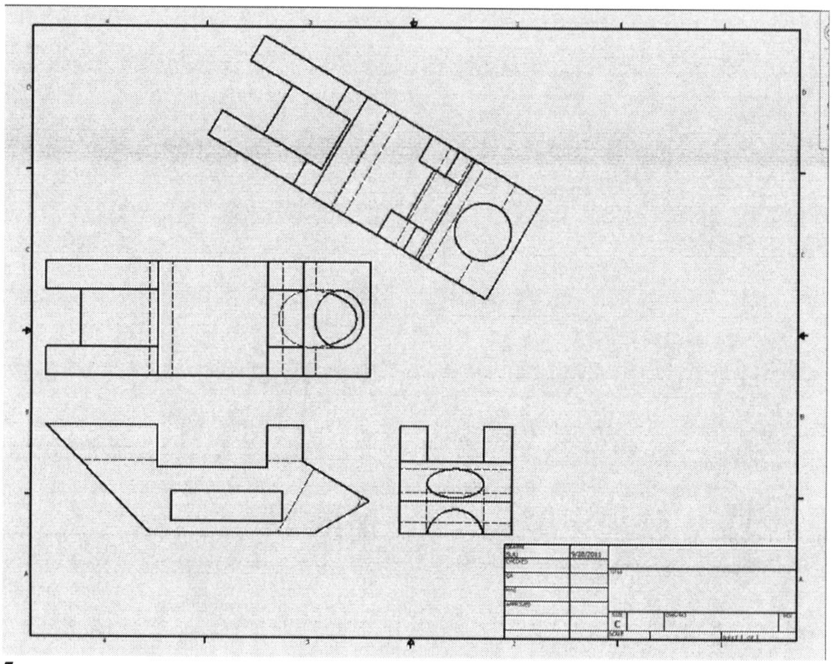

Figure 15

17. Move the cursor to the side view causing red dots to appear as shown in Figure 16.

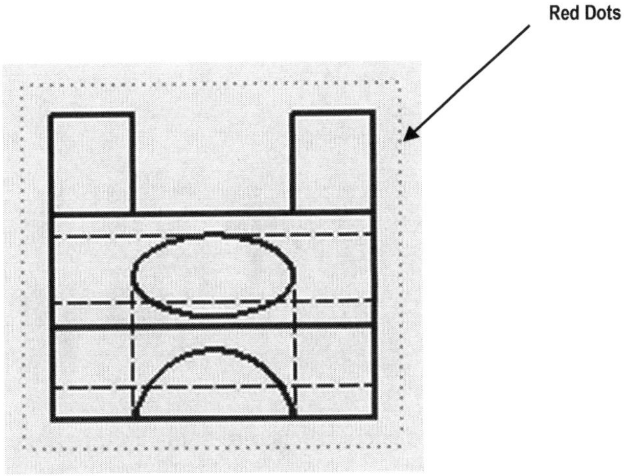

Figure 16

18. Right click on the view. A pop-up menu will appear. Left click on **Delete** as shown in Figure 17.

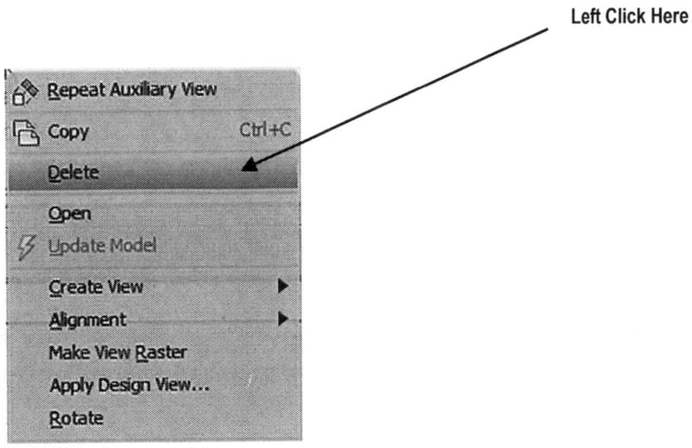

Figure 17

19. A Delete dialog box will appear. Left click on **OK** as shown in Figure 18.

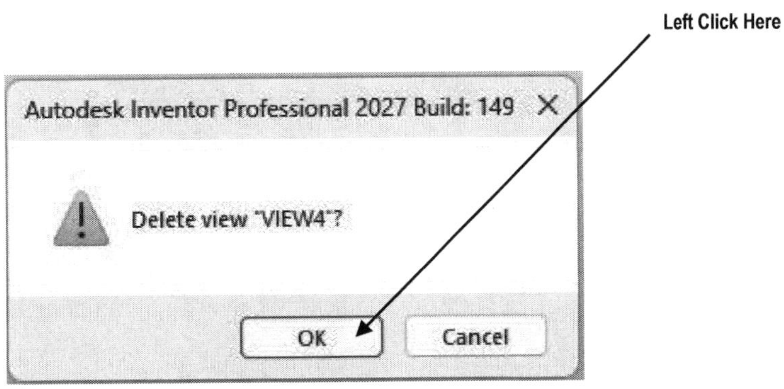

Figure 18

Create a Section View using the Drawing Views Panel

20. Move the cursor to the upper left portion of the screen and left click on **Section** as shown in Figure 19.

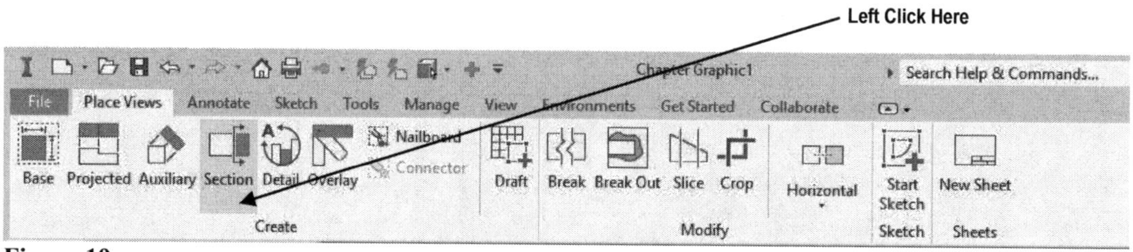

Figure 19

21. Move the cursor over the front view causing red dots to appear around the view as shown in Figure 20.

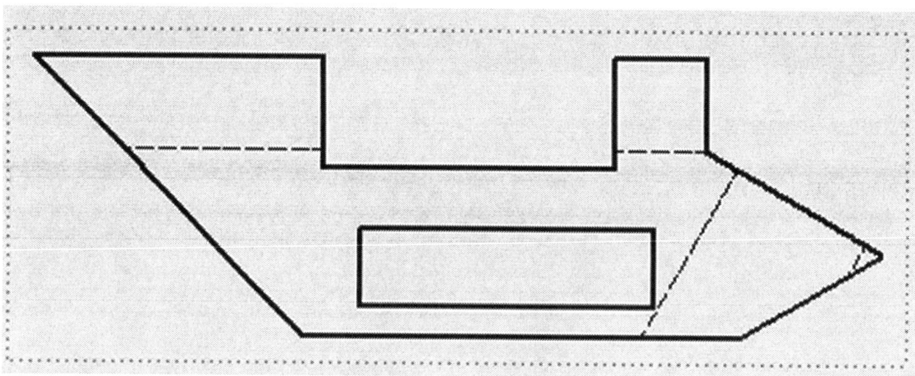

Figure 20

22. Left click inside the red dots as shown in Figure 21.

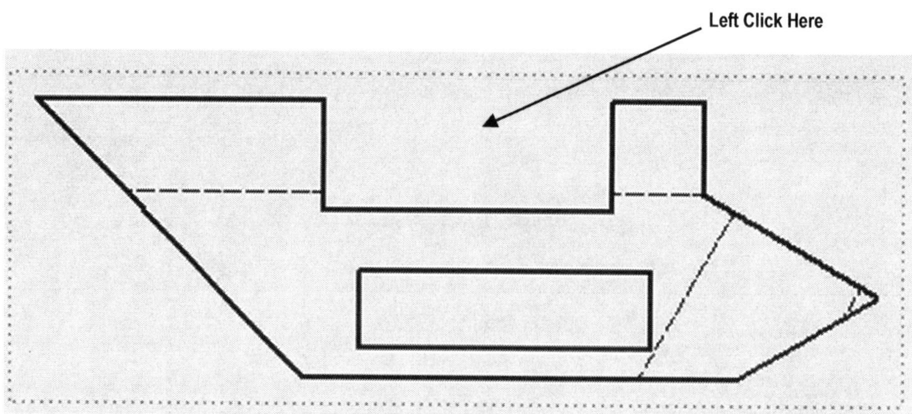

Figure 21

23. Move the cursor up from the previous location and left click once as shown in Figure 22.

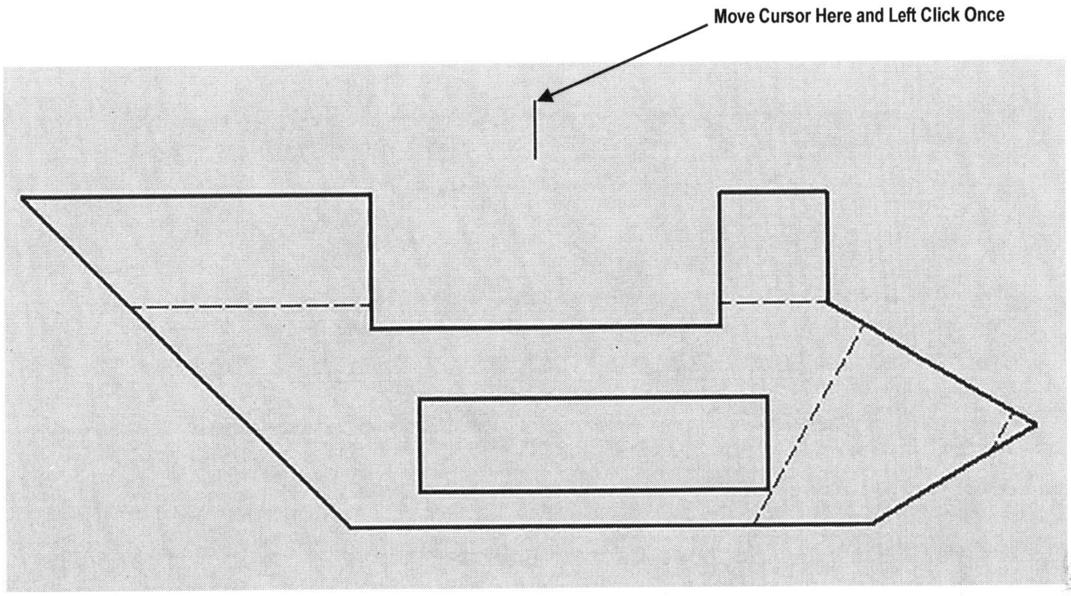

Figure 22

24. Move the cursor down creating a cutting plane line and left click again as shown in Figure 23.

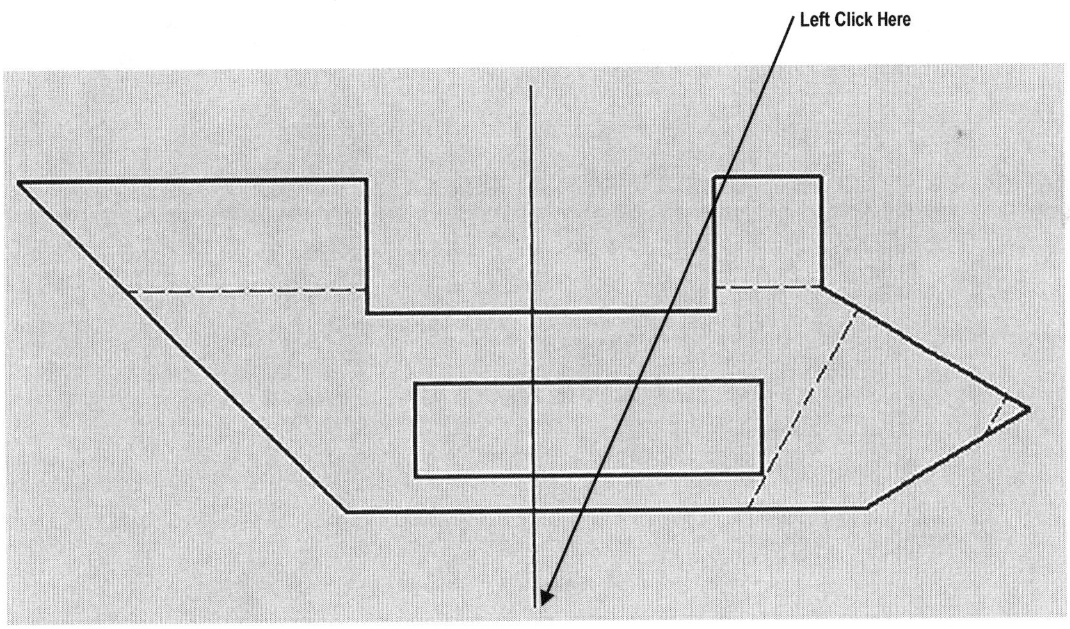

Figure 23

25. Right click once. Left click on **Continue** as shown in Figure 24.

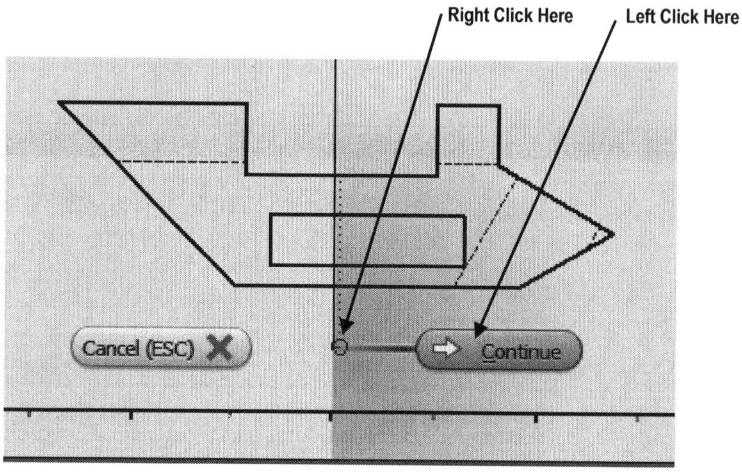

Figure 24

26. The Section View dialog box will appear as shown in Figure 25. The section view will be attached to the cursor. Move the cursor to the right where the side view was located and left click once. The Section View dialog box will close.

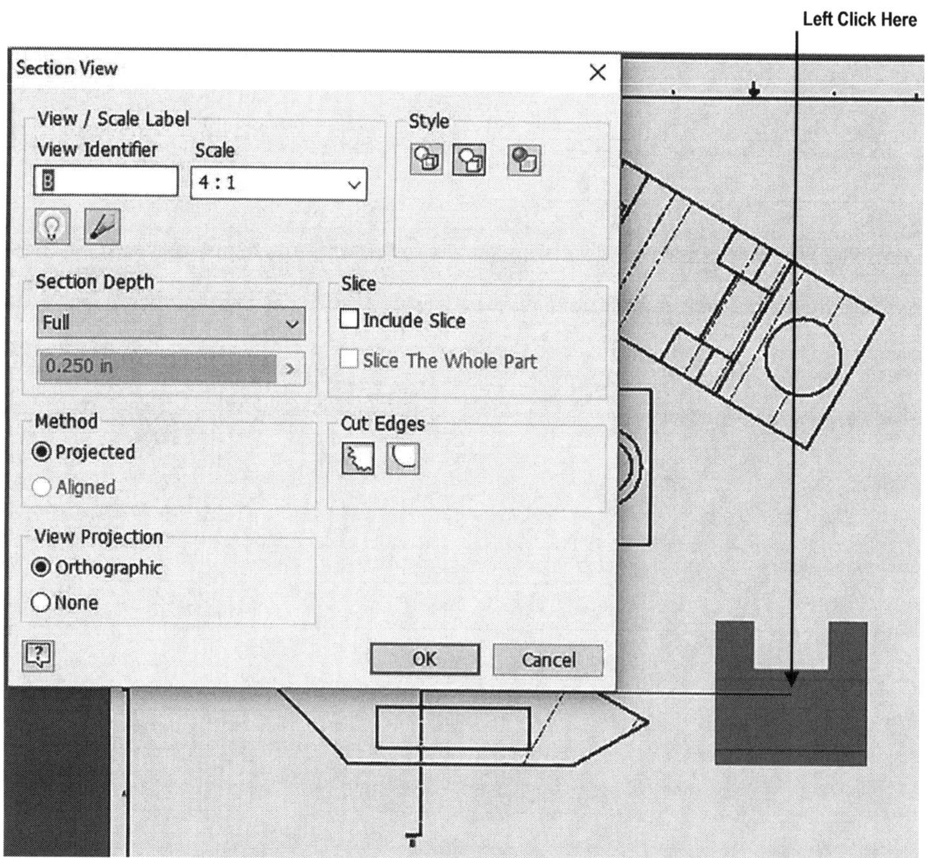

Figure 25

27. Inventor will create a section view to the right as shown in Figure 26.

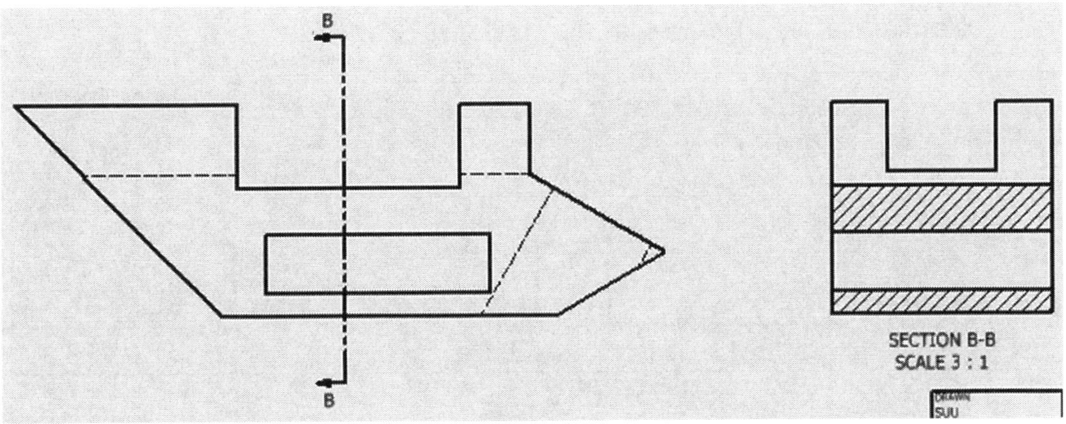

Figure 26

28. Inventor will create a section view. The cross hatch in the section view represents wherever the cutting plane line cuts through the part. Move the cursor over the center of the cutting plane line causing it to turn red as shown in Figure 27.

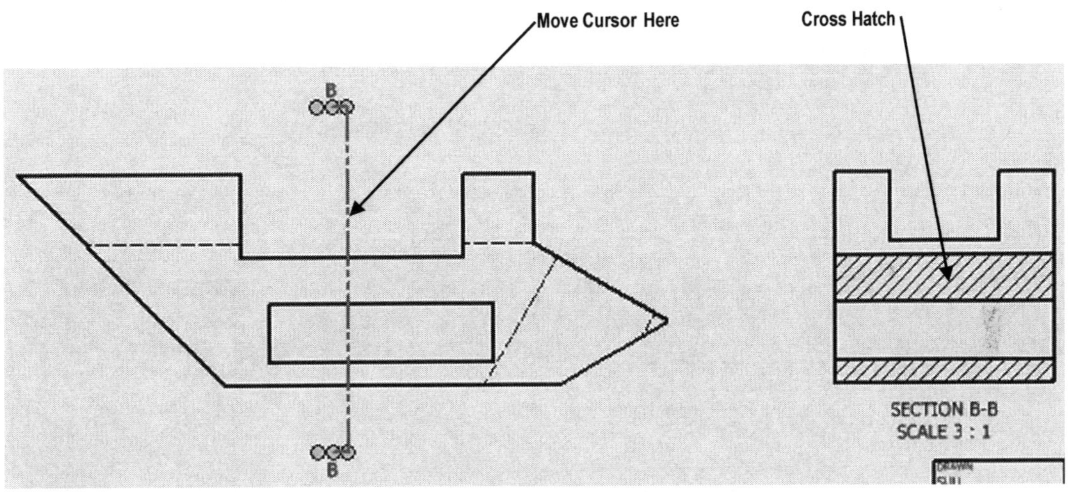

Figure 27

29. Once the line becomes highlighted (turns red) left click (holding the left mouse button down) and drag the cursor to the right. The cutting plane line will become a normal looking line while attached to the cursor as shown in Figure 28.

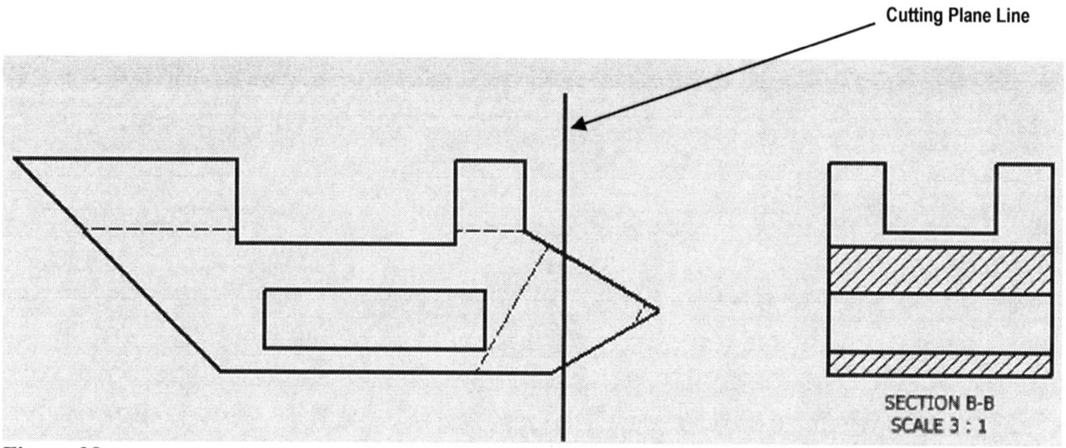

Figure 28

30. Once the cutting plane line has been moved to a new location release the left mouse button. The section view now reflects the new location of the cutting plane line as shown in Figure 29.

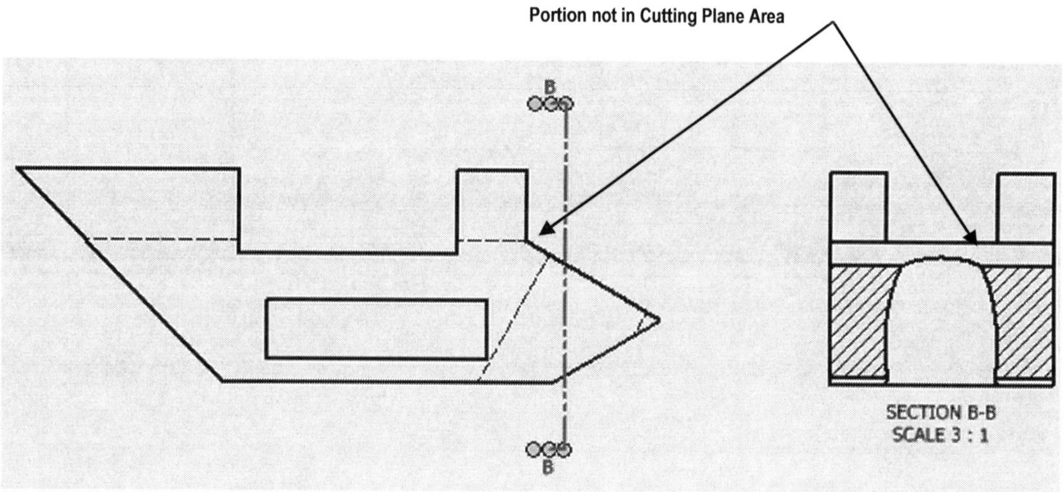

Figure 29

Create a broken view using the Break command

31. Left click (holding the left mouse button down) on the cutting plane line and move it back to its original location. Notice that the cross hatch in the section view will update to reflect the location of the cutting plane line as shown in Figure 30.

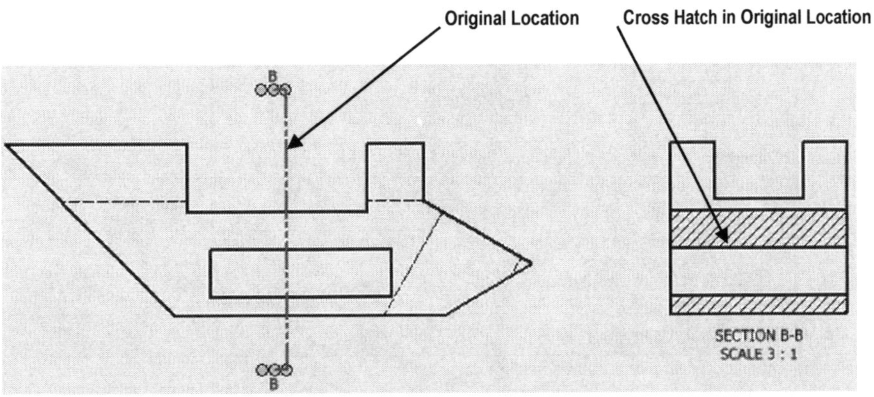

Figure 30

32. Move the cursor to the middle left portion of the screen and left click on **Break** as shown in Figure 31.

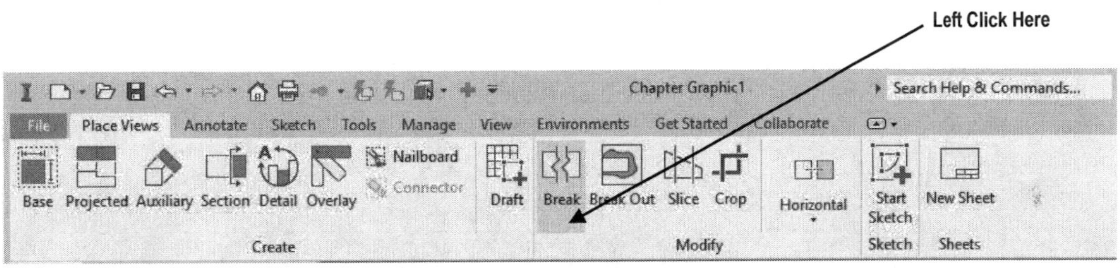

Figure 31

33. Move the cursor to the front view causing red dots to appear. Left click once as shown in Figure 32.

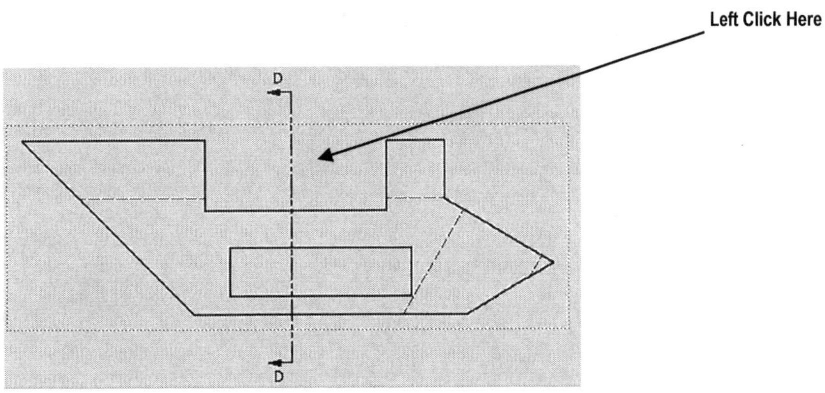

Figure 32

34. The Break Dialog box will appear.

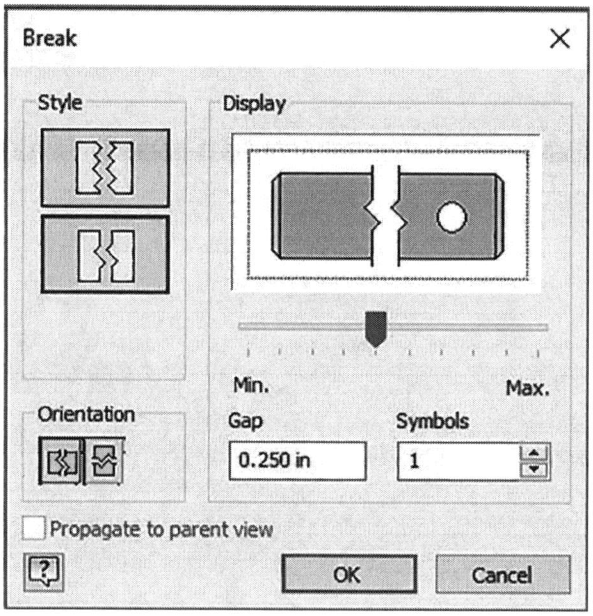

Figure 33

35. Left click on the part causing a red box to appear as shown in Figure 34.

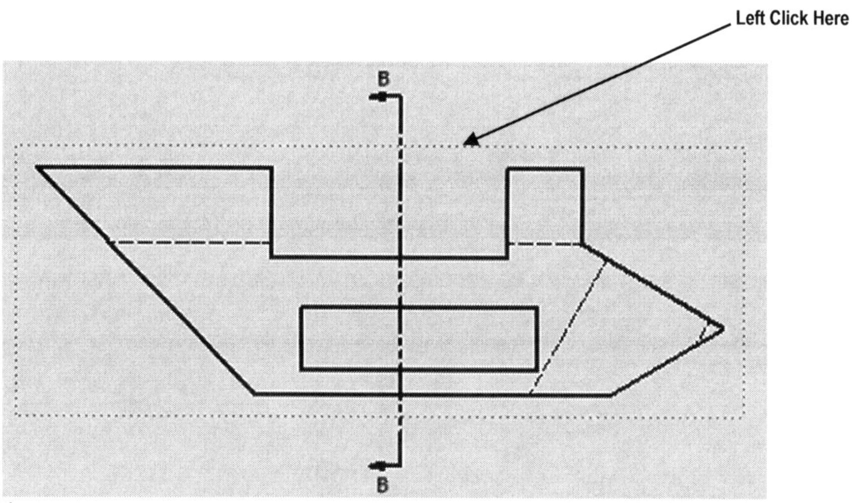

Figure 34

36. Move the cursor to the left side of the cutting plane line and left click once. Move the cursor to the left. Another line will appear next to the first line. These two lines represent the size of the gap that Inventor will create in the part. A third line will be attached to the cursor. This line represents how much of the part will be removed from the view. Move the cursor to the far left portion of the part and left click as shown in Figure 35.

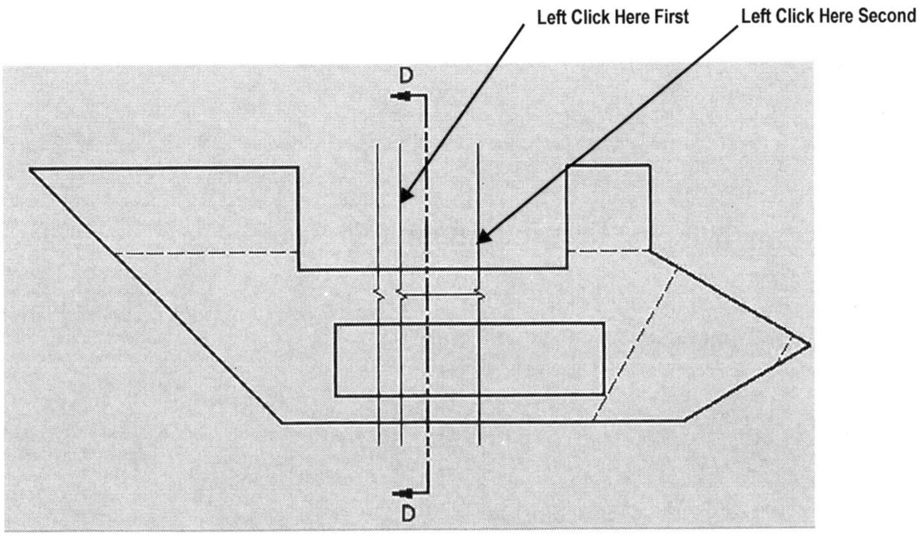

Figure 35

37. Inventor will remove sections from both the front and top views as shown in Figure 36.

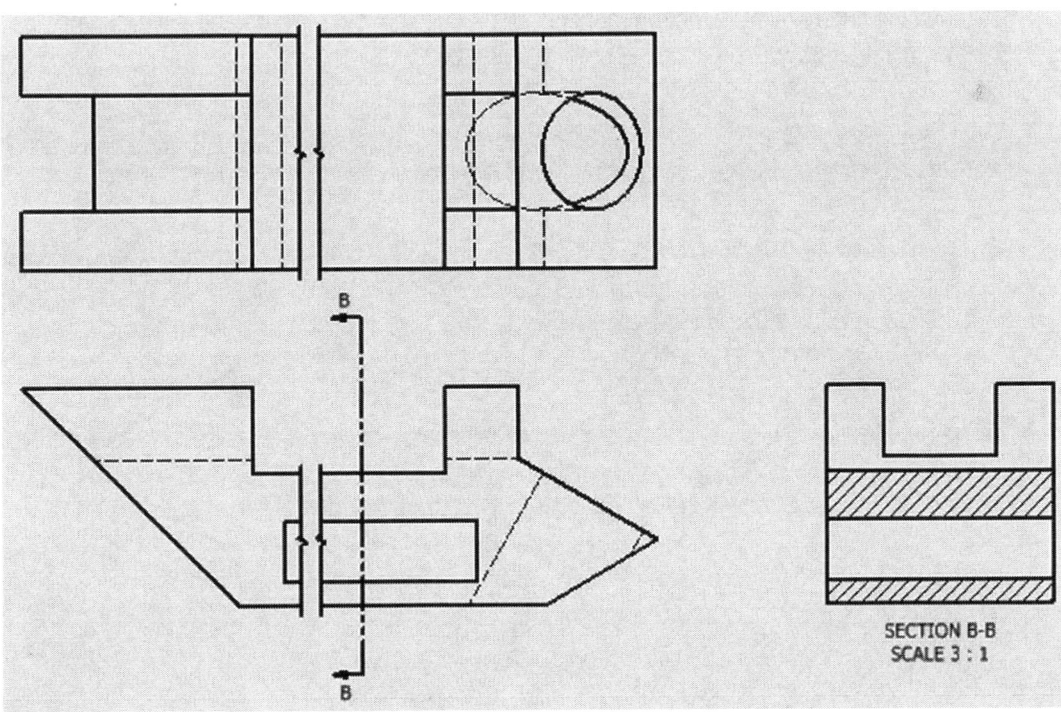

Figure 36

38. Move the cursor to the upper left portion of the screen and left click on **Undo** as shown in Figure 37.

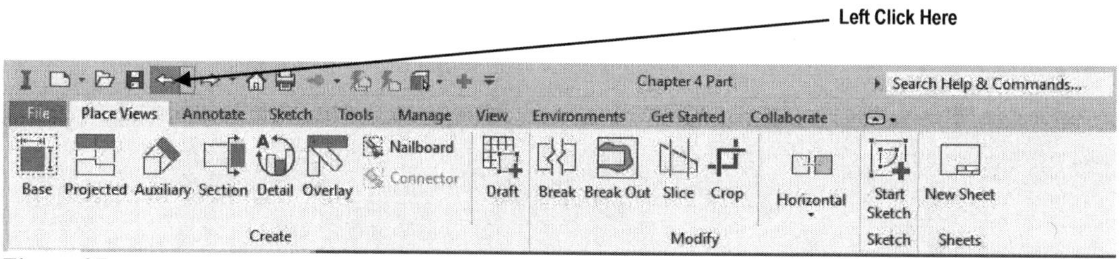

Figure 37

Dimension views using the Drawing Annotation Panel

39. Move the cursor to the upper left portion of the screen and left click on the **Annotate** tab. Left click on **Dimension** as shown in Figure 38.

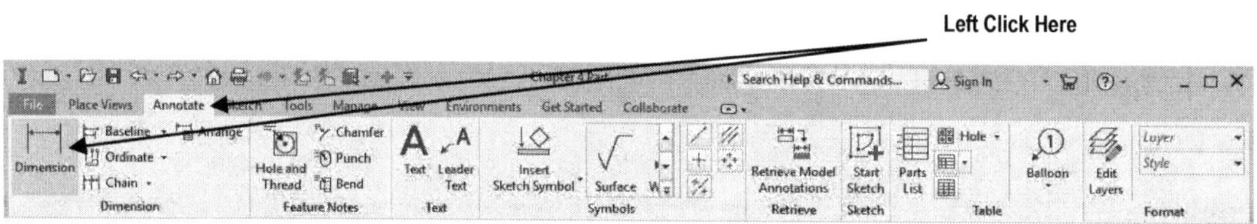

Figure 38

40. Move the cursor over the top horizontal line causing it to turn red and left click once. Then move the cursor over the bottom horizontal line causing it to turn red and left click once as shown in Figure 39. The dimension will be attached to the cursor.

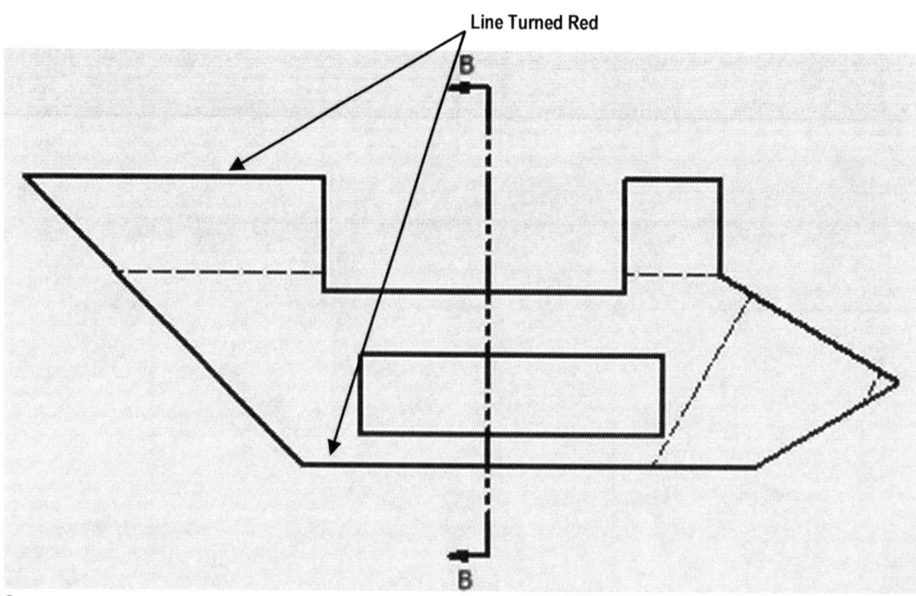

Figure 39

41. Move the cursor to the left and left click once. The actual dimension of the line will appear as shown in Figure 40. The Edit Dimension dialog box (not shown) will appear. Left click on **OK**. If there is a need to change the size of the dimensions, left click on the **Manage** tab, **Styles Editor**, scroll down to, and left click on the Plus sign to the left of **Text**, then left click on **Note Text (ANSI)**. Just below "Text Height" is the size of the dimension text. Enter .500 (or larger) to increase the dimension text height.

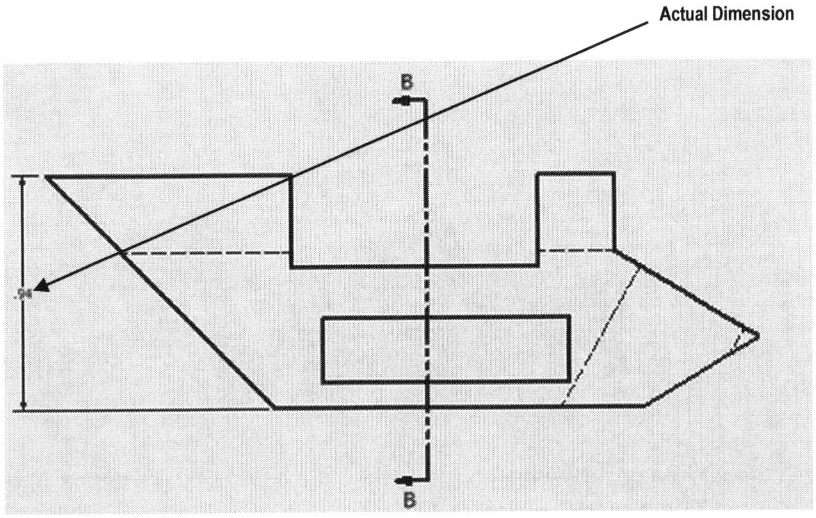

Figure 40

42. Finish dimensioning the part to your own satisfaction. When the part is satisfactorily dimensioned, save the file to a location where it can easily be retrieved.

43. To delete an unwanted dimension, move the cursor over the dimension. The dimension will turn red and several green dots will appear as shown in Figure 41.

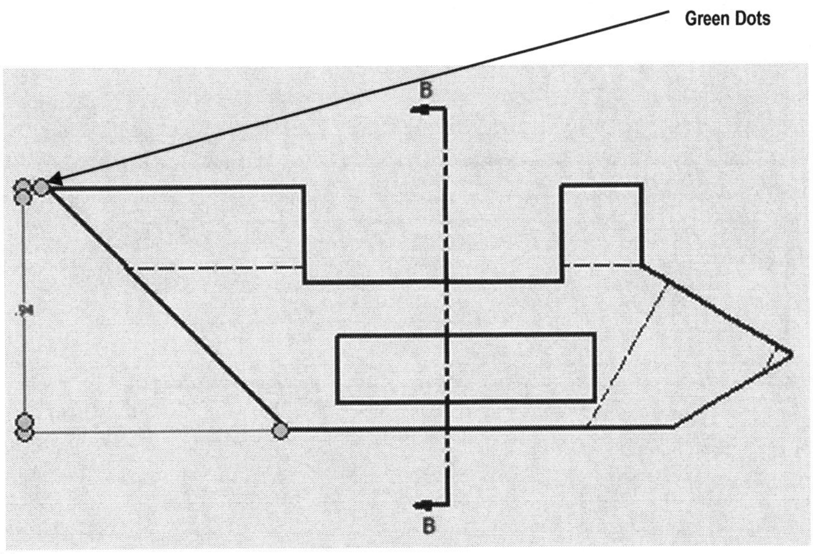

Figure 41

Create Text using the Drawing Annotation Panel

44. Right click on the dimension. A pop-up menu will appear. Left click on **Delete** as shown in Figure 42.

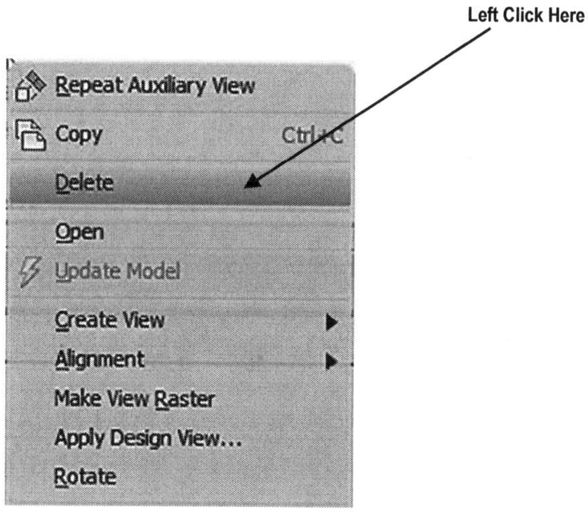

Figure 42

45. Move the cursor to the upper middle portion of the screen and left click on the **Annotate** tab. Left click on **Text** as shown in Figure 43.

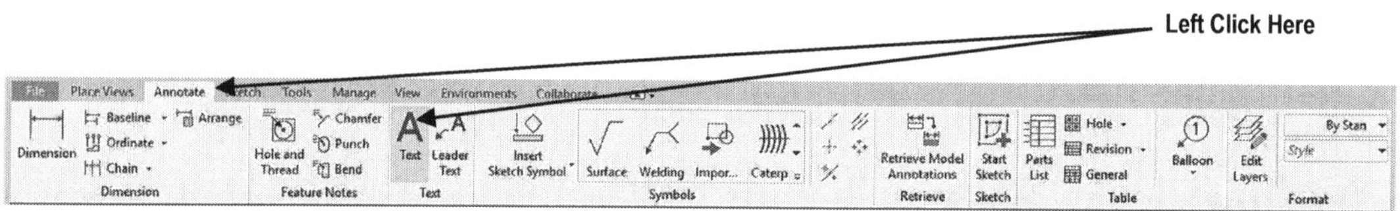

Figure 43

46. Move the cursor to the title block location as shown in Figure 44. Left click once when the yellow dot appears.

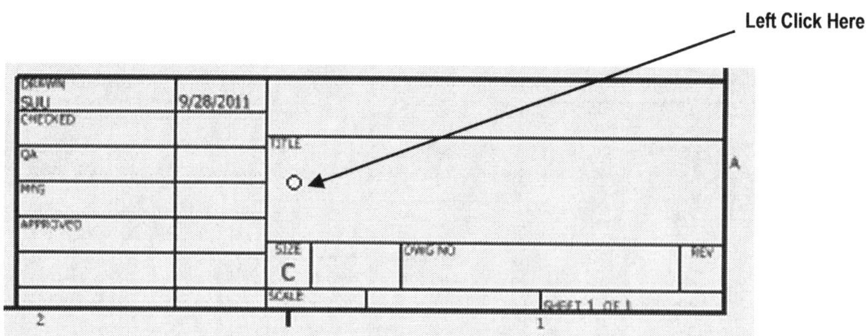

Figure 44

47. The Format Text dialog box will appear. Left click on the drop-down box and change the text height to **.240** inches as shown in Figure 45.

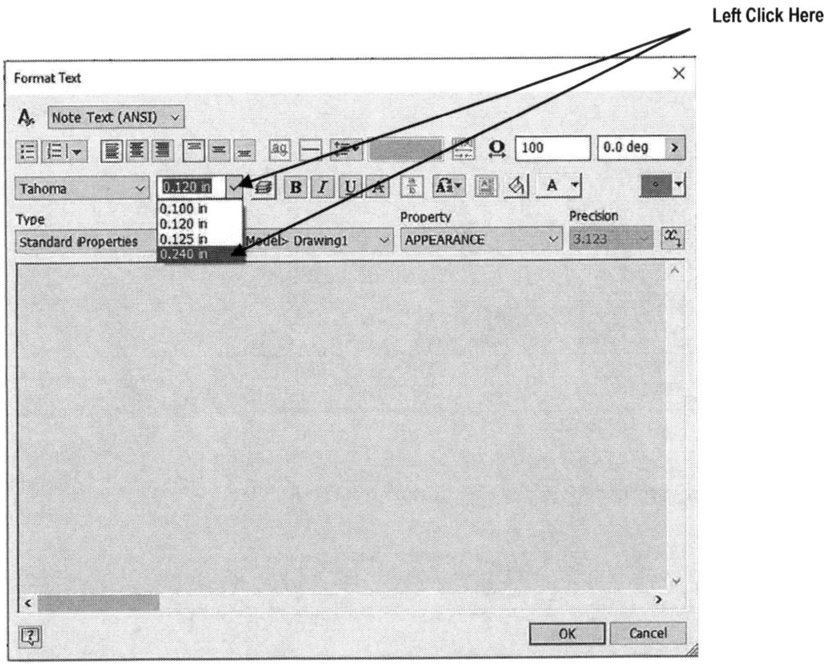

Figure 45

48. Move the cursor to the open area located in the lower half of the Format Text dialog box and enter your first and last name. Text will appear near the flashing cursor as shown in Figure 46.

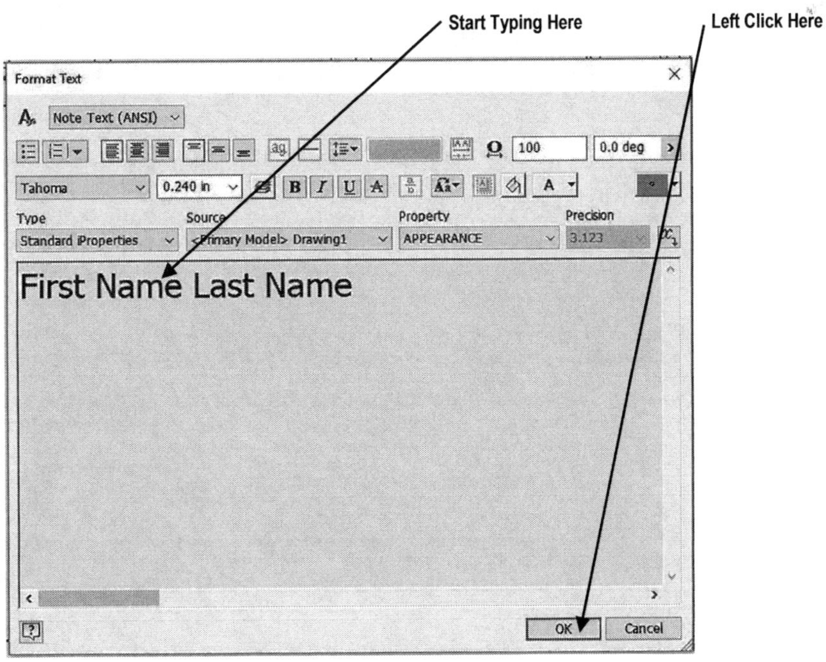

Figure 46

49. After text has been entered, left click on **OK** as shown in Figure 46.

50. The Format Text dialog box will close.

51. Text will appear in the title block as shown in Figure 47.

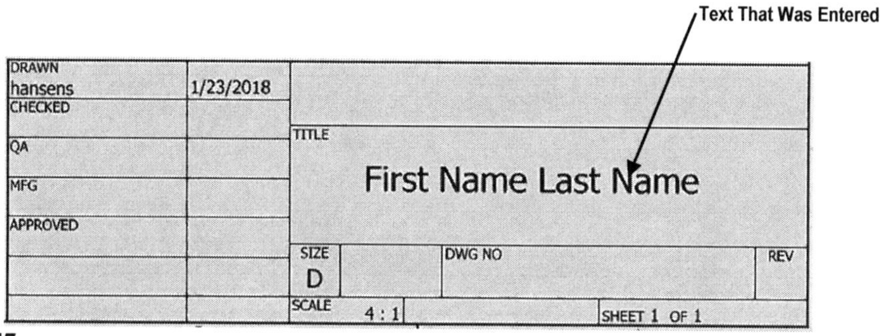

Figure 47

52. Right click near the text. A pop-up menu will appear as shown in Figure 48.

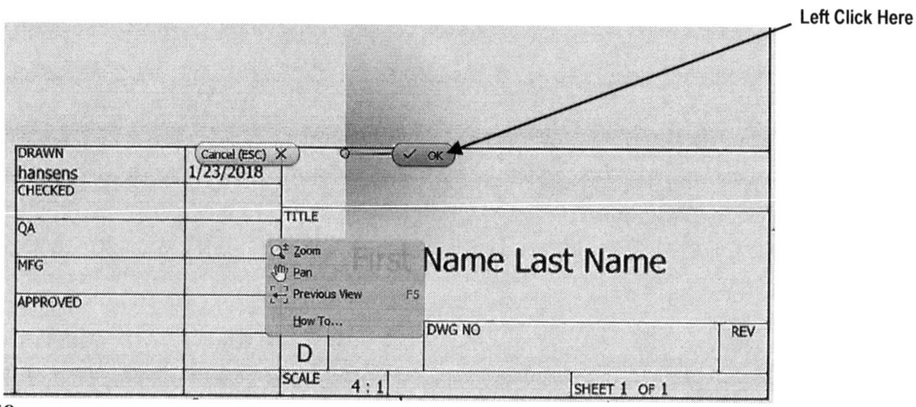

Figure 48

53. If the text needs to be moved, move the cursor over the text causing several green dots to appear as shown in Figure 49.

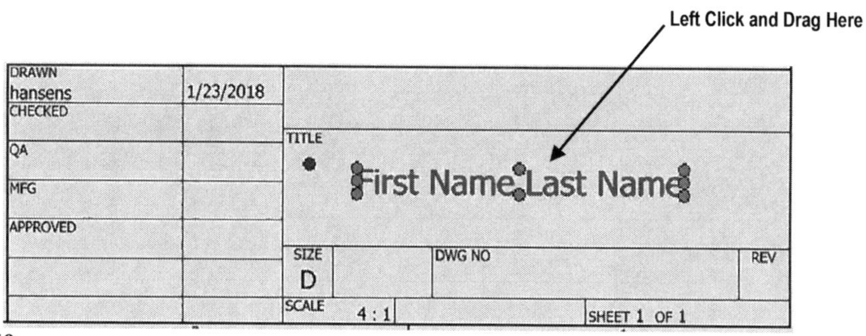

Figure 49

54. While the text is highlighted, left click (holding the left mouse button down) and drag the text to the desired location. After the text is in the desired location, release the left mouse button, move the cursor away from the text, and left click once.

55. Move the cursor to the upper left portion of the screen and left click on the **Place Views** tab as shown in Figure 50. This will return Inventor to the Place View tool bar.

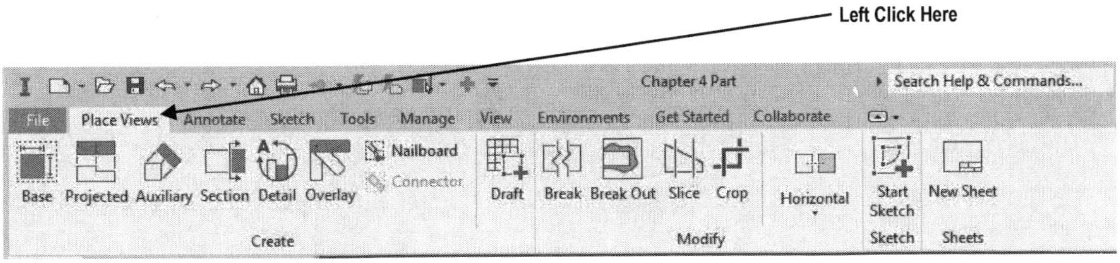

Figure 50

56. Your screen should look similar to Figure 51.

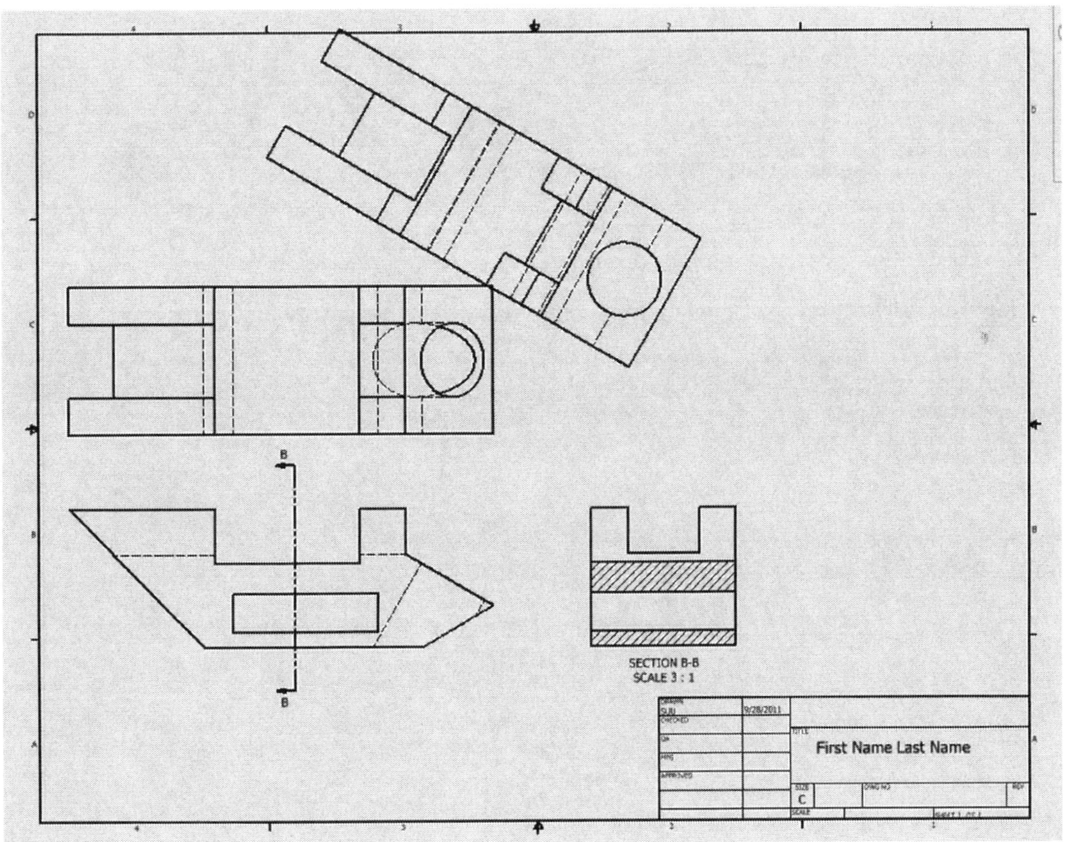

Figure 51

57. Before starting a new sheet of detail drawings, make sure to first save the current sheet. **Caution: Once a new sheet has been created the old sheet is not retrievable unless it has been saved. If a new sheet is created before the old sheet was saved, left click on the Undo icon located at the upper left portion of the screen as shown in Figure 52.**

Figure 52

58. Move the cursor to the left middle portion of the screen and left click on **New Sheet** as shown in Figure 53.

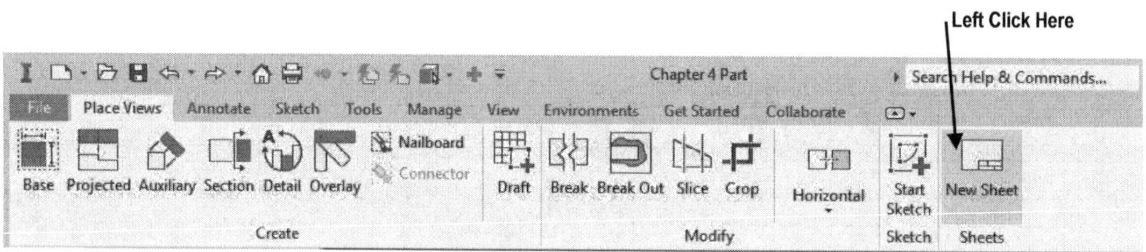

Figure 53

59. This will begin a new sheet for more detail drawings if necessary.

Chapter Problems

Create Section View Drawings for the following problems.

Problem 4-1

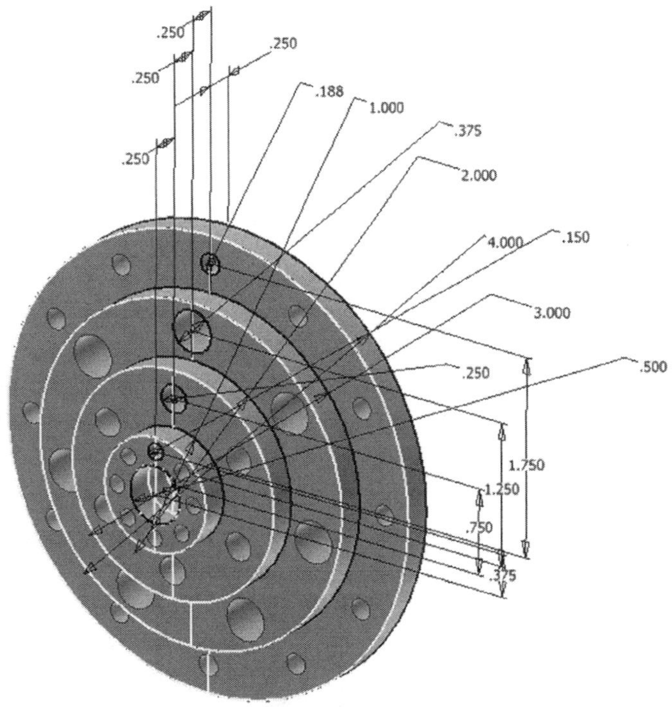

Problem 4-2

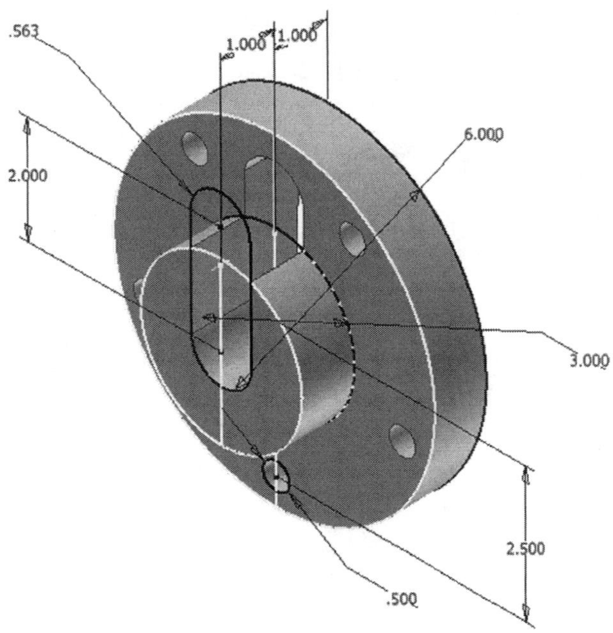

Problem 4-3 Create the sketch shown below. Use the Revolve command to revolve the sketch into a 3D Solid (shown at the bottom of the page) then create a Section View

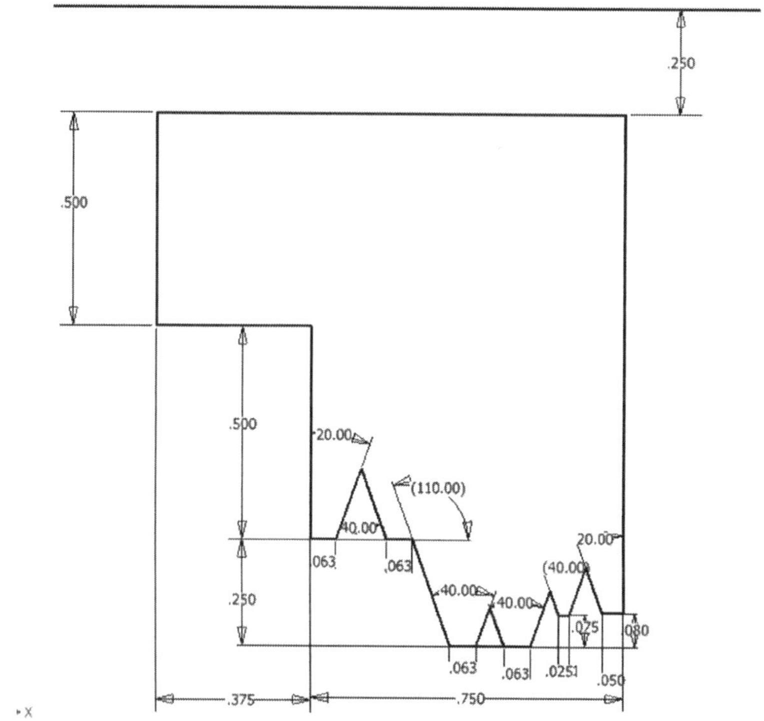

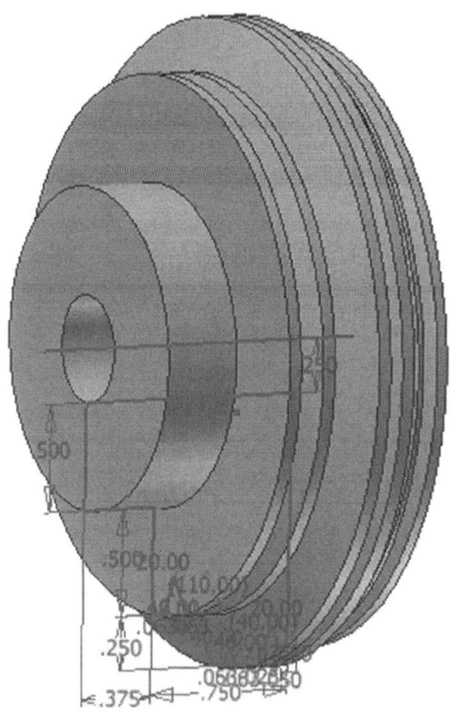

Problem 4-4 Create the sketch shown below. Use the Revolve command to revolve the sketch into a 3D Solid (shown at the bottom of the page) then create a Section View

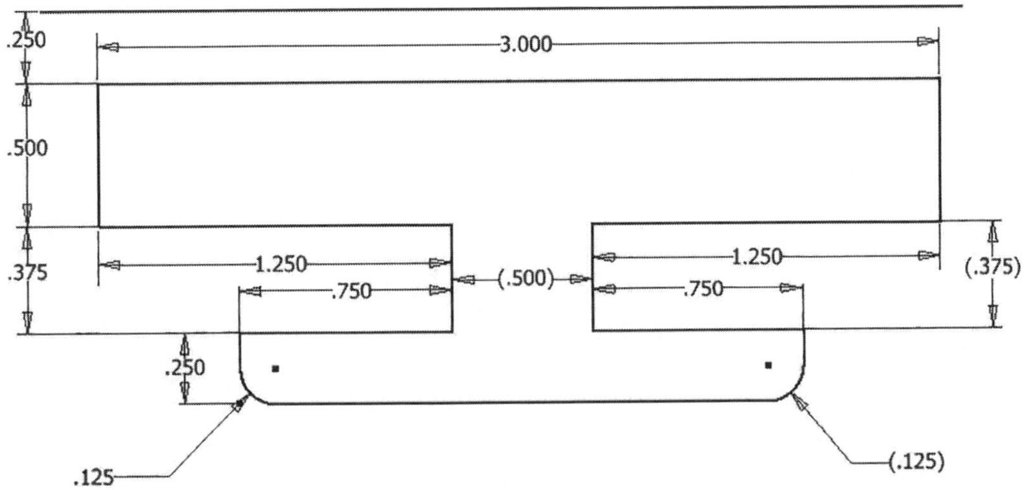

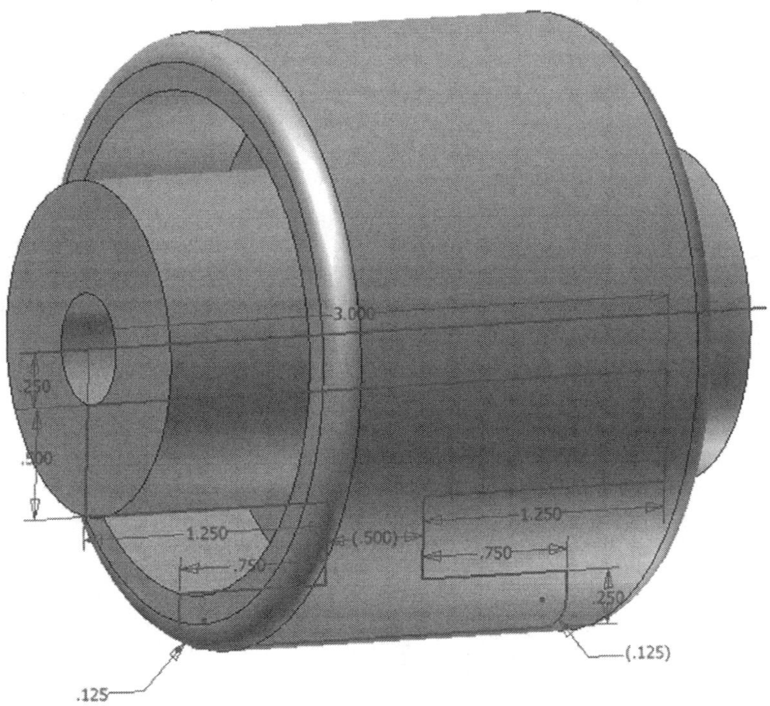

Problem 4-5 Create Section View Drawings for the following problems

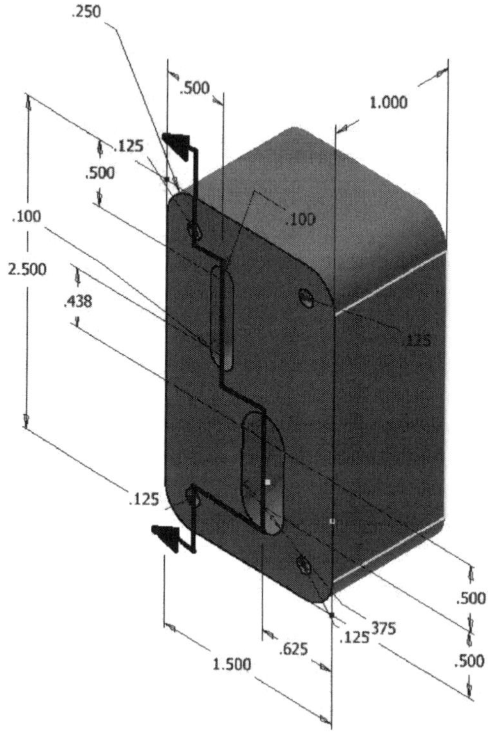

Problem 4-6

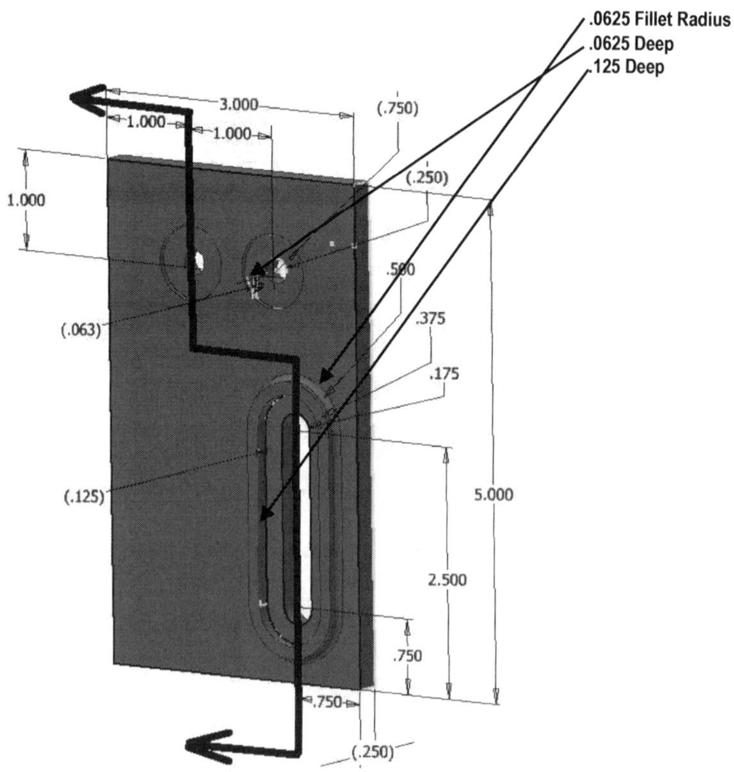

Problem 4-7

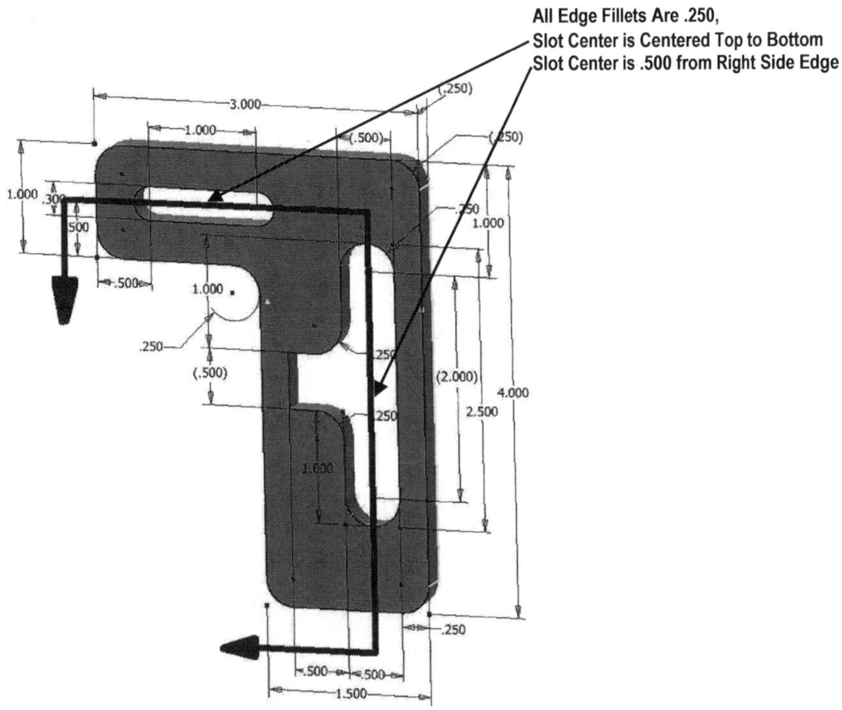

Problem 4-8

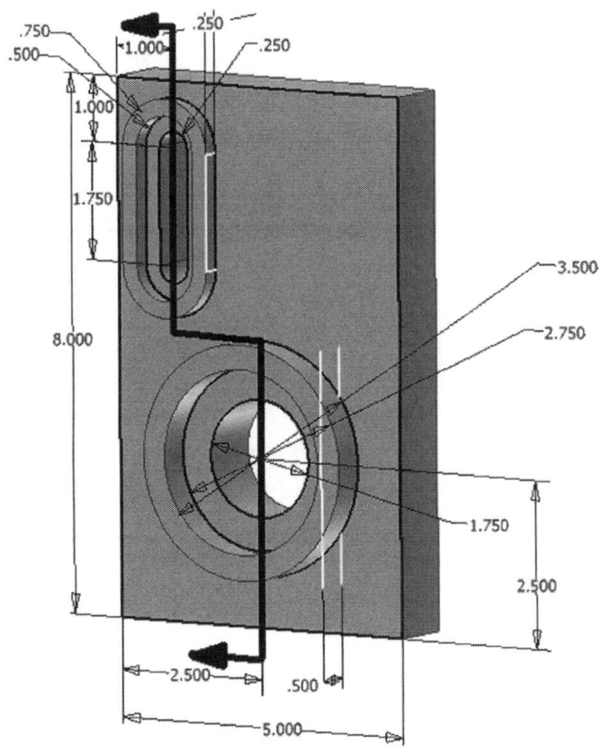

CHAPTER 5

Learning to Edit Existing Solid Models

Objectives:

1. Design a simple part
2. Learn to use the Circular Pattern Command
3. Edit the part using the Sketch Panel
4. Edit the part using the Extrude Command
5. Edit the part using the Fillet Command

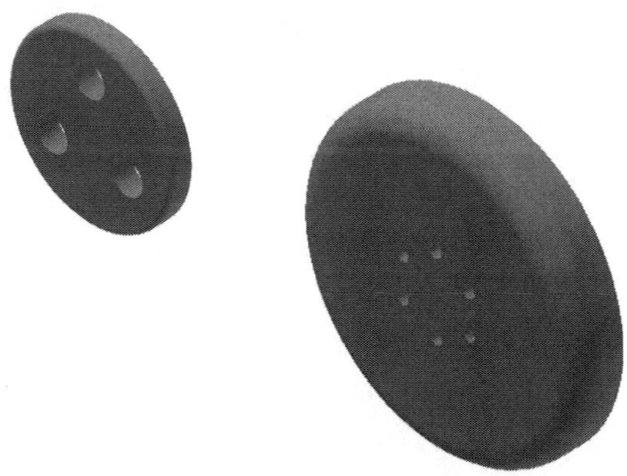

Chapter 5 includes instruction on how to design and edit the part shown.

1. Start Autodesk Inventor 2027 by referring to "Chapter 1 Getting Started."
2. After Autodesk Inventor 2027 is running, begin a new sketch.
3. Create the sketch on the **XY Plane** as shown in Figure 1.

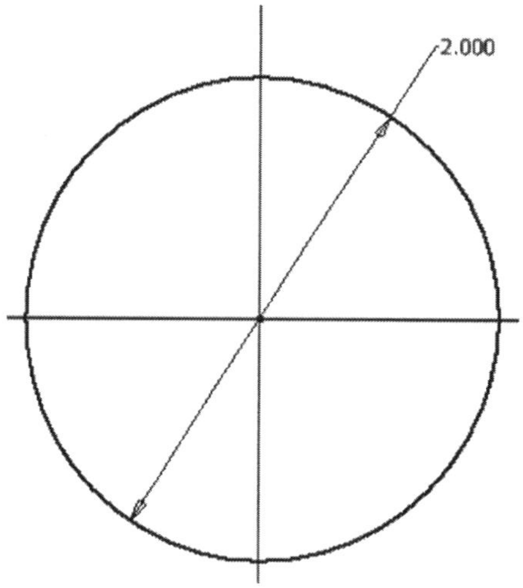

Figure 1

4. Change the view to Isometric/Home View as shown in Figure 2.

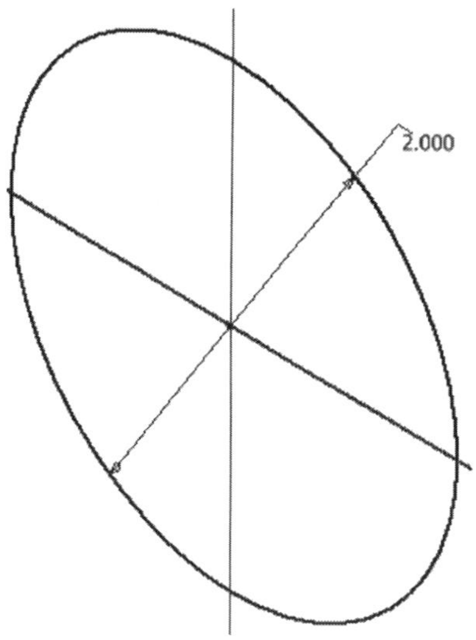

Figure 2

5. Extrude the sketch to a distance of .25 inches as shown in Figure 3.

6. Once a solid has been created, begin a New Sketch on the front surface as shown in Figure 3.

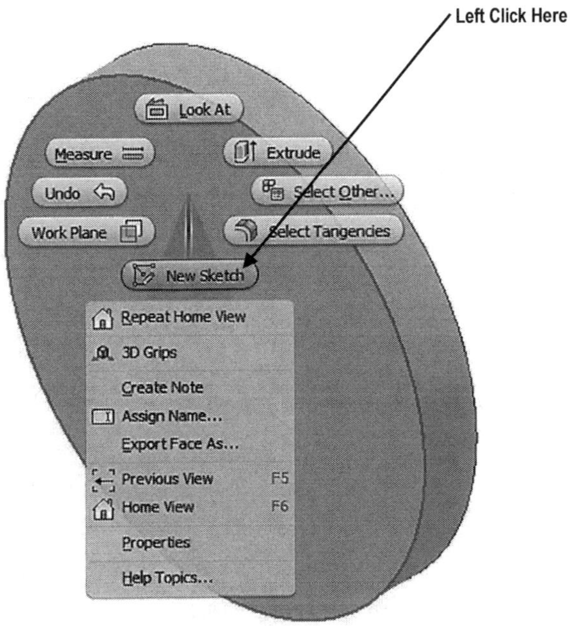

Figure 3

7. Complete the following sketch as shown in Figure 4.

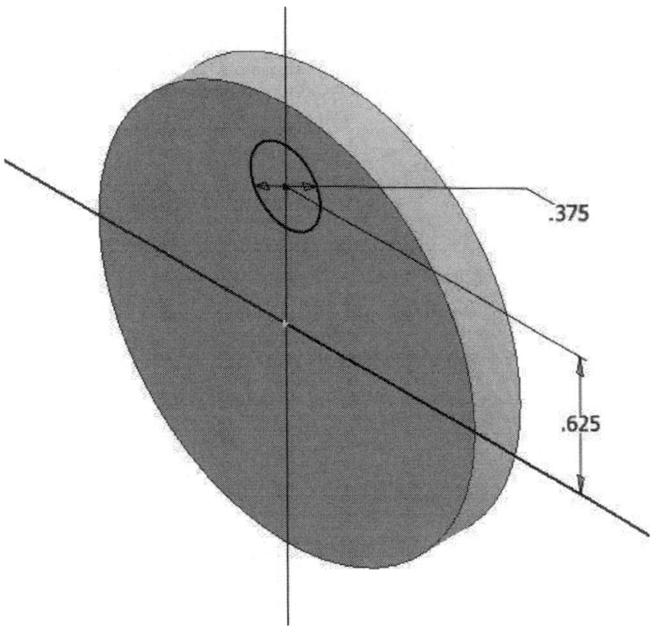

Figure 4

8. Exit out of the Sketch Panel. Change the view to Isometric/Home View as shown in Figure 5.

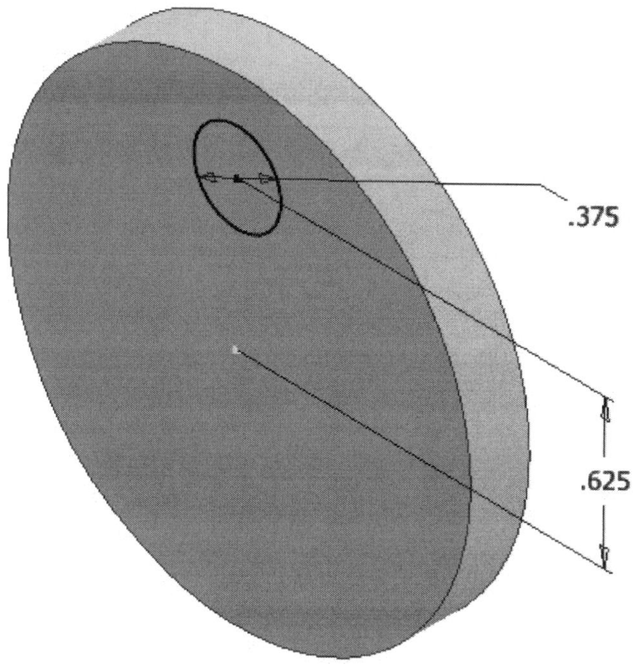

Figure 5

9. Use the Extrude-Cut command to cut a hole in the part as shown in Figure 6.

Figure 6

10. Use the Circular Pattern command to create 3 holes in the part as shown in Figure 7.

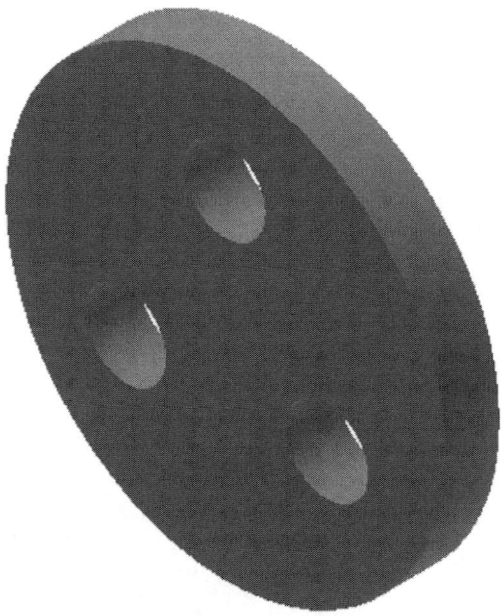

Figure 7

11. Use the Fillet command to create a fillet with .0625 radius as shown in Figure 8.

Figure 8

Edit the part using the Sketch Panel

12. If for some reason a change needs to be made to this part, it can be accomplished by editing either a sketch or a feature located in the browser at the upper left corner of the screen as shown in Figure 9.

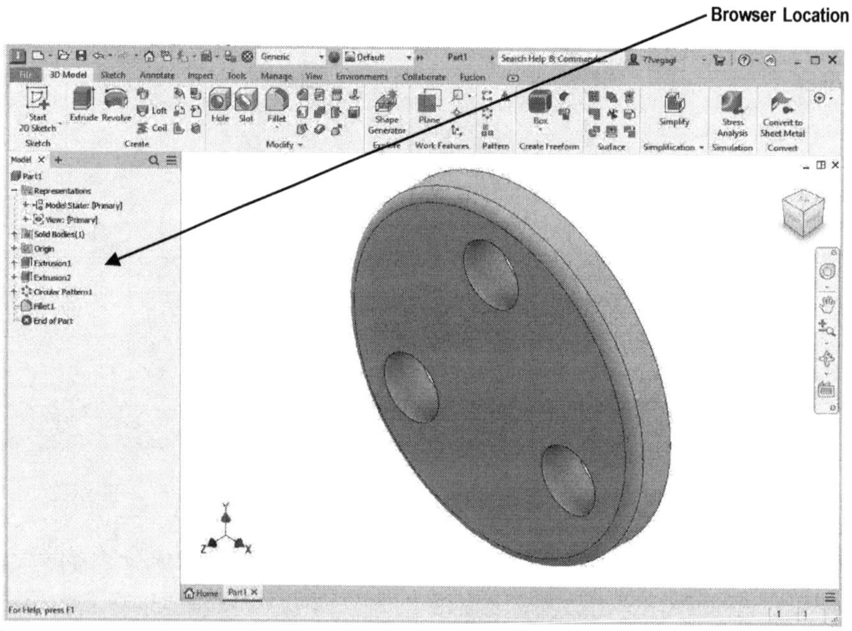

Figure 9

13. A close-up of the browser is shown in Figure 10. Left click on each of the "plus signs" in the browser. The browser will expand showing more details for part construction.

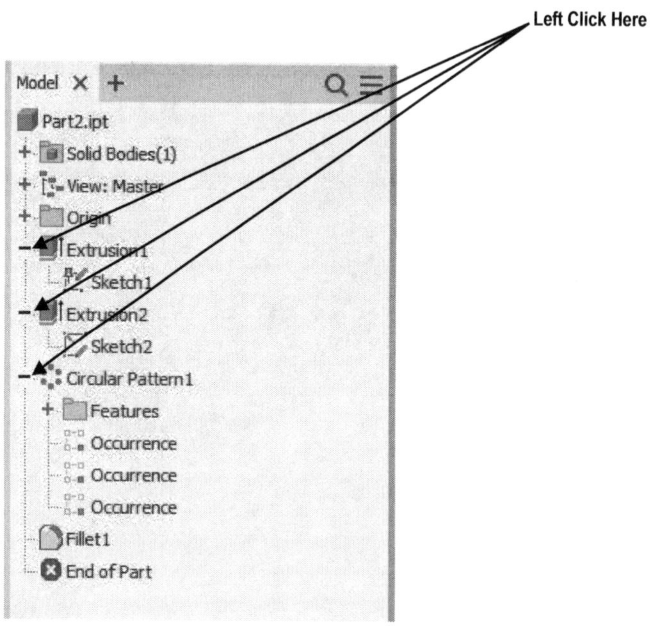

Figure 10

14. If a change needs to be made to any portion of the part that was constructed using Sketch1, the change can be made here.

15. Move the cursor over Sketch1. A box will appear around the text “Sketch1” as shown in Figure 11.

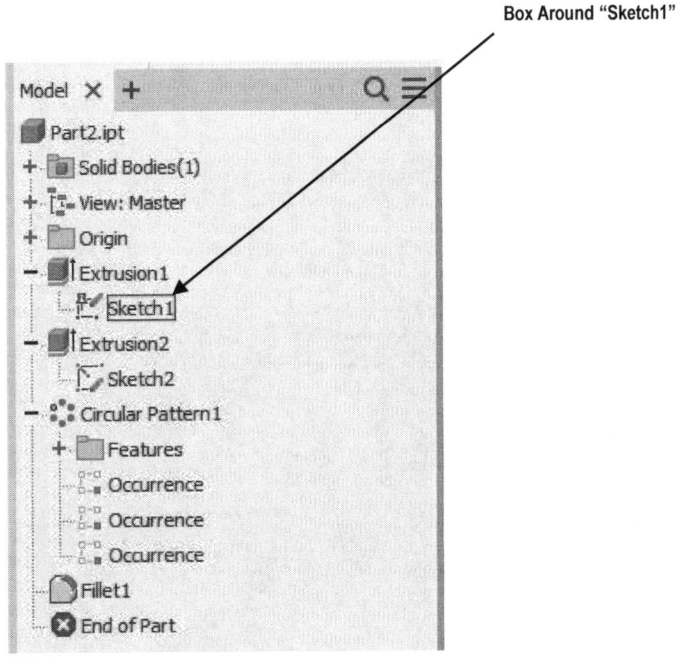

Figure 11

16. The original sketch will also appear as shown in Figure 12.

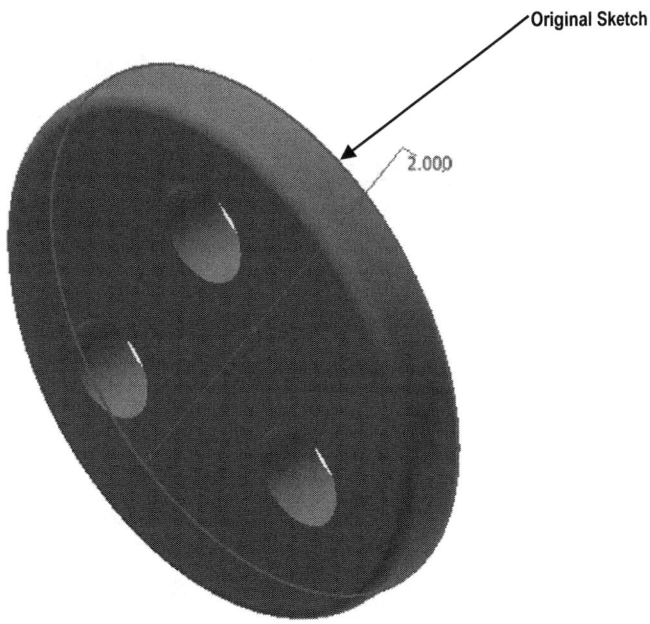

Figure 12

17. Right click on **Sketch1**. The text "Sketch1" will become highlighted. A pop-up menu will appear. Left click on **Edit Sketch** as shown in Figure 13.

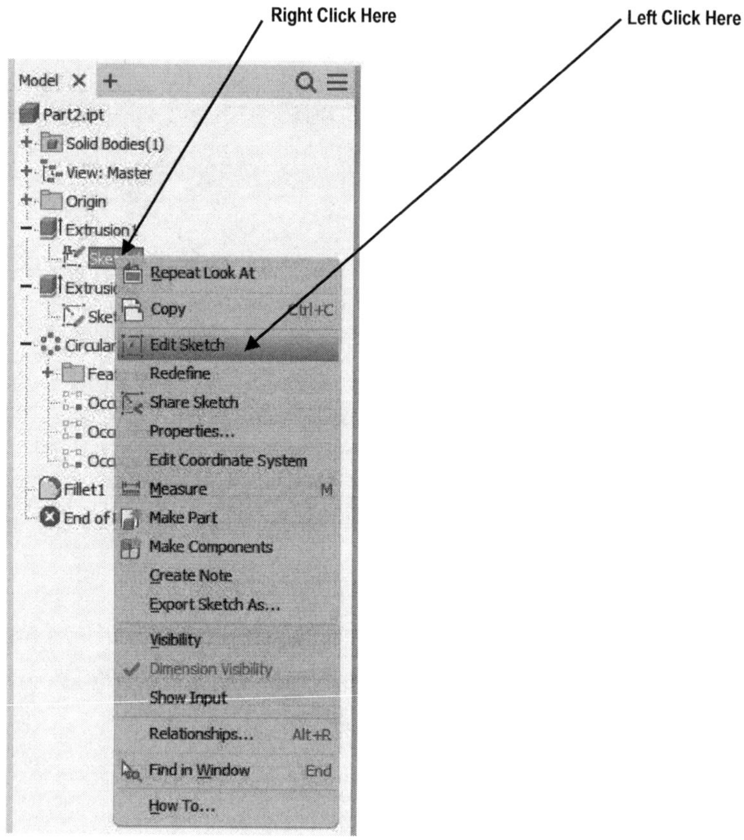

Figure 13

18. The original sketch will appear as shown in Figure 14.

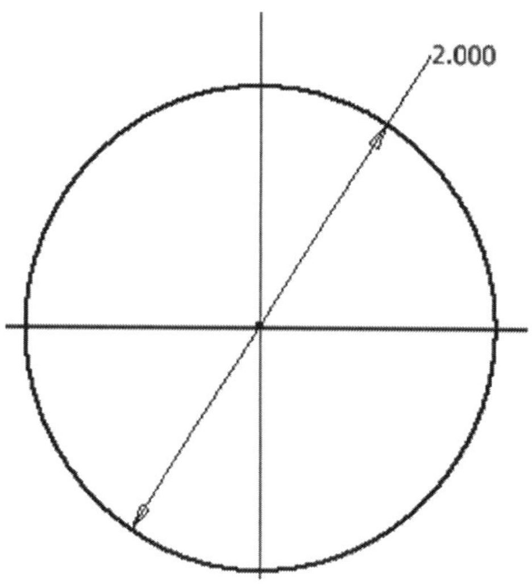

Figure 14

19. If Inventor rotated the part to provide a perpendicular view then skip to Number 22. If the sketch is not a perpendicular view, move the cursor to the upper right portion of the screen and left click on the "Face View/Look At" icon as shown in Figure 15.

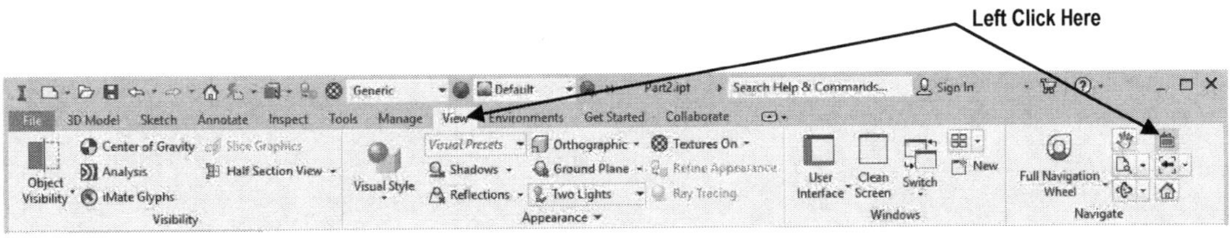

Figure 15

20. Move the cursor over to the browser and left click on the "plus" sign to the left of Origin. The browser will expand displaying all three workplanes. Move the cursor over the text "XY Plane." A box will appear around XY Plane and the sketch itself. After the box appears, left click once on the **XY Plane** as shown in Figure 16.

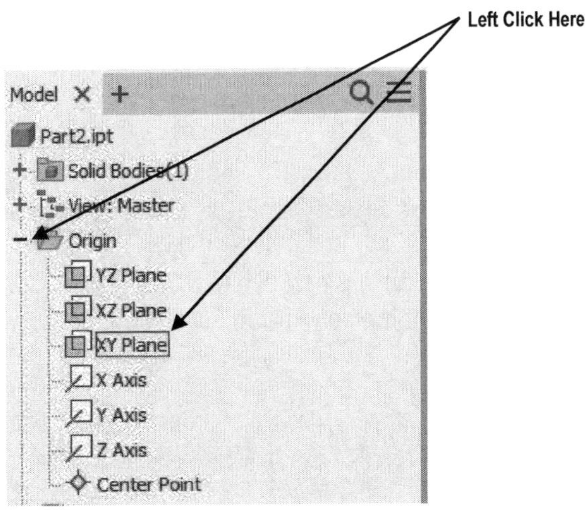

Figure 16

21. Inventor will provide a perpendicular view of the sketch similar to when the sketch was first constructed. Your screen should look similar to Figure 17.

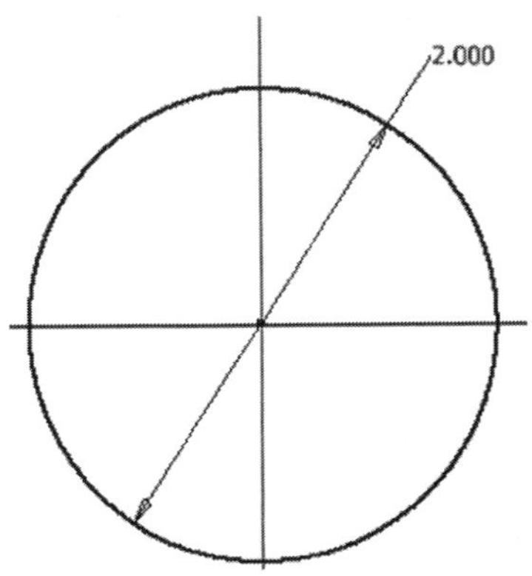

Figure 17

22. Start by modifying the diameter of the part. First, double click on the overall dimension. The Edit Dimension dialog box will appear as shown in Figure 18.

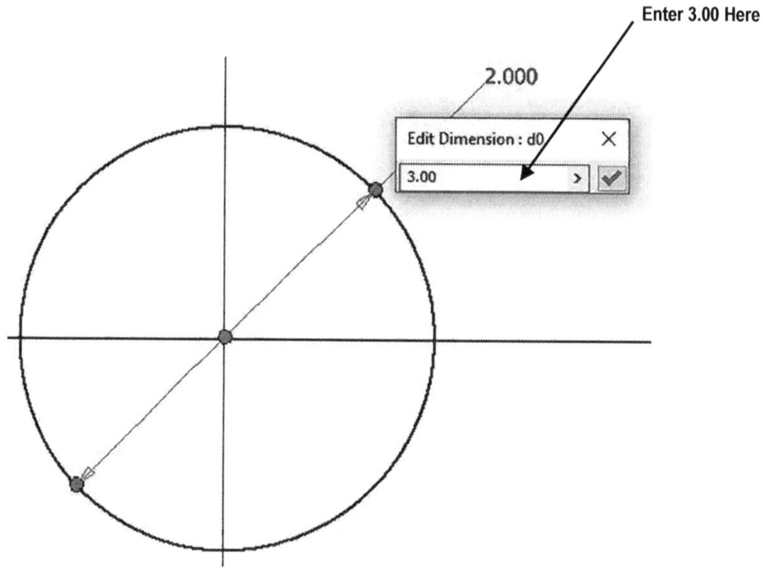

Figure 18

23. Enter **3.00** as shown in Figure 18. Press **Enter** on the keyboard.

24. The diameter of the part will increase to 3.00. Right click around the sketch. A pop-up menu will appear. Left click on **Finish 2D Sketch** as shown in Figure 19.

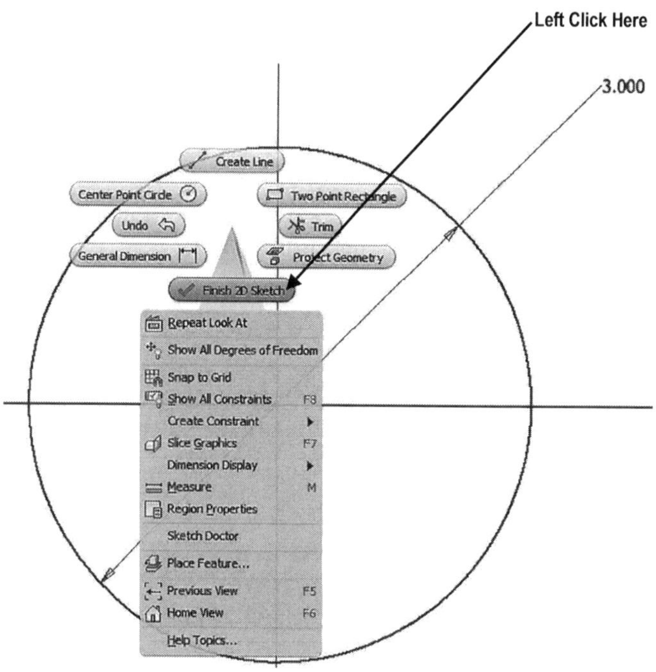

Figure 19

25. Exiting out of the Sketch Panel Inventor should update to reflect the changes made to the part. If the part did not update, move the cursor to the upper left portion of the screen and left click on the **Manage** tab. Left click on **Update** as shown in Figure 20.

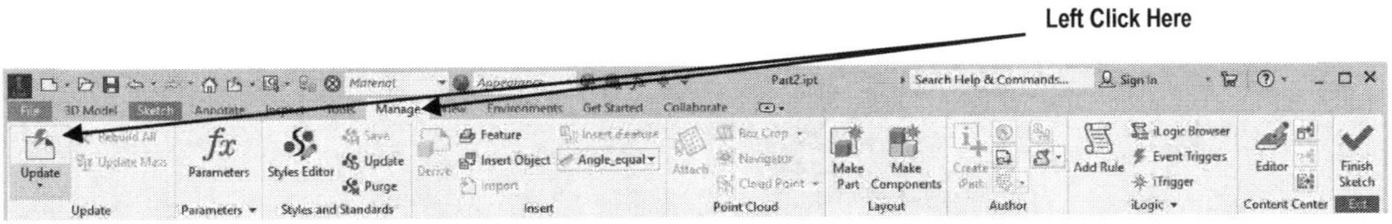

Figure 20

26. Inventor will automatically update the part as shown in Figure 21. The part will be updated without the need to repeat any of the steps that created the original part.

Figure 21

Edit the part using the Extrude command

27. Move the cursor over the text “Extrusion1.” A box will appear around the text. After the box appears, right click once on **Extrusion1** as shown in Figure 22.

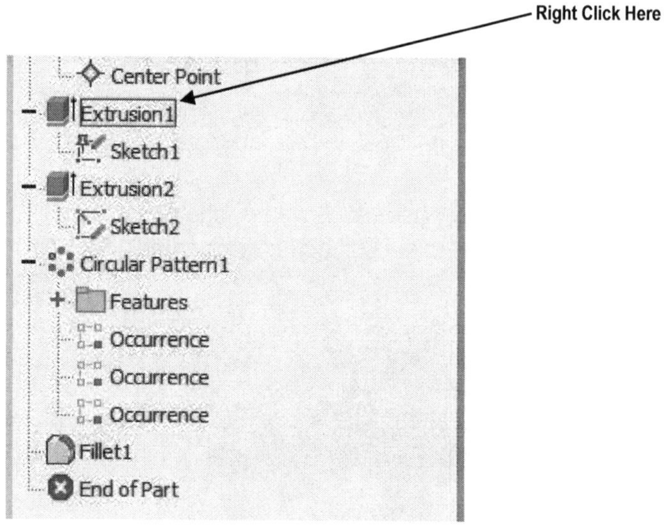

Figure 22

28. A pop-up menu will appear. Left click on **Edit Feature** as shown in Figure 23.

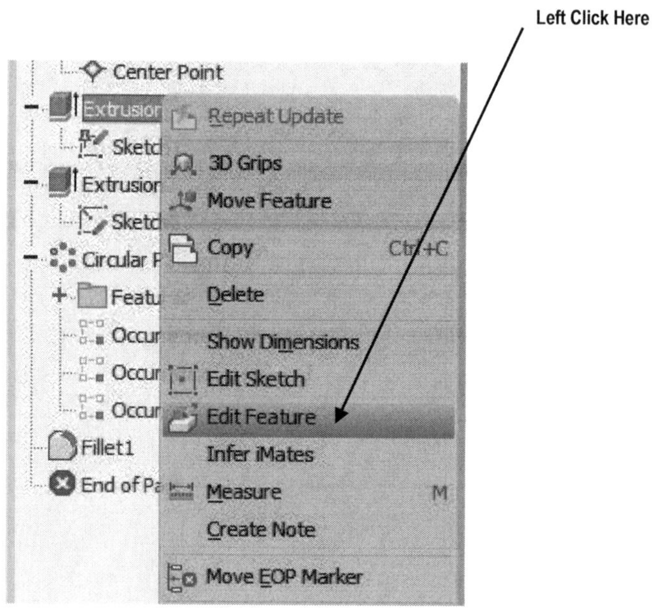

Figure 23

29. The Extrusion dialog box will appear. Enter **.500** for the extrusion distance and left click on **OK** as shown in Figure 24.

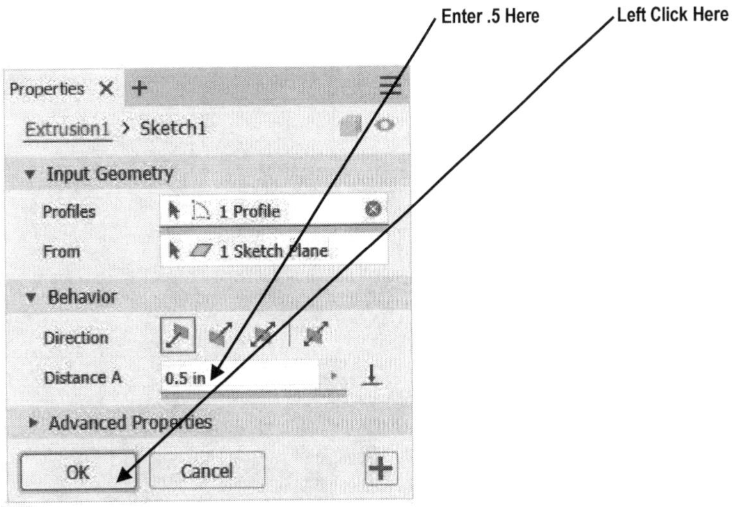

Figure 24

30. Exiting out of the Sketch Panel Inventor should update to reflect the changes made to the part. If the part did not update, move the cursor to the upper left portion of the screen and left click on the **Manage** tab. Left click on **Update** as shown in Figure 25.

Figure 25

31. Inventor will automatically update the part. Notice that the holes are no longer thru holes as shown in Figure 26.

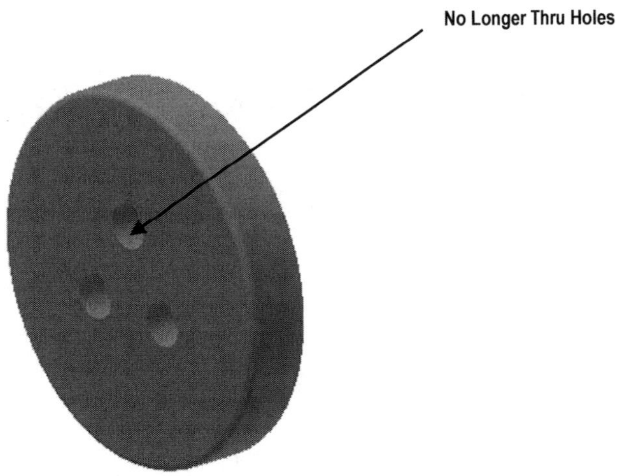

Figure 26

32. Rotate the view around close to perpendicular using "Face View/Look At" command to see that the holes are no longer thru as shown in Figure 27.

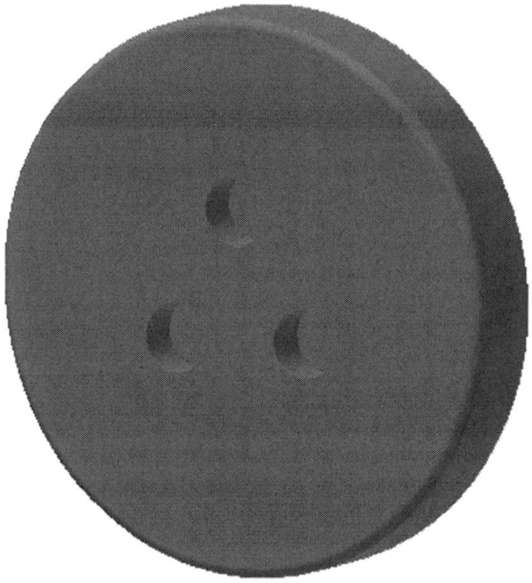

Figure 27

33. Move the cursor over the text "Sketch2." A box will appear around the text. After the box appears, right click once on **Sketch2** as shown in Figure 28.

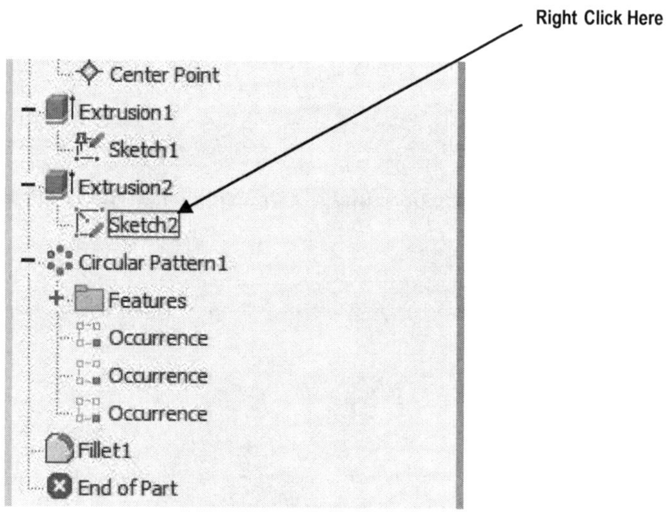

Figure 28

34. A pop-up menu will appear. Left click on **Edit Sketch** as shown in Figure 29.

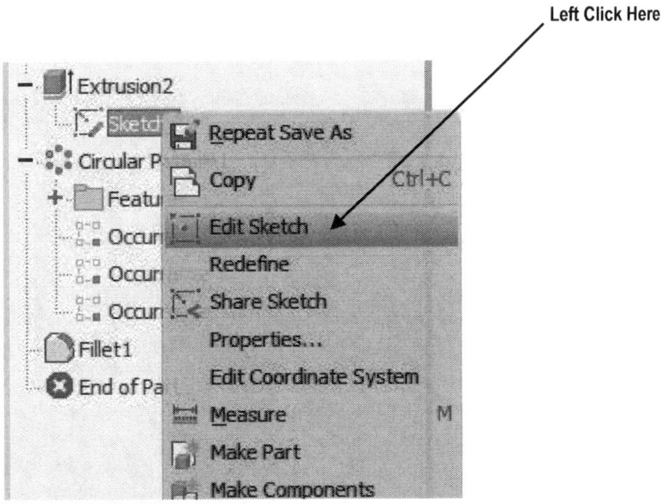

Figure 29

35. The original sketch will appear as shown in Figure 30.

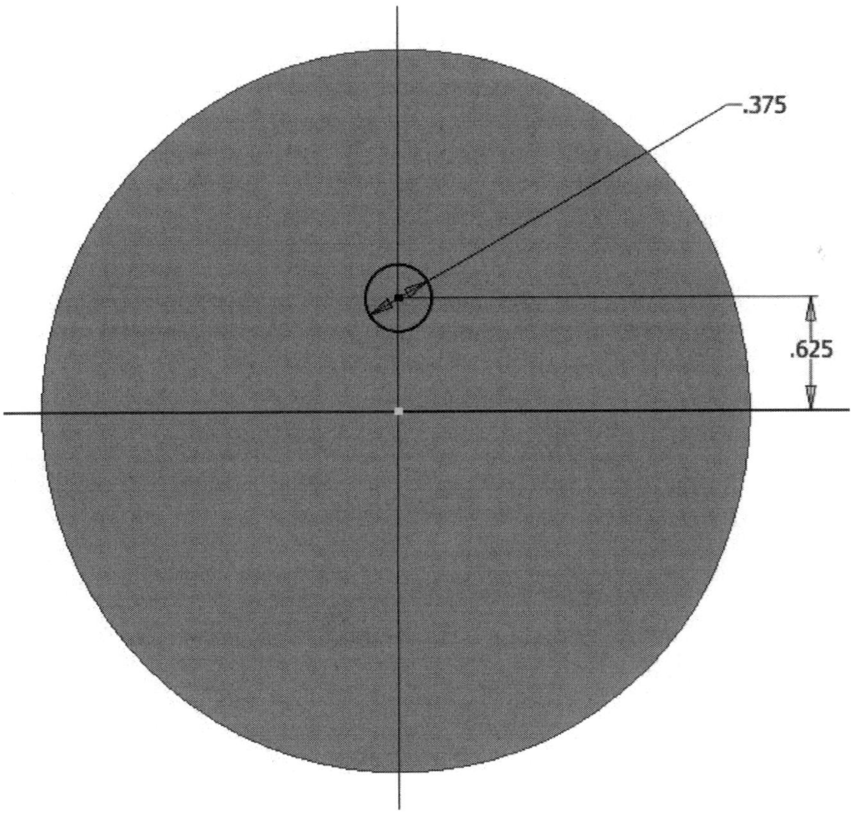

Figure 30

36. Modify the diameter of the holes by double clicking on the overall dimension. The Edit Dimension dialog box will appear as shown in Figure 31.

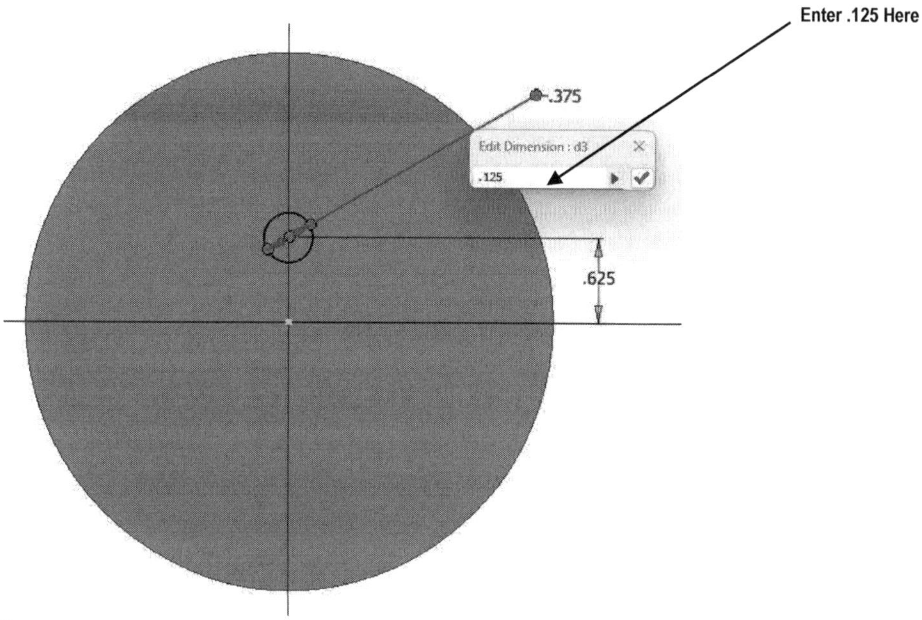

Figure 31

37. Enter **.125** and press **Enter** on the keyboard as shown in Figure 31.

38. The diameter of the holes will be reduced to .125. Right click around the sketch. A pop-up menu will appear. Left click on **Finish 2D Sketch** as shown in Figure 32.

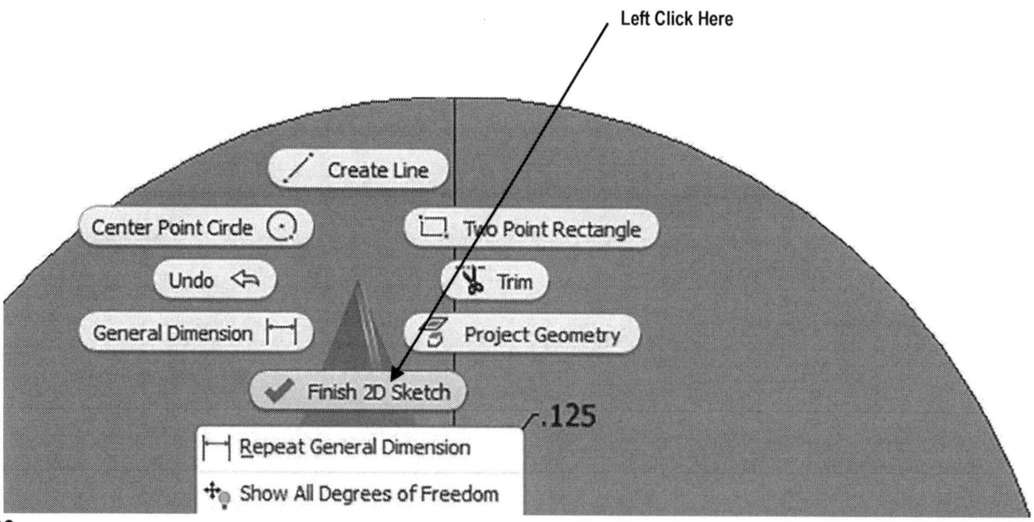

Figure 32

39. The part should update to reflect the changes. If the part did not update, move the cursor to the upper left portion of the screen and left click on the **Manage** tab. Left click on **Update** as shown in Figure 33.

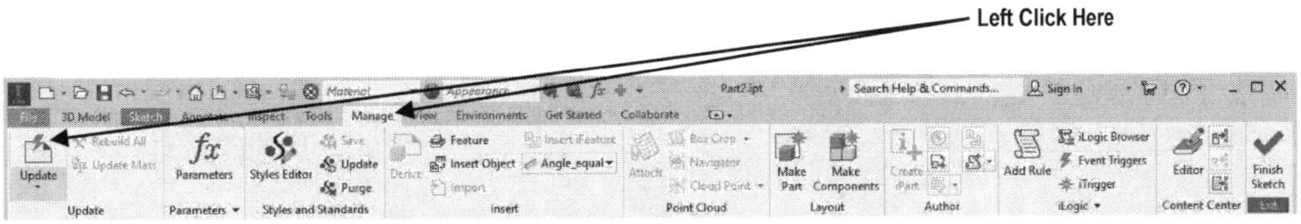

Figure 33

40. Inventor will automatically update the part as shown in Figure 34.

Figure 34

41. Move the cursor over the text "Extrusion2." A box will appear around the text. After the box appears, right click once on **Extrusion2** as shown in Figure 35.

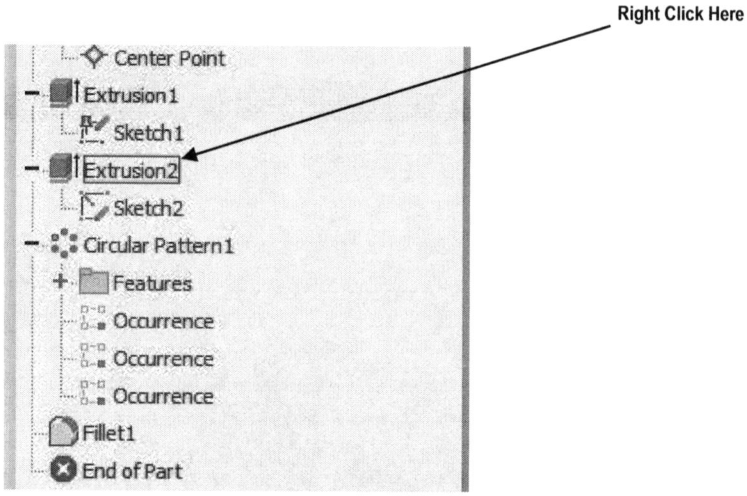

Figure 35

42. A pop-up menu will appear. Left click on **Edit Feature** as shown in Figure 36.

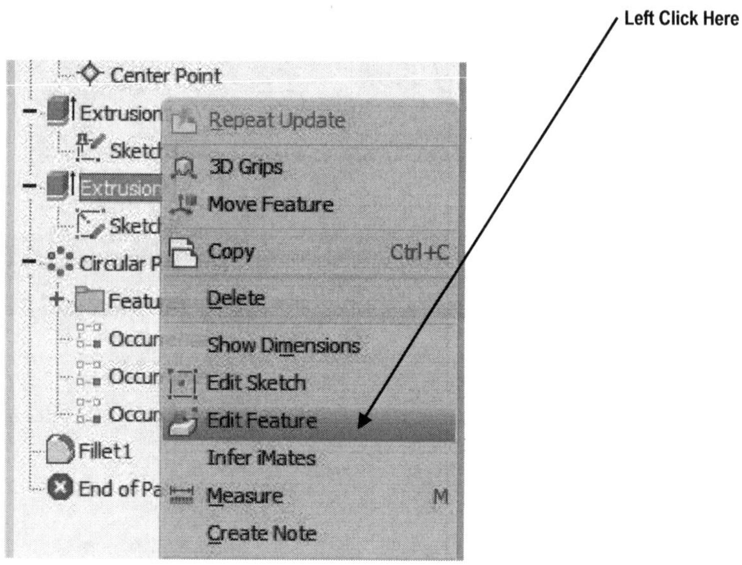

Figure 36

43. The Extrusion dialog box will appear. Enter **.5** for the extrusion distance and left click on **OK** as shown in Figure 37.

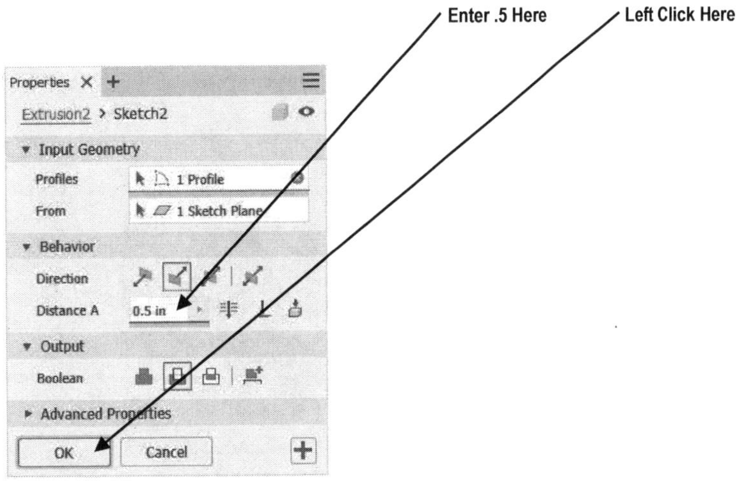

Figure 37

44. The part should update to reflect the changes. If the part did not update, move the cursor to the upper left portion of the screen and left click on the **Manage** tab. Left click on **Update** as shown in Figure 38.

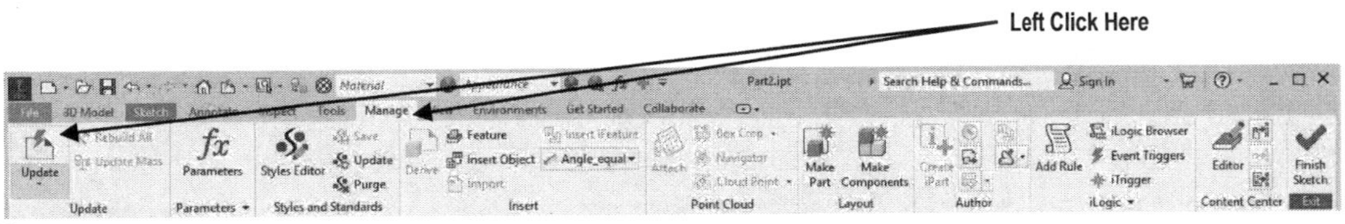

Figure 38

45. Inventor will automatically update the part. Notice that the holes are now thru holes as shown in Figure 39.

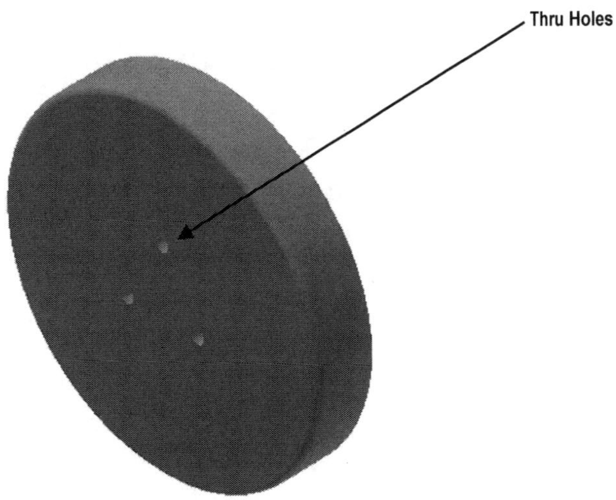

Figure 39

46. Use the Free Orbit/Rotate command to rotate the part as shown in Figure 40.

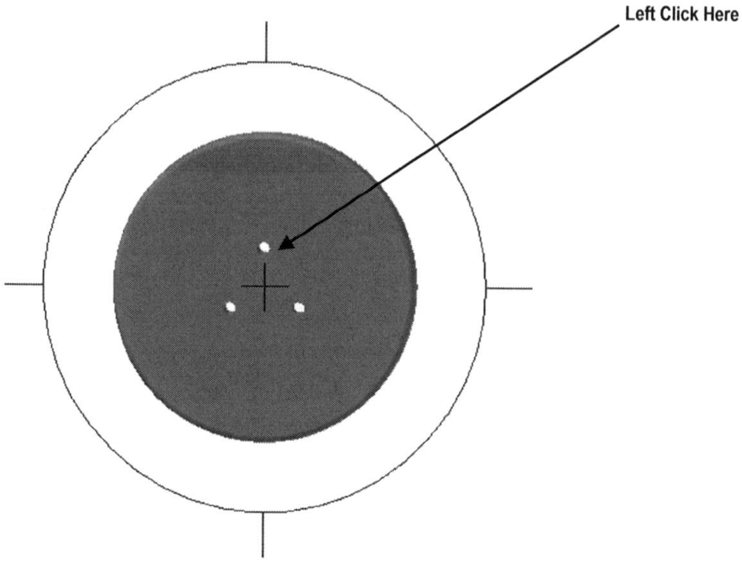

Figure 40

Edit the part using the Circular Pattern command

47. Move the cursor over the text “Circular Pattern1.” A box will appear around the text. After the box appears, right click once on **Circular Pattern 1** as shown in Figure 41.

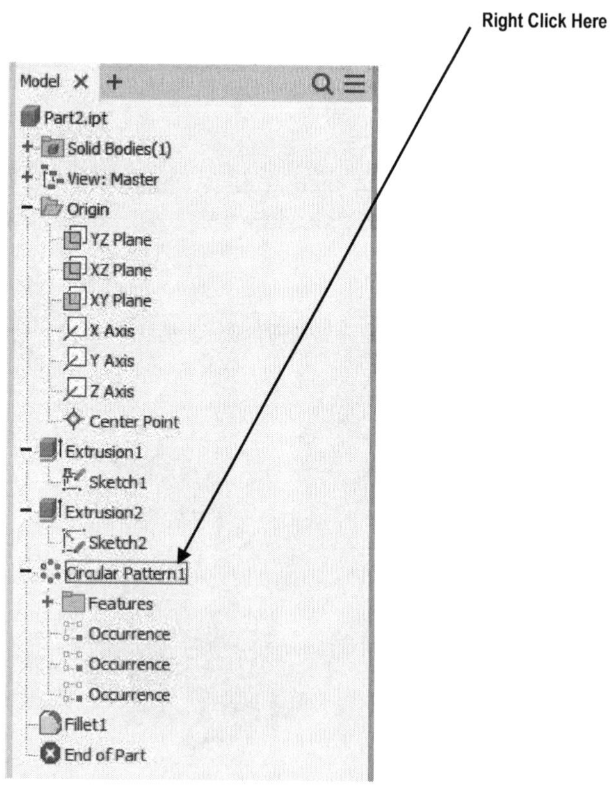

Figure 41

48. A pop-up menu will appear. Left click on **Edit Feature** as shown in Figure 42.

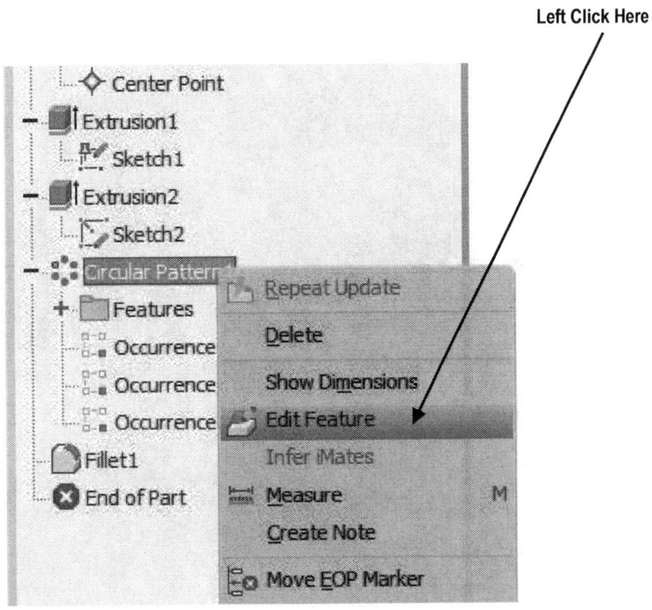

Figure 42

49. The Circular Pattern dialog box will appear. Enter **6** under "Placement" as shown in Figure 43.

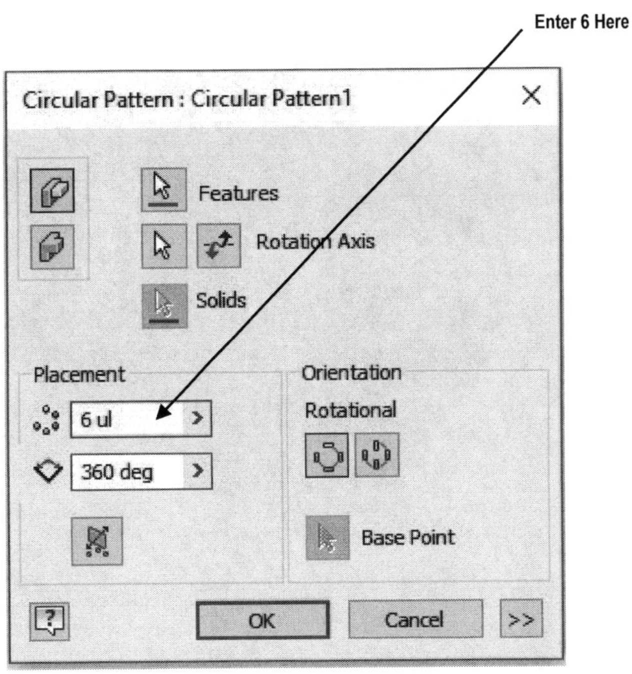

Figure 43

50. Inventor will provide a preview as shown in Figure 44.

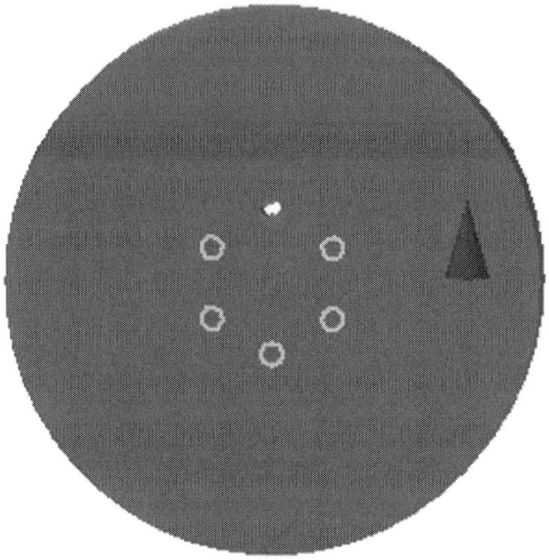

Figure 44

51. Left click on **OK** in the Circular Pattern dialog box. Your screen should look similar to Figure 45.

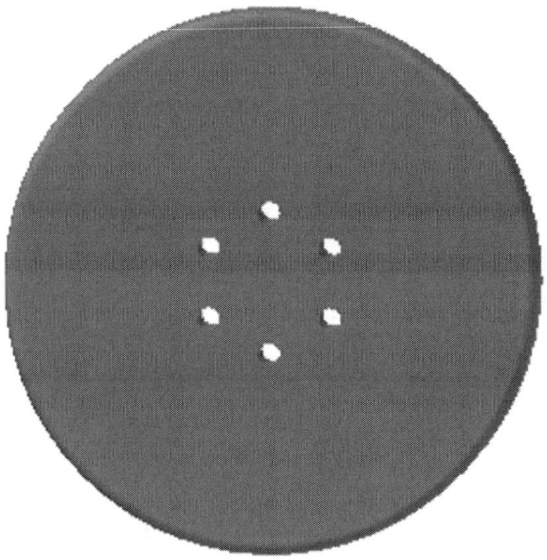

Figure 45

52. Change the view to **Home/Isometric View** as shown in Figure 46.

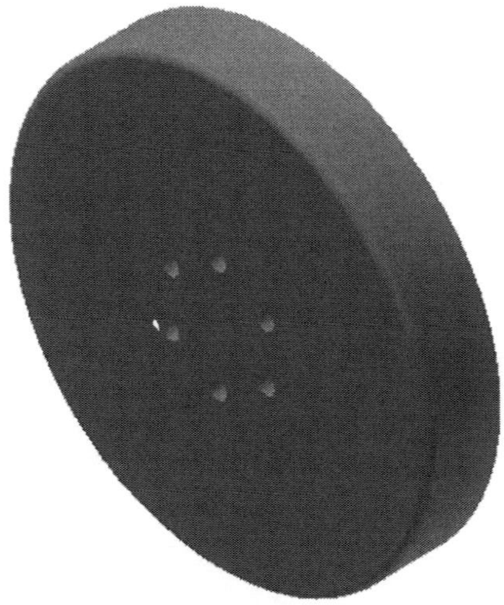

Figure 46

Edit the part using the Fillet command

53. Move the cursor over the text "Fillet1." A box will appear around the text. After the box appears, left click once on **Fillet1** as shown in Figure 47.

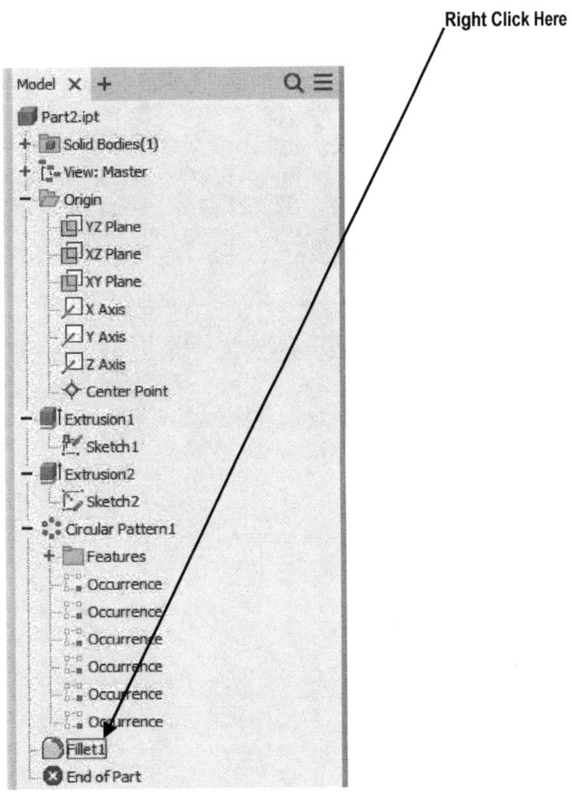

Figure 47

54. Right click on **Fillet1**. A pop-up menu will appear. Left click on **Edit Feature** as shown in Figure 48.

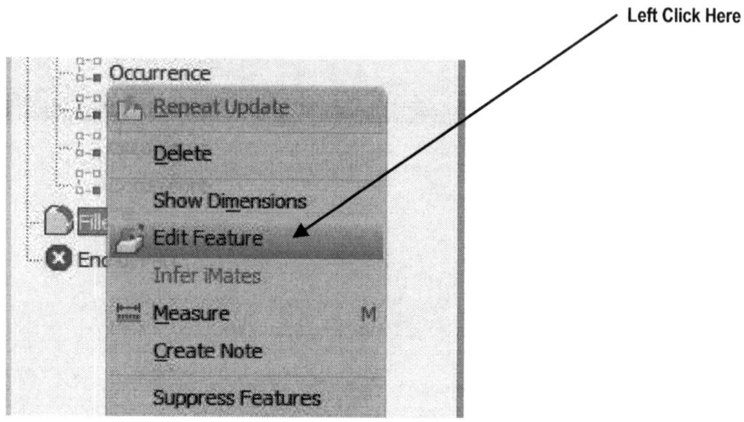

Figure 48

55. The Fillet dialog box will appear. Enter **.250** for the Radius and left click on **OK** as shown in Figure 49.

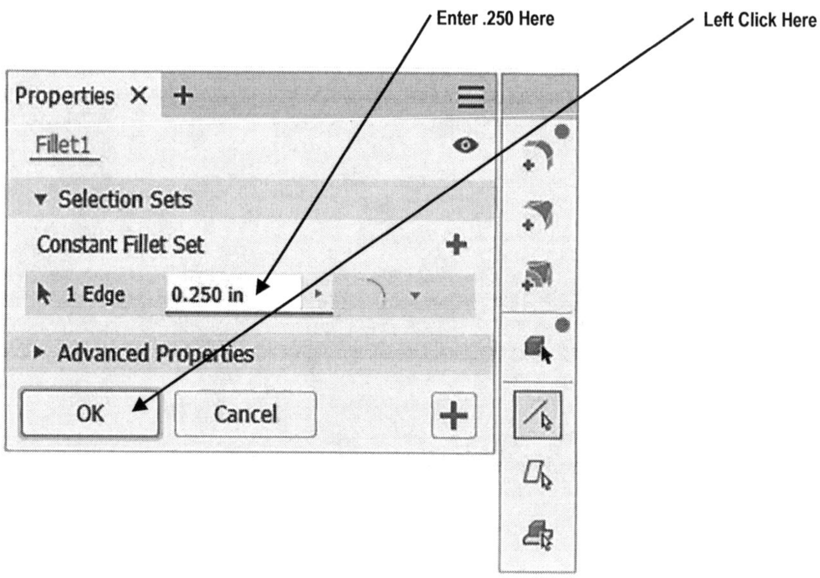

Figure 49

56. Your screen should look similar to Figure 50.

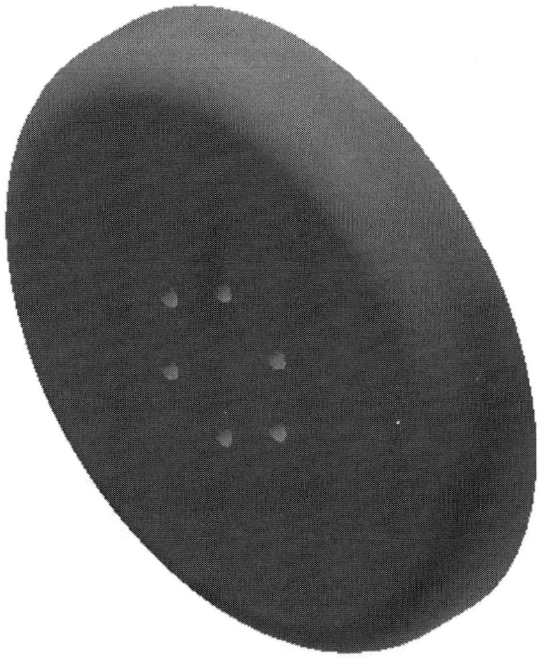

Figure 50

57. Move the cursor over the second listed text "Occurrence". A box will appear around the text. After the box appears, left click once on **Occurrence** as shown in Figure 51.

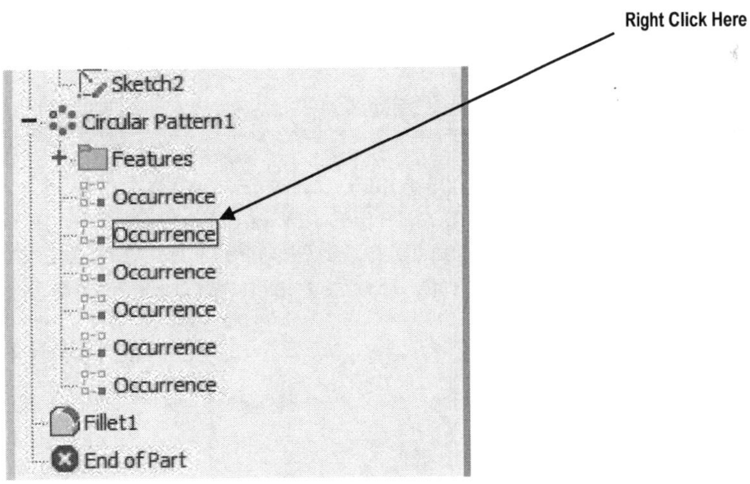

Figure 51

58. Right click once. A pop-up menu will appear. Left click on **Suppress** as shown in Figure 52. Inventor will suppress that particular occurrence while leaving all others active.

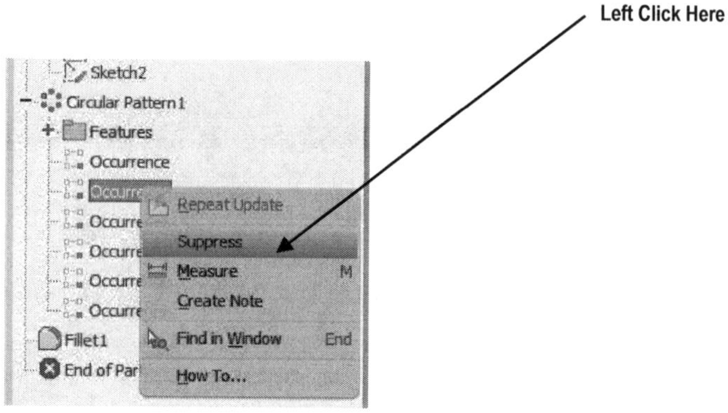

Figure 52

59. Inventor will draw a line through and gray the text as shown in Figure 53. You will notice that the second hole created using the Circular Pattern command is not visible. Repeat the previous steps to un-suppress the occurrence.

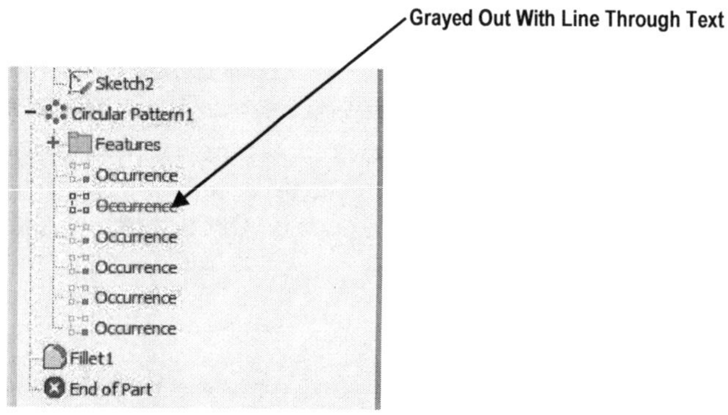

Figure 53

60. The names of all branches in the browser can also be edited. Move the cursor to the lower left portion of the screen where the browser is located. Move the cursor over **Extrusion1** and left click once causing the text to become highlighted. After the text is highlighted, left click one time. The text may be edited as shown in Figure 54.

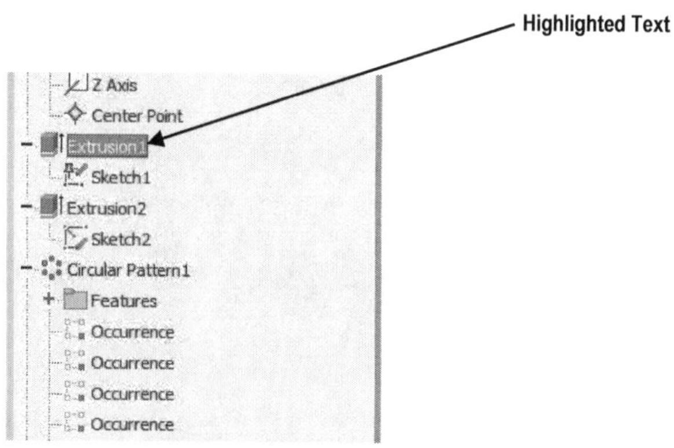

Figure 54

61. Enter the text **Base Extrusion** as shown in Figure 55. Press **Enter** on the keyboard. Text for each individual operation can be edited if desired.

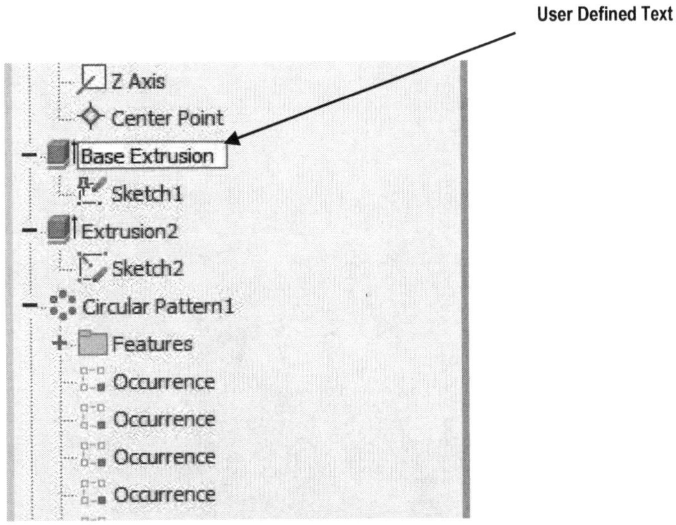

Figure 55

62. Notice that the final design looks significantly different than the original design. The part was redesigned by modifying the existing part as shown in Figure 56.

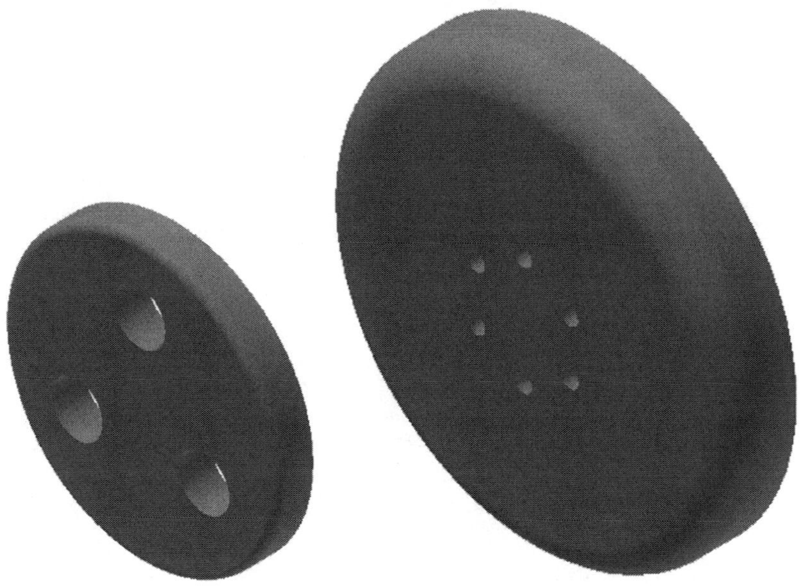

Figure 56

Chapter Problems

Use the previously created parts shown below from Chapters 1-3 to perform the required edits. Edit at least 1 Sketch dimension and at least 1 Feature dimension making the part recognizably different.

Problem 5-1

Problem 1-4

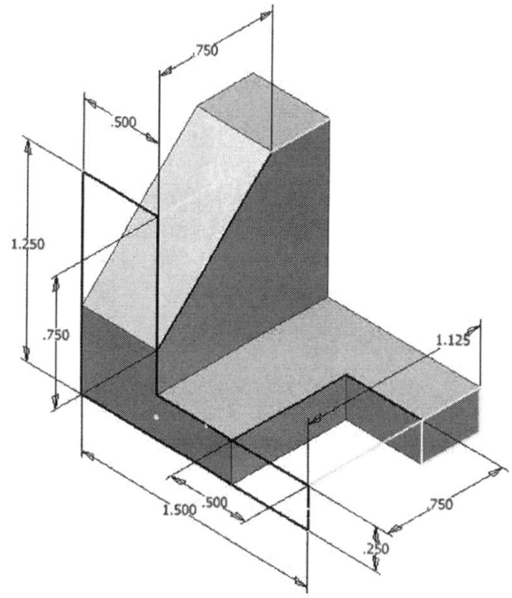

Problem 5-2

Problem 1-10

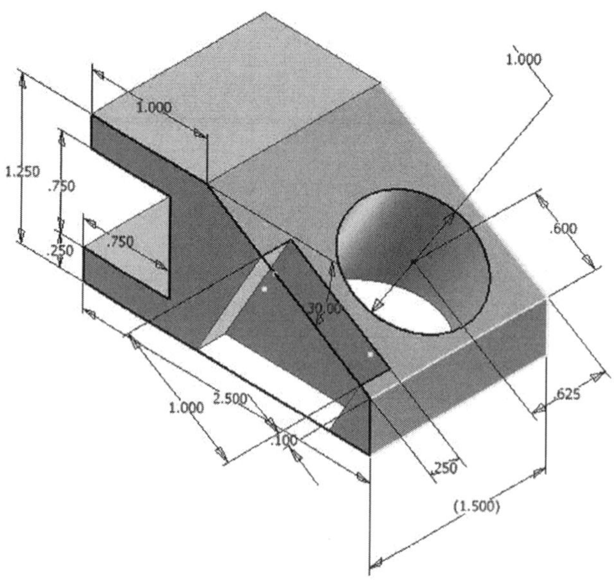

Problem 5-3

Problem 1-11

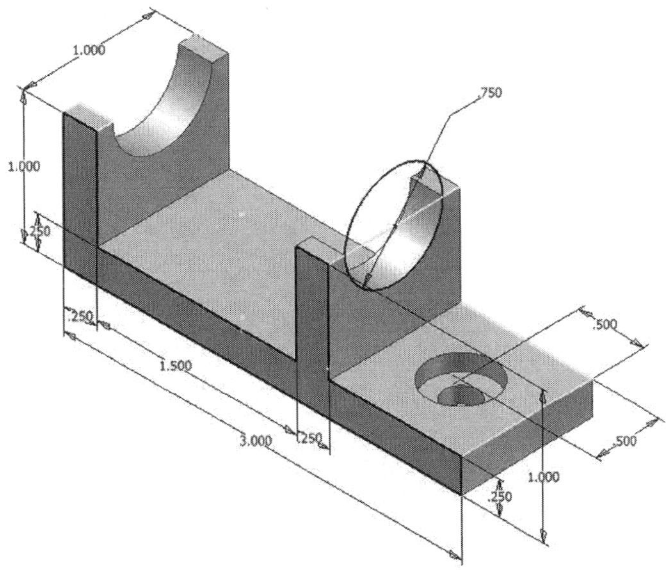

Problem 5-4

Problem 1-14

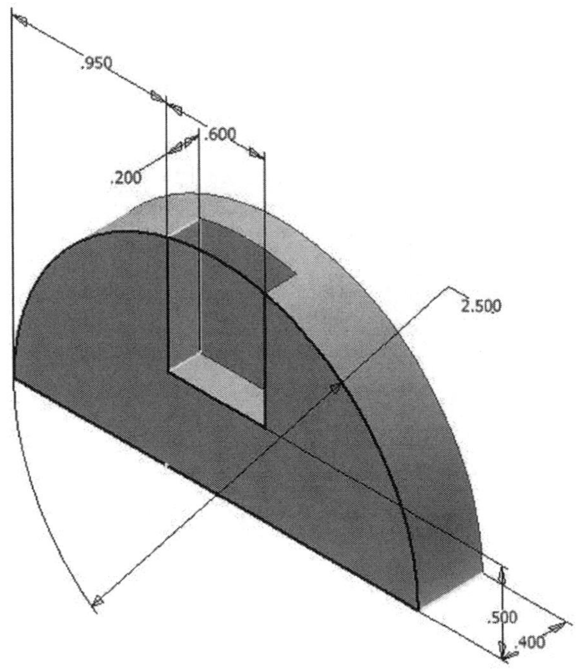

Problem 5-5

Problem 2-9

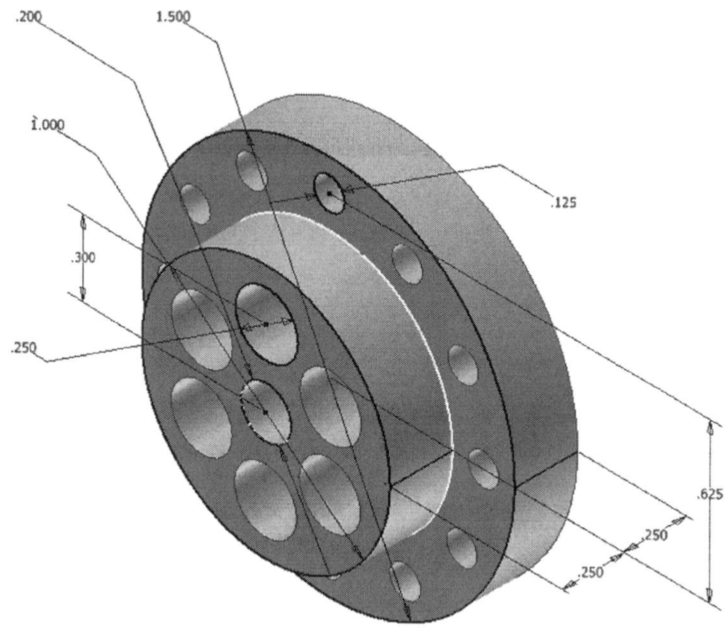

Problem 5-6

Problem 2-10

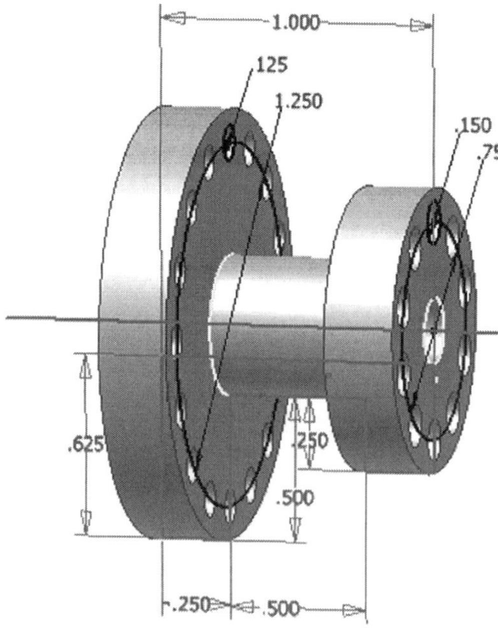

Problem 5-7

Problem 3-4

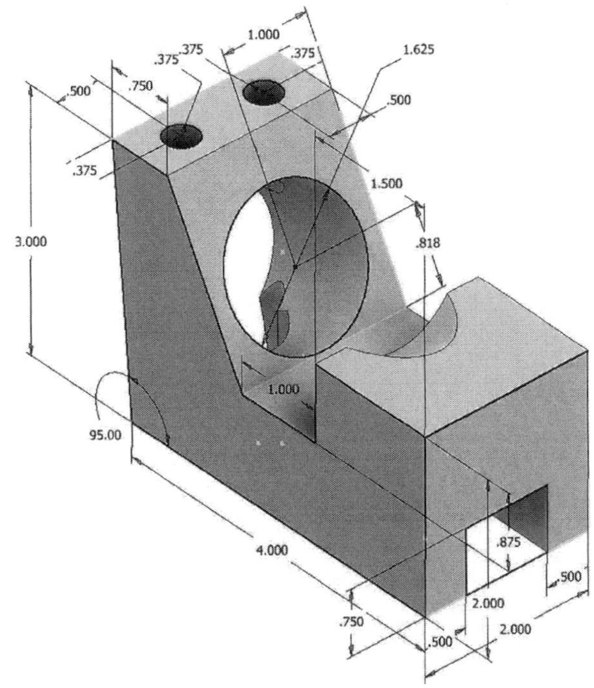

Problem 5-8

Problem 3-5

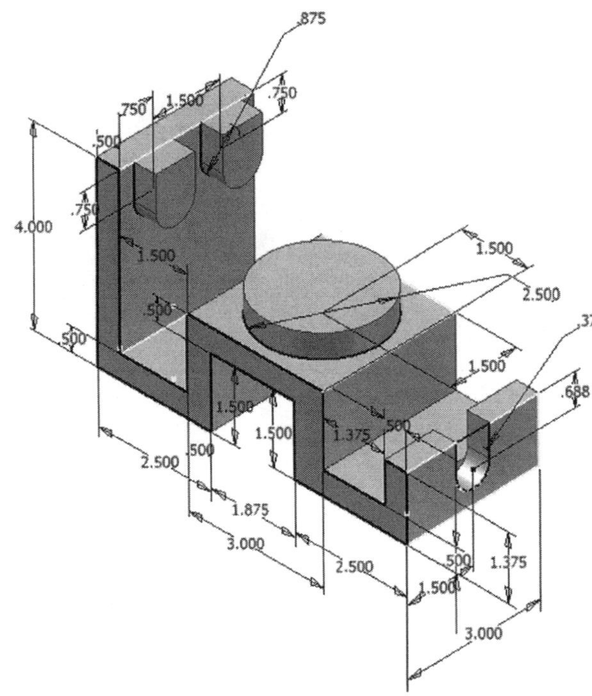

CHAPTER 6

Designing Part Models for Assembly

Objectives:

1. Design multiple sketch parts
2. Learn to use the XY, YZ, and ZX Planes
3. Learn to use the Wireframe viewing command
4. Learn to project geometry on to a new sketch
5. Learn to use the Shell command
6. Learn to use Constraints while constructing a Sketch

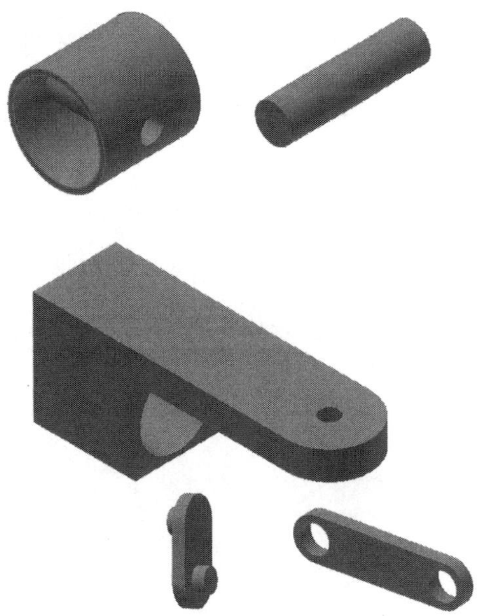

Chapter 6 includes instruction on how to design the parts shown.

1. Start Autodesk Inventor 2027 by referring to "Chapter 1 Getting Started."

2. After Autodesk Inventor 2027 is running, begin a new sketch.

3. Complete the sketch on the **XY Plane** with the center of the circle on the origin as shown in Figure 1. This will ensure that the YZ and ZX planes will cut through the part.

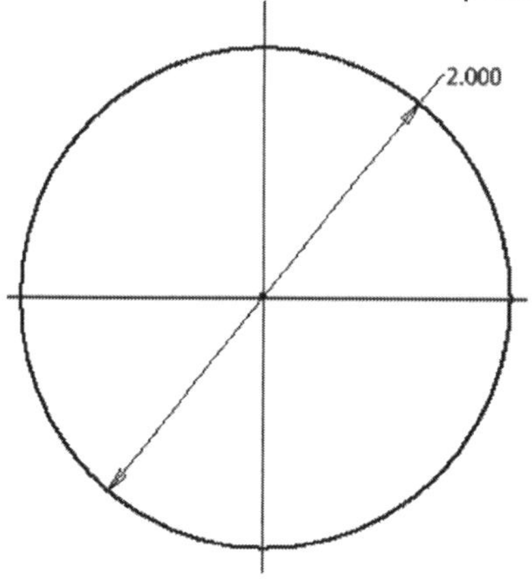

Figure 1

4. Exit out of the Sketch Panel and change the view to Isometric as shown in Figure 2.

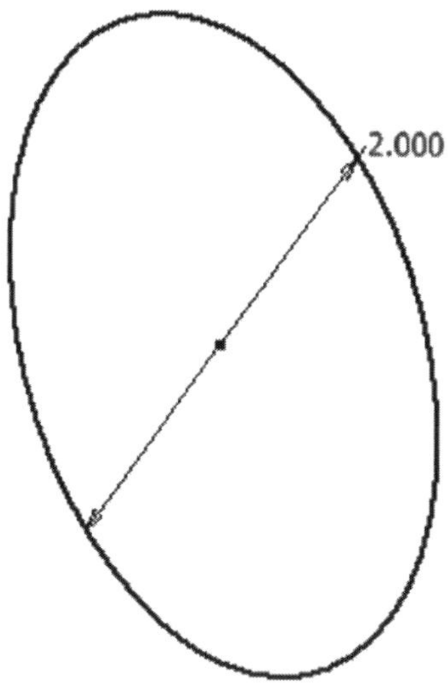

Figure 2

5. Extrude the sketch a distance of 2 inches as shown in Figure 3.

Figure 3

6. Move the cursor over to the Browser and left click on the plus sign next to the text "Origin" as shown in Figure 4.

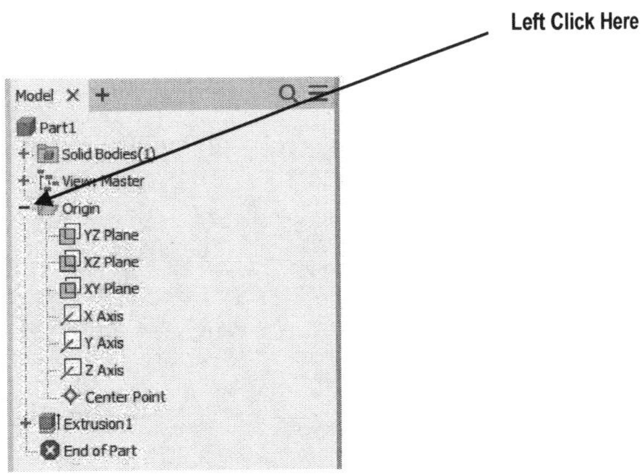

Figure 4

Learn to use the YZ, XZ, and XY Planes

7. The list will expand. Move the cursor over the text "YZ Plane" causing a box to appear around the text as shown in Figure 5.

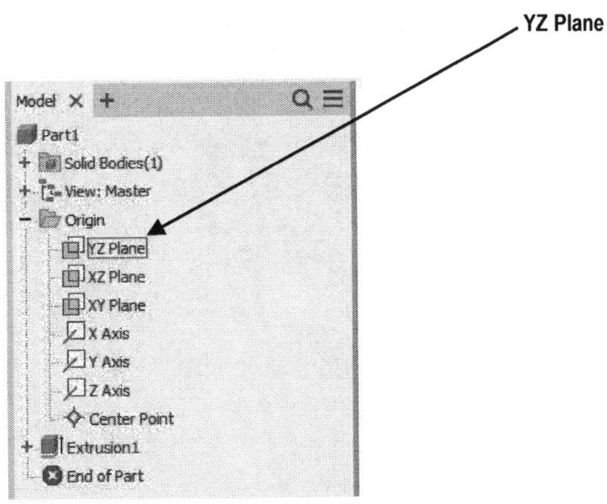

Figure 5

8. The YZ plane will become visible as shown in Figure 6.

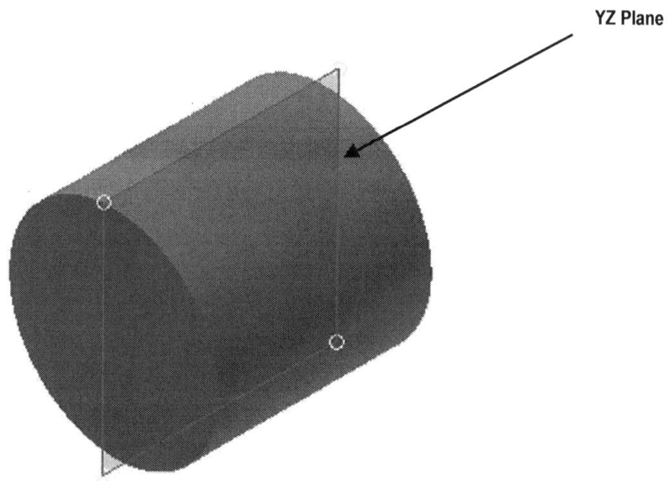

Figure 6

9. Right click on the text **YZ Plane**. A pop-up menu will appear. Left click on **New Sketch** as shown in Figure 7.

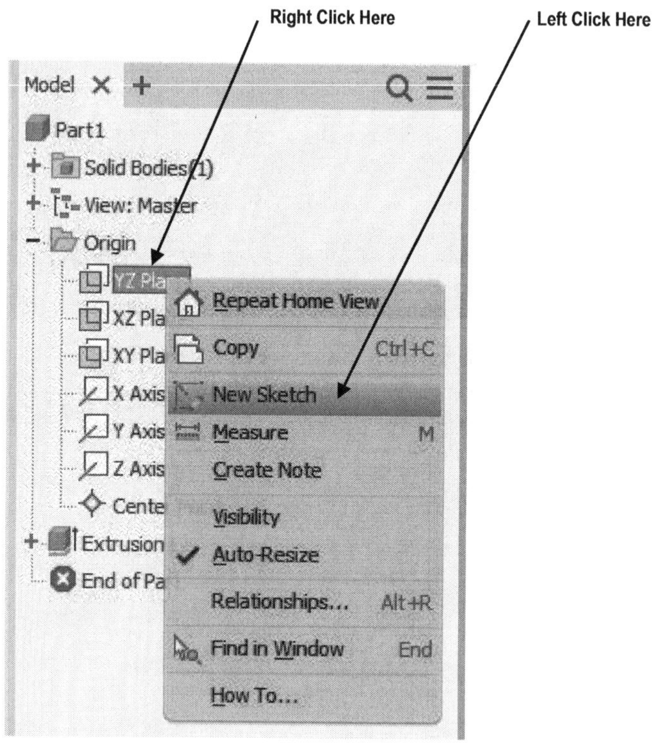

Figure 7

10. Use the Home View command to rotate the part as shown. Your screen should look similar to Figure 8.

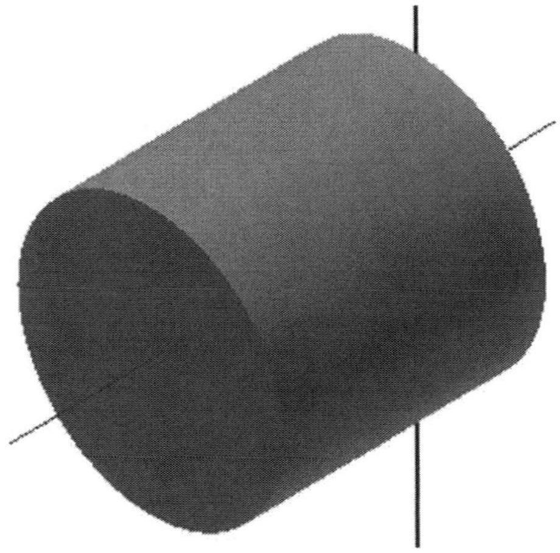

Figure 8

Learn to use the Wireframe viewing command

11. Move the cursor to the upper left portion of the screen and left click on the **View** tab. Left click on the drop-down arrow below the "Visual Style" icon. A drop-down menu will appear. Left click on **Wireframe Model edges only** as shown in Figure 9.

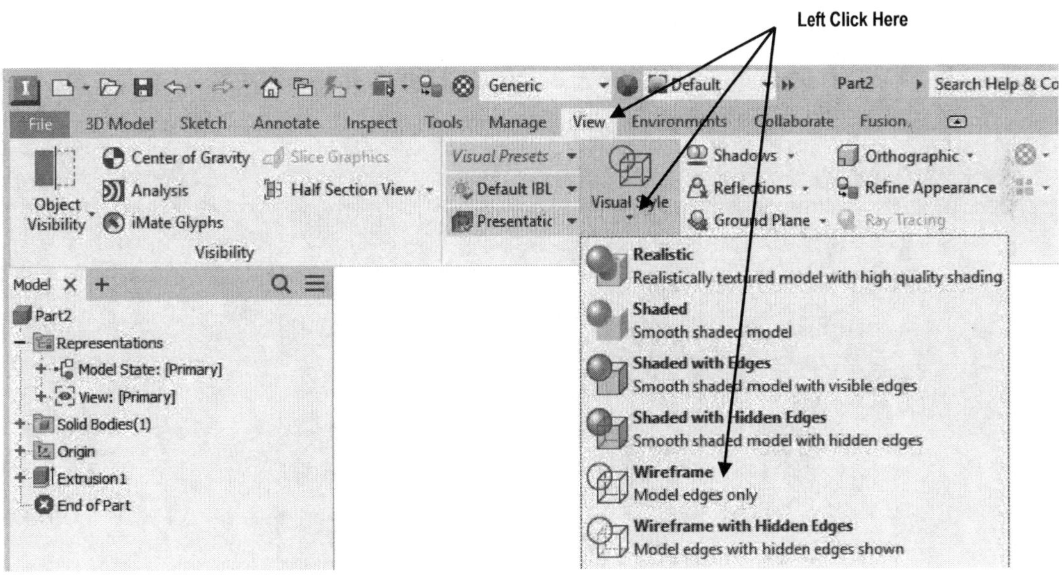

Figure 9

12. Your screen should look similar to Figure 10.

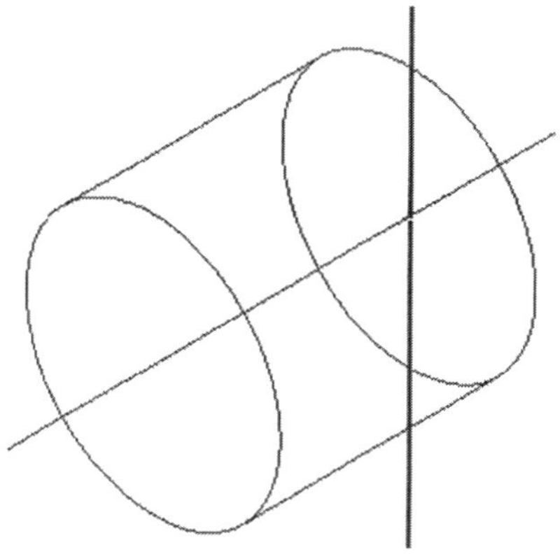

Figure 10

13. Move the cursor to the upper right portion of the screen and left click on the **View** tab. Left click on the **Look At** icon as shown in Figure 11.

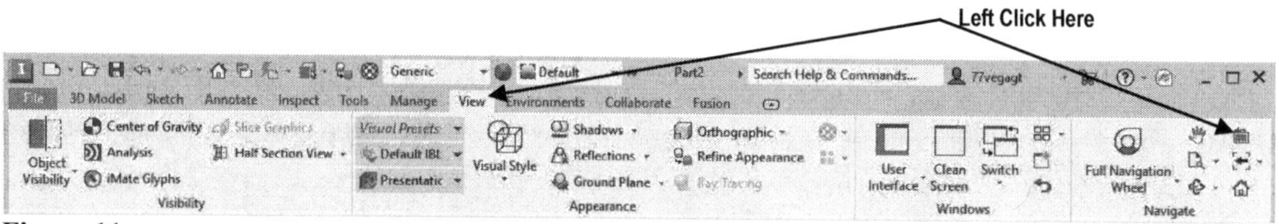

Figure 11

14. Move the cursor to the upper left portion of the screen and left click on the text **YZ Plane** in the Browser as shown in Figure 12.

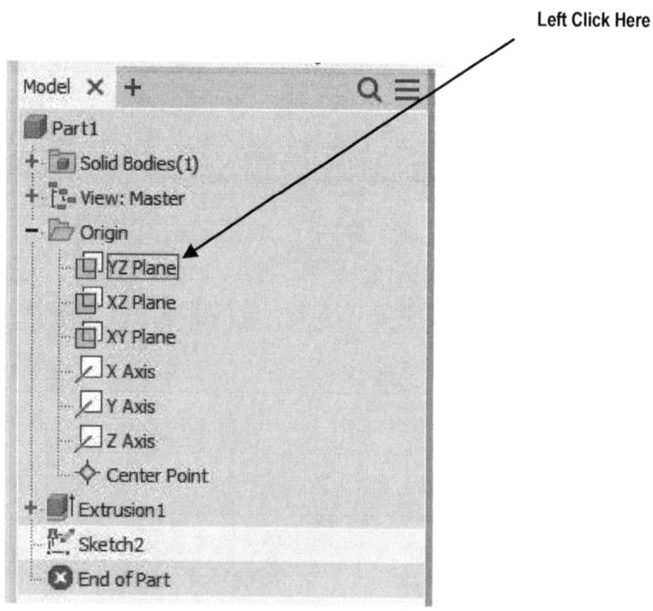

Figure 12

15. Notice the YZ plane becoming visible through the part as shown in Figure 13.

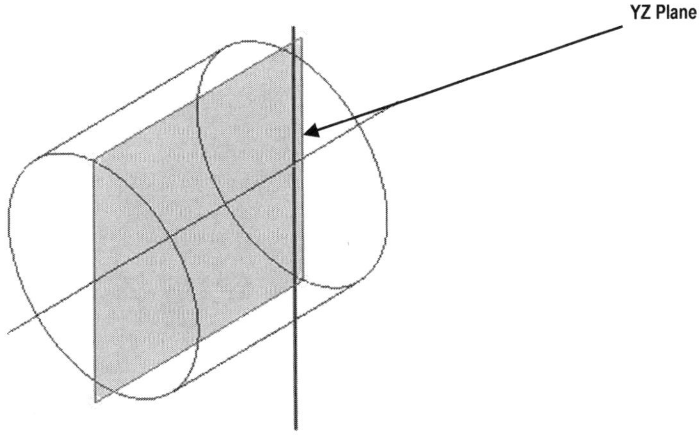

Figure 13

Learn to project geometry to a new sketch

16. Inventor will rotate the YZ plane to provide a perpendicular view as shown in Figure 14.

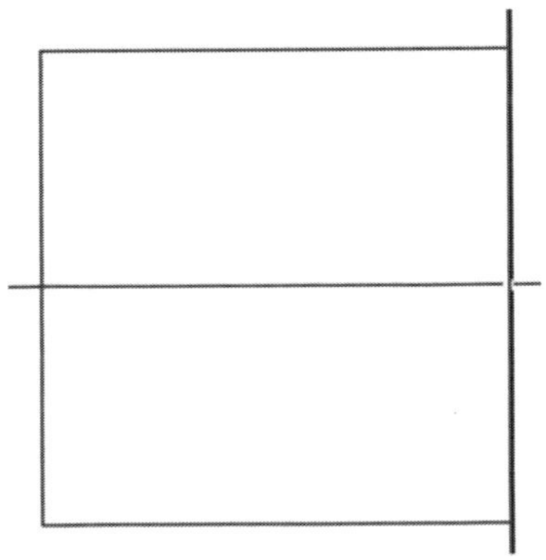

Figure 14

17. Move the cursor to the upper middle portion of the screen and left click on the **Sketch** tab. Left click on **Project Geometry** as shown in Figure 15.

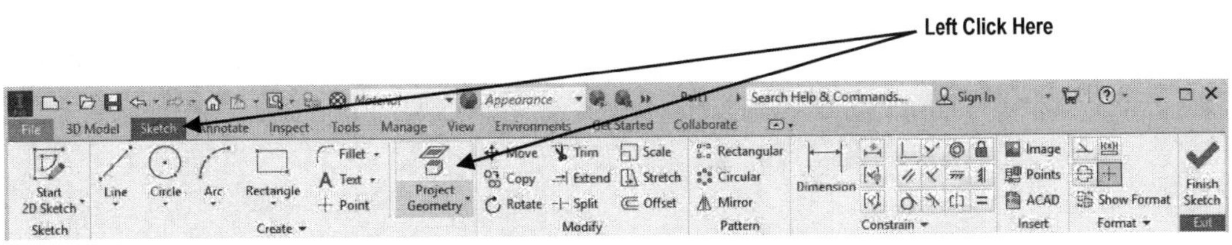

Figure 15

18. Move the cursor over the top and bottom lines and left click. Inventor will project these lines onto the sketch for reference purposes as shown in Figure 16. They will need to be deleted before exiting the sketch.

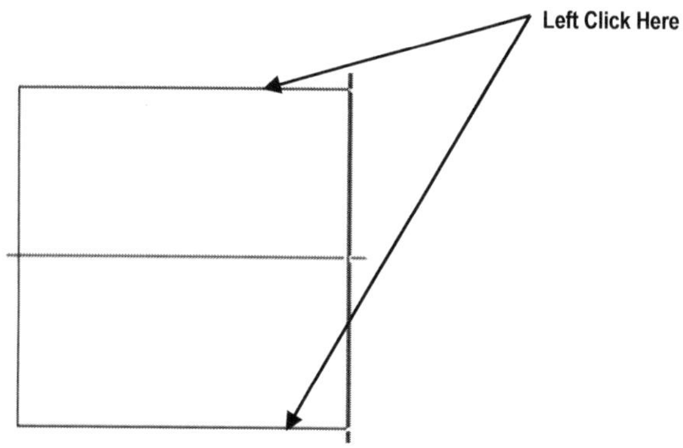

Figure 16

19. Use the Line command to draw a line from the midpoint of the top line to the midpoint of the bottom line. Create a .50 inch diameter circle on the midpoint of the line as shown in Figure 17.

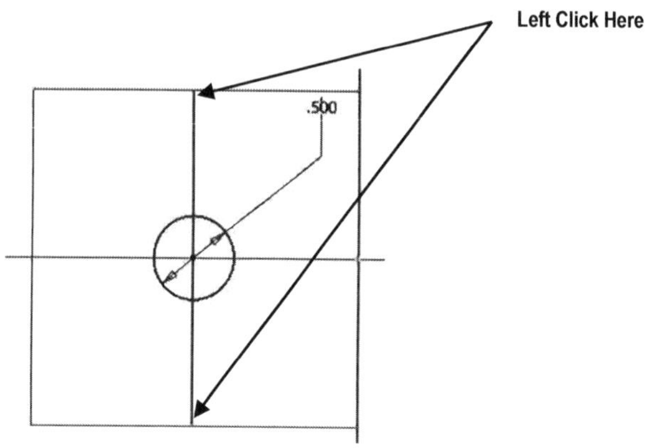

Figure 17

20. Right click on the center line causing a pop up menu to appear. Left click on **Construction** as shown in Figure 18.

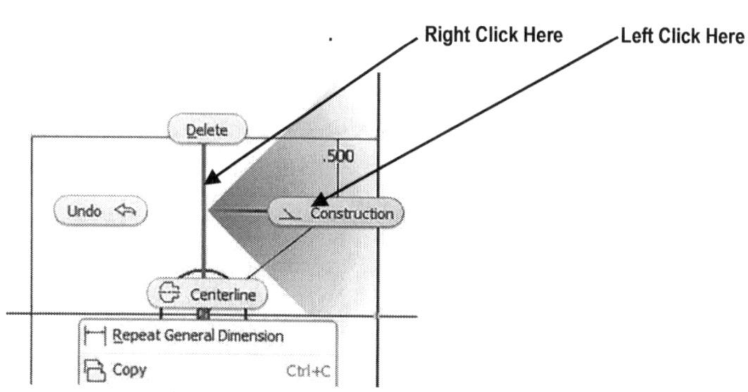

Figure 18

21. Delete the lines that were projected onto the sketch. If after trying to delete the lines they are still visible, don't worry about them since they will not affect any upcoming operations as shown in Figure 19.

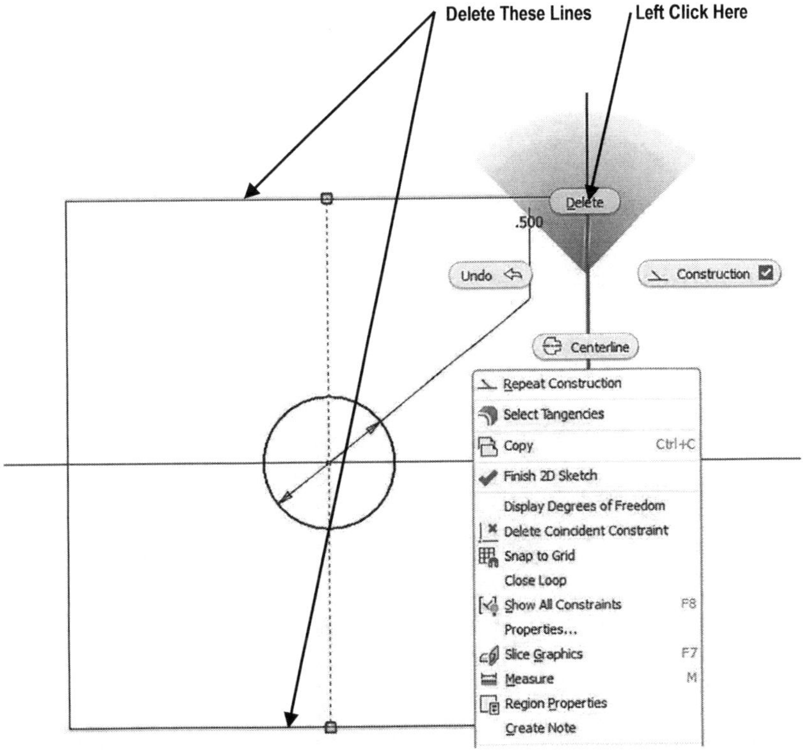

Figure 19

22. Exit out of the Sketch Panel and change the view to Isometric/Home as shown in Figure 20.

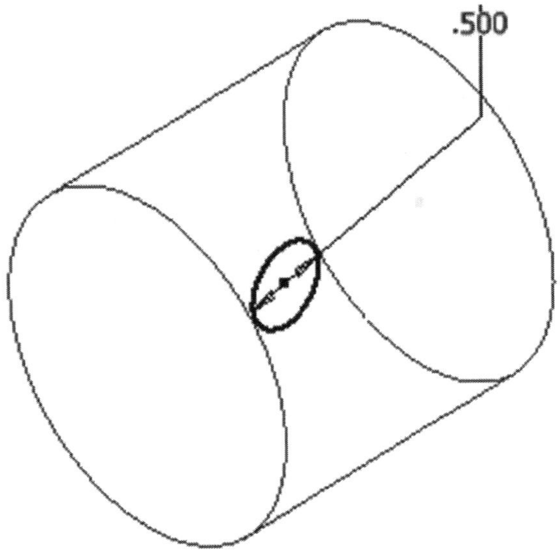

Figure 20

23. Left click on the **3D Model** tab if not already selected. Use the Extrude command to create a hole in the part using the newly created circle. Left click on the "Cut" icon. Enter **2.00** for the distance. Left click on the "Bi-directional" icon. Inventor will provide a preview of the extrusion. Left click on **OK** as shown in Figure 21.

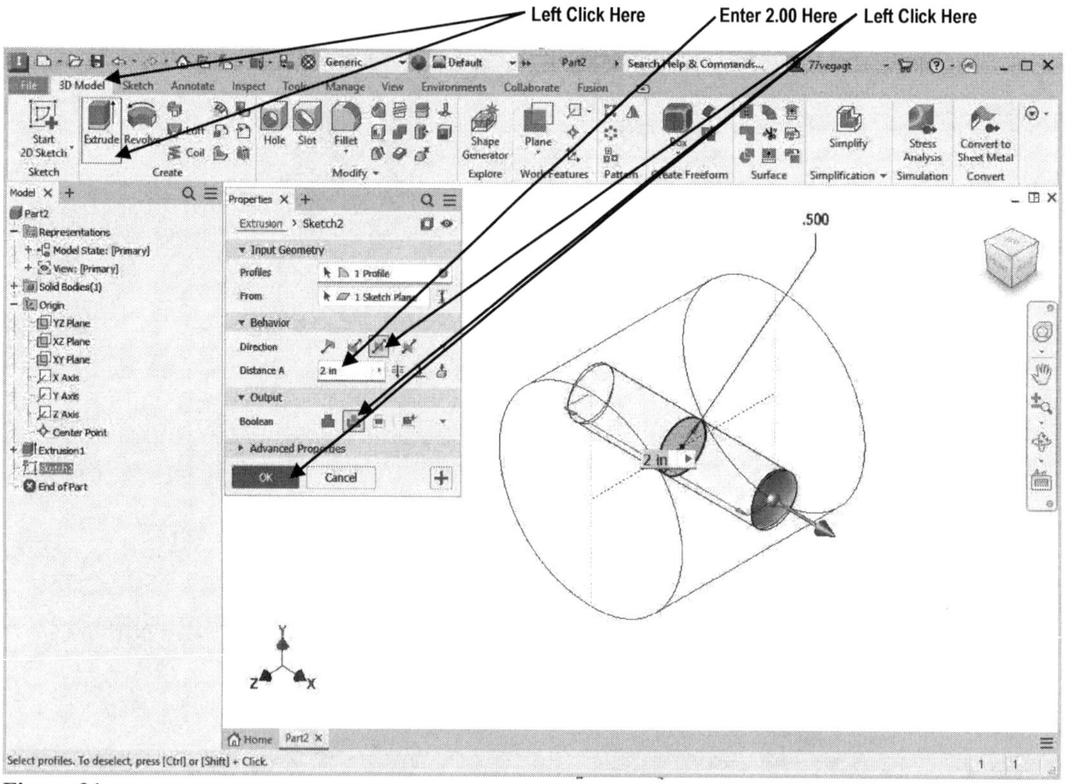

Figure 21

24. Your screen should look similar to Figure 22.

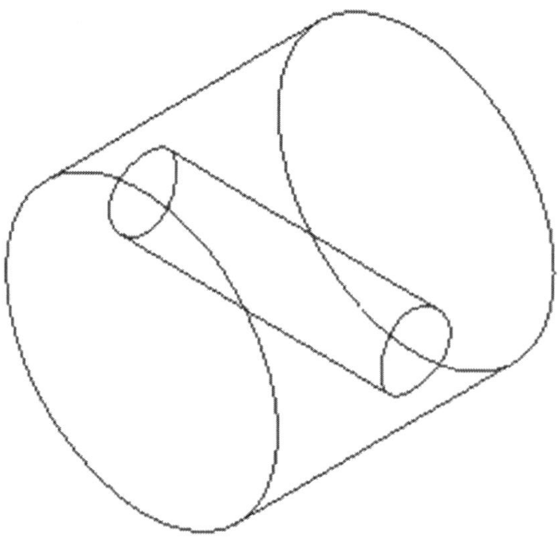

Figure 22

25. Move the cursor to the upper middle portion of the screen and left click on the **View** tab. Left click on the drop-down arrow underneath "Visual Style." Left click on **Shaded with Edges** as shown in Figure 23.

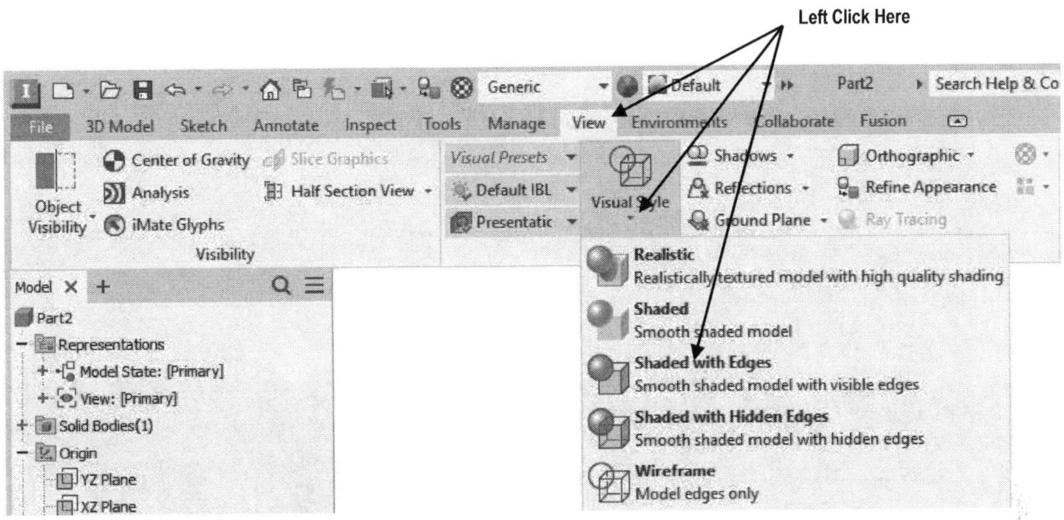

Figure 23

26. Your screen should look similar to Figure 24.

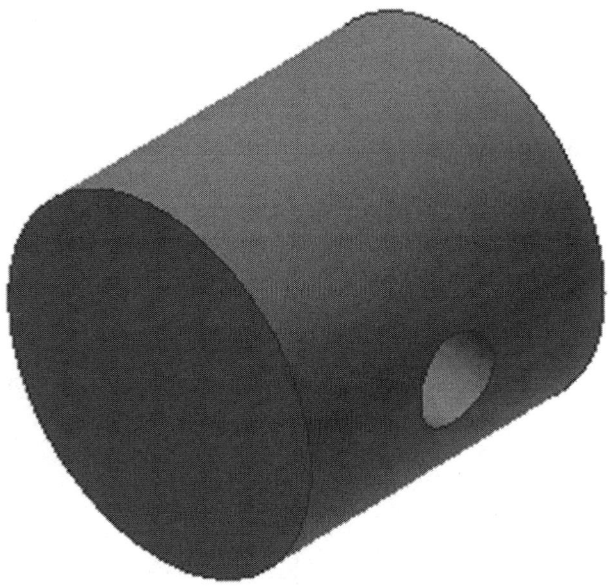

Figure 24

Learn to use the Shell command

27. Move the cursor to the upper left portion of the screen and left click on the 3D Model tab. Left click on the **Shell** icon. The Shell dialog box will appear as shown in Figure 25.

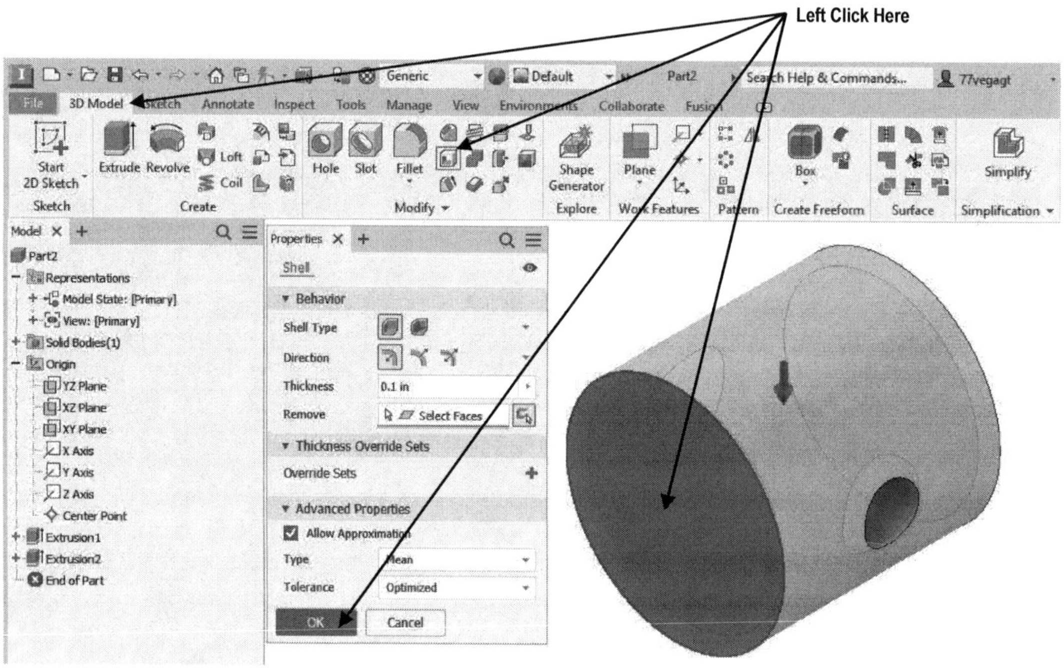

Figure 25

28. Left click on the lower surface of the part and left click on **OK** as shown in Figure 25.

29. Your screen should look similar to Figure 26.

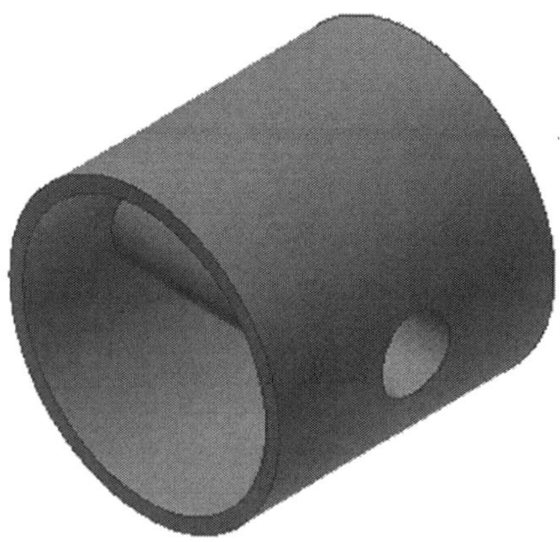

Figure 26

30. Move the cursor to the upper middle portion of the screen and left click on the **View** tab. Left click on the **Look At** icon as shown in Figure 27.

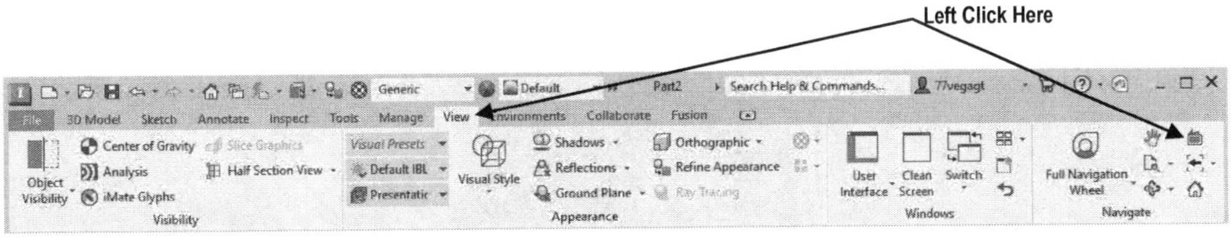

Figure 27

31. Move the cursor to the lower surface of the part causing the inside and outside edges to turn red and left click as shown in Figure 28.

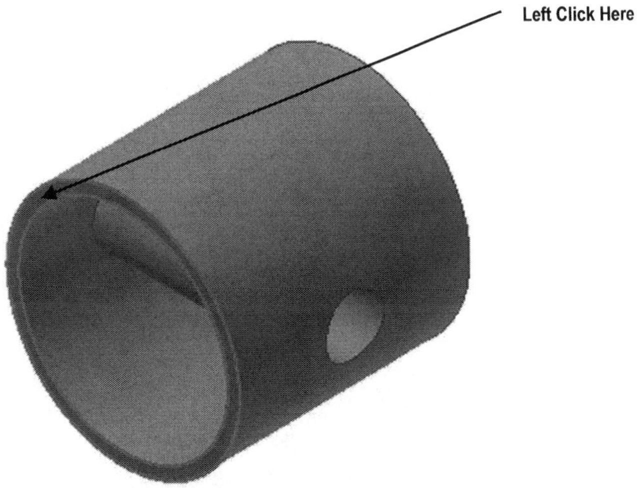

Figure 28

32. After both edges turn red, left click once. Inventor will rotate the part providing a perpendicular view of the inside as shown in Figure 29.

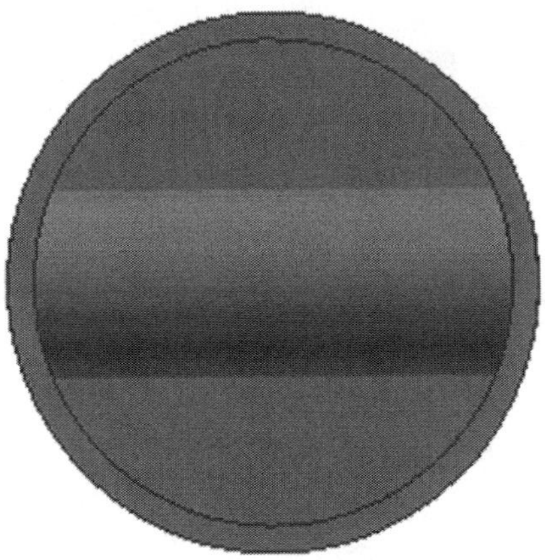

Figure 29

33. Begin a new sketch on the surface shown in Figure 30.

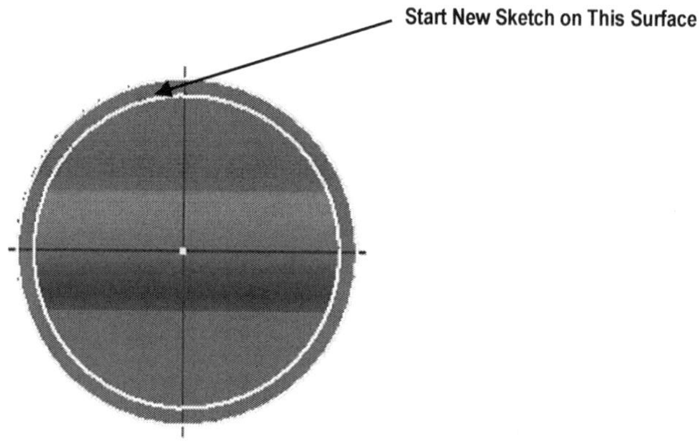

Figure 30

34. Use the rectangle command to complete the following sketch. Dimension the rectangle from the origin as shown in Figure 31.

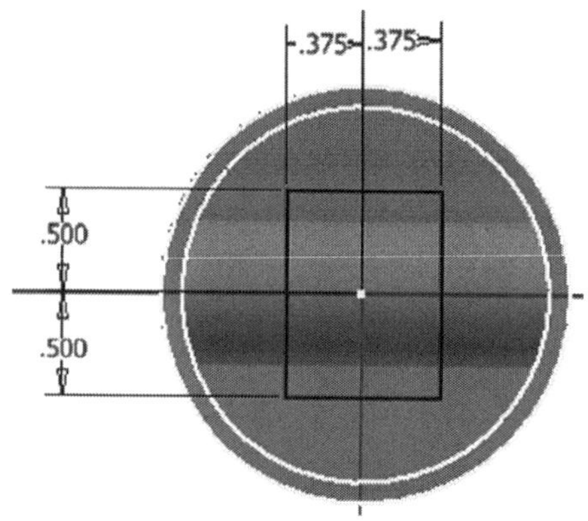

Figure 31

35. Exit the Sketch Panel and change the view to Isometric/Home View as shown in Figure 32.

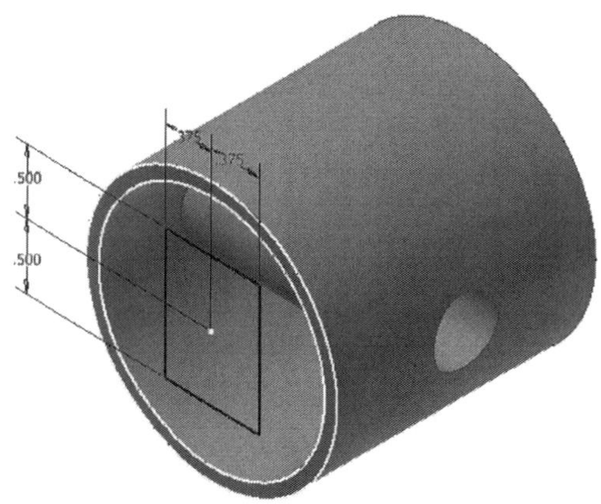

Figure 32

36. Use the Extrude Cut command to "cut" back into the part a distance of 1.875 as shown in Figure 33.

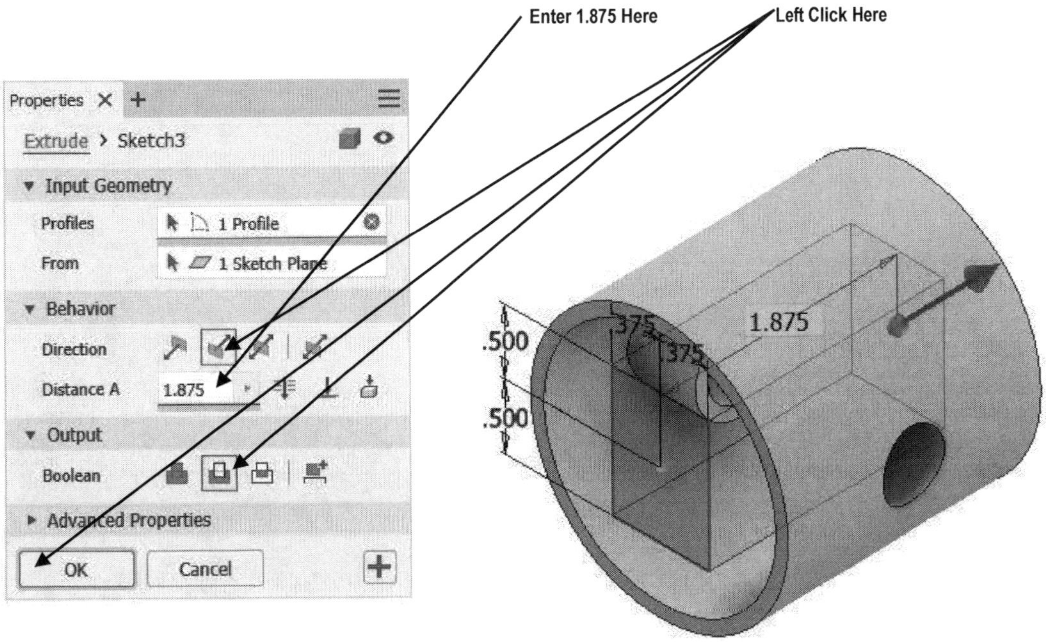

Figure 33

37. Save the part as Piston1.ipt where it can be easily retrieved later.

38. Begin a new drawing as described in Chapter 1.

39. Draw a circle on the **XY Plane** in the center of the grid as shown in Figure 34.

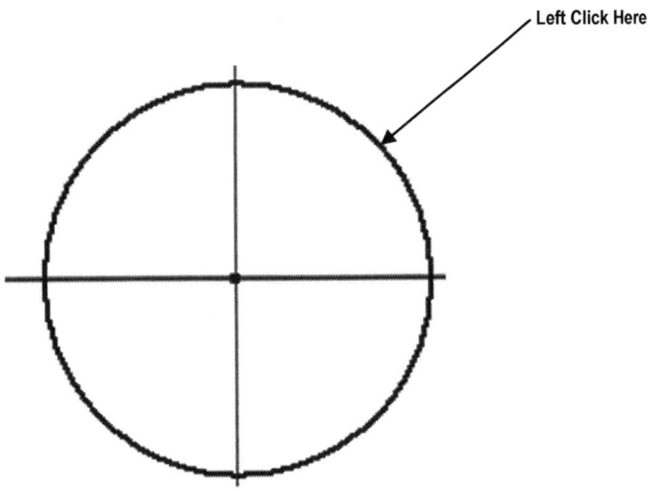

Figure 34

40. Use the **Dimension** command to dimension the circle to **.5** inches as shown in Figure 35.

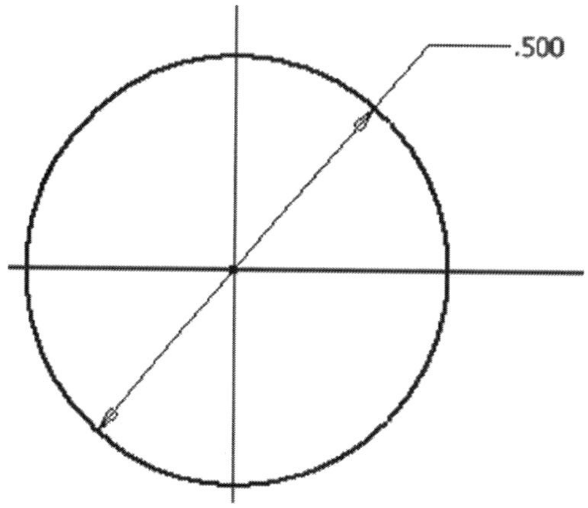

Figure 35

41. Use the **Home View** command to view the sketch in Isometric. Exit the Sketch Panel and Extrude the circle to a length of **1.875** inches as shown in Figure 36.

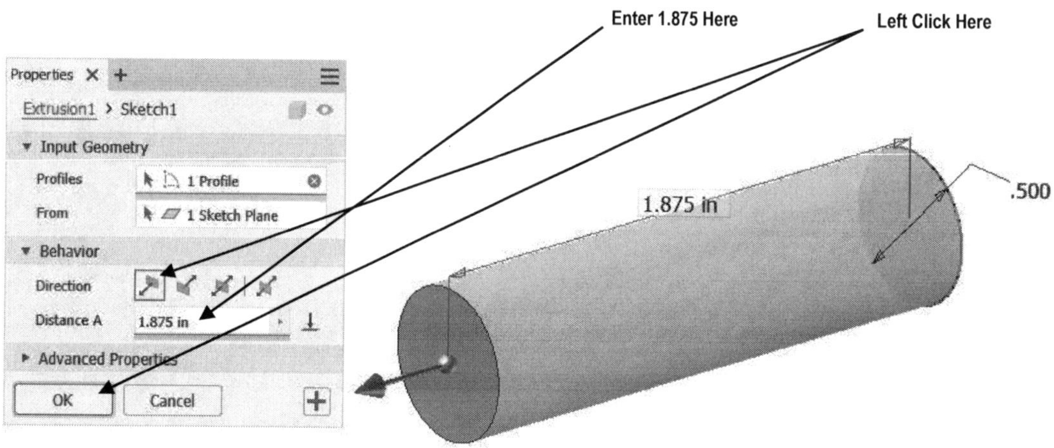

Figure 36

42. Your screen should look similar to Figure 37.

Figure 37

43. Save the part as Wristpin1.ipt where it can be easily retrieved later.

44. Begin a new sketch as described in Chapter 1.

45. Complete the sketch shown in Figure 38.

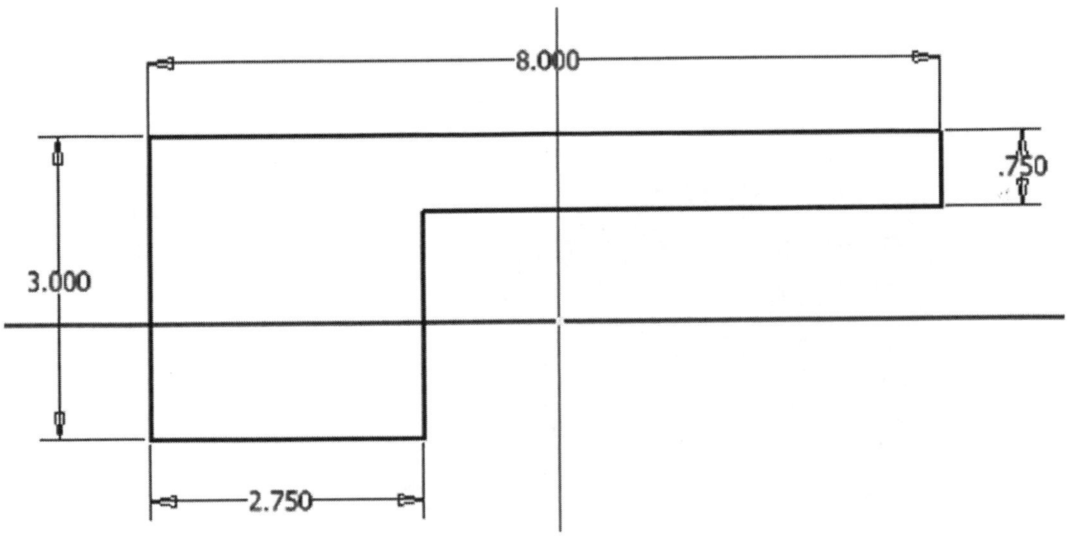

Figure 38

46. Exit the Sketch Panel and change the view to Isometric as shown in Figure 39.

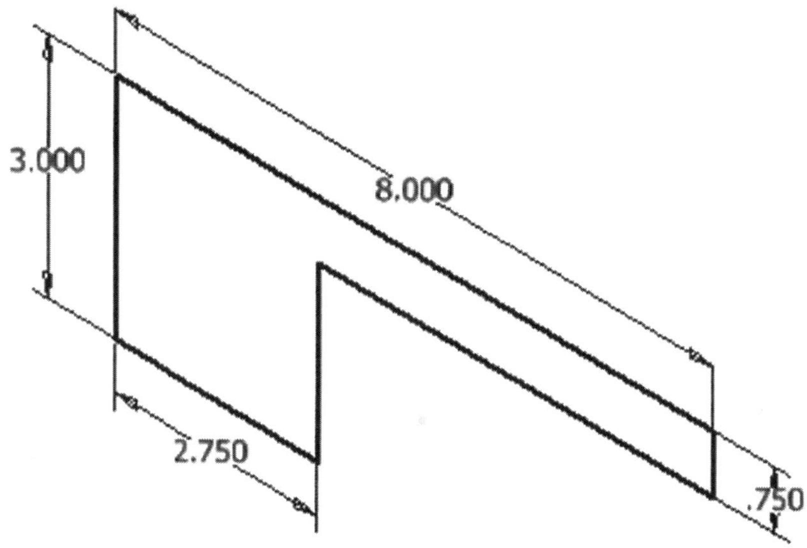

Figure 39

47. Extrude the sketch to a distance of **2.25** inches. Your screen should look similar to what is shown in Figure 40.

Figure 40

48. Use the Fillet command to create **1.125** inch fillets on the front portion of the part as shown in Figure 41.

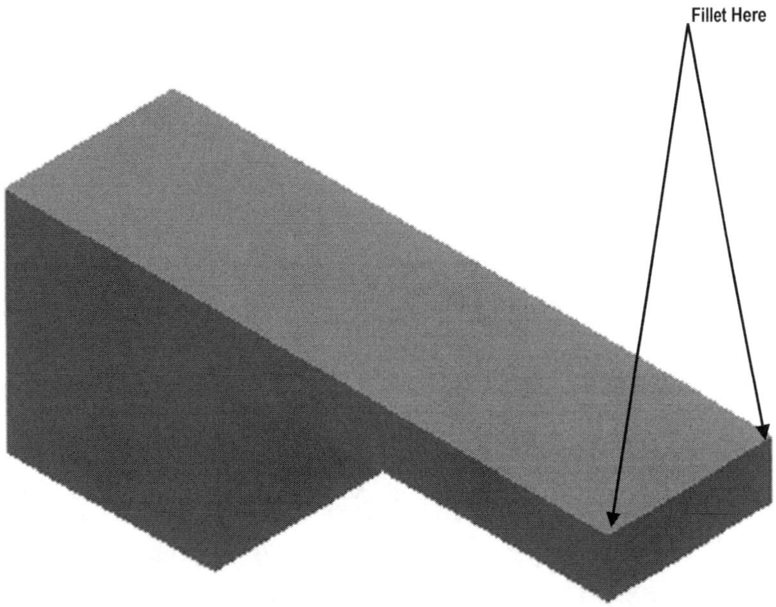

Figure 41

49. Your screen should look similar to Figure 42.

Figure 42

50. Move the cursor to the upper middle portion of the screen and left click on the **View** tab. Left click on the **Look At** icon as shown in Figure 43.

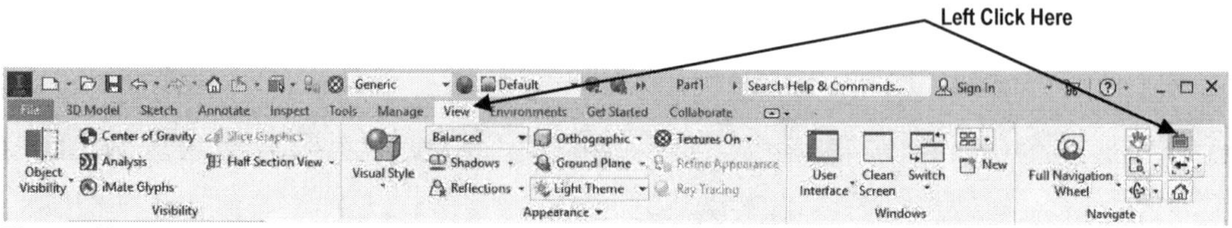

Figure 43

51. Move the cursor to the surface shown in Figure 44 causing it to turn red. Left click once.

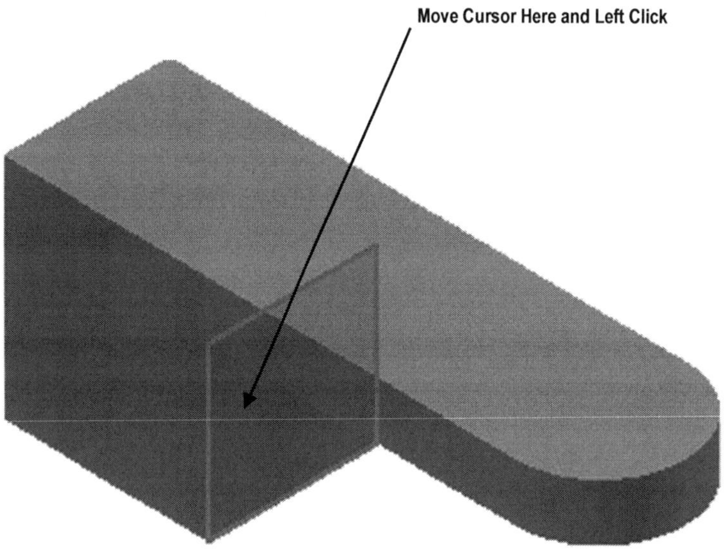

Figure 44

52. Complete the sketch shown in Figure 45.

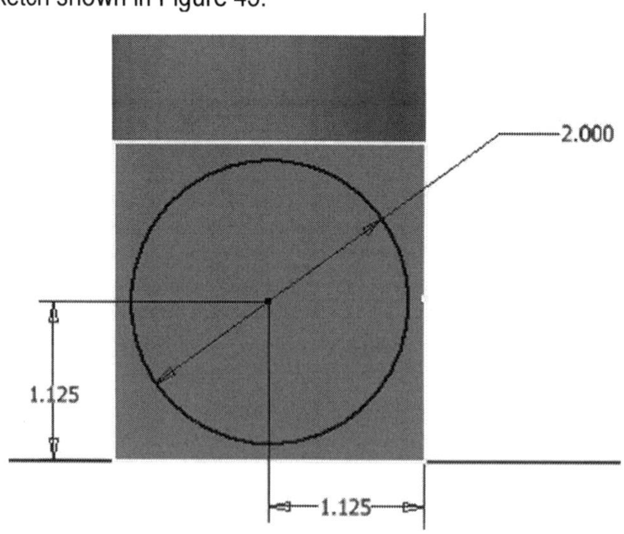

Figure 45

53. Change the view to Isometric as shown in Figure 46.

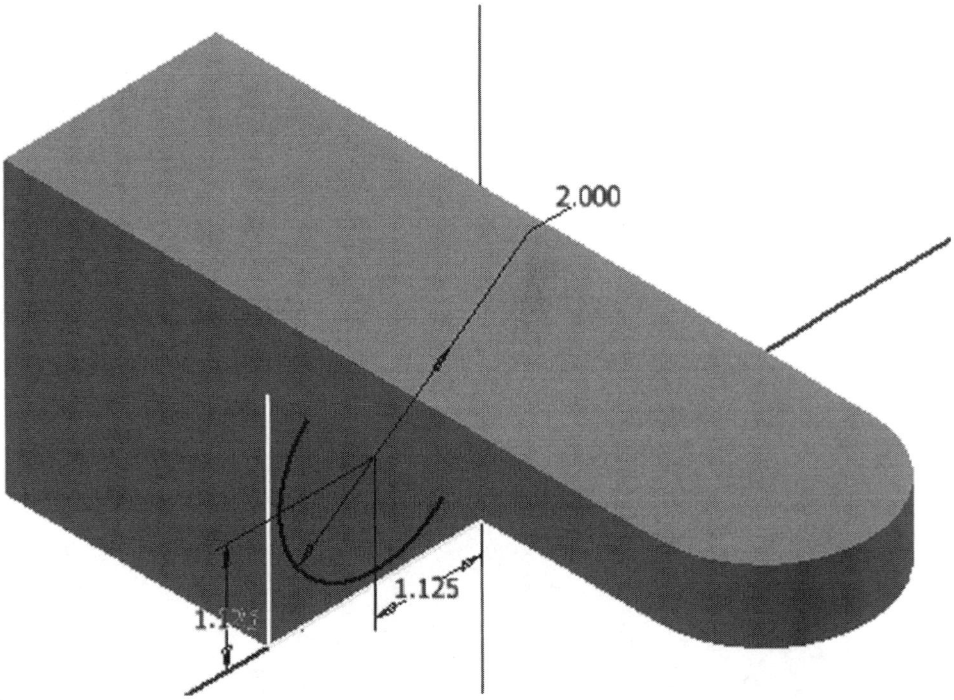

Figure 46

54. Use the Extrude command to extrude cut the circle that was just completed, creating a thru hole. Your screen should look similar to Figure 47.

Figure 47

55. Move the cursor to the upper middle portion of the screen and left click on the **View** tab. Left click on the **Look At** icon as shown in Figure 48.

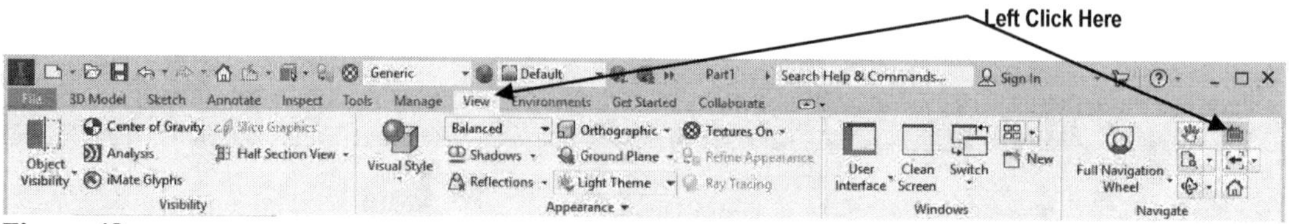

Figure 48

56. Left click on the surface shown in Figure 49.

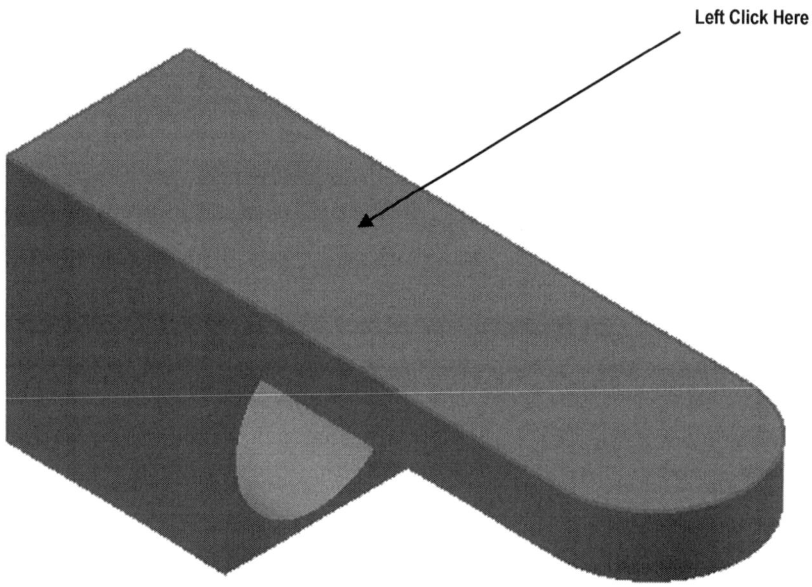

Figure 49

57. Complete the sketch shown in Figure 50.

Figure 50

58. Use the Extrude command to extrude or cut out the circle that was just completed. Change the view to Isometric as shown in Figure 51.

Figure 51

59. Save the part as Pistoncase1.ipt where it can be easily retrieved later.

60. Begin a new drawing as described in Chapter 1.

61. Begin a sketch on the **XY Plane** as shown in Figure 52. Make sure that the circles are located on the endpoint of a line. Also make sure the circles are NOT the same diameter.

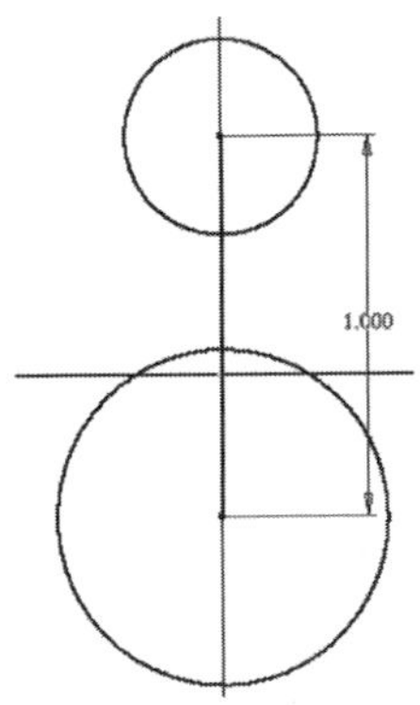

Figure 52

62. Move the cursor to the upper middle portion of the screen and left click on the Equal Constraint icon as shown in Figure 53.

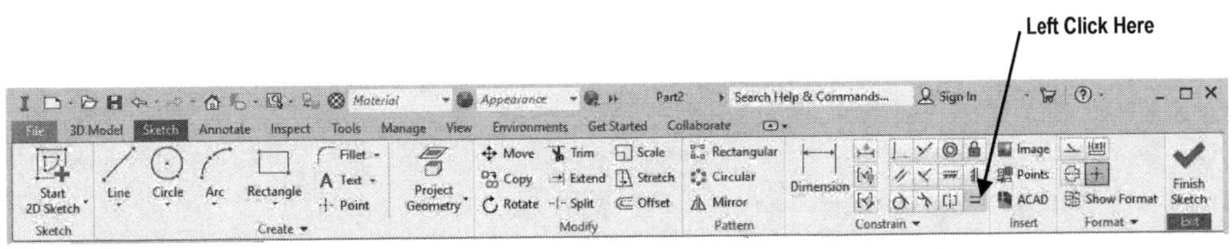

Figure 53

63. Left click on each of the circles as shown in Figure 54.

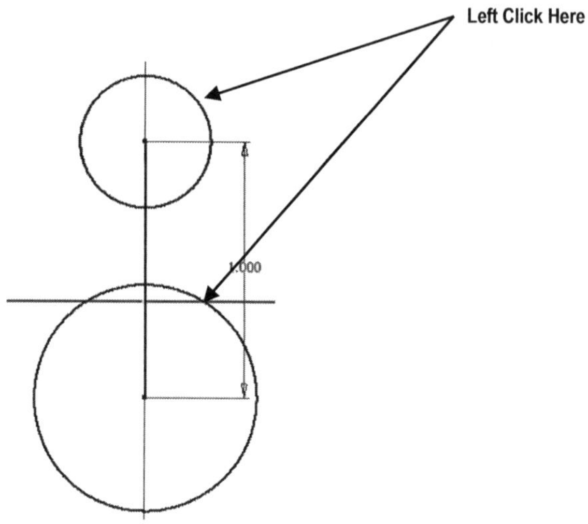

Figure 54

64. Inventor will create two circles of the same size as shown in Figure 55. When one circle is dimensioned, Inventor will automatically update the size of the other circle.

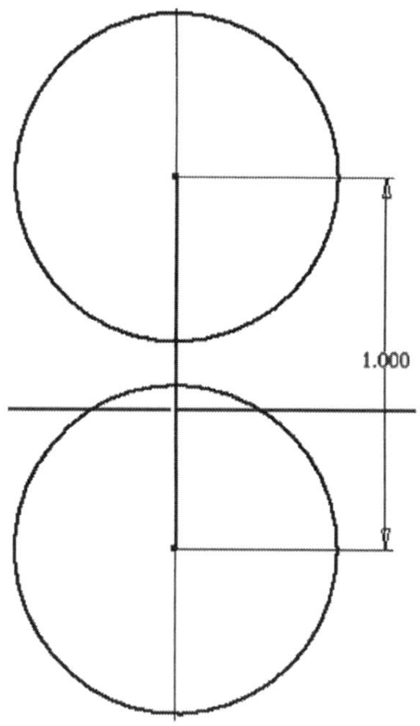

Figure 55

65. Finish completing the sketch shown in Figure 56.

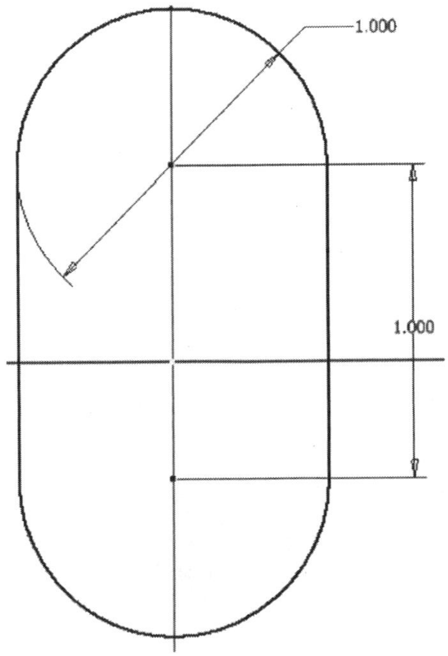

Figure 56

66. Extrude the sketch into a solid with a thickness of **.25** as shown in Figure 57.

Figure 57

67. Complete the following sketch. Use the center of the outside fillet radius as the center of the circle as shown in Figure 58.

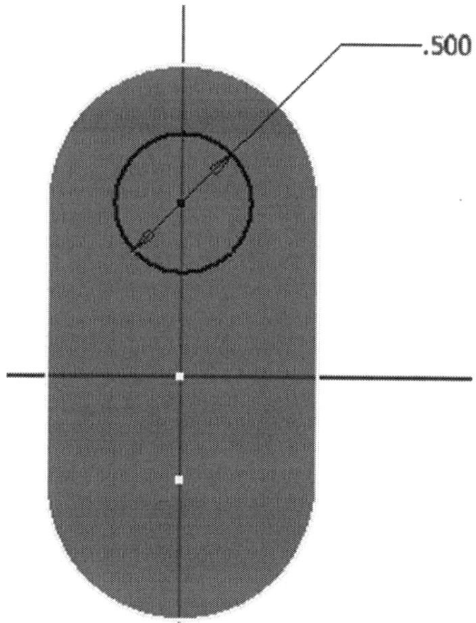

Figure 58

68. Extrude the sketch into a solid with a thickness of **.25** as shown in Figure 59.

Figure 59

69. Rotate the part around to gain access to the opposite side as shown in Figure 60.

Figure 60

70. Complete the following sketch as shown in Figure 61.

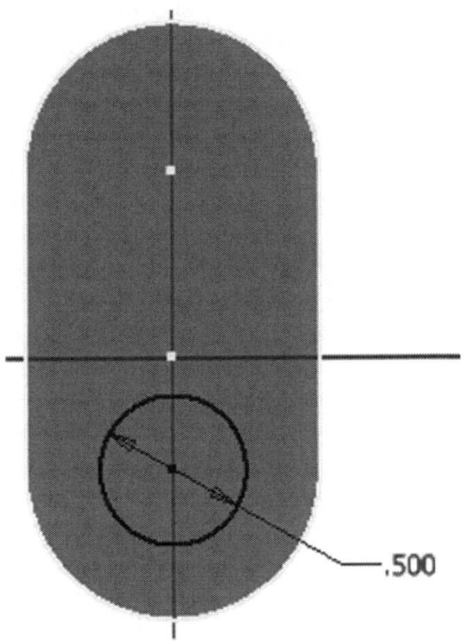

Figure 61

71. Extrude the sketch into a solid with a thickness of **.25** as shown in Figure 62.

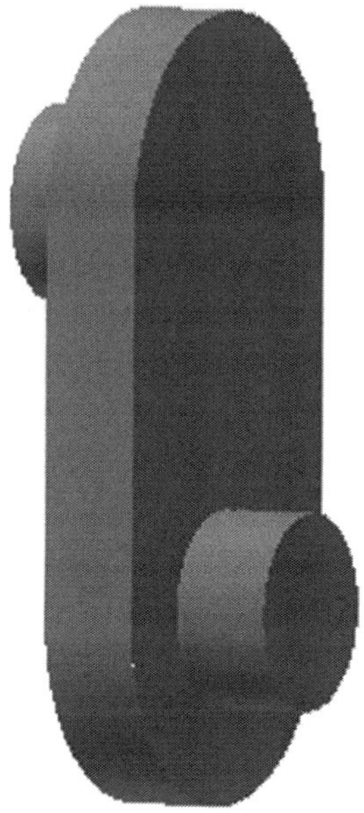

Figure 62

72. Save the part as Crankshaft1.ipt where it can be easily retrieved later.

73. Begin a new drawing as described in Chapter 1.

74. Create a new sketch on the **XY Plane** as shown. Make sure each of the circles are NOT sharing the same center and are NOT in line with each other as shown in Figure 63.

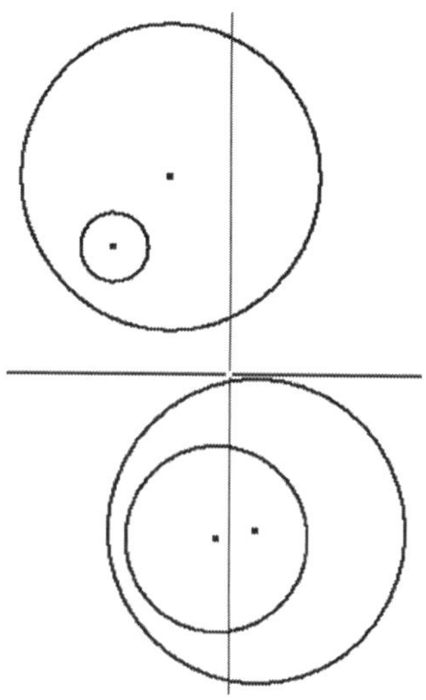

Figure 63

75. Move the cursor to the upper middle portion of the screen and left click on the Concentric Constraint icon as shown in Figure 64.

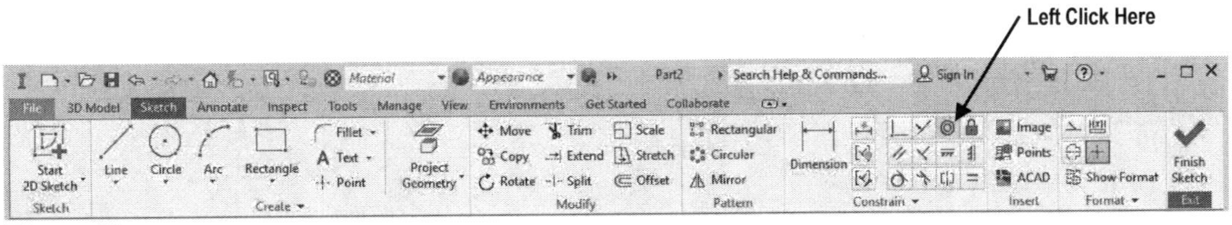

Figure 64

76. Holding the Shift key down, left click on each circle as shown in Figure 65.

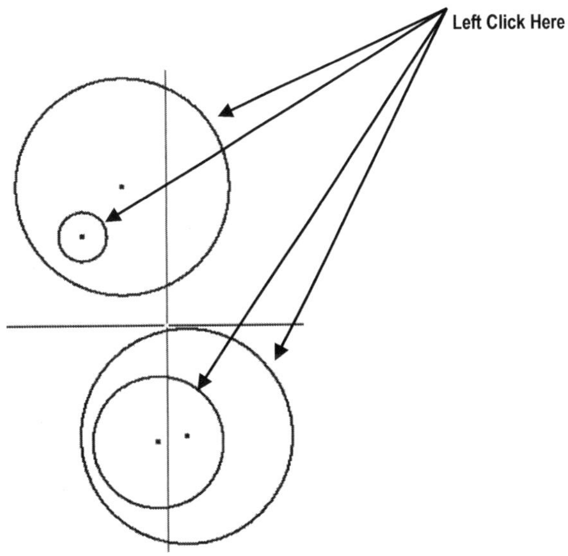

Figure 65

77. Inventor will create concentric circles as shown in Figure 66.

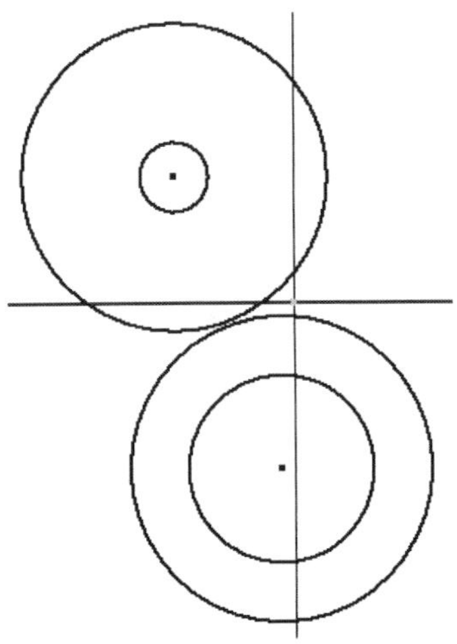

Figure 66

78. Move the cursor to the upper middle portion of the screen and left click on the Vertical Constraint icon as shown in Figure 67.

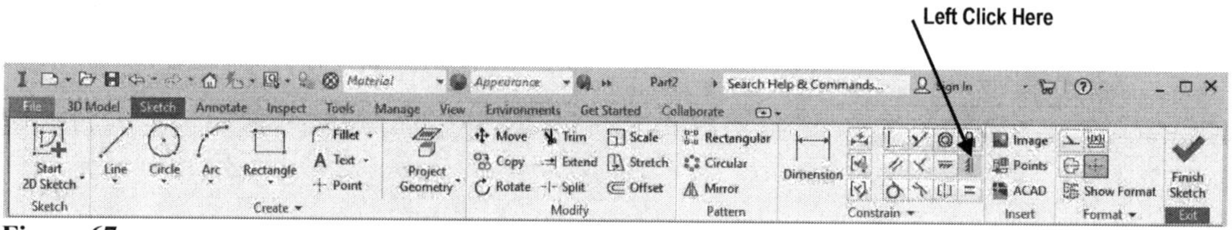

Figure 67

79. Left click on the centers of the circles as shown in Figure 68.

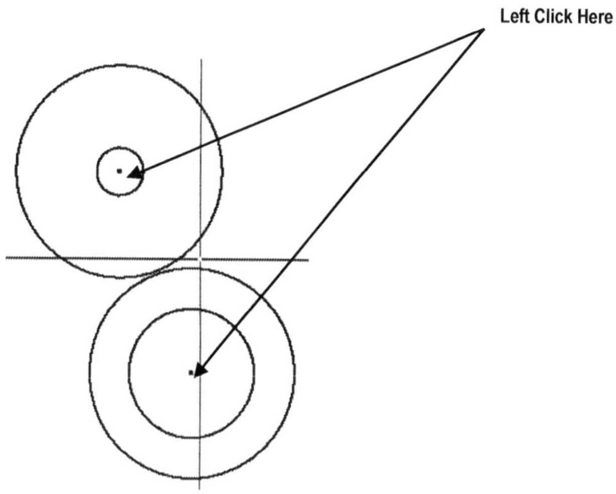

Figure 68

80. Inventor will create a vertical constraint between the centers of the circles as shown in Figure 69.

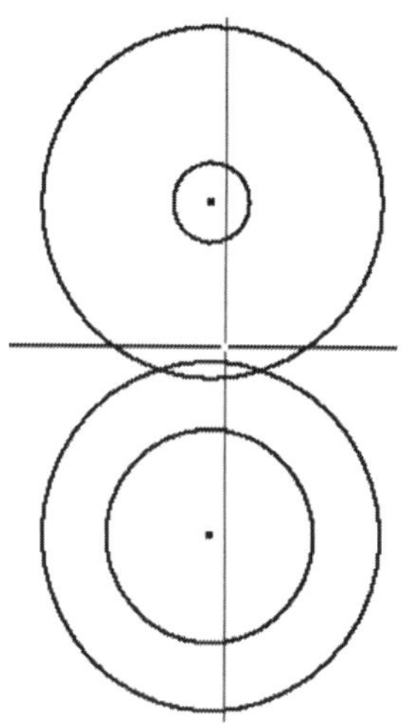
Figure 69

81. Use the Free Orbit/Rotate command to rotate the sketch around on to its side as shown in Figure 70.

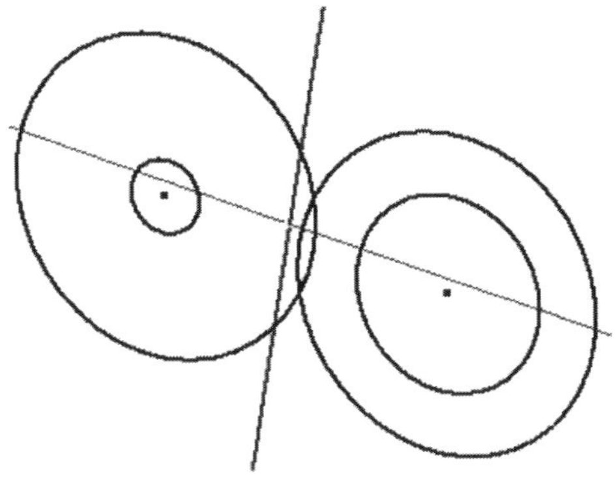

Figure 70

82. Using the geometry created above, complete the sketch shown. Extrude the sketch to a thickness of **.25** inches as shown in Figure 71.

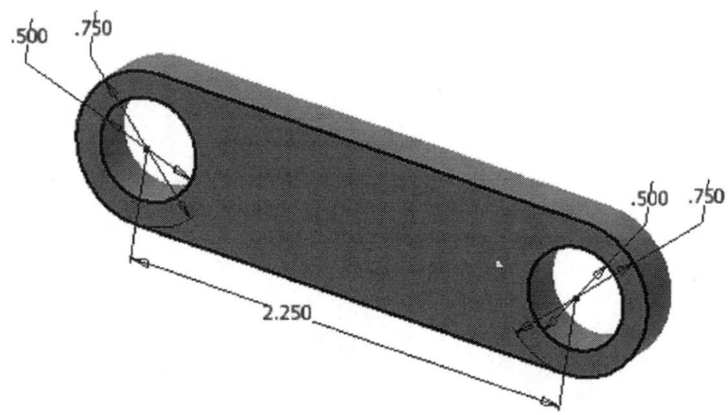

Figure 71

83. Save the part as Conrod1.ipt where it can be easily retrieved later.

84. Be sure to save all parts. Each of these parts will be used in following chapters.

CHAPTER 7

Introduction to Assembly View Procedures

Objectives:

1. Learn to import existing solid models into the Assembly Panel
2. Learn to constrain all parts in the Assembly Panel
3. Learn to edit/modify parts while in the Assembly Panel
4. Learn to assign colors to different parts in the Assembly Panel
5. Learn to drive a Constraint to animate/simulate motion
6. Learn to create an .avi or .wmv file while in the Assembly Panel

Chapter 7 includes instruction on how to construct the assembly shown.

1. Start Inventor 2027 by referring to "Chapter 1 Getting Started."

2. After Autodesk Inventor 2027 is running, left click on the New icon. The Create New File dialog box will appear. Left click on the **English** folder as shown in Figure 1.

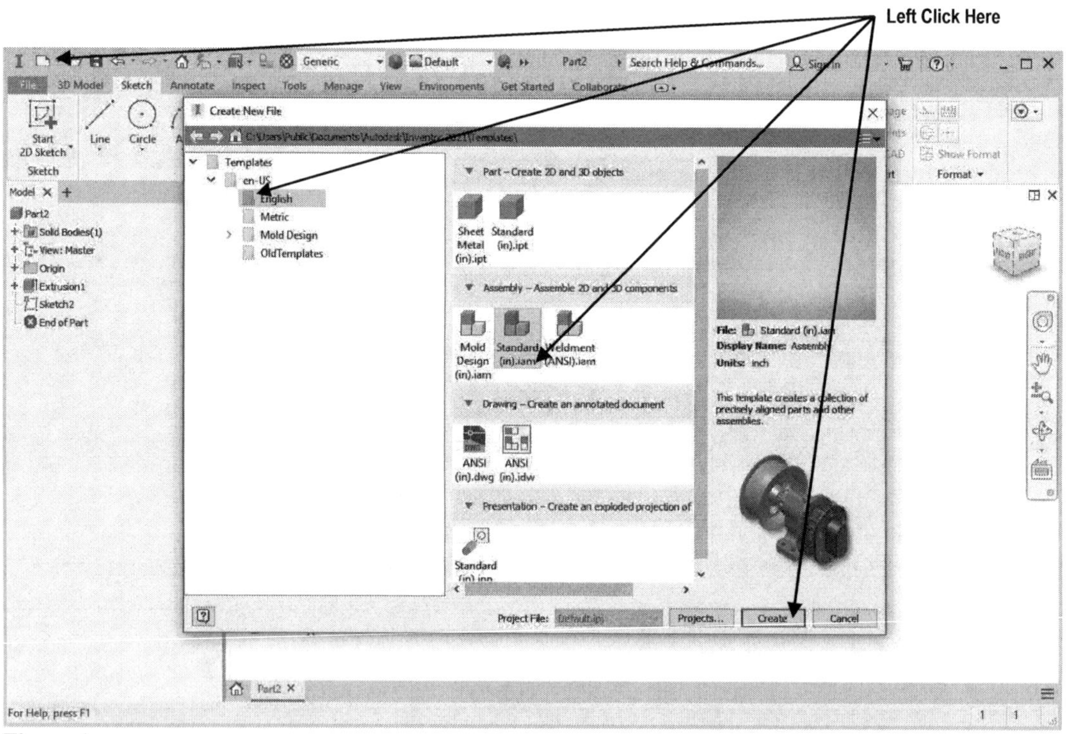

Figure 1

3. Left click on **Standard (in).iam**. Left click on **Create** as shown in Figure 1.

Learn to import existing solid models into the Assemble Panel

4. The Assemble Panel will open. Your screen should look similar to Figure 2.

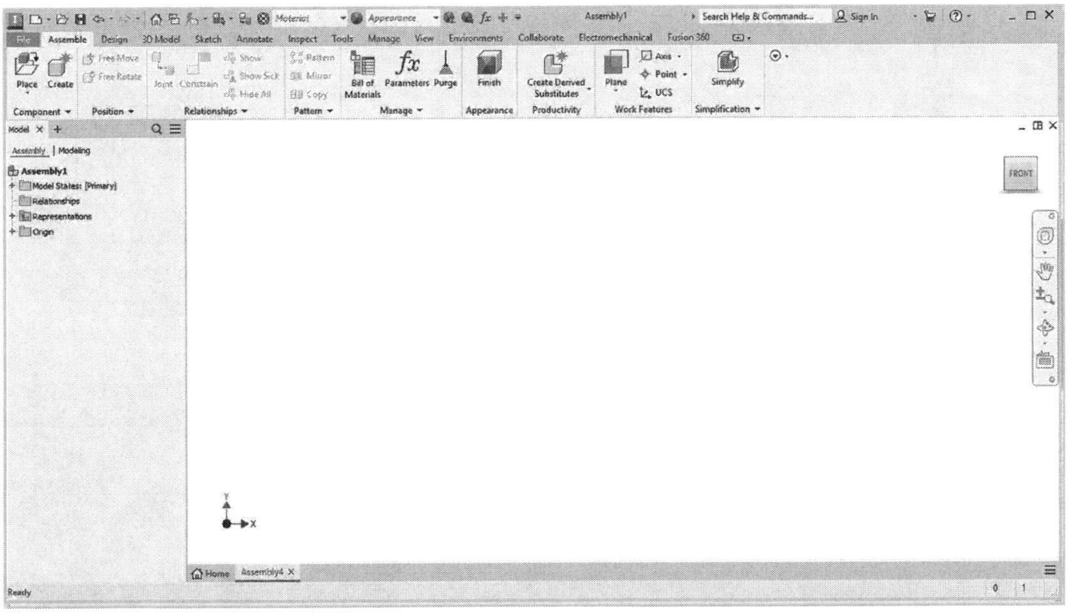

Figure 2

5. Move the cursor to the upper left portion of the screen. Left click on the drop-down arrow underneath Place. A drop-down menu will appear. Left click on **Place** as shown in Figure 3.

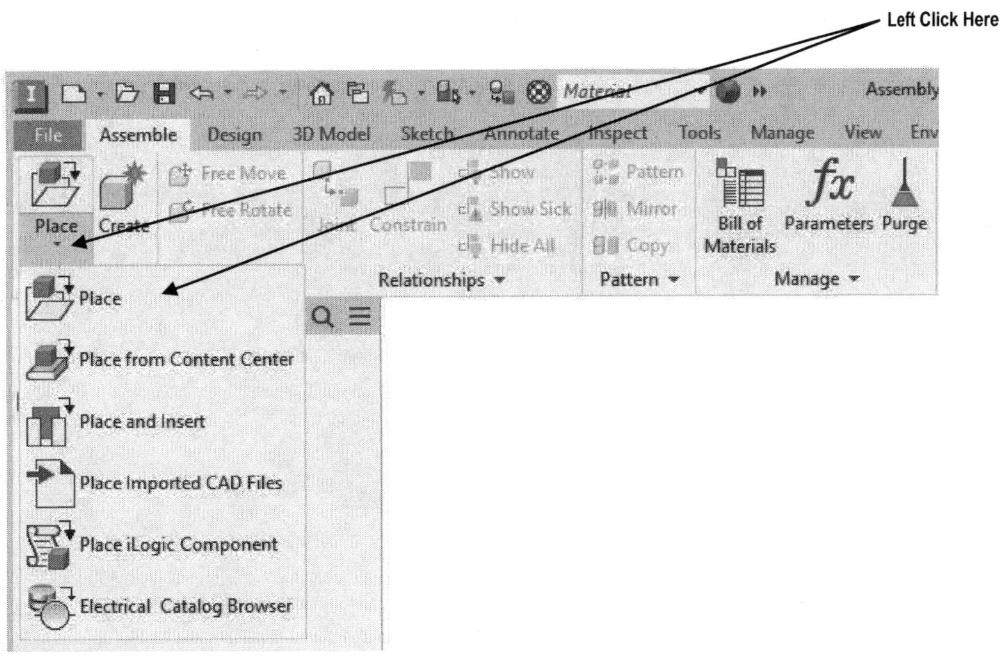

Figure 3

6. The Place Component dialog box will appear. Locate the PistonCase1.ipt file and left click on **Open** as shown in Figure 4.

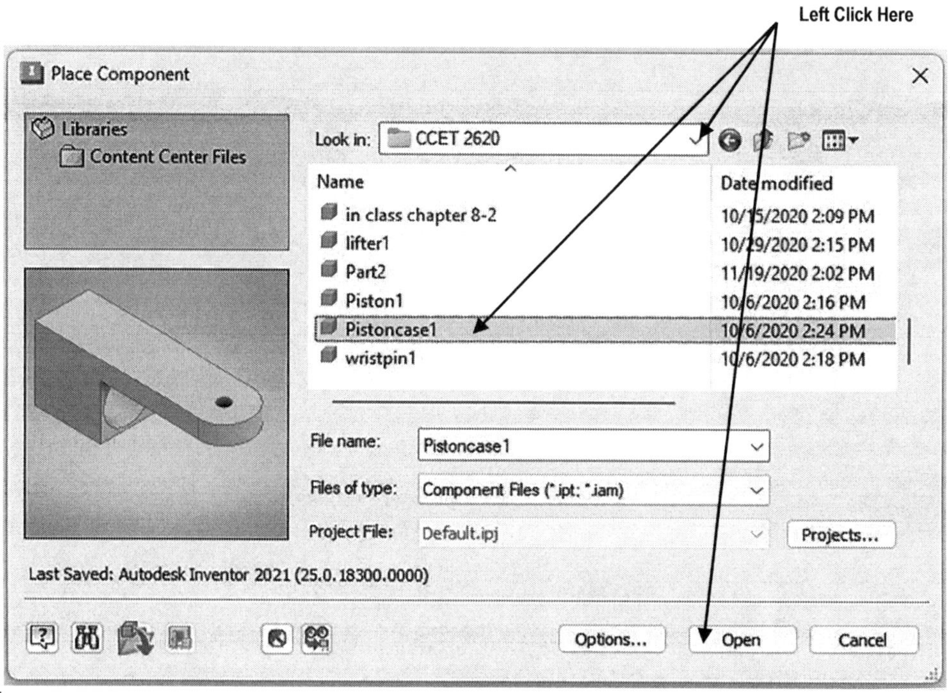

Figure 4

7. Left click once. Inventor will place one piston case in the drawing space while another piston case will be attached to the cursor as shown in Figure 5.

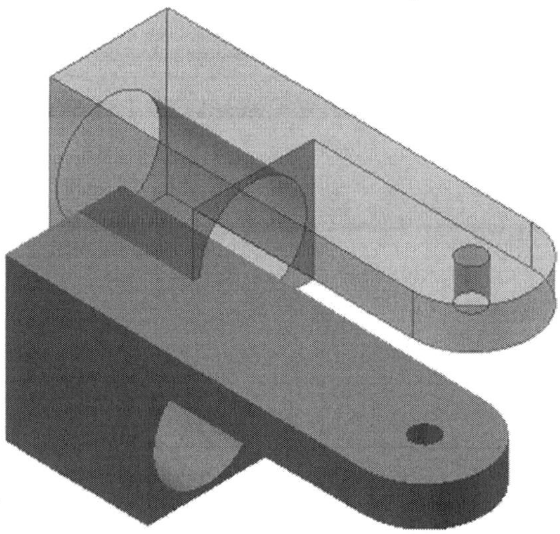

Figure 5

8. Press the **Esc** key on the keyboard. This will cancel placing a 2nd piston case. Your screen should look similar to Figure 6.

Figure 6

9. Move the cursor to the upper left portion of the screen and left click on **Place** as shown in Figure 7.

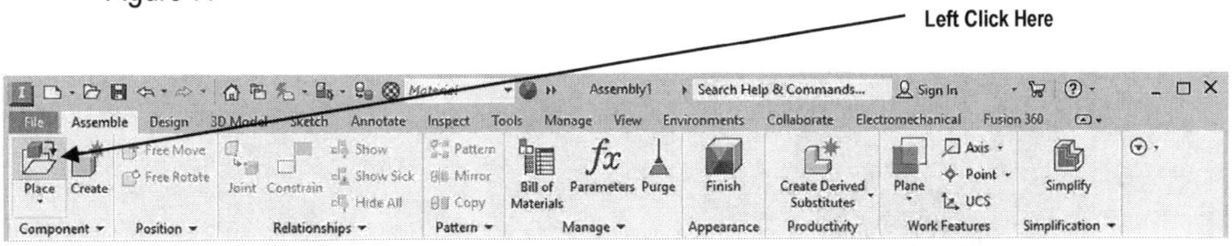

Figure 7

10. The Place Component dialog box will appear. Locate the Piston1.ipt file and left click on **Open** as shown in Figure 8.

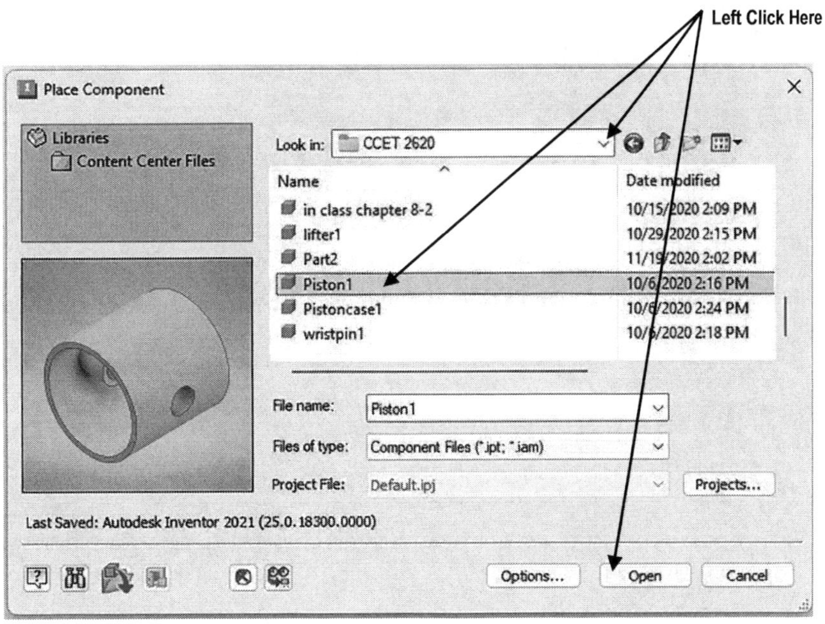

Figure 8

11. The piston will be attached to the cursor. Place the piston anywhere near the piston case and left click once. Another piston will be attached to the cursor in case another will be used. In this drawing there is no need to import the same part multiple times. Press the **Esc** key once. Your screen should look similar to Figure 9.

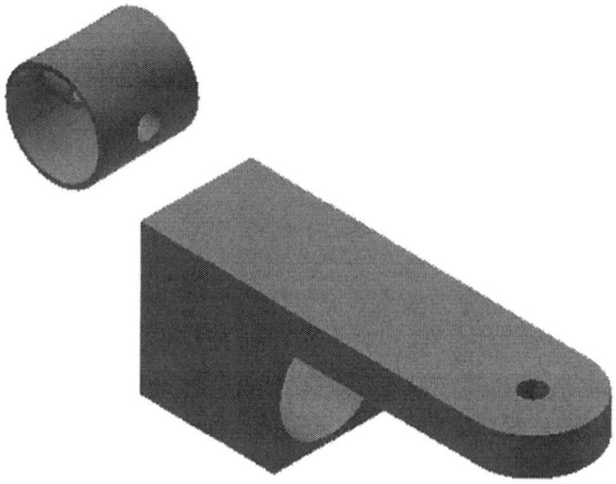

Figure 9

12. Continue to "Place" the remaining parts into the Assembly area as shown in Figure 10.

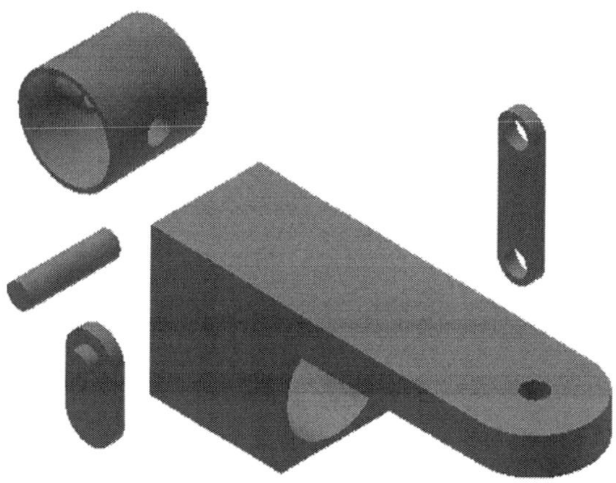

Figure 10

13. Move the cursor to the upper middle portion of the screen and left click on the **Free Rotate** icon as shown in Figure 11.

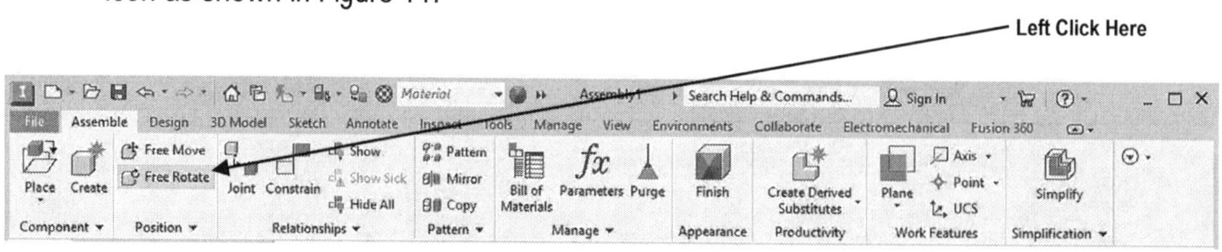

Figure 111

14. Move the cursor to the piston case and left click once. A white circle will appear around the piston case. Rotate the piston case upward as shown in Figure 12.

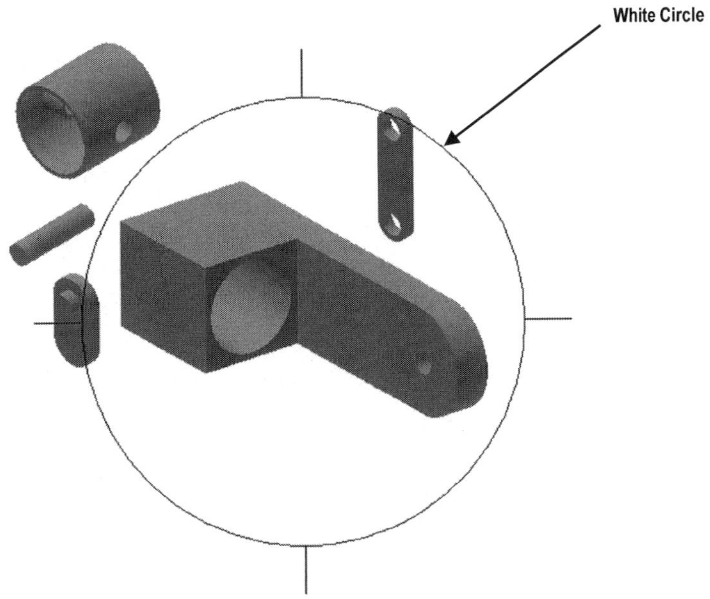

Figure 12

15. Your screen should look similar to Figure 13.

16. After the piston case is rotated as shown in Figure 13, right click once. A pop-up menu will appear. Left click on **Done** as shown in Figure 13.

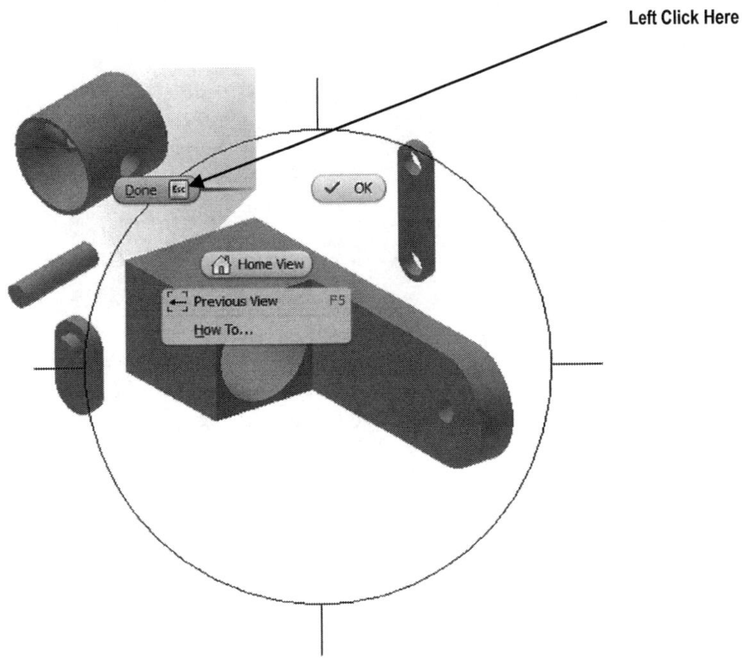

Figure 13

17. Move the cursor to the lower left portion of the screen in the browser. Move the cursor over the text **Pistoncase1** and left click once. The text box will turn blue. Right click once. A pop-up menu will appear. Left click on **Grounded** as shown in Figure 14. Inventor will "Ground" the Pistoncase preventing it from moving. A push pin will appear in the browser next to the Pistoncase text as shown in Figure 14. Only ground the Pistoncase. All other parts will need to be "Ungrounded".

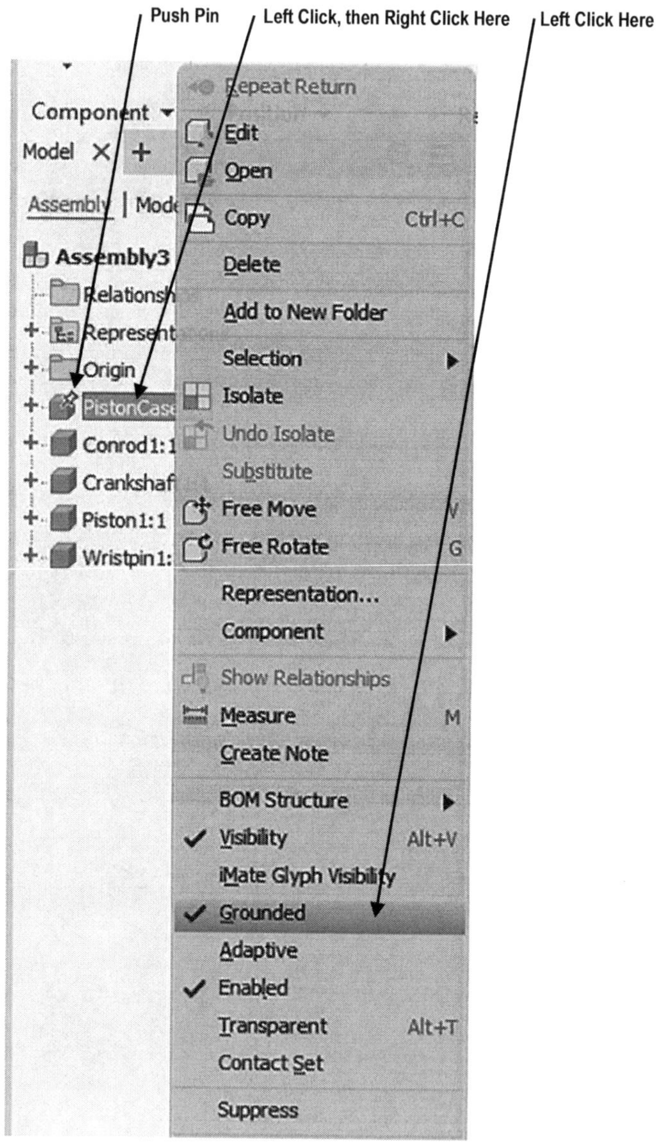

Figure 124

18. Your screen should look similar to Figure 15.

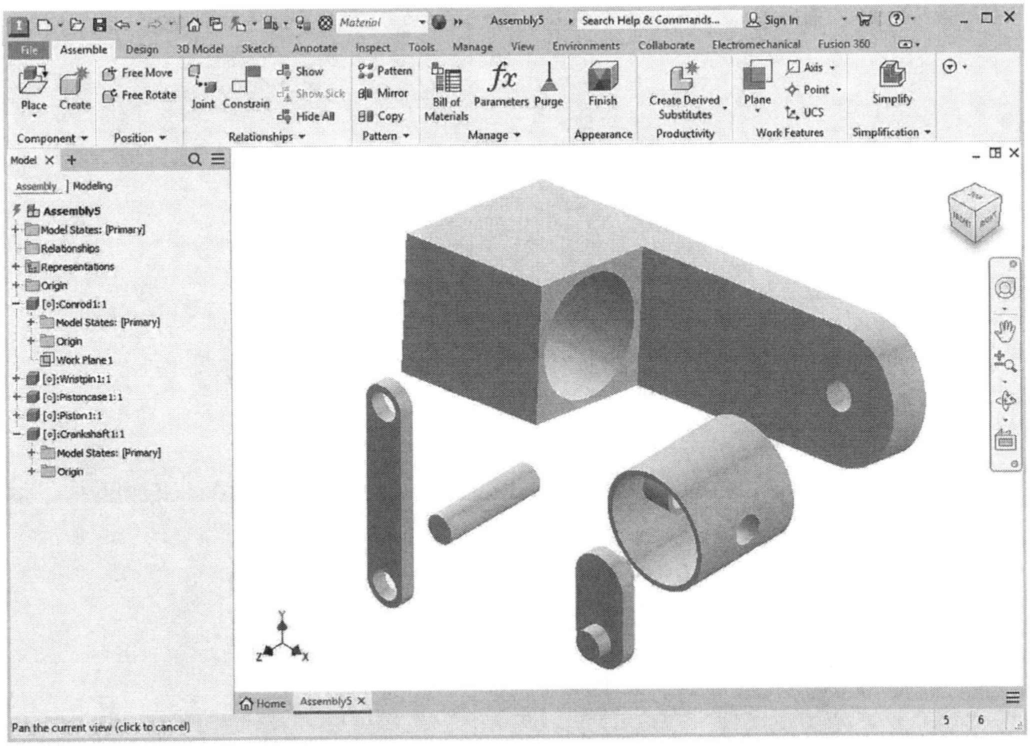

Figure 135

Learn to constrain all parts in the Assemble Panel

19. Move the cursor to the upper middle portion of the screen and left click on **Constrain**. The Place Constraint dialog box will appear as shown in Figure 16.

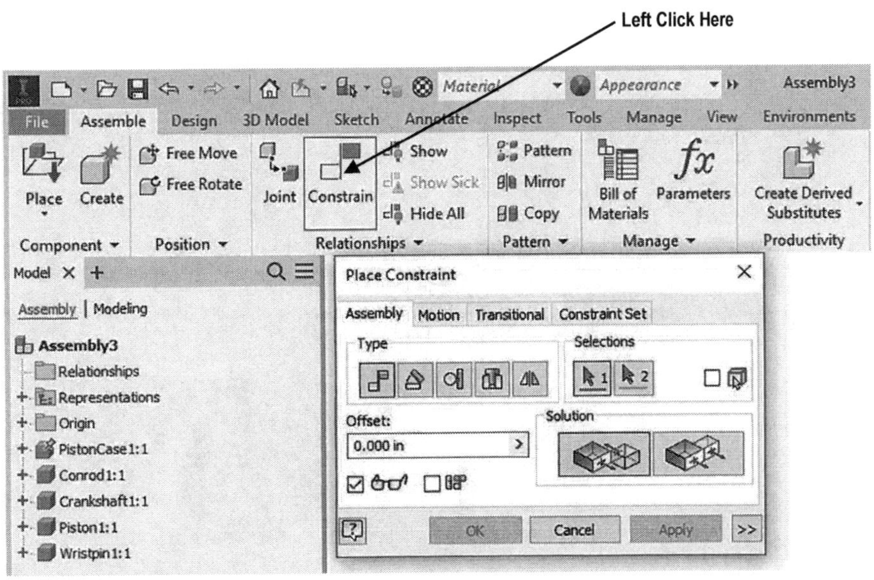

Figure 14

20. Move the cursor over the piston until a center line appears and left click on the center line as shown in Figure 17.

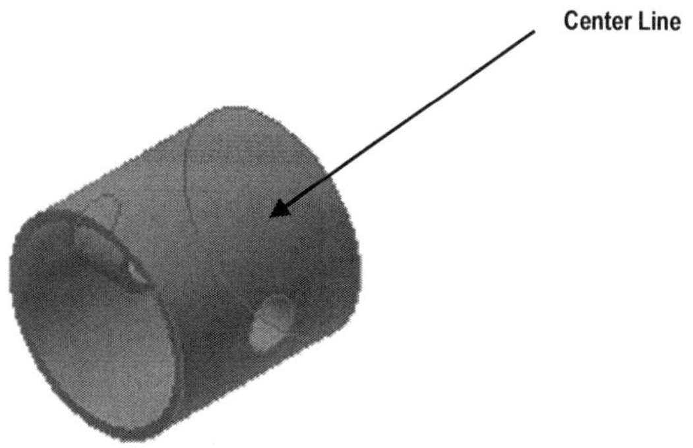

Figure 15

21. Move the cursor over the piston case until a center line appears and left click on the center line as shown in Figure 18.

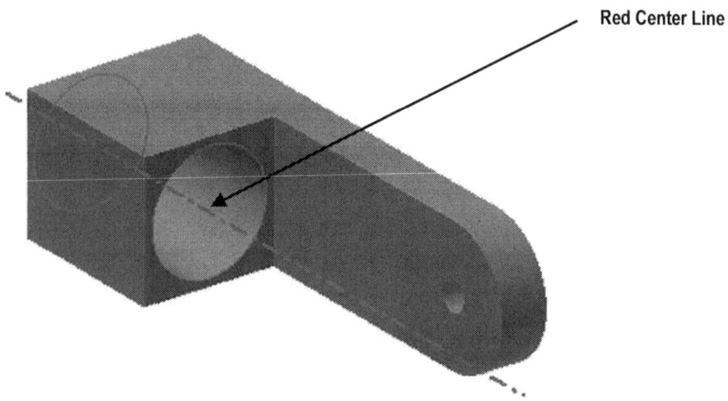

Figure 16

22. Inventor will align the centers of the piston and the piston case. Your screen should look similar to Figure 19.

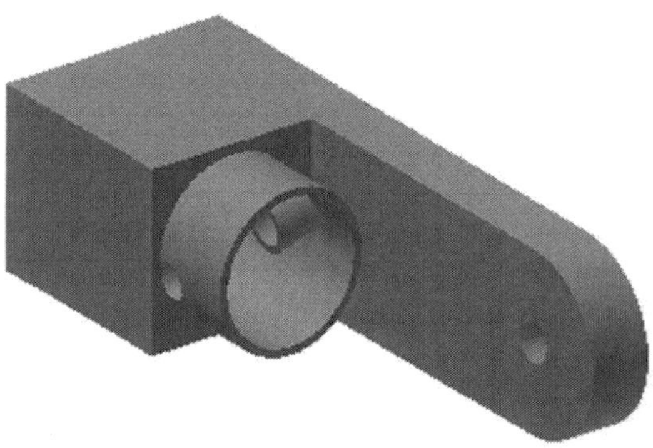

Figure 17

23. If Inventor installed the piston upside down, (open side of the piston is facing upward) left click on the Opposed icon as shown in Figure 20.

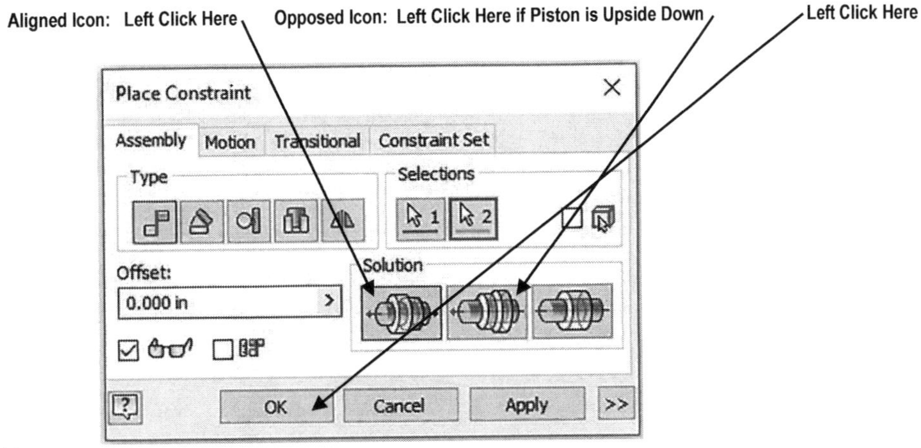

Figure 18

24. Left click on **OK** as shown in Figure 20.

25. Your screen should look similar to Figure 21.

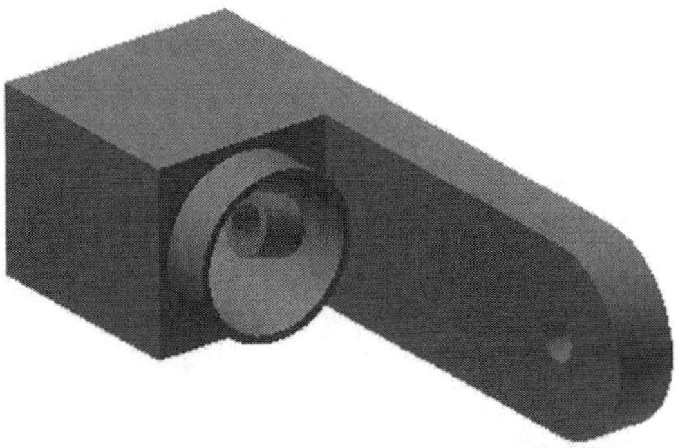

Figure 19

26. Move the cursor to the lower left portion of the piston. Left click (holding the left mouse button down) and slide the piston down out below the bore as shown in Figure 22.

Figure 20

27. Move the cursor to the upper middle portion of the screen and left click on **Constrain**. The Place Constraint dialog box will appear as shown in Figure 23.

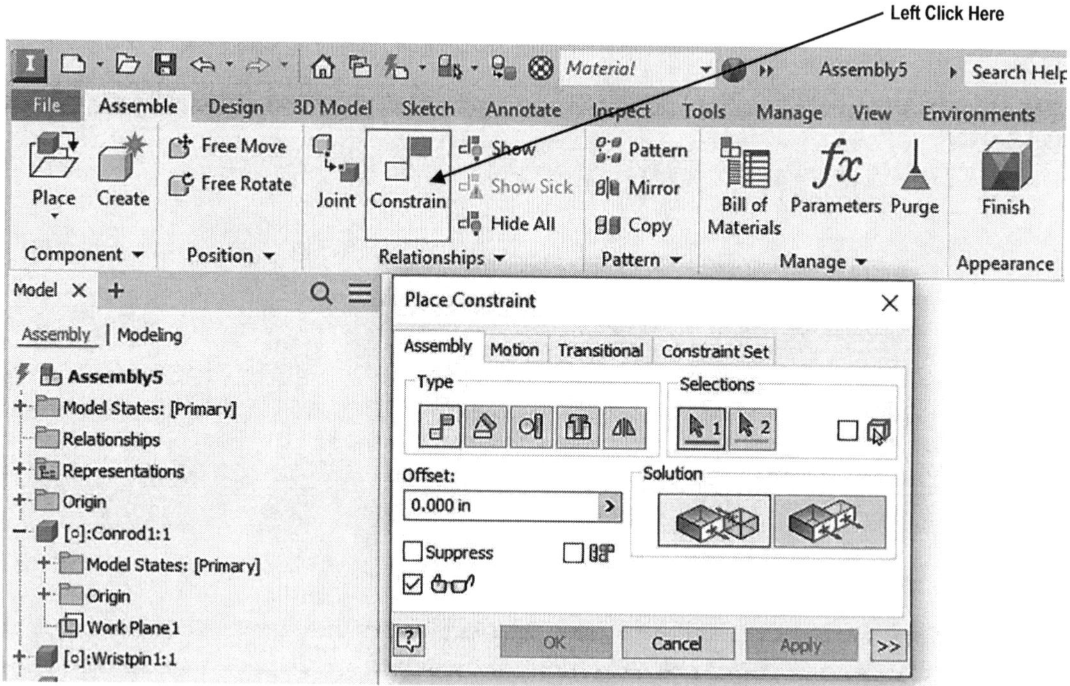

Figure 21

28. Move the cursor to the wristpin hole on the piston. A center line will appear. Left click once as shown in Figure 24.

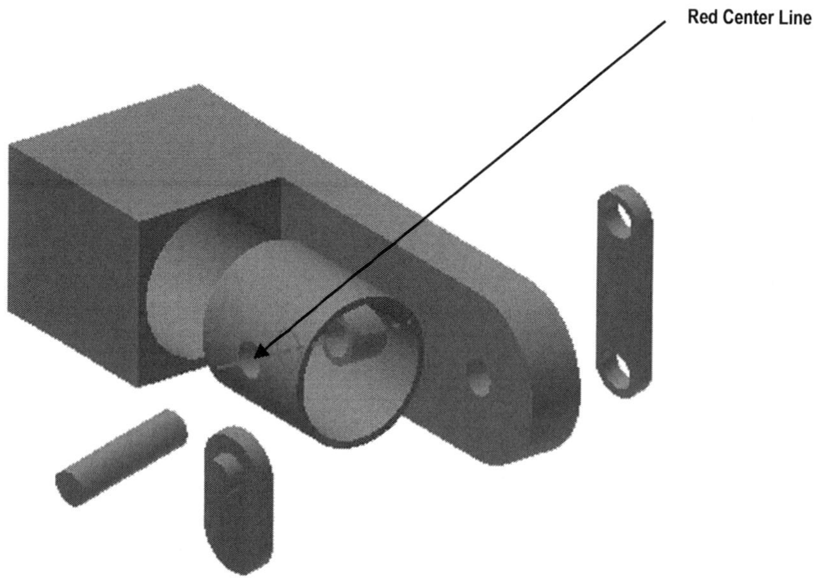

Figure 22

29. Move the cursor to the upper portion of the connecting rod. Move the cursor inside the hole in the connecting rod causing a center line to appear. Left click once as shown in Figure 25. You may have to zoom in to accomplish this.

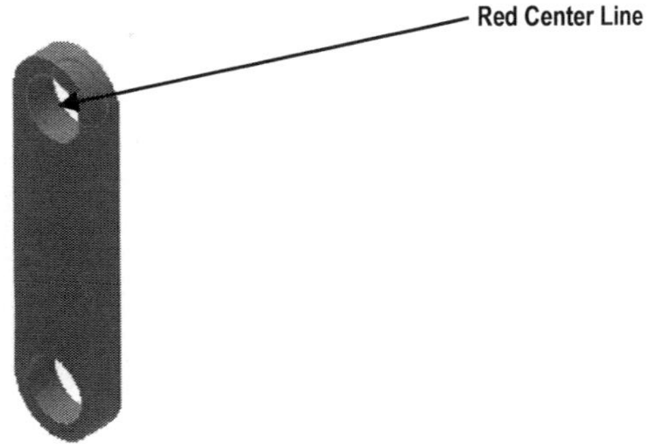

Figure 23

30. Left click on the Aligned icon. Left click on **OK** as shown in Figure 26.

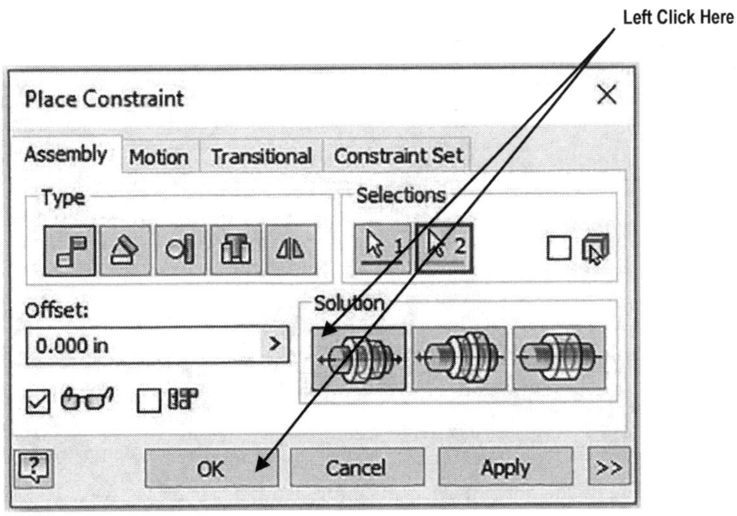

Figure 24

31. Your screen should look similar to Figure 27.

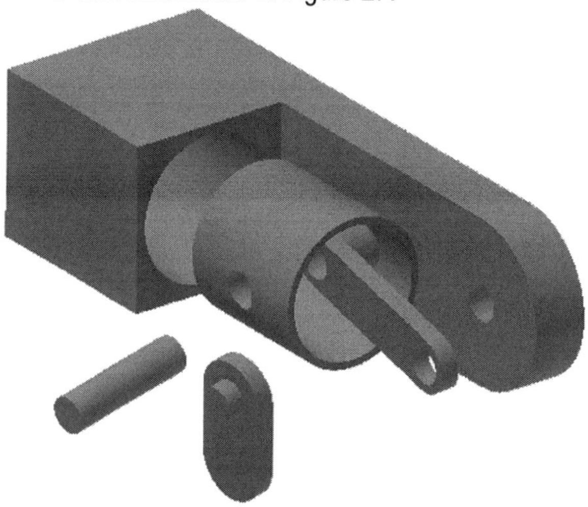

Figure 25

32. Use the Free Orbit/Rotate command to rotate the entire assembly to gain access to the underside of the piston as shown in Figure 28.

Figure 26

33. Move the cursor to the upper middle portion of the screen and left click on **Constrain**. The Place Constraint dialog box will appear as shown in Figure 29.

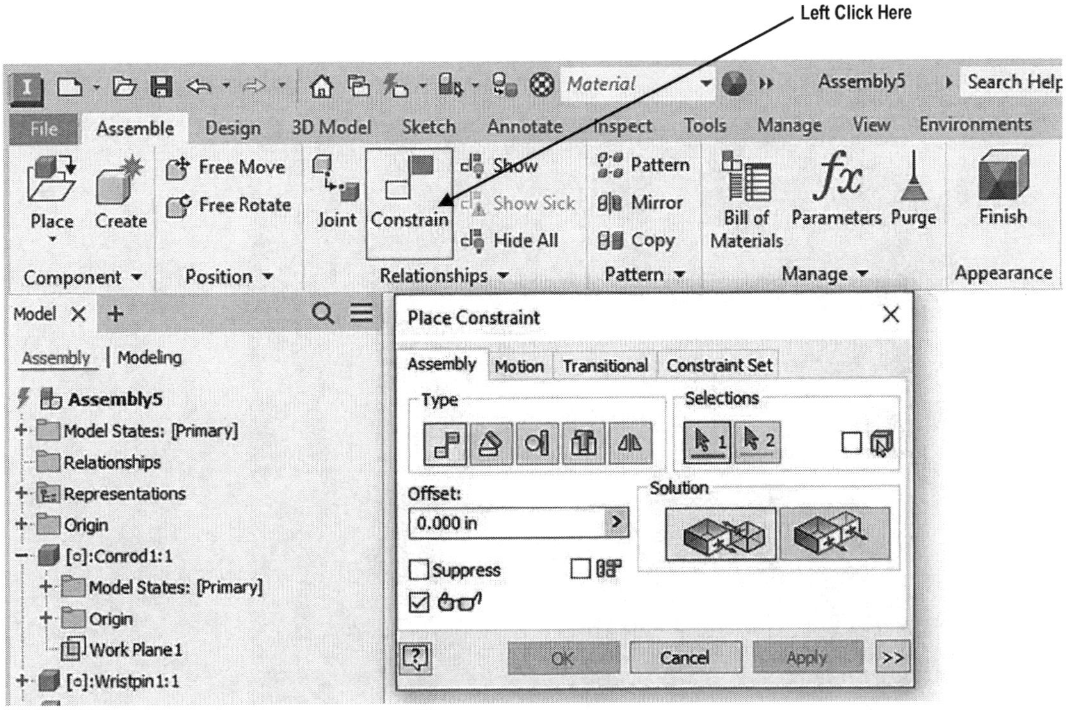

Figure 27

34. Move the cursor to the left side of the connecting rod causing an arrow to appear. Left click as shown in Figure 30. You may have to zoom in so that Inventor will find the proper surface.

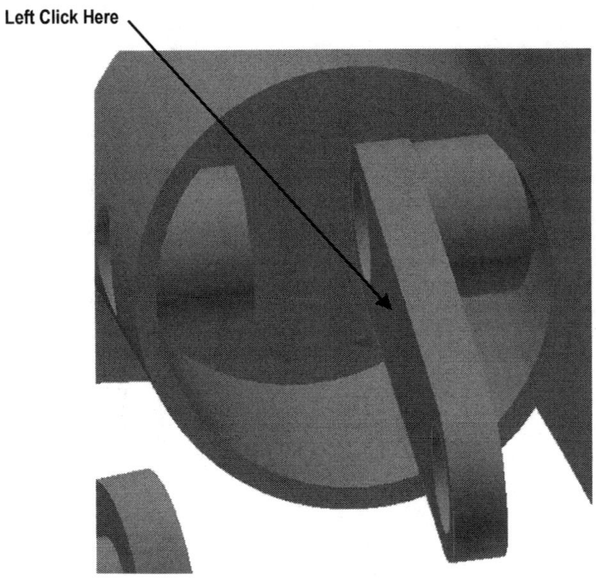

Figure 28

35. Use the Rotate command to turn the piston in order to gain access to the surface opposite the previously selected surface. Hit the **Esc** key once or right click and select **Done** to get out of the Rotate command. Left click on the surface opposite the previously selected surface as shown in Figure 31.

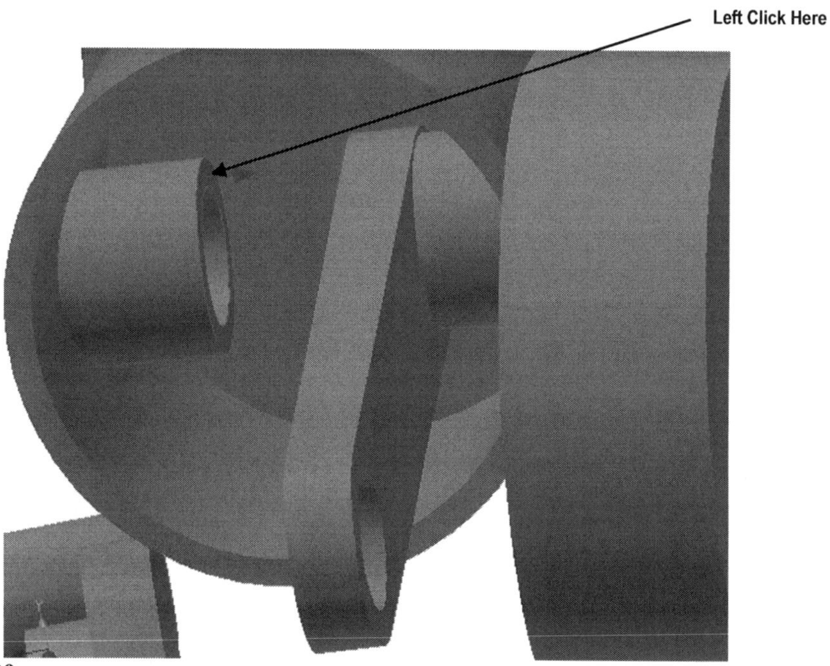

Figure 29

36. Left click on the Mate icon. Enter **.250** for the Offset as shown in Figure 32.

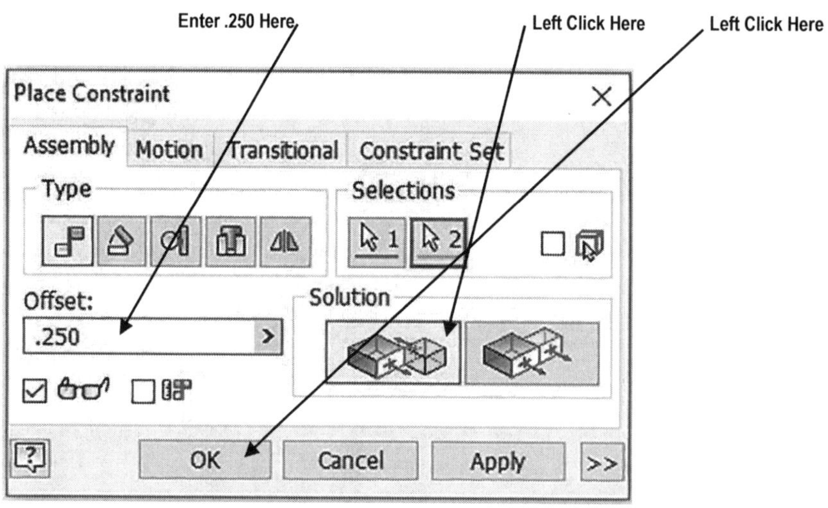

Figure 30

37. Left click on **OK**.

38. The connecting rod should be centered in the piston. Your screen should look similar to Figure 33.

Figure 31

39. Right click anywhere around the drawing. A pop-up menu will appear. Left click on **Home View** as shown in Figure 34.

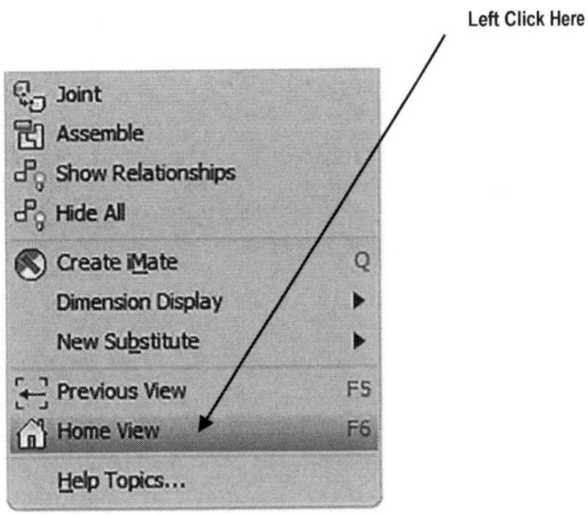

Figure 32

40. Inventor will provide an isometric view of the assembly as shown in Figure 35.

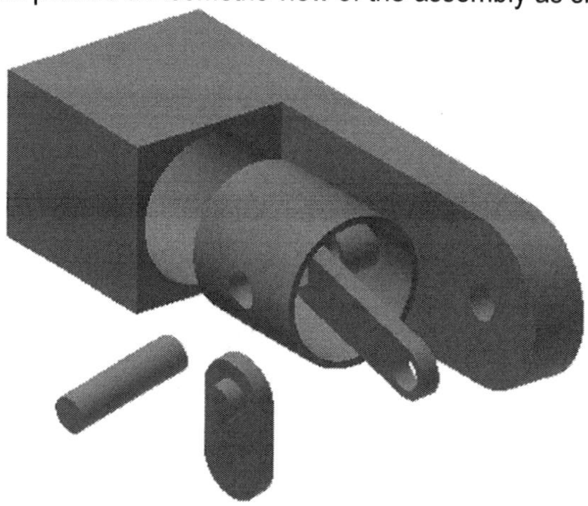

Figure 33

41. Move the cursor to the upper middle portion of the screen and left click on **Constrain**. The Place Constraint dialog box will appear as shown in Figure 36.

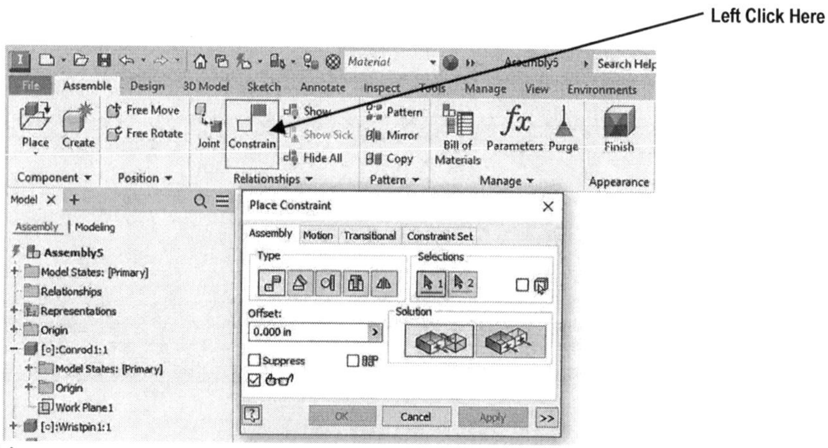

Figure 34

42. Move the cursor to the wrist pin causing a center line to appear. After the center line appears, left click once as shown in Figure 37.

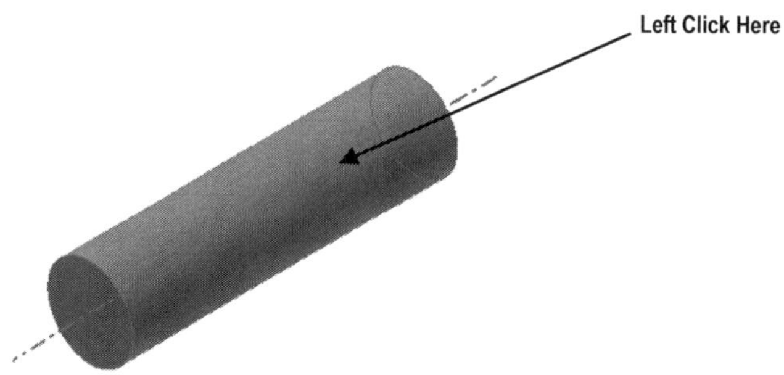

Figure 35

43. Move the cursor to the piston causing a center line to appear. After the center line appears, left click once as shown in Figure 38.

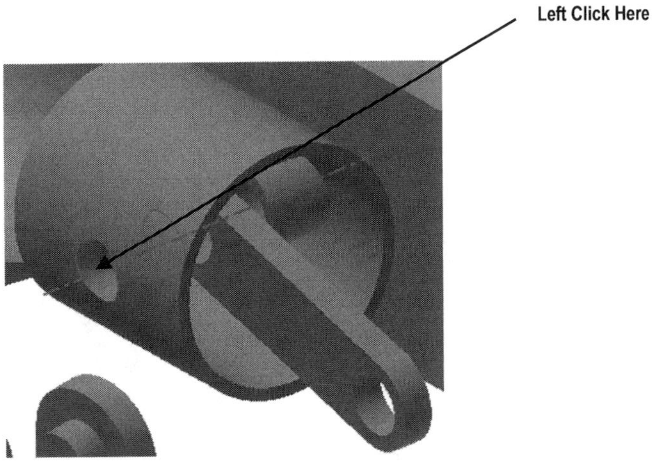

Figure 36

44. Left click on the Aligned icon. Left click on **OK** as shown in Figure 39.

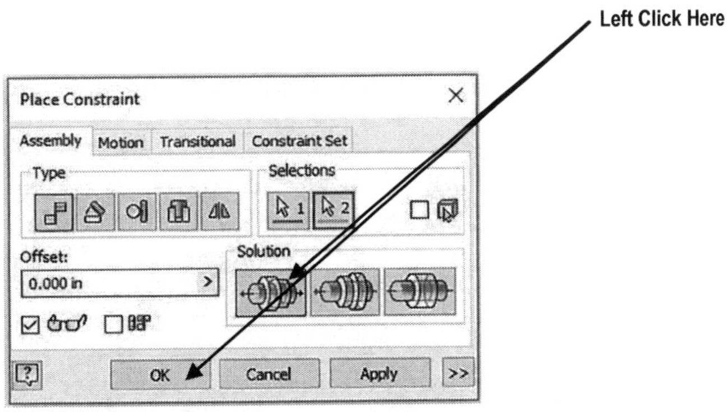

Figure 37

45. Move the cursor to the upper middle portion of the screen and left click on **Constrain**. The Place Constraint dialog box will appear as shown in Figure 40.

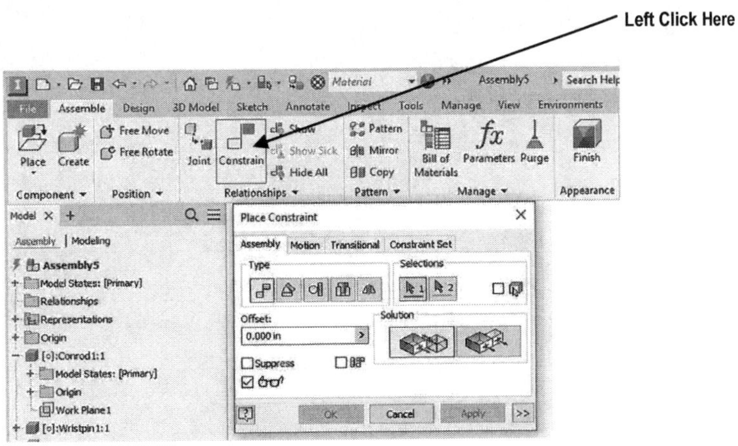

Figure 38

46. Left click on the Flush icon as shown in Figure 41.

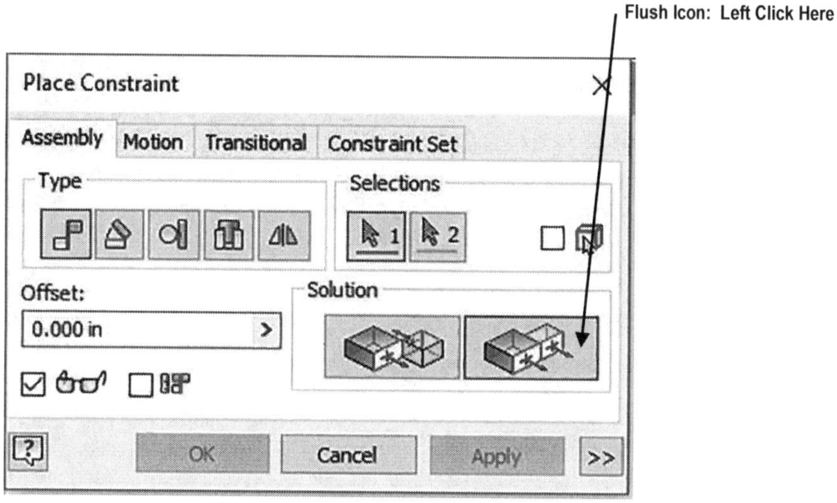

Figure 39

47. Move the cursor to the side of the wrist pin causing an arrow to appear. After the arrow appears, left click once as shown in Figure 42.

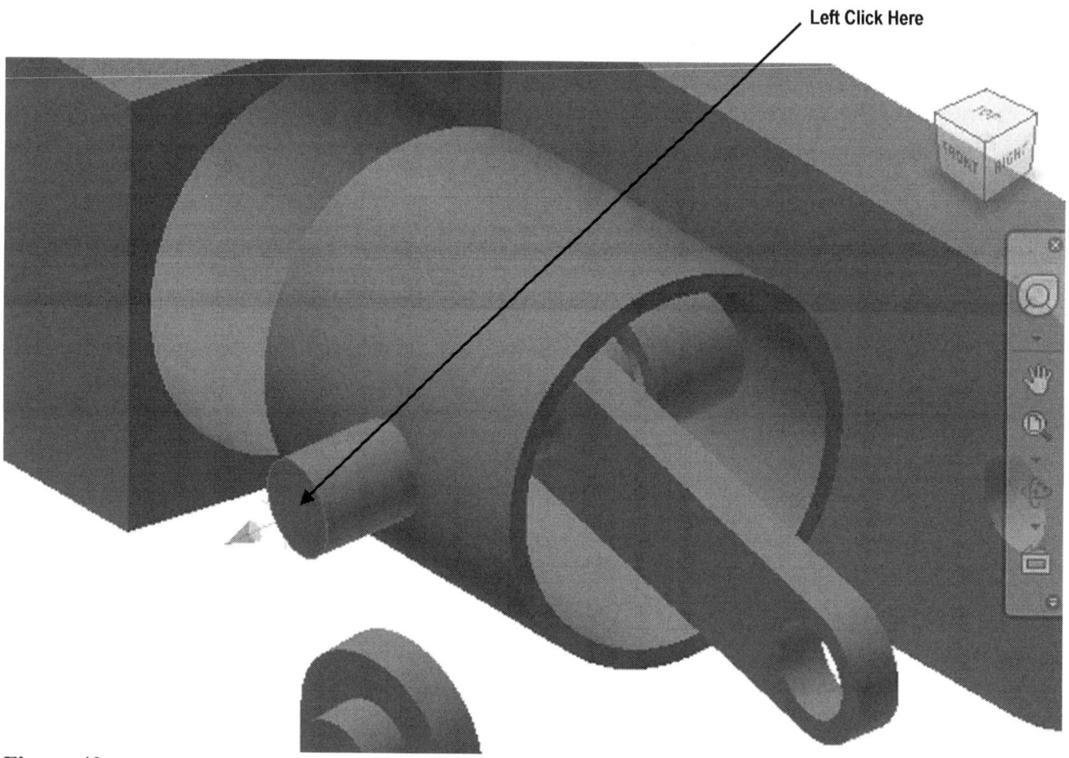

Figure 40

48. Move the cursor to the side of the connecting rod causing an arrow to appear. After the arrow appears, left click once as shown in Figure 43.

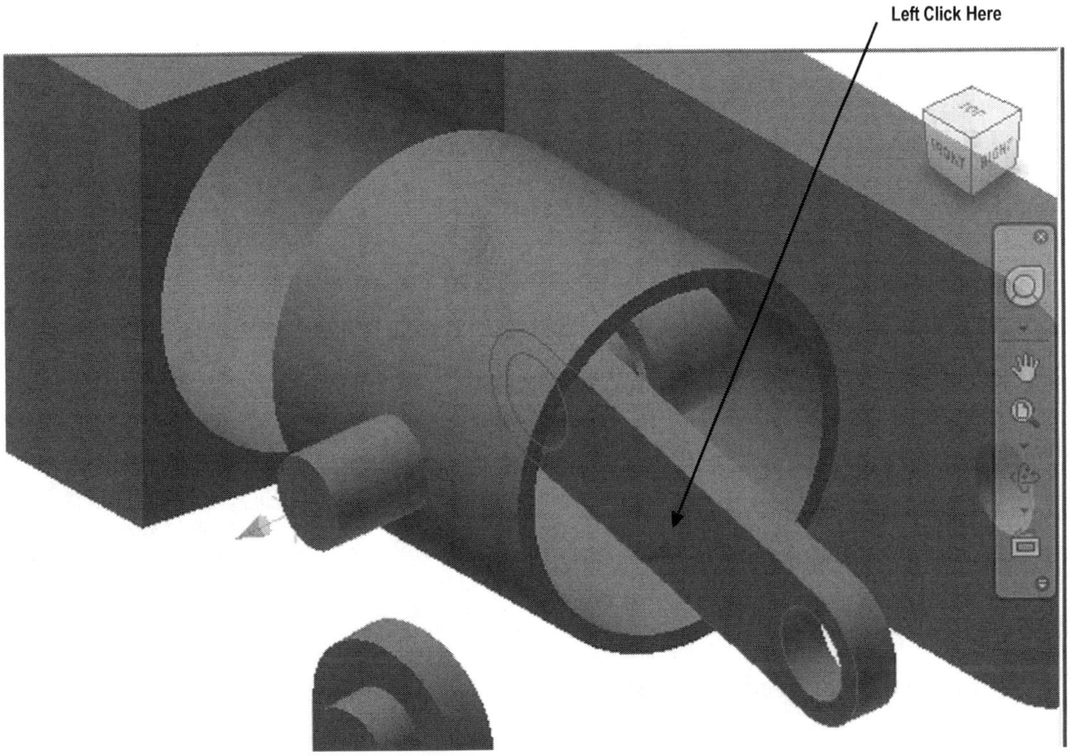

Figure 41

49. Enter **-.7825** under Offset. Left click on **OK** as shown in Figure 44.

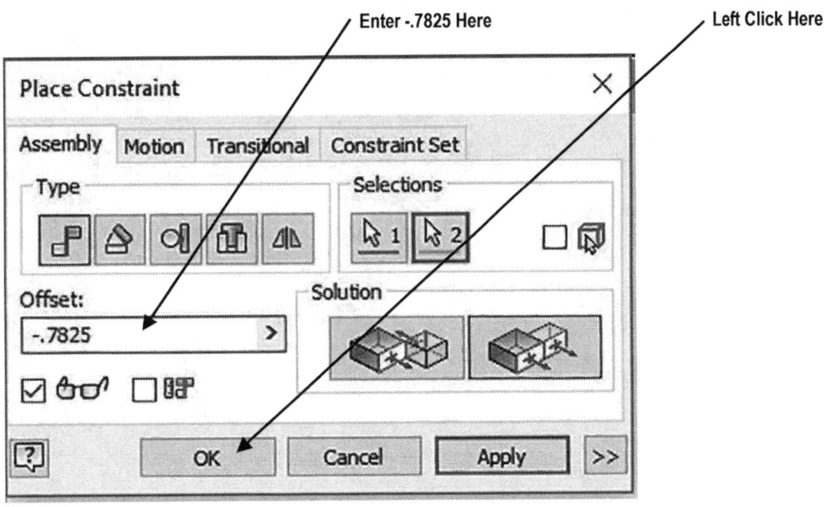

Figure 42

50. Your screen should look similar to Figure 45.

Figure 43

51. Move the cursor to the upper middle portion of the screen and left click on **Constrain**. The Place Constraint dialog box will appear as shown in Figure 46.

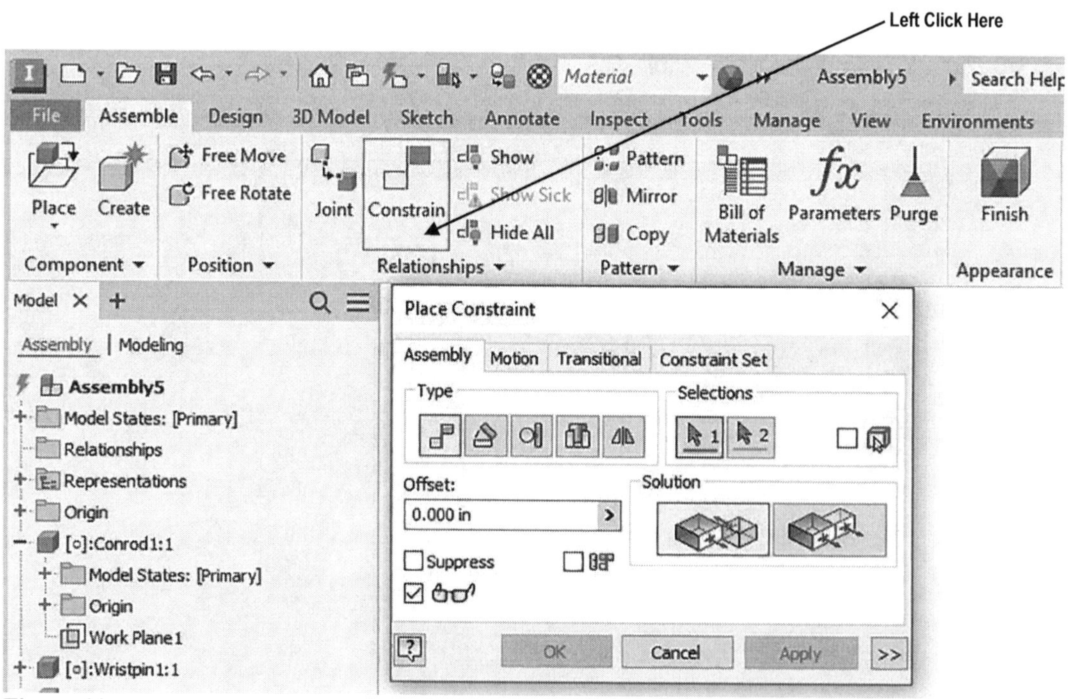

Figure 44

52. Move the cursor to the crankshaft pin causing a center line to appear. After a center line appears, left click once as shown in Figure 47. The crankshaft pin will be secured to the connecting rod.

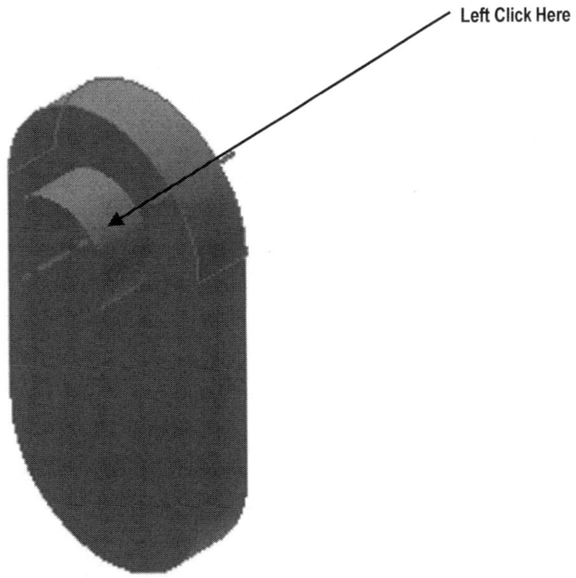

Figure 45

53. Move the cursor to the connecting rod end causing a center line to appear. The connecting rod will be secured to the crankshaft. After the center line appears, left click once as shown in Figure 48.

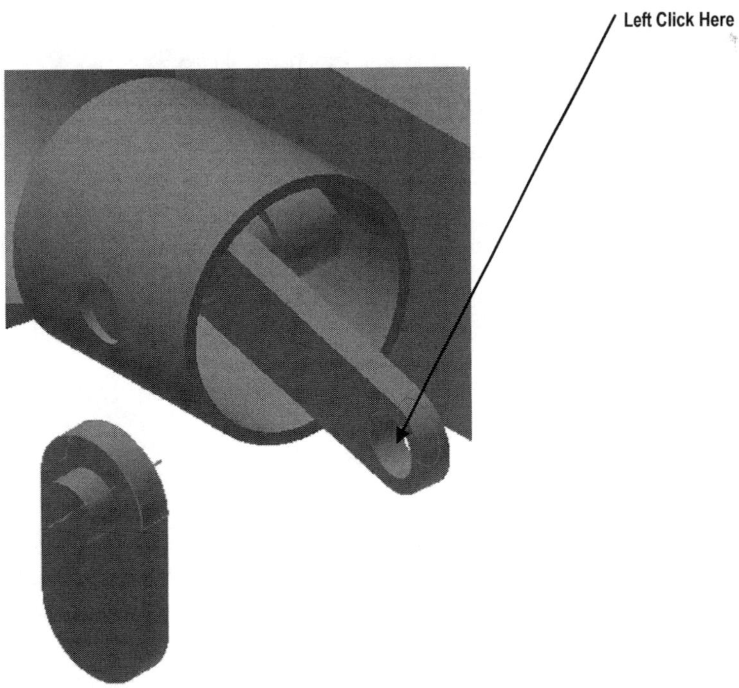

Figure 46

54. Inventor will place the connecting rod and crankshaft together as shown in Figure 49.

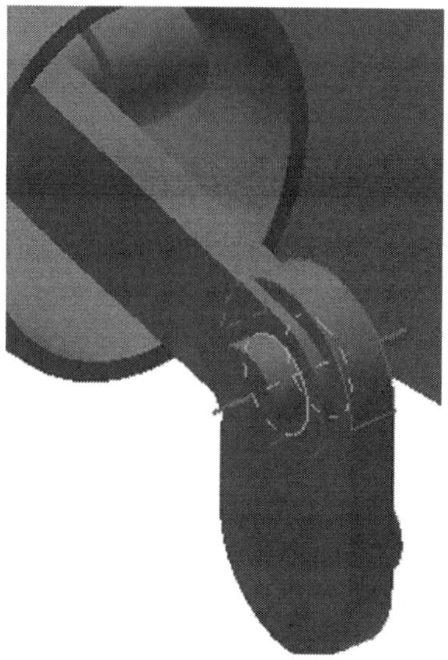

Figure 47

55. Left click on the Aligned icon. Left click on **OK** as shown in Figure 50.

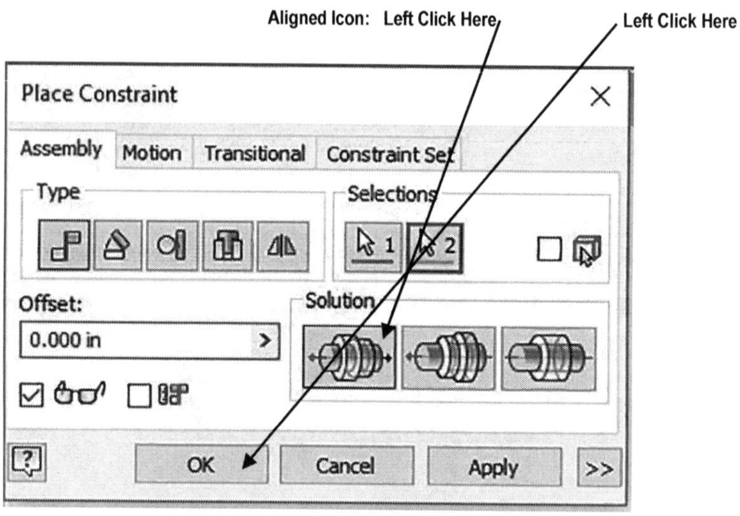

Figure 48

56. Move the cursor over the piston. Left click (holding the left mouse button down) and drag the piston upward toward the bottom of the bore as shown in Figure 51.

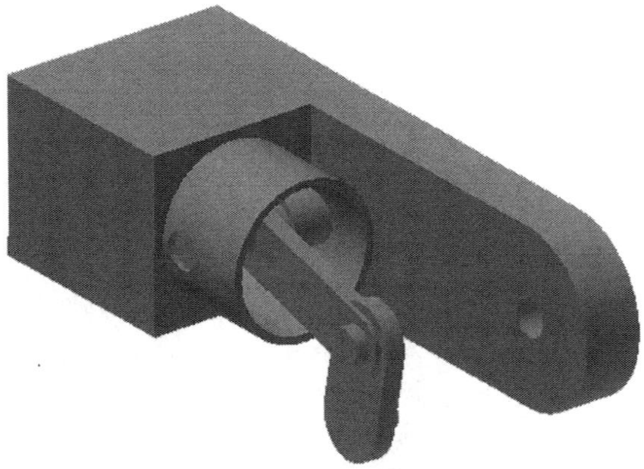

Figure 49

57. Use the Rotate command and roll the assembly around to gain access to the opposite side as shown in Figure 52.

Figure 50

58. Move the cursor to the upper middle portion of the screen and left click on **Constrain**. The Place Constraint dialog box will appear as shown in Figure 53.

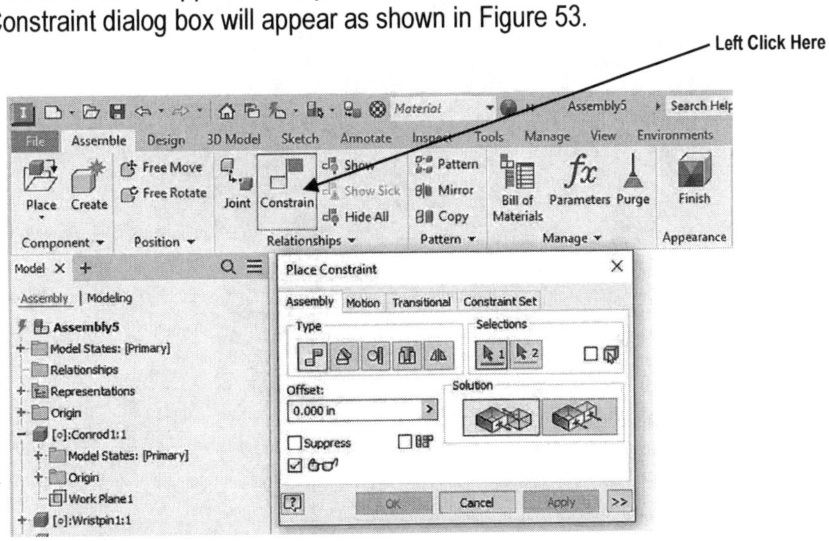

Figure 51

59. Move the cursor to the crankshaft pin causing a center line to appear. After the center line appears, left click once as shown in Figure 54.

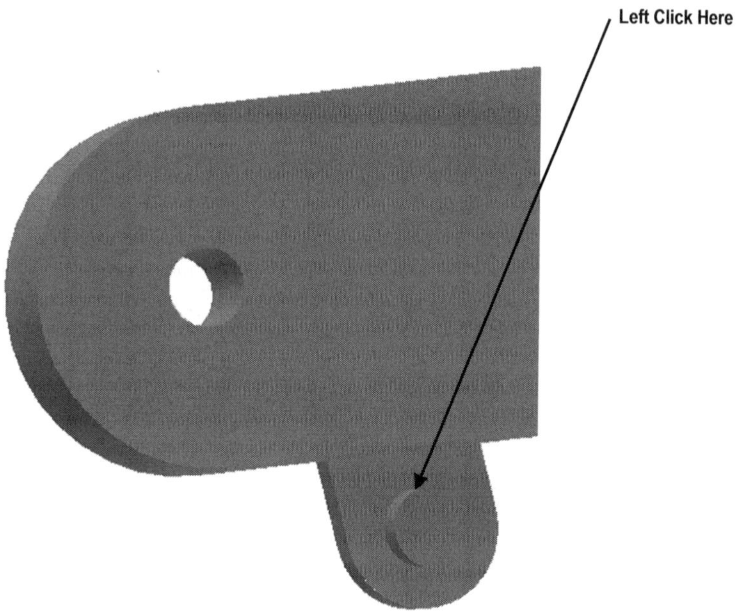

Figure 52

60. Move the cursor to the piston case hole causing a center line to appear. After the center line appears, left click once as shown in Figure 55.

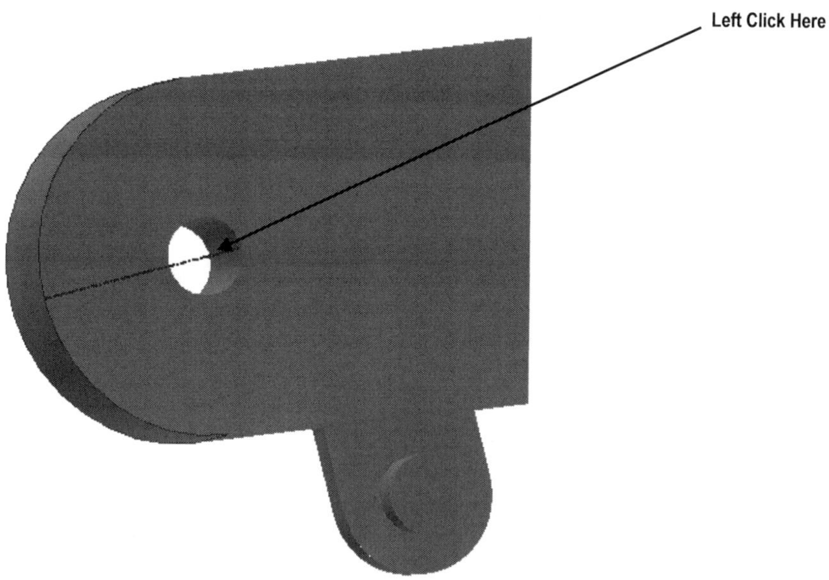

Figure 53

61. Inventor will place the crankshaft pin into the piston case as shown in Figure 56.

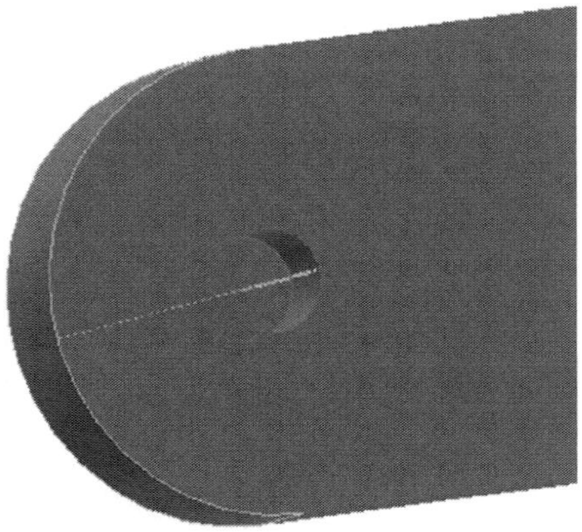

Figure 54

62. Left click on the Aligned Icon. Left click on **OK** as shown in Figure 57.

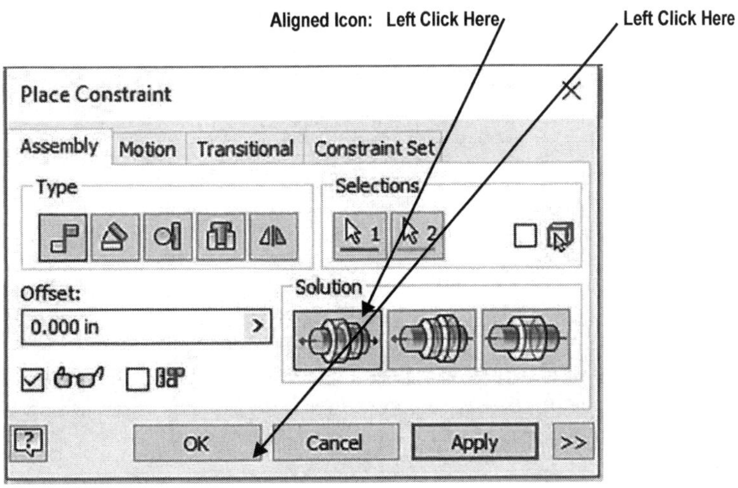

Figure 55

63. Your screen should look similar to Figure 58.

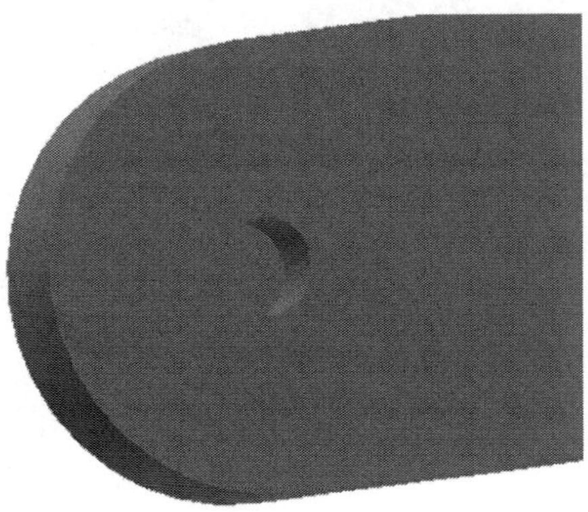

Figure 56

64. Right click anywhere around the drawing. A pop-up menu will appear. Left click on **Home View** as shown in Figure 59.

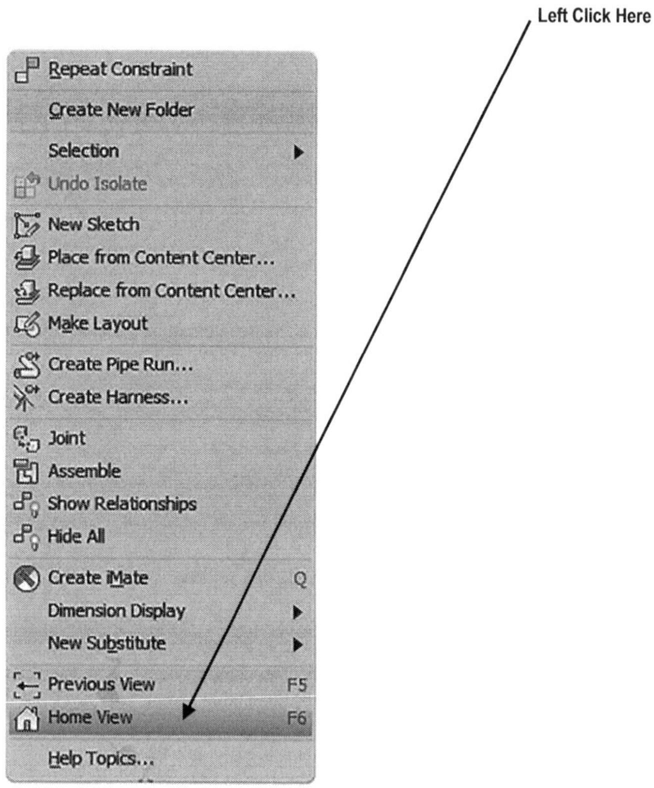

Figure 57

65. Your screen should look similar to Figure 60. If the crankshaft is not visible, it is embedded into the piston case. Simply left click on it (holding the left mouse button down) and move the crank out of the piston case.

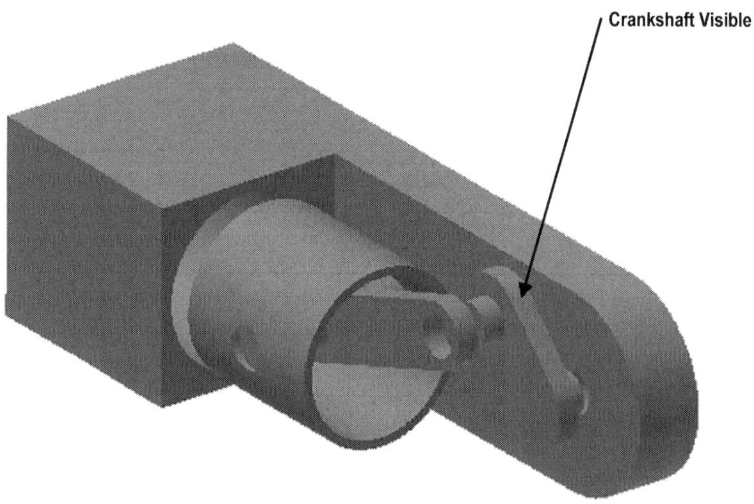

Figure 58

66. Move the cursor to the upper middle portion of the screen and left click on **Constrain**. The Place Constraint dialog box will appear as shown in Figure 61.

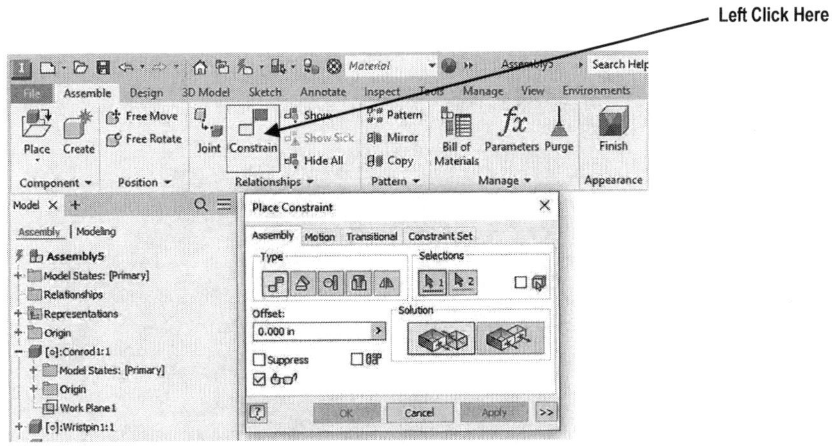

Figure 59

67. Left click on the "Flush" icon as shown in Figure 62.

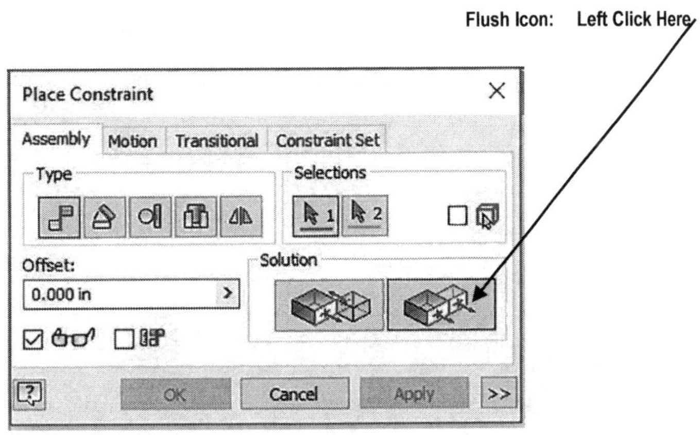

Figure 60

68. Move the cursor to the left side of the connecting rod causing an arrow to appear. After the arrow appears, left click once as shown in Figure 63.

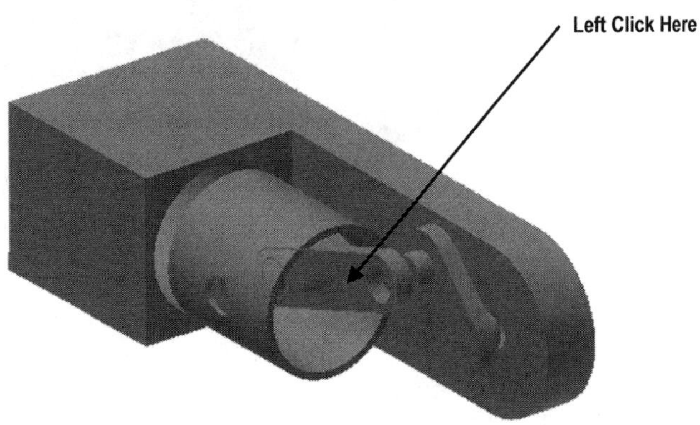

Figure 61

69. Move the cursor to the crankshaft connecting rod pin face causing an arrow to appear. Once the arrow appears, left click once as shown in Figure 64.

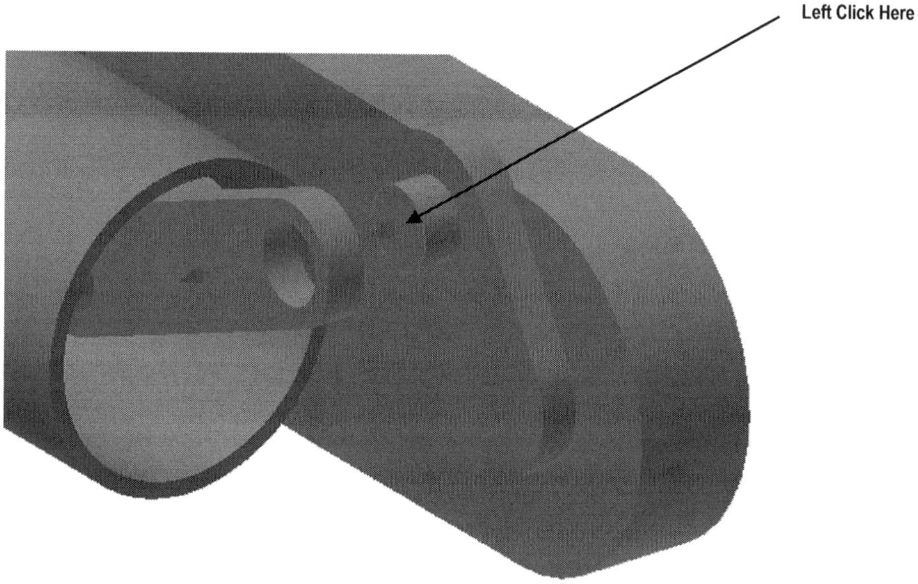

Figure 62

70. Inventor will place the connecting rod flush with the crankshaft connecting rod pin as shown in Figure 65.

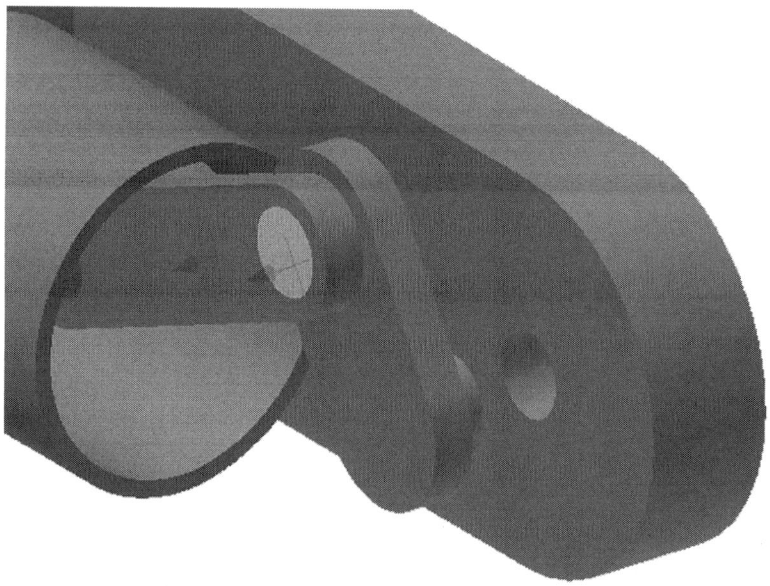

Figure 63

71. Left click on the Flush icon. Left click on **OK** as shown in Figure 66.

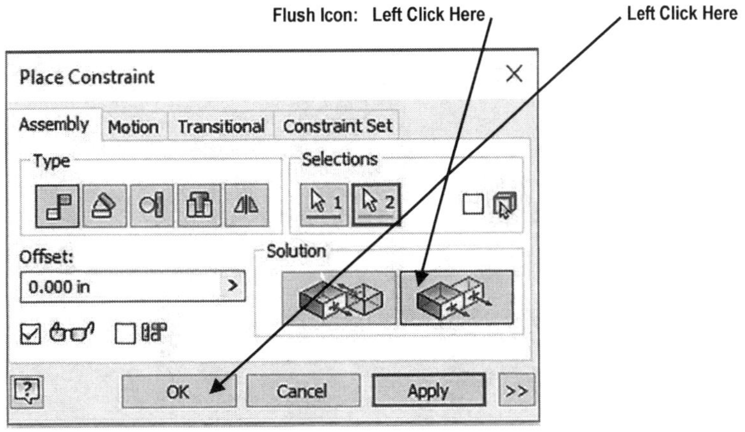

Figure 64

Learn to edit/modify parts while in the Assemble Panel

72. Your screen should look similar to Figure 67.

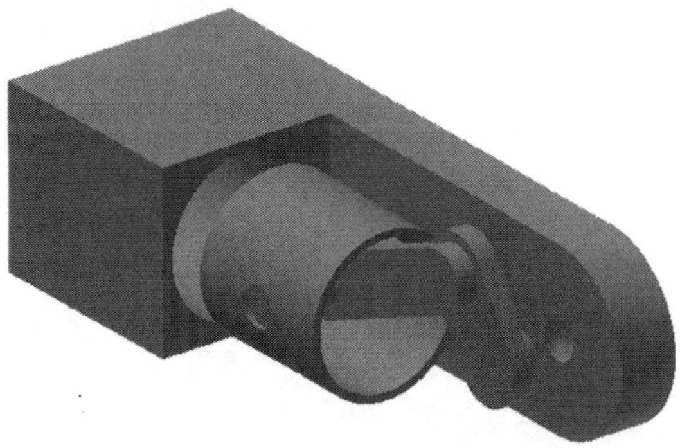

Figure 65

73. The length of the connecting rod is too short and must be modified. Move the cursor over the connecting rod causing the edges to become highlighted as shown in Figure 68.

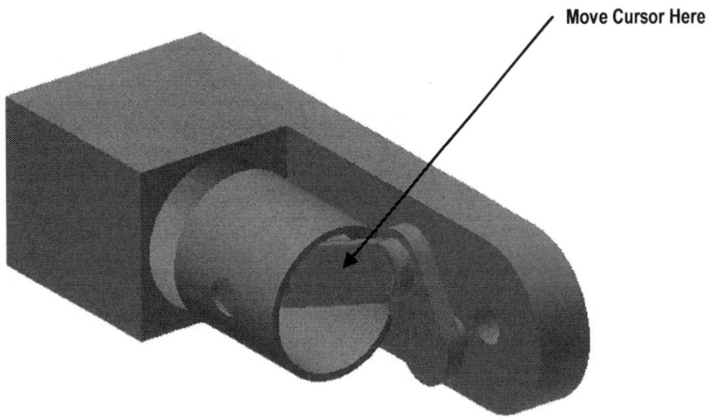

Figure 66

74. Double left click on the connecting rod. All other parts will become grayed as shown in Figure 69.

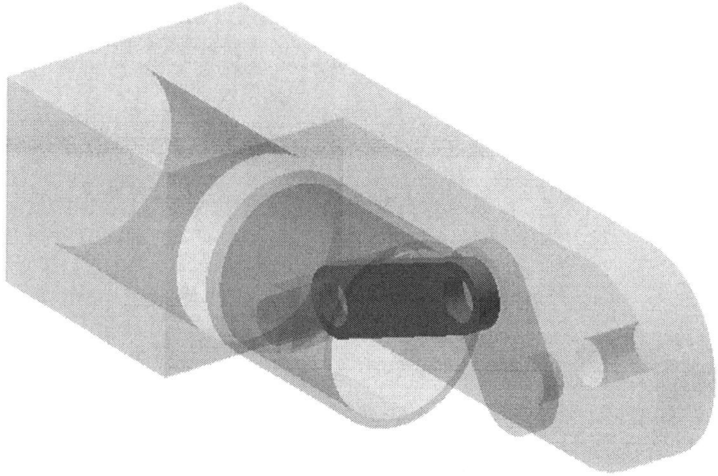

Figure 67

75. Notice the browser at the lower left of the screen has changed. All items related to all other parts are grayed (inactive). The items that illustrate the connecting rod are white (active) as shown in Figure 70.

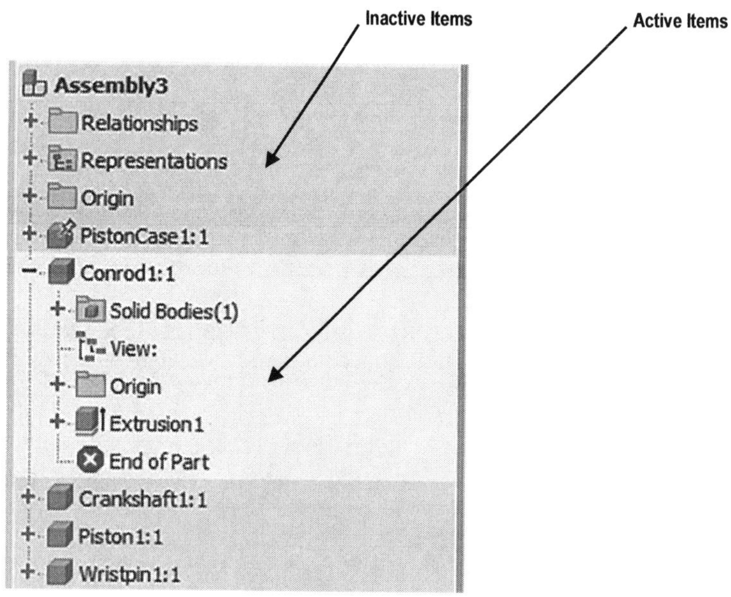

Figure 68

76. Left click on the "plus sign" next to the text "Extrusion1" as shown in Figure 71.

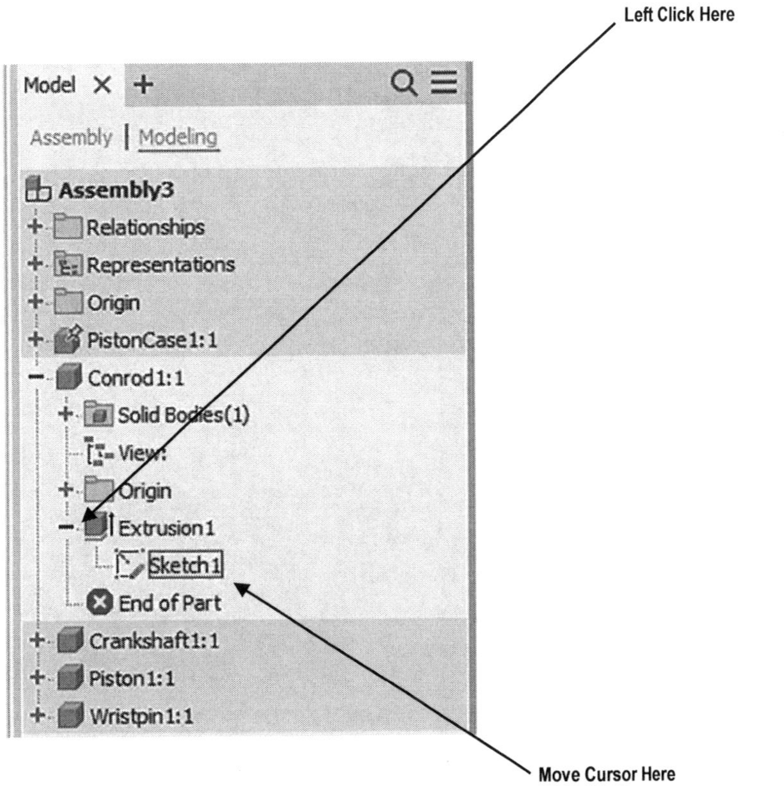

Figure 69

77. Move the cursor over the text "Sketch1" causing a box to appear around the text. Notice at the same time the sketch will become highlighted on the connecting rod as shown in Figure 72.

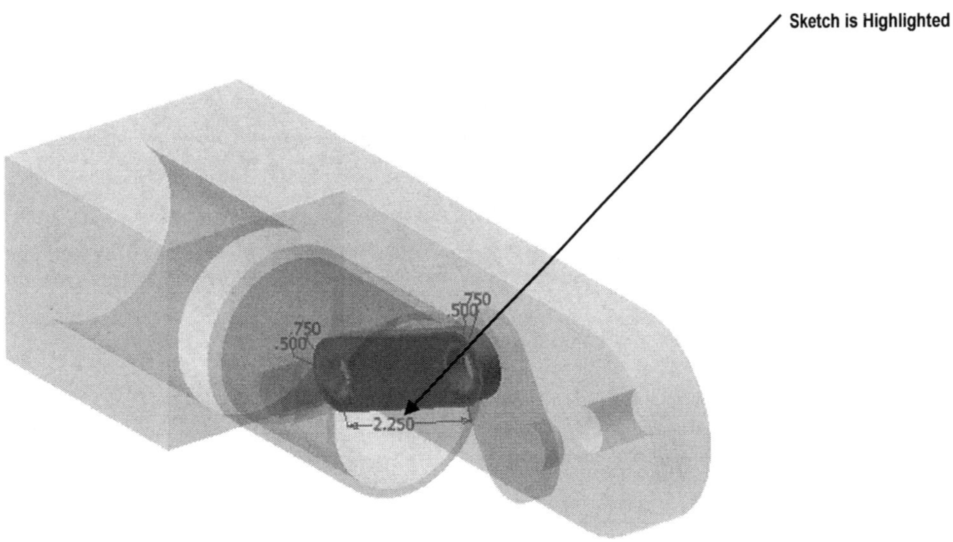

Figure 70

78. Right click on **Sketch1** while the box is visible around the text. A pop-up menu will appear. Left click on **Edit Sketch** as shown in Figure 73.

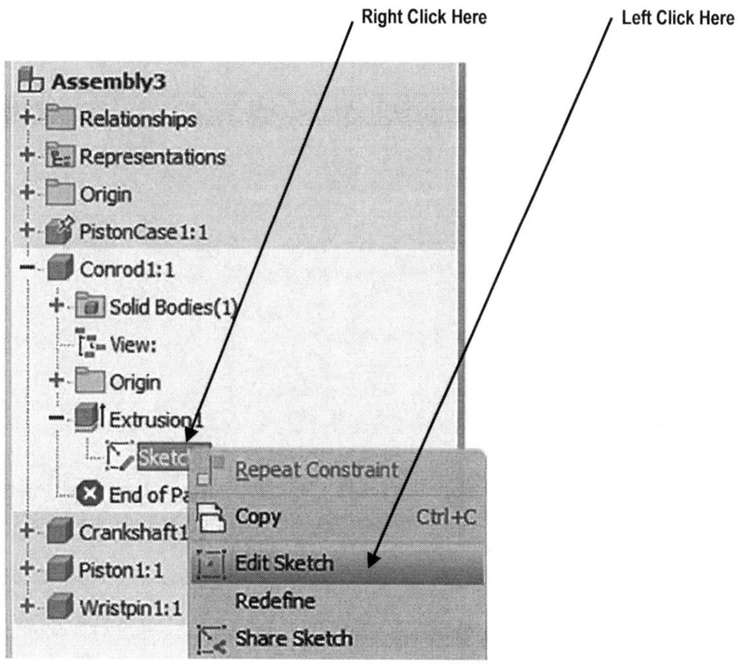

Figure 71

79. Your screen should look similar to Figure 74.

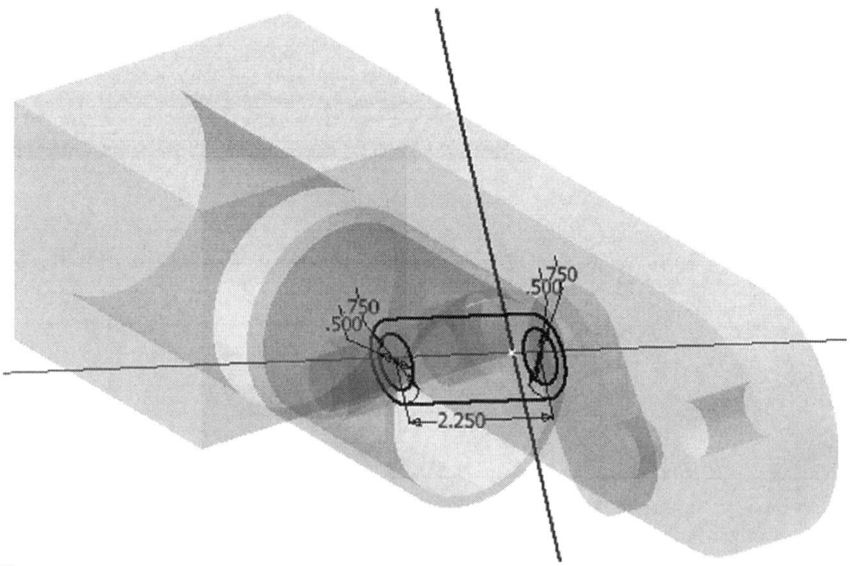

Figure 72

80. Move the cursor over the 2.250 dimension. After it becomes highlighted, double left click the mouse button. The Edit Dimension dialog box will appear as shown in Figure 75.

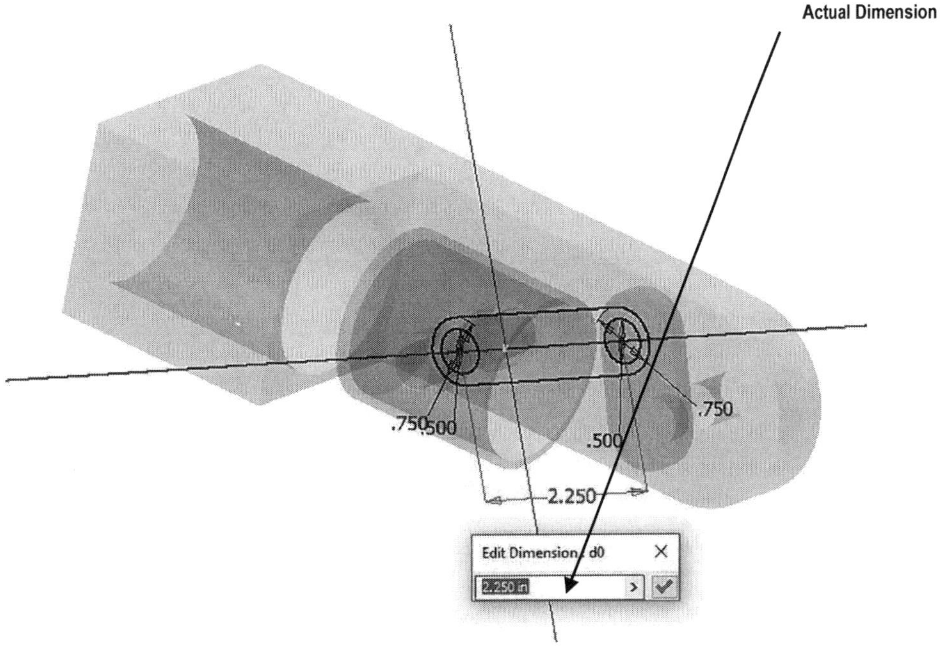

Figure 73

81. While the text is still highlighted, enter **4.75** and press **Enter** on the keyboard or left click the green check mark as shown in Figure 76.

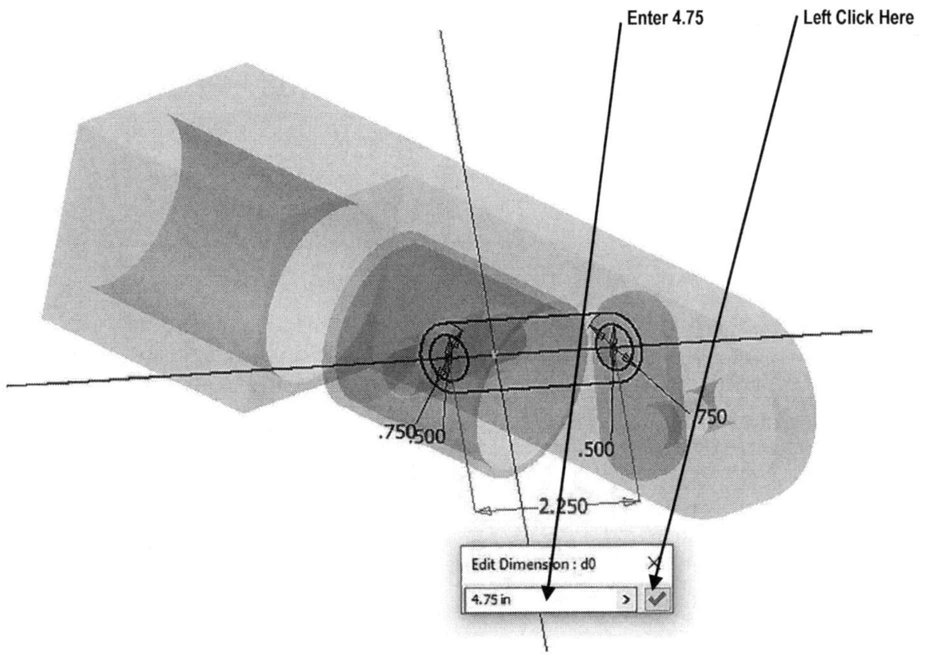

Figure 74

82. The length of the connecting rod will become 4.75 inches as shown in Figure 77.

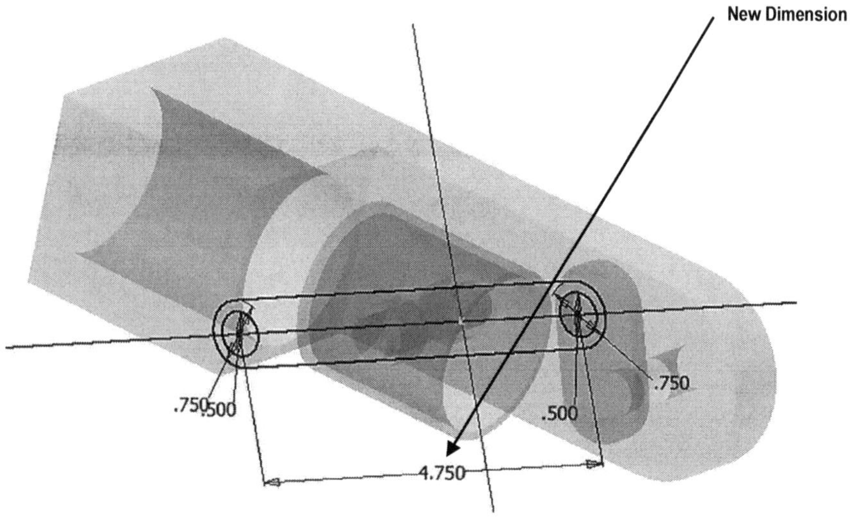

Figure 75

83. Move the cursor to the upper middle portion of the screen and left click on the **Manage** tab. Left click on the **Update** icon as shown in Figure 78.

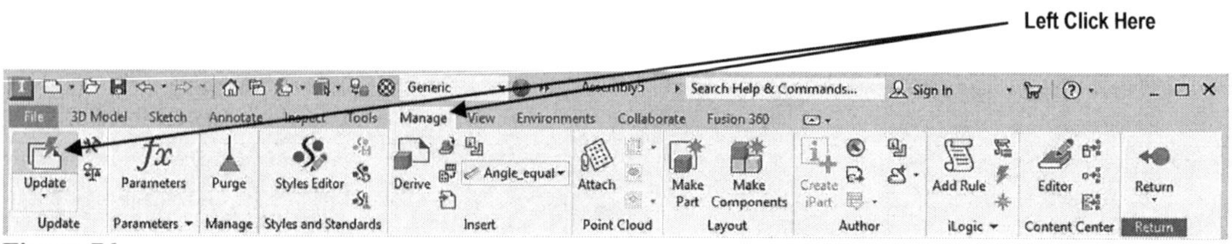

Figure 76

84. Inventor will update the change made to the sketch in the 3D Model Panel as shown in Figure 79.

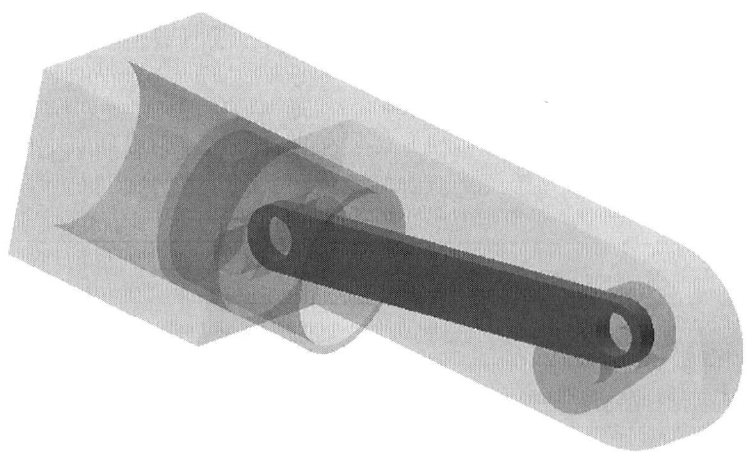

Figure 77

85. Move the cursor to the upper right portion of the screen and left click on **Return** as shown in Figure 80.

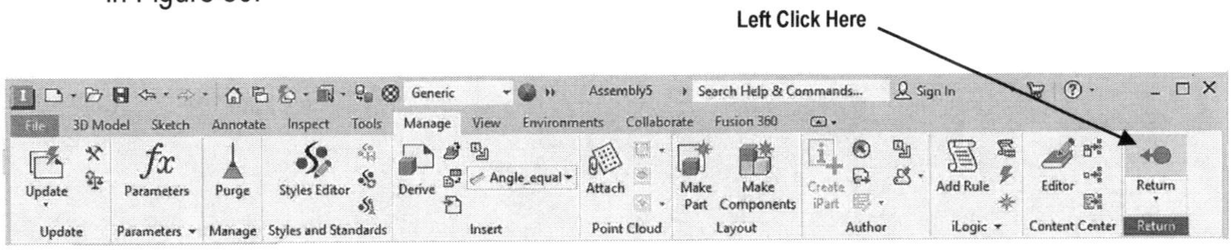

Figure 78

86. Inventor will return to the Assembly Panel displaying the changes made to the connecting rod. Your screen should look similar to Figure 81.

Figure 79

87. The length of the crankshaft pin must also be modified. Move the cursor over the crankshaft as shown in Figure 82. The edges will become highlighted.

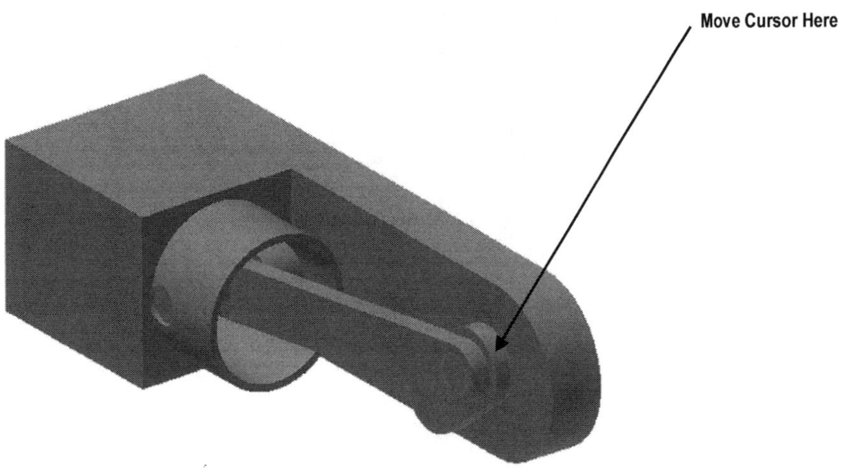

Figure 80

88. Double left click on the crankshaft. All other parts will become grayed as shown in Figure 83.

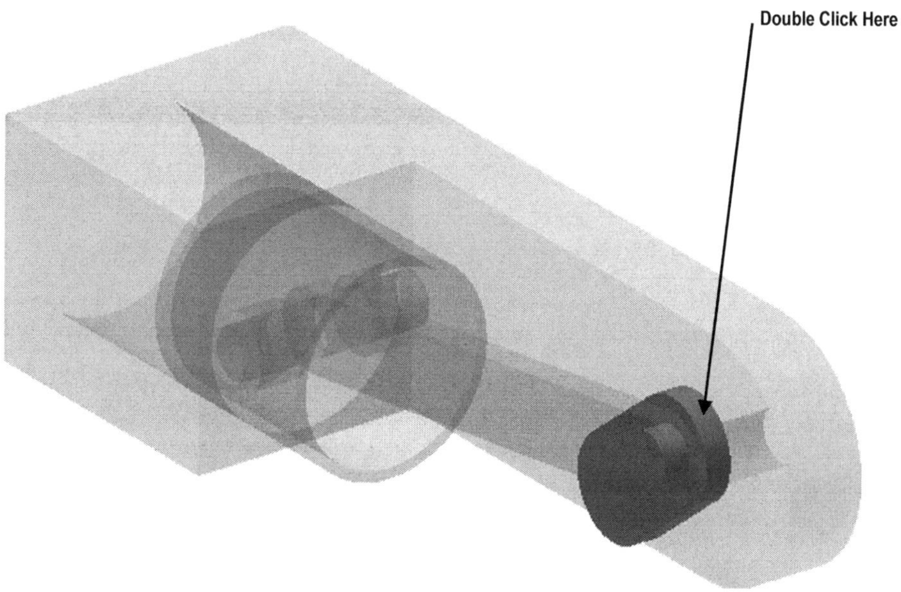

Figure 81

89. Notice the browser at the lower left of the screen has changed. All of the items related to all other parts are grayed (inactive). The items that illustrate the crankshaft are white (active) as shown in Figure 84.

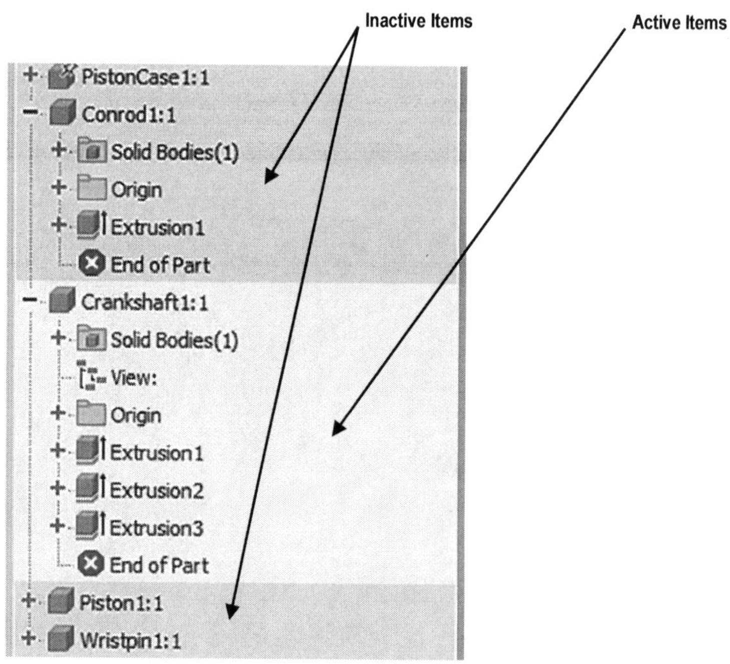

Figure 82

90. Right click on **Extrusion3** (or Extrusion2 depending on whichever Extruded pin protrudes through the piston case). A pop-up menu will appear. Left click on **Edit Feature** as shown in Figure 85.

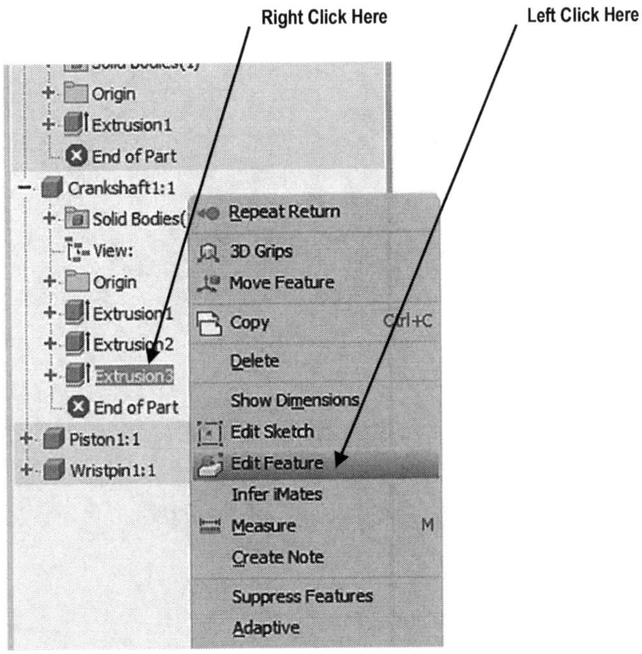

Figure 83

91. The Extrude dialog box will appear. Enter **2.00** for the extrusion distance and left click on **OK** as shown in Figure 86.

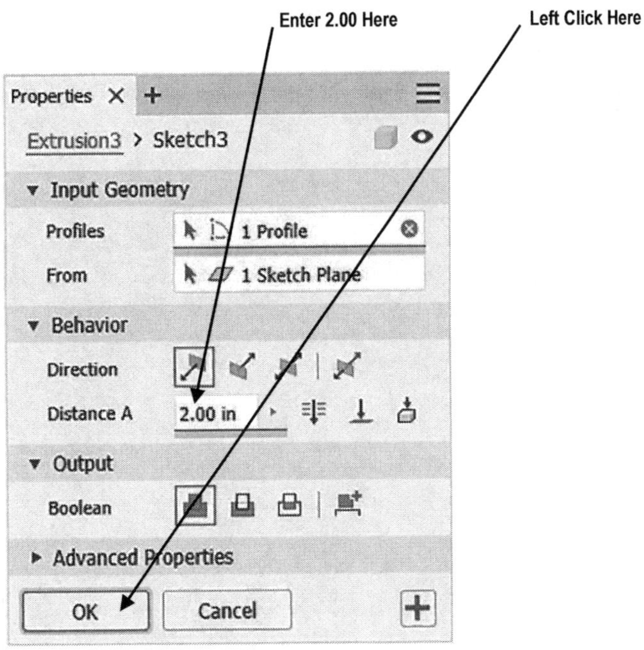

Figure 84

92. Inventor will update the change made to the sketch in the 3D Model Panel as shown in Figure 87.

Figure 85

93. Move the cursor to the upper left portion of the screen and left click on the **Manage** tab. Left click on **Update** as shown in Figure 88.

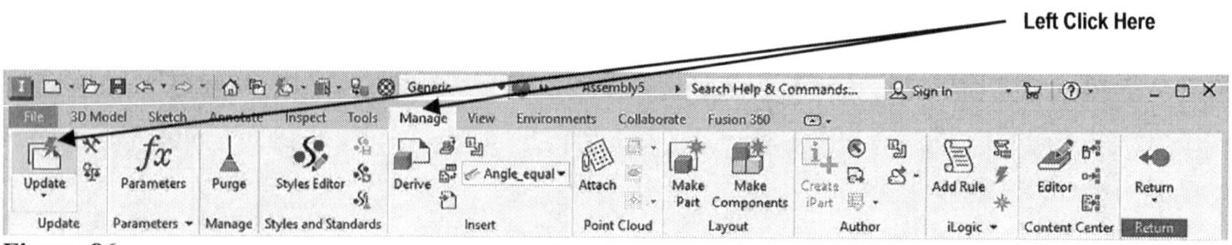

Figure 86

94. Move the cursor to the upper right portion of the screen and left click **Return** as shown in Figure 89.

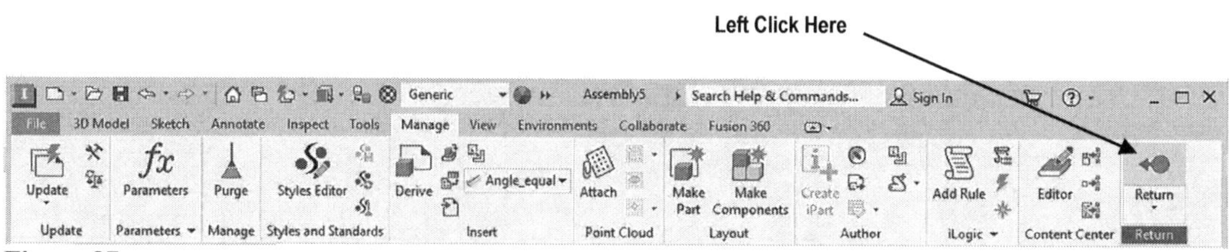

Figure 87

95. Inventor will return to the Assembly Panel displaying the changes made to the crankshaft. Your screen should look similar to Figure 90.

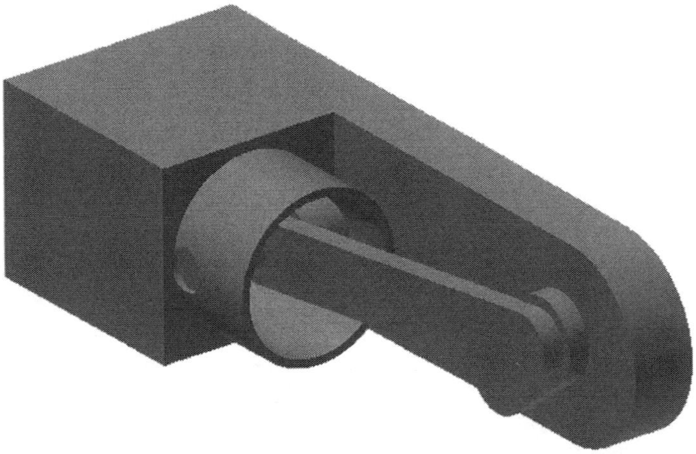

Figure 88

Learn to assign colors to different parts in the Assemble Panel

96. Left click on the side of the piston case. Then move the cursor to the upper middle portion of the screen and left click on the drop-down arrow to the right of Default as shown in Figure 91.

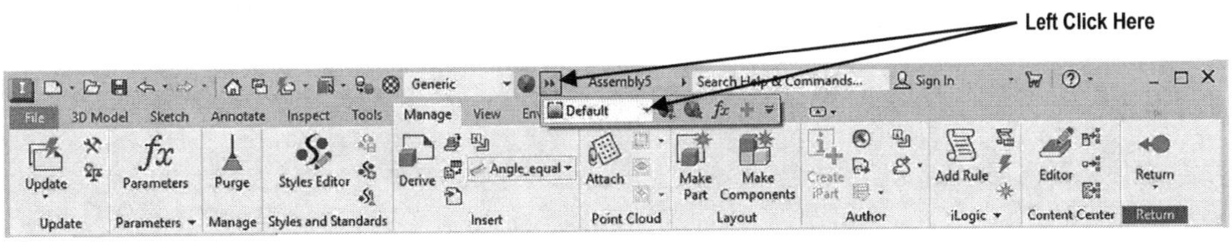

Figure 89

97. Place a check next to “Inventor Material Library” as shown in Figure 92 if needed.

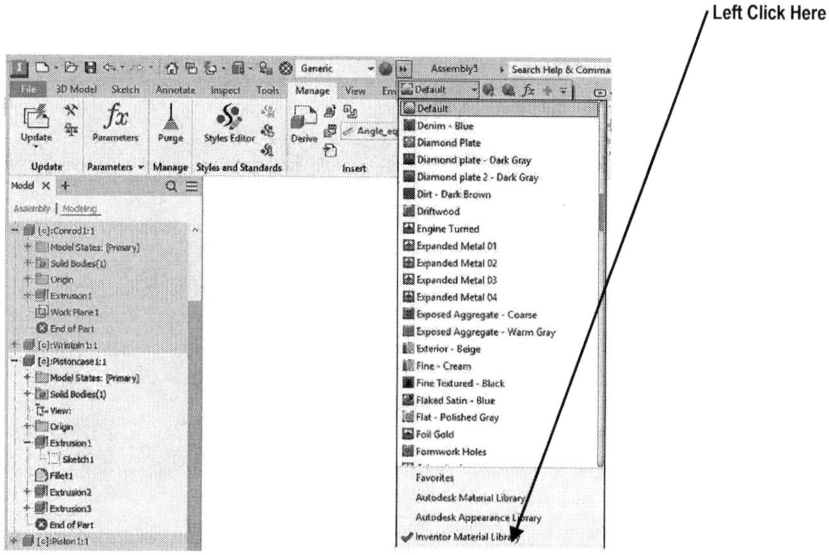

Figure 90

98. Scroll down to **Polycarbonate, Clear** and left click once as shown in Figure 93.

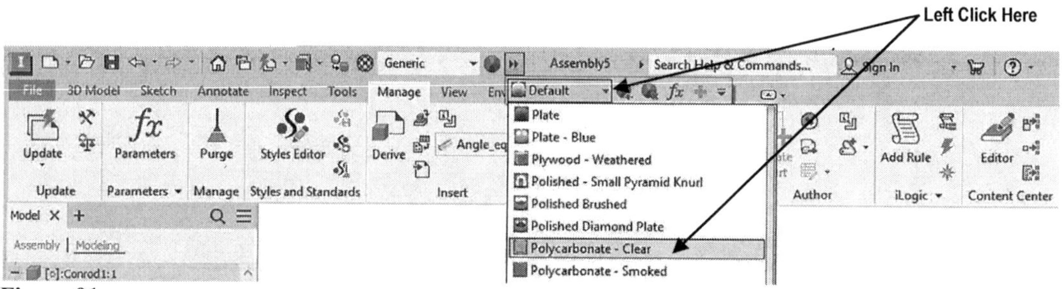

Figure 91

99. Inventor will change the color of the piston case to Polycarbonate, Clear as shown in Figure 94.

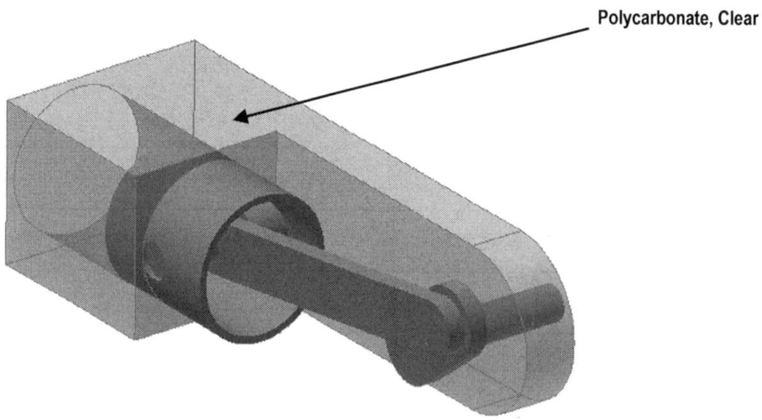

Figure 92

100. Move the cursor to any portion of the piston causing the edges to become highlighted and left click as shown in Figure 95.

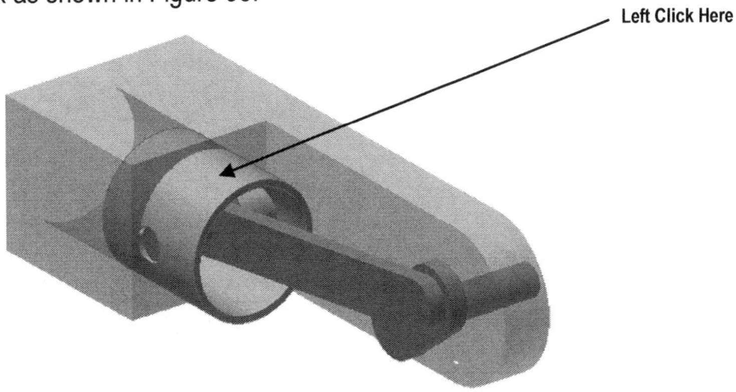

Figure 93

101. Move the cursor to the upper right portion of the screen and left click on the drop-down arrow next to Default. A drop-down menu will appear. Scroll down to **Stainless Brushed** and left click as shown in Figure 96.

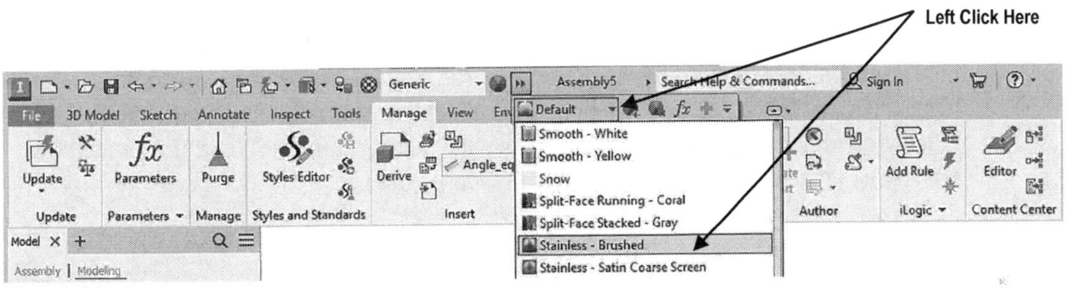

Figure 94

102. Inventor will change the color of the piston to Stainless Brushed as shown in Figure 97.

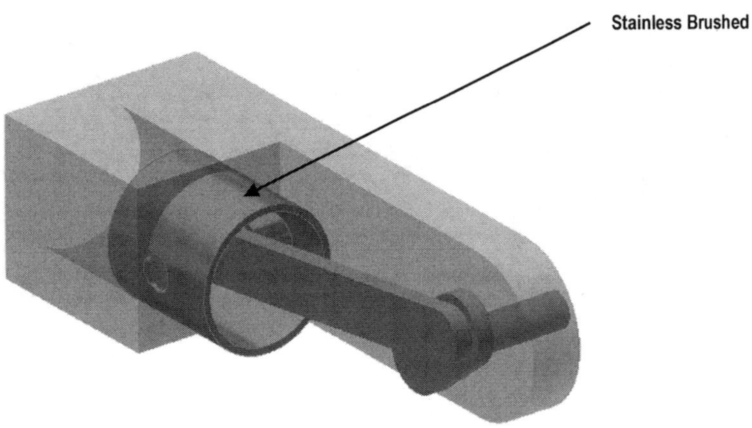

Figure 95

103. Using the same procedure, change the connecting rod color to **Clear Yellow** as shown in Figure 98.

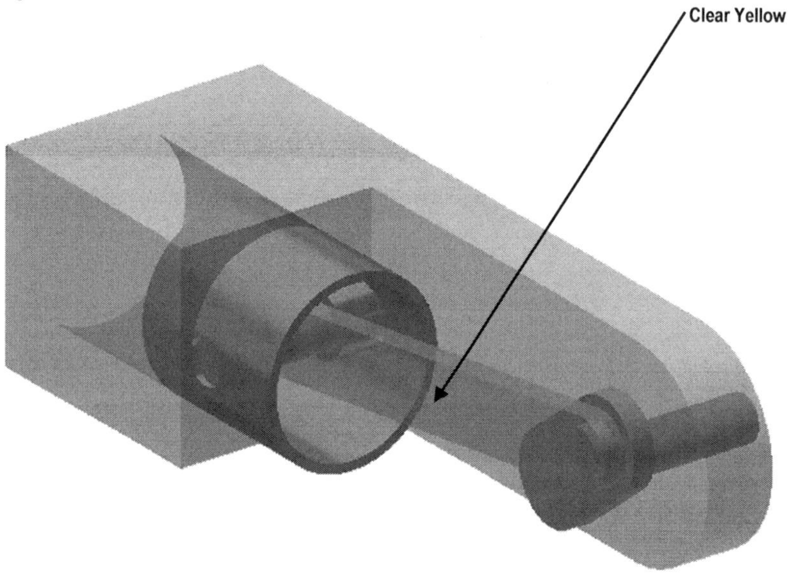

Figure 96

104. Move the cursor to the face of the connecting rod causing the edges to become highlighted. After the edges have become highlighted, left click (holding the left mouse button down) and drag the cursor in a circle causing the crankshaft to turn. Rotate the crankshaft upward to the position shown in Figure 99.

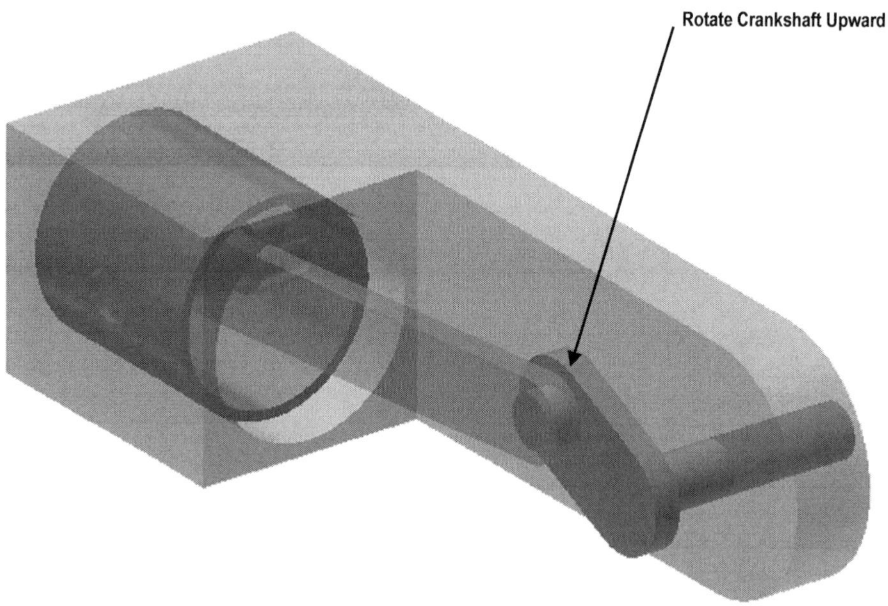

Figure 97

Learn to drive constraints to simulate motion

105. Move the cursor to the upper left portion of the screen and left click on the **Assemble** tab. Left click on **Constrain.** The Place Constraint dialog box will appear. Left click on the "Angle Constraint" icon and select the Directed Angle option as shown in Figure 100.

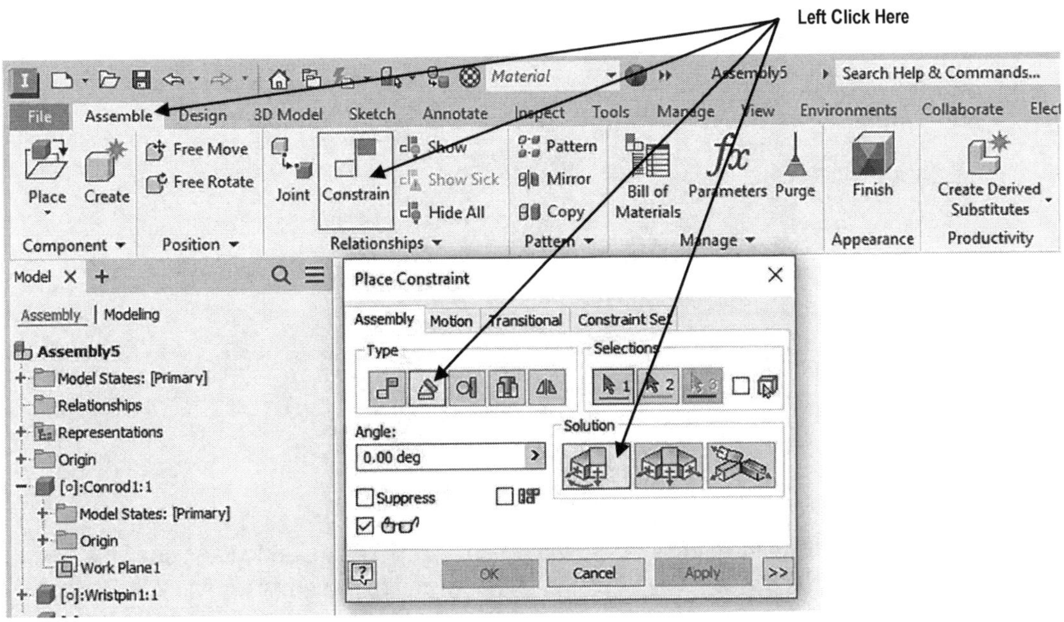

Figure 98

106. Move the cursor to the top portion of the crankshaft causing an arrow to appear. Left click as shown in Figure 101. You may have to zoom in to select the surface.

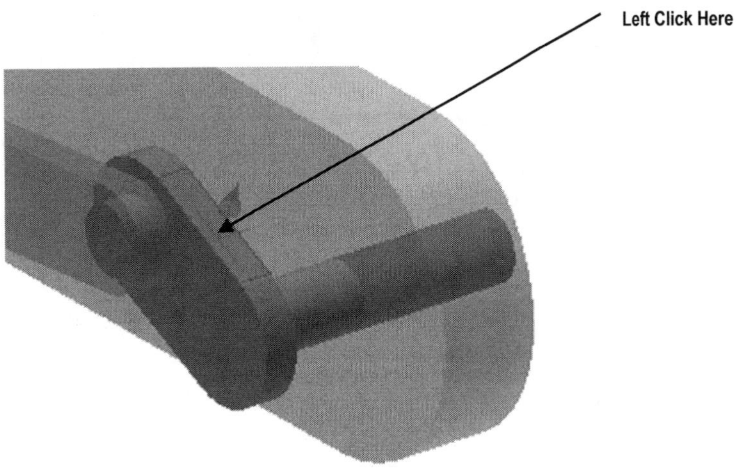

Figure 99

107. Move the cursor to the side of the piston case causing an arrow to appear. Left click once as shown in Figure 102.

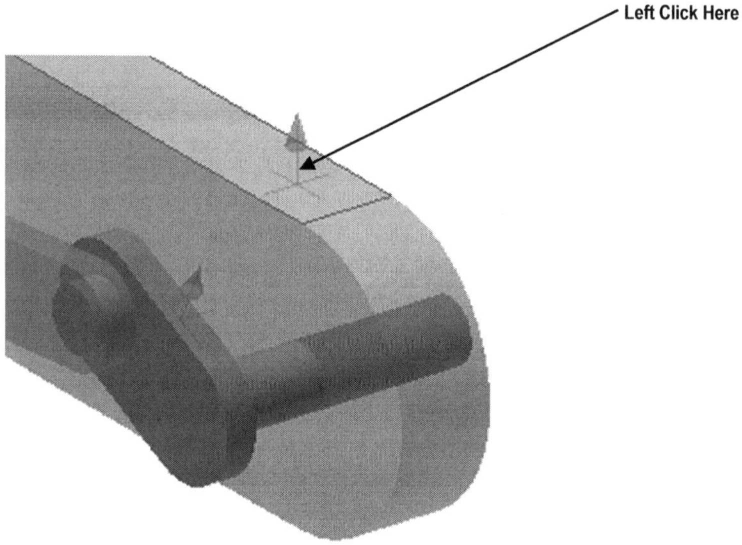

Figure 100

108. Inventor will rotate the crankshaft so that it is parallel (0 degrees) to the side of the piston case. If 20 or 30 degrees were entered in the Angle box, Inventor would rotate the crankshaft to a position 20 or 30 degrees from the side of the piston case. When 0 is entered into the Angle box, Inventor will rotate the crankshaft parallel to the piston case side as shown in Figure 103.

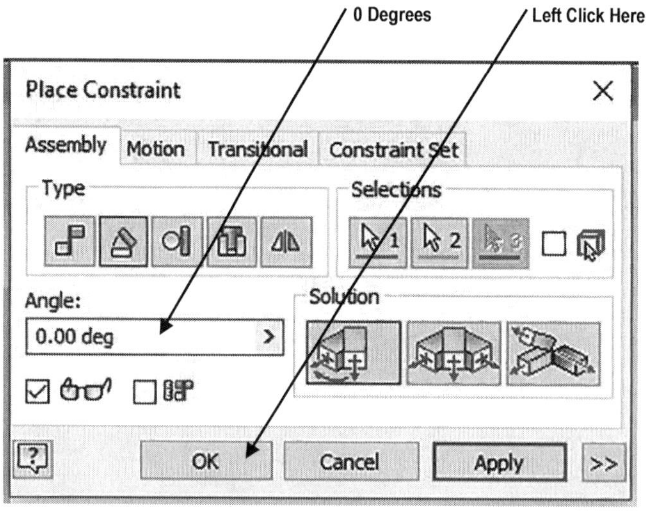

Figure 101

109. Left click on **OK** as shown in Figure 103.

110. Move the cursor to the lower left portion of the browser. Left click on the plus sign next to Crankshaft. Scroll down to **Angle:1** and right click once. A pop-up menu will appear. Left click on **Drive** as shown in Figure 104.

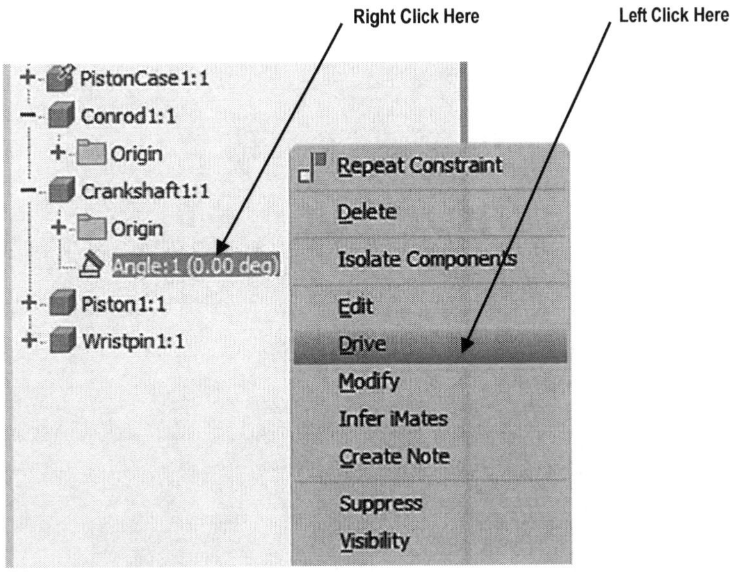

Figure 102

111. The Drive Constraint dialog box will appear. Enter **0** degrees under "Start." Enter **360000** degrees under "End." Left click on the double arrows at the far right lower corner of the dialog box as shown in Figure 105.

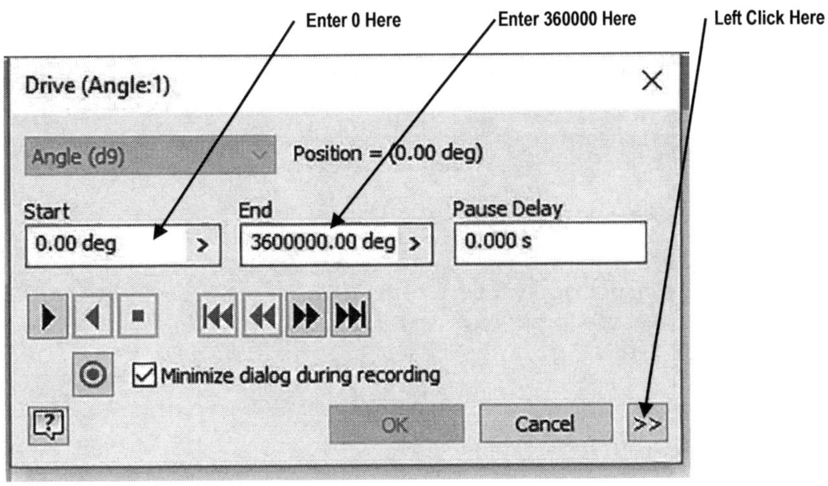

Figure 103

112. The Drive Constraint dialog box will expand, providing more options. Enter **10** for number of degrees and place a dot next to Start/End/Start as shown in Figure 106.

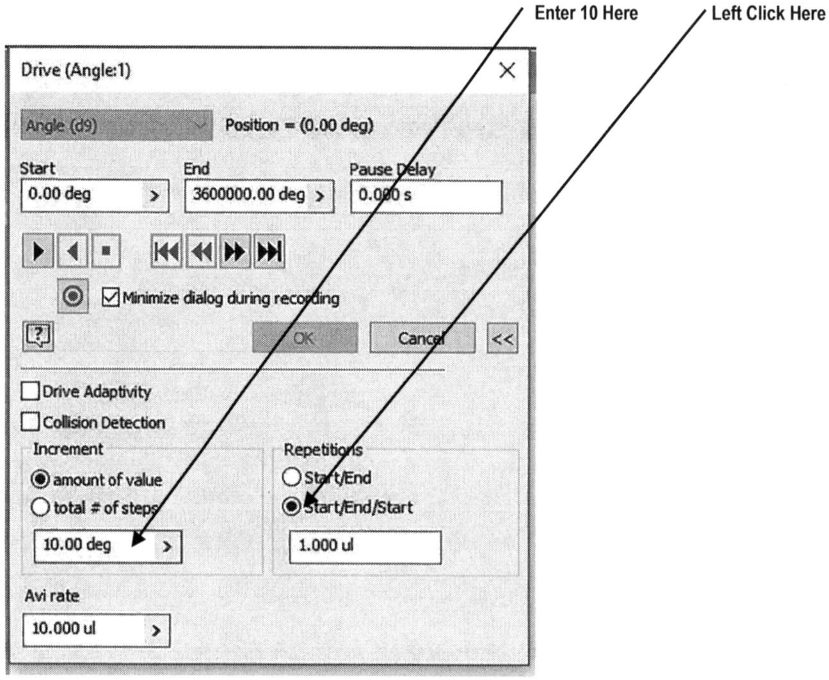

Figure 104

113. Use the Zoom option to zoom out. Use the Pan option to move the assembly off to the side. Left click on the "Play" icon as shown in Figure 107.

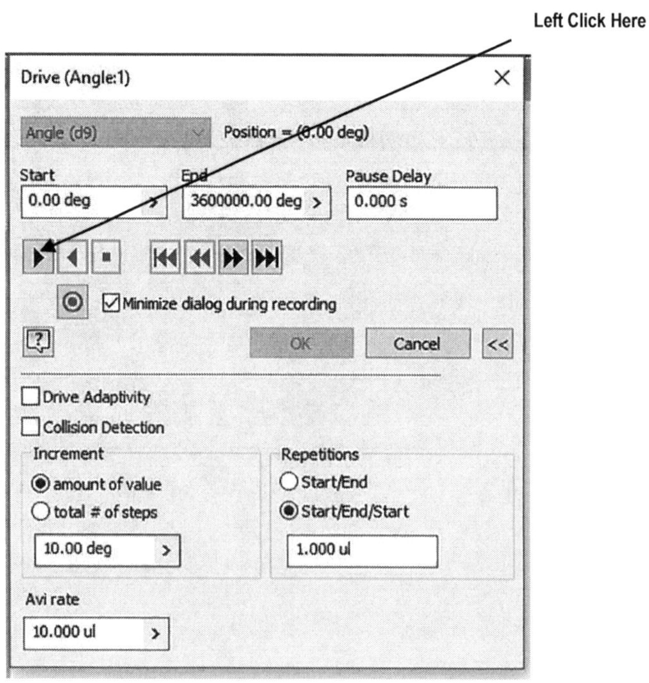

Figure 105

114. Inventor will animate the part causing the crankshaft to rotate.

115. Left click on the "Stop" icon. The animation will stop. Left click on the "Minimize" icon. The Drive Constraint dialog box will get smaller. Left click on the "Rewind" icon. This will rewind the animation back to 0 degrees as shown in Figure 108.

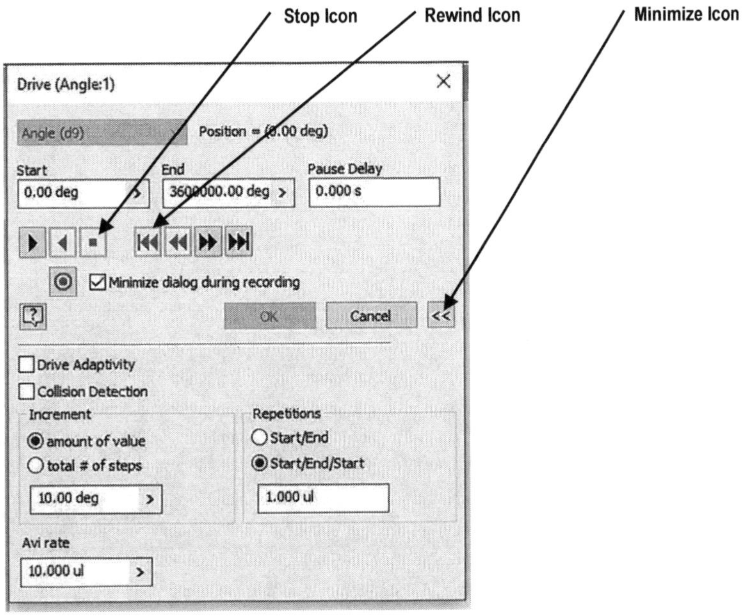

Figure 106

Learn to create an .avi or .wmv file while in the Assemble Panel

116. Left click on the "Record" icon as shown in Figure 109.

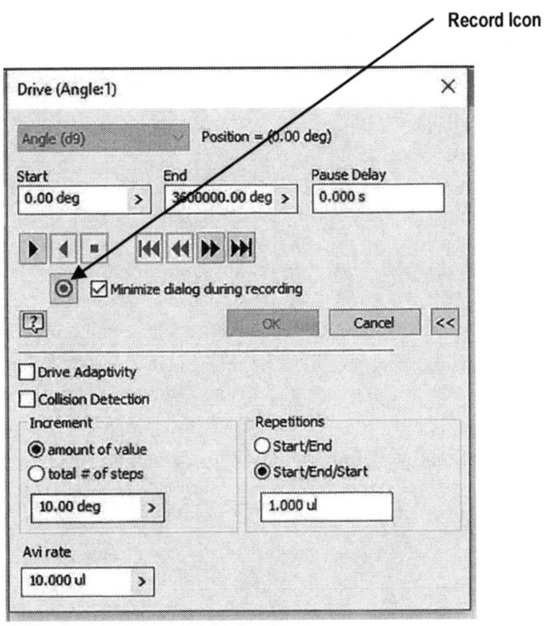

Figure 107

117. The Save As dialog box will appear as shown in Figure 110. Save the file where it can be easily retrieved later.

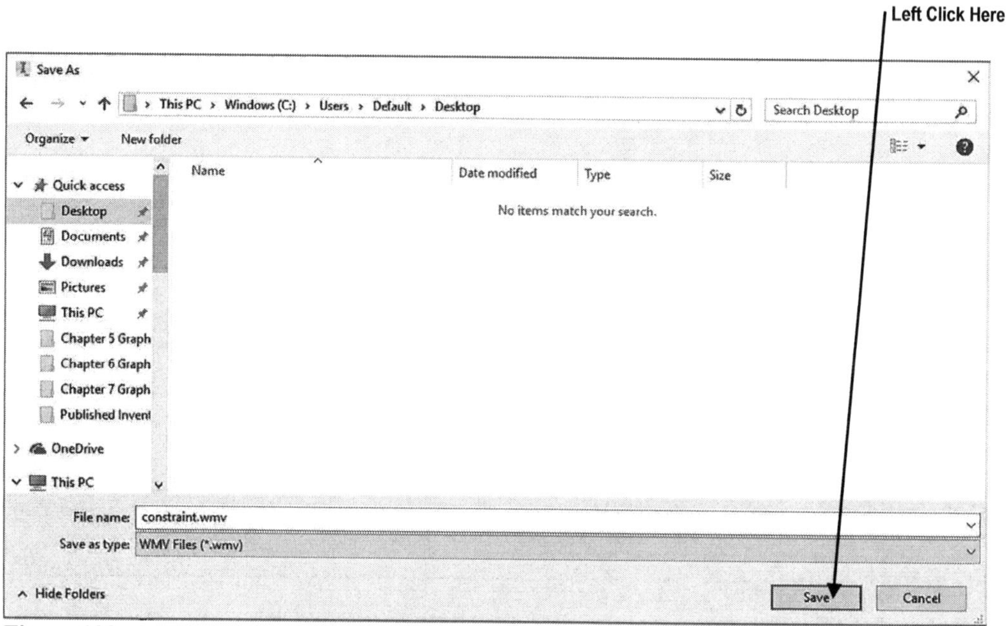

Figure 108

118. The WMV Export Properties dialog box will appear. Left click on **OK** as shown in Figure 111.

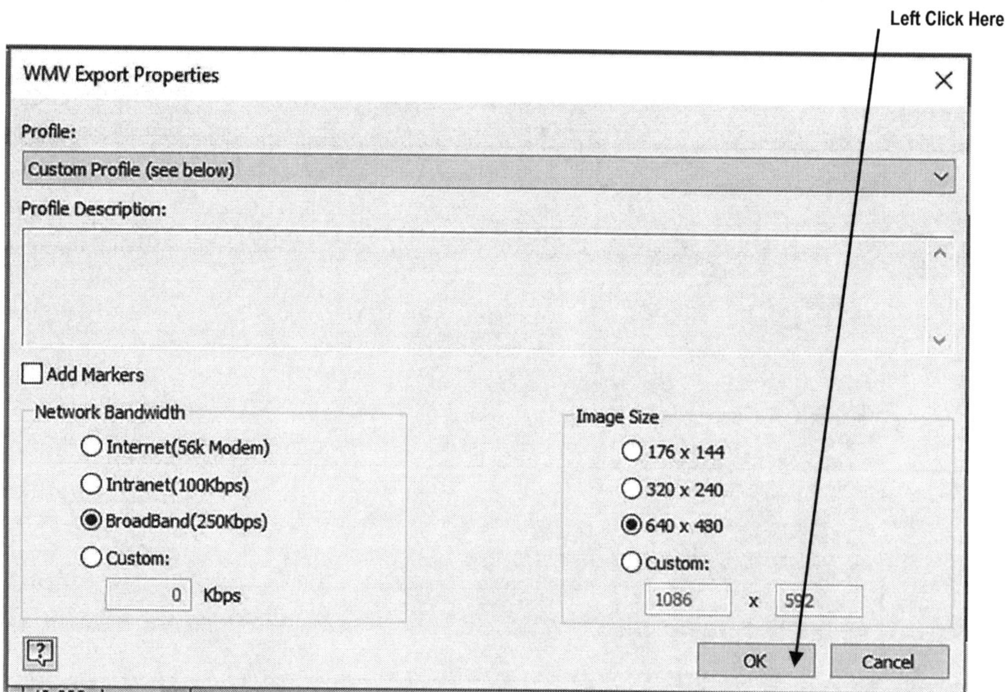

Figure 109

119. Left click on the "Play" icon as shown in Figure 112. Inventor will begin animating the piston assembly while recording a simulation (creating a .wmv file).

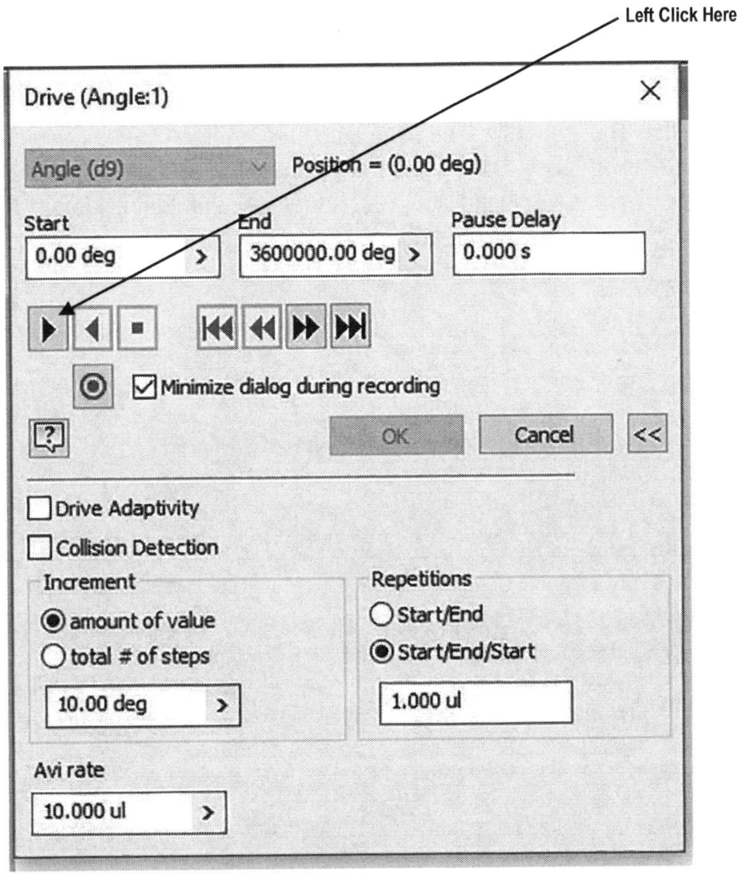

Figure 110

120. While Inventor is recording the simulation, the Drive Constraint dialog box will minimize in the lower left corner of the screen. If you are using dual screens, the Drive dialog box may be in the lower left corner of the opposite screen. The speed of the animation will decrease during the recording time. Allow Inventor to record for approximately 15-30 seconds. Inventor is in the process of creating a .wmv file that can be viewed in Windows Media Player. After about 30 seconds, left click on the Close symbol in the upper right corner of the dialog box as shown in Figure 113. The Drive Constraint dialog box will close and the recording will be complete.

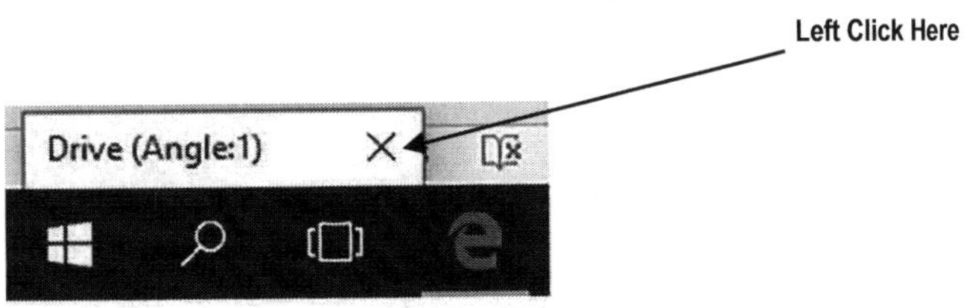

Figure 111

121. Go to the location where the file was saved and double click on it.

122. Windows Media Player or Real Player will play the file. The file may have to be opened in either Windows Media Player or Real Player.

123. Save the Inventor file (.iam) as Chapter 7 Assembly1.iam where it can be easily retrieved at a later time. These parts will be used again in Chapter 17. The Save dialog box will appear. The dialog box will ask if you want to save the assembly itself along with any changes that were made to individual parts that make up the assembly. Left click on **OK** to save the changes that were made as shown in Figure 114.

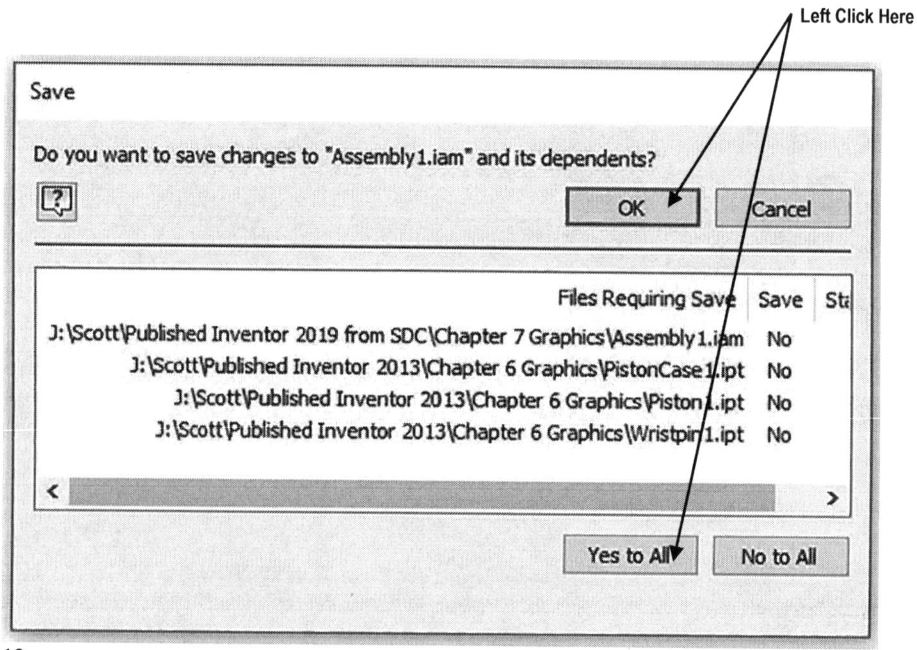

Figure 112

Chapter Problems

Using the dimensions from Chapter 6, modify the PistonCase1 housing to accept 2 pistons. The length of the shorter crankshaft pin will need to be increased by .25 inches to .50 inches in order to accommodate the additional connection rod as shown.

Start by opening the original Pistoncase1 part file and editing the housing. Save the part as Pistoncase2. Then open the original Crankshaft1 part file and increase the extrusion distance of the shorter crankshaft pin to 0.50 inches. Save the part as Crankshaft2.

Problem 7-1

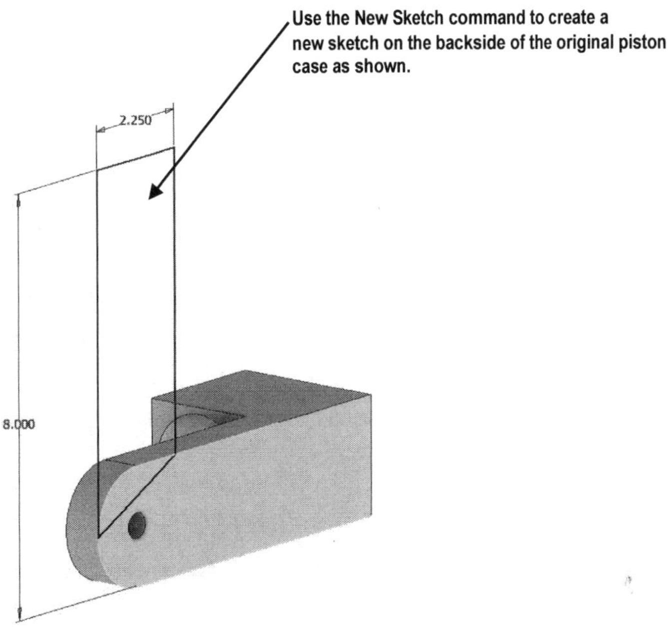

Problem 7-2

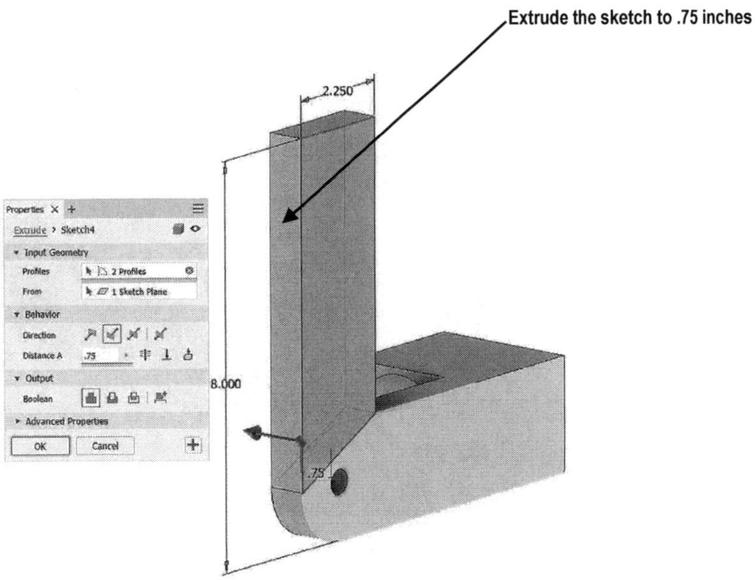

Problem 7-3 Use the Rectangle command in the Sketch Panel to create a new sketch 2.75 inches long and extrude it to 2.750 inches. Then complete the sketch shown below.

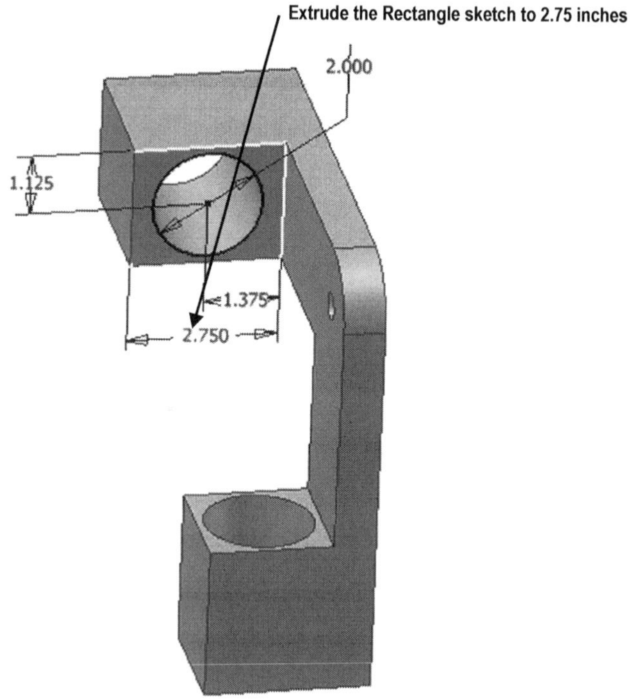

Problem 7-4 Increase the Extrusion distance on one crankshaft pin from .25 to 2.00 inches (if this was not already completed from Chapter 7). Increase the extrusion distance from .25 inches to .50 inches on the other pin as shown.

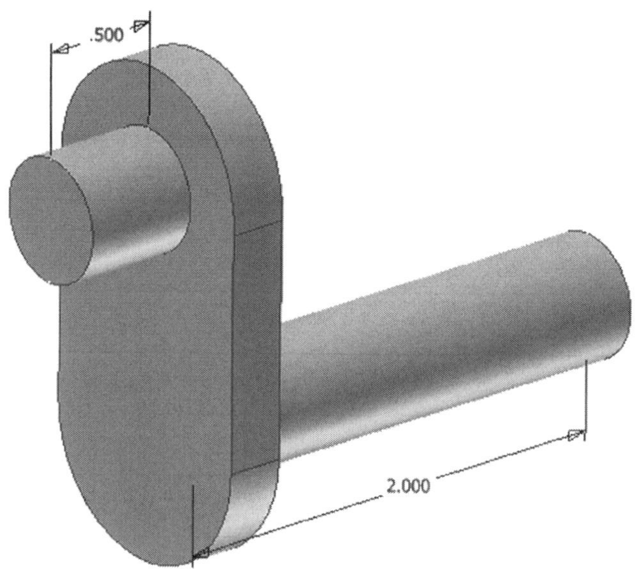

Problem 7-5 Using the Place command, import the parts shown below into the Assembly Panel. You will need 2 pistons, 2 connecting rods, 2 wrist pins, the modified piston case and the modified crank shaft.

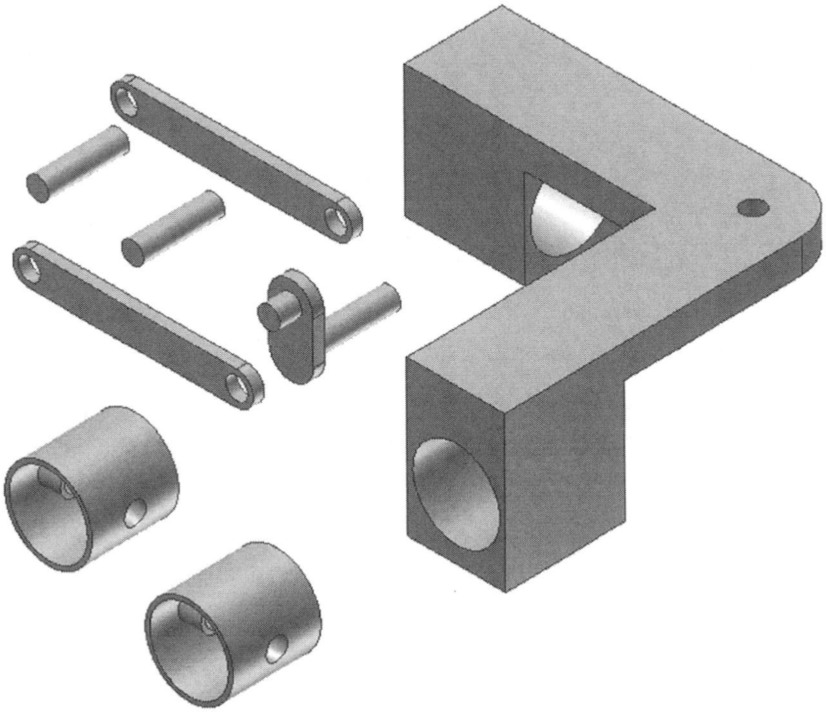

Problem 7-6 Using the dimensions from Chapter 6, assemble all the parts in the same manner into a new assembly. When finished, your screen should look similar to what is shown below.

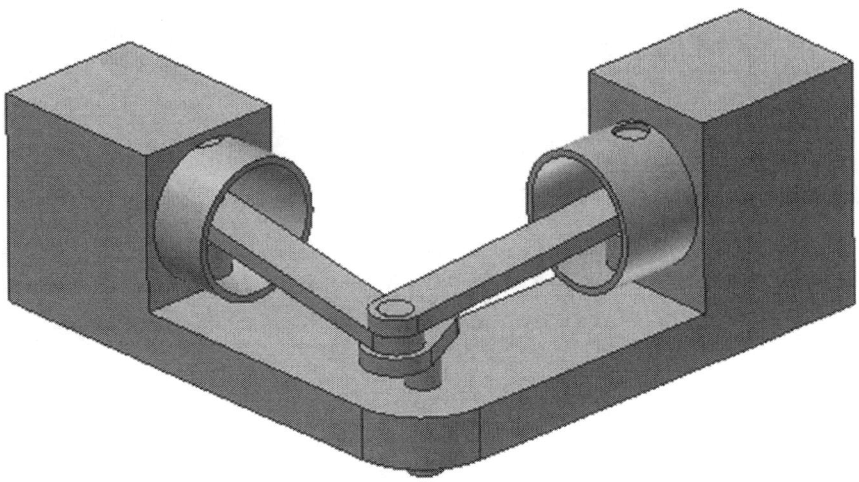

CHAPTER 8

Introduction to the Presentation Panel

Objectives:

1. Learn to import existing solid models into the Presentation Panel
2. Learn to Tweak Components in the Presentation Panel

Chapter 8 includes instruction on how to design the presentation shown.

1. Start Inventor 2027 by referring to "Chapter 1 Getting Started."

2. After Inventor is running, begin by creating the parts shown in Figure 1 (pin diameter is .500 inches).

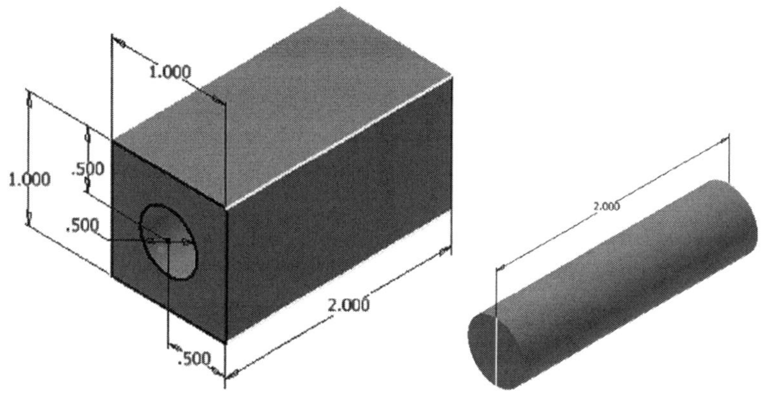

Figure 1

3. Save the block as block1.ipt. and save the pin as pin1.ipt where they can easily be retrieved at a later time. Close both files.

4. Move the cursor to the upper left portion of the screen and left click on **File**. A pop up menu will appear. Move the cursor over New (without left clicking). Another pop up menu will appear. Left click on **Assembly** as shown in Figure 2.

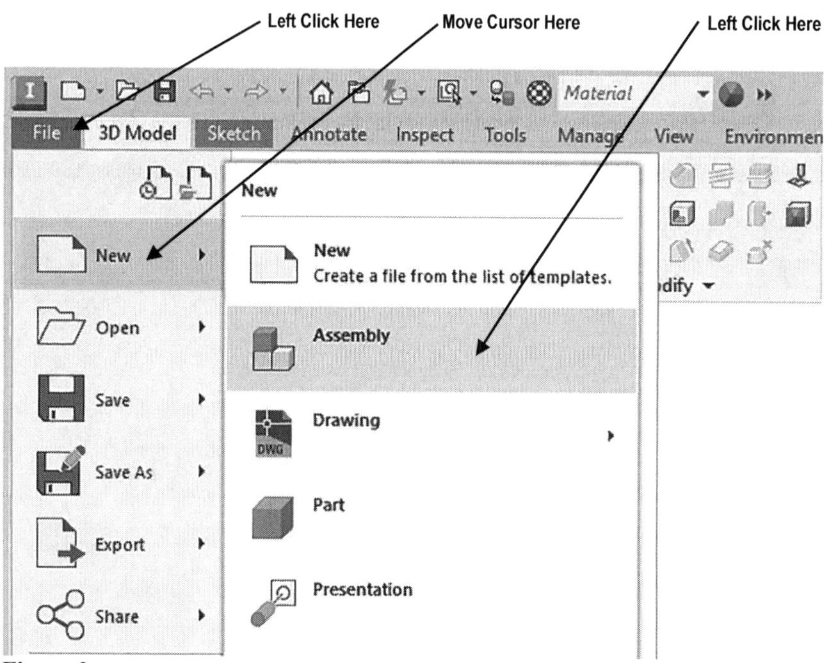

Figure 2

5. The Assemble Panel will open as shown in Figure 3.

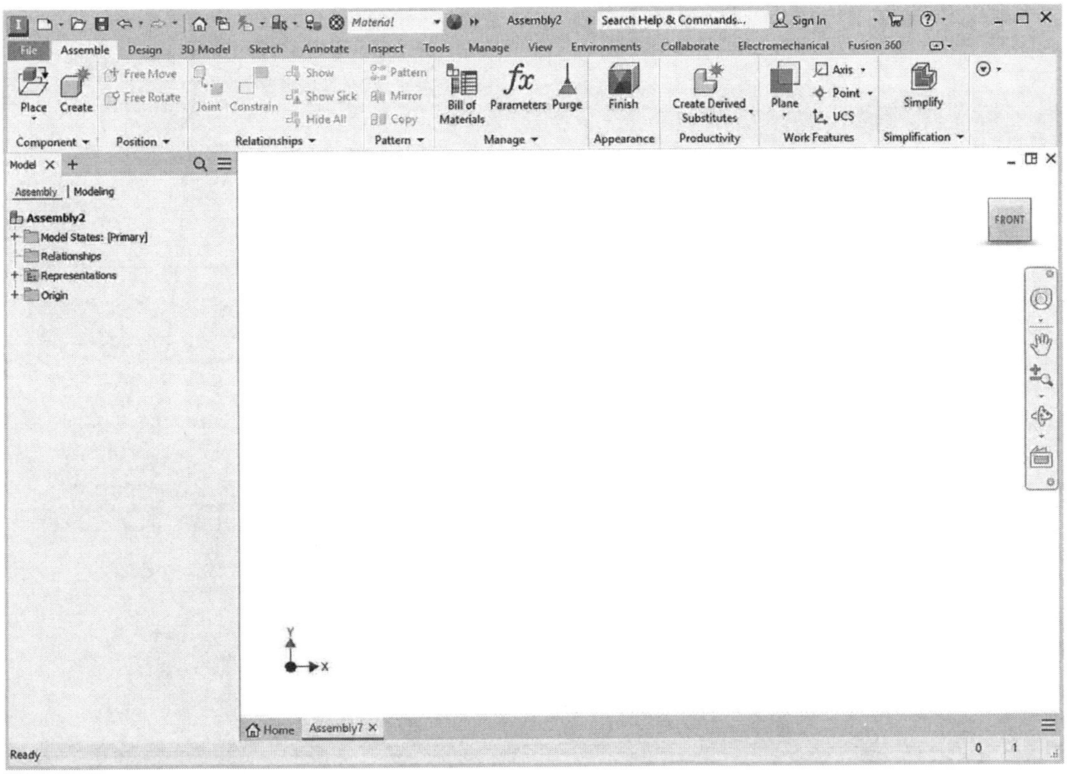

Figure 3

6. Your screen should look similar to Figure 3.

7. Move your cursor to the **Assemble** tab and left click as shown in Figure 4.

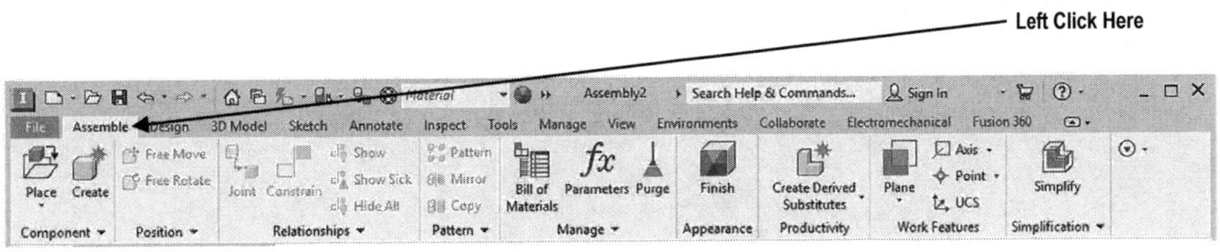

Figure 4

8. Move the cursor to the upper left portion of the screen and left click on **Place** as shown in Figure 5.

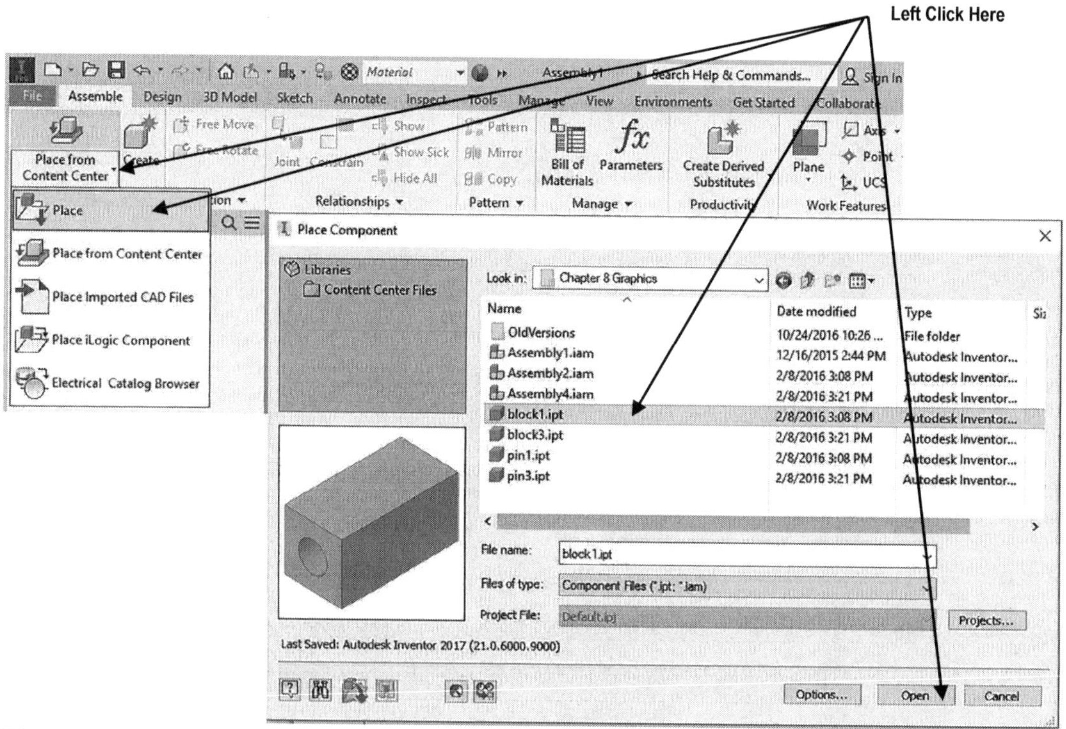

Figure 5

9. The Place Component dialog box will appear. Left click on **block1.ipt**. Left click on **Open** as shown in Figure 5.

10. The block will appear attached to the cursor. Left click once. Press **Esc** on the keyboard. Your screen should look similar to Figure 6.

Figure 6

11. Move the cursor to the upper left portion of the screen and left click on **Place** as shown in Figure 7.

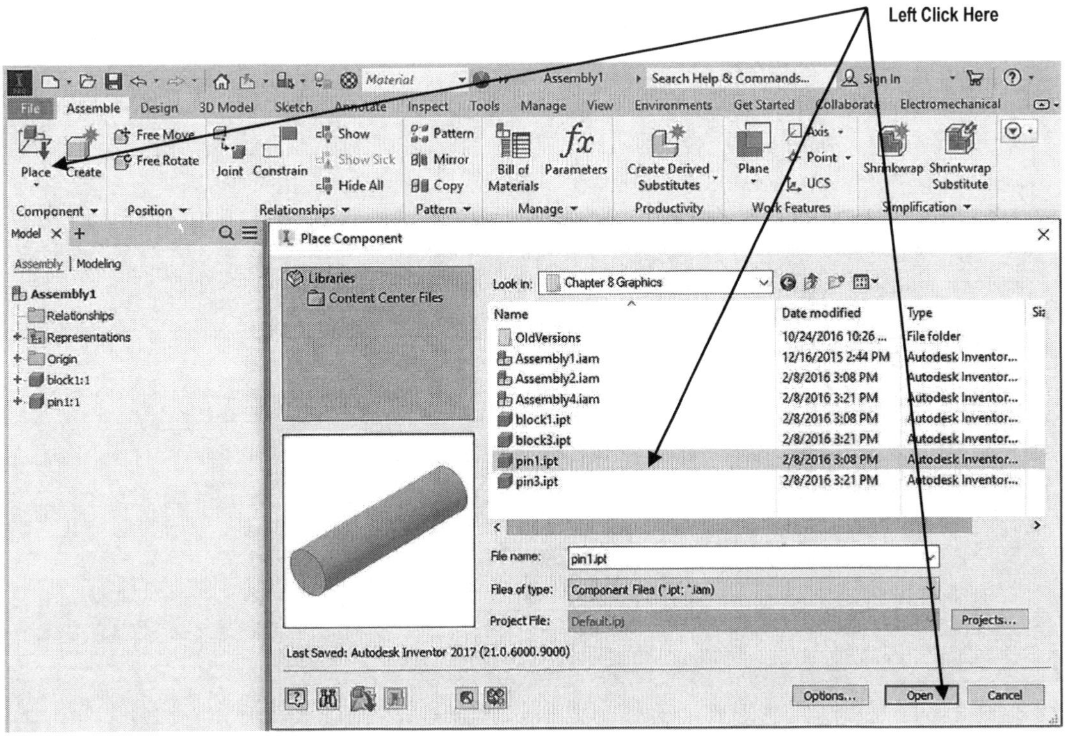

Figure 7

12. The Place Component dialog box will appear. Left click on **pin1.ipt**. Left click on **Open** as shown in Figure 7.

13. The pin will appear attached to the cursor. Place the pin near the block and left click once. Press **Esc** on the keyboard. Your screen should look similar to Figure 8.

Figure 8

14. Move the cursor to the middle left portion of the screen and left click on **Constrain.** The Place Constraint dialog box will appear as shown in Figure 9.

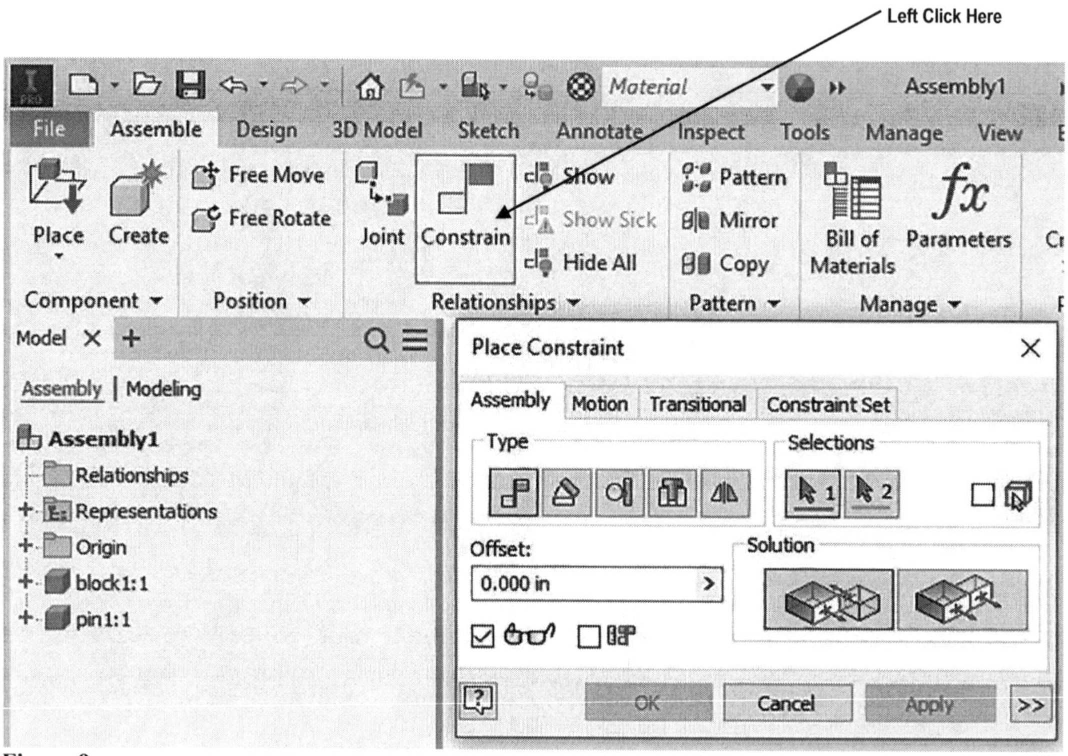

Figure 9

15. Move the cursor over the hole in the block. A center line will appear. Left click once as shown in Figure 10.

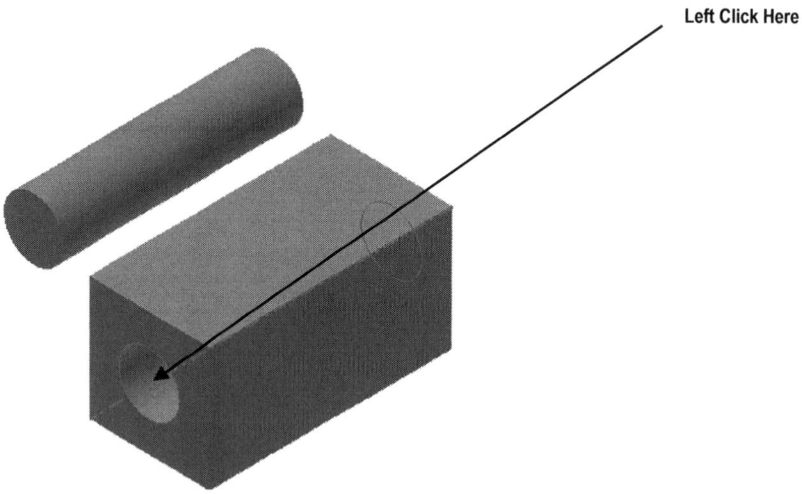

Figure 10

16. Move the cursor over the pin. A center line will appear. Left click once as shown in Figure 11.

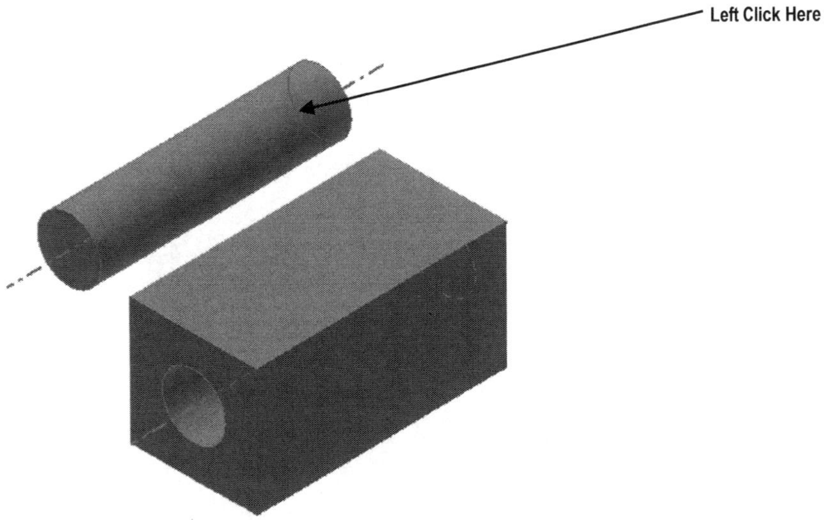

Figure 11

17. Inventor will insert the pin into the block. Left click on **OK**. Your screen should look similar to Figure 12.

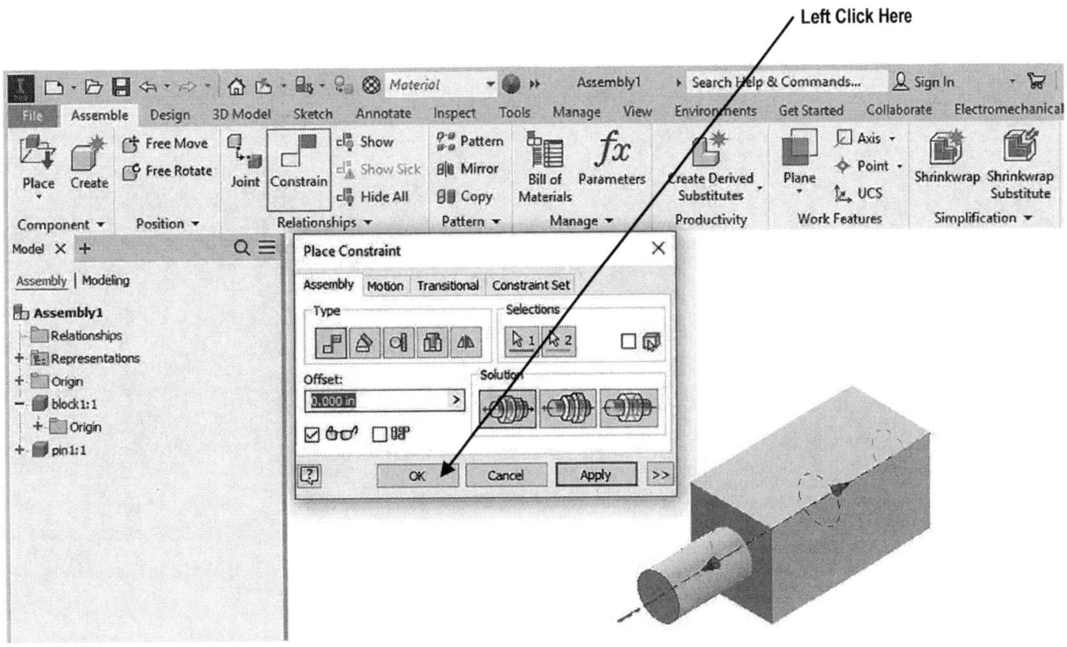

Figure 12

18. Typically a surface constraint would be added to prevent the pin from sliding back and forth in the block. However, this assembly will be used in the Presentation Panel. A surface constraint will not be added because the pin must slide in and out of the block. An Assembly does not need Constraints to be used in the Presentation Panel.

19. Move the cursor to the center of the pin. Left click (holding down the left mouse button) and slide the pin flush with the outside of the block as shown in Figure 13.

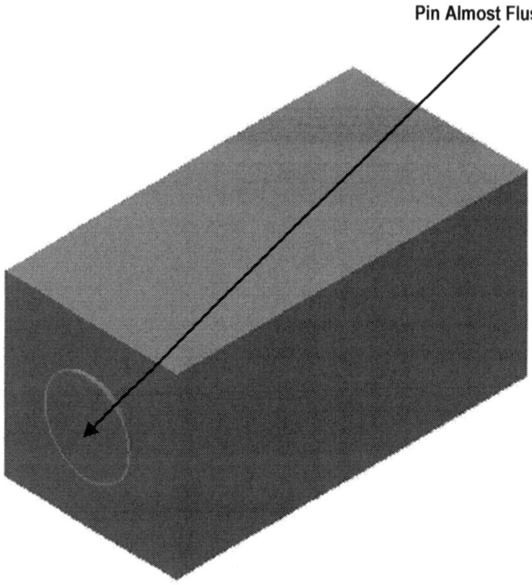

Figure 13

20. Save the parts as Chapter 8 Assembly1.iam where it can be easily retrieved later. Leave the file open at this time.

Learn to import existing assembly models into the Presentation Panel

21. Move the cursor to the upper left portion of the screen and left click on the "New" icon. Left click on **Presentation** as shown in Figure 14.

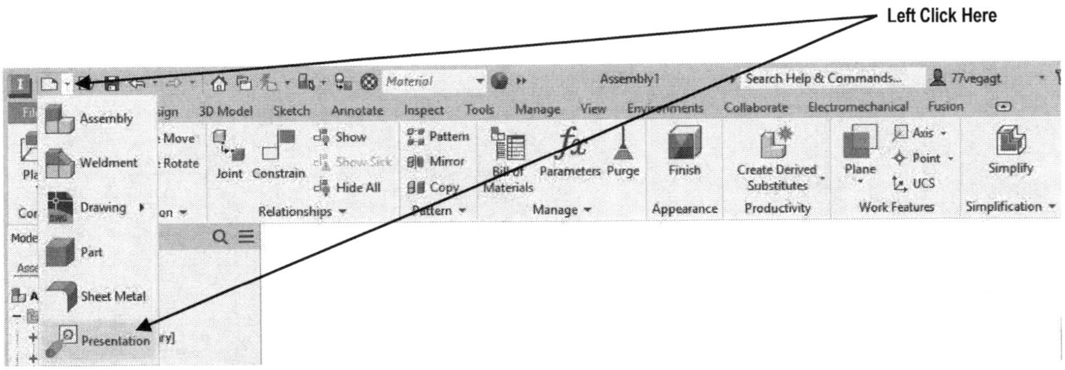

Figure 14

22. Inventor should now be in the Presentation Panel as shown in Figure 15. The Open dialog box will appear. Left click on the assembly that was previously created. Left click on **Open** as shown in Figure 15.

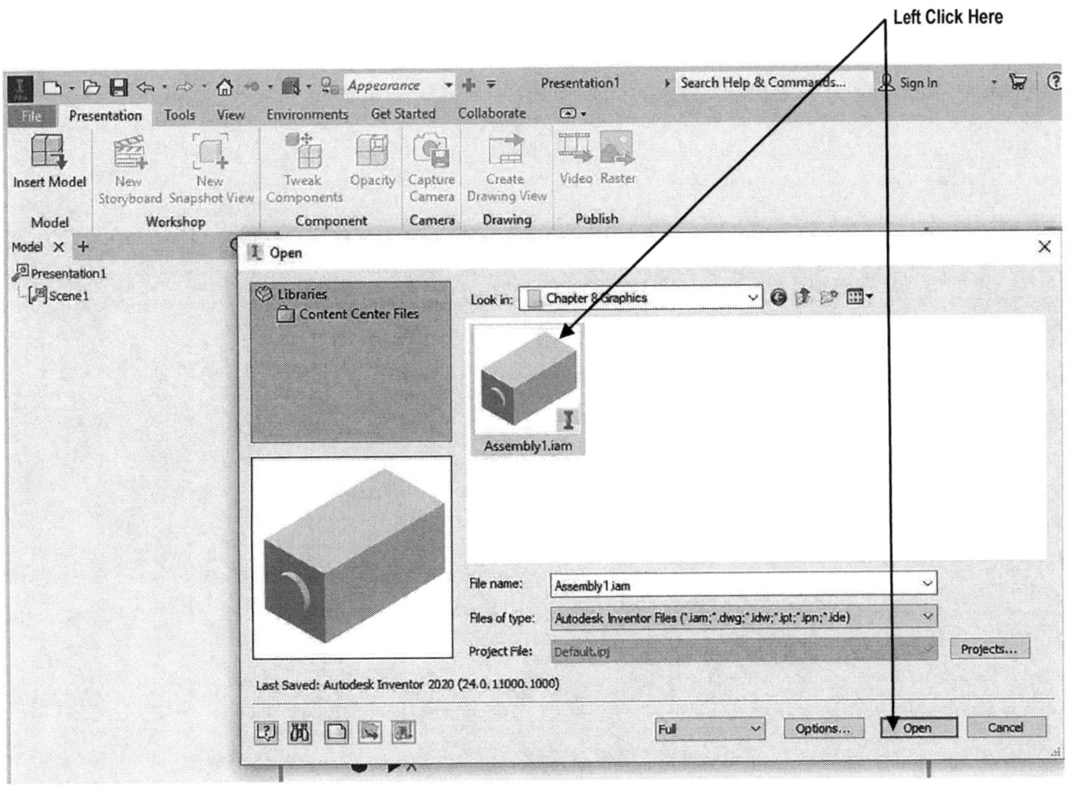

Figure 15

23. The Presentation Panel will open as shown in Figure 16.

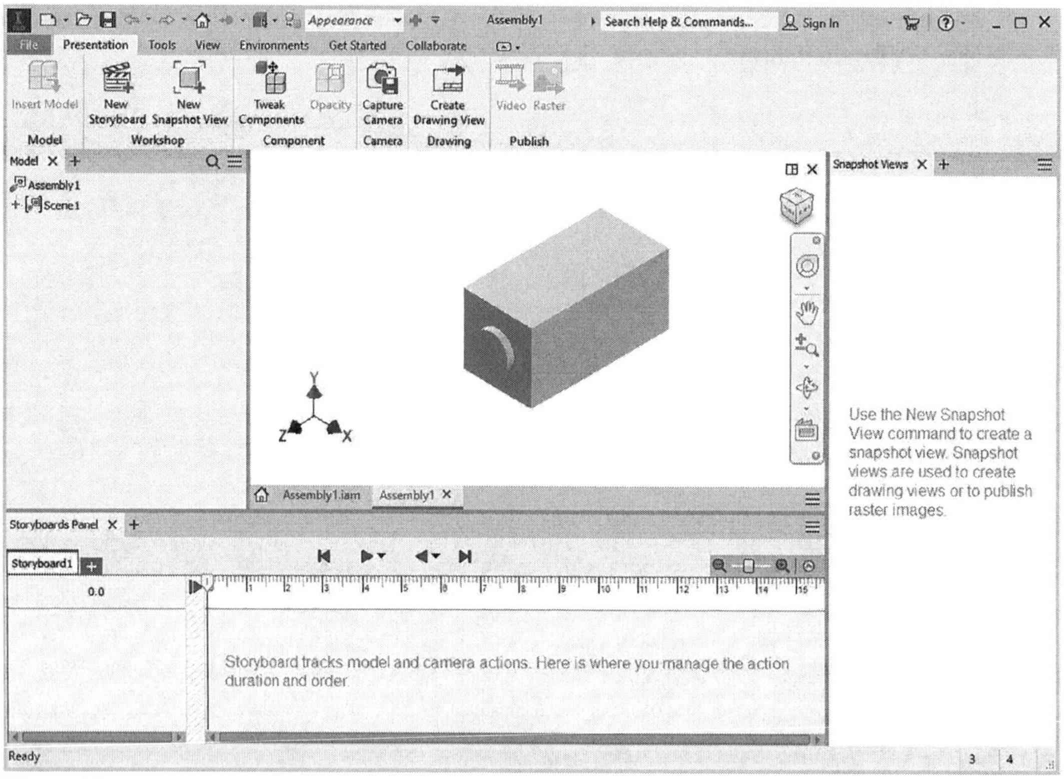

Figure 16

Learn to Tweak Components in the Presentation Panel

24. Move the cursor to the upper left portion of the screen and left click on **Tweak Components**. Left click on the drop-down arrow next to Local. Left click on **World** as shown in Figure 17.

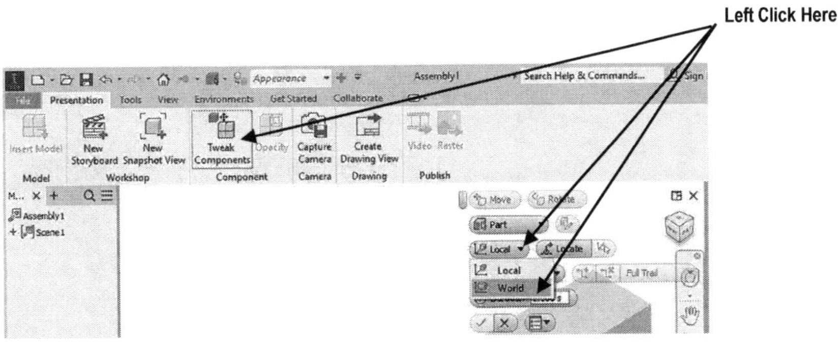

Figure 17

25. Move the cursor to the face of the pin and left click once. The origin will appear as shown in Figure 18.

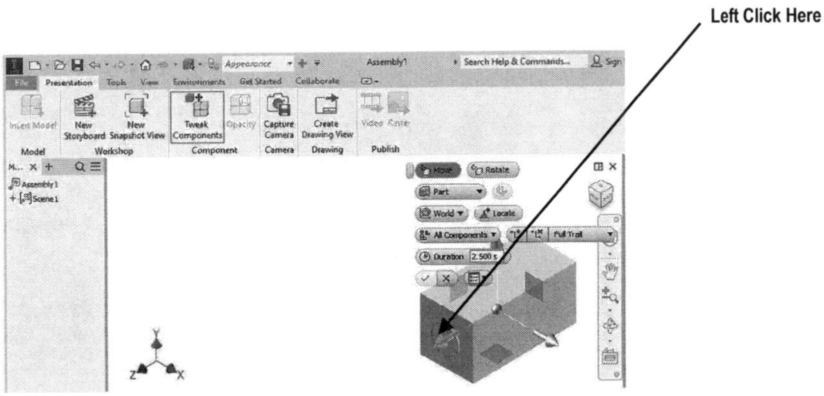

Figure 18

26. Move the cursor over the Z axis arrow causing it to become highlighted as shown in Figure 19.

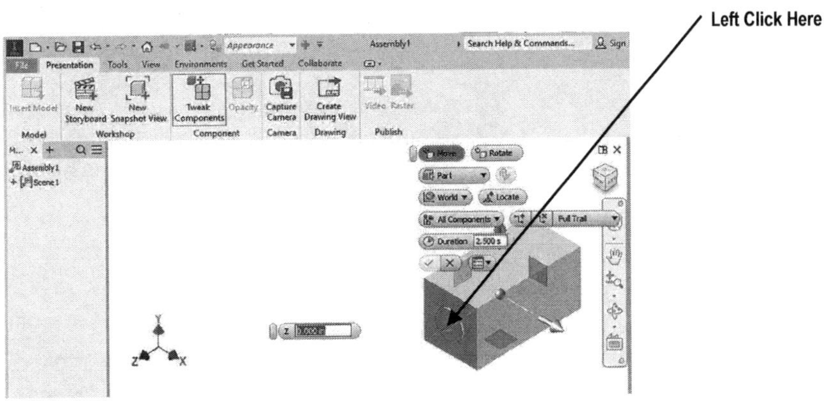

Figure 19

27. Left click on the "Z" axis arrow (holding the left mouse button down) and drag the pin out of the block towards the lower left portion of the screen as shown in Figure 20.

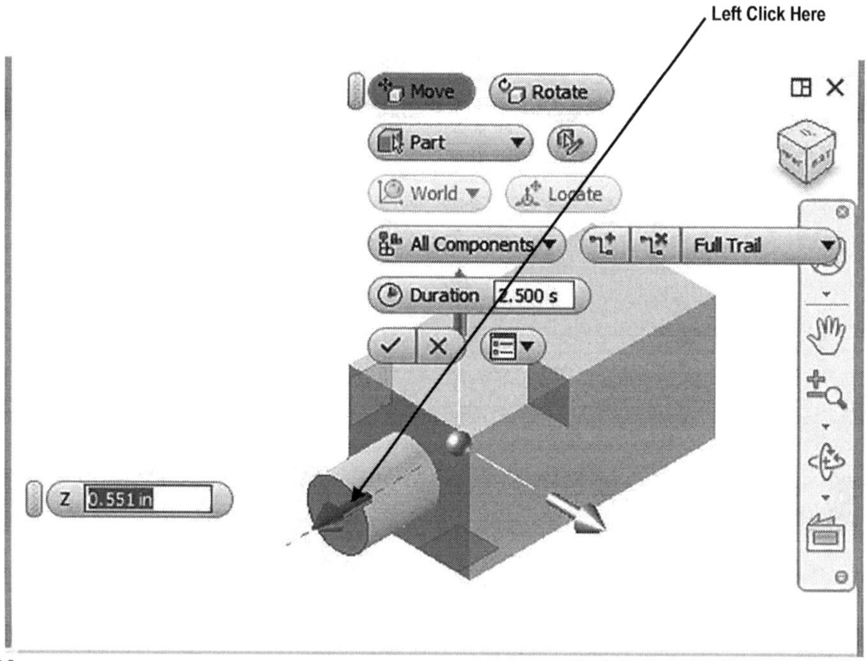

Figure 20

28. Drag the pin to the location as shown in Figure 21.

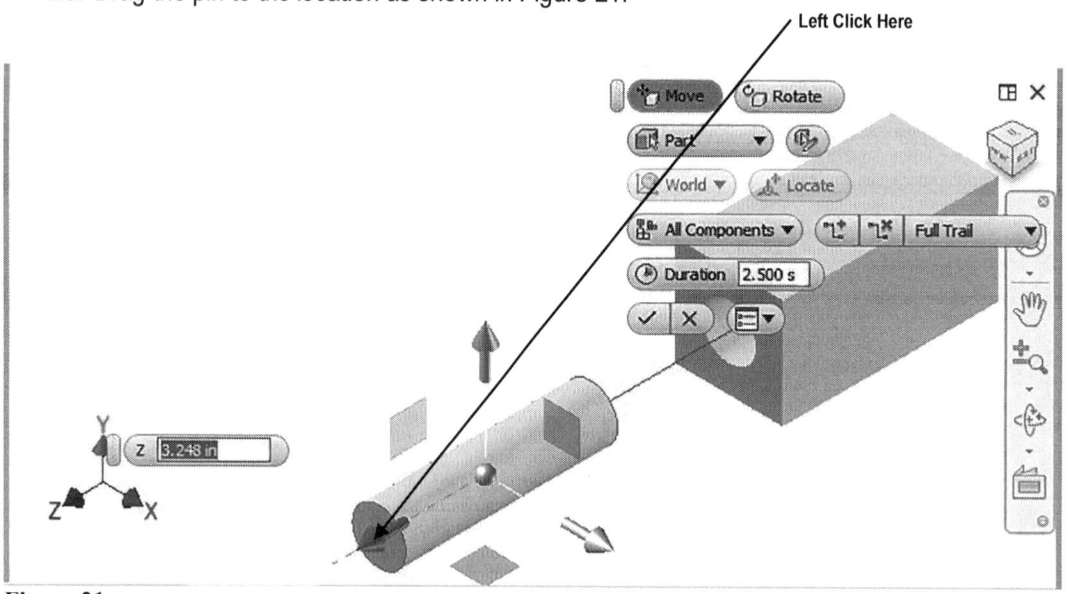

Figure 21

29. Your screen should look similar to Figure 22.

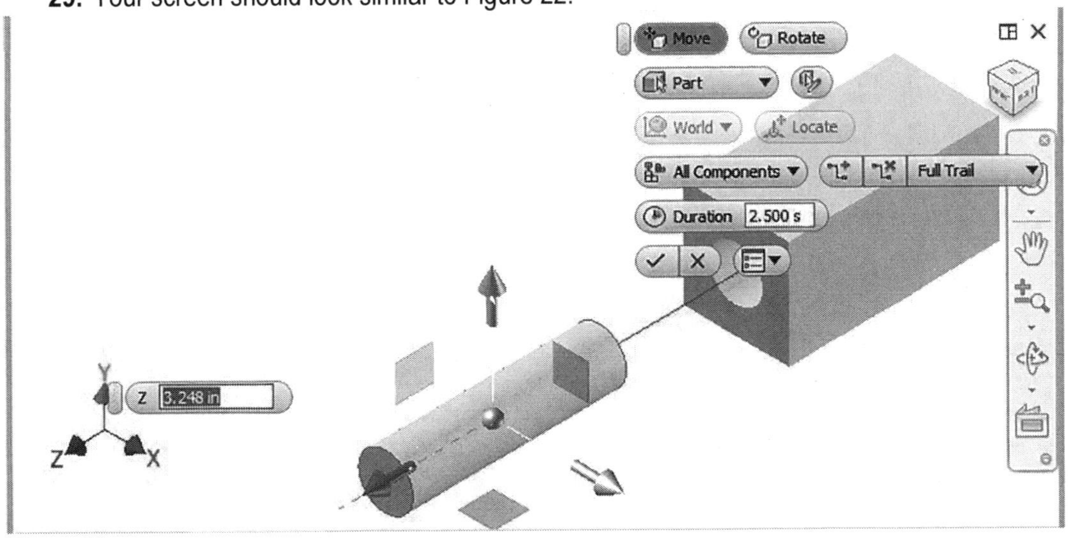

Figure 22

30. Left click on the "Y" axis arrow as shown in Figure 23.

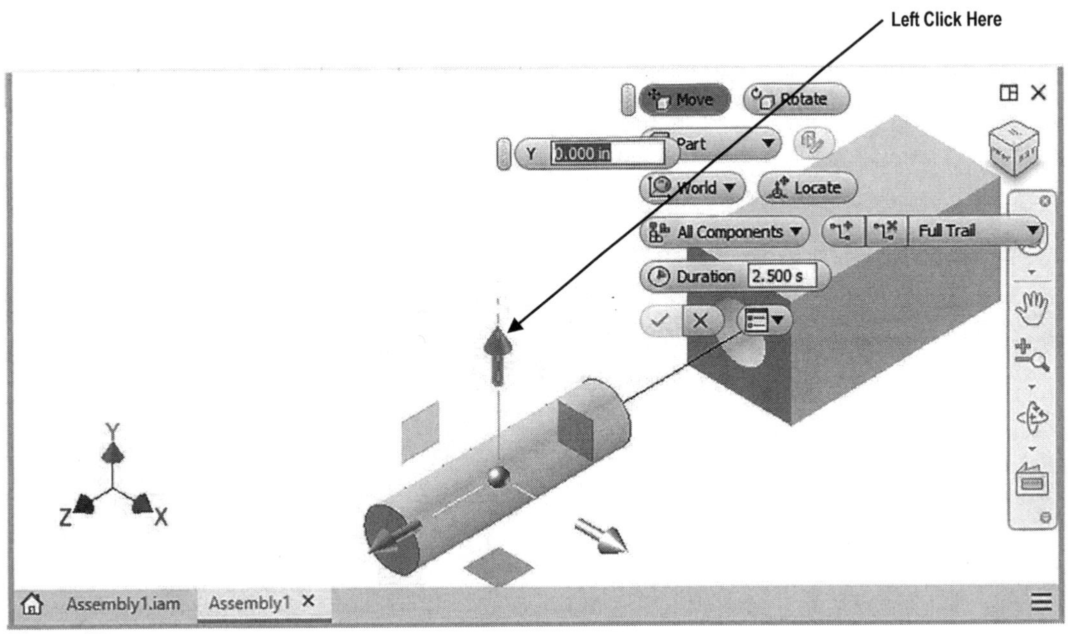

Figure 23

31. Left click (holding the left mouse button down) and drag the pin upwards along the "Y" axis as shown in Figure 24.

Left Click Here

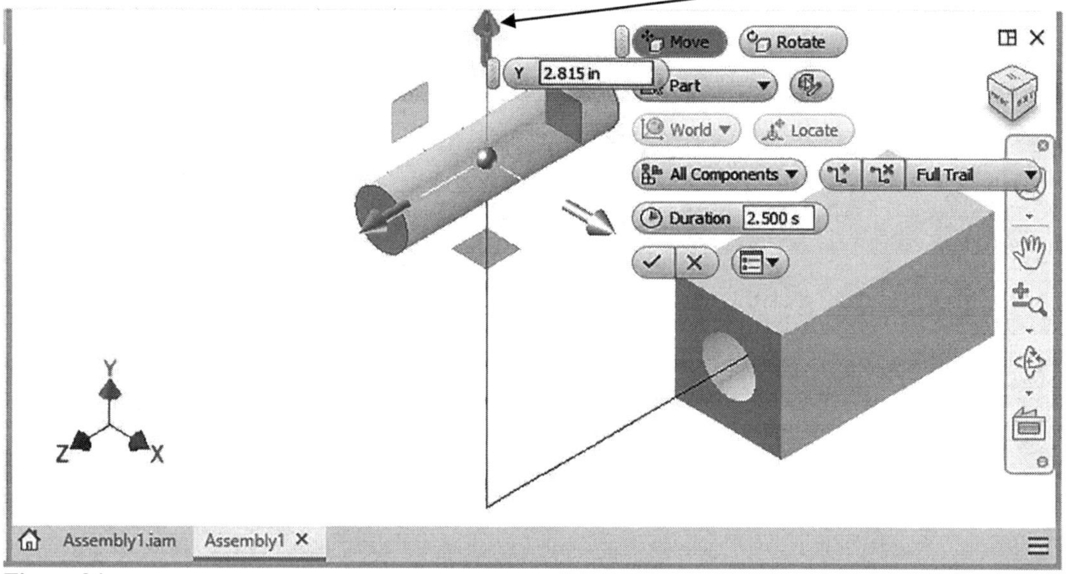

Figure 24

32. Left click on the "X" axis arrow as shown in Figure 25.

Left Click Here

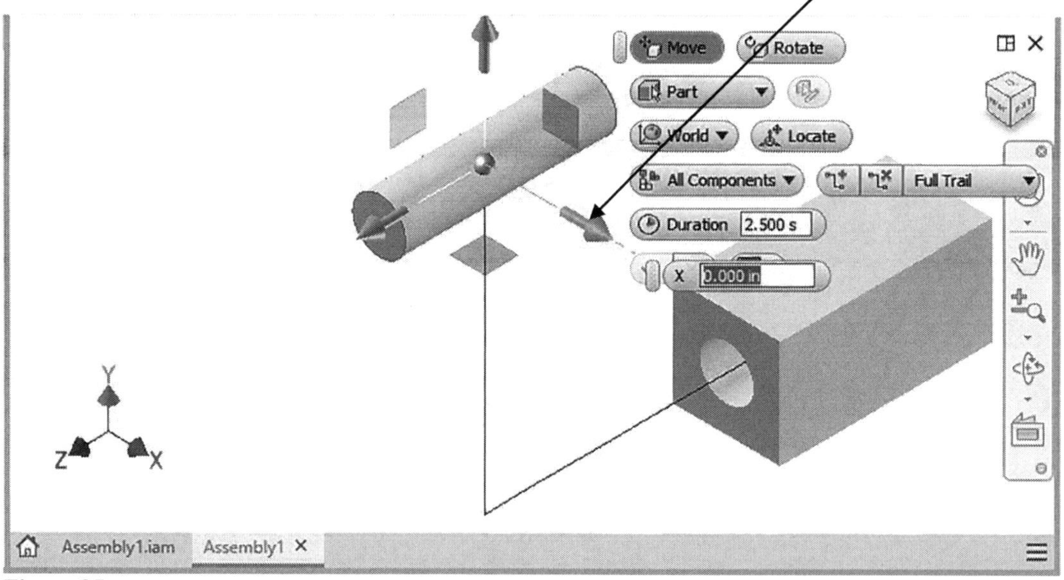

Figure 25

33. Left click (holding the left mouse button down) and drag the pin along the "X" axis. Left click on the green check mark as shown in Figure 26.

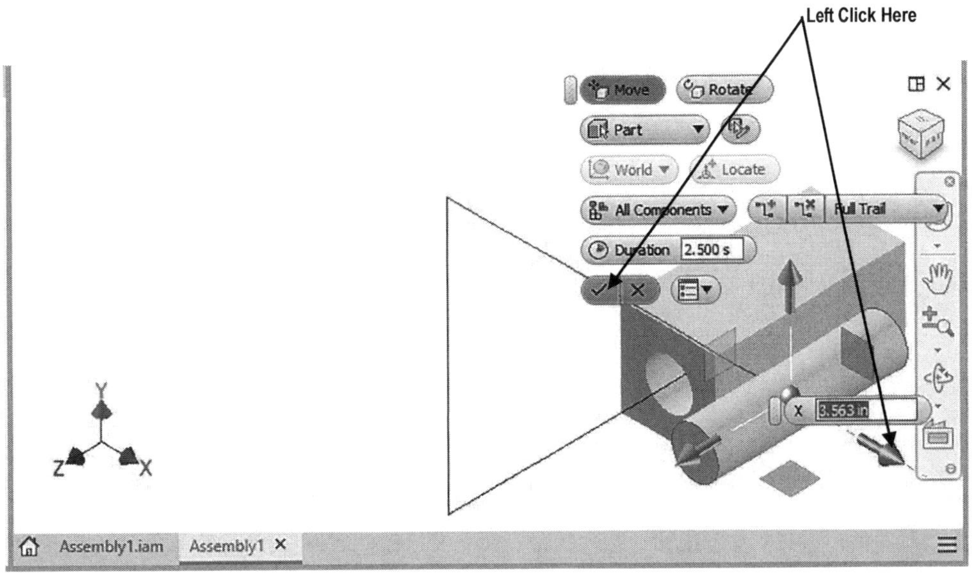

Figure 26

34. Left click on the "Rewind" icon. Inventor will move the pin inside the hole. Then left click on the "Play" icon. Inventor will animate the parts. Left click on the opposite "Rewind" and "Play" icons and Inventor will animate the parts in reverse order as shown in Figure 27.

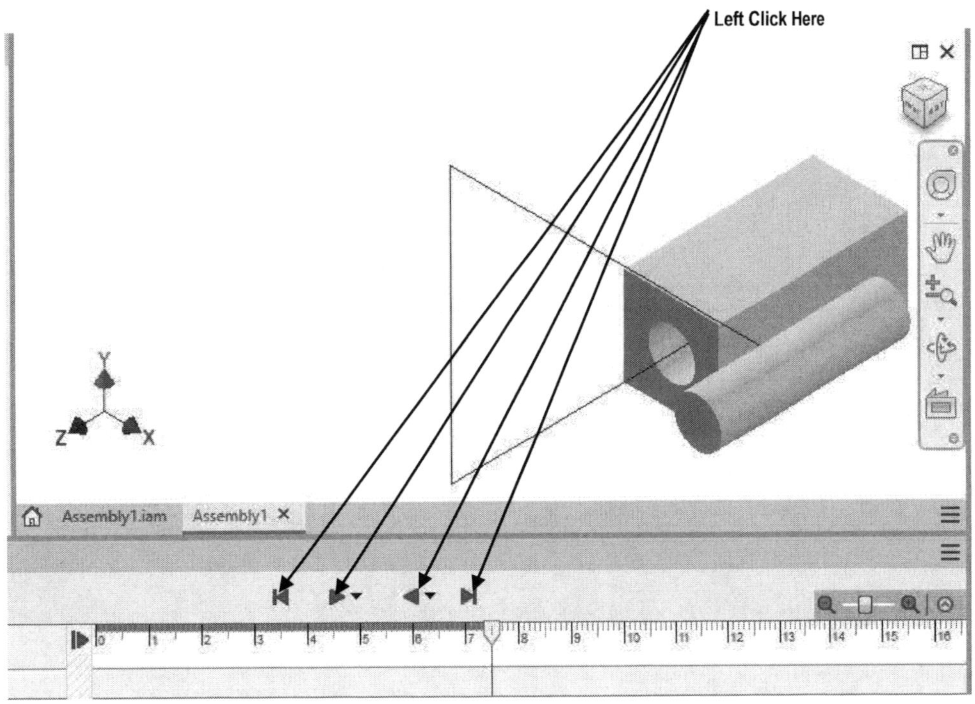

Figure 27

35. Your screen should look similar to Figure 28.

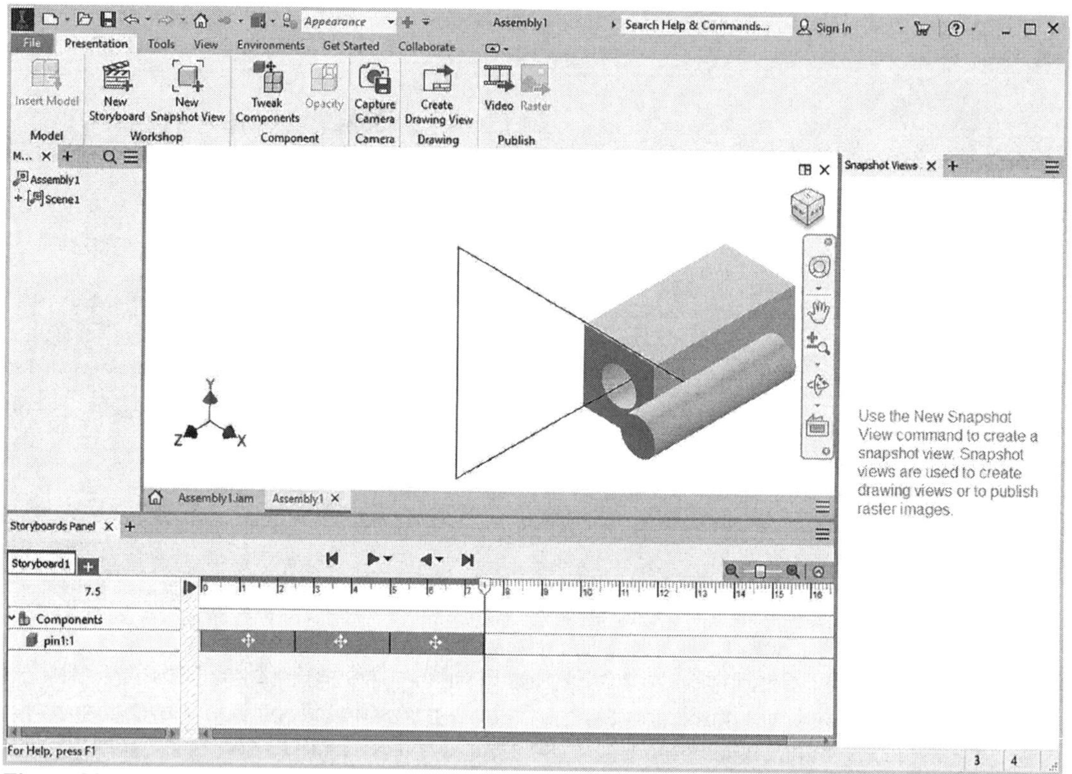

Figure 28

Chapter Problems

Create the following parts and use them to design Presentations. They are all mating parts.

Problem 8-1

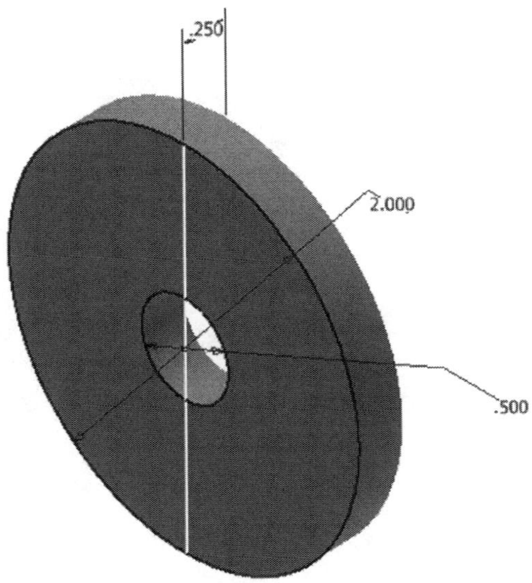

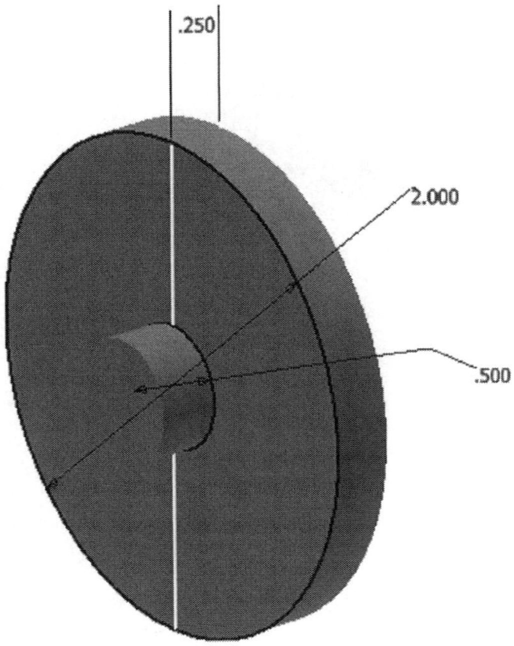

Problem 8-2

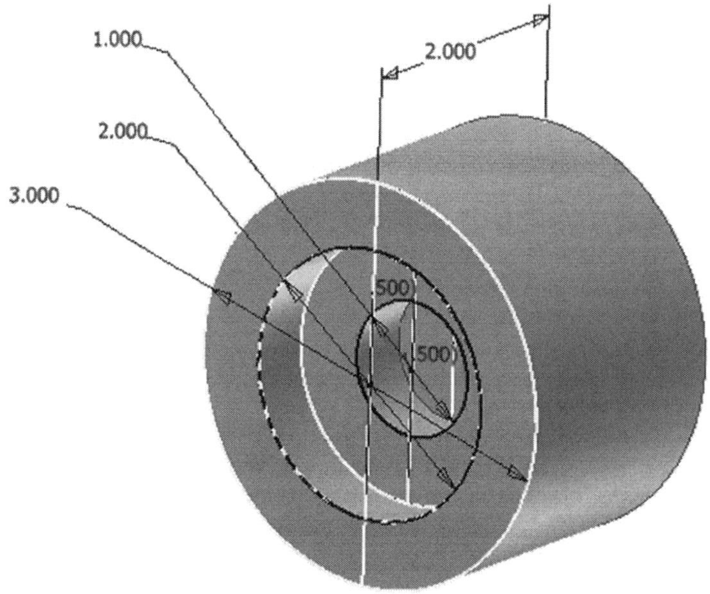

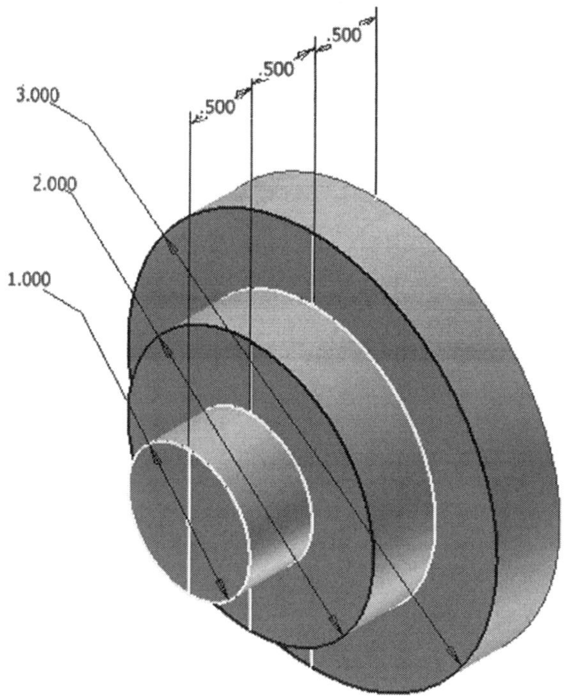

Problem 8-3

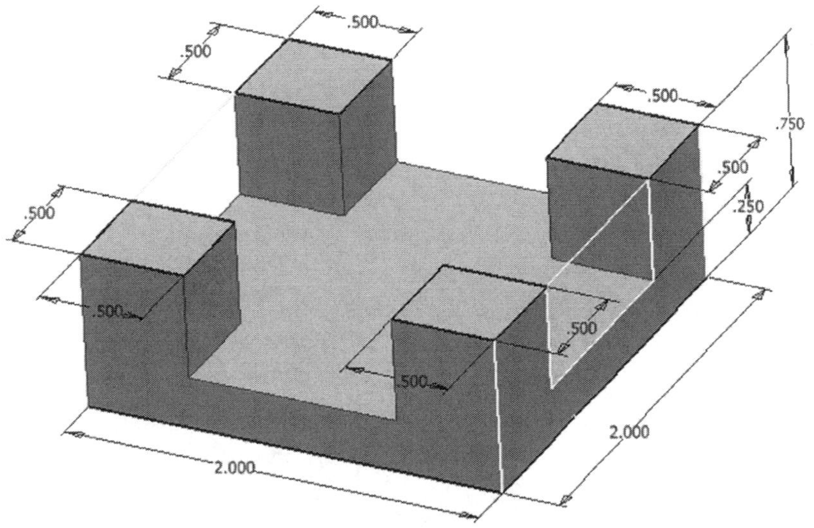
.500
.500
.500
.750
.500
.250
.500
.500
.500
.500
2.000
2.000

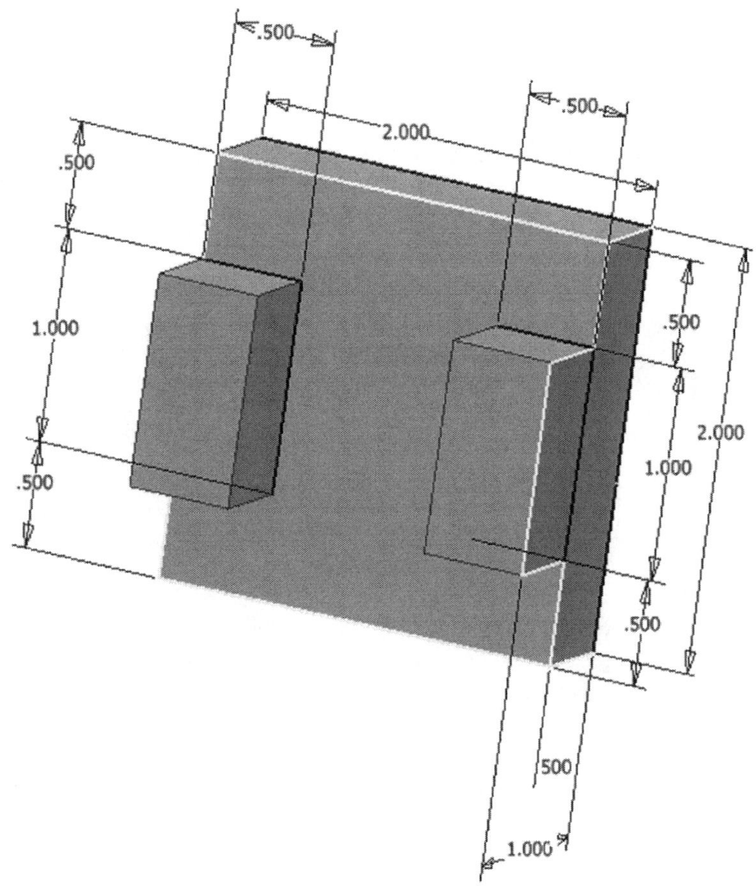
.500
2.000
.500
.500
1.000
.500
.500
2.000
1.000
.500
.500
1.000

Problem 8-4 Import the following part twice into the Assembly Panel and create an Assembly and then create a Presentation in the Presentation Panel.

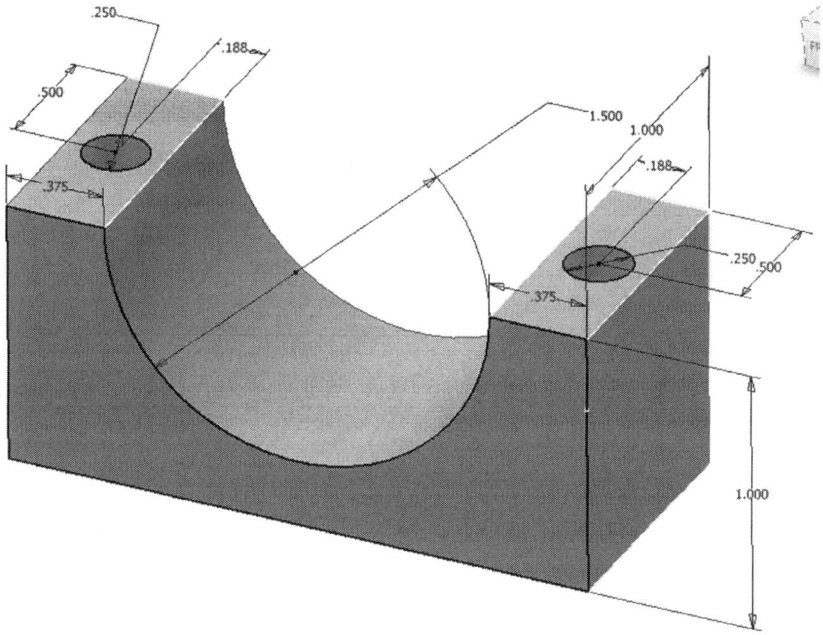

When completed, your screen should look similar to what is shown below.

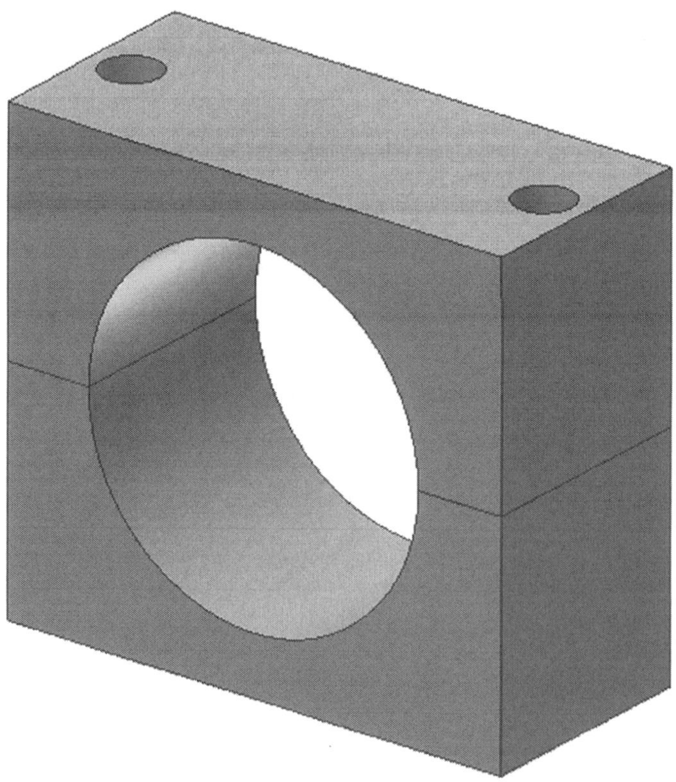

CHAPTER 9

Introduction to Advanced Commands

Objectives:

1. Learn to use the Sweep command
2. Learn to use the Rectangular Pattern command
3. Learn to use the Loft command
4. Learn to use the Work Plane command
5. Learn to use the Coil command

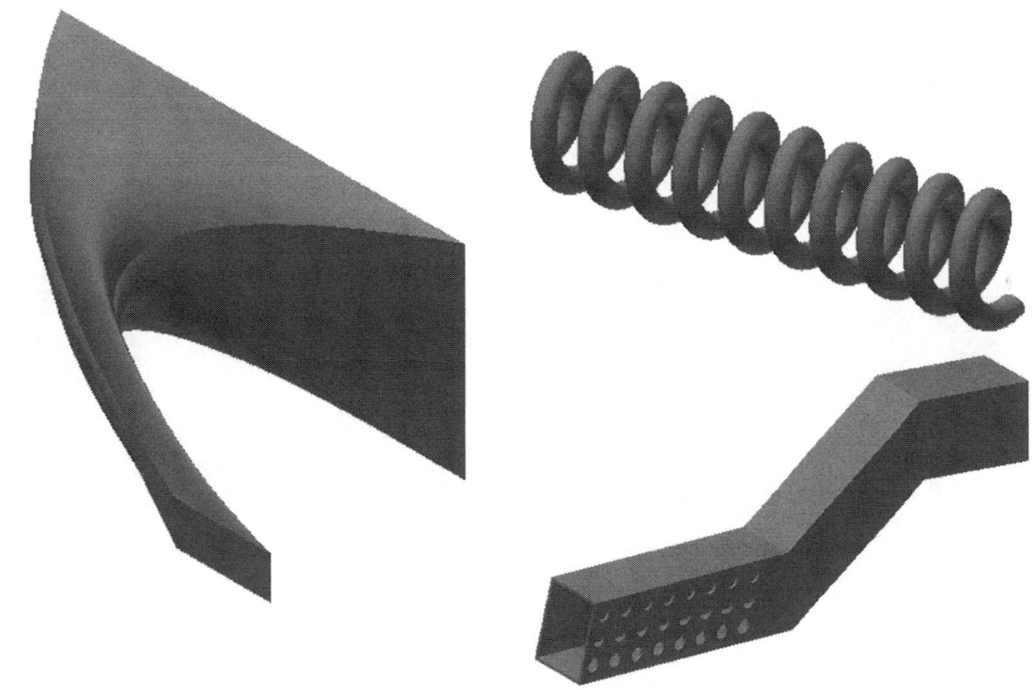

Chapter 9 includes instruction on how to design the parts shown.

Learn to create a sweep using the Sweep command

1. Start Inventor by referring to "Chapter 1 Getting Started."

2. After Inventor is running, begin a New Sketch.

3. Move the cursor to the upper left portion of the screen and left click on **Rectangle** as shown in Figure 1.

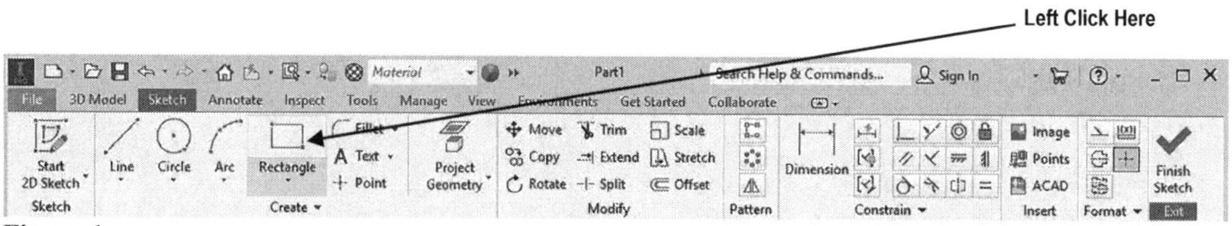

Figure 1

4. Complete the sketch shown below. Once the sketch is complete, right click anywhere on the screen. A pop-up menu will appear. Left click **Finish 2D Sketch** as shown in Figure 2.

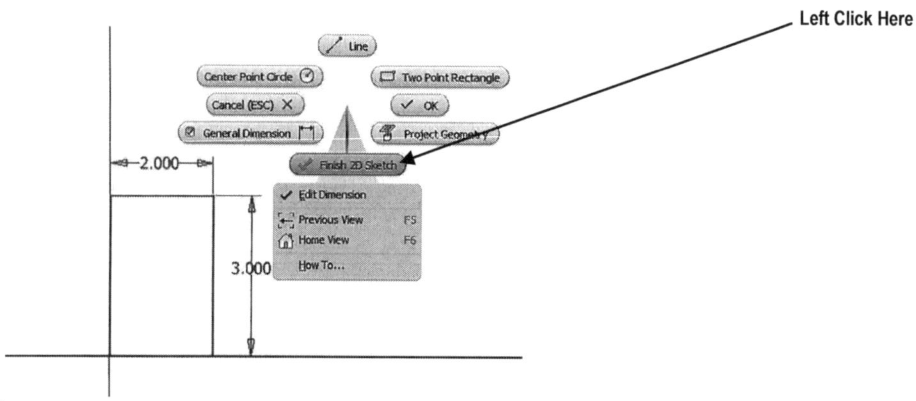

Figure 2

5. Your screen should look similar to Figure 3.

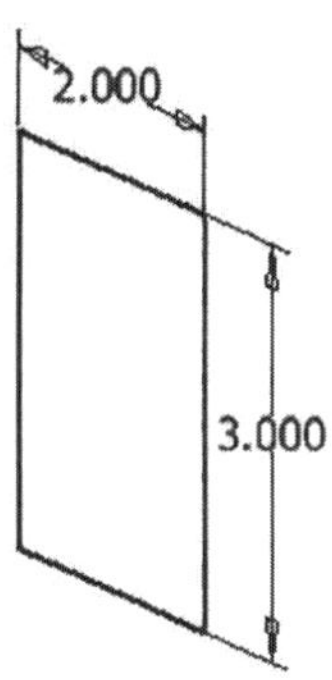

Figure 3

6. Move the cursor over the text "YZ Plane" causing a red box to appear. Right click once. A pop-up menu will appear. Left click on **New Sketch** as shown in Figure 4.

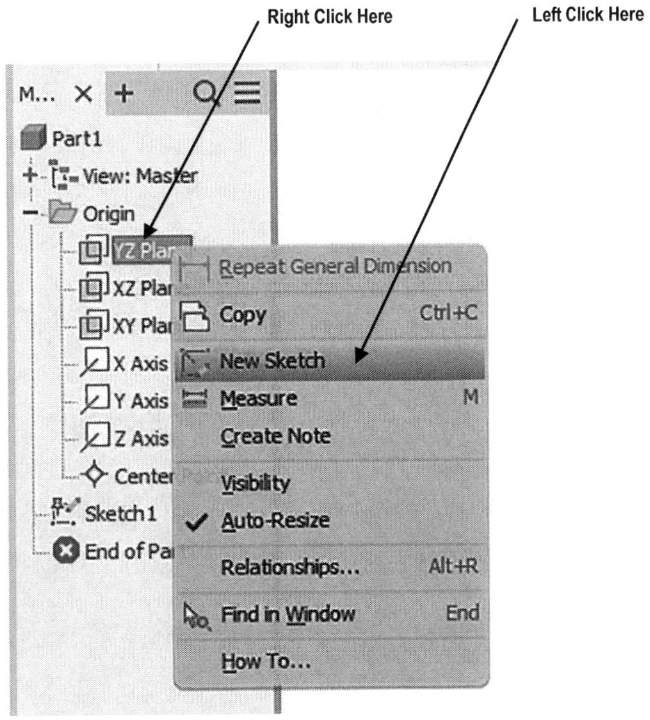

Figure 4

7. Your screen should look similar to Figure 5.

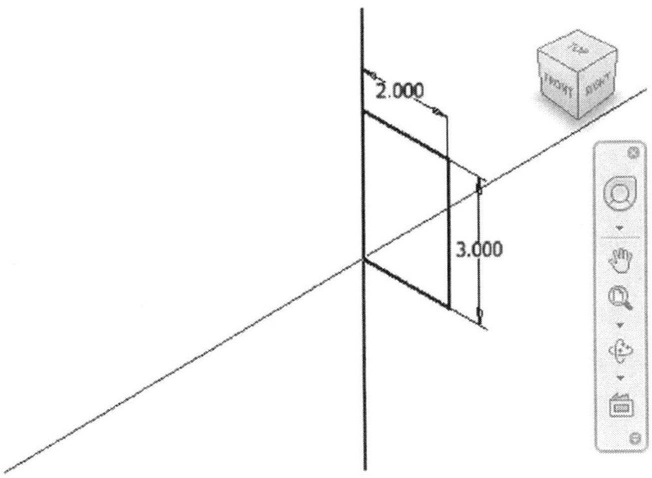

Figure 5

8. Complete the following sketch. The angle of the lines can be estimated. The sketch lines must intersect with the corner of the 2 inch by 3 inch box as shown in Figure 6. Remember to use the **Aligned** dimension function (while the dimension is attached to the cursor right click causing a pop-up menu to appear then left click on **Aligned**). Exit out of the Sketch Panel.

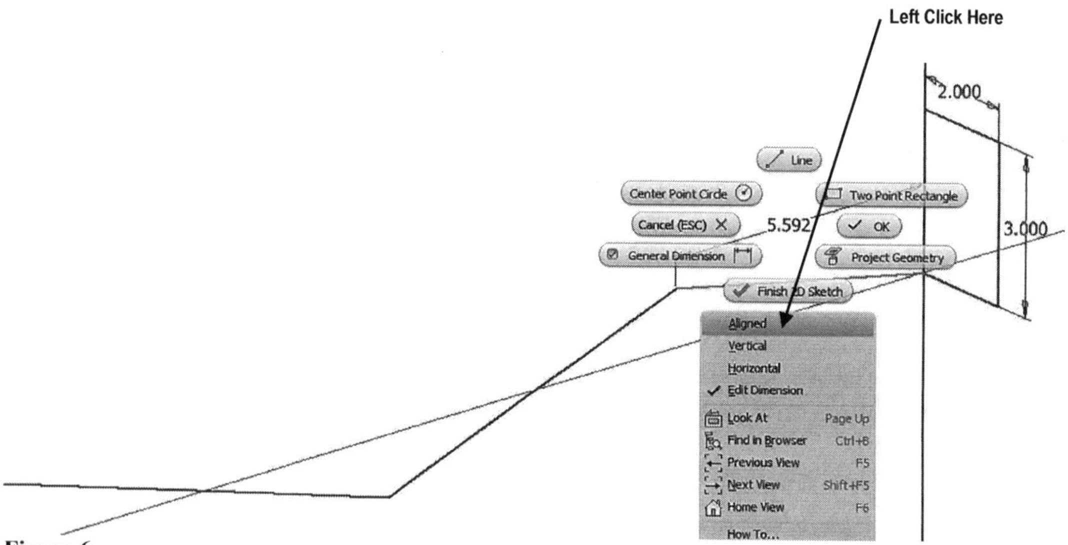

Figure 6

9. Your screen should look similar to Figure 7.

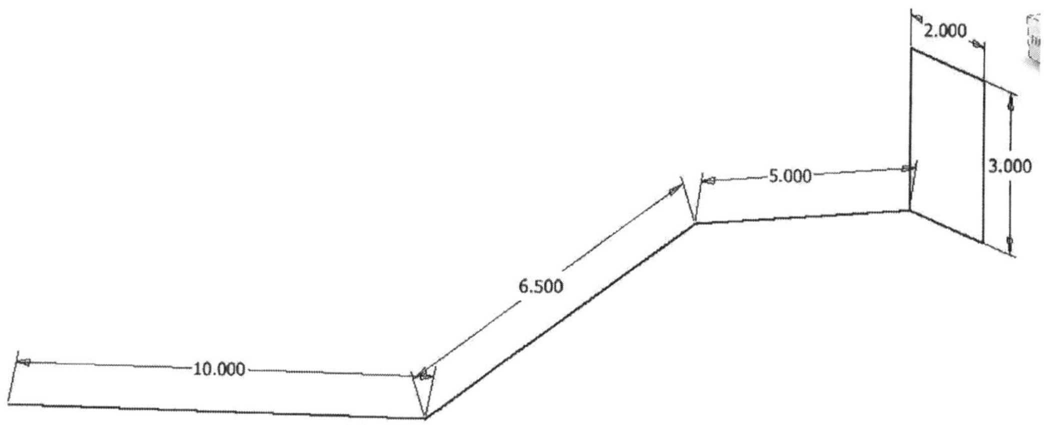

Figure 7

10. Move the cursor to the upper left portion of the screen and left click on **Sweep**. Move the cursor over the sweep line causing it to turn red and left click once as shown in Figure 8.

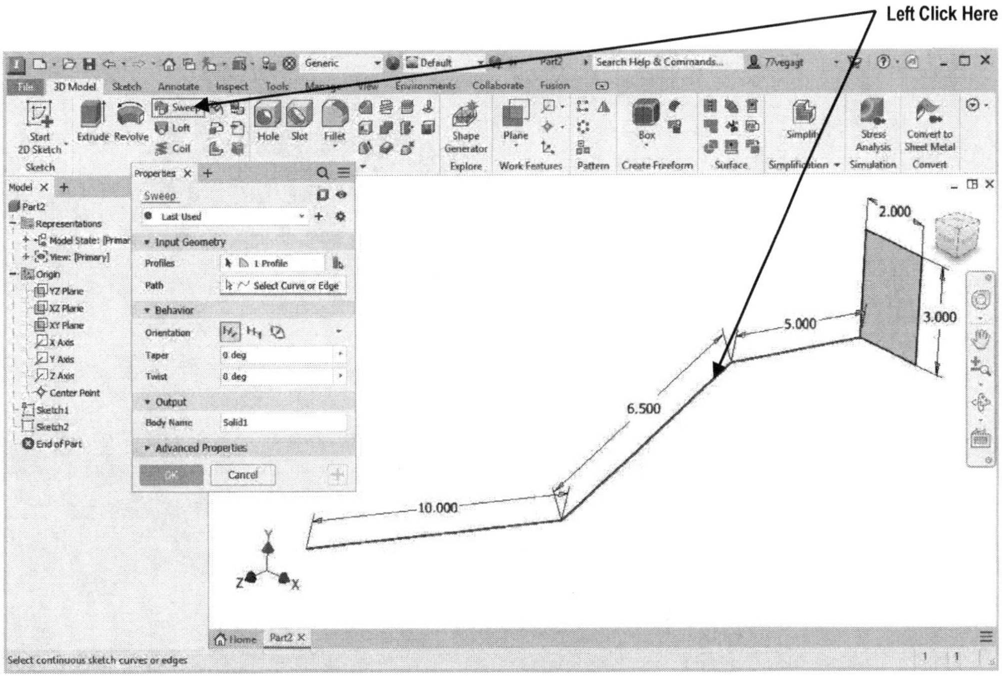

Figure 8

11. A preview of the sweep will appear as shown in Figure 9.

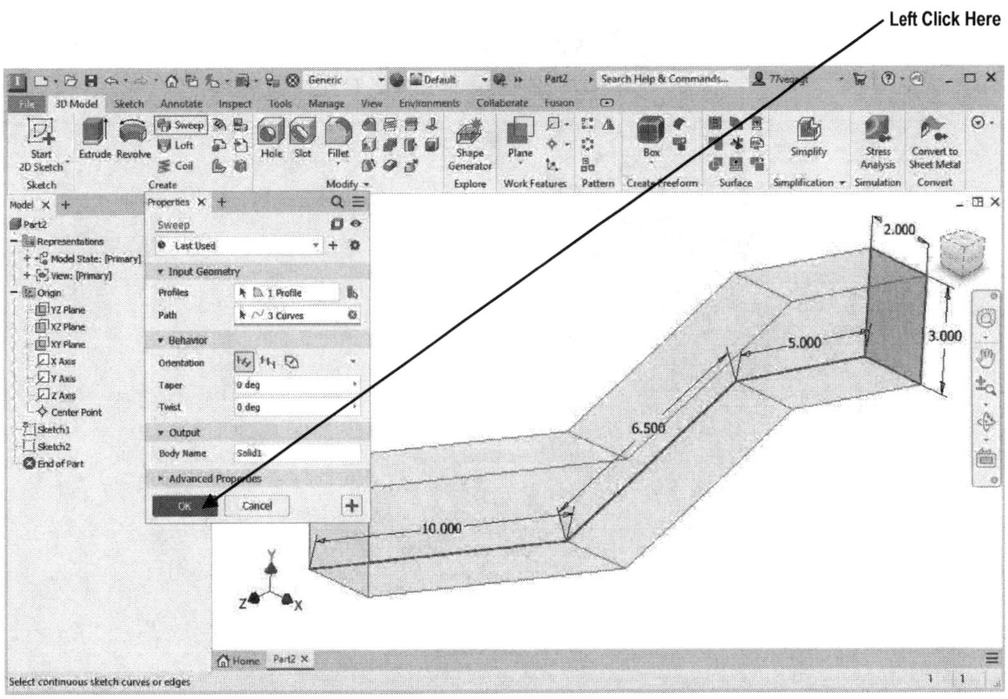

Figure 9

12. Left click on **OK** as shown in Figure 9.

13. Your screen should look similar to Figure 10.

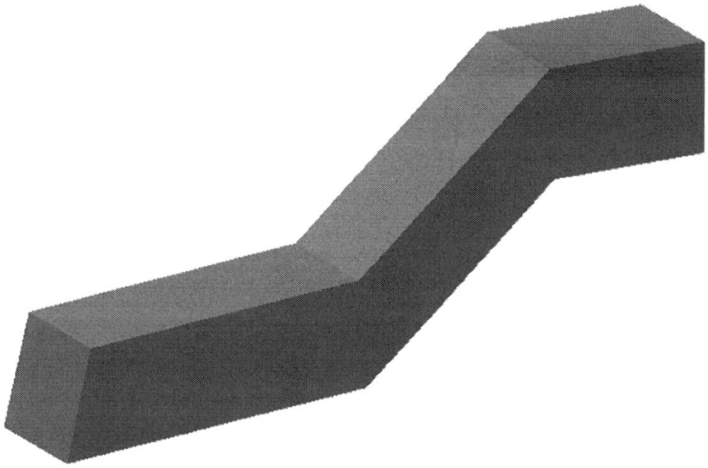

Figure 10

14. Use the **Shell** command to shell the tubing as shown in Figure 11.

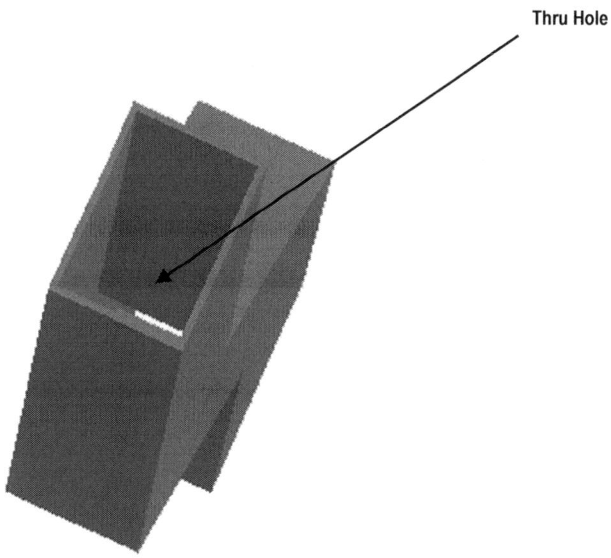

Figure 11

15. Begin a new sketch as shown in Figure 12. Use the Look At command to gain a perpendicular view of the surface.

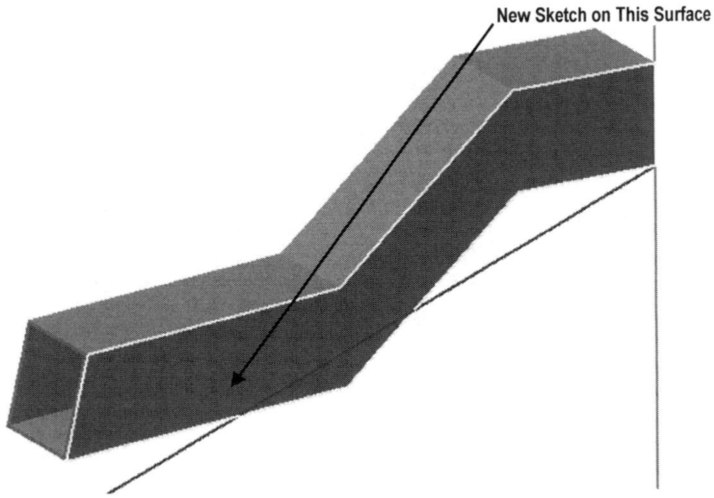

Figure 12

16. Your screen should look similar to Figure 13.

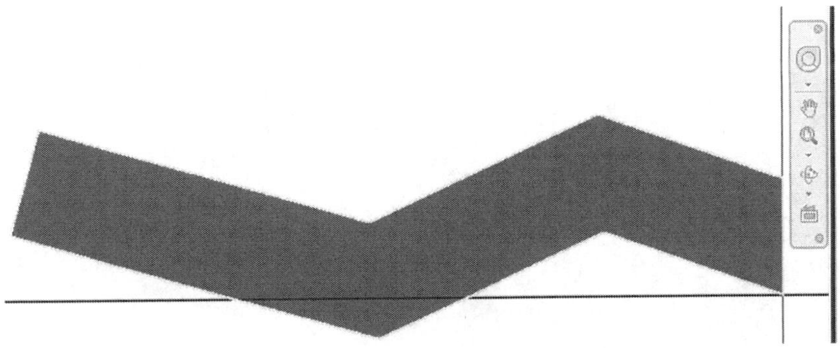

Figure 13

17. Complete the following sketch. You may have to zoom in as shown in Figure 14.

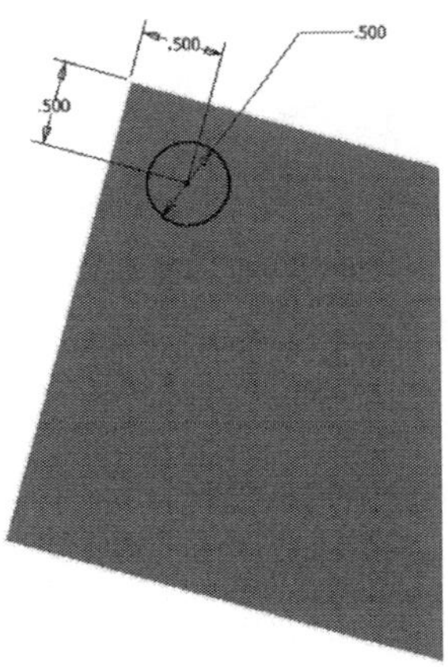

Figure 14

18. Exit out of the Sketch area and change the view to Home View as shown in Figure 15.

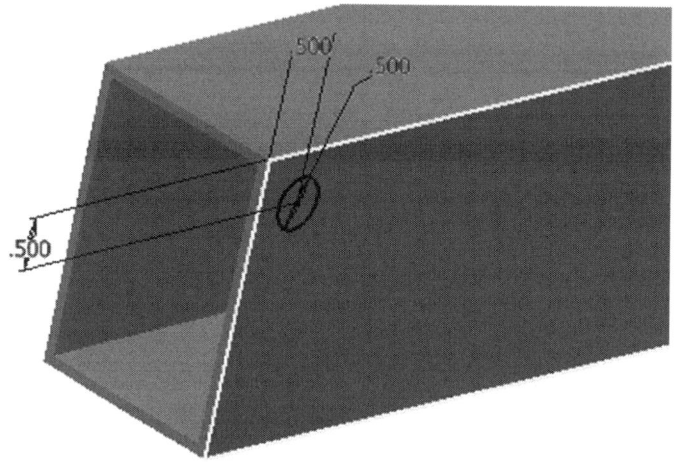

Figure 15

Learn to use the Rectangular Pattern command

19. Use the **Extrude** command to cut the hole out as shown in Figure 16.

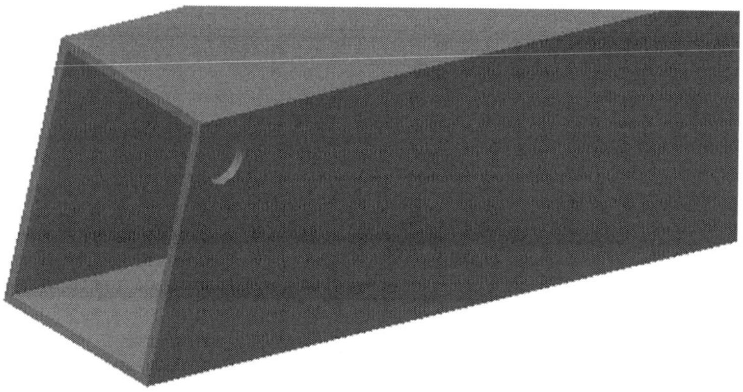

Figure 16

20. Move the cursor to the upper middle portion of the screen and left click on the Rectangular Pattern icon. The Rectangular Pattern dialog box will appear as shown in Figure 17.

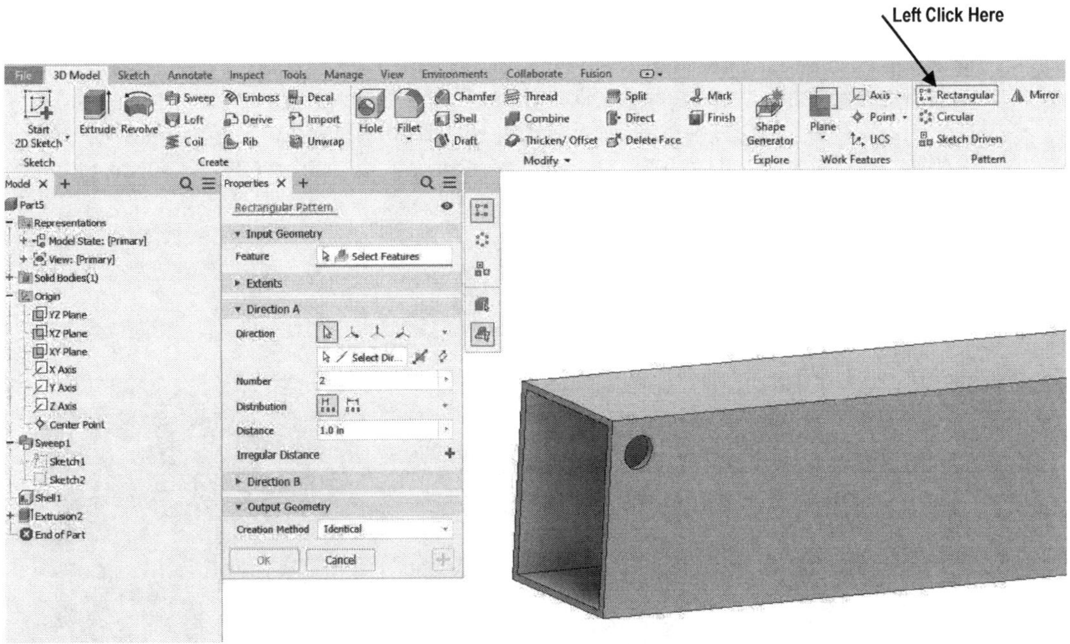

Figure 17

21. Left click next to Feature to select the hole. Move the cursor inside the hole and left click once as shown in Figure 18.

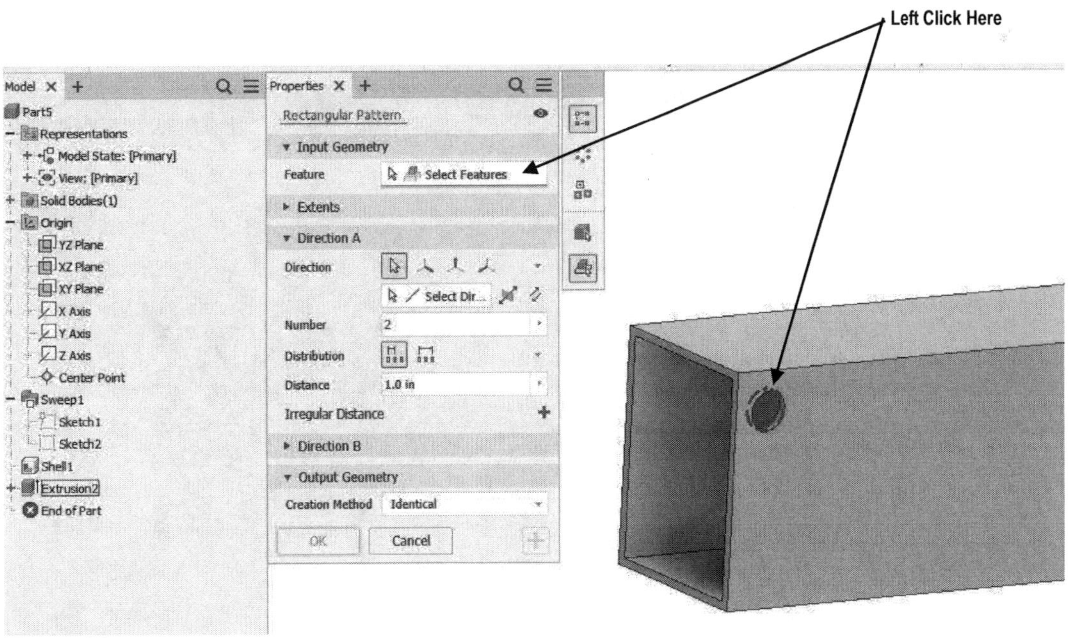

Figure 18

22. Left click on the arrow under Direction A. Now left click on the top edge of the part. If there is a need to reverse the direction of the pattern (so the pattern does not travel off the part), left click on the Flip icon (icon with arrows pointing up and down). Inventor will provide a preview of the holes it will pattern in the X direction. Now left click on the arrow under Direction B. Now left click on the side edge of the part. Inventor will provide a preview of the holes it will pattern in the Y direction. Enter **8** for the number of occurrences (rows) in Direction 1, and **3** for the number of occurrences (columns) in Direction B. Enter **1.0** and **.875** for the distance between the circles respectively. Left click on **OK** as shown in Figure 19.

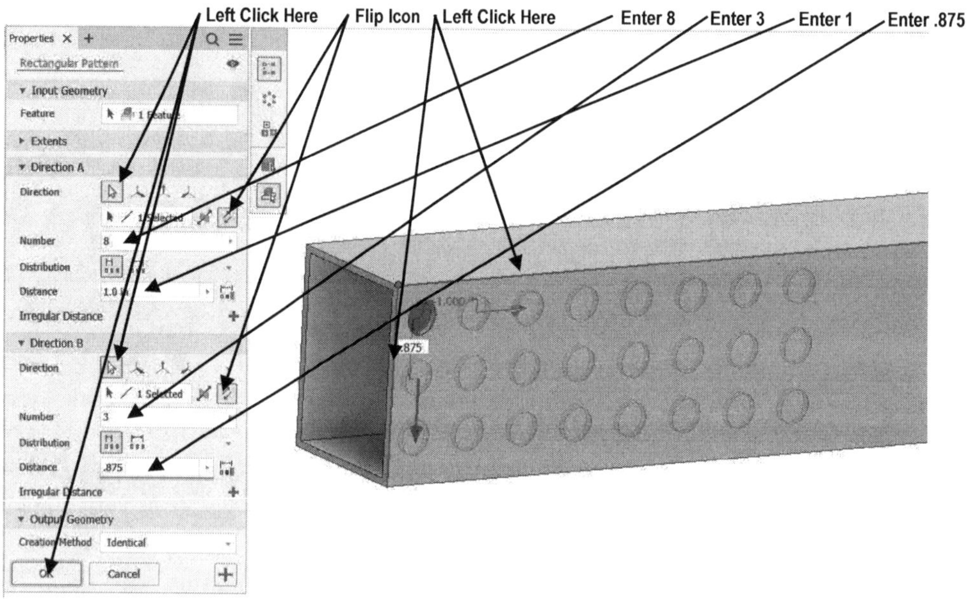

Figure 19

Learn to create a loft using the Loft command

23. Your screen should look similar to Figure 20.

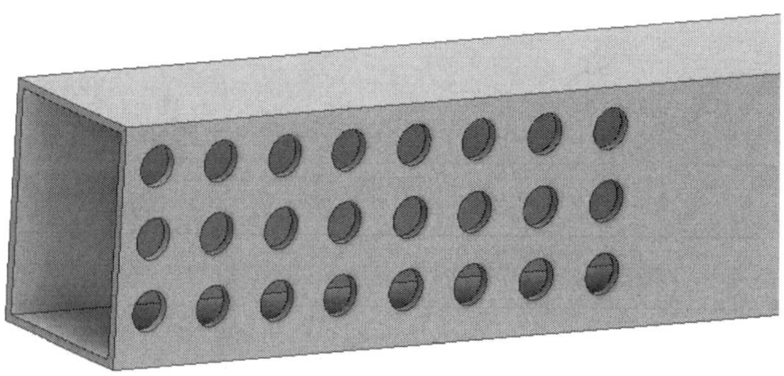

Figure 20

24. Begin a new drawing. Complete the sketch shown below. Exit out of the Sketch Panel as shown in Figure 21.

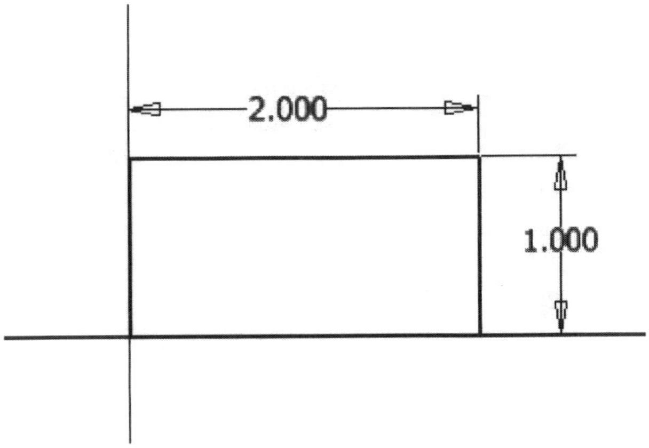

Figure 21

25. Left click on the plus sign to the left of the text "Origin." The browser will expand as shown in Figure 22.

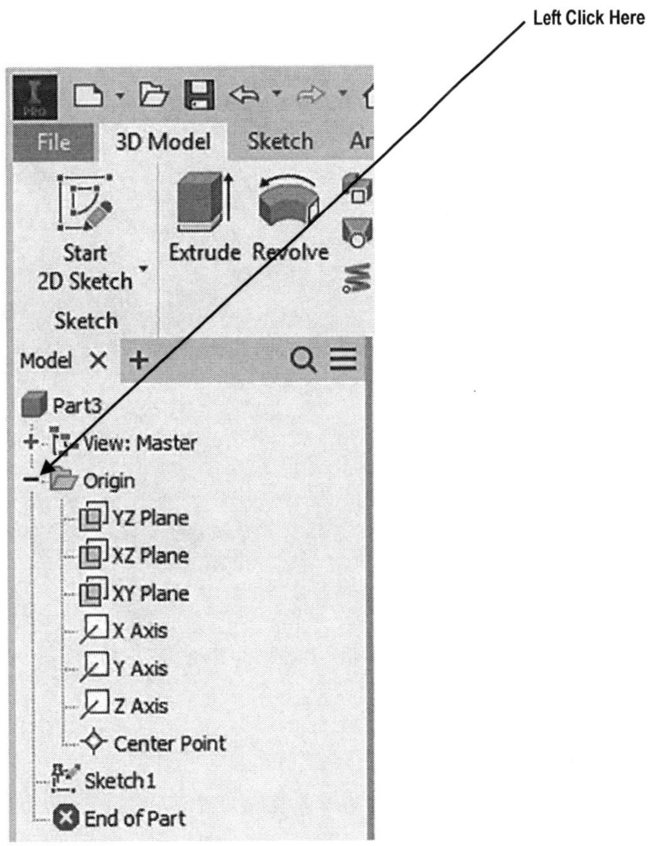

Figure 22

26. Move the cursor to the upper right portion of the screen and left click on **Plane** as shown in Figure 23.

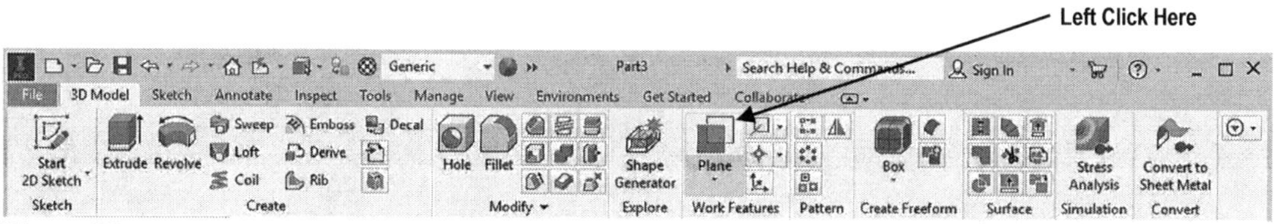

Figure 23

27. Left click on **XY Plane** in the browser. The "XY Plane" text will become highlighted. Left click once as shown in Figure 24.

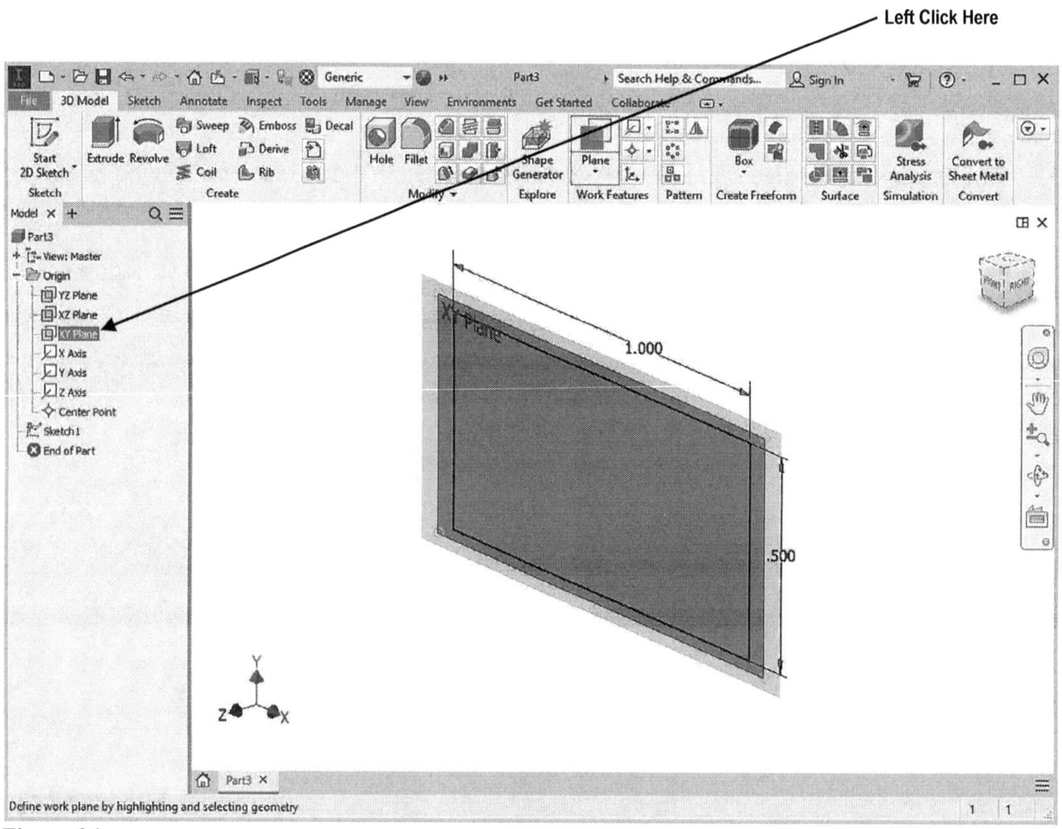

Figure 24

28. Move the cursor to the center of the sketch and left click (holding the left mouse button down) dragging the cursor to the lower left portion of the screen. Enter **.500** as shown in Figure 25 and press the **Enter** key on the keyboard.

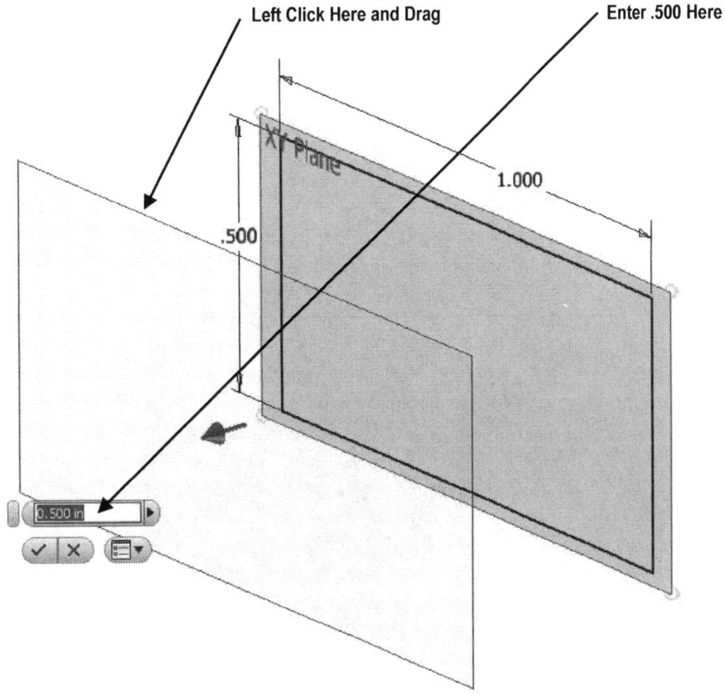

Figure 25

29. Your screen should look similar to Figure 26.

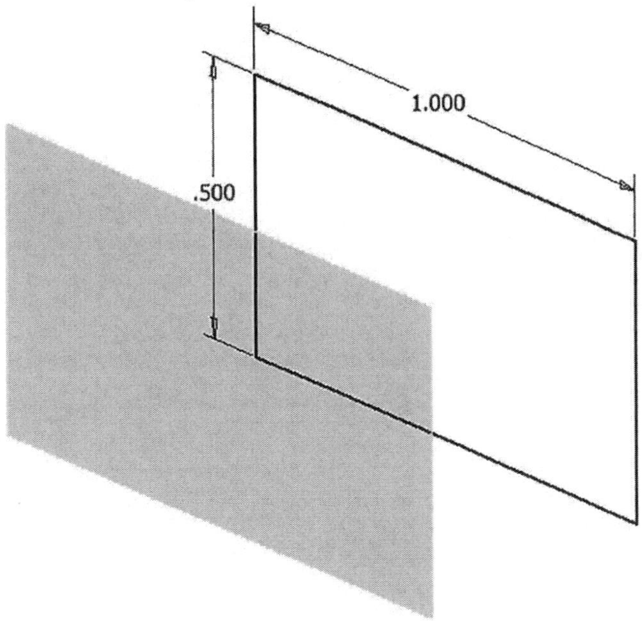

Figure 26

30. Begin a New Sketch on the newly created Workplane as shown in Figure 27.

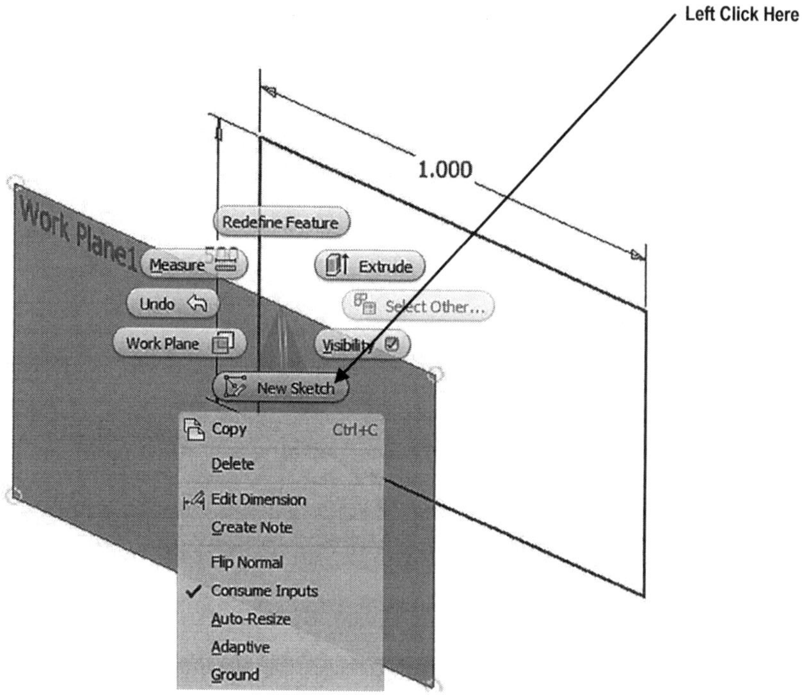

Figure 27

31. Complete the sketch shown in Figure 28. Estimate the location and size of the circle and exit the Sketch Panel.

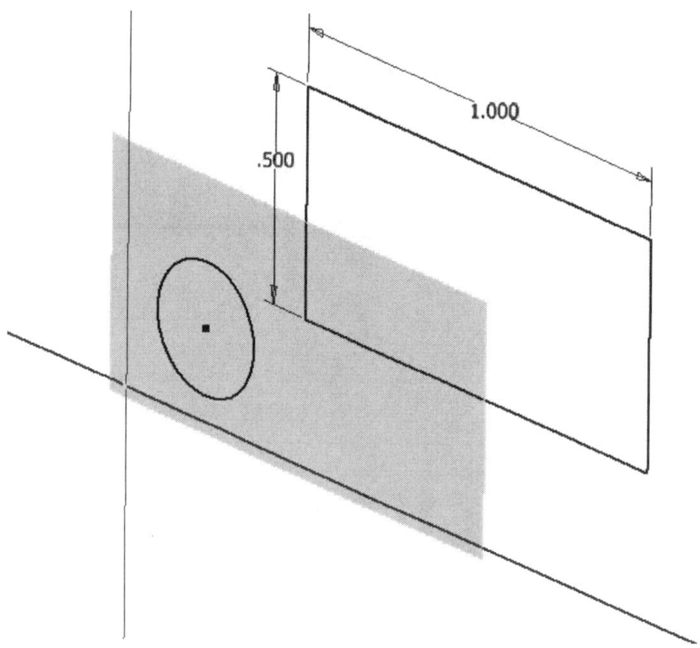

Figure 28

32. Move the cursor to the upper right portion of the screen and left click **Plane** as shown in Figure 29.

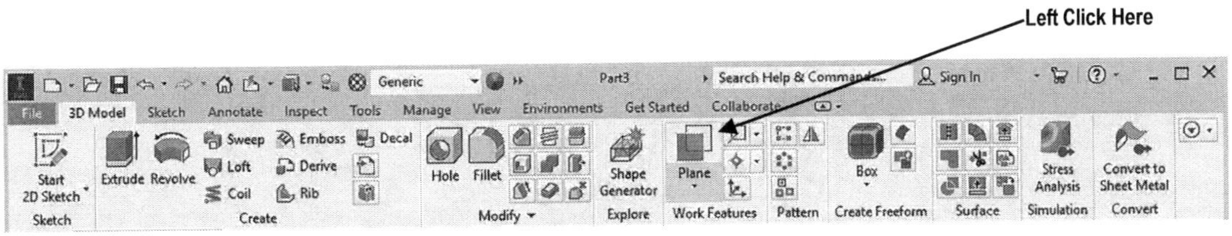

Figure 29

33. Left click on **XY Plane** in the browser. The “XY Plane” text will become highlighted as shown in Figure 30.

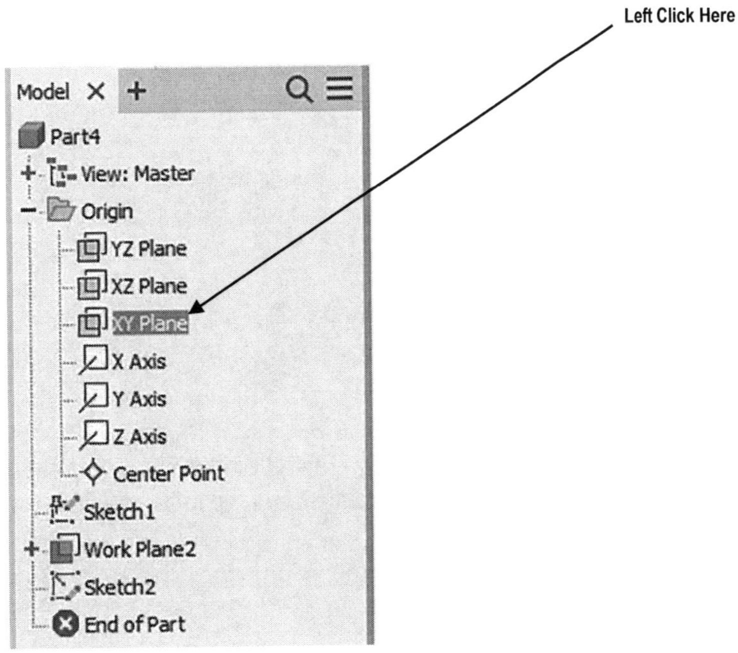

Figure 30

34. Move the cursor to the center of the sketch and left click (holding the left mouse button down) dragging the cursor to the lower left portion of the screen. Enter **1.000** as shown in Figure 31 and press the **Enter** key on the keyboard.

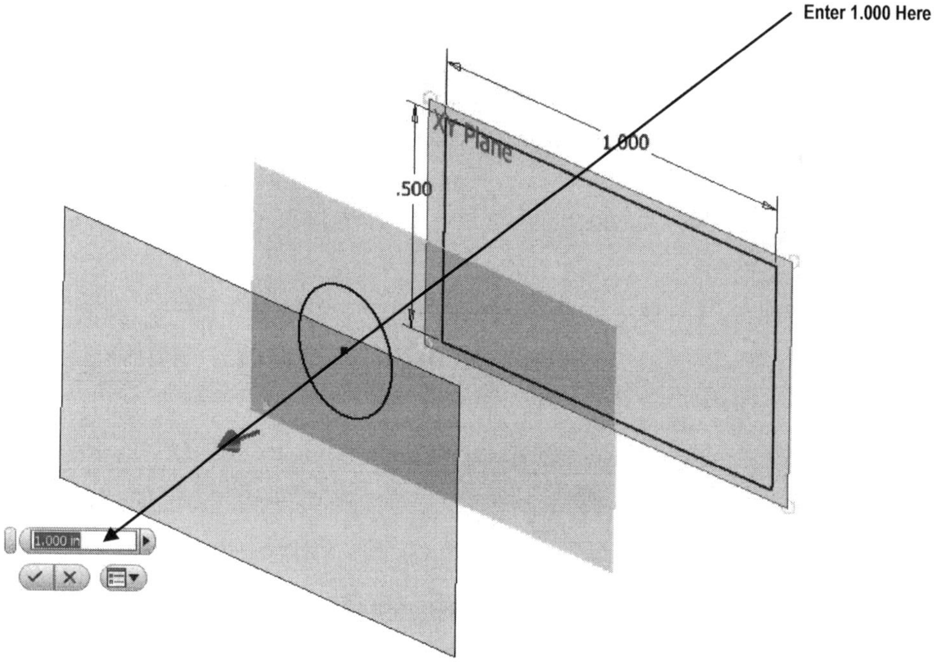

Figure 31

35. Begin a New Sketch on the newly created Workplane. Complete the sketch shown in Figure 32. Estimate the location and size of the rectangle and exit the Sketch Panel.

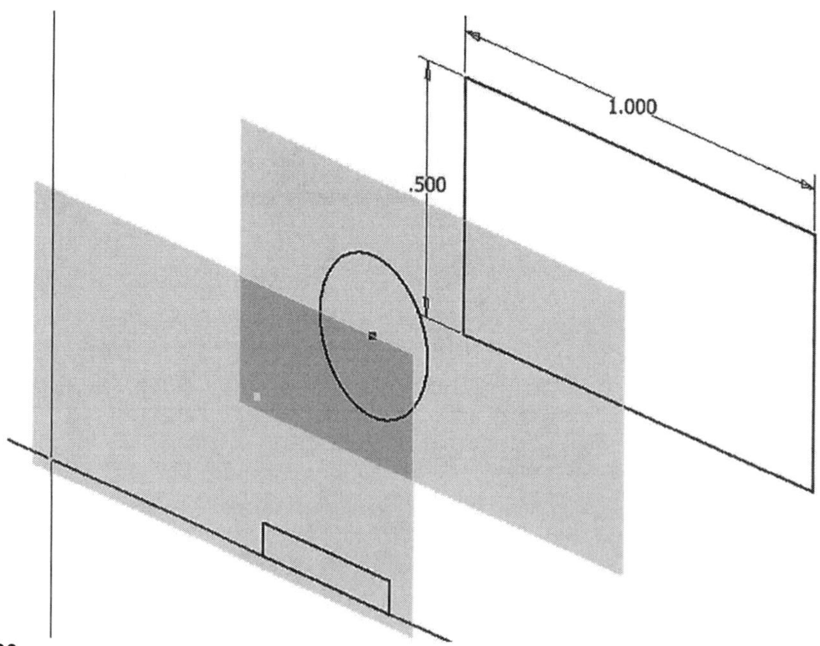

Figure 32

36. Move the cursor to the upper left portion of the screen and left click on the **Loft** icon as shown in Figure 33.

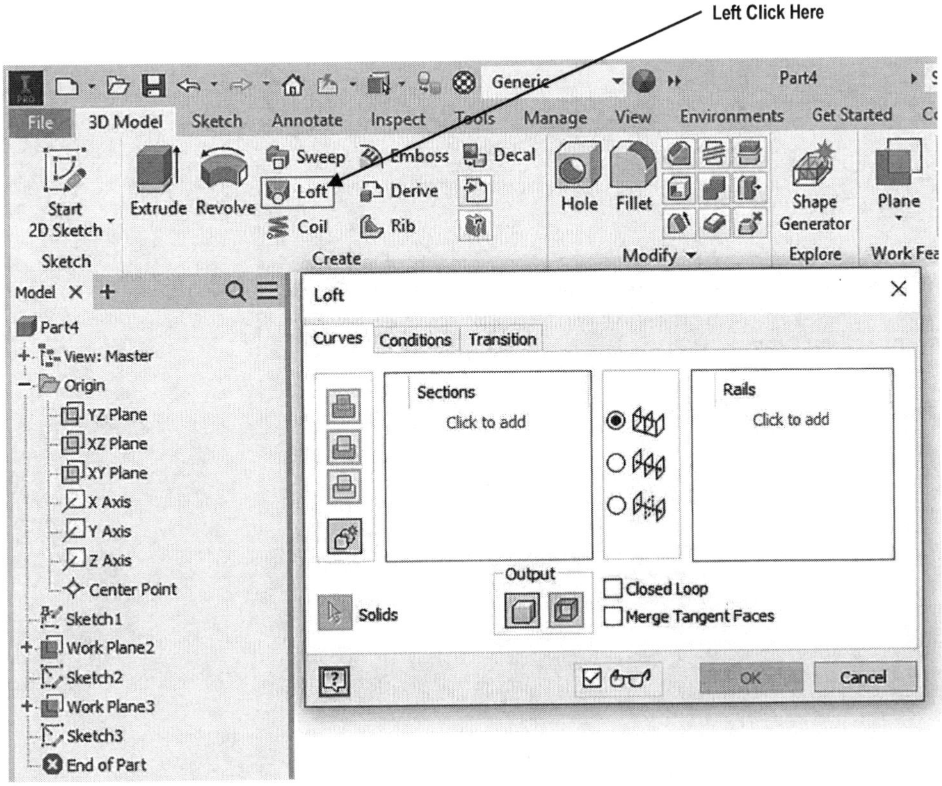

Figure 33

37. The Loft dialog box will appear as shown in Figure 34.

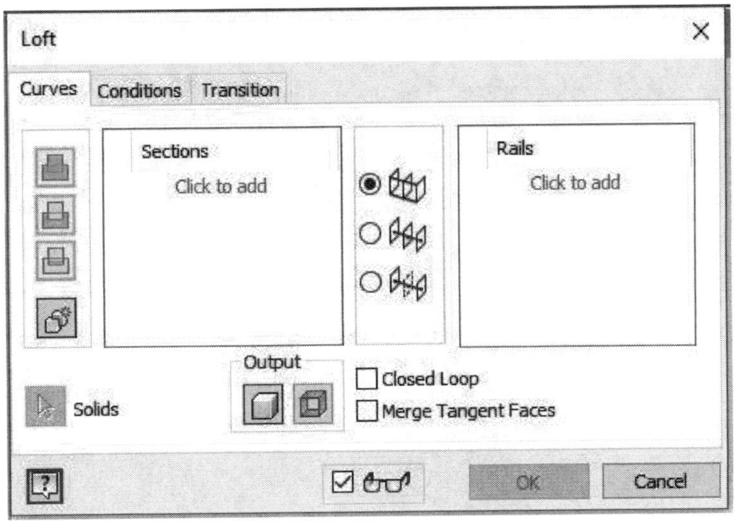

Figure 34

38. Left click on each of the sketches as shown in Figure 35.

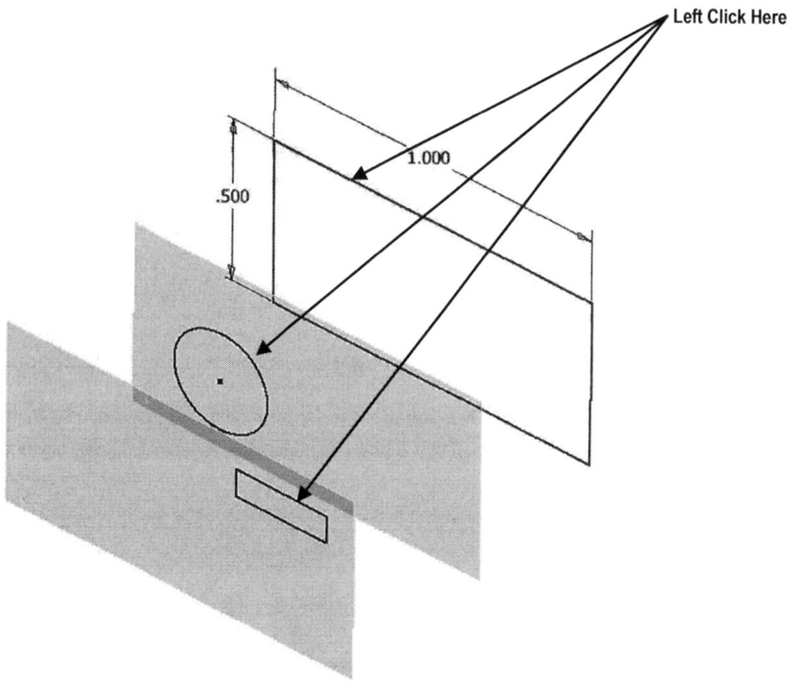

Figure 35

39. Inventor will provide a preview of the loft as shown in Figure 36.

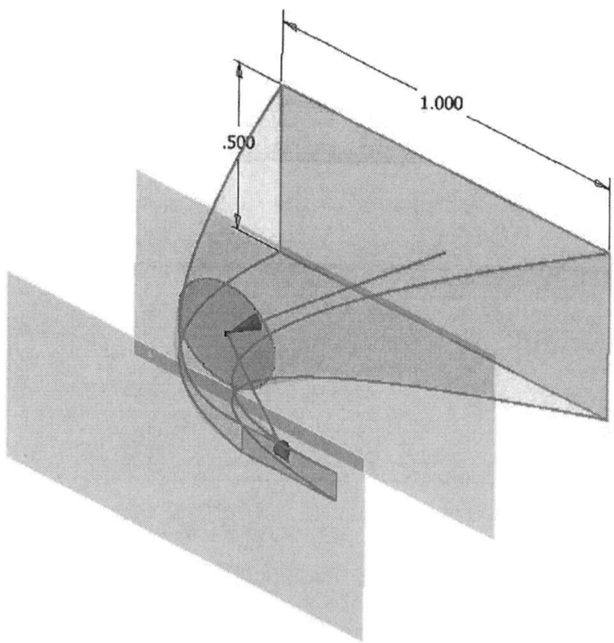

Figure 36

40. Left click on **OK**.

41. Your screen should look similar to Figure 37.

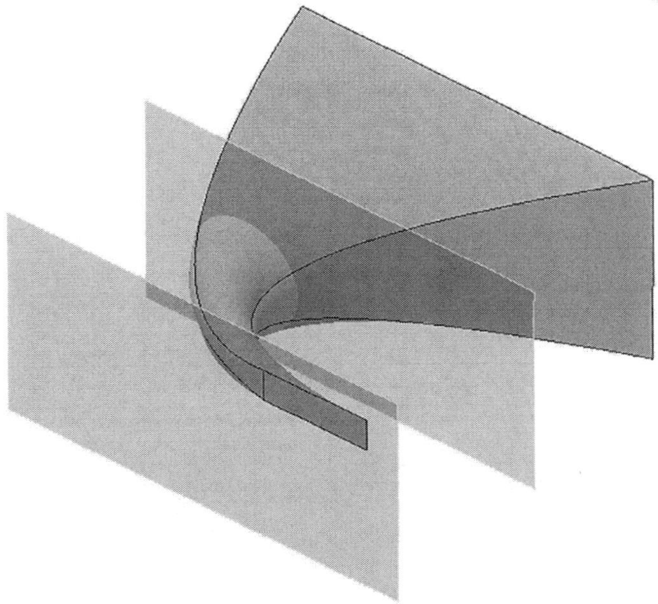

Figure 37

42. To hide the work planes, move the cursor over the edge of the work plane causing the edges to become highlighted red. Right click once. A pop-up menu will appear. Left click on **Visibility**. Hide both work planes as shown in Figure 38.

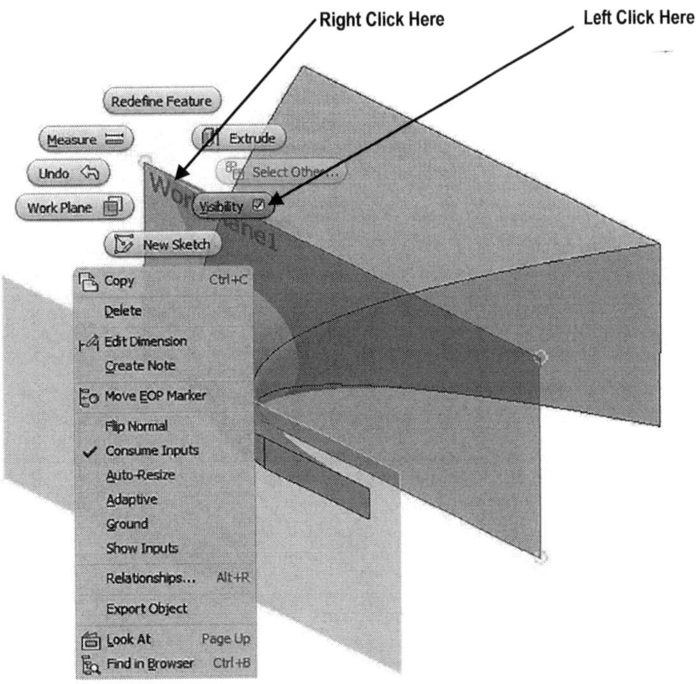

Figure 38

43. Your screen should look similar to Figure 39.

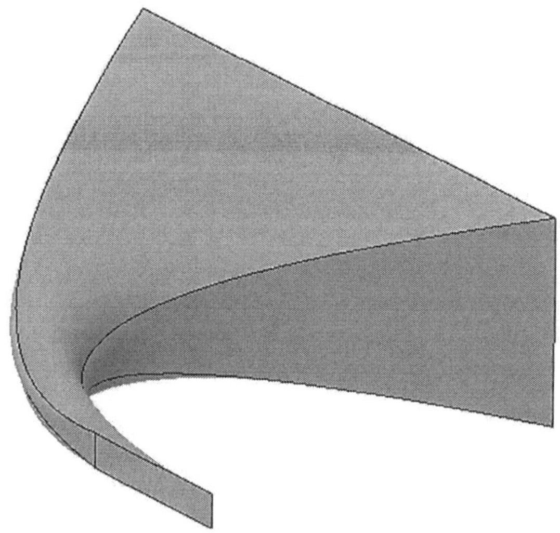

Figure 39

44. If more accuracy is required for each sketch, geometry can be projected from one work plane to another as previously described in Chapter 6. Geometry can also be sized and located using the Dimension command as discussed in previous chapters.

Learn to create a coil using the Coil command

45. Begin a new drawing.

46. Complete the sketch shown in Figure 40 and exit the Sketch Panel.

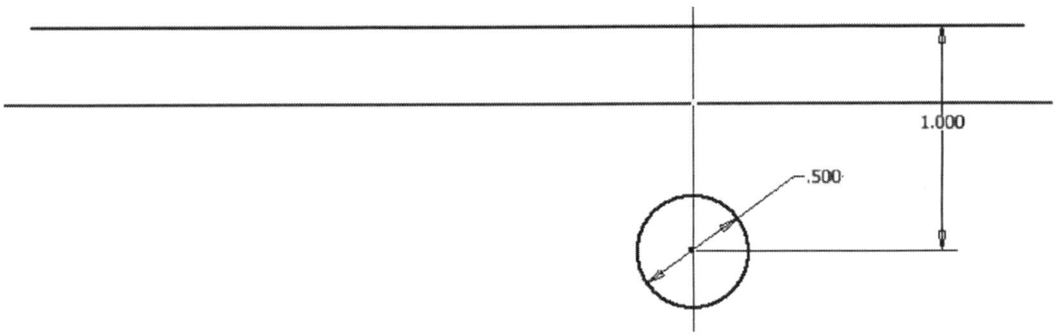

Figure 40

47. Move the cursor to the middle left portion of the screen and left click on the **Coil** icon. Left click on the "Axis" icon. Left click on the horizontal line above the circle as shown in Figure 41.

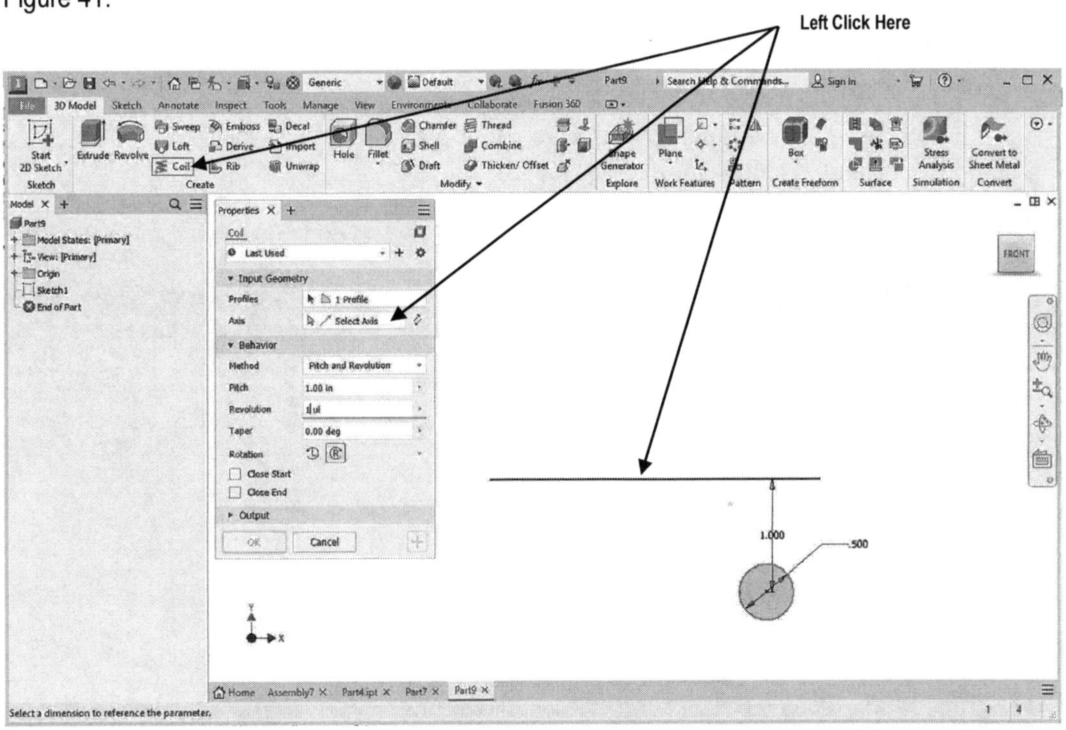

Figure 41

48. Inventor will provide a preview of the coil. Left click on the Axis icon (if needed) to reverse the direction of the coil as shown in Figure 42.

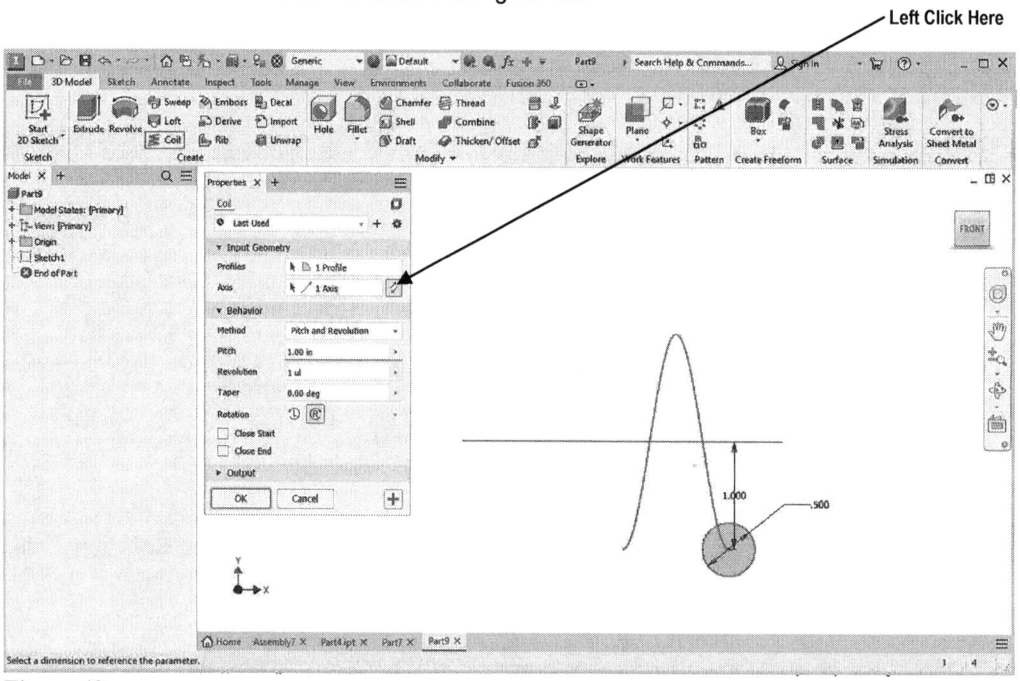

Figure 42

49. Under the Behavior options, Enter **10** for the number of Revolutions. Left click on **OK** as shown in Figure 43.

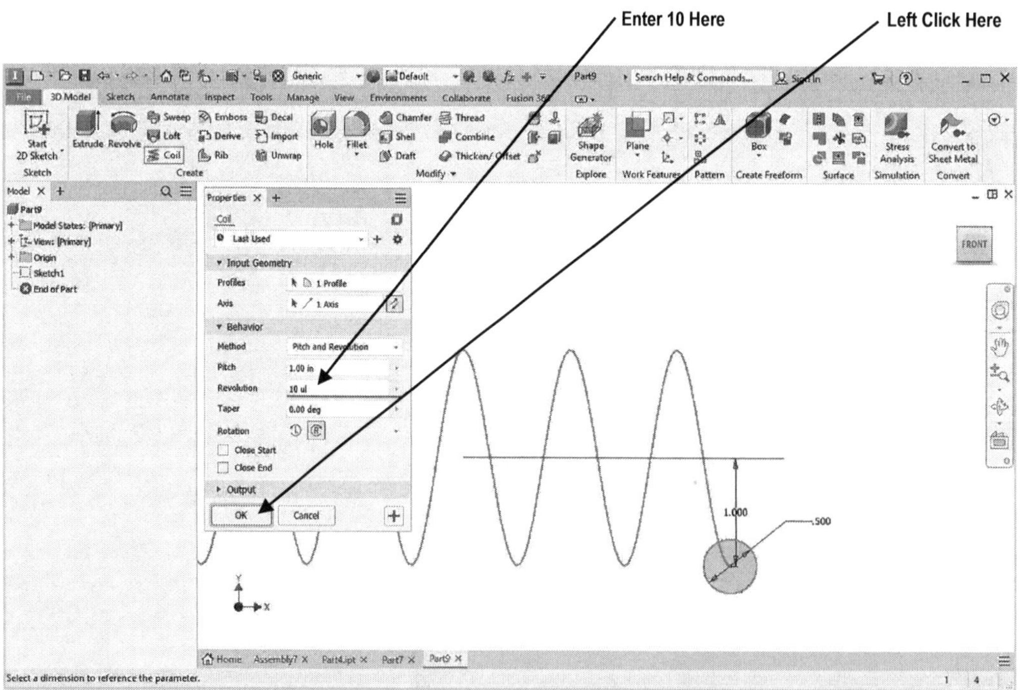

Figure 43

50. Your screen should look similar to Figure 44.

Figure 44

Chapter Problems

Complete the following problem sketches.

Problem 9-1

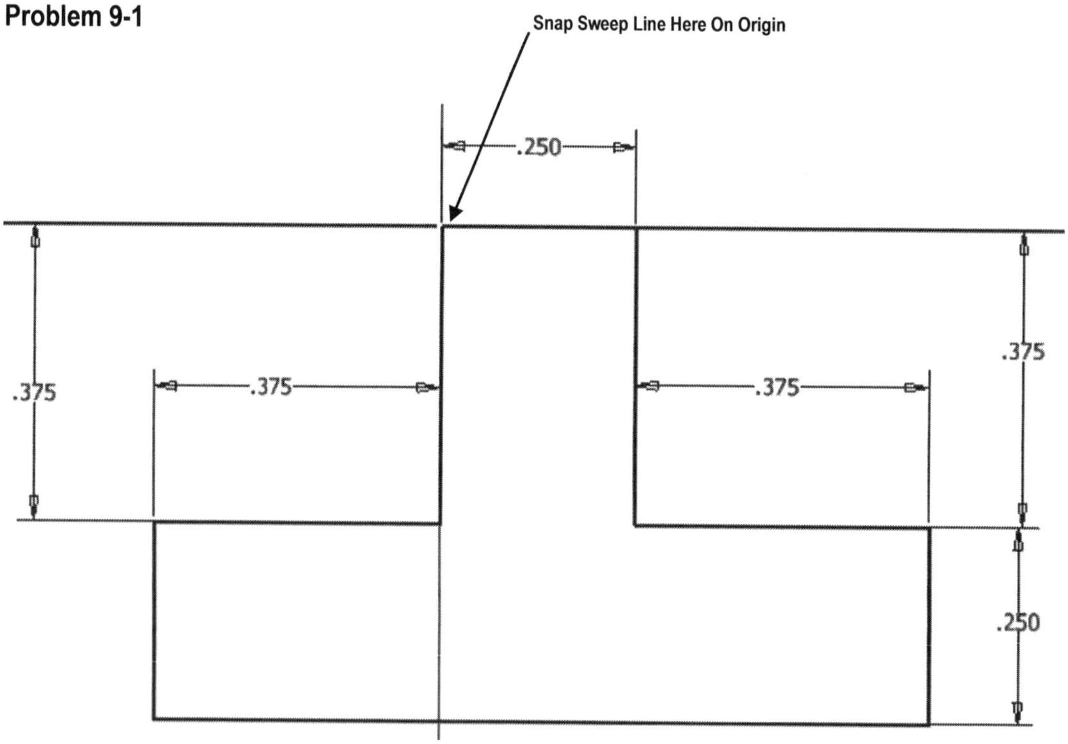

Create the following Sweep line. Sweep the sketch along the sweep line shown below.

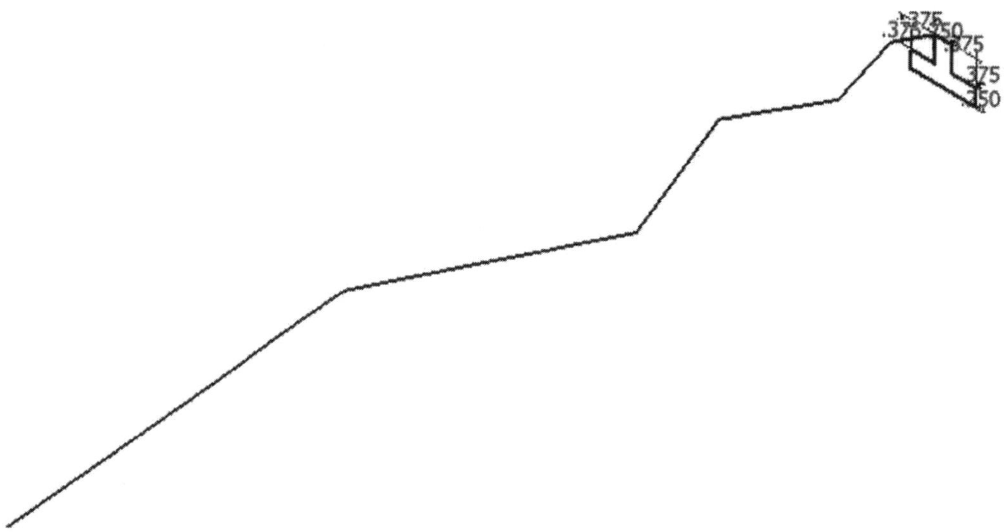

Problem 9-2

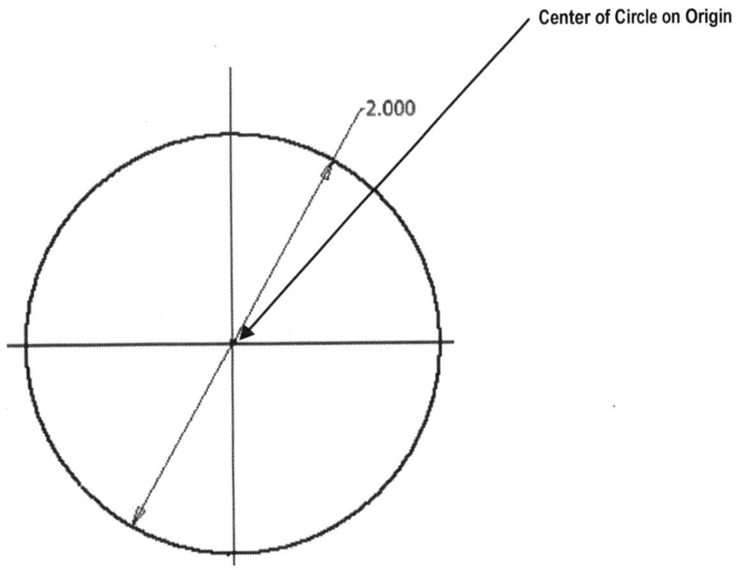

Create the following Sweep line. The center of the circle must intersect the sweep line as shown.

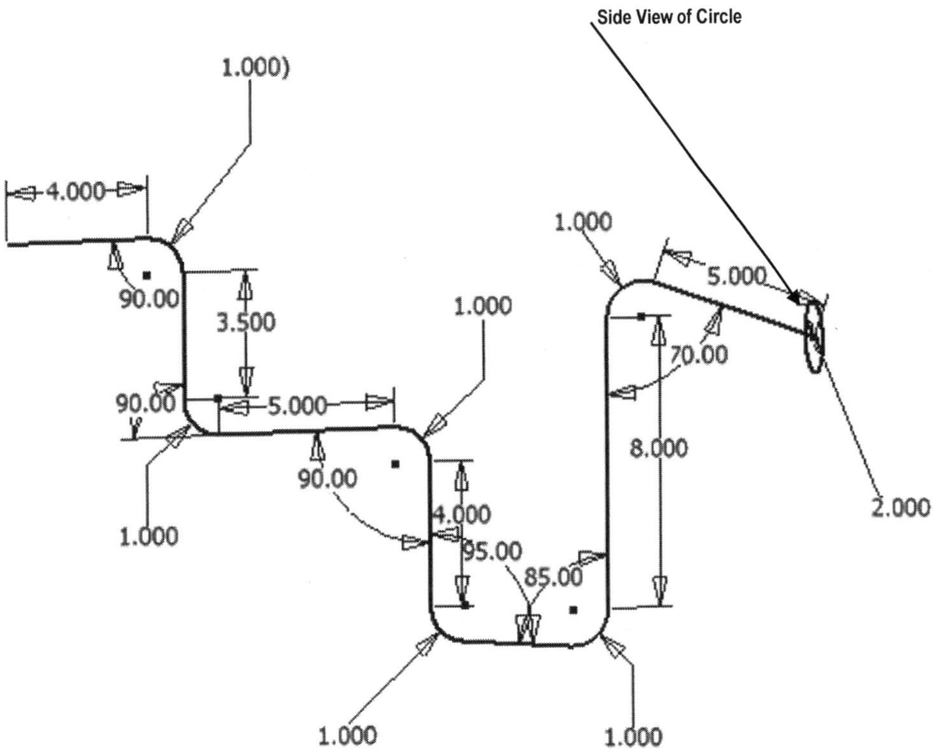

CHAPTER 10

Introduction to Creating Threads

Objectives:

1. Learn to use the Polygon command
2. Learn to create threads in a solid model
3. Learn to interpret threads specs

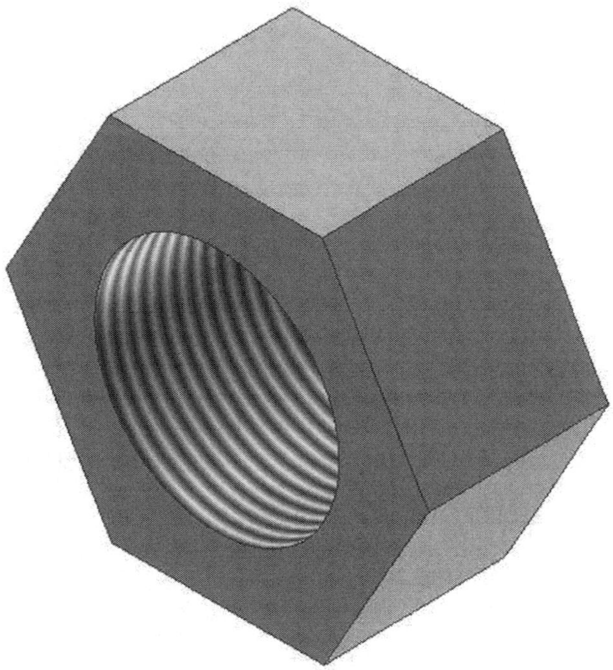

Chapter 10 includes instruction on how to create threads in the part shown.

Learn to create a Polygon

1. Start Inventor by referring to "Chapter 1 Getting Started." After Inventor is running, begin a New Sketch.

2. Move the cursor to the middle left portion of the screen and left click on the drop-down arrow under Rectangle. Left click on **Polygon** as shown in Figure 1.

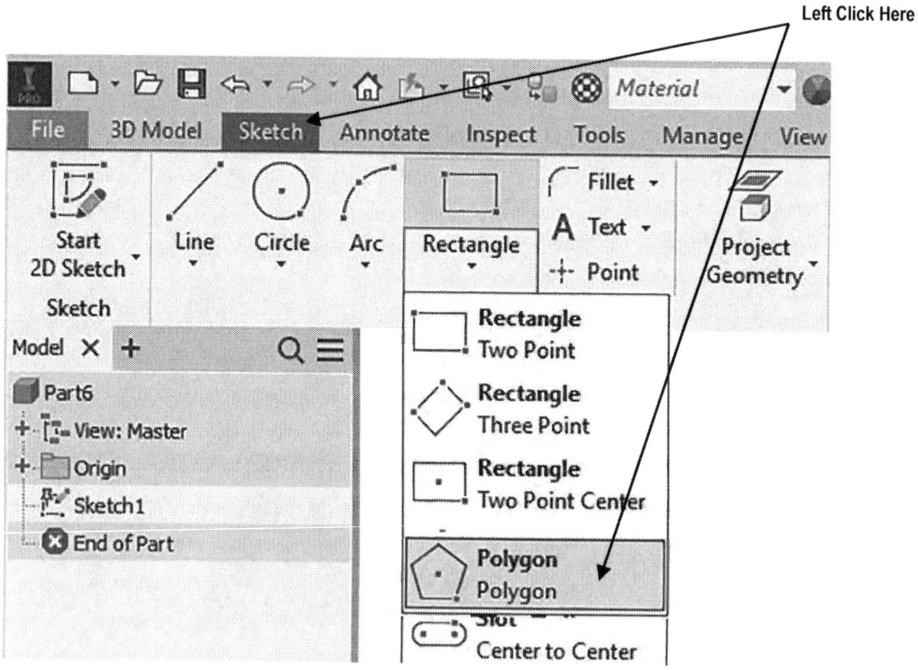

Figure 1

3. The Polygon dialog box will appear. Left click on the **Circumscribed** icon. This will be used to define the distance across the flats (basically what size wrench or socket would be required to loosen or tighten the nut). Enter **6** for the number of sides as shown in Figure 2.

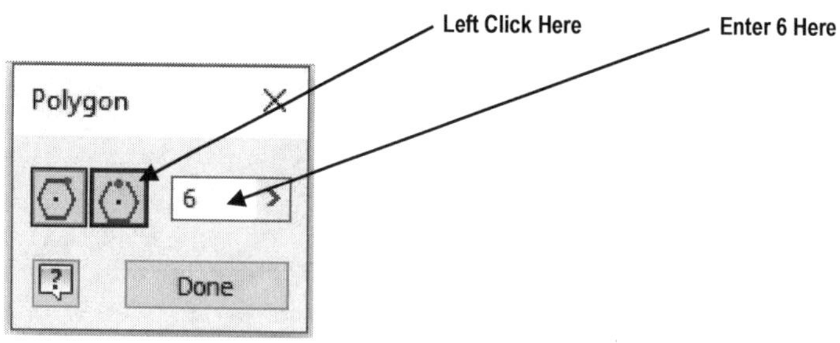

Figure 2

4. Left click on the origin and drag the cursor out to the side similar to creating a circle as shown in Figure 3.

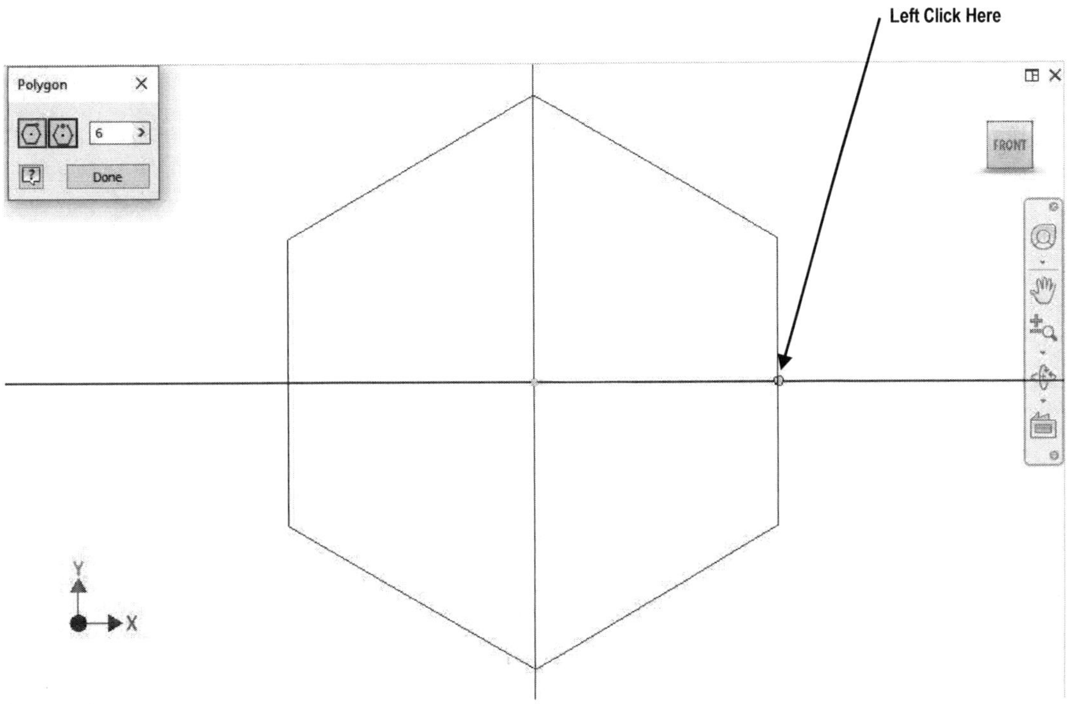

Figure 3

5. Left click on **Done** as shown in Figure 4.

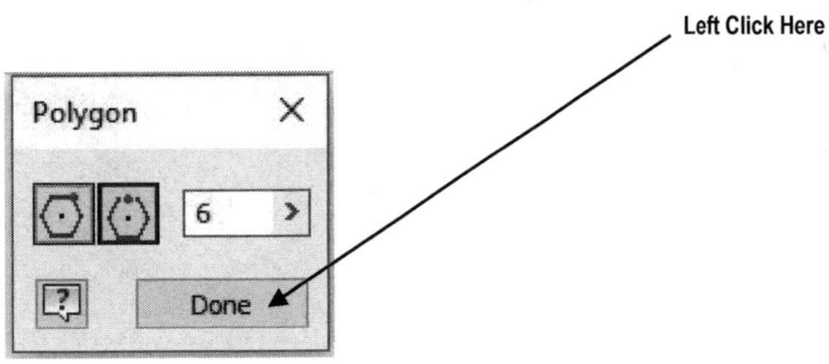

Figure 4

6. Complete and dimension the sketch as shown in Figure 5.

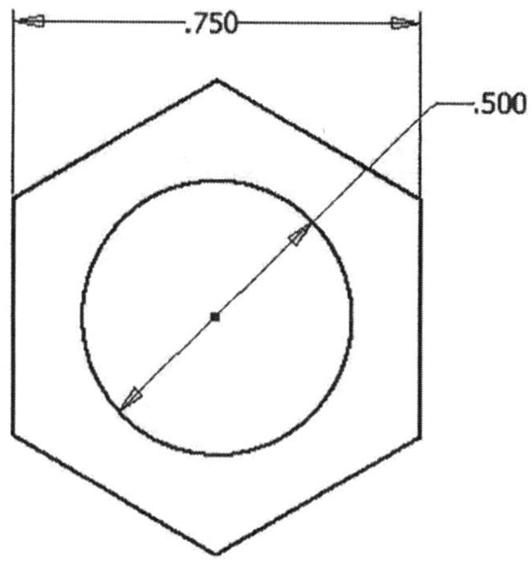

Figure 5

7. Exit out of the Sketch Panel as shown in Figure 6.

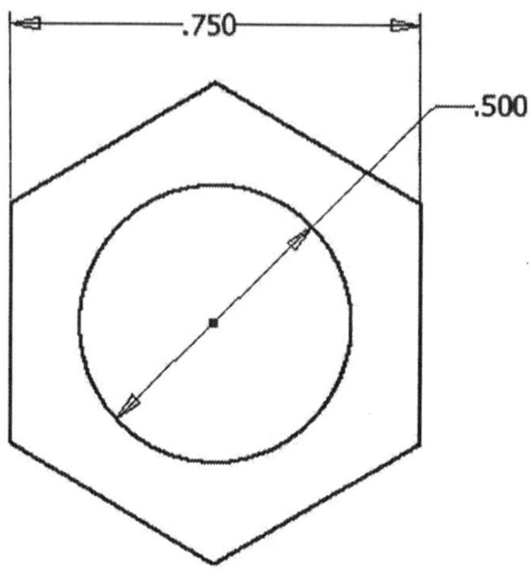

Figure 6

8. Rotate the part around to gain an isometric view of the part as shown in Figure 7.

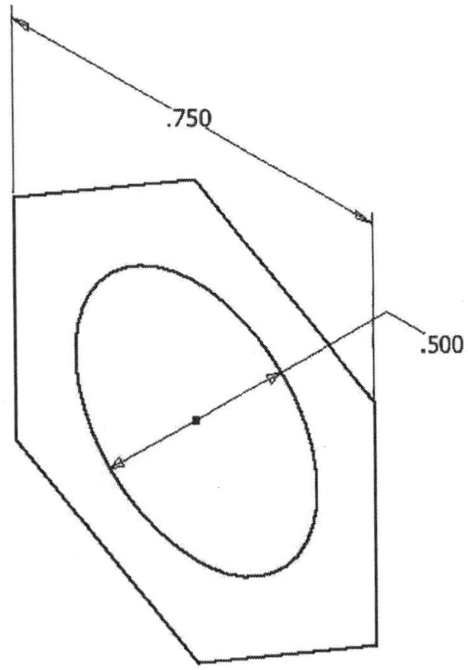

Figure 7

9. Extrude the part a distance of **.375** inches as shown in Figure 8.

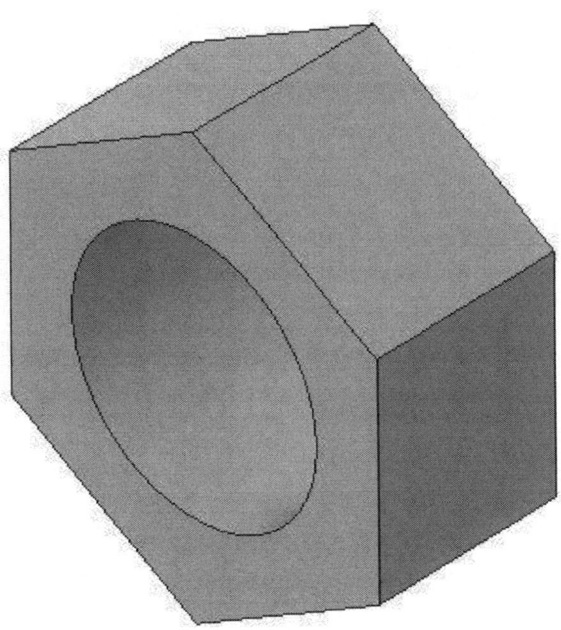

Figure 8

Learn to create Threads

10. Move the cursor to the upper middle portion of the screen and left click **Thread**. The Thread dialog box will appear as shown in Figure 9.

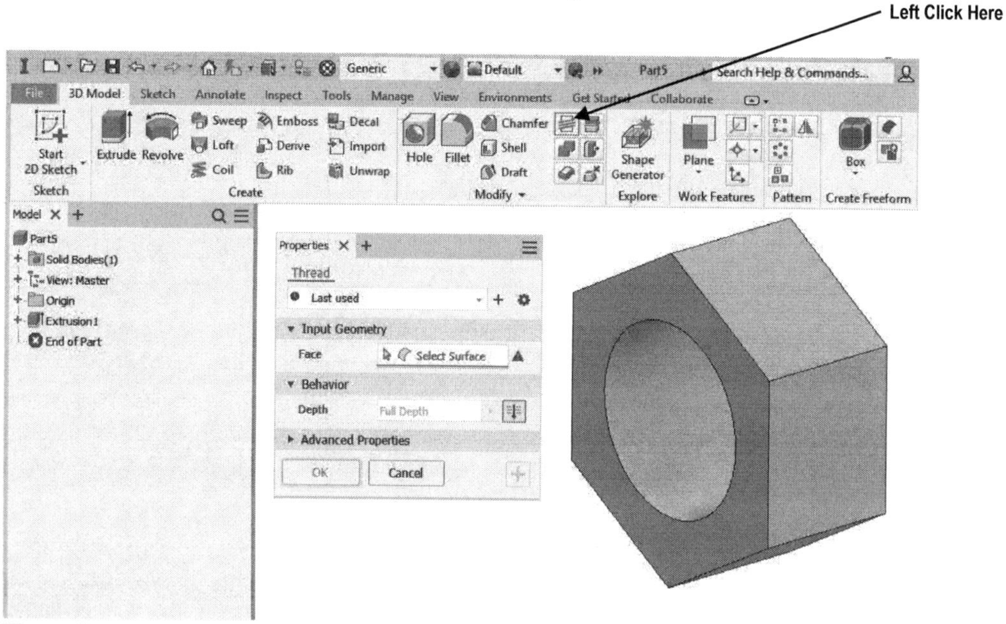

Figure 9

11. The default is right handed threads (threads that turn clockwise to tighten). Move the cursor inside the hole and left click once as shown in Figure 10.

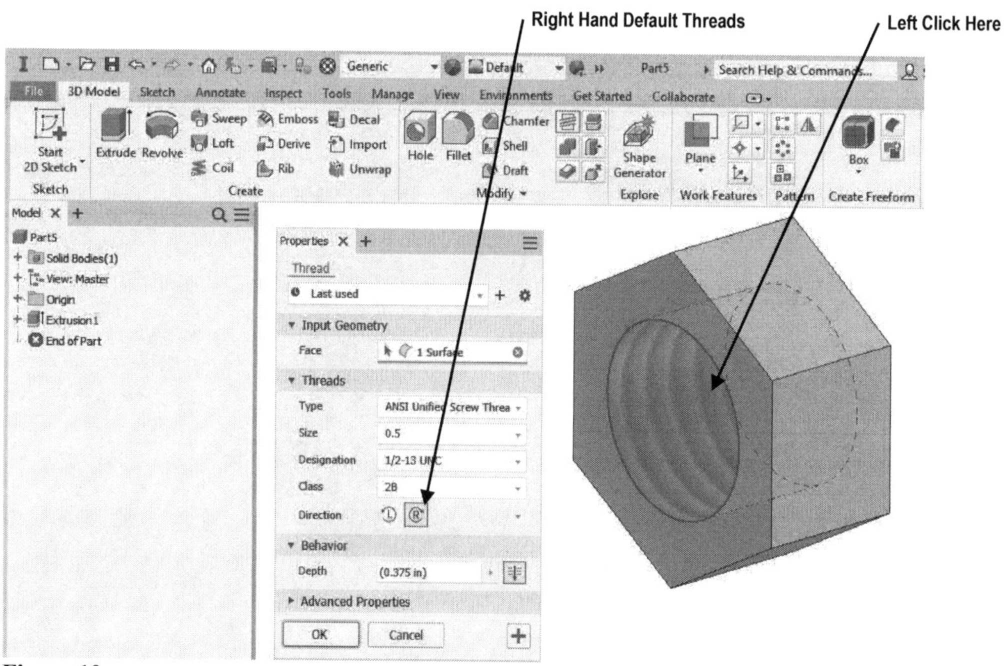

Figure 10

12. Left click on the drop-down arrow to the right of Designation. A drop-down menu will appear. A list of compatible threads will appear. The first number refers to the diameter of the thread (bolt or hole). The second number refers to the pitch (in this case, the number of threads per inch). The letters indicate what type of thread and whether the threads are coarse or fine (UNC means Coarse and UNF means Fine) as shown in Figure 11.

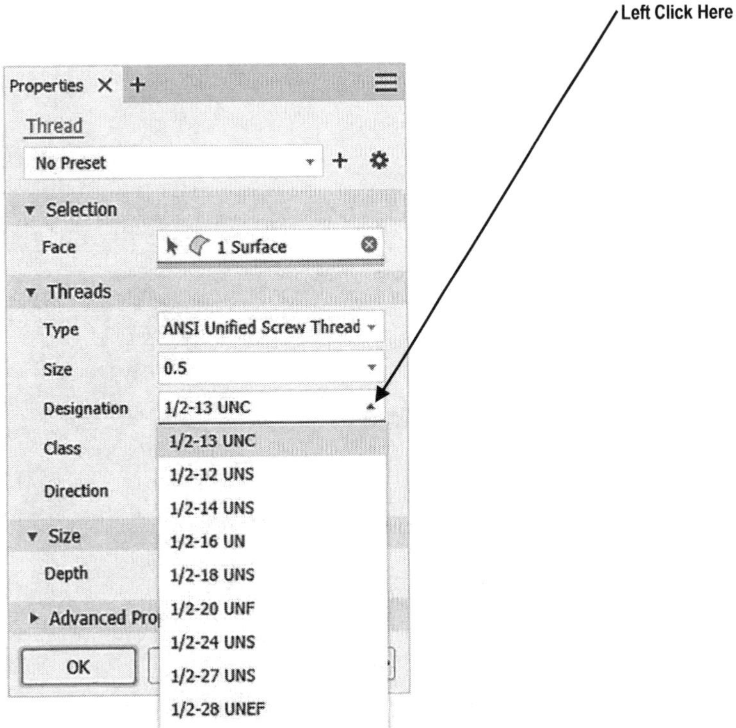

Figure 11

13. Left click on **1/2 - 20 UNF**. Inventor will provide a preview of the different thread types selected as shown in Figure 12.

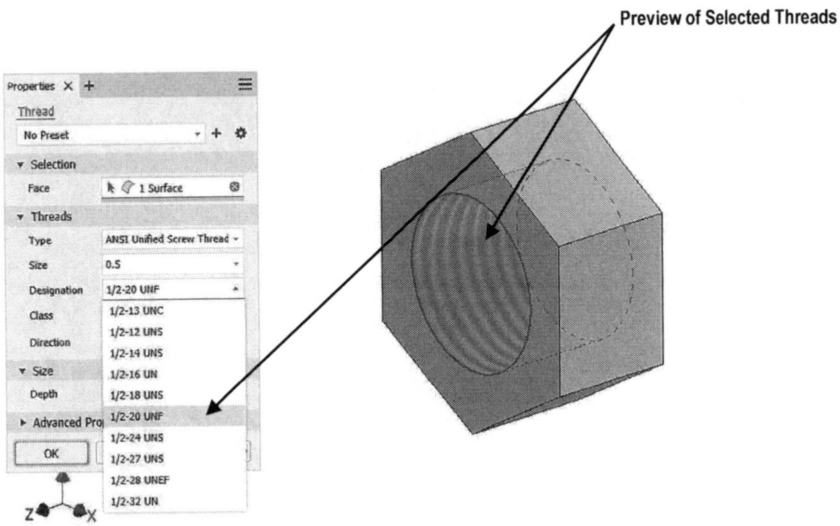

Figure 12

14. Left click on **OK** as shown in Figure 13.

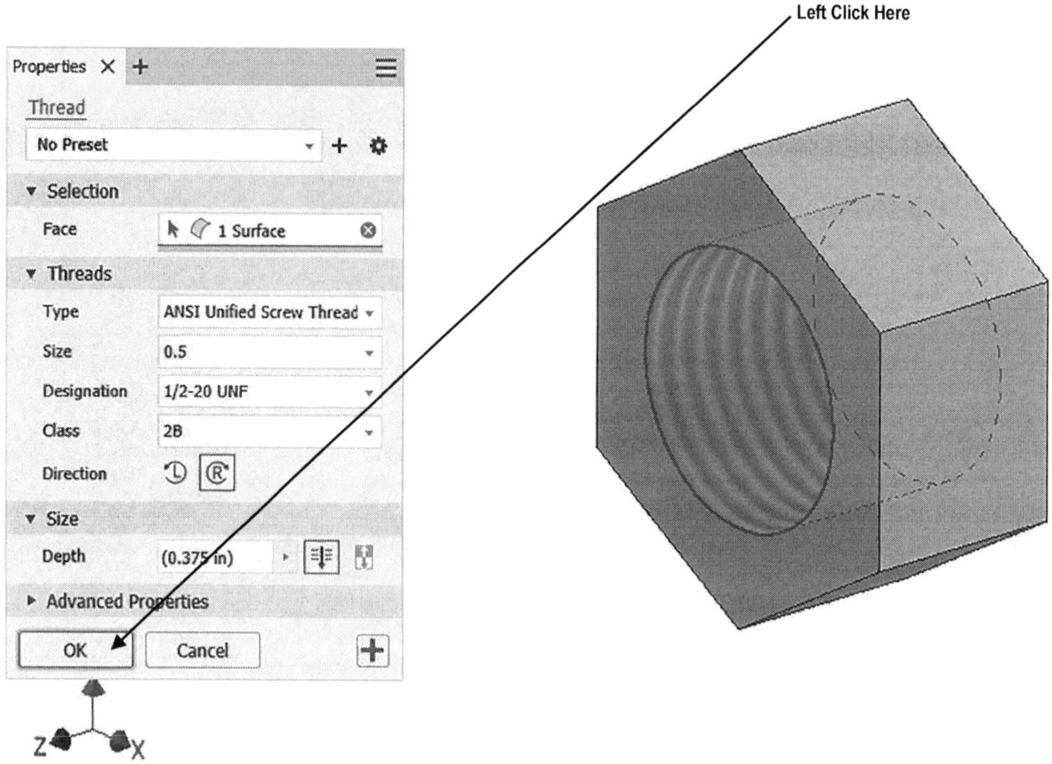

Figure 13

15. Your screen should look similar to Figure 14.

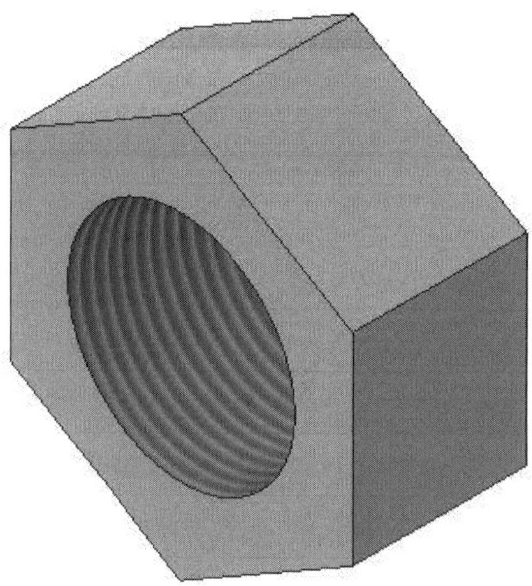

Figure 14

CHAPTER 11

Advanced Work Plane Procedures

Objectives:

1. Learn to create points on a solid model
2. Learn to use the Split command
3. Learn to create an offset/oblique Work Plane

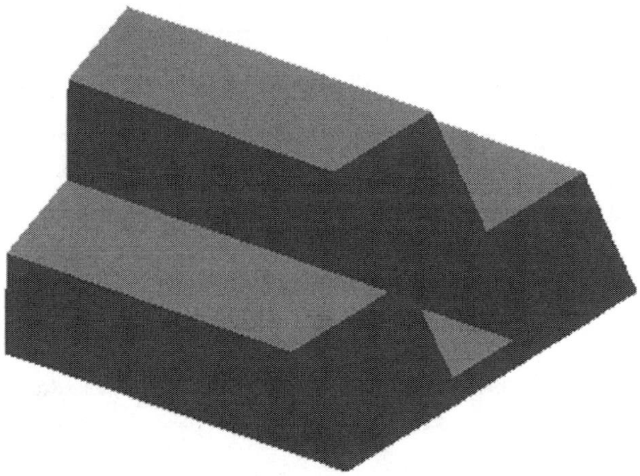

Chapter 11 includes instruction on how to design the part shown.

1. Start Inventor by referring to "Chapter 1 Getting Started." After Inventor is running, begin a New Sketch.

2. Complete the sketch shown in Figure 1.

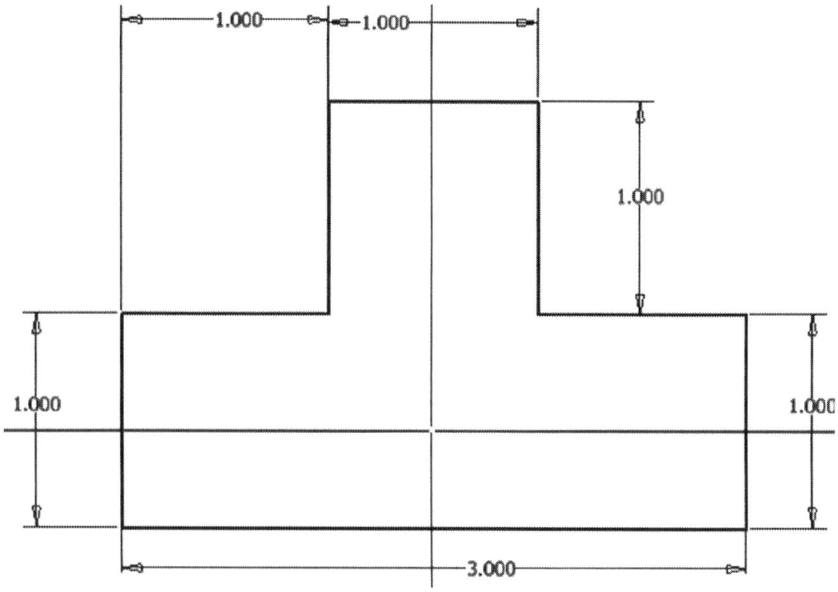

Figure 1

3. Exit the Sketch Panel. Extrude the sketch to a thickness of **4.00** inches as shown in Figure 2.

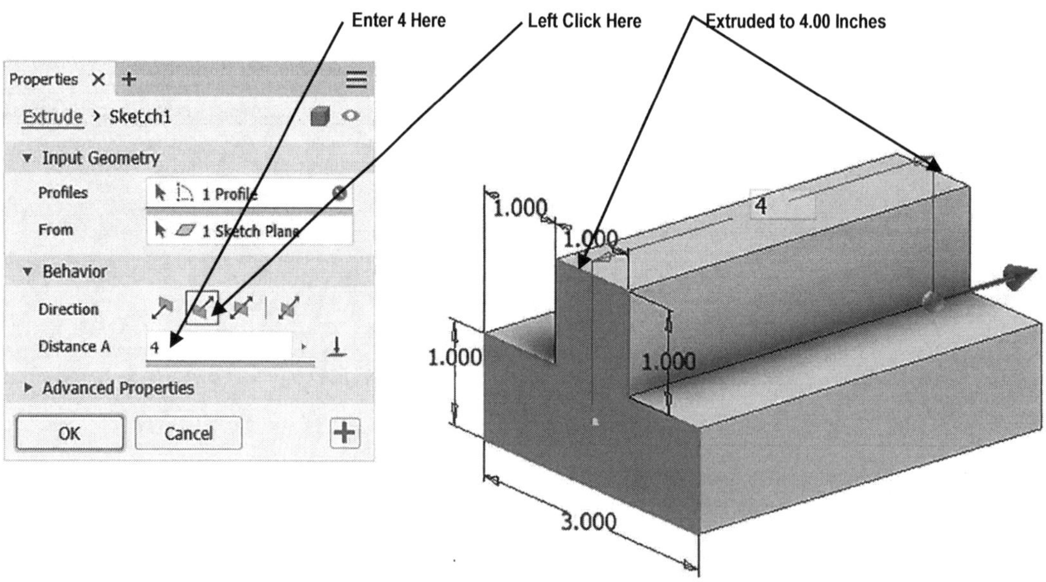

Figure 2

4. Your screen should look similar to Figure 3.

Figure 3

5. Use the **Rotate** command to rotate the part to gain a perpendicular view of the front surface as shown in Figure 4.

Figure 4

6. Use the **Rectangle** command to complete the sketch as shown in Figure 5. All dimensions are .188.

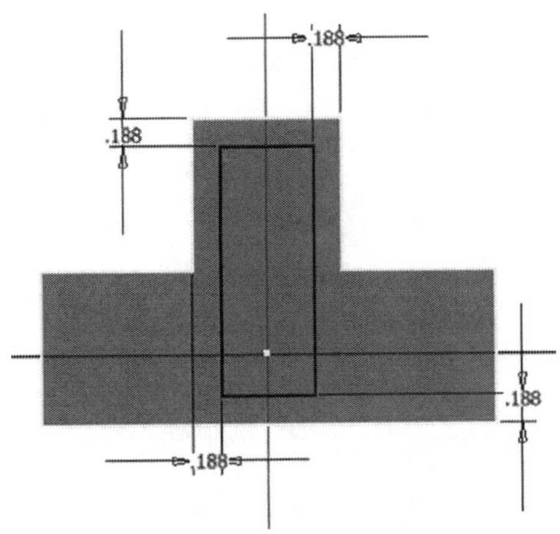

Figure 5

7. Extrude (cut) the rectangle a distance of **4.00** inches creating a square hole as shown in Figure 6.

Figure 6

8. Rotate the part around to gain an isometric (Home View) of the part as shown in Figure 7.

Figure 7

9. Rotate the part around to gain an isometric view of the left side of the part as shown in Figure 8.

Figure 8

10. Begin a **New Sketch** on the front surface of the part as shown in Figure 9.

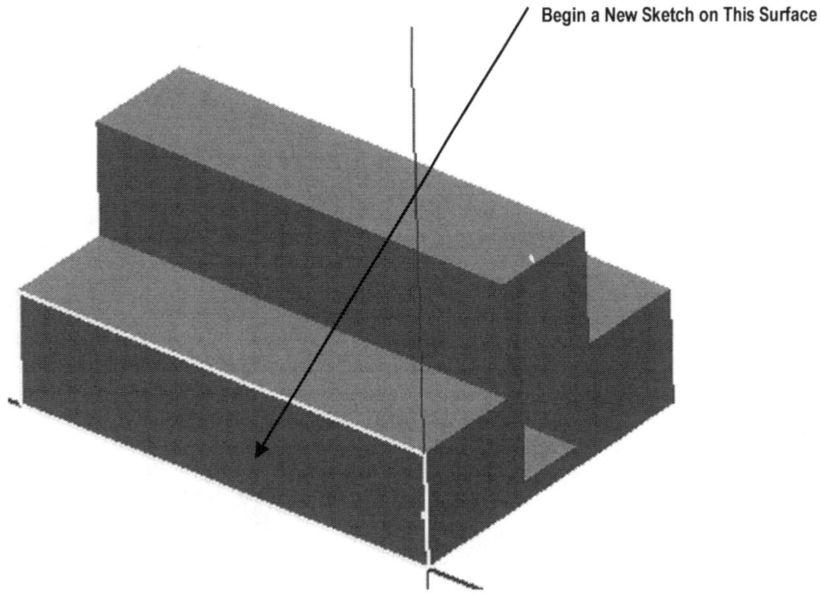

Figure 9

Learn to create points on multiple sketches

11. Create 2 Points on the side of the part as shown in Figure 10.

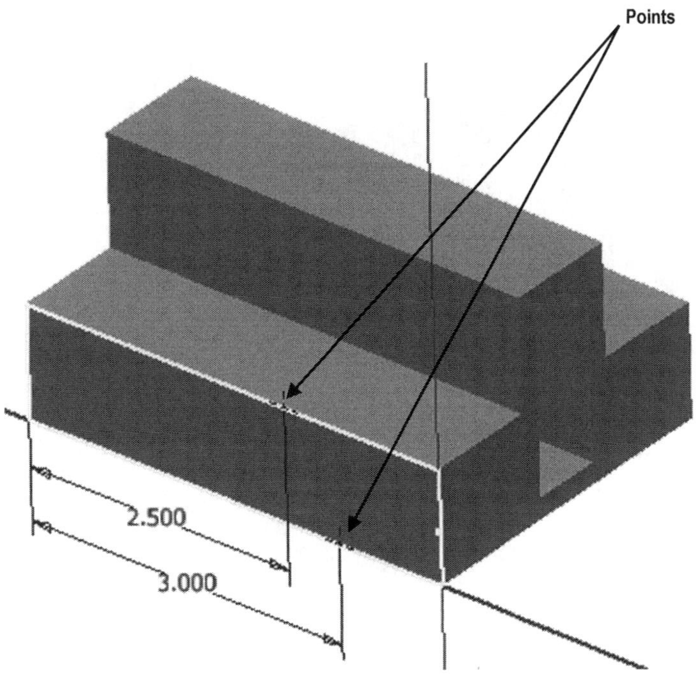

Figure 10

12. Exit out of the Sketch. Right click on **Sketch3** in the browser. A pop-up menu will appear. Left click on **Visibility** in order to see the points as shown in Figure 11.

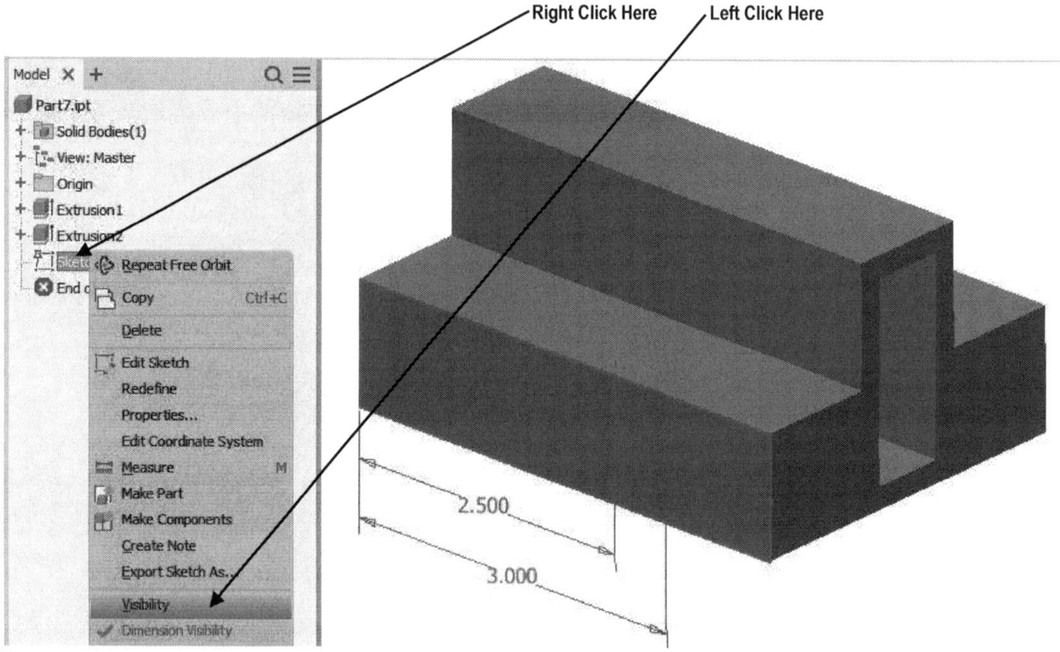

Figure 11

13. Rotate the part upward as shown in Figure 12.

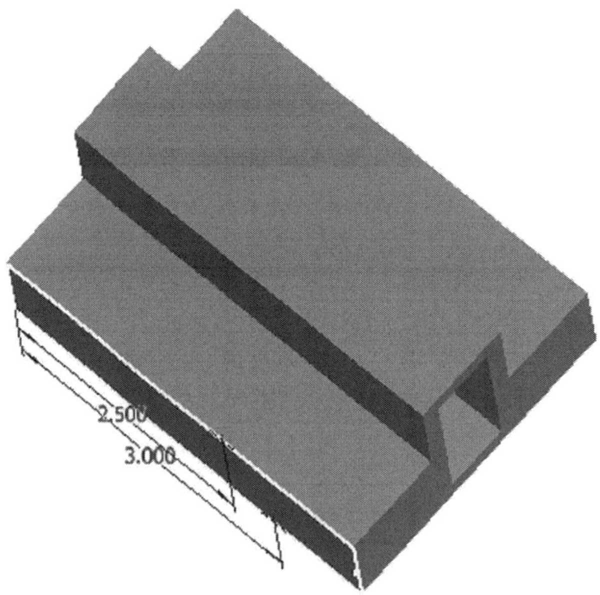

Figure 12

14. Begin a **New Sketch** on the surface shown in Figure 13.

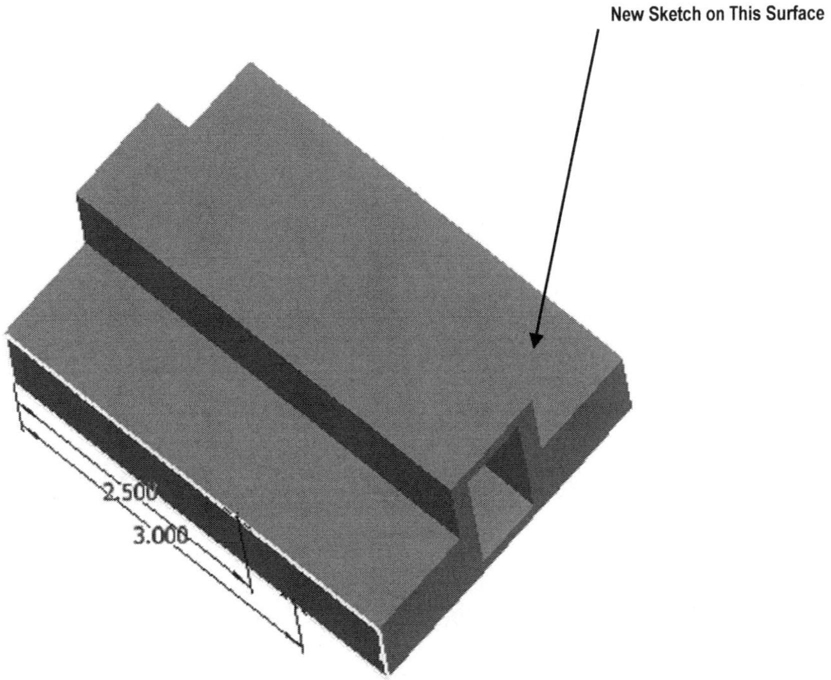

Figure 13

15. Create a **Point** on the surface as shown in Figure 14.

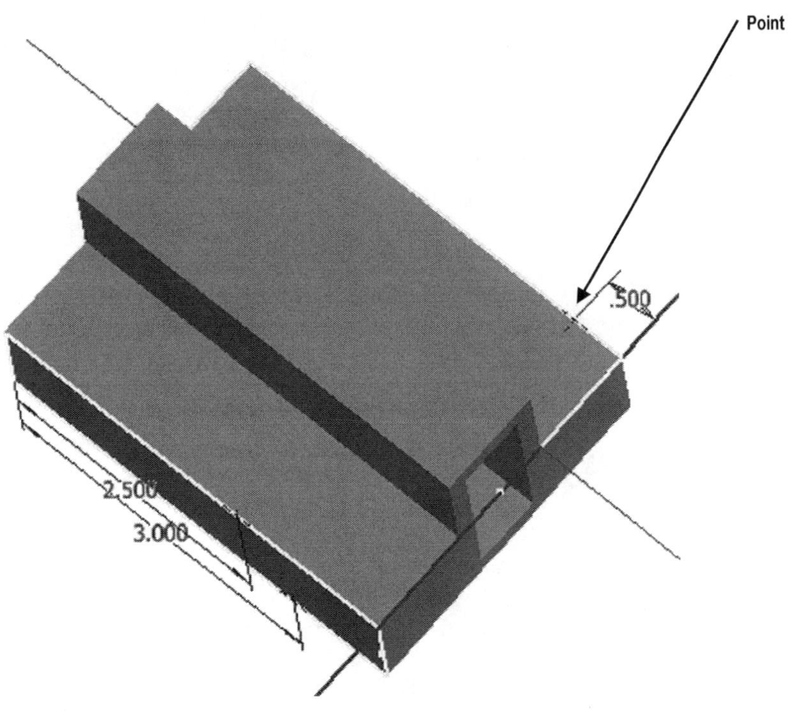

Figure 14

16. Exit the Sketch. If the Sketch is not visible use the instruction found in Step 12 to make it visible as shown in Figure 15.

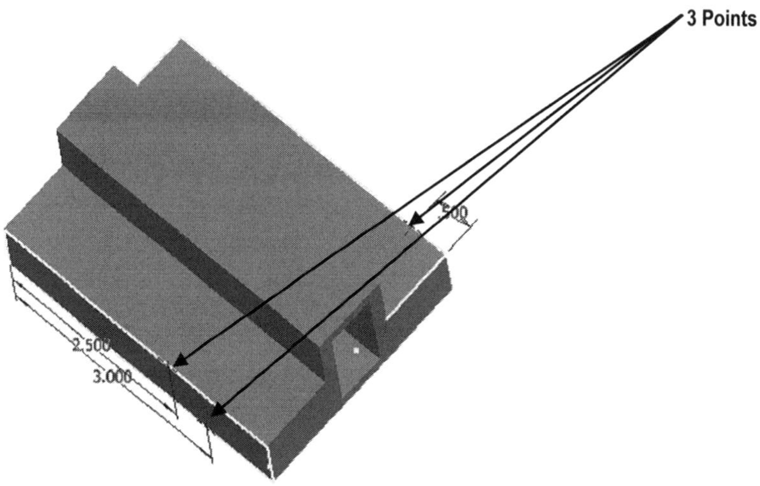

Figure 15

Learn to use these points to create an offset work plane

17. Move the cursor to the upper middle portion of the screen and left click on **Plane** as shown in Figure 16.

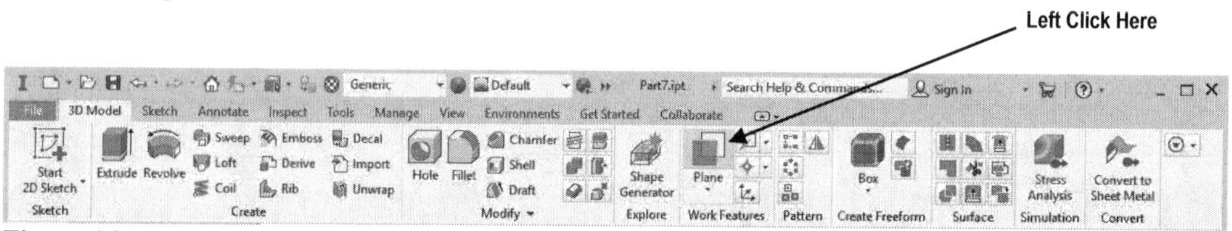

Figure 16

18. Left click on each of the 3 points as shown in Figure 17.

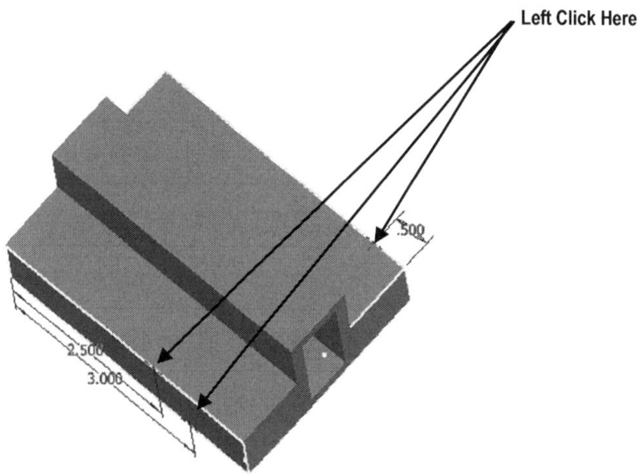

Figure 17

19. Inventor will create a Work Plane from the 3 points as shown in Figure 18.

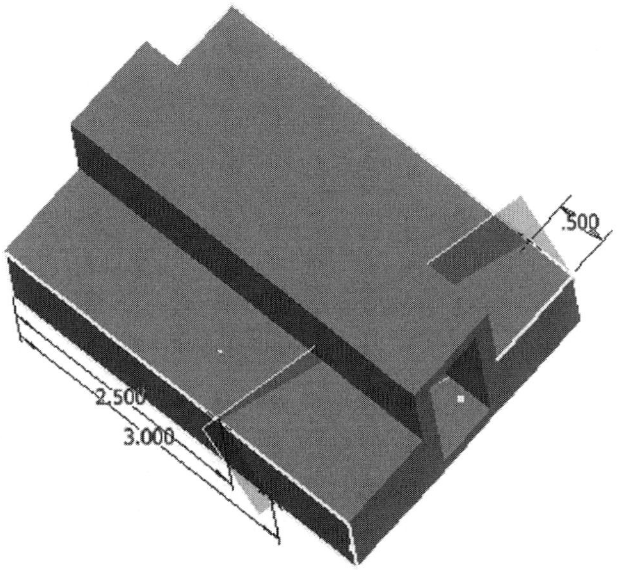

Figure 18

20. Move the cursor to the upper middle portion of the screen and left click on the **Split** icon as shown in Figure 19. The Split command is used to remove part of a Model from either side of a work plane.

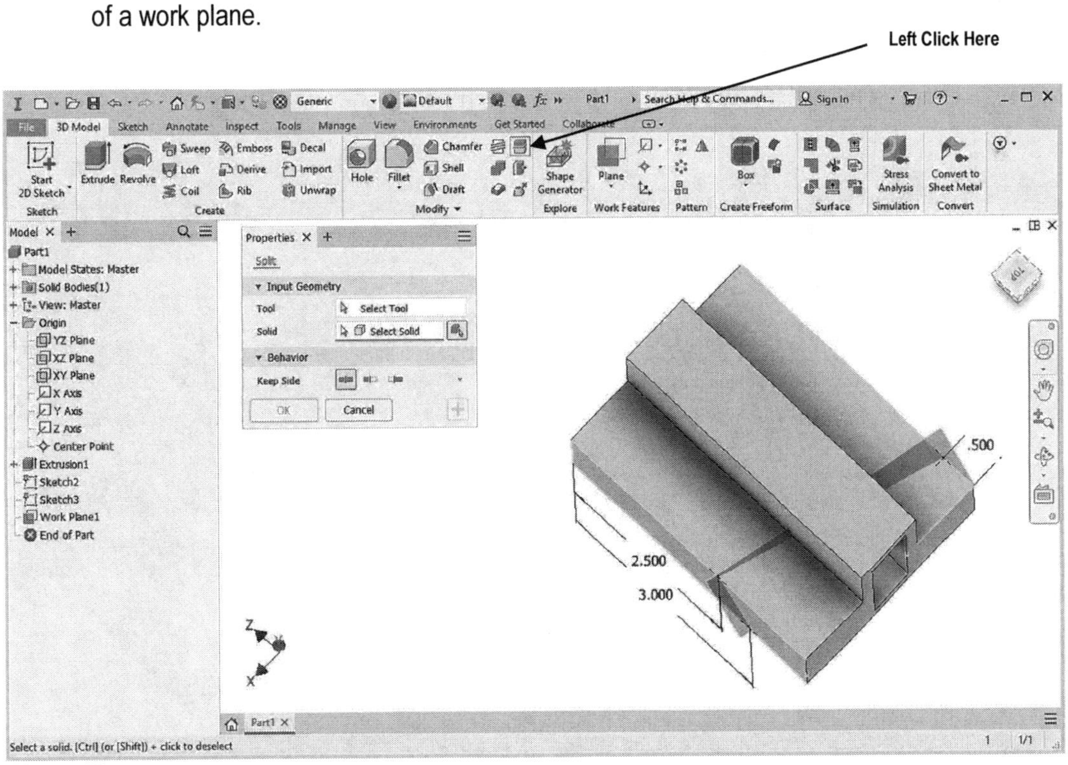

Figure 19

21. Left click to the right of Select Tool. Move the cursor over the edge of the newly created plane causing it to turn red and left click as shown in Figure 20.

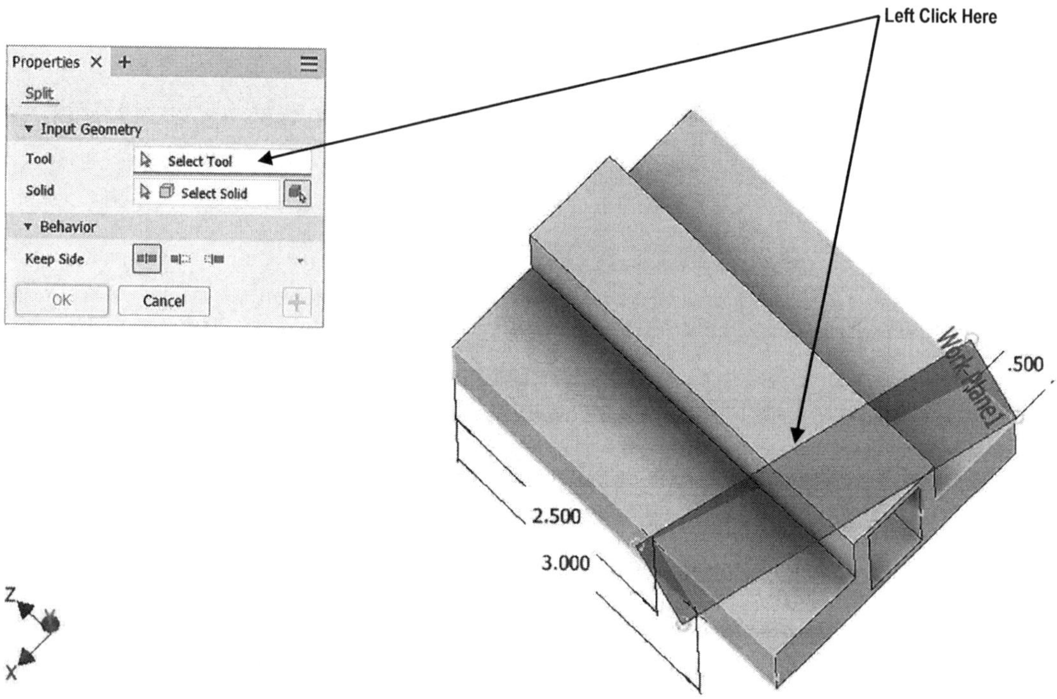

Figure 20

22. Left click on the right side face, causing it to turn red as shown in Figure 21.

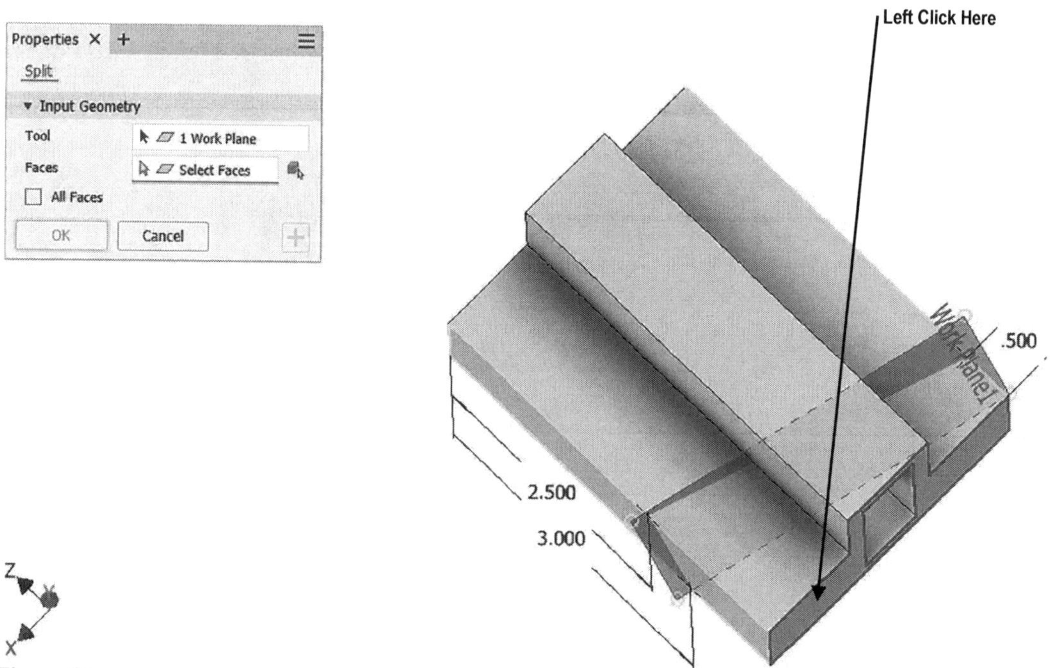

Figure 21

23. Left click on the Solid Section icon (green cube with box around it indicates that it is On). Left click on the drop-down arrow to the left of Behavior. The first type of Split, splits the model in half. Left click on Keep Opposite Side icon. Left click on **OK** as shown in Figure 22.

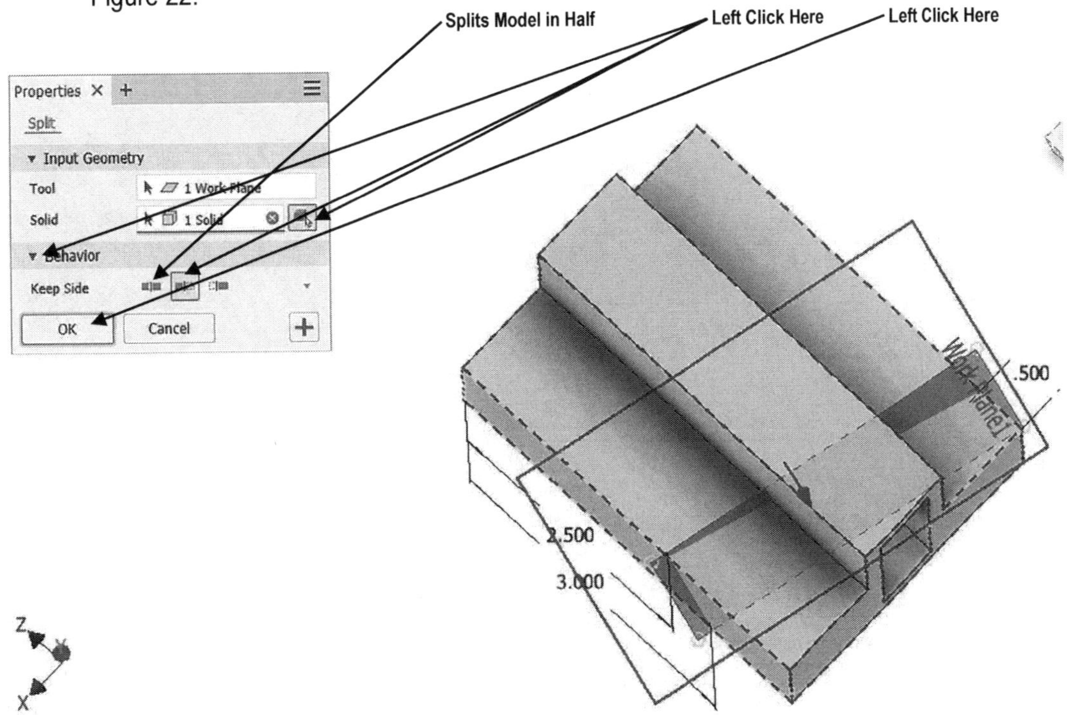

Figure 22

24. Your screen should look similar to Figure 23.

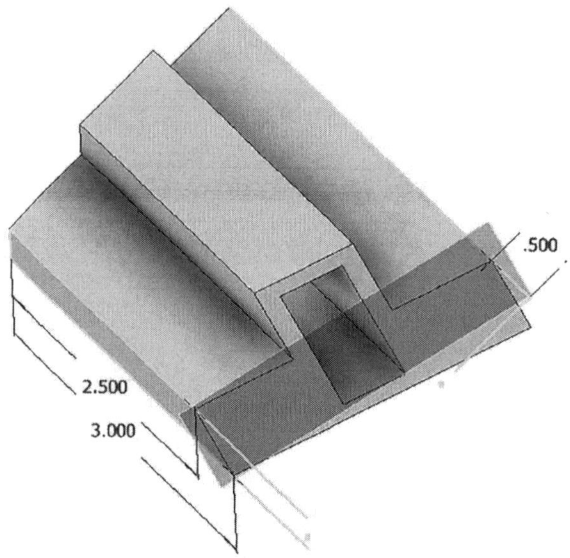

Figure 23

25. To clean up the appearance of the part, move the cursor to the left portion of the screen and left click, then right click on each of the Sketches and the Work Plane, and turn off the **Visibility** on each item as shown in Figure 24.

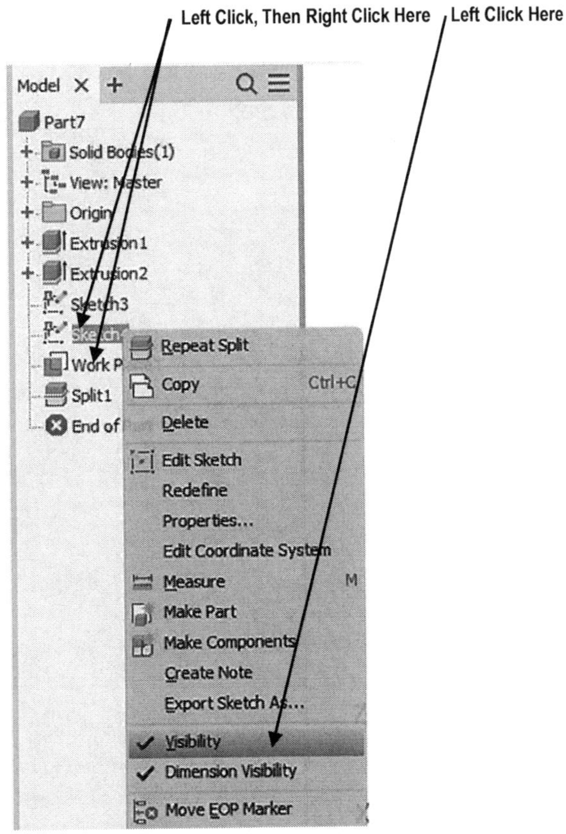

Figure 24

26. Your screen should look similar to Figure 25.

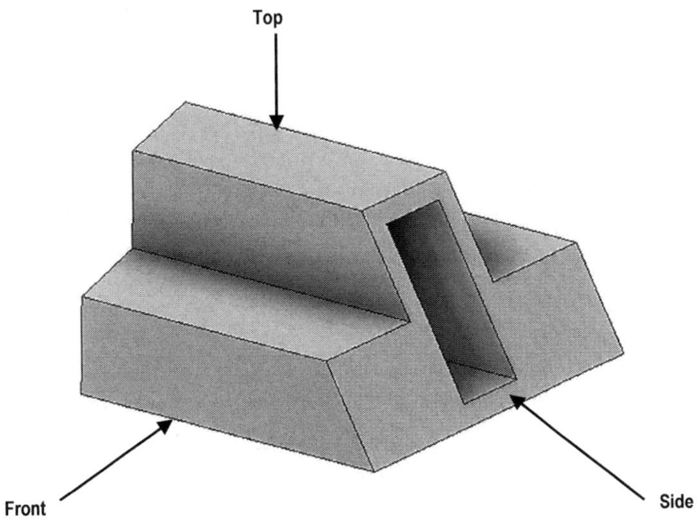

Figure 25

Chapter Problems

To test your Orthographic skills, create a 3 view Orthographic drawing of the part shown above (Top, Front and Right Hand side views) in either a 2 Dimensional CAD package (such as AutoCAD) or by hand on a Drafting board. Show all hidden lines in your 2D drawing. Once you have completed your 2 Dimensional drawing, refer to Chapter 3 on how to create a 3 View drawing using Inventor (showing all hidden lines), and then compare your “hand drawing” to the Inventor 3 view drawing.

CHAPTER 12

Introduction to Stress Analysis

Objectives:

1. Learn to Create a simple part
2. Learn to run Stress Analysis
3. Learn to interpret Stress Analysis results

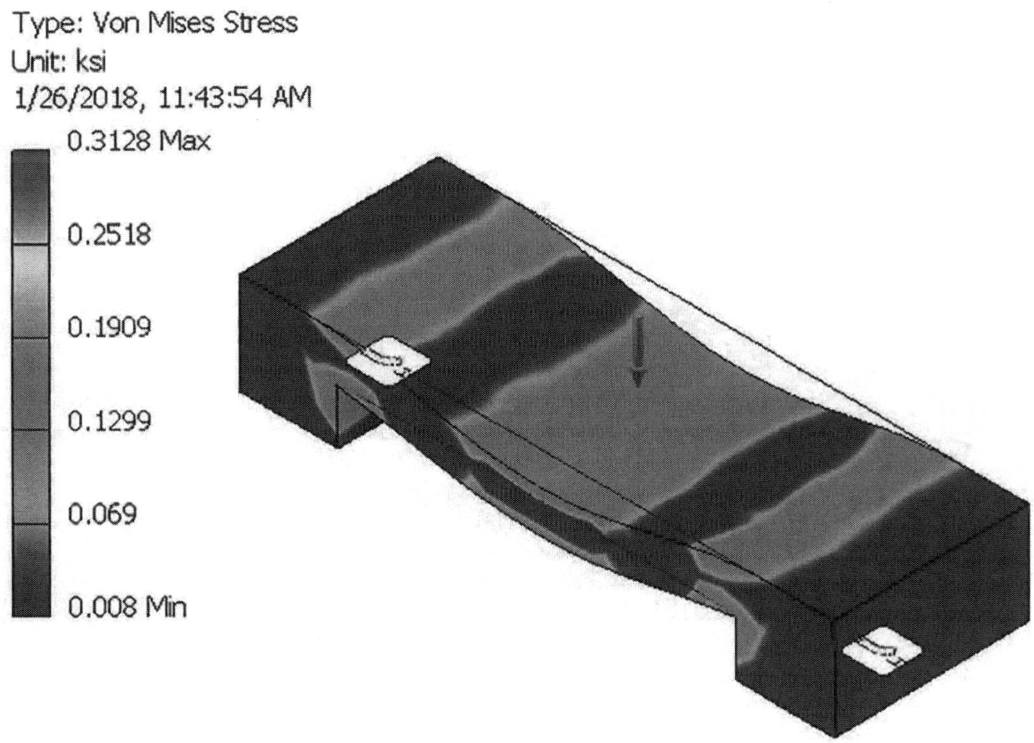

Chapter 12 includes instruction on how to perform a stress analysis on the part shown.

Learn to create a simple part

1. Start Inventor by referring to "Chapter 1 Getting Started."

2. After Inventor is running, begin a New Sketch.

3. Complete the sketch shown in Figure 1.

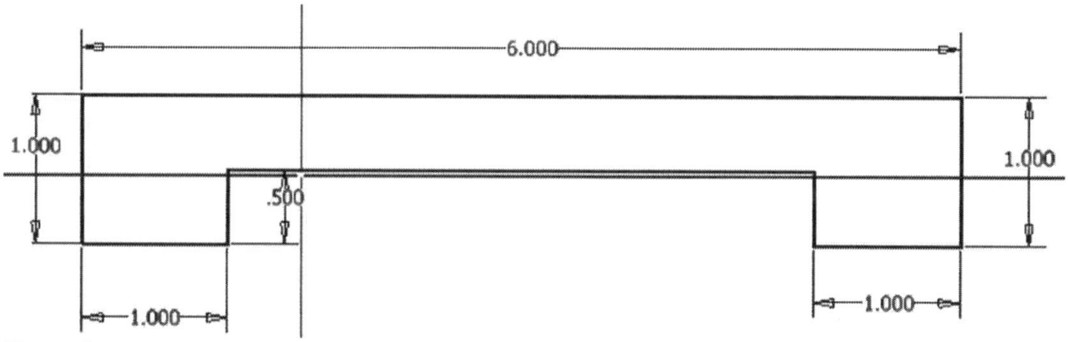

Figure 1

4. Exit the Sketch Panel. Extrude the sketch to a thickness of **2.00** inches as shown in Figure 2. Save the part where it can be easily retrieved later.

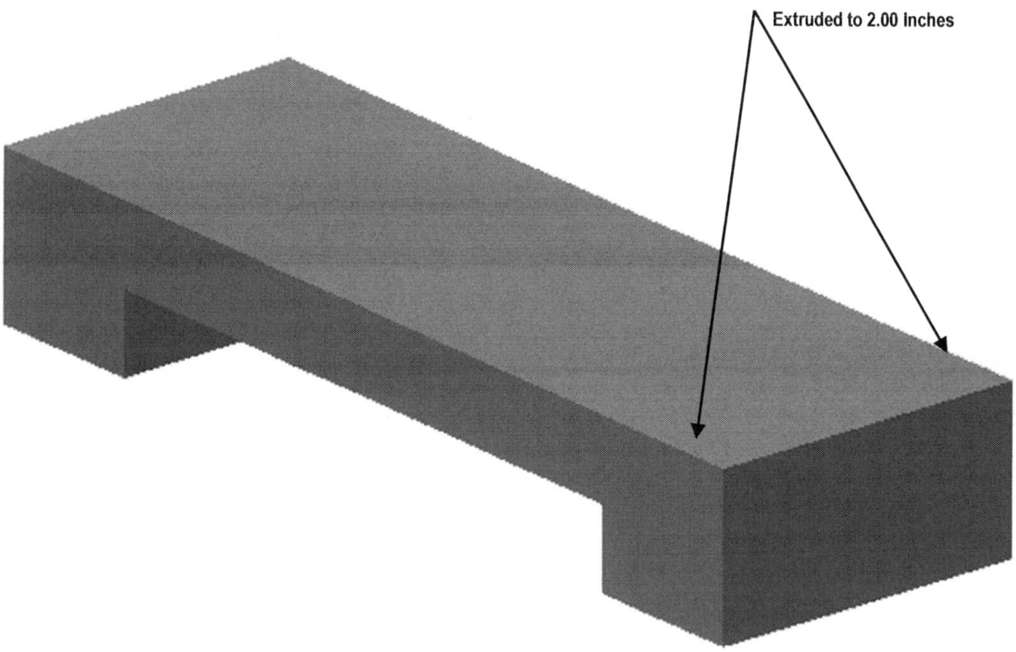

Figure 2

Learn to apply material to a simple part

5. Move the cursor to the right portion of the screen and left click on **Stress Analysis** as shown in Figure 3.

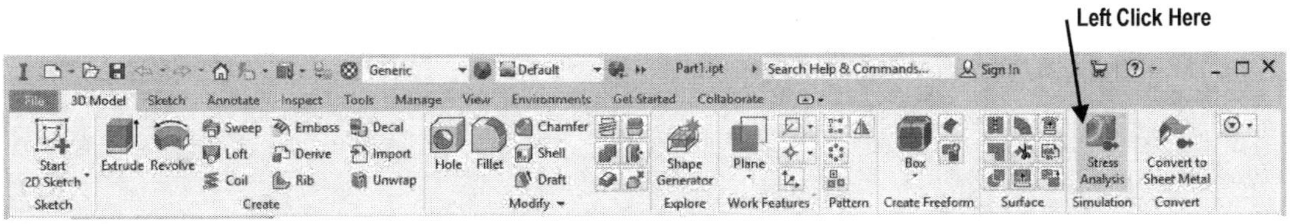

Figure 3

6. The Analysis tab will become active. Move the cursor to the upper left portion of the screen and left click on **Create Simulation** as shown in Figure 4.

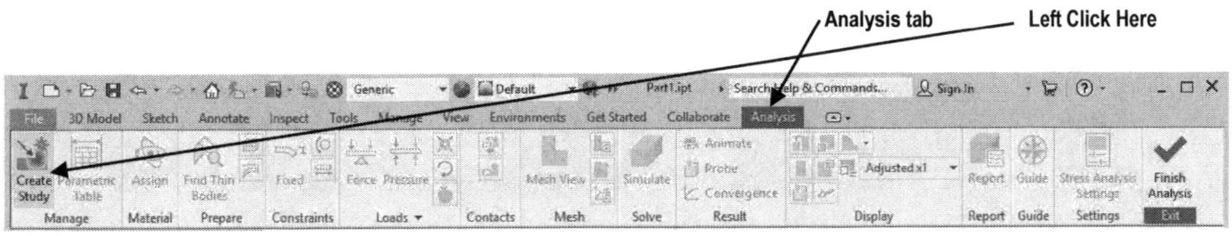

Figure 4

7. The Create New Study dialog box will appear. Left click on **OK** as shown in Figure 5.

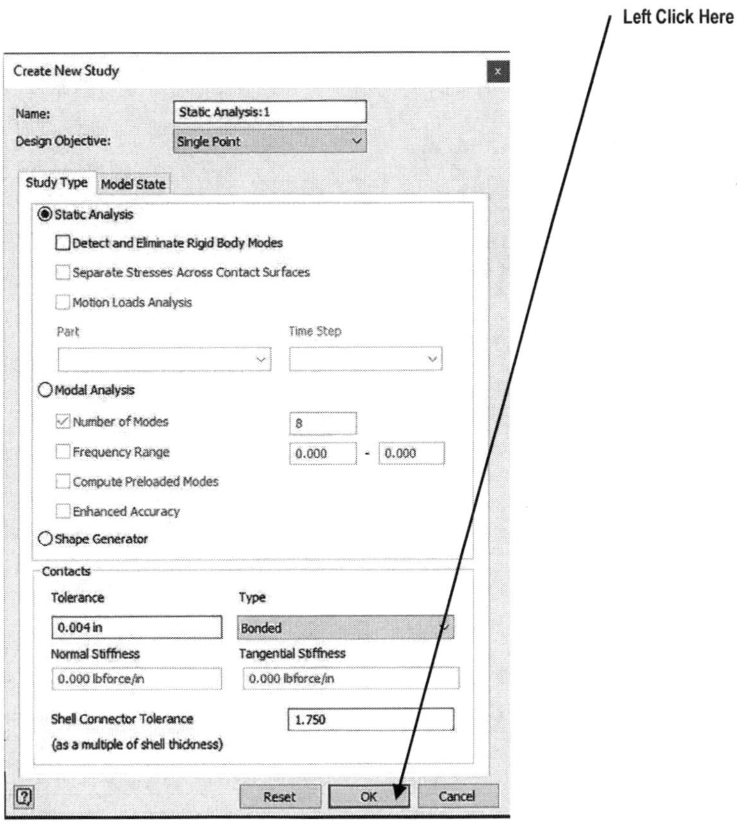

Figure 5

8. Move the cursor to the upper left portion of the screen and left click on **Assign**. This "assigns" material to the solid model for analysis as shown in Figure 6.

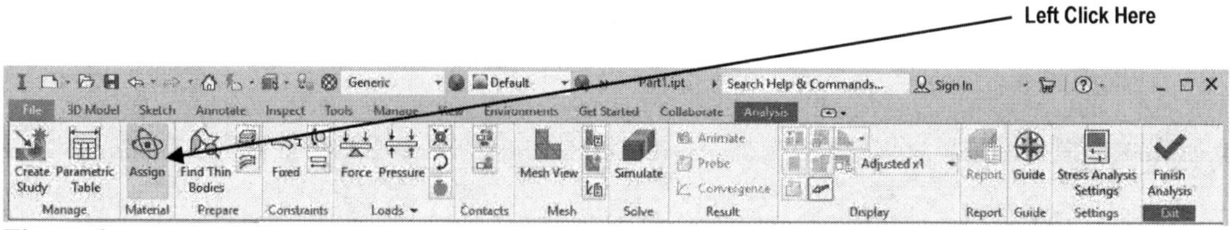

Figure 6

9. The Assign Materials dialog box will appear. Left click on **Materials** as shown in Figure 7.

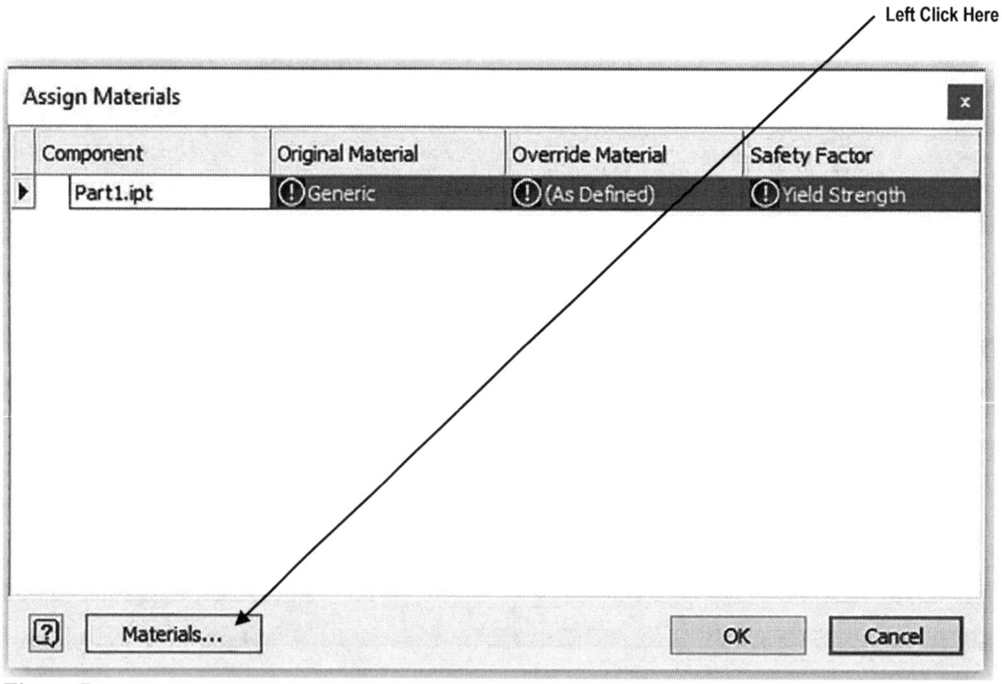

Figure 7

10. The Material Browser dialog box will appear. Left click on **Aluminum 6061**. Now, right click on **Aluminum 6061**. A pop-up menu will appear. Left click on **Assign to Selection**. Left click on Close as shown in Figure 8.

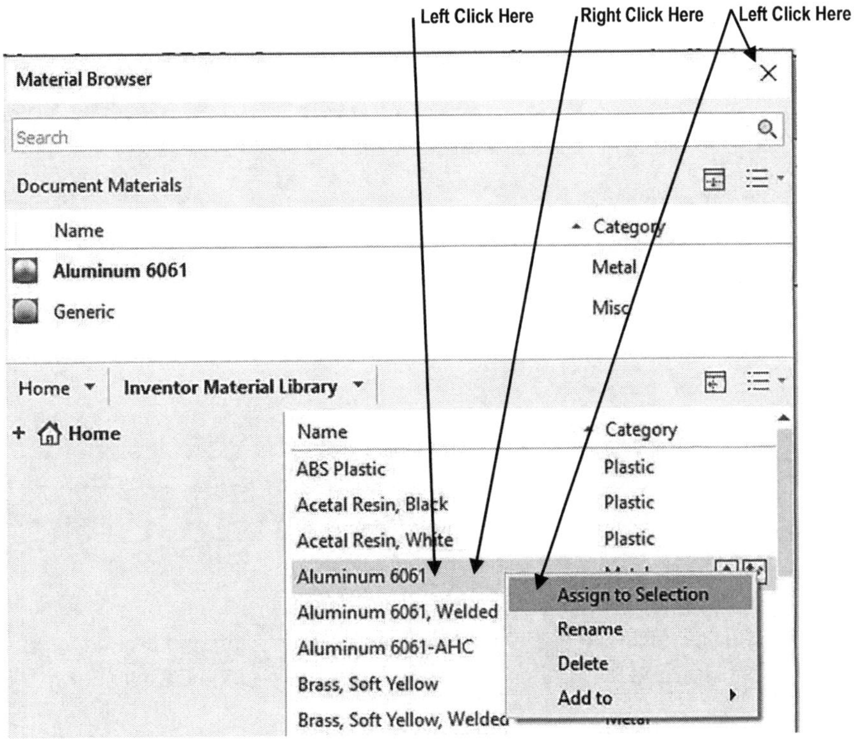

Figure 8

11. Close the Material Browser dialog box. The Assign Materials dialog box will re-appear with Aluminum 6061 listed in the Original Material column. Left click on **OK** as shown in Figure 9.

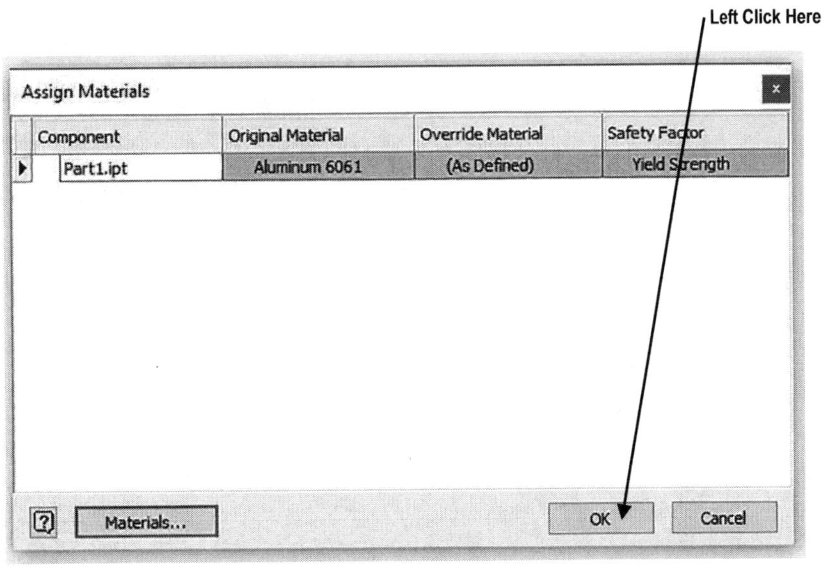

Figure 9

Learn to apply a fixture to a simple part

12. Move the cursor to the upper middle portion of the screen and left click on **Fixed** as shown in Figure 10.

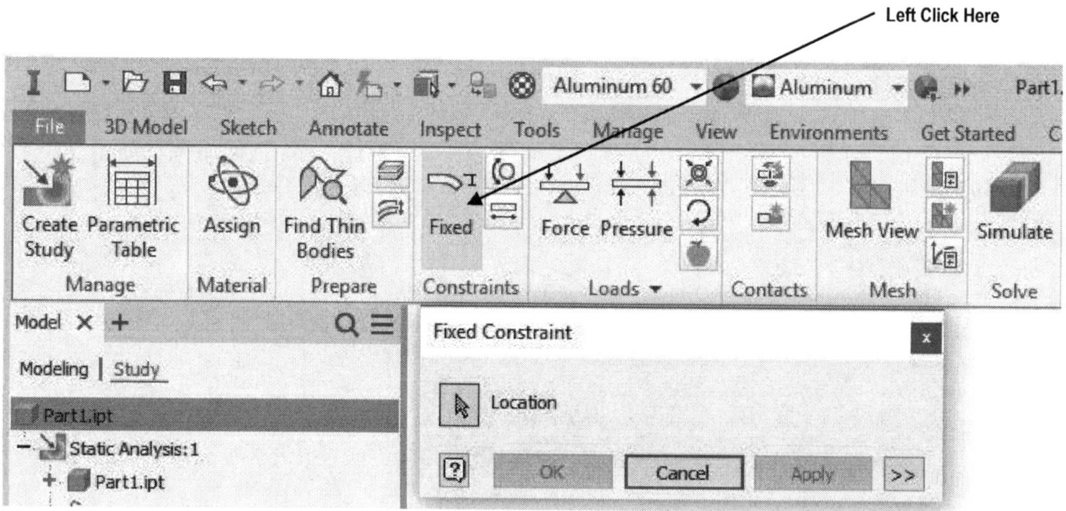

Figure 10

13. The Fixed Constraint dialog box will appear. Rotate the part around to gain access to the bottom side and left click on the "feet." Then, left click on **OK** as shown in Figure 11.

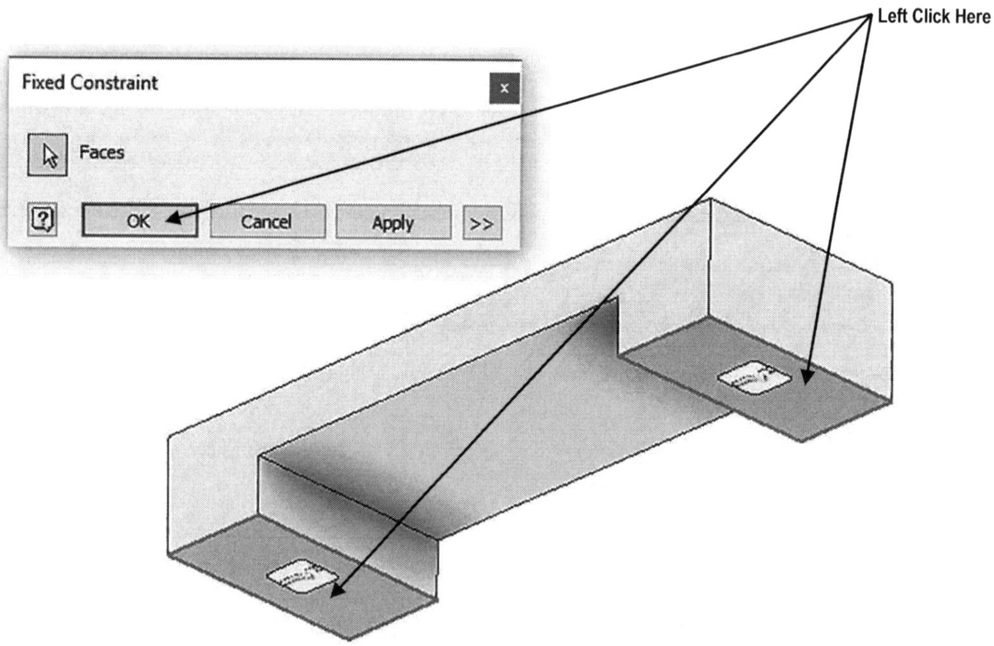

Figure 11

Learn to apply force to a simple part

14. Move the cursor to the upper middle portion of the screen and left click on the drop-down arrow located under **Loads**. A drop-down menu will appear. Left click on **Force** as shown in Figure 12.

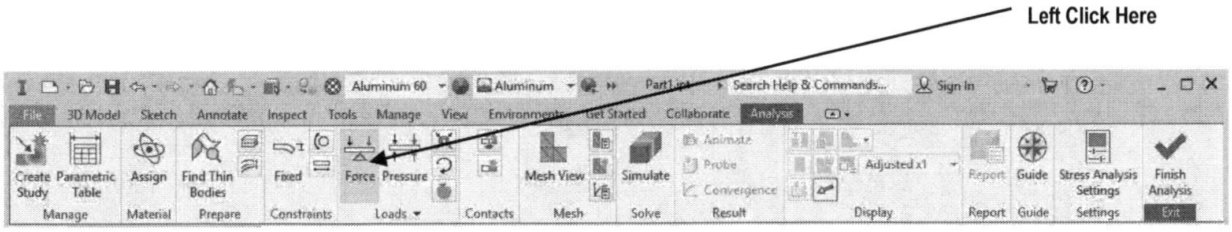

Figure 12

15. The Force dialog box will appear. Enter **100 lbs** for the amount of force as shown in Figure 13.

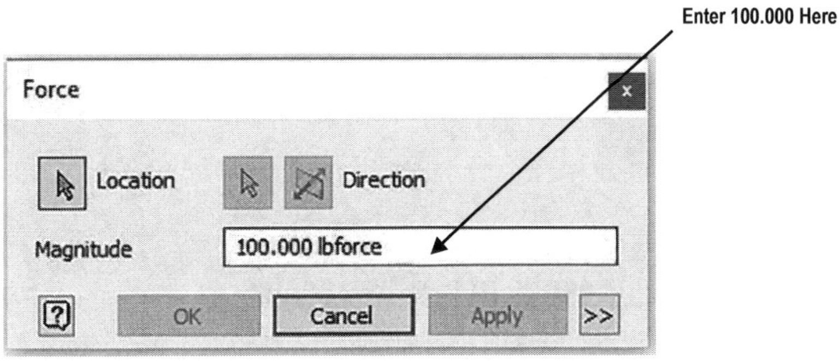

Figure 13

16. Rotate the part around to gain access to the top portion. Left click on the top portion. Left click on **OK** as shown in Figure 14.

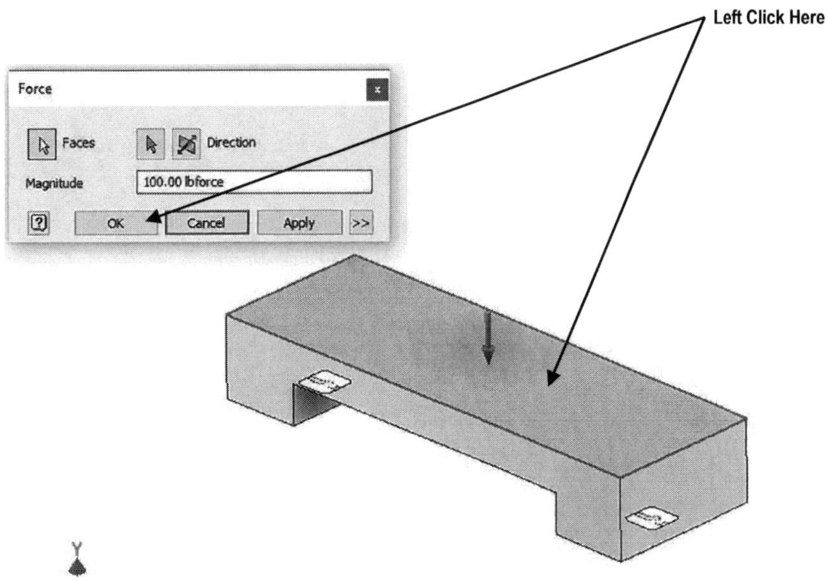

Figure 14

Learn to perform a stress analysis on a simple part

17. Move your cursor to the upper middle portion of the screen and left click on **Simulate**. The Simulate dialog box will appear. Left click on **Run** as shown in Figure 15.

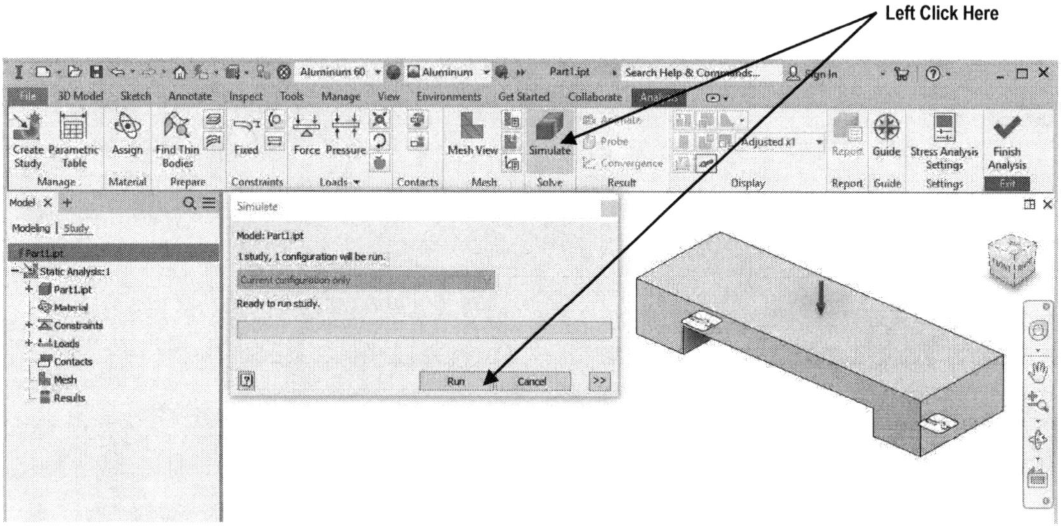

Figure 15

Learn to interpret results of a stress analysis

18. Inventor is in the process of analyzing the stress on this part with a force of 100 lbs as shown in Figure 16.

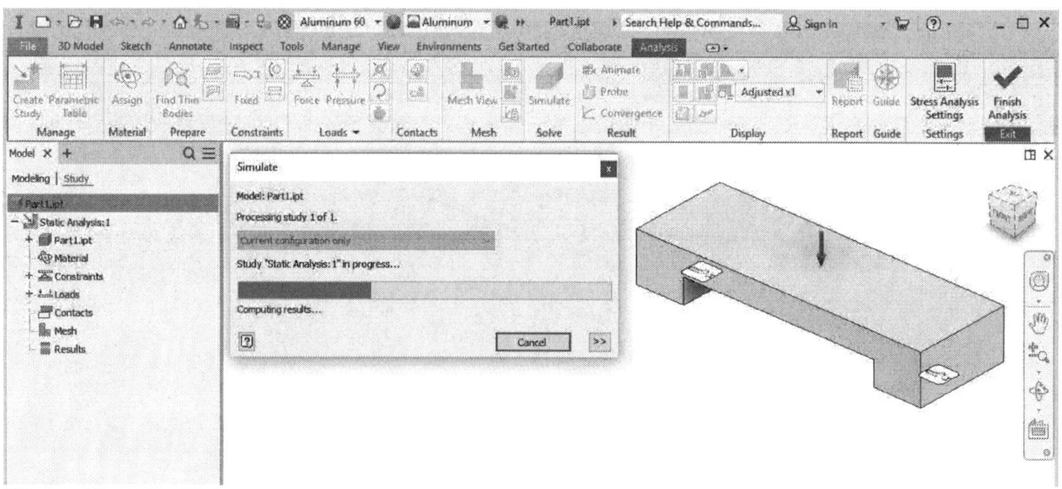

Figure 16

19. Inventor will display the results of the analysis. High stress areas are identified by any reddish orange areas that appear on the model as shown in Figure 17. Rotate the part around to examine any high stress areas on the underside.

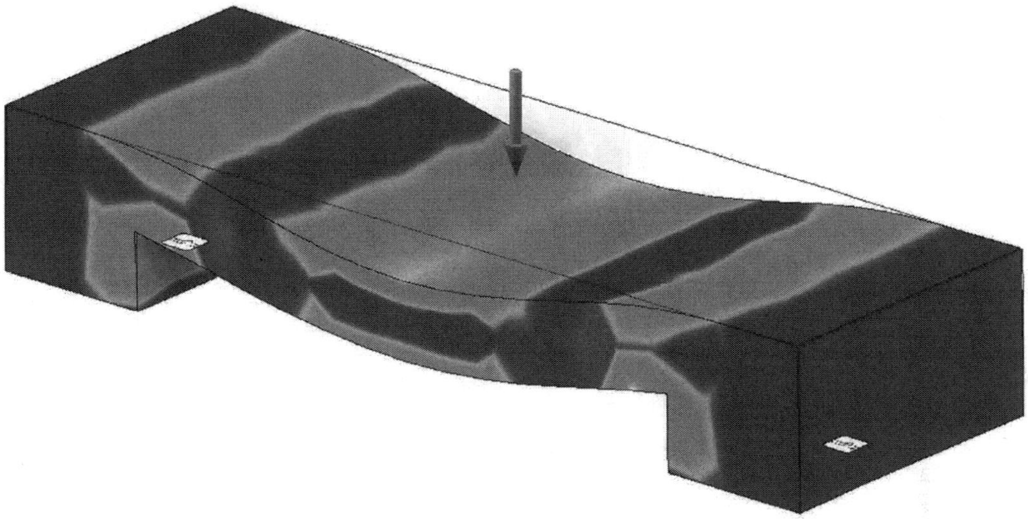

Figure 17

20. Move the cursor to the upper middle portion of the screen and left click on the Animate icon. The Animate Results dialog box will appear. Left click on "Play." Inventor will animate the stress analysis as shown in Figure 18.

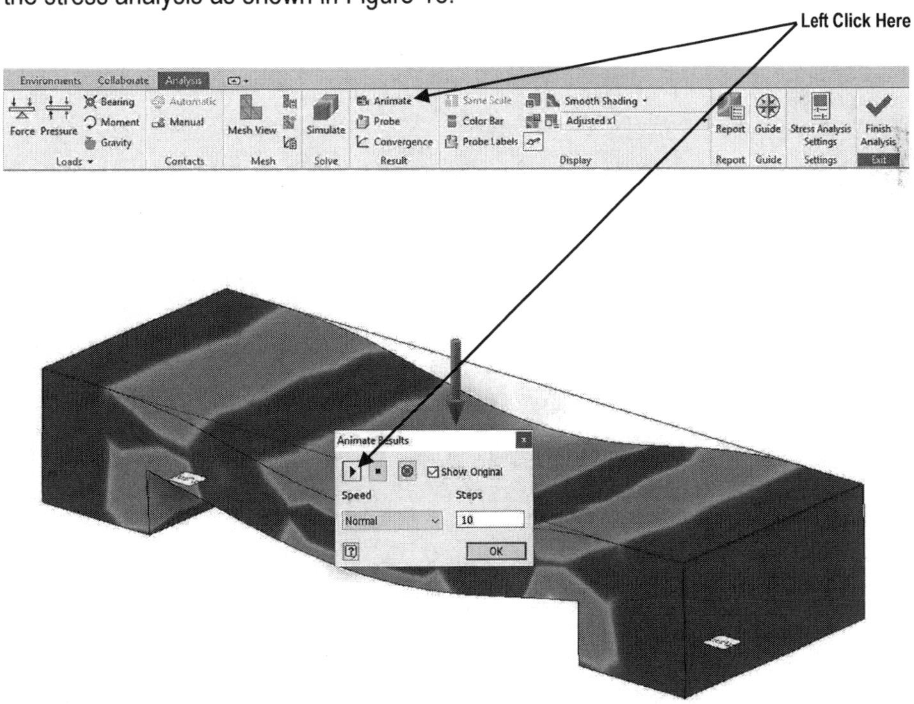

Figure 18

21. Results of the analysis can be viewed by selecting the **Probe** icon or the **Convergence** plot. Results can also be viewed by selecting the **Report** icon. Left click on **Finish Stress Analysis** as shown in Figure 19.

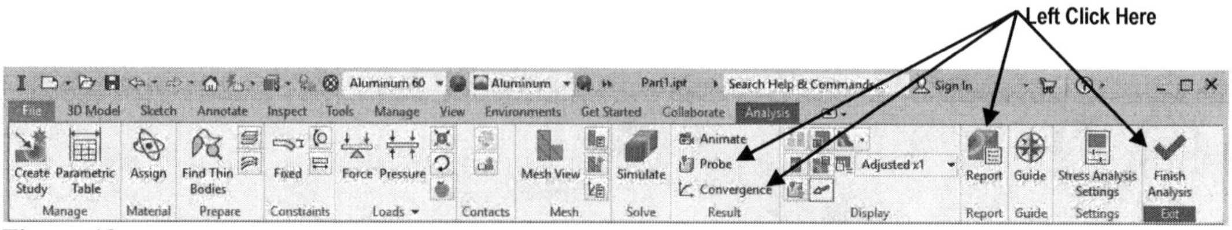

Figure 19

Chapter Problems

Problem 12-1

Complete the following sketch.

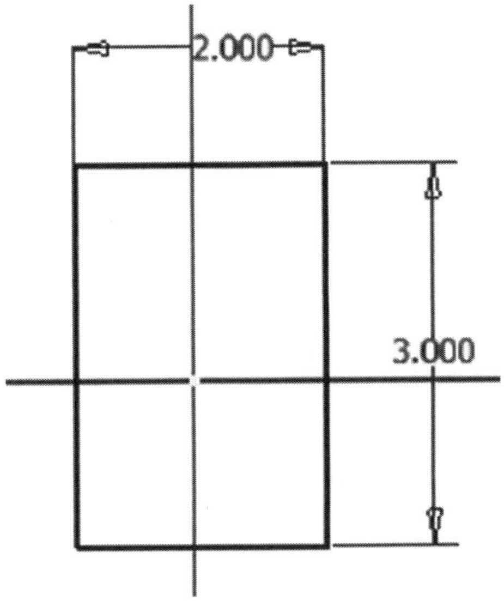

Extrude the sketch to a distance of 96 inches.

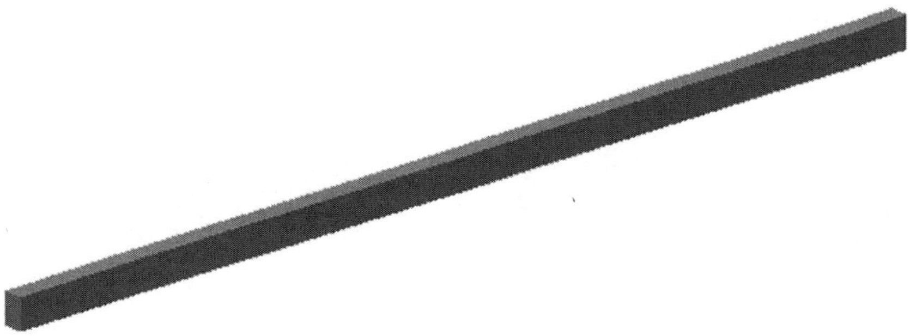

Use the Shell command to create a wall thickness of .10.

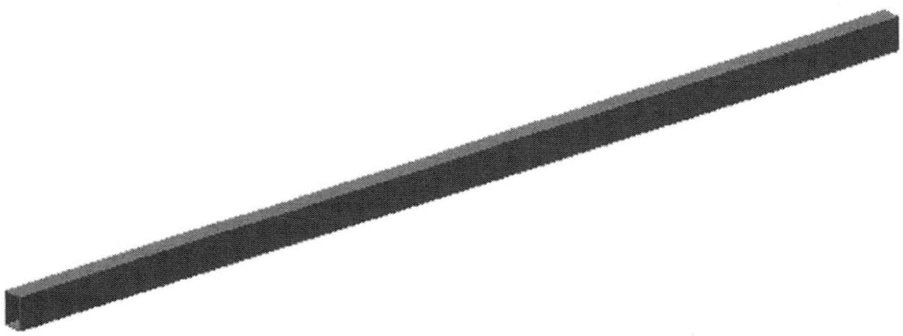

Run a stress analysis on the part using Acetal Resin, White Plastic. Use the left open edge for the Fixed edge. Use a load of 500 pounds along the top. The end result will be the creation of a Cantilever as shown.

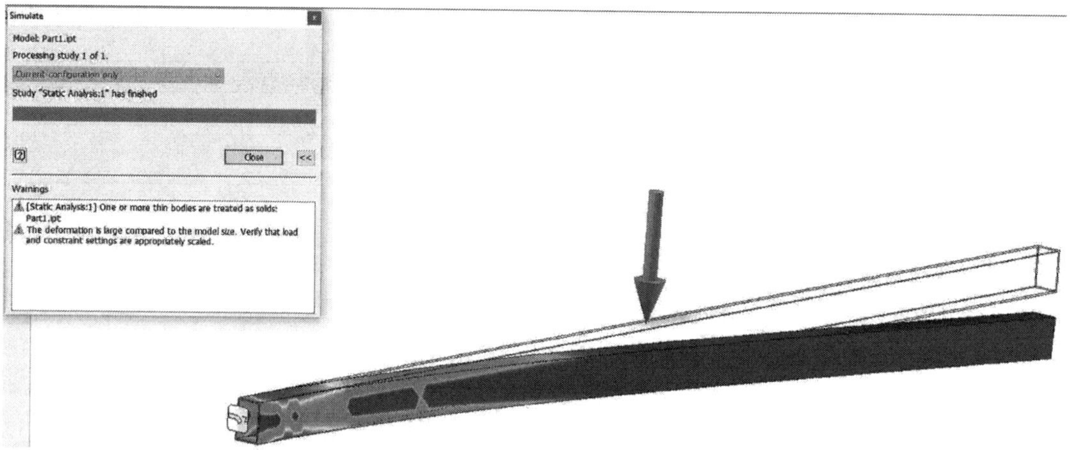

CHAPTER 13

Introduction to the Design Accelerator

Objectives:

1. Learn to create a Disc Cam
2. Learn to edit the Disc Cam
3. Learn to constrain the Disc Cam in an Assembly file
4. Learn to animate the Disc Cam using the Drive Constraint command

Chapter 10 includes instruction on how to design the part shown. This chapter contains a brief introduction to the Design Accelerator. The Design Accelerator contains numerous predefined parts. This chapter will cover one of these parts.

1. Start Inventor by referring to "Chapter 1 Getting Started."

2. After Inventor is running, begin a New Sketch.

3. Complete the sketch shown in Figure 1.

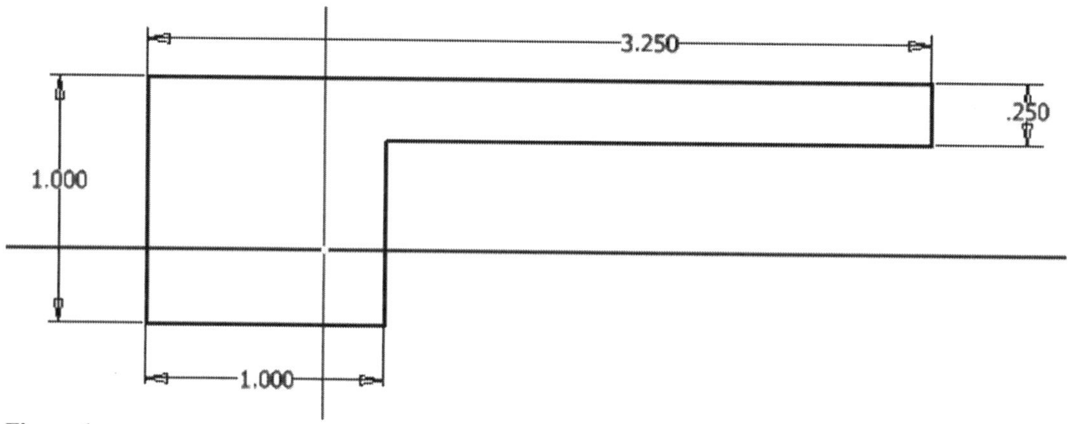

Figure 1

4. Exit the Sketch Panel. Extrude the sketch to a thickness of **1.00** inch as shown in Figure 2.

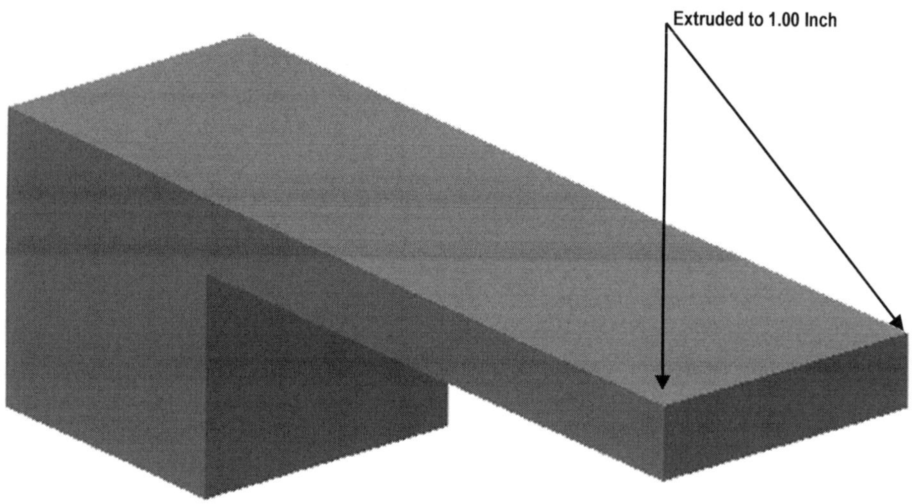

Figure 2

5. Use the **Fillet** command (.5 inch fillets) to radius the lower edge(s) as shown in Figure 3.

Figure 3

6. Use the **Rotate** command to rotate the part upward as shown in Figure 4.

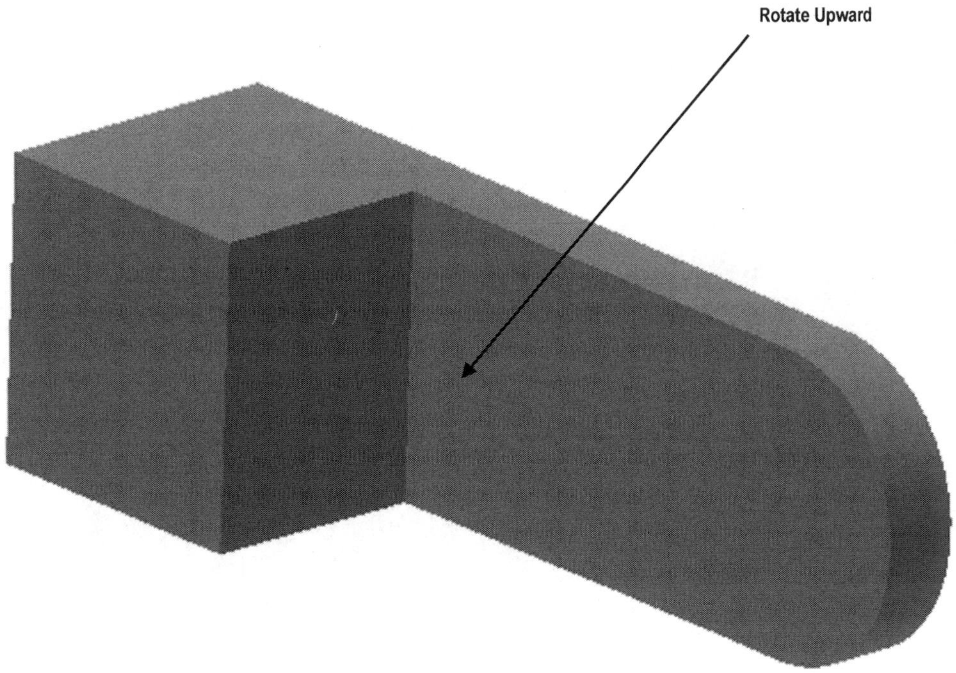

Figure 4

7. Complete the sketch as shown in Figure 5. The center of the circle is located on the center of the fillet radius.

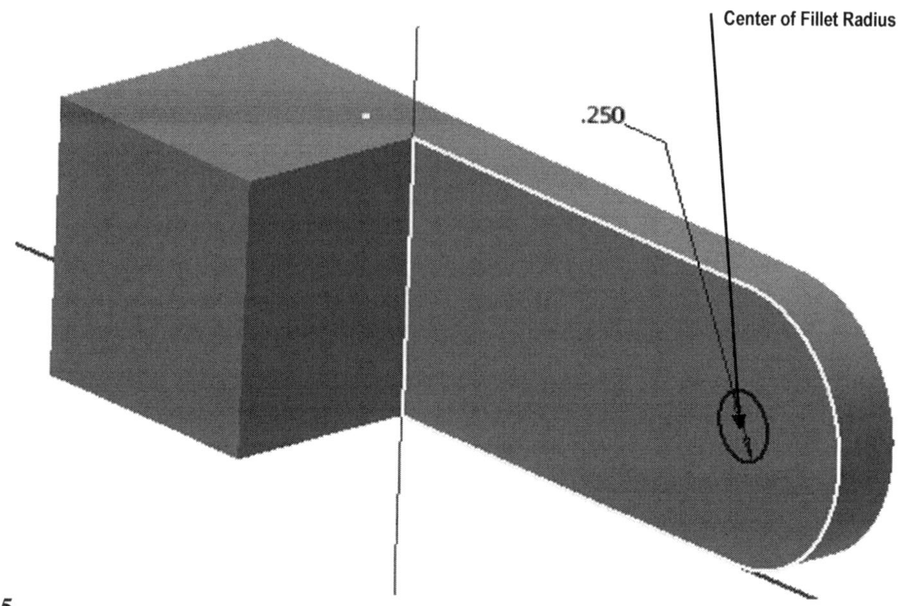

Figure 5

8. Extrude the circle to a distance of **.75** inches as shown in Figure 6.

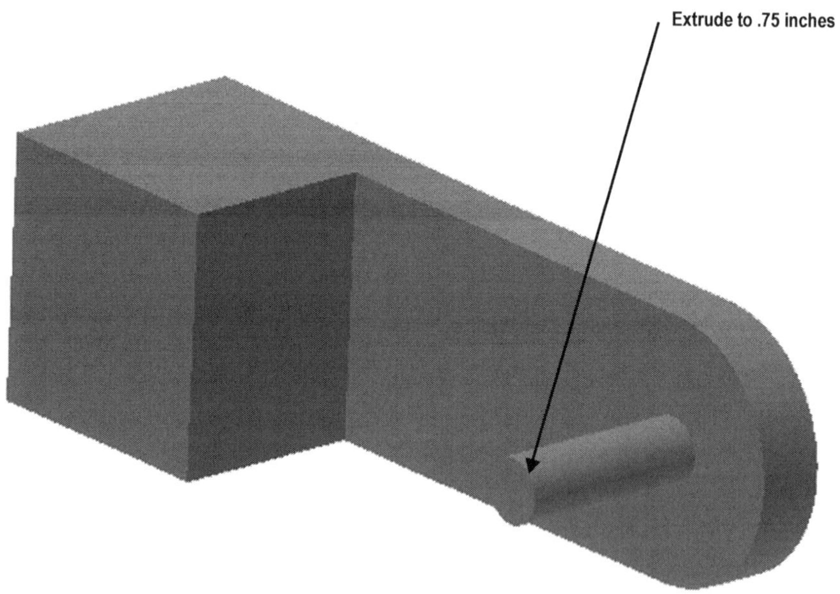

Figure 6

9. Complete the sketch as shown in Figure 7.

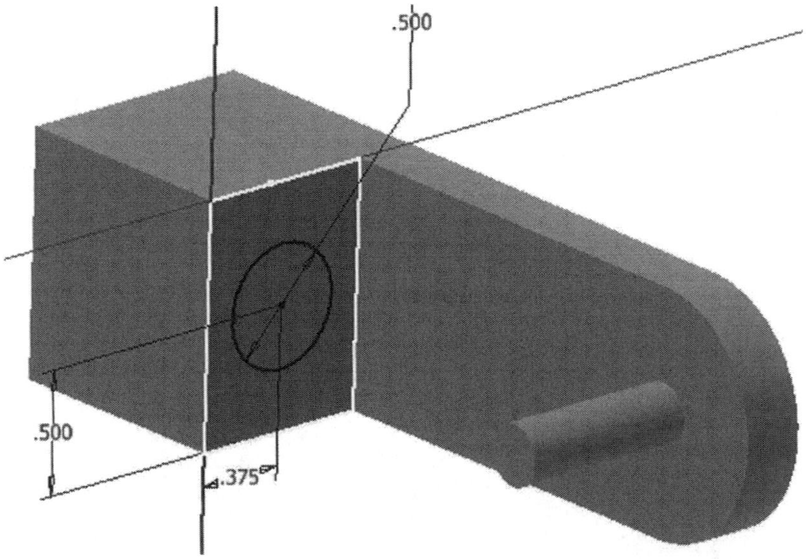

Figure 7

10. Use the "cut" option in the **Extrude** command to cut a hole a distance of 1.00 inch as shown in Figure 8.

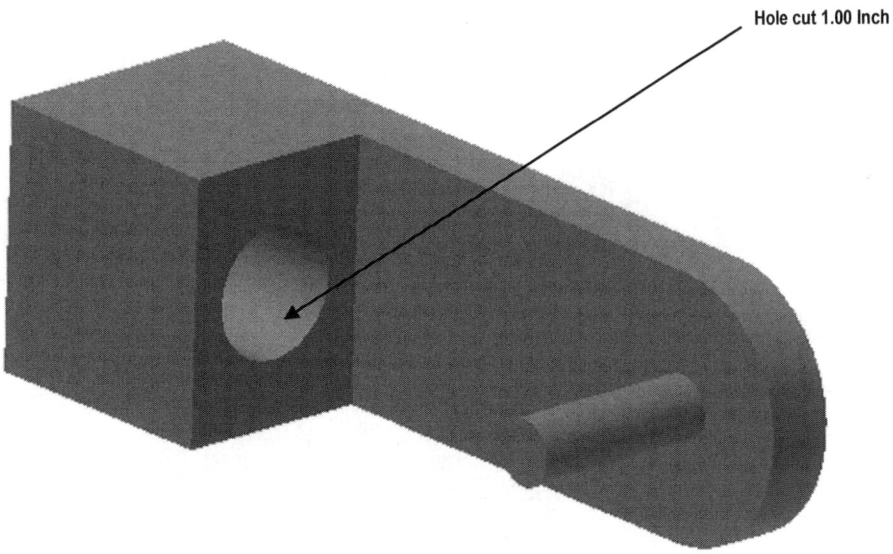

Figure 8

11. Save the part as Camcase1.ipt where it can be easily retrieved later.

12. Begin a new drawing as described in Chapter 1.

13. Complete the sketch shown. Extrude the .500 inch diameter circle to a distance of 1 inch and the .625 inch diameter circle to a distance of .125 inches as shown in Figure 9.

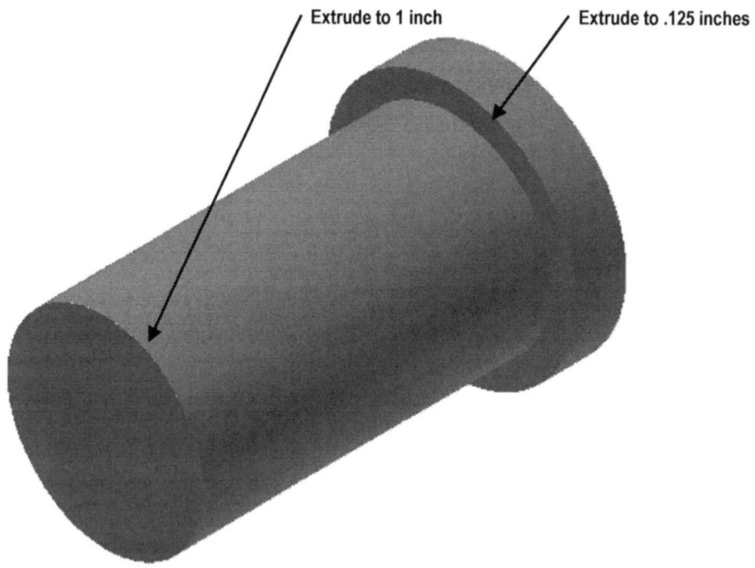

Figure 9

14. The bottom of the part needs to be flat as shown in Figure 10.

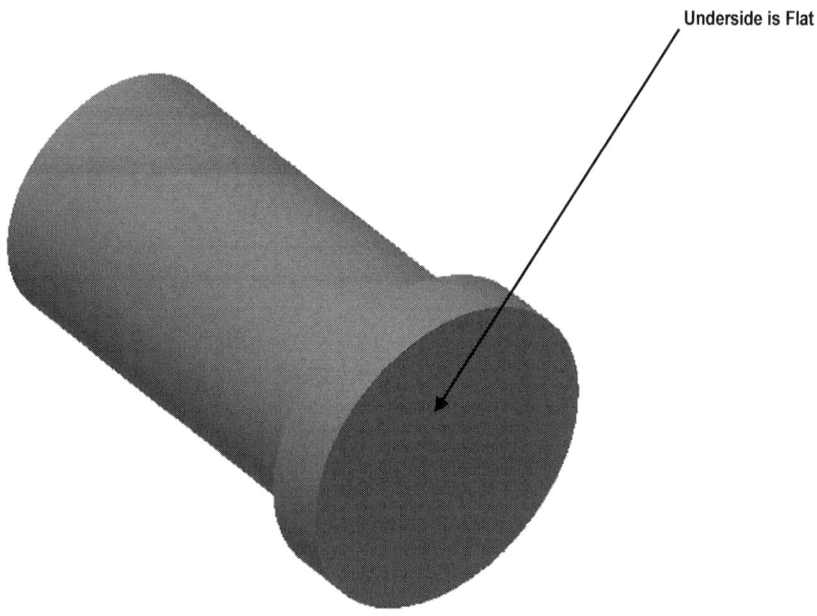

Figure 10

15. Save the part as Lifter1.ipt where it can be easily retrieved later.

16. Begin a new Assemble drawing as described in Chapter 7 and shown in Figure 11.

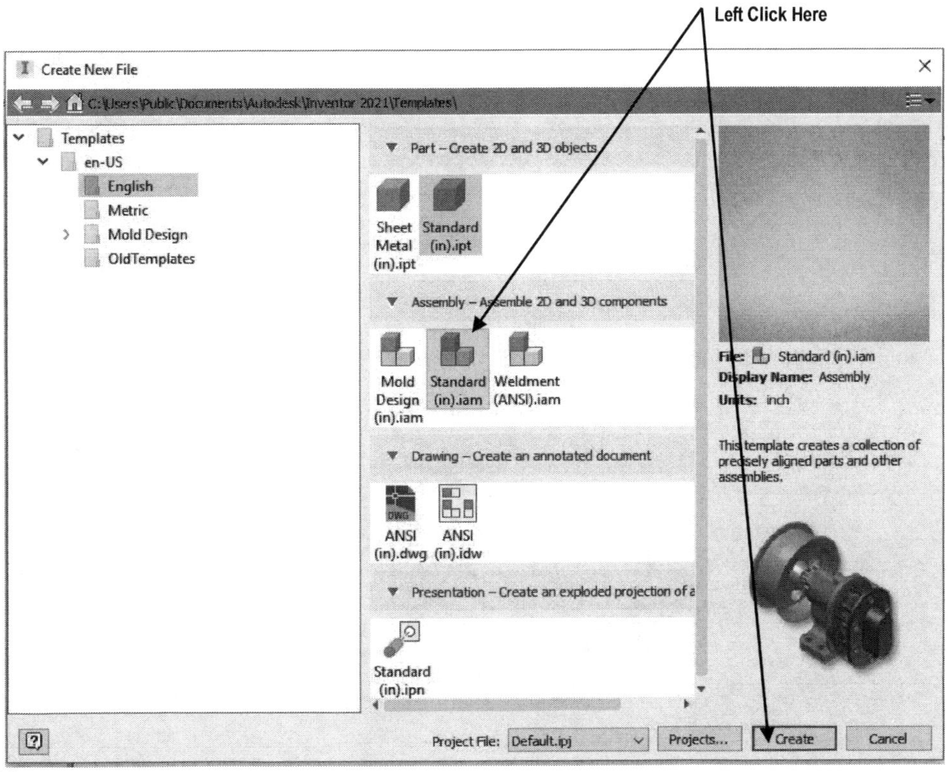

Figure 11

17. The Assemble Panel will appear as shown in Figure 12.

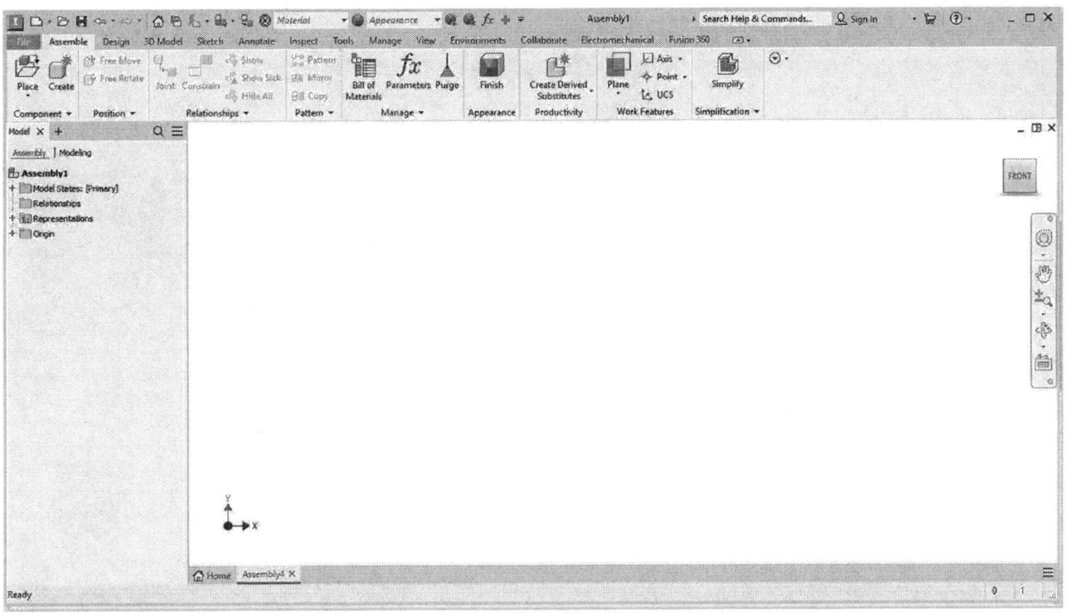

Figure 12

18. Use the **Place** command to place the Camcase1.ipt file into the assembly as shown in Figure 13.

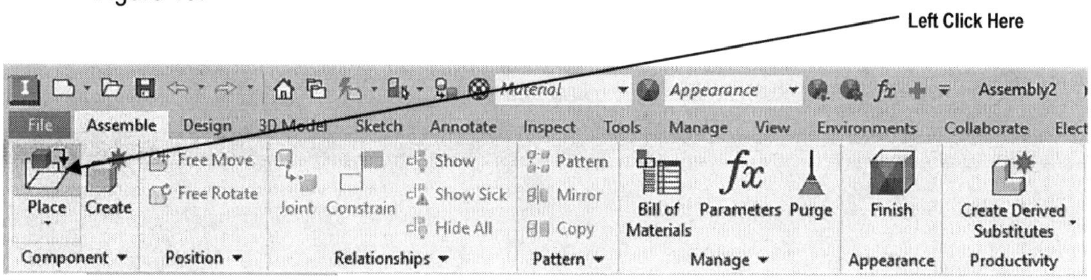

Figure 13

19. The Place Component dialog box will appear as shown in Figure 14.

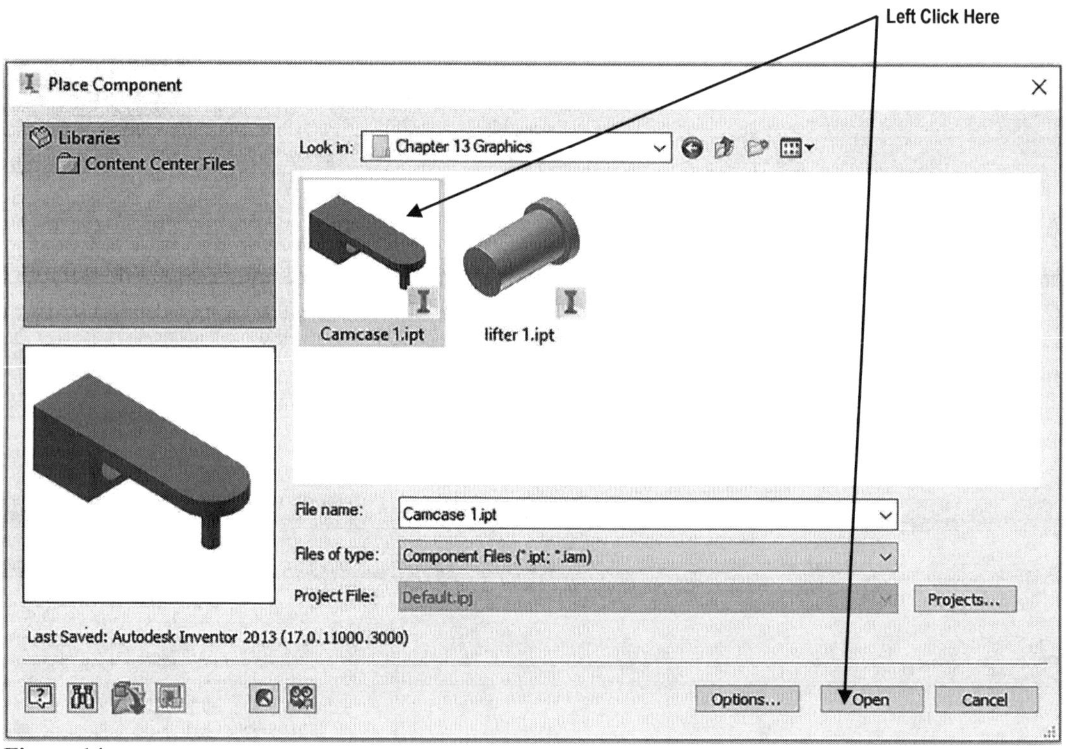

Figure 14

20. Repeat the same steps to place the Lifter1.ipt file into the assembly. Your screen should look similar to Figure 15.

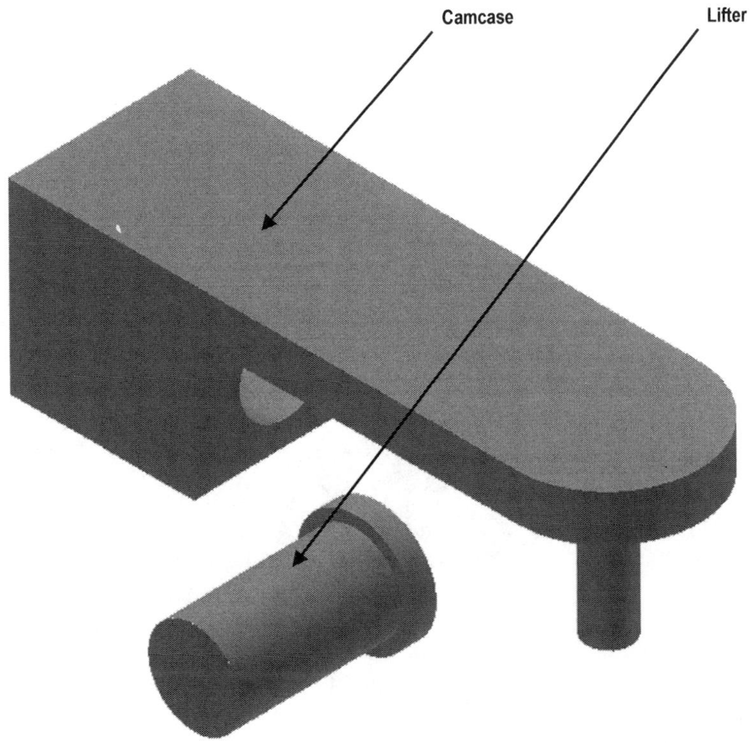

Figure 15

21. Use the **Rotate** command to rotate the case around for better access. Use the **Constraint** command to place the lifter into the lifter bore with the foot towards the bottom of the case as shown in Figure 16. Save the file before proceeding.

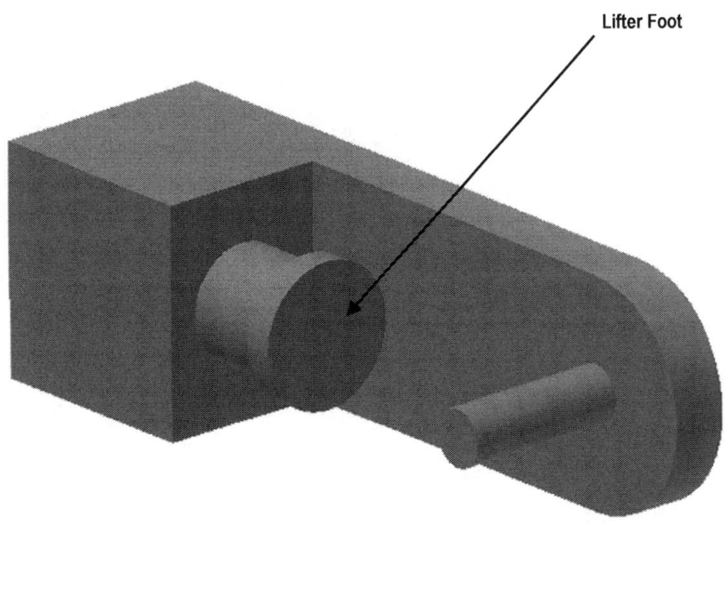

Figure 16

Learn to create a Disc Cam

22. Move the cursor to the upper left portion of the screen and left click on the **Design** tab as shown in Figure 17.

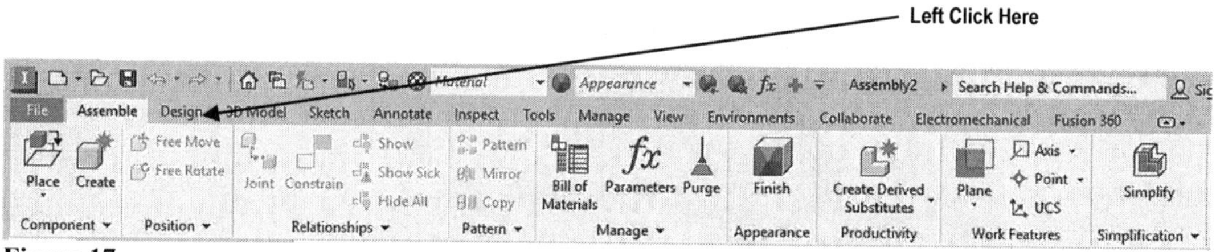

Figure 17

23. The Design Accelerator panel will open as shown in Figure 18.

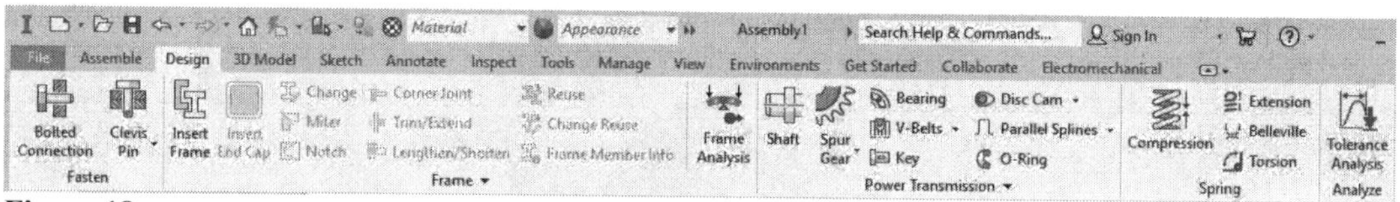

Figure 18

24. After left clicking on the Design tab, the Bearing, V-Belts and Disc Cam icons will appear. Move the cursor to the upper right portion of the screen and left click on the **Disc Cam** icon as shown in Figure 19.

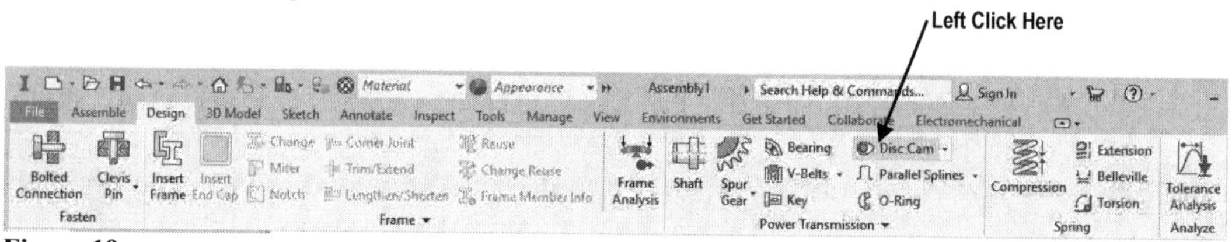

Figure 19

25. The Disc Cam Component Generator dialog box will appear as shown in Figure 20.

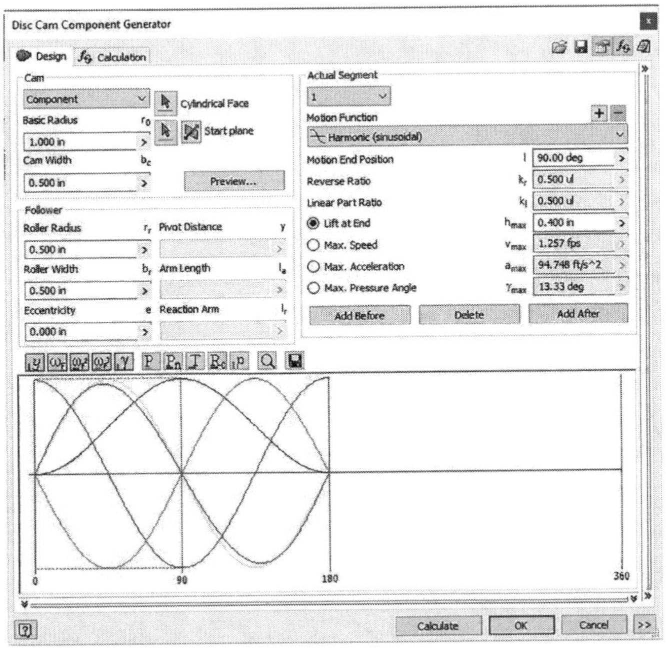

Figure 20

26. Highlight the text below Roller Radius and enter **2.000**. This will create a more pointed disc cam. Left click on **Calculate** and **OK** as shown in Figure 21.

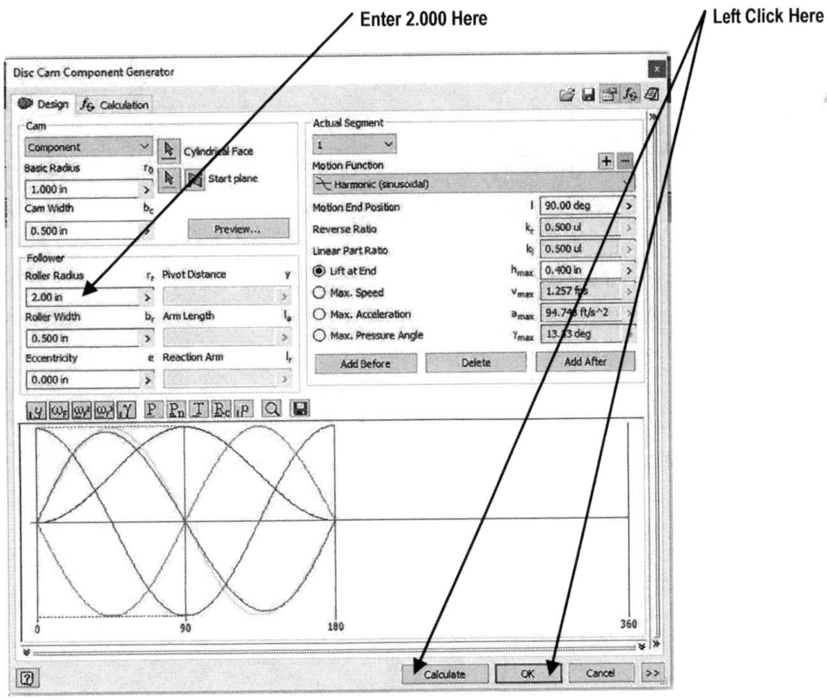

Figure 21

27. The disc cam will be attached to the cursor. If the "File Naming" dialog box (not shown) appears, left click on OK. Left click as shown in Figure 22.

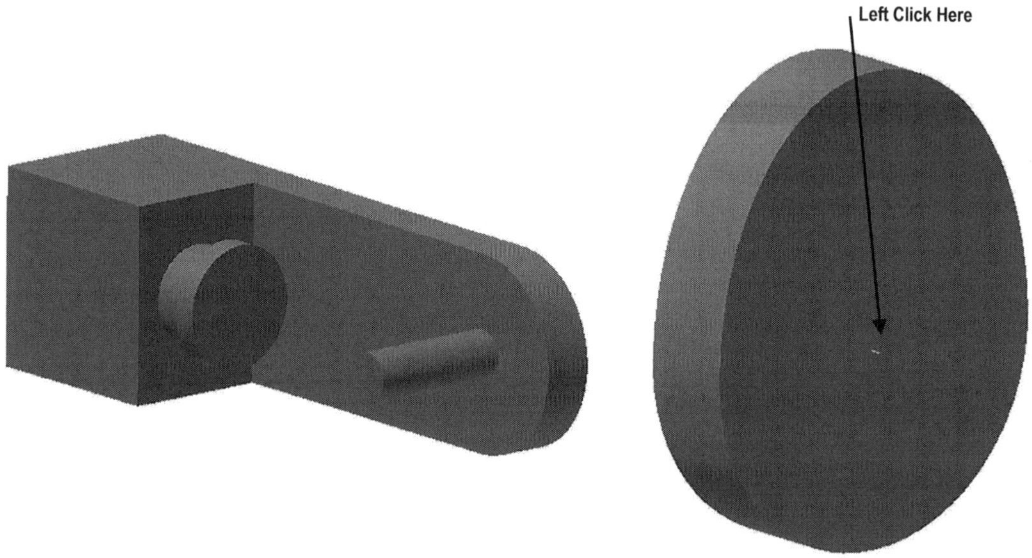

Figure 22

28. Your screen should look similar to Figure 23.

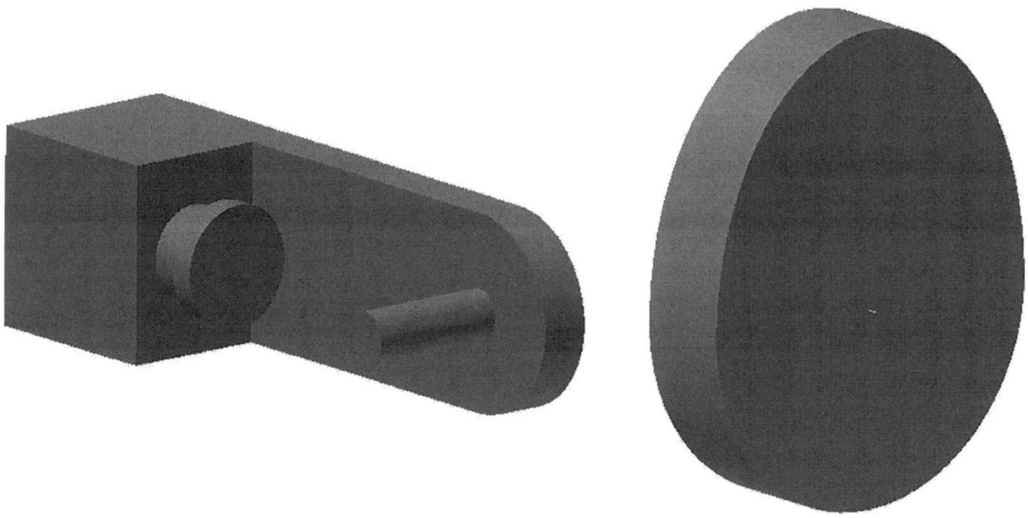

Figure 23

Learn to edit a Disc Cam

29. The disc cam will need the addition of a center hole and key slot. Move the cursor of the upper face of the disc cam causing the edges to become highlighted, and double click once as shown in Figure 24.

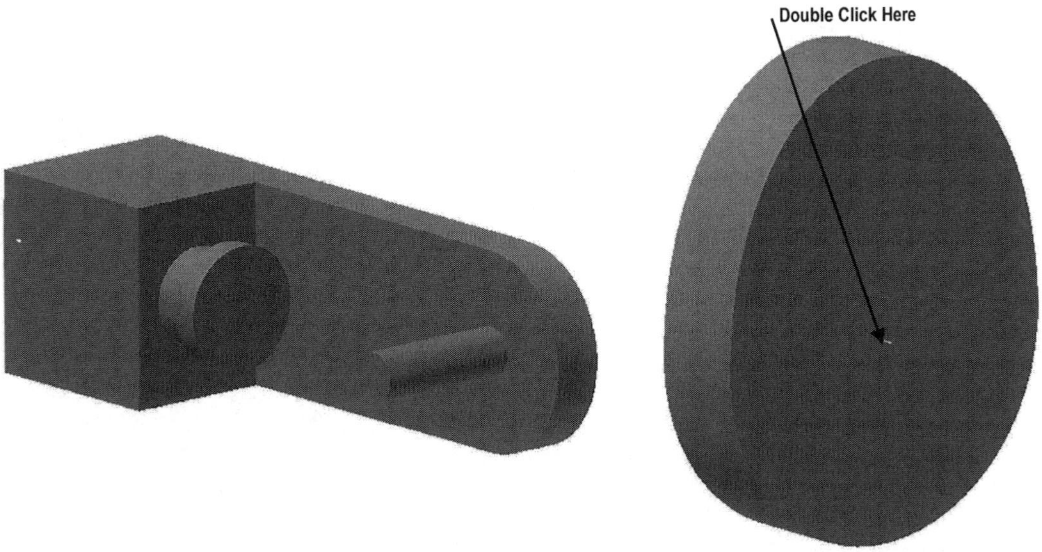

Figure 24

30. The rest of the parts in the assembly will become inactive as shown in Figure 25.

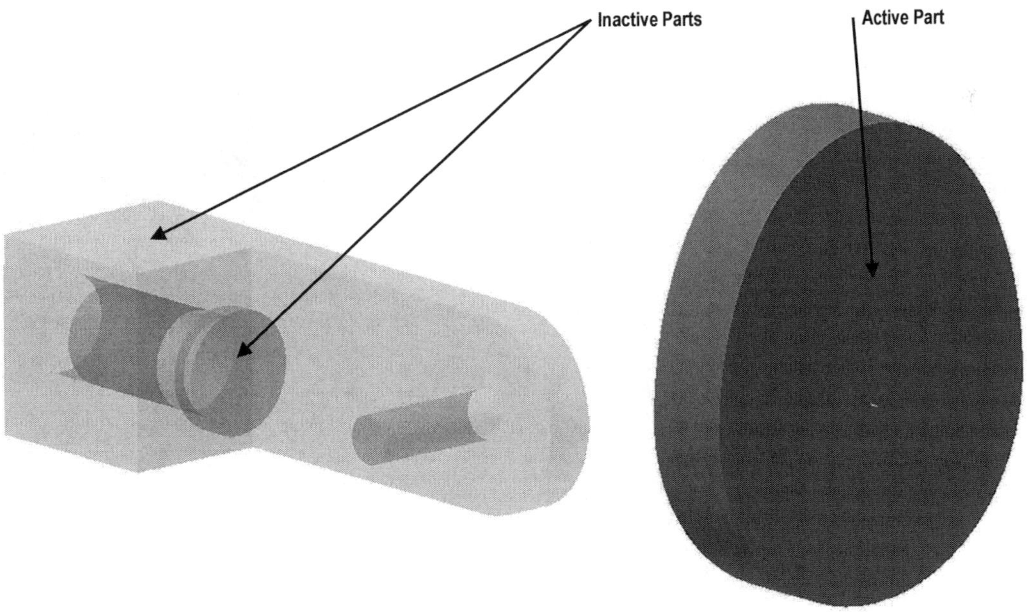

Figure 25

31. Your screen should look similar to Figure 26.

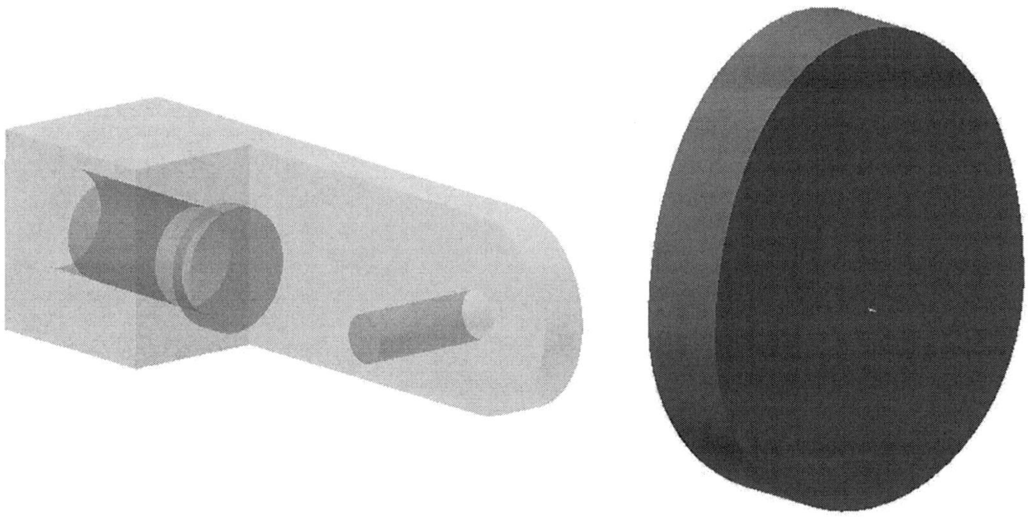

Figure 26

32. Move the cursor to the front face of the cam disc causing the edges to turn red and right click once. A pop-up menu will appear. Left click on **New Sketch** as shown in Figure 27.

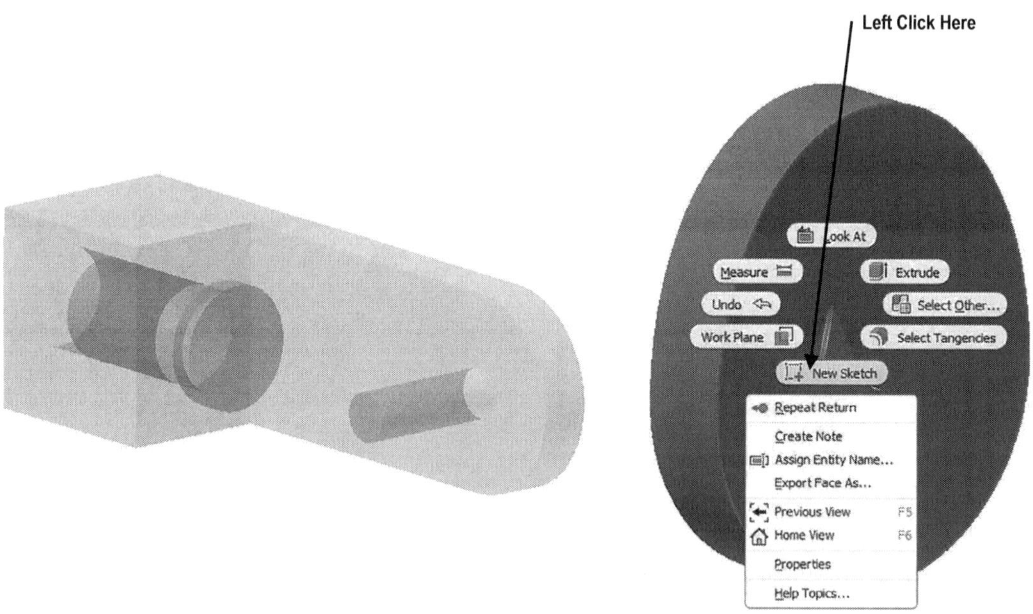

Figure 27

33. Inventor will return to the Sketch Panel as shown in Figure 28.

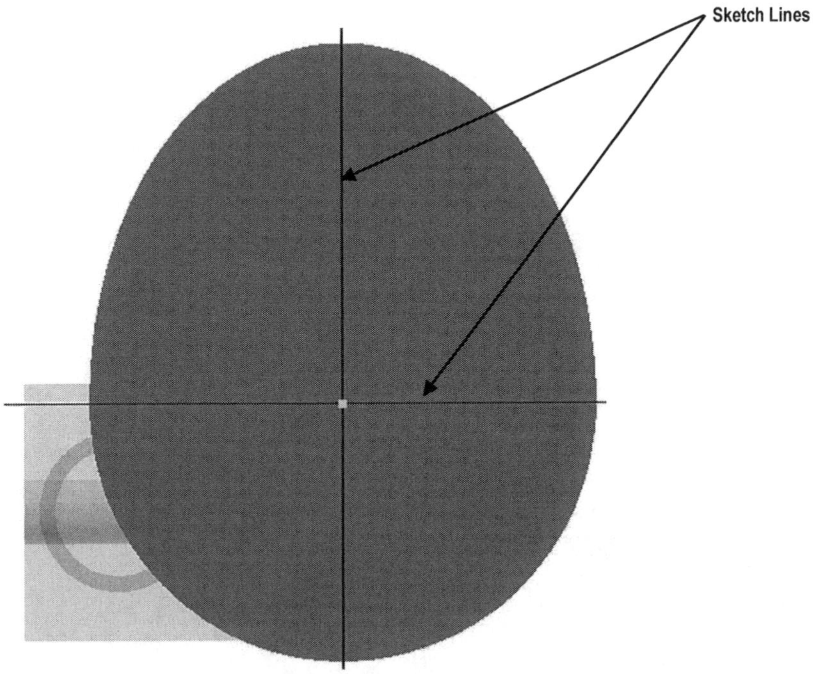

Figure 28

34. Your screen should look similar to what is shown in Figure 29.

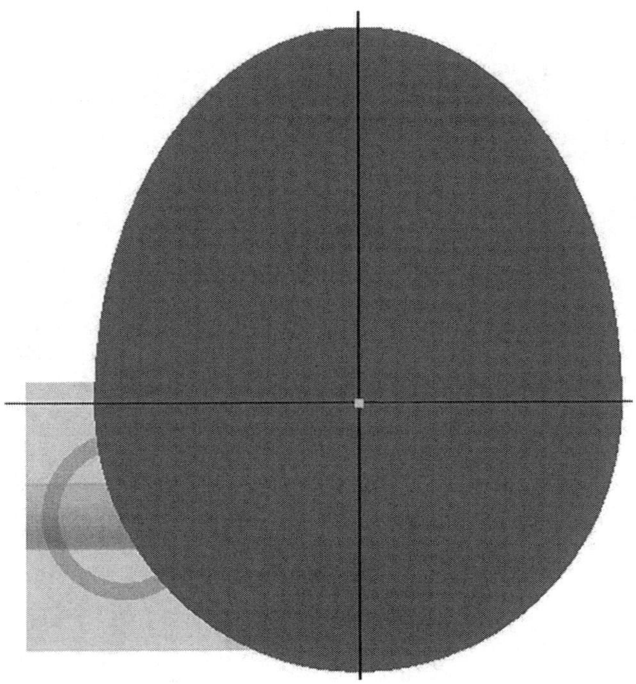

Figure 29

35. Complete the sketch as shown in Figure 30.

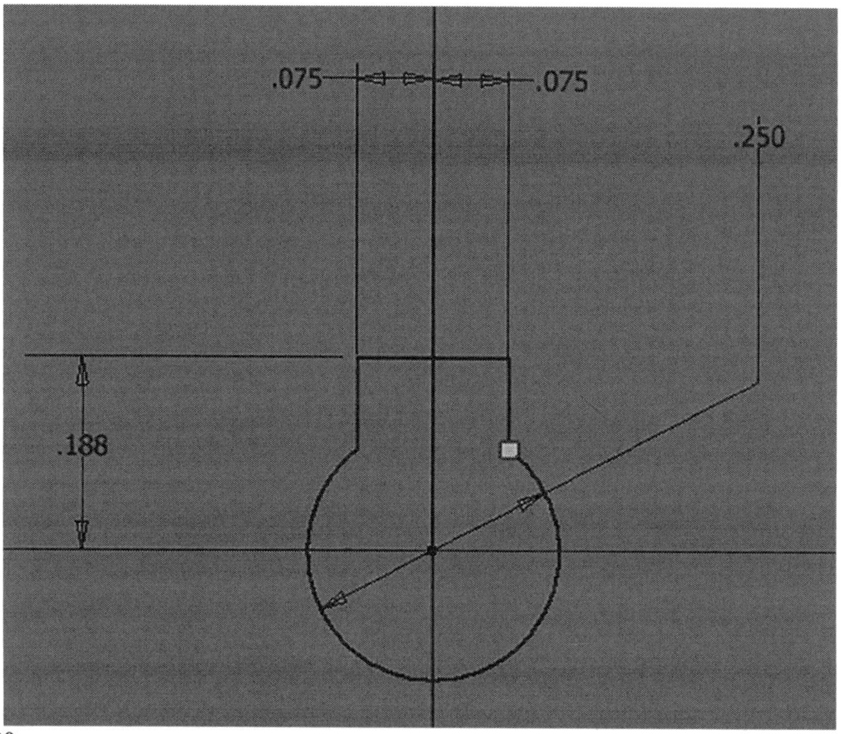

Figure 30

36. Once the sketch is complete, exit out of the Sketch Panel as shown in Figure 31.

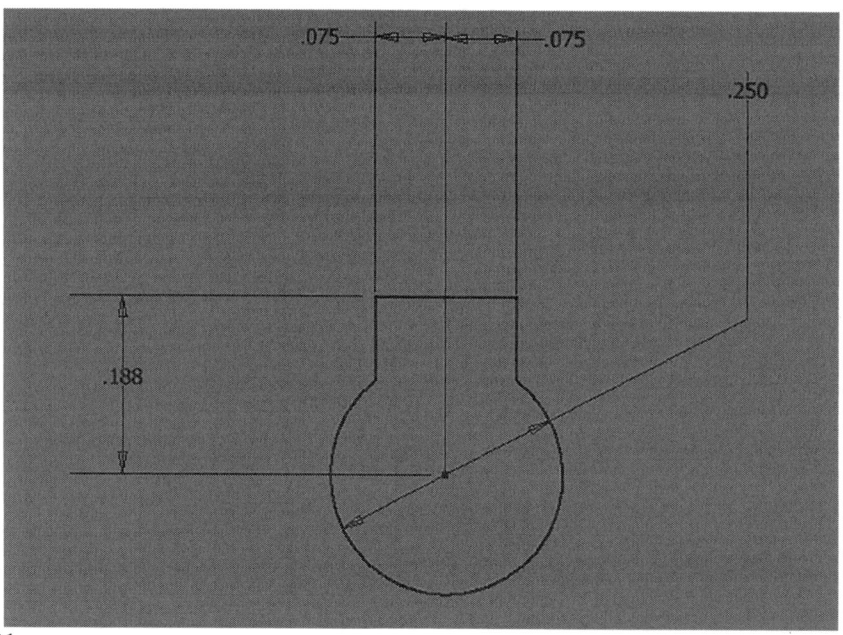

Figure 31

37. Use the **Rotate** command to rotate the part around as shown. Use the **Extrude** cut command to cut a hole and key slot as shown in Figure 32.

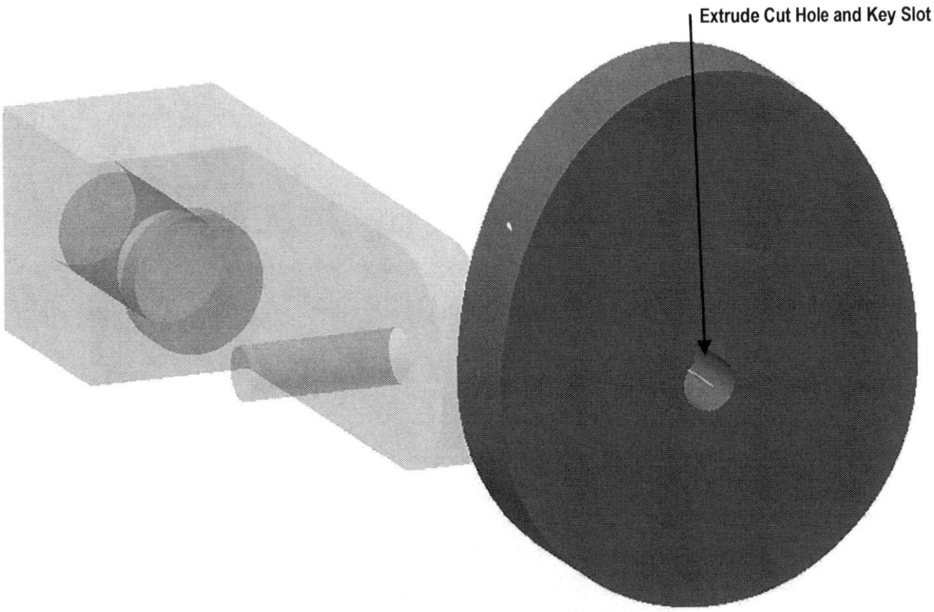

Figure 32

38. Left click on **Return** twice (if needed) as shown in Figure 33.

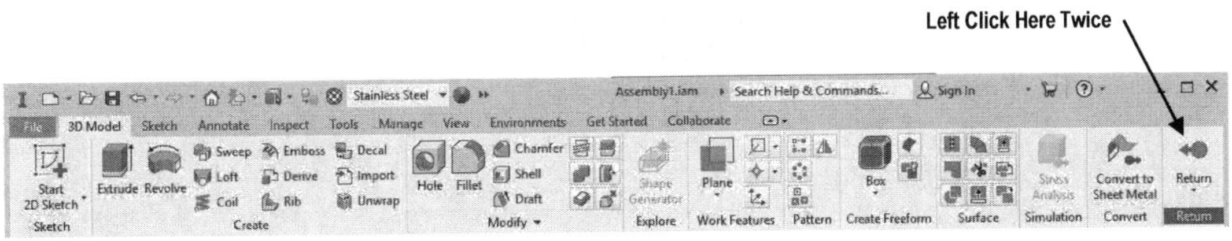

Figure 33

39. Your screen should look similar to Figure 34.

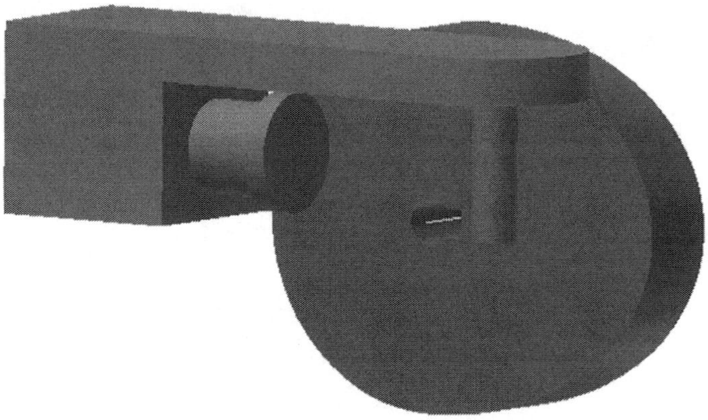

Figure 34

40. Move the cursor to the upper left portion of the screen and left click on the **Assemble** tab. Inventor will return to the Assemble Panel if not already in the Assemble Panel.

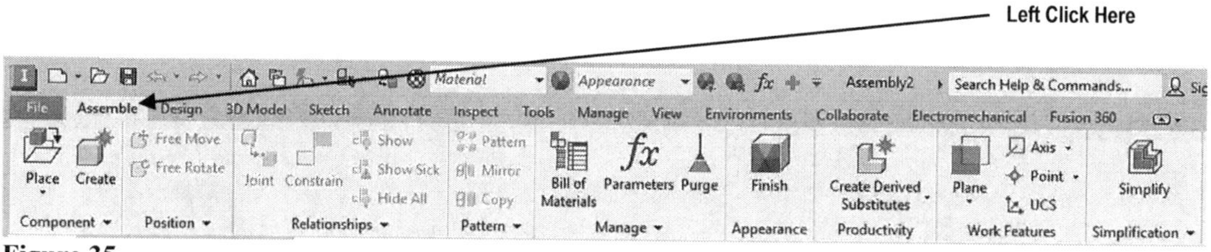

Figure 35

41. Use the **Constrain** command to constrain the center of the disc cam to the center of the shaft as shown in Figure 36.

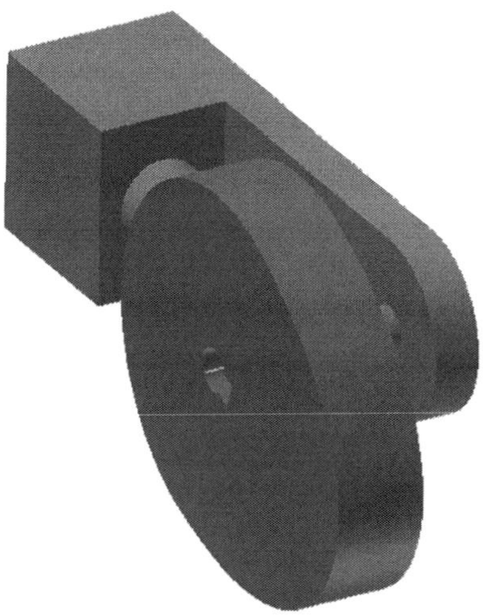
Figure 36

42. Rotate the assembly around to gain access to the side of the disc cam. Use the **Constraint** command to constrain the disc cam an offset distance of **.125** inches from the inside of the cam case as shown in Figure 37.

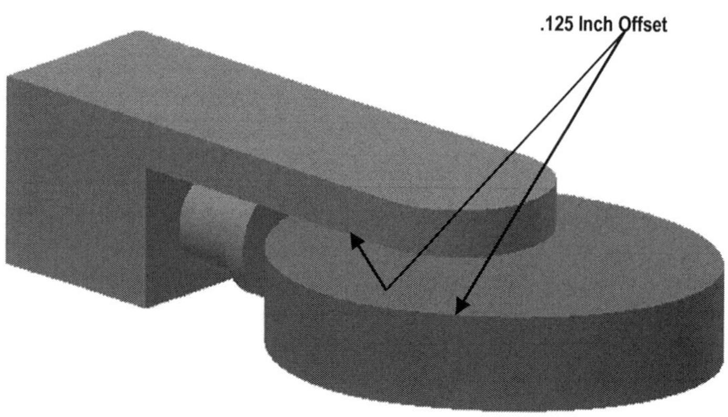

Figure 37

43. Use the **Rotate** command to rotate the part as shown. The disc cam's location on the shaft should be similar to Figure 38.

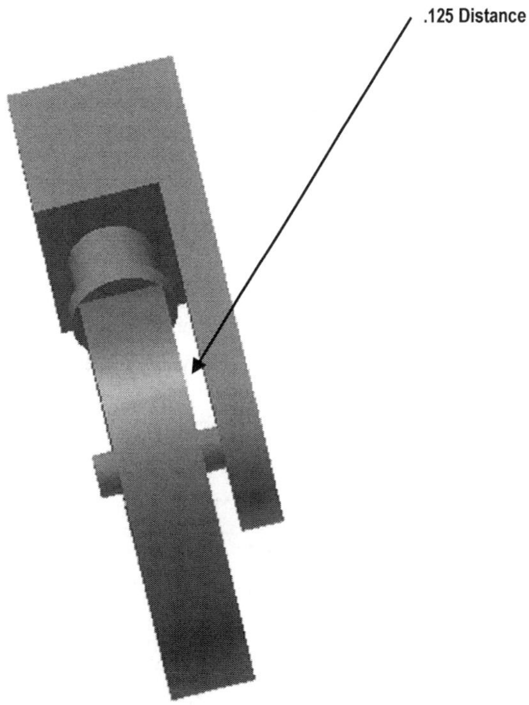

Figure 38

44. Use the **Rotate** command to rotate the assembly around as shown in Figure 39.

Figure 39

45. Move the cursor to the upper left portion of the screen and left click on **Constrain** as shown in Figure 40.

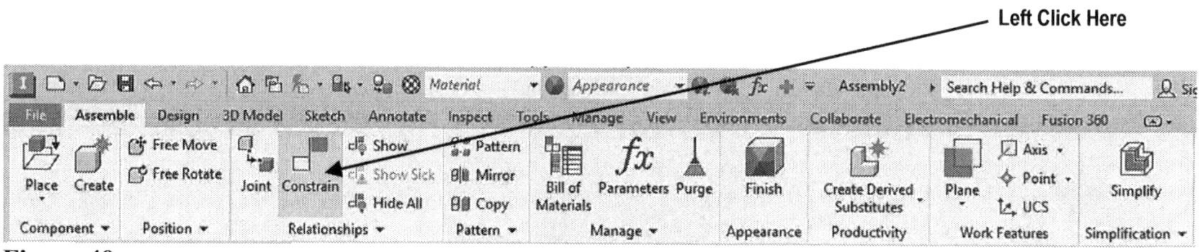

Figure 40

46. The Place Constraint dialog box will appear. Left click on the **Tangent** icon. Left click on the “Outside Tangent” solution as shown in Figure 41.

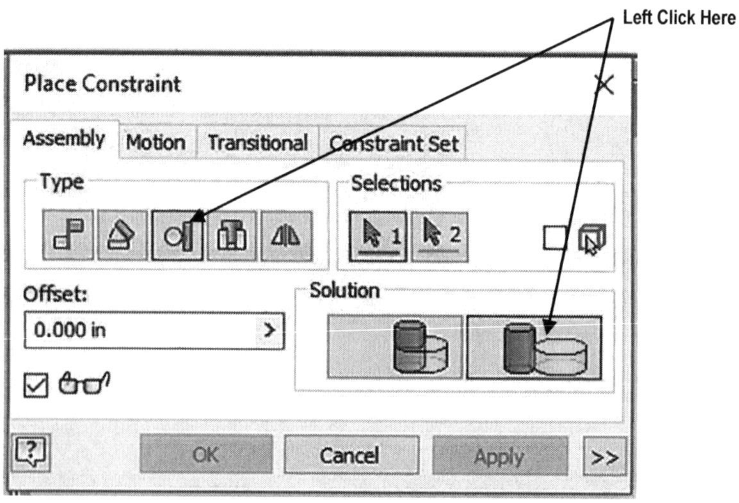

Figure 41

47. Left click on the lifter foot as shown in Figure 42.

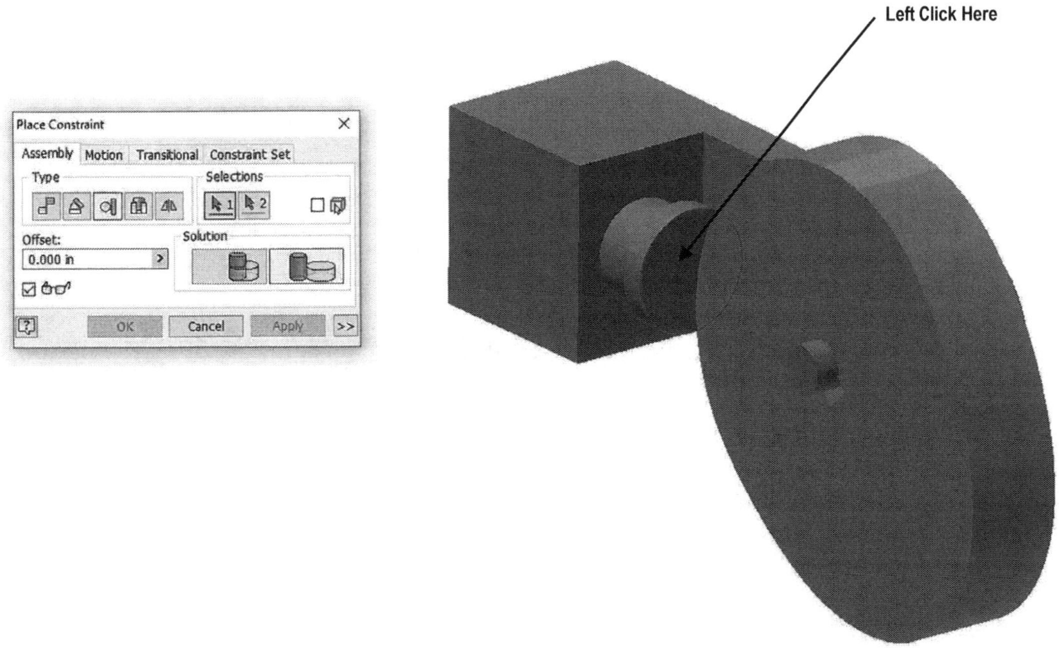

Figure 42

48. Left click on the surface of the disc cam as shown in Figure 43.

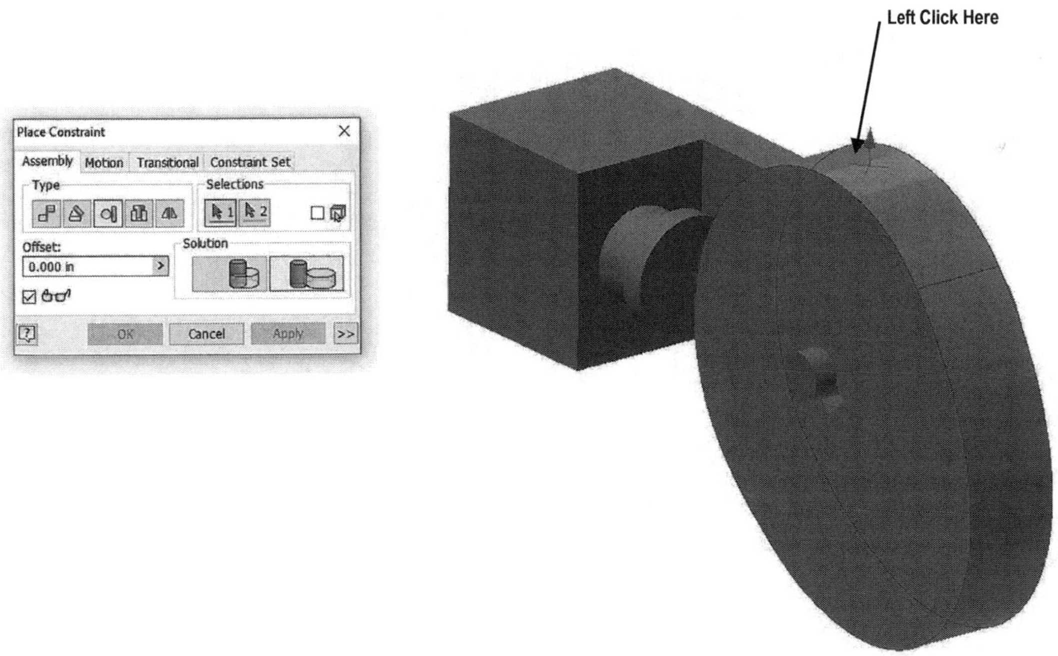

Figure 43

49. Left click on **OK** as shown in Figure 44.

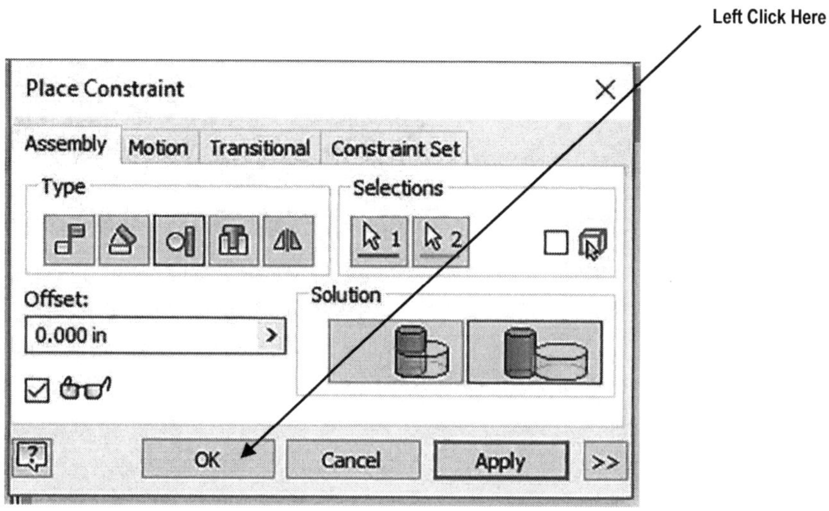

Figure 44

50. Use the cursor to rotate the disc cam upward as shown in Figure 45.

Figure 45

51. Move the cursor to the upper left portion of the screen and left click on **Constrain** as shown in Figure 46.

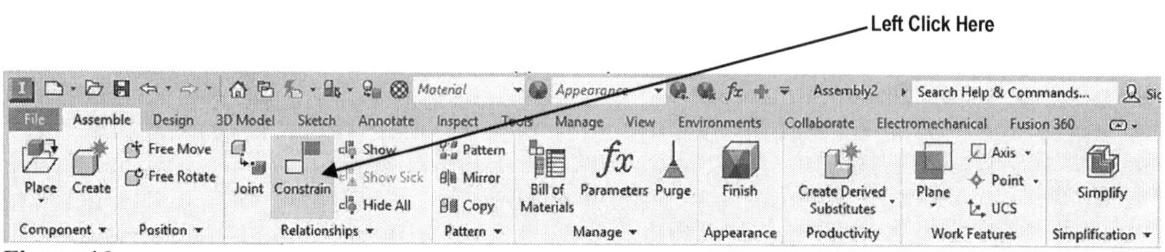

Figure 46

52. The Place Constraint dialog box will appear. Left click on the **Angle** icon. Left click on the "Directed Angle" solution as shown in Figure 47.

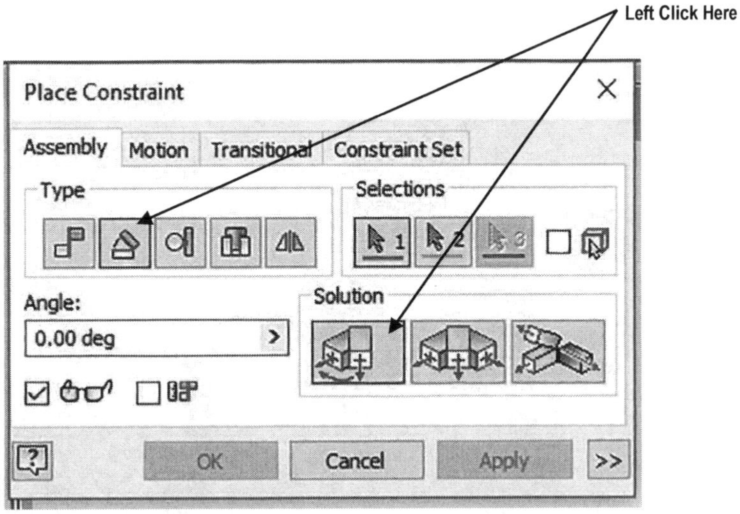

Figure 47

53. Use the **Zoom** command to zoom in on the key slot. Left click on the back (inside) of the key slot as shown in Figure 48.

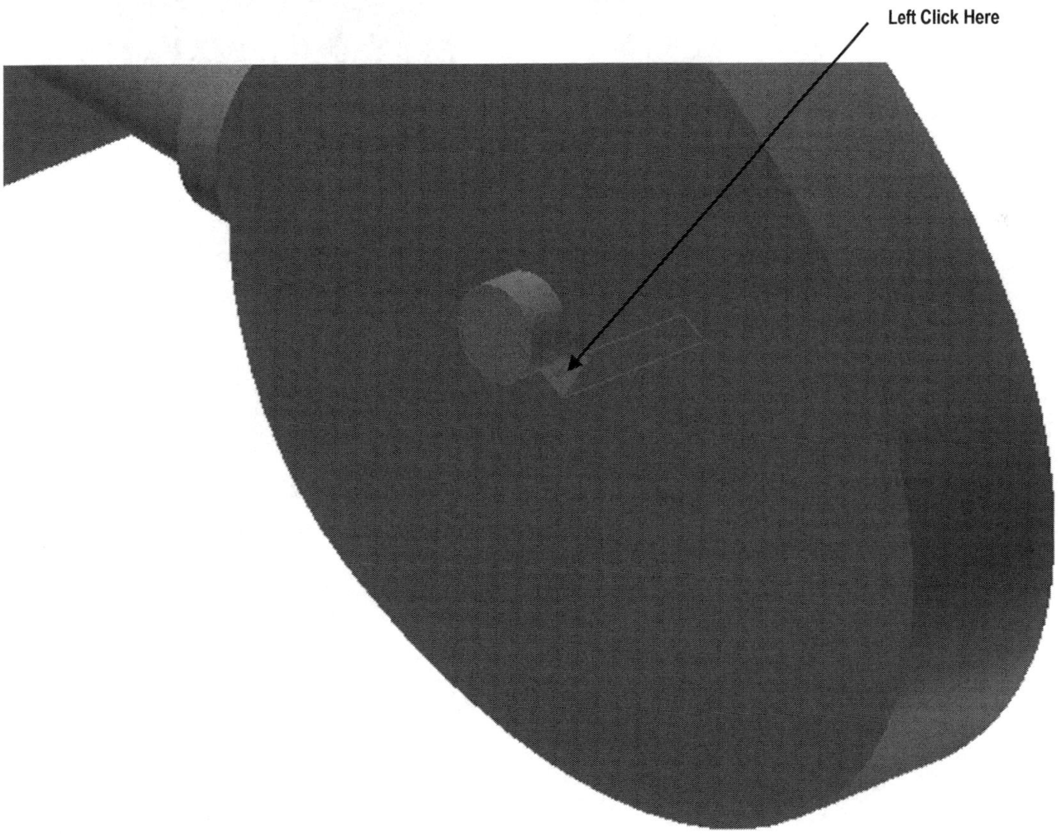

Figure 48

Learn to animate the assembly

54. Left click on the underside of the cam case as shown in Figure 49.

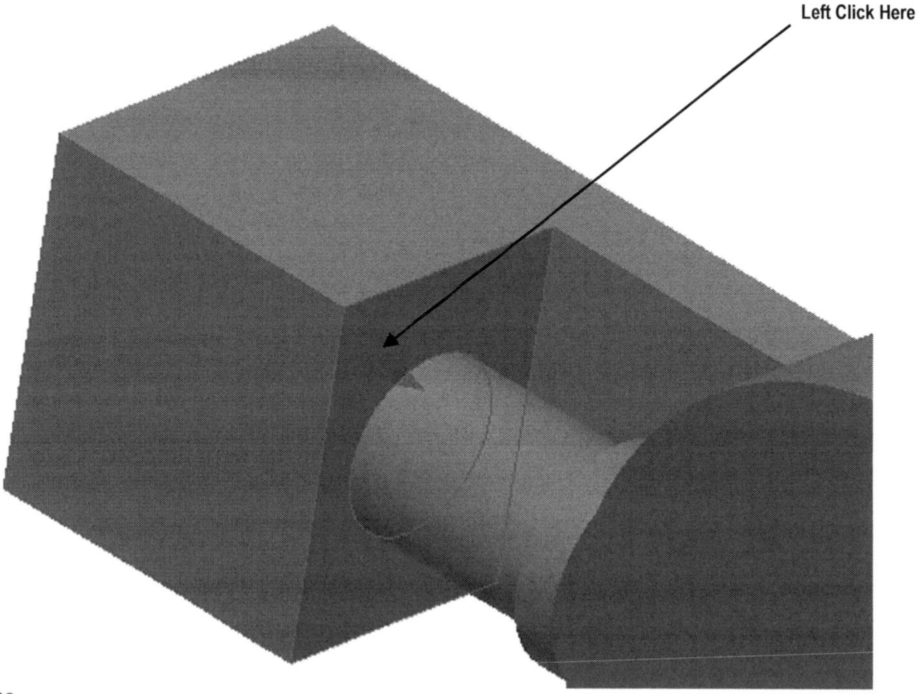

Figure 49

55. Left click on **OK** as shown in Figure 50.

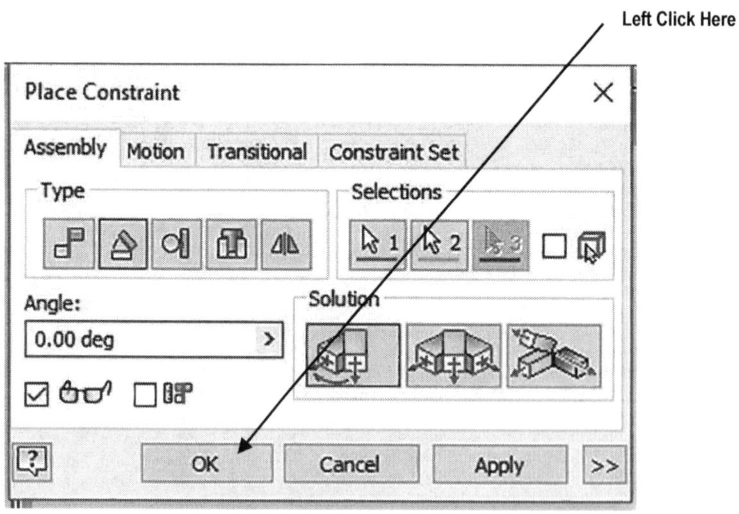

Figure 50

56. Move the cursor to the lower left portion of the screen to the part tree. Scroll down to **Angle:1** and right click once. A pop-up menu will appear. Left click on **Drive** as shown in Figure 51.

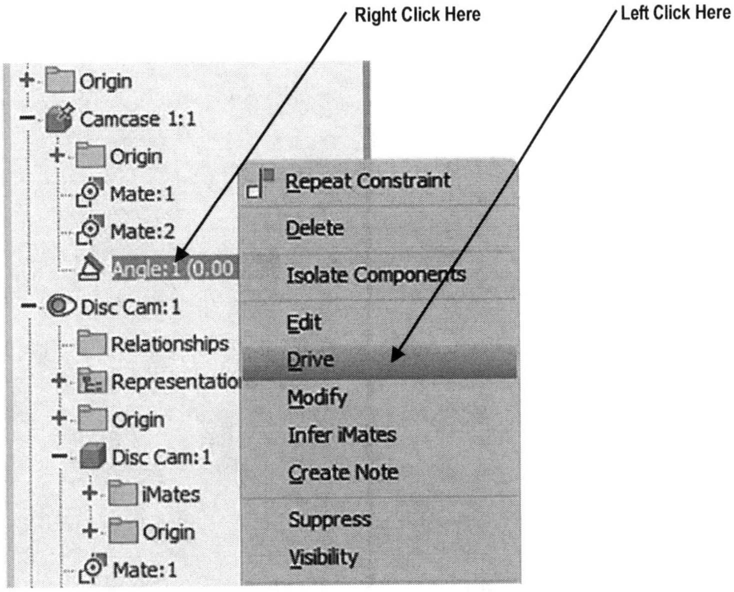

Figure 51

57. The Drive Constraint dialog box will appear. Enter **0** degrees under "Start." Enter **360000** degrees under "End." Left click on the double arrows at the far lower right corner of the dialog box as shown in Figure 52.

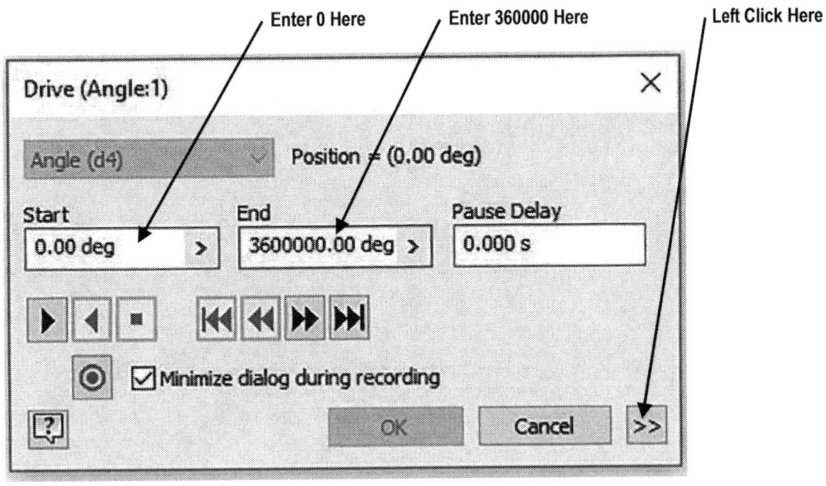

Figure 52

58. The Drive Constraint dialog box will expand providing more options. Enter **10** for the number of degrees. Place a dot next to Start/End/Start as shown in Figure 53.

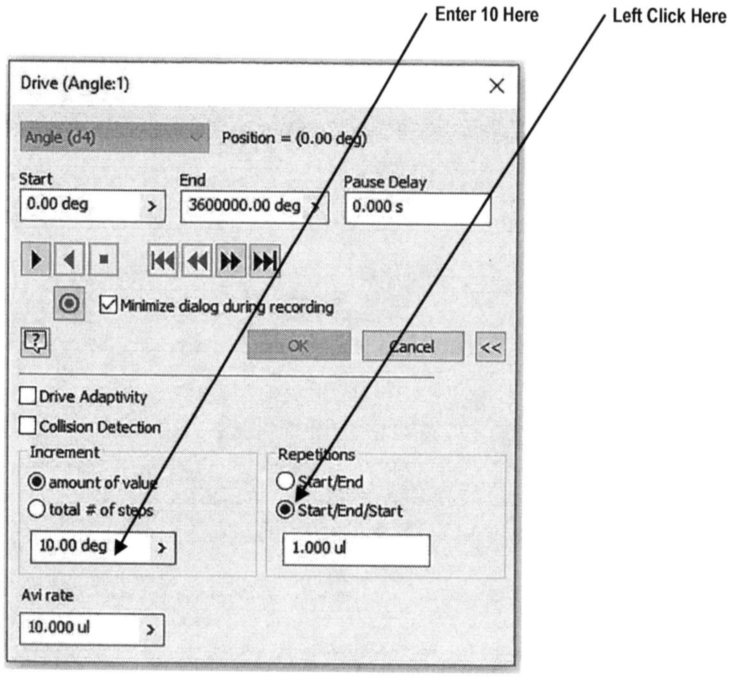

Figure 53

59. Use the **Zoom** option to zoom out if needed. Use the **Pan** option to move the assembly off to the side. Left click on the "Play" icon as shown in Figure 54.

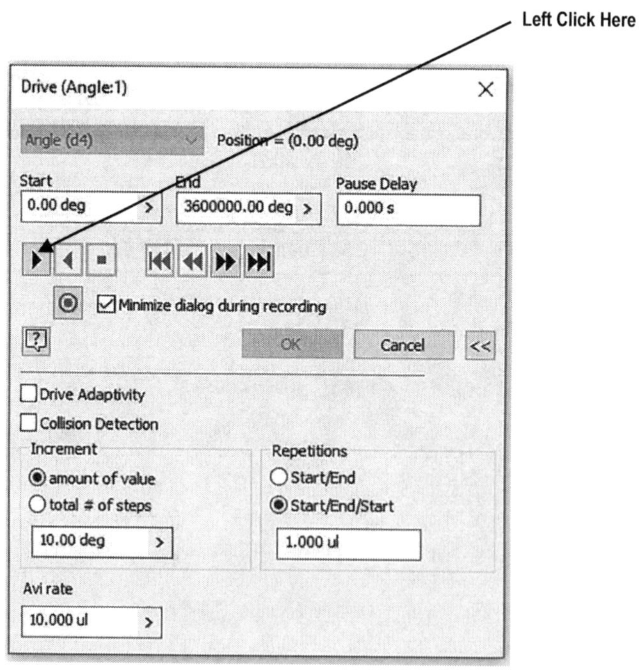

Figure 54

60. Inventor will animate the assembly causing the disc cam to rotate.

61. Left click on the "Stop" icon. The animation will stop. Left click on the "Minimize" icon. The Drive Constraint dialog box will get smaller. Left click on the "Rewind" icon. This will rewind the animation back to 0 degrees as shown in Figure 55. Refer to Chapter 7 for instructions on how to create an .avi or .wmv file.

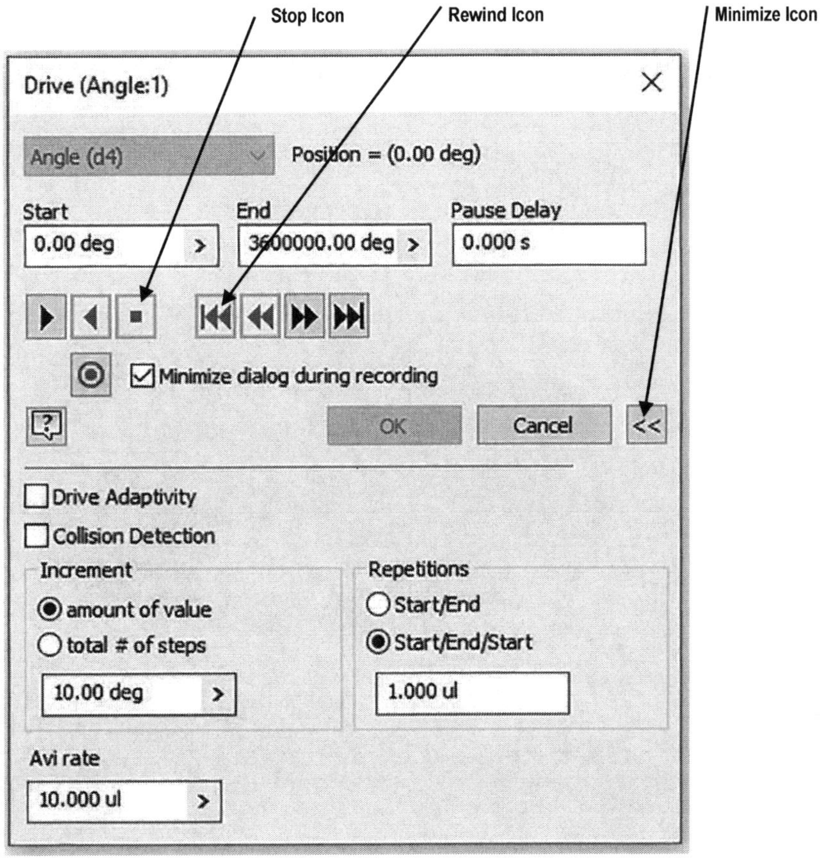

Figure 55

Chapter Problems

Problem 13-1

Create the following roller lifter and use it to replace the flat bottom lifter and constrain it to the Disc Cam as described in the chapter.

Using the existing flat bottom lifter, modify the base to utilize a small roller wheel. Use the Rectangle command to cut a .375 inch portion of the lifter as shown. Center the .063 hole on the lifter body.

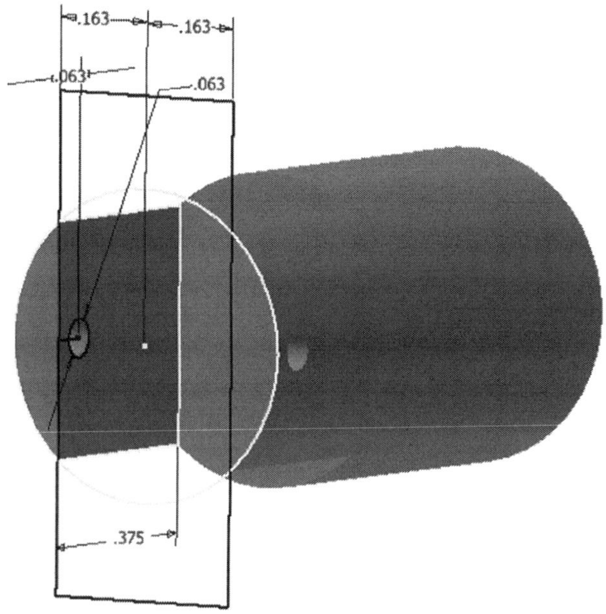

Create the roller pin as shown.

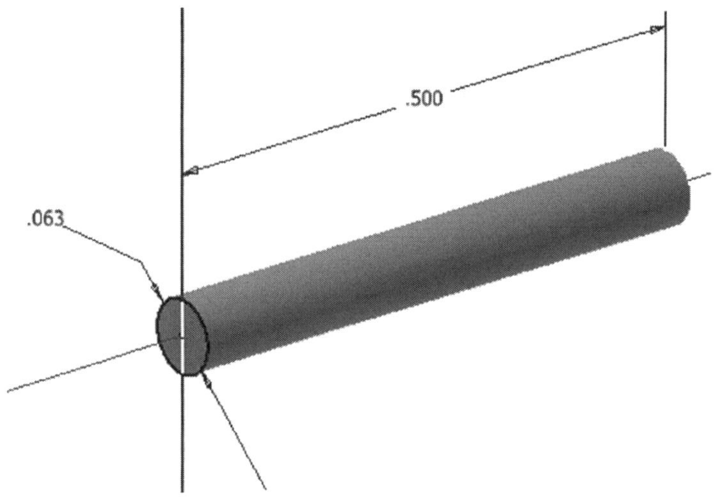

Create the roller wheel as shown.

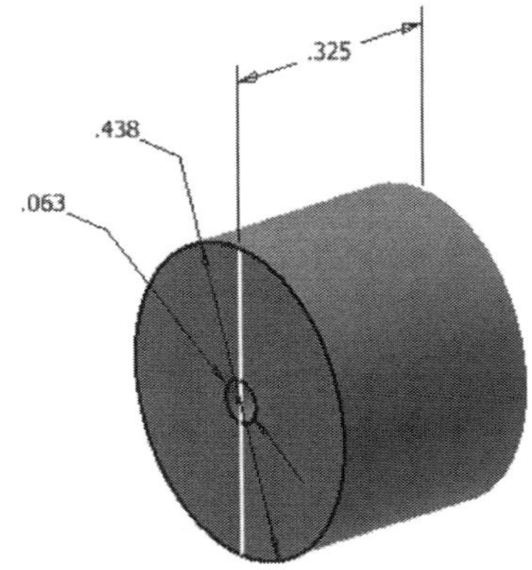

Your screen should look similar to what is shown.

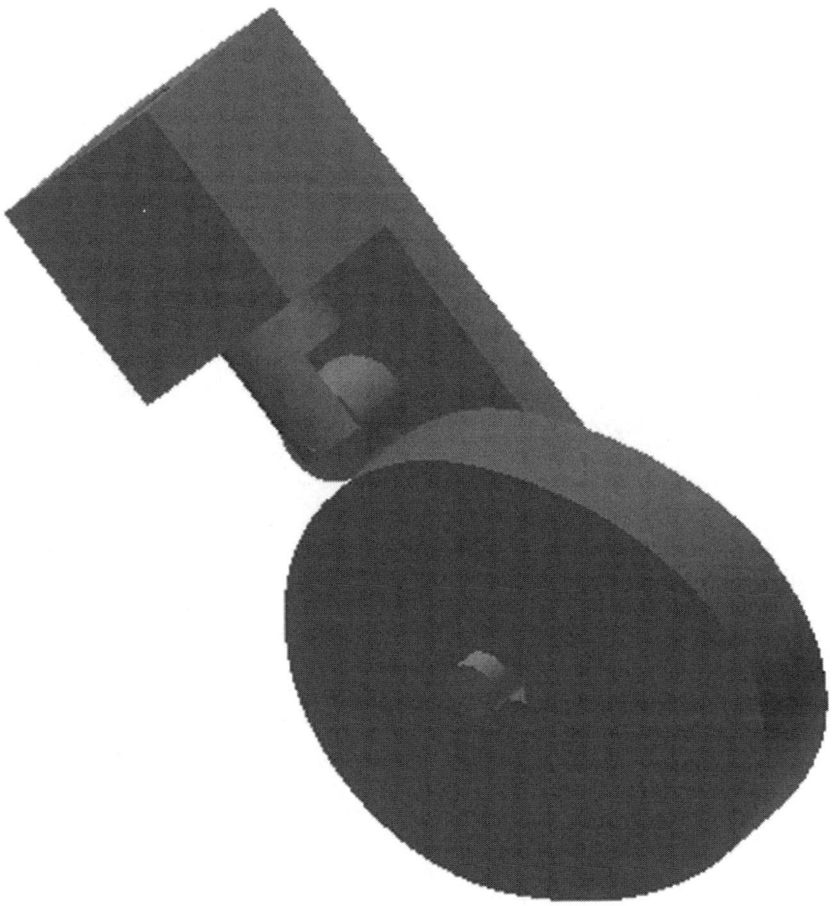

CHAPTER 14

Introduction to Sheet Metal

Objectives:

1. Learn to create a simple sheet metal part
2. Learn to create simple bends
3. Learn to create an angled bend

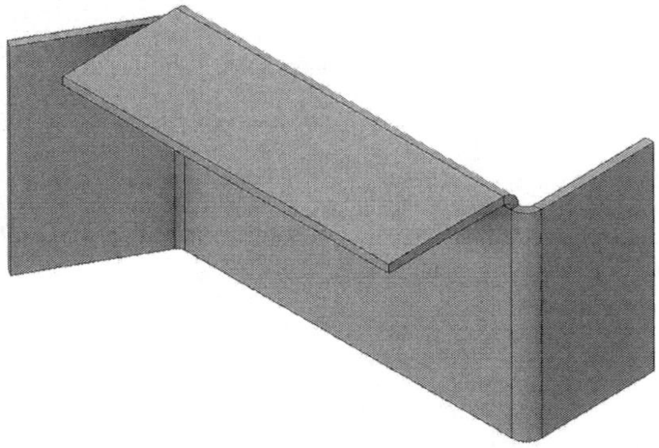

Chapter 14 includes instruction on how to create the part shown.

1. Start Inventor by referring to "Chapter 1 Getting Started."
2. After Inventor is running, left click on the "New" icon. The Create New File dialog box will appear. Left click on the en-US folder. Left click on **Sheet Metal.ipt**. Left click on **Create** as shown in Figure 1.

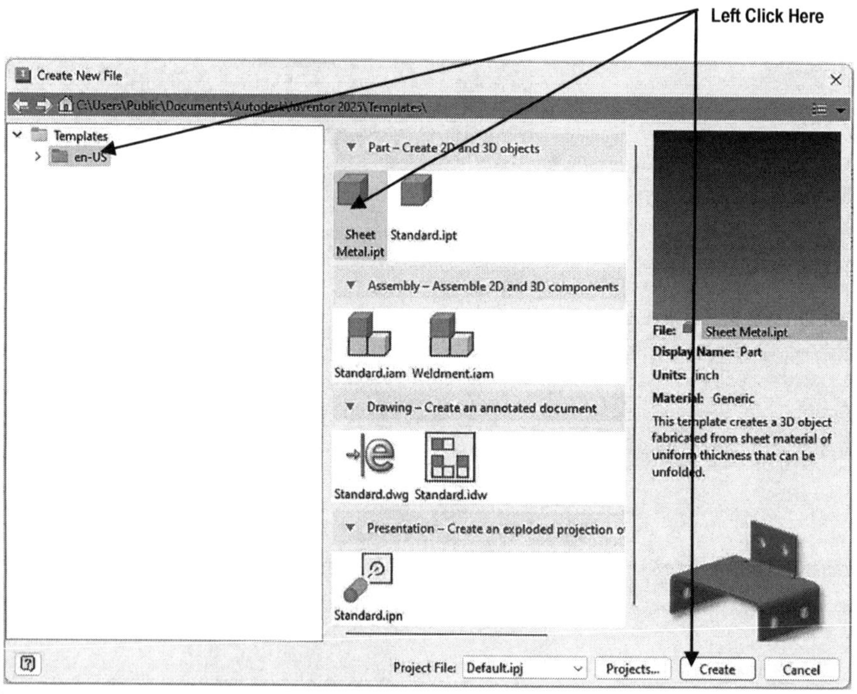

Figure 1

3. Your screen should look similar to Figure 2.

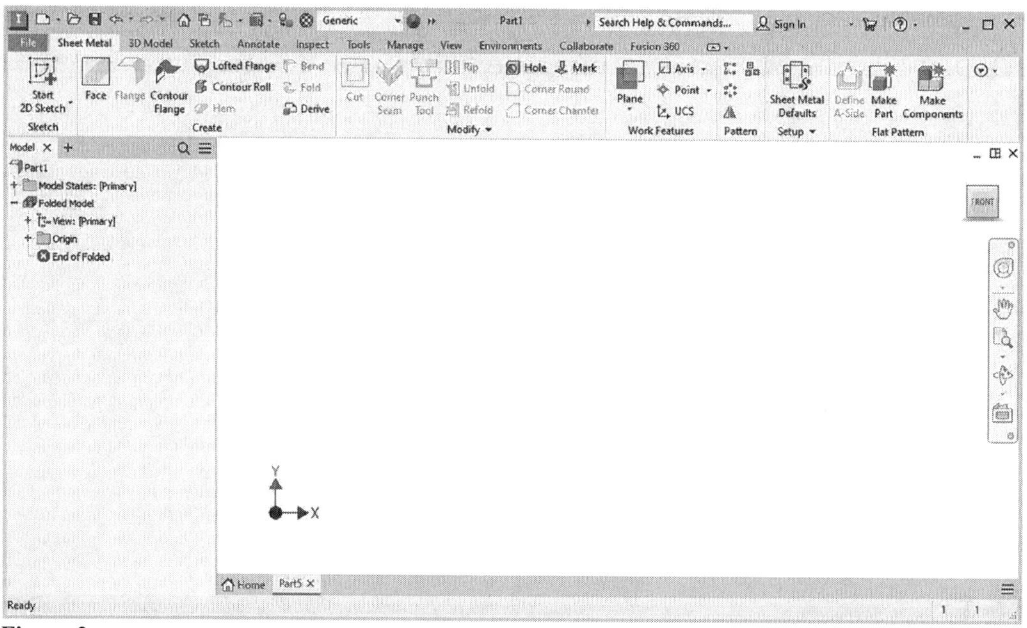
Figure 2

Learn to create a simple sketch

4. Move the cursor to the upper left portion of the screen and left click on the **Start 2D Sketch** icon. Move the cursor to the middle portion of the screen and left click on the **XY Plane** as shown in Figure 3.

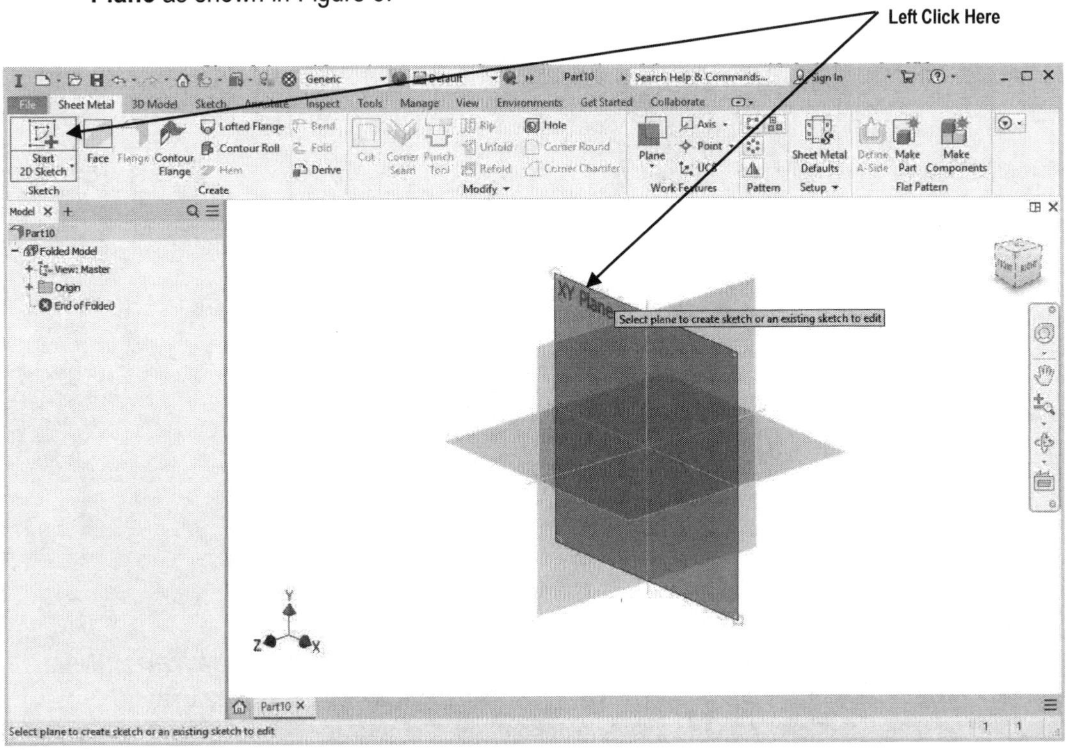

Figure 3

5. Use the Rectangle command to create the following sketch as shown in Figure 4.

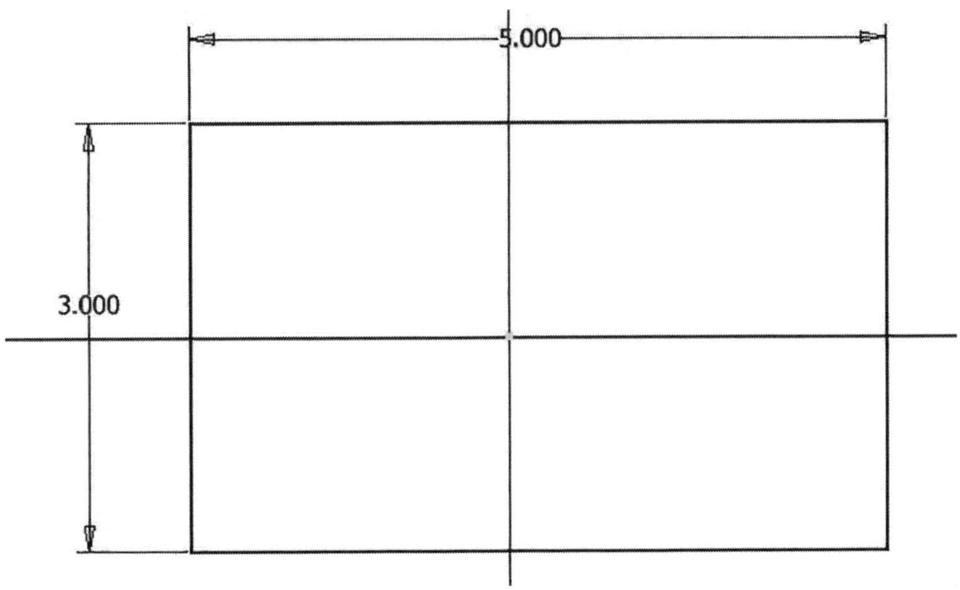

Figure 4

6. Exit out of the Sketch as shown in Figure 5.

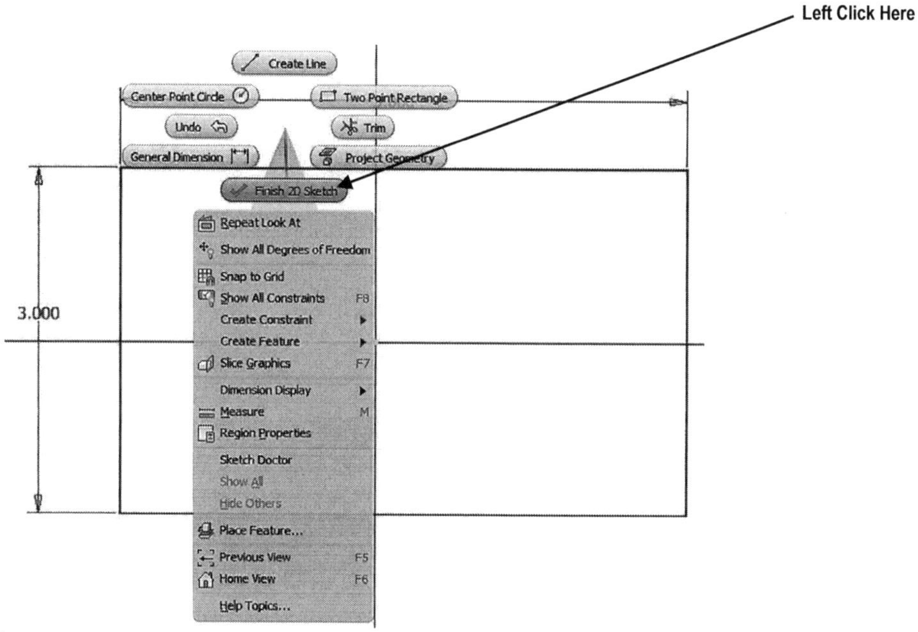

Figure 5

Learn to create a Face

7. Move the cursor to the upper left portion of the screen and left click on the **Sheet Metal** tab. Left click on the **Face** icon. The Face command works similar to the Extrude command. Left click on **OK** as shown in Figure 6.

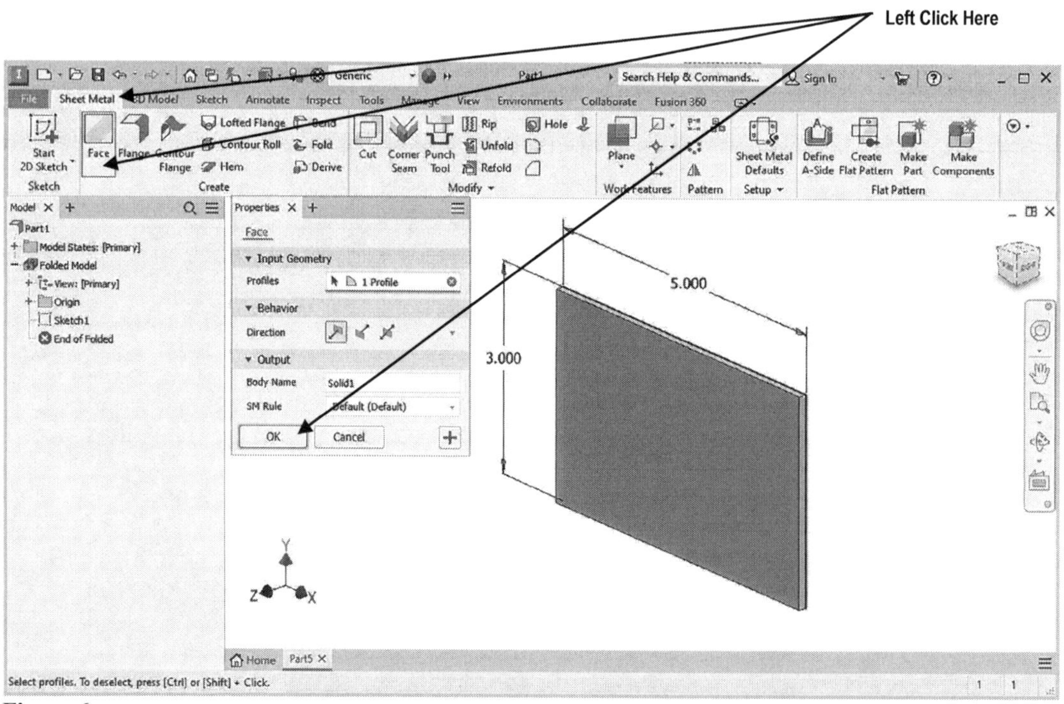

Figure 6

8. Your screen should look similar to Figure 7.

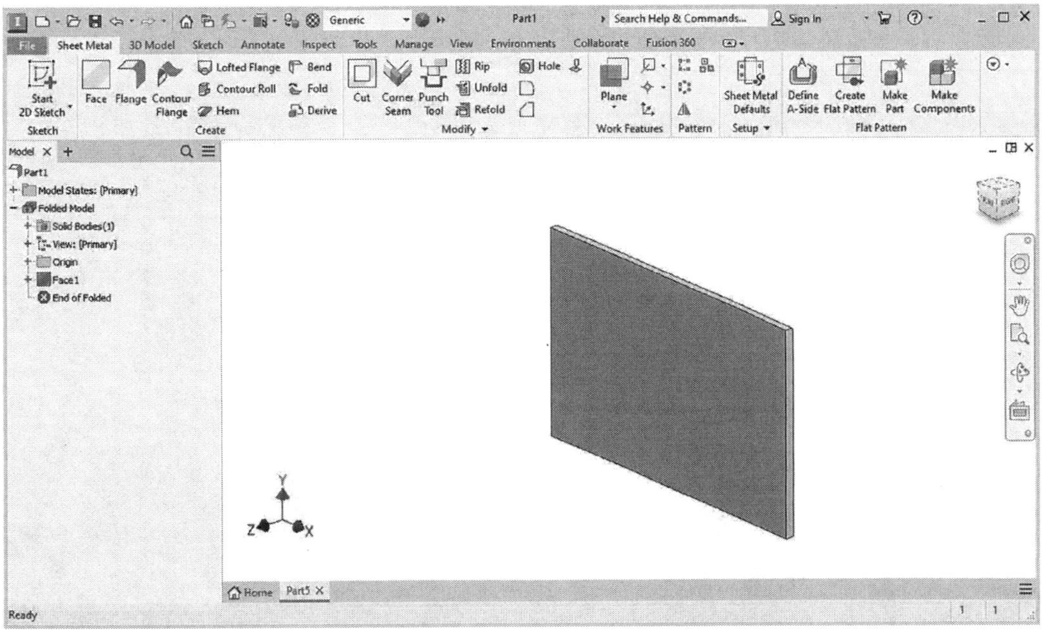

Figure 7

Learn to create a Flange

9. Move the cursor to the upper left portion of the screen and left click on the **Flange** icon. The Flange dialog box will appear as shown in Figure 8.

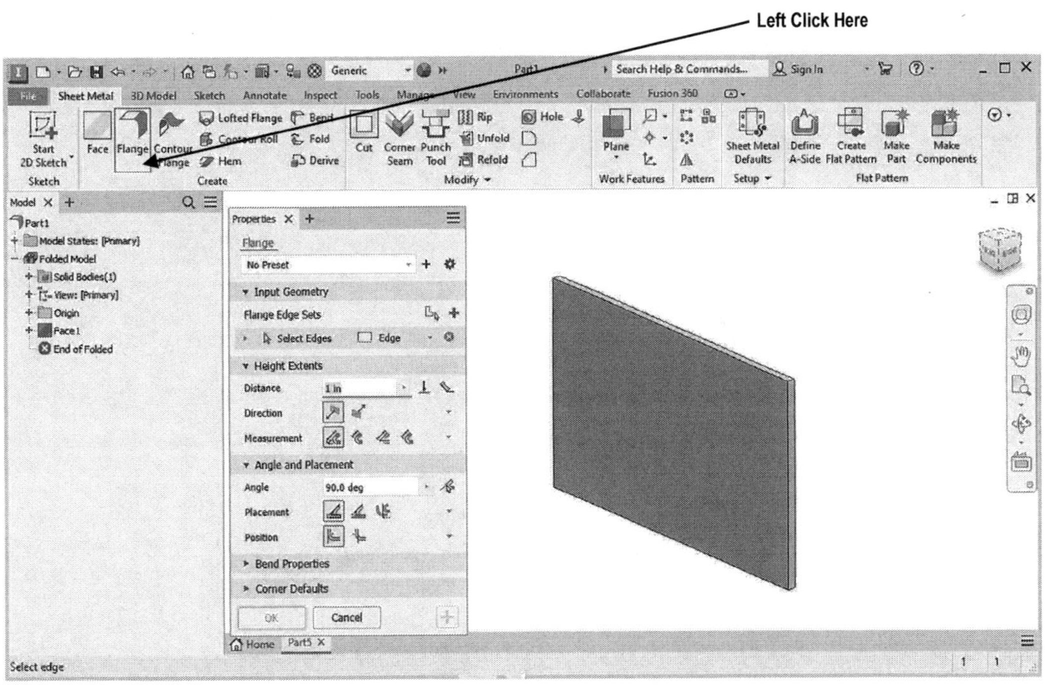

Figure 8

Learn to create a sheet metal bend

10. Left click on the edge of the part. Inventor will create a preview of the flange and bend position on the outside edge (default) as shown in Figure 9.

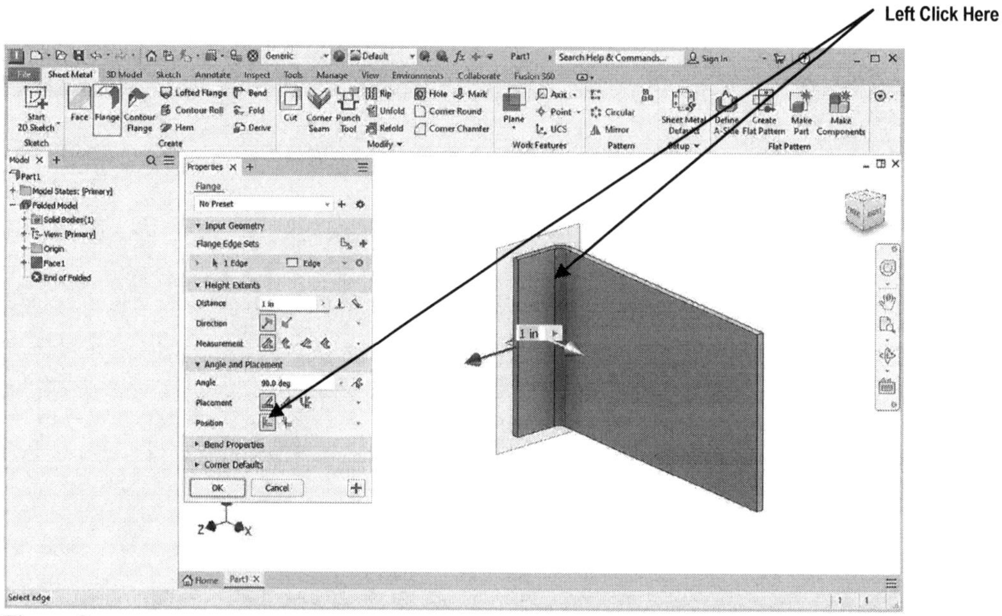

Figure 9

Learn to create a Bend from the adjacent face

11. Left click on the Bend Position icon. Inventor will move the bend position from the inside edge to the outside edge (Bend from the adjacent face). This is done to accommodate the thickness of the material as shown in Figure 10.

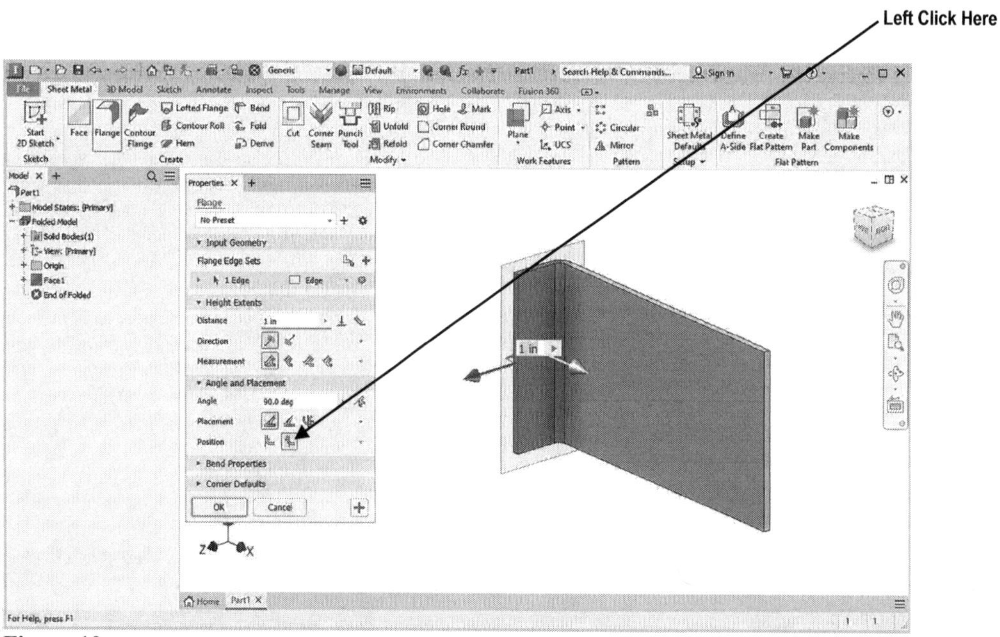

Figure 10

12. Enter **2.0** inches for the Distance as shown in Figure 11.

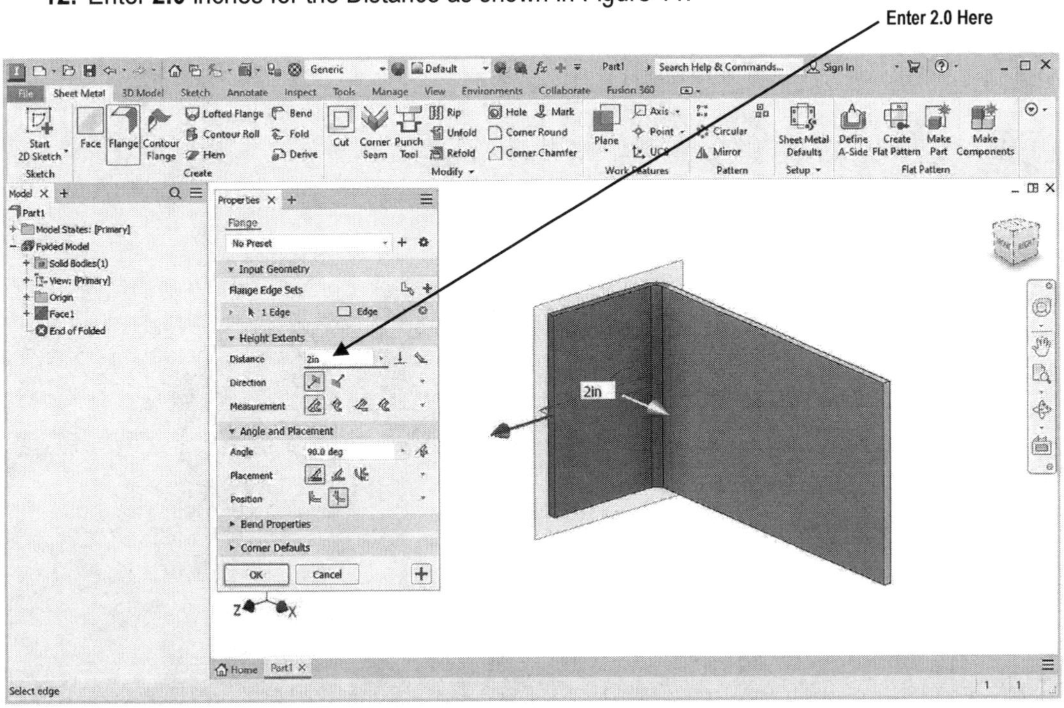

Figure 11

Learn to create an Angular Flange

13. Enter **60.0** for the Flange Angle. Left click on **OK** as shown in Figure 12.

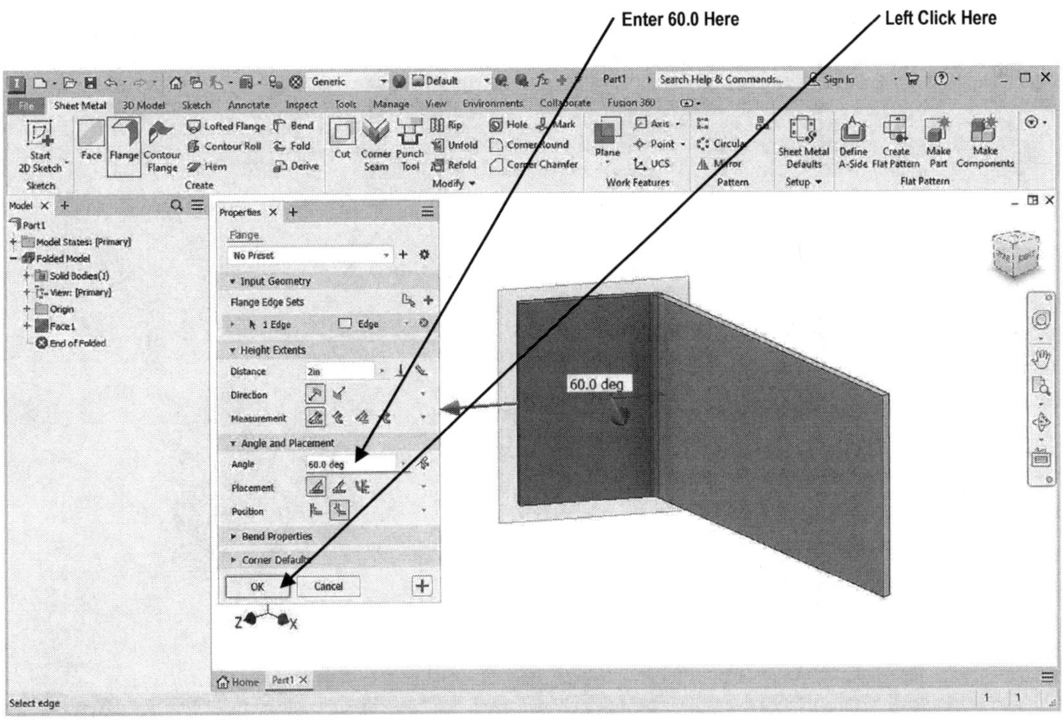

Figure 12

14. Your screen should look similar to Figure 13.

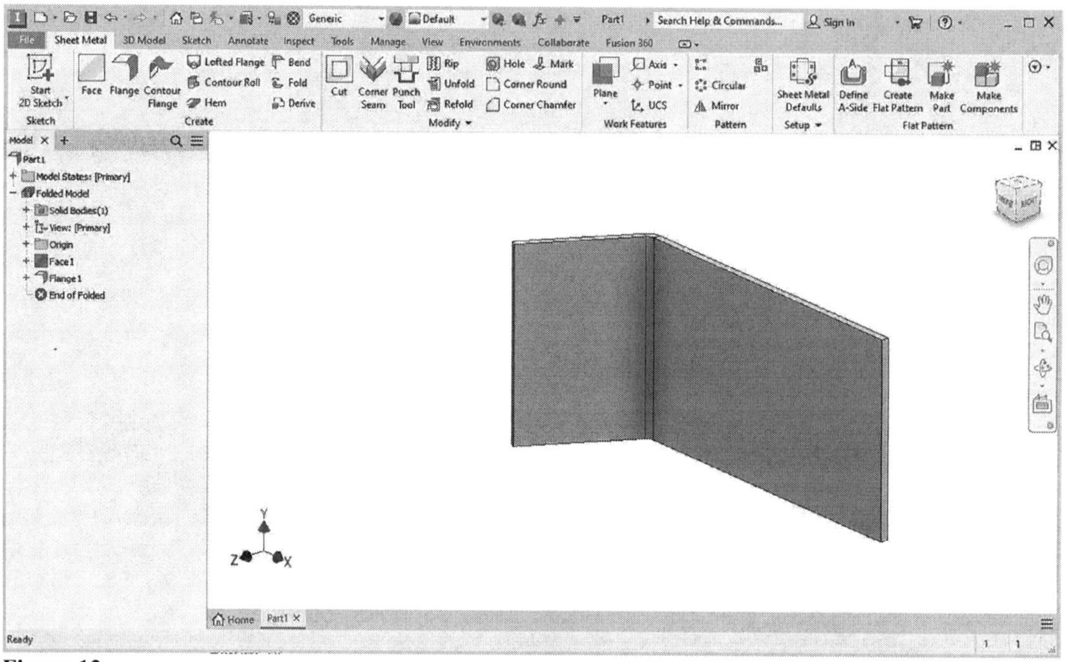

Figure 13

15. Left click on the Flange icon. Enter **90.0** for the Flange Angle. Left click on **OK** as shown in Figure 14.

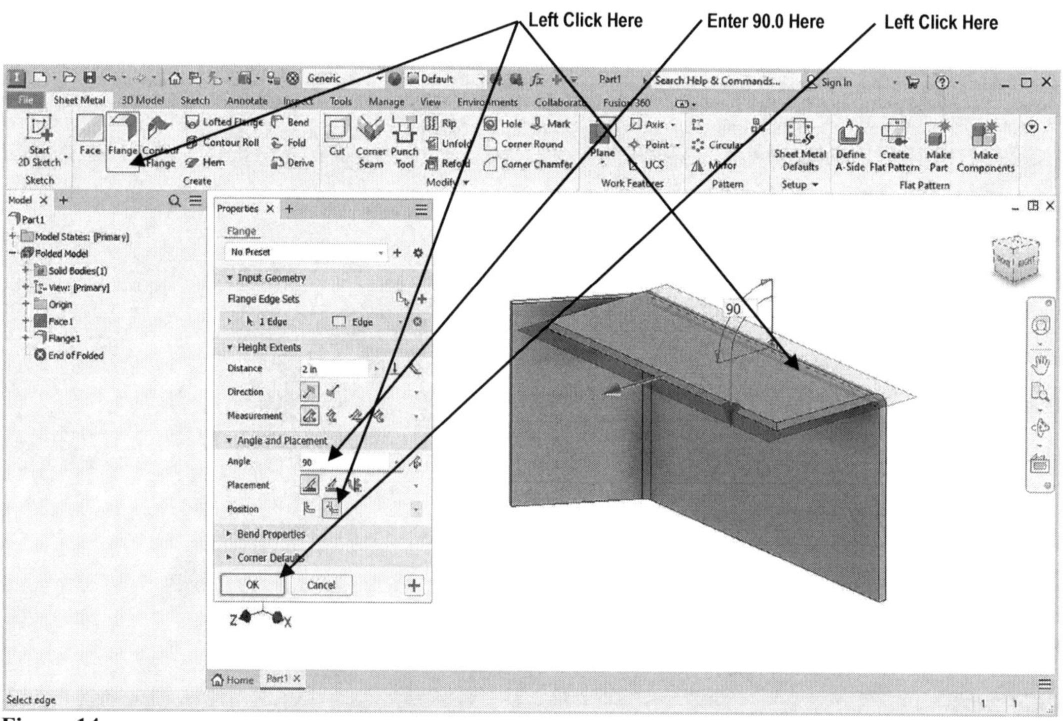

Figure 14

16. Repeat the same steps to create a flange facing to the rear as shown in Figure 15.

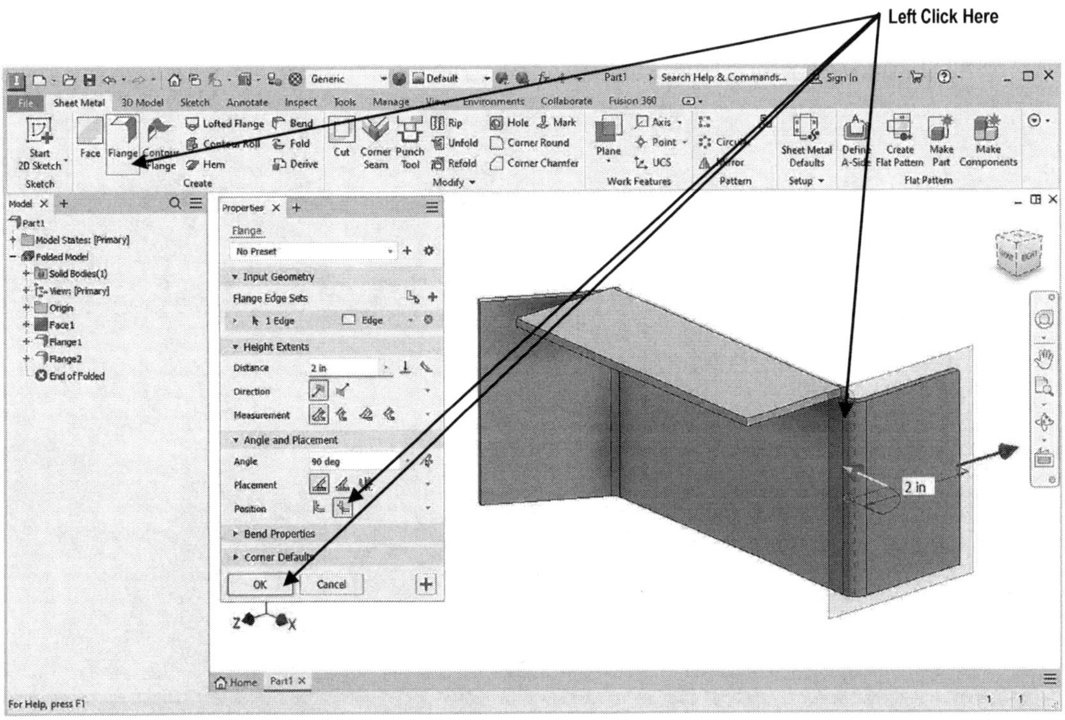

Figure 15

17. Your screen should look similar to Figure 16.

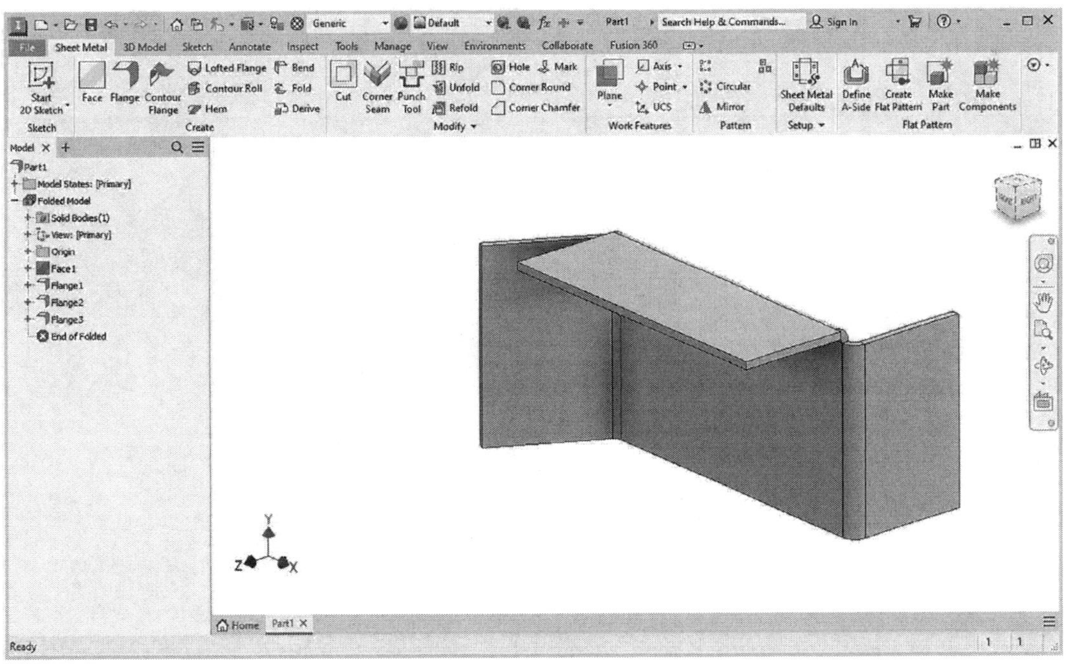

Figure 16

Learn to create a Flat Pattern

18. Move the cursor to the upper right portion of the screen and left click on the **Create Flat Pattern** icon as shown in Figure 17. The Create Flat Pattern command will "flatten" the part to show what it will look like when stamped from a piece of sheet metal.

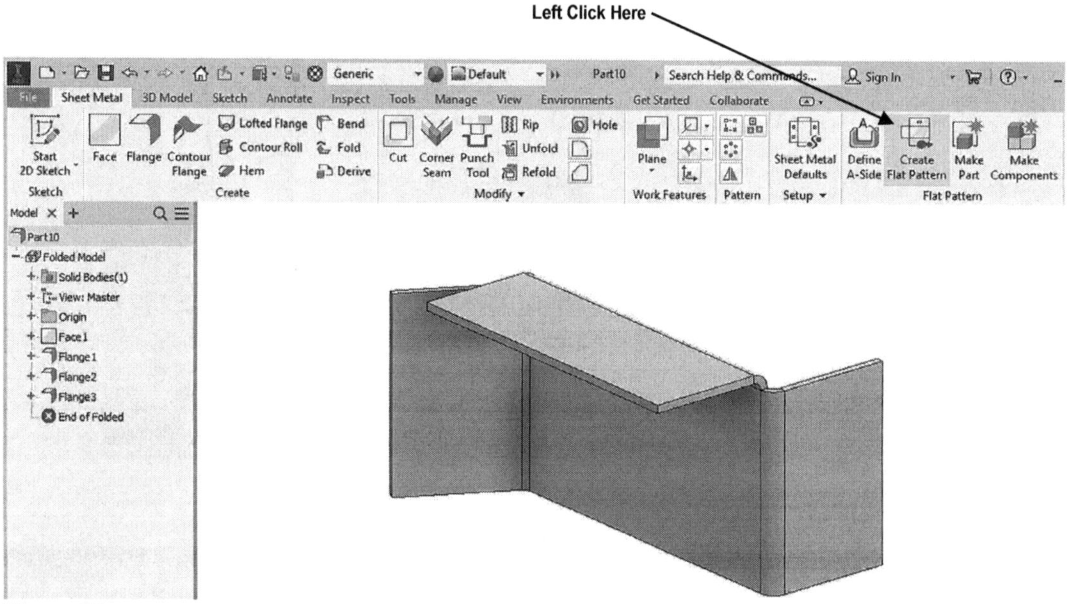

Figure 17

19. Your screen should look similar to Figure 18.

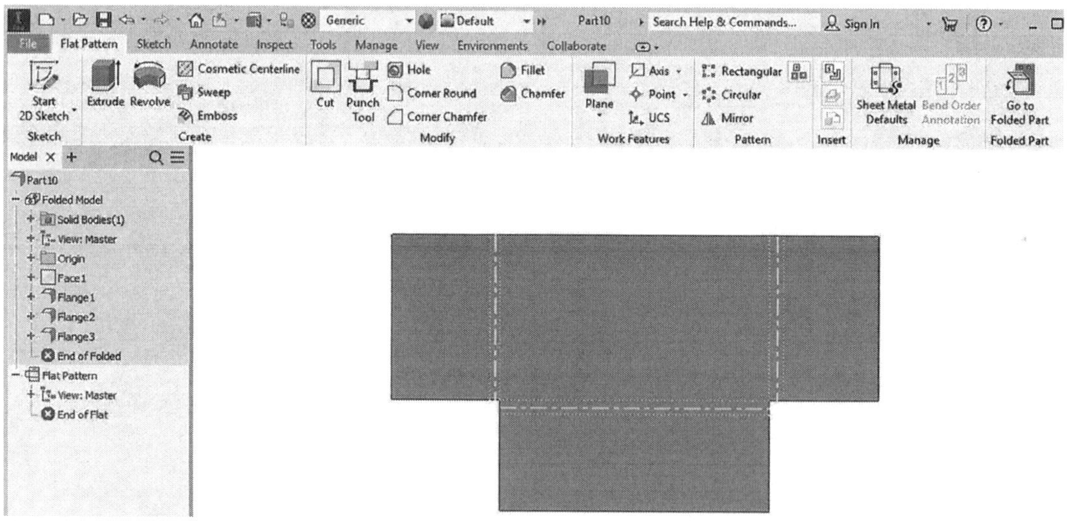

Figure 18

Learn to create a Bend Order Annotation

20. Left click on the **Bend Order Annotation** icon. Inventor will show the order the bends need to be made as shown in Figure 19.

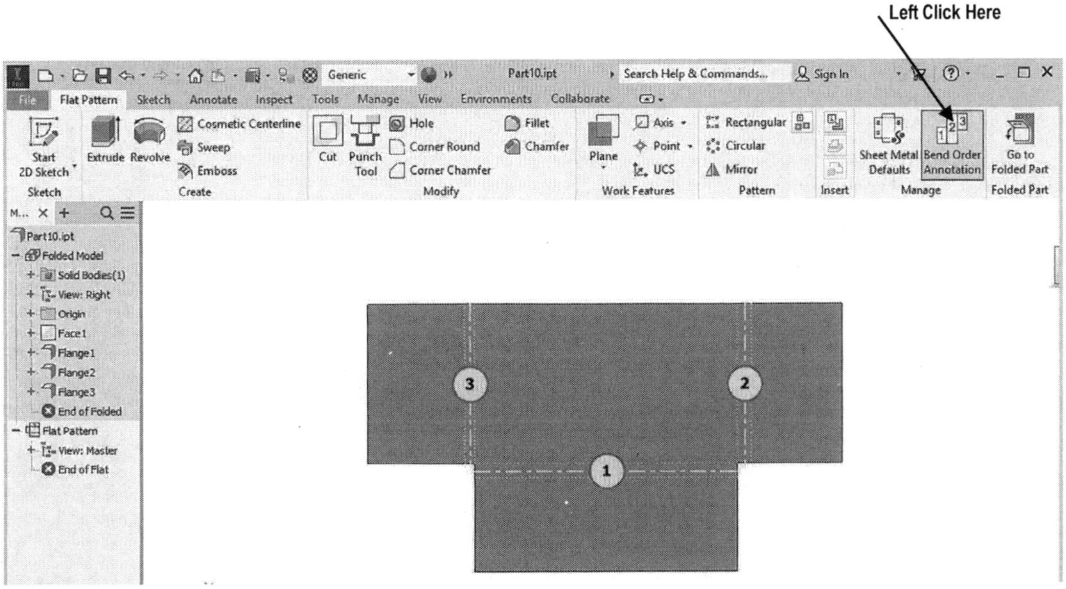

Figure 19

21. Left click on the **Go to Folded Part** icon as shown in Figure 20.

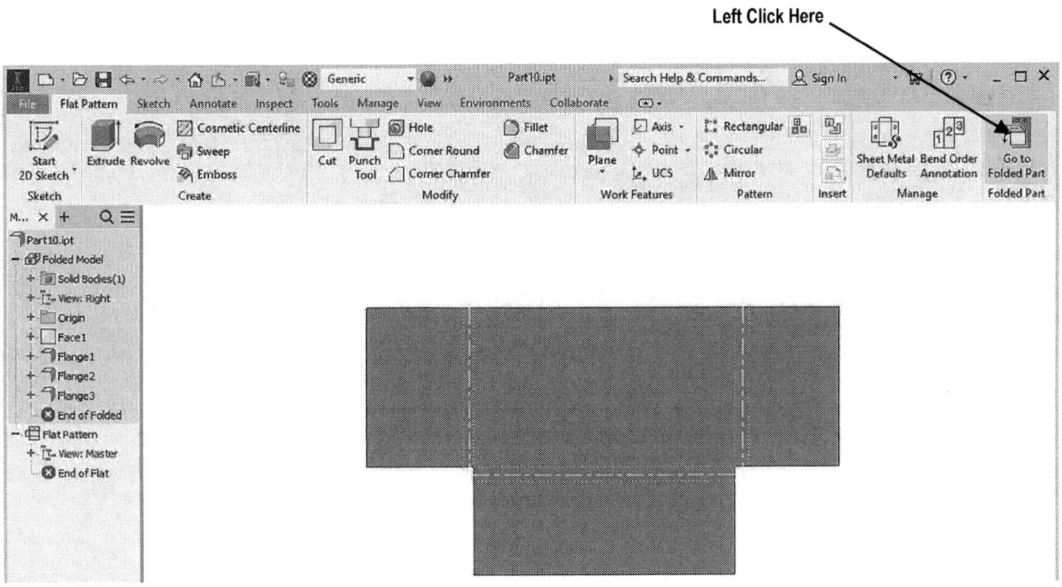

Figure 20

22. Your screen should look similar to Figure 21.

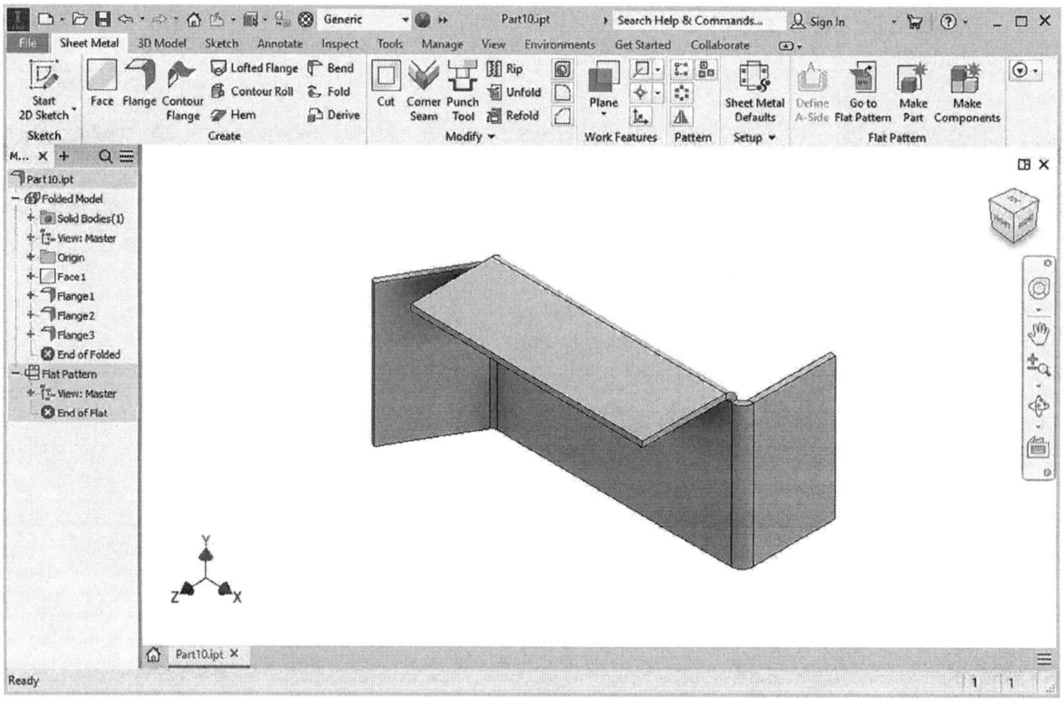

Figure 21

Learn to create a 3 view drawing of a Flat Pattern

23. Left click on the drop-down arrow to the right of the New icon. A drop-down menu will appear. Left click on **Drawing** as shown in Figure 22.

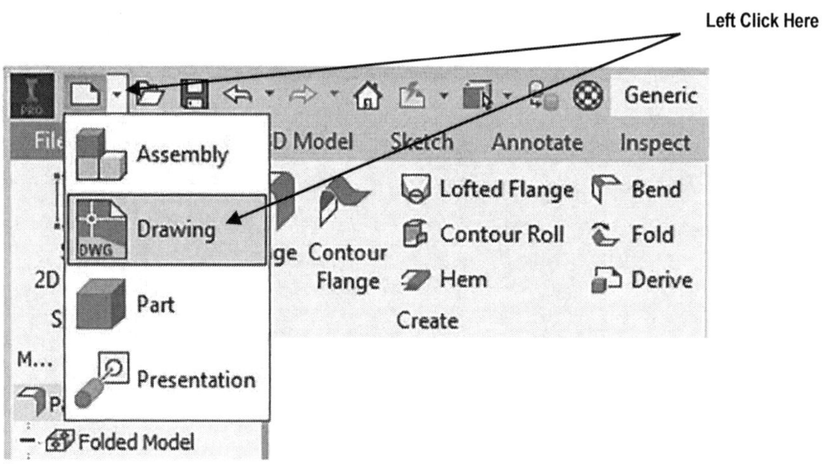

Figure 22

24. The Drawing Panel will appear as shown in Figure 23.

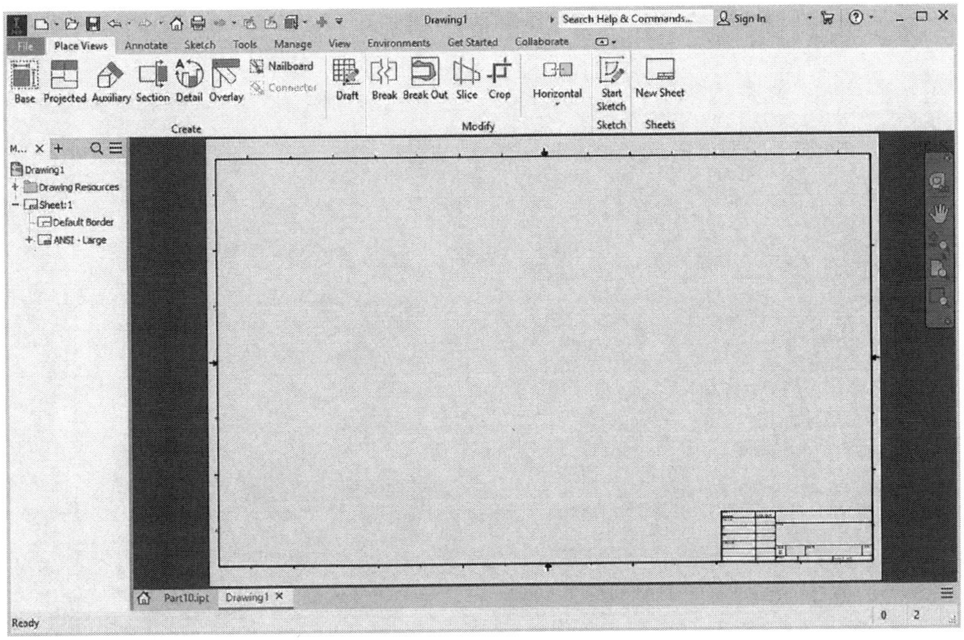

Figure 23

25. Left click on the **Base** icon. The Drawing View dialog box will appear. Left click on the dot to the left of Flat Pattern. Inventor will create a preview of the flat pattern. Left click on **OK** as shown in Figure 24.

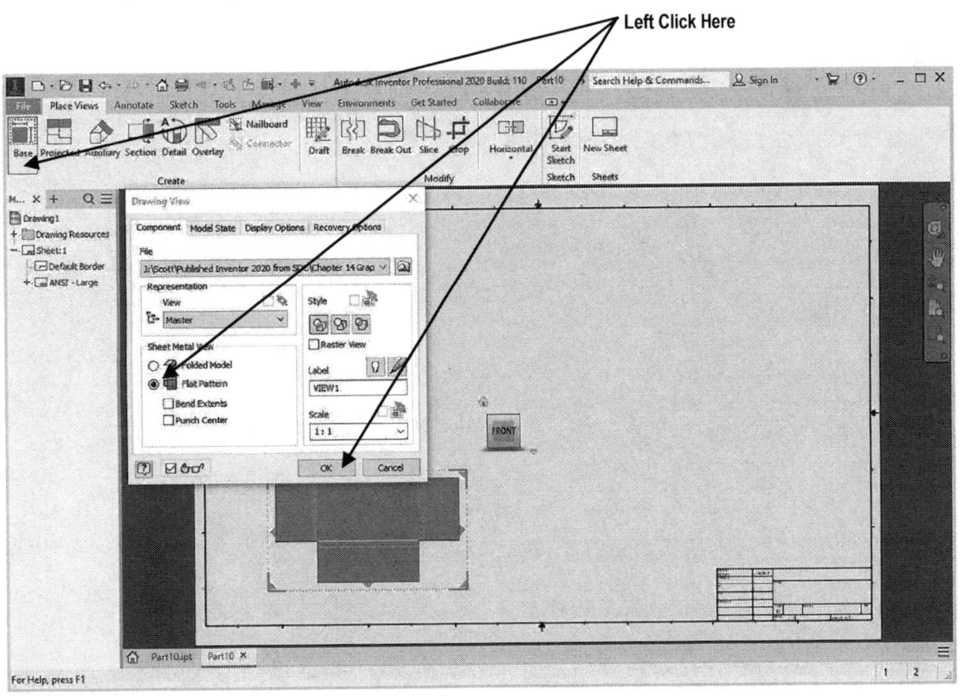

Figure 24

26. Your screen should look similar to Figure 25.

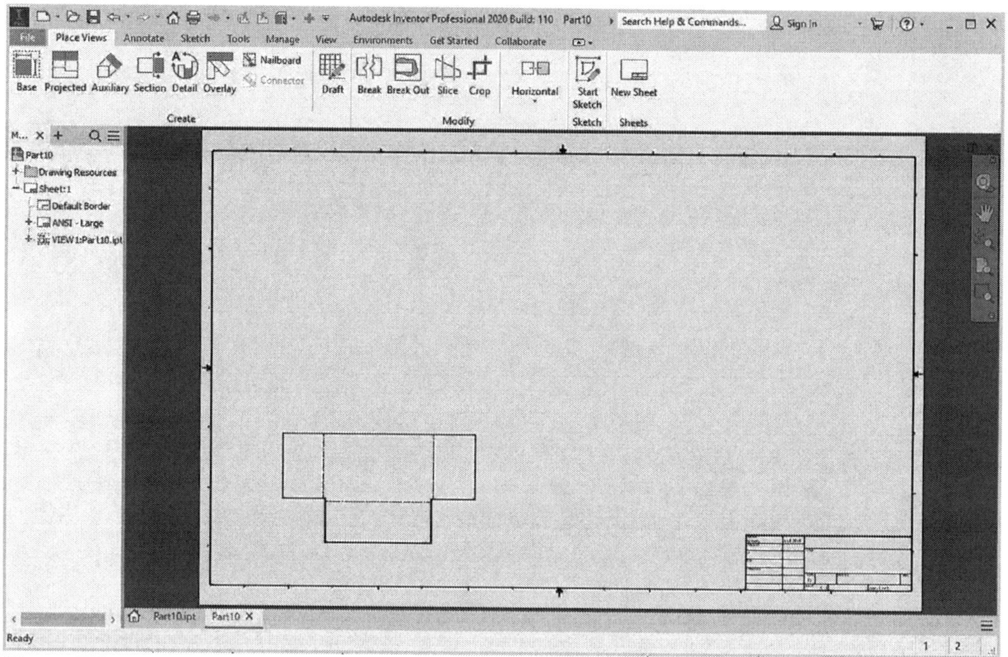

Figure 25

27. Left click on the **Annotate** tab. Add dimensions as shown in Figure 26.

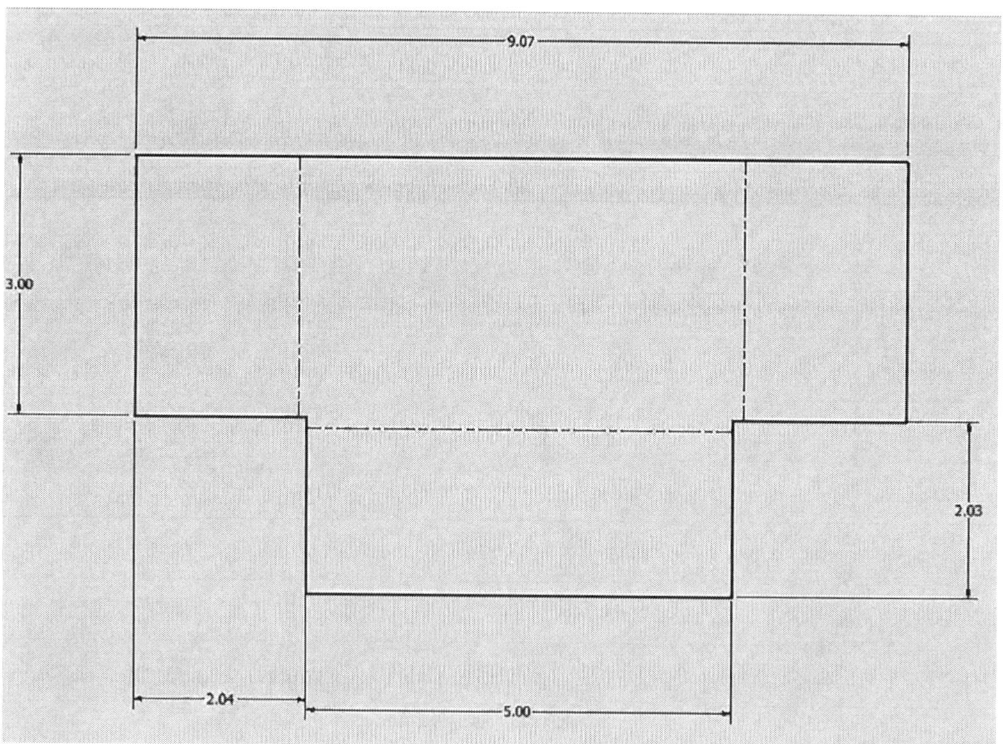

Figure 26

Learn to create a 3 view drawing of a folded part

28. Move the cursor to the lower left portion of the screen and left click on the Part.ipt tab as shown in Figure 27.

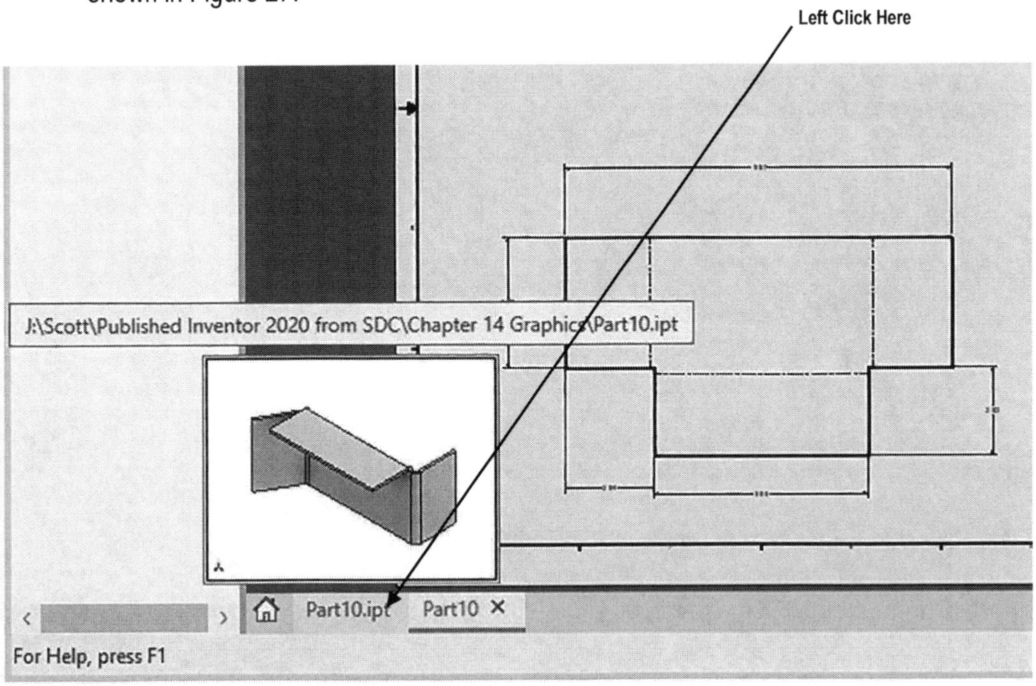

Figure 27

29. Your screen should look similar to Figure 28.

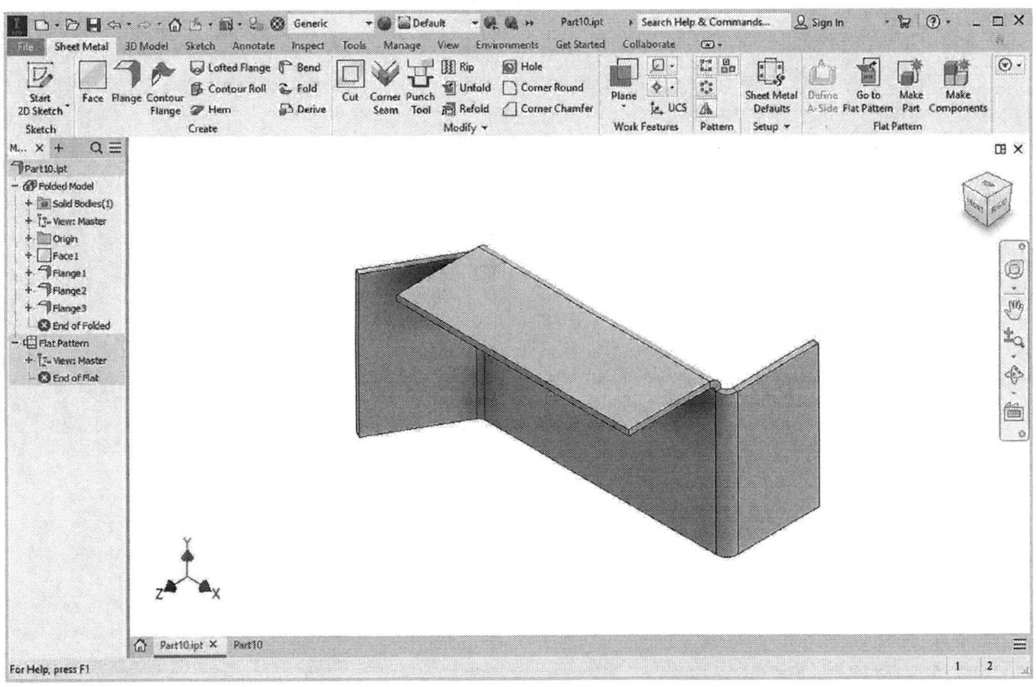

Figure 28

30. Left click on the drop-down arrow to the right of the New icon. A drop-down menu will appear. Left click on **Drawing** as shown in Figure 29.

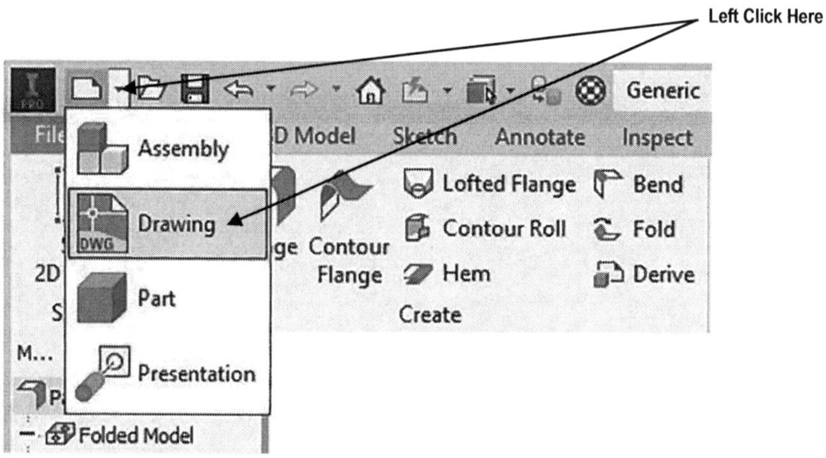

Figure 29

31. Your screen should look similar to Figure 30.

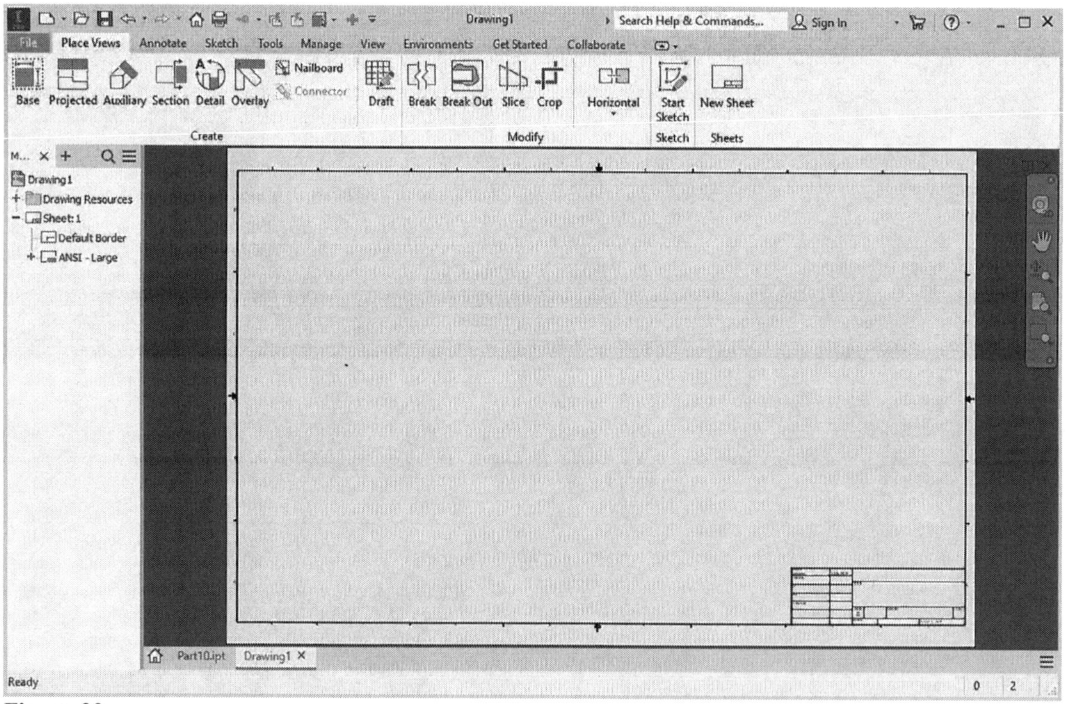

Figure 30

32. Left click on the **Base** icon. The Drawing View dialog box will appear. Place a dot to the left of Folded Model. Inventor will create a preview of the folded model. Left click on **OK** as shown in Figure 31.

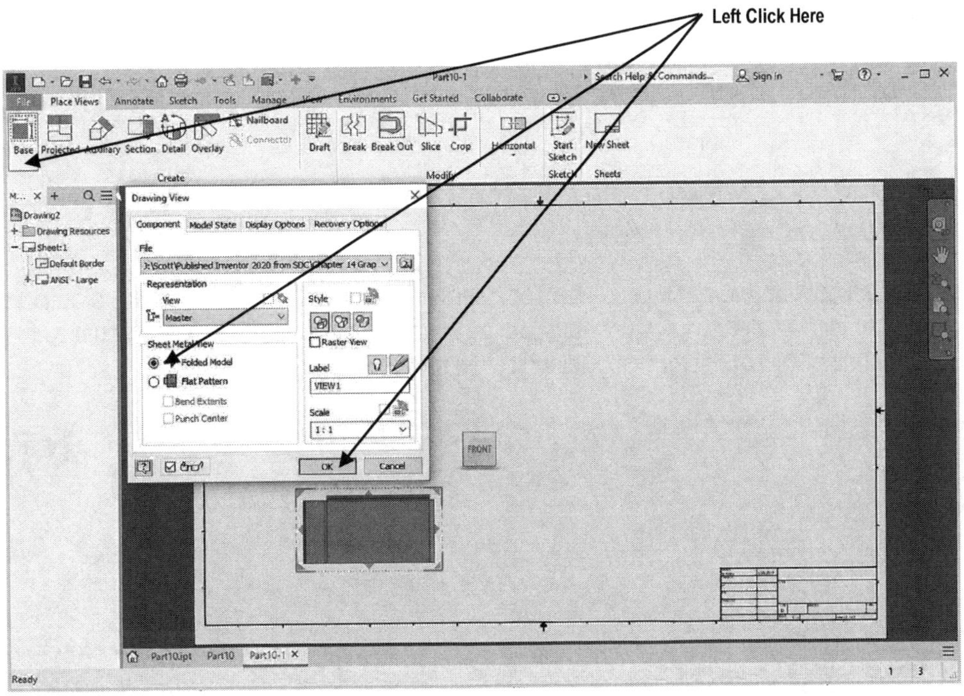

Figure 31

33. Your screen should look similar to Figure 32.

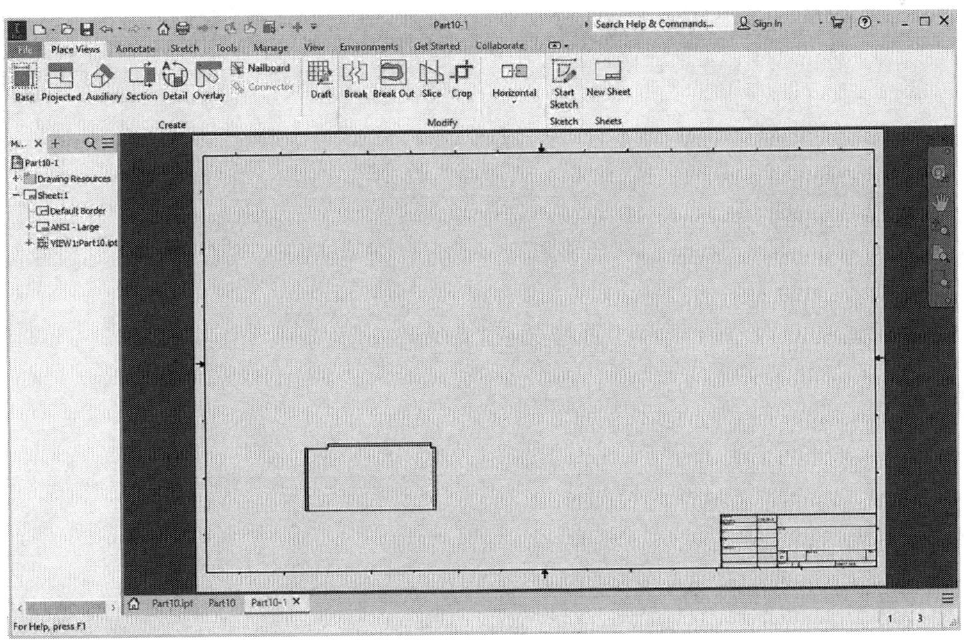

Figure 32

34. Left click on the **Projected** icon as shown in Figure 33.

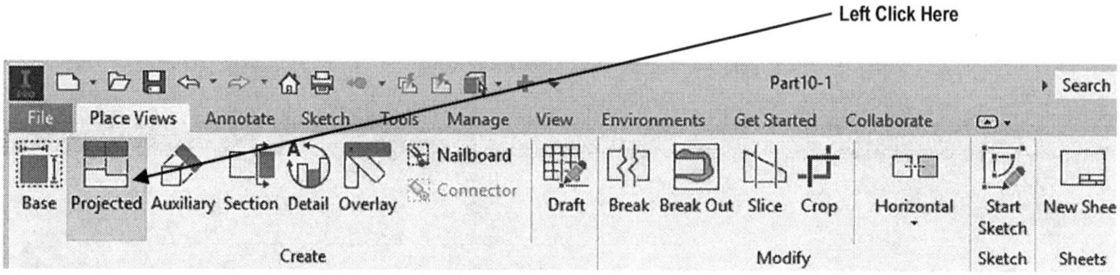

Figure 33

35. Left click on the front view. The Top, Isometric and Right side views will be attached to the cursor. Create a 3 view drawing with an isometric view as previously discussed in Chapter 3. Your screen should look similar to Figure 34.

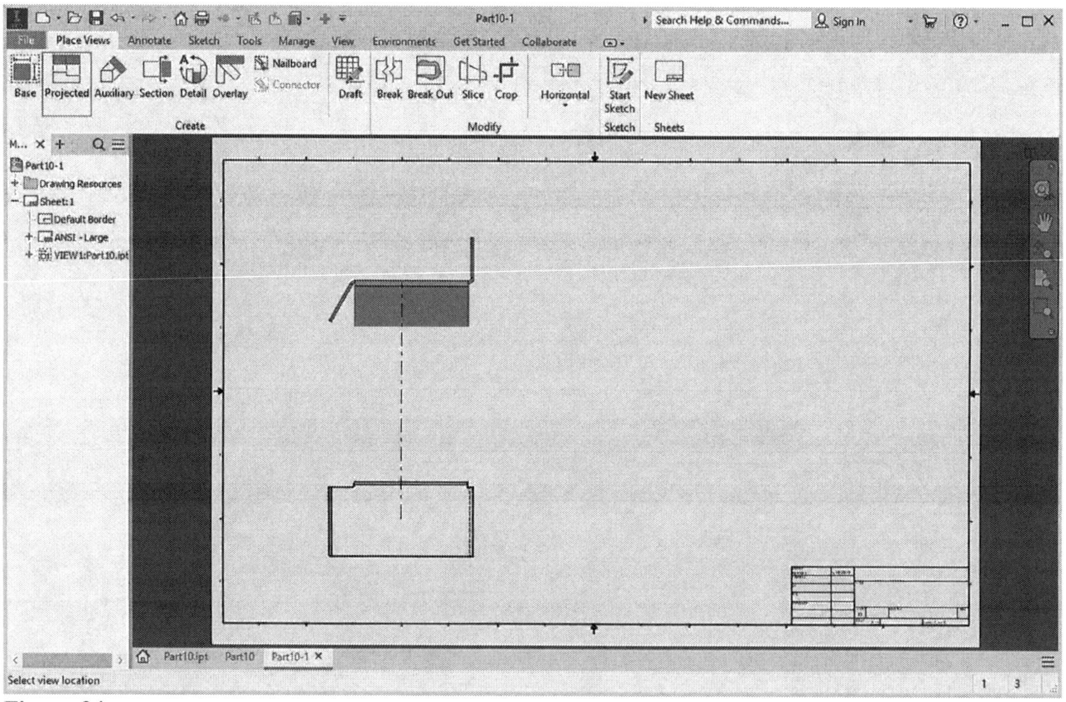

Figure 34

36. Your screen should look similar to Figure 35.

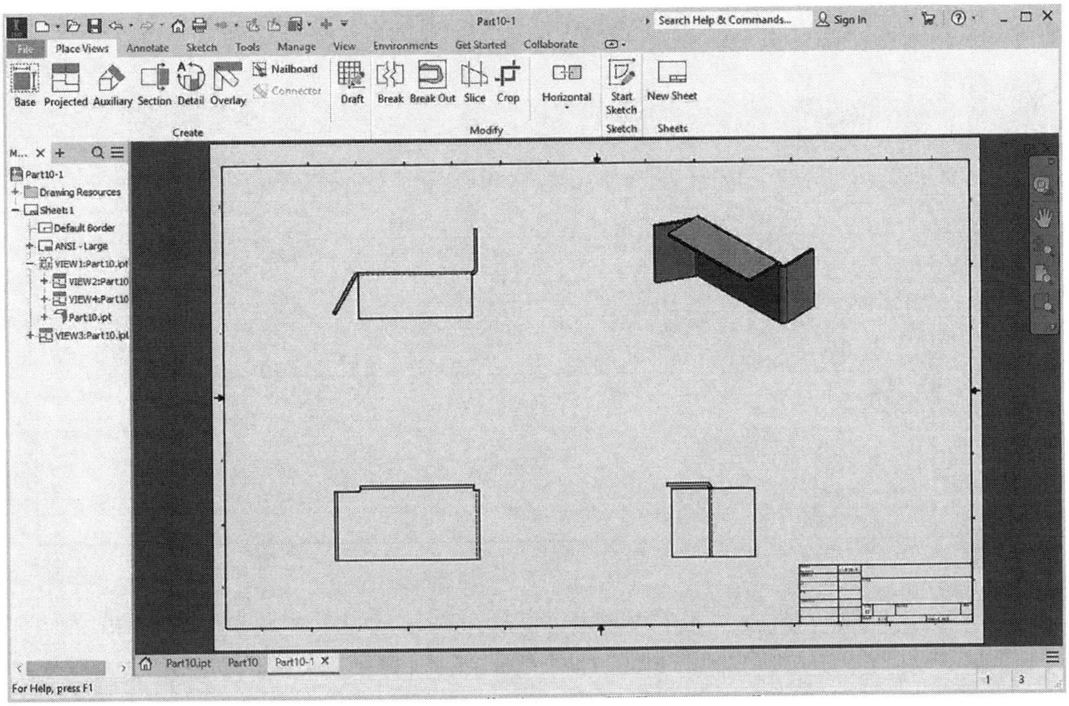

Figure 35

37. Dimension the part as shown in Figure 36.

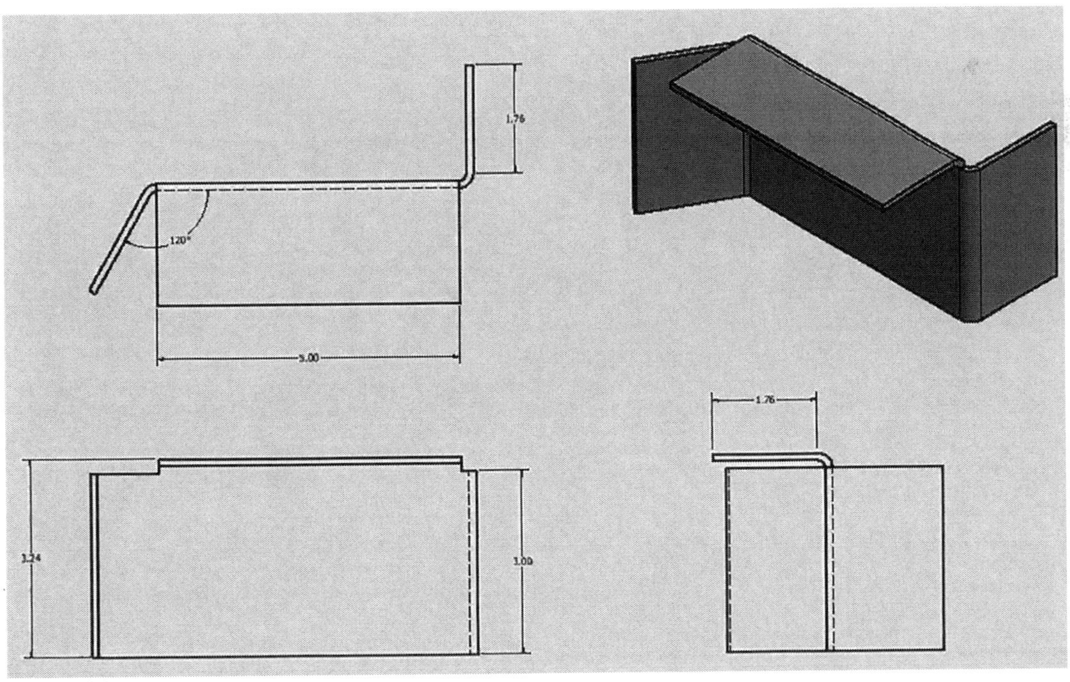

Figure 36

Chapter Problems

Problem 14-1

Complete the following sketch.

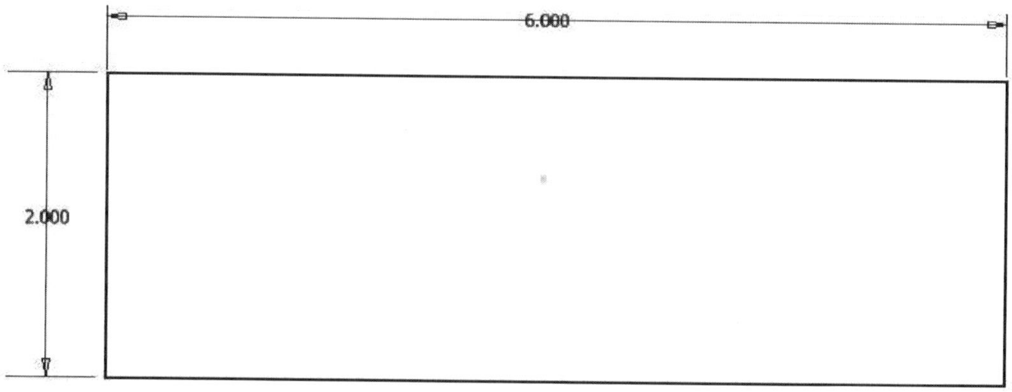

Use the Face command to create an Extruded body. Create a 1 inch Flange on both sides and a 2 inch Flange on top. Use "Bend from the adjacent face" for all bends.

Your screen should look similar to what is shown below. Create a Flat Pattern Drawing with dimensions.

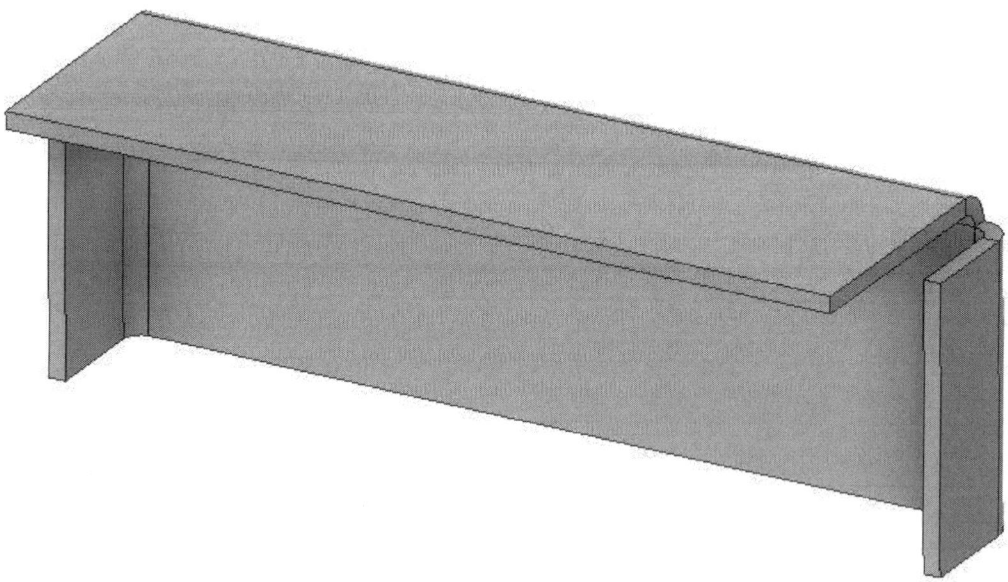

Complete the following sketch.

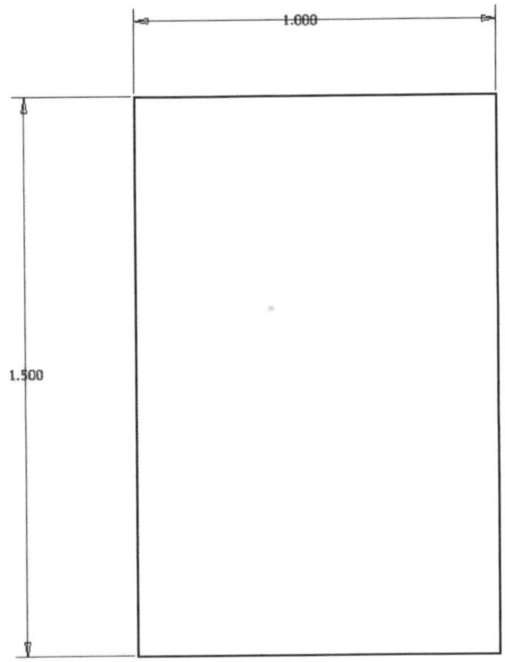

Use the Face command to create an Extruded body. Create a 2 inch flange on top, a 1 inch flange on the right side and a 1 inch flange (facing backwards) on the left side. Use "Inside bend face extents" for all bends.

Your screen should look similar to what is shown below. Create a Flat Pattern Drawing with dimensions.

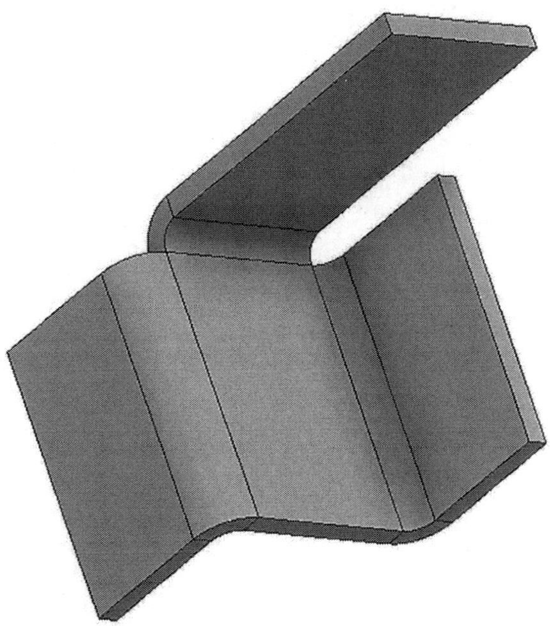

CHAPTER 15

Introduction to Weldment

Objectives:

1. Learn to create a Flat weld
2. Learn to create a Convex weld
3. Learn to create a Concave weld
4. Learn to create a Cosmetic weld

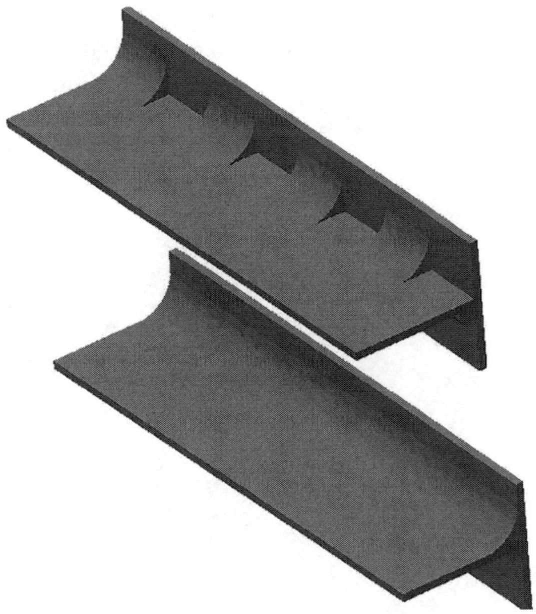

Chapter 15 includes instruction on how to create the parts shown.

1. Start Inventor by referring to "Chapter 1 Getting Started."

2. Complete the following sketch and Extrude to a thickness of .0625 inches as shown in Figure 1 and save as Part1.ipt.

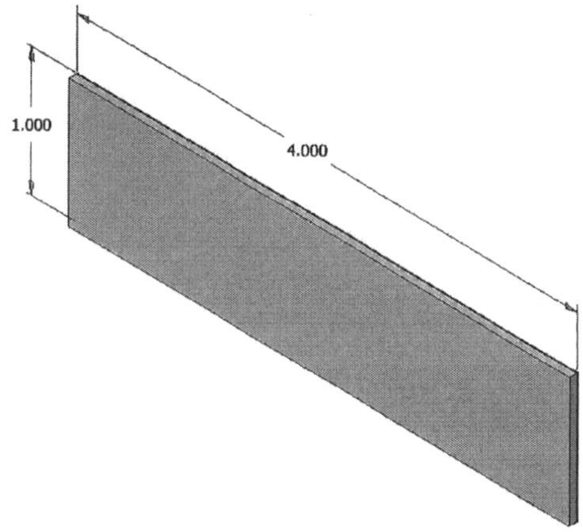

Figure 1

3. Move the cursor to the upper left portion of the screen and left click on the New icon (not shown). Left click on the en-US folder. Left click on the **Weldment (ANSI).iam** icon. Left click on **Create** as shown in Figure 2.

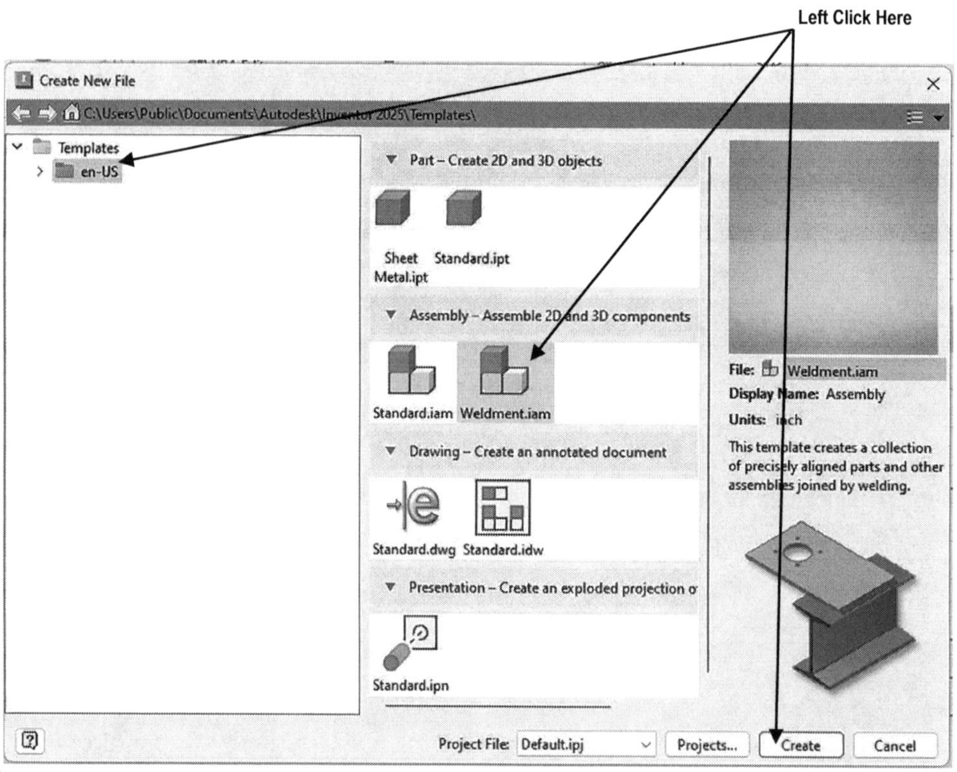

Figure 2

4. Inventor will open the Weldment Panel (which also includes tools found in the Assemble Panel). Your screen should look similar to what is shown in Figure 3.

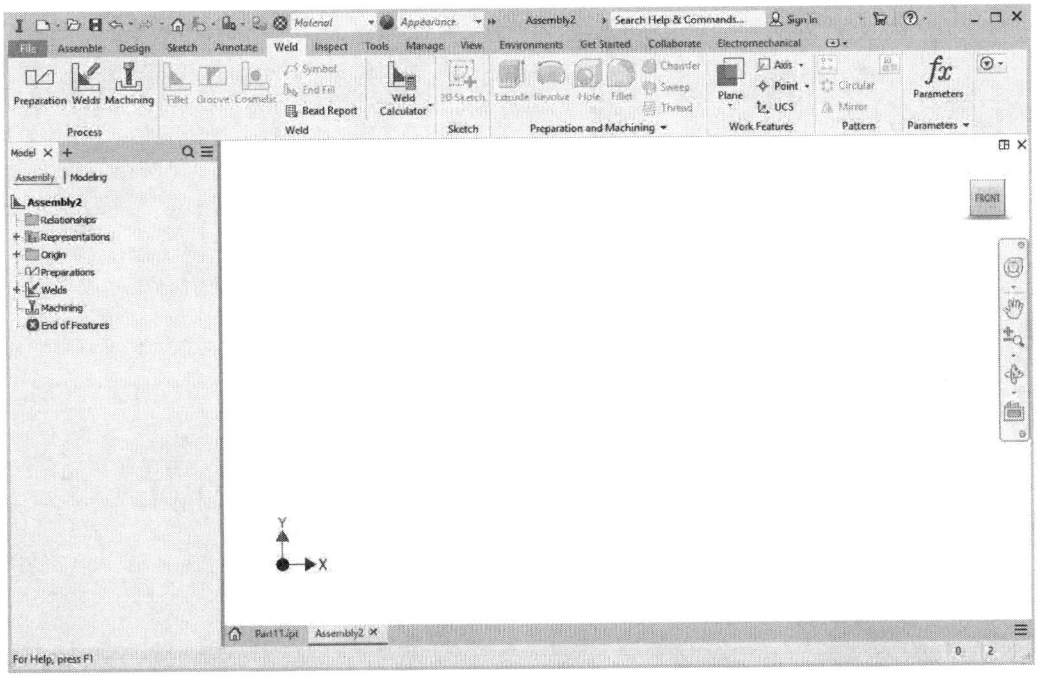

Figure 3

5. Left click on the **Assemble** tab as shown in Figure 4.

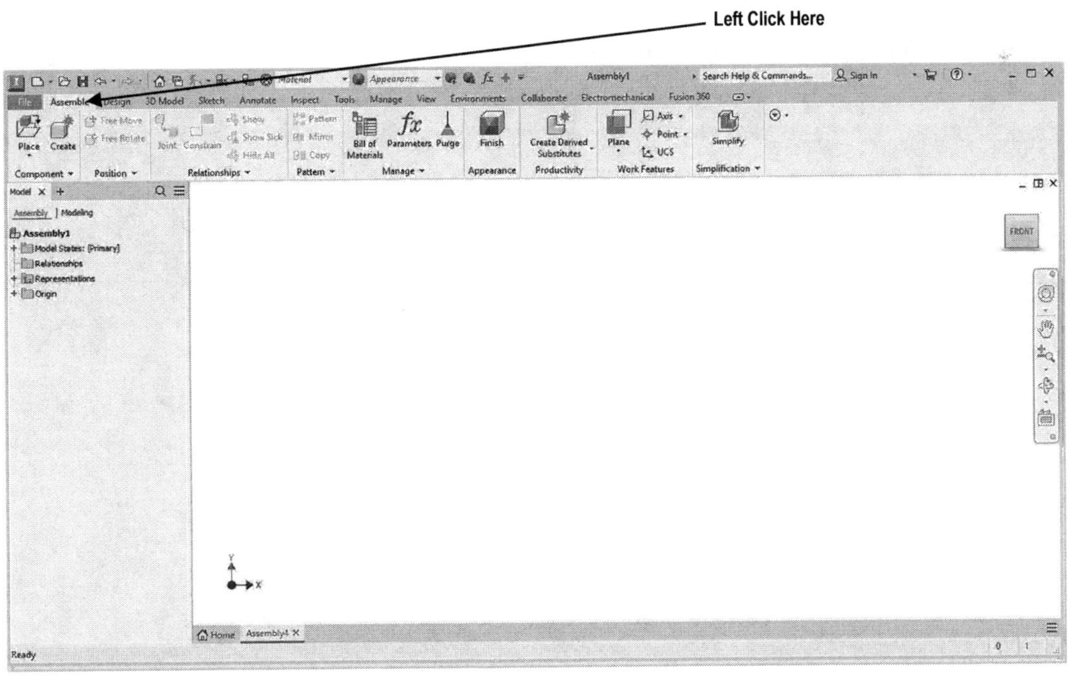

Figure 4

6. Move your cursor to the upper left portion of the screen and left click on the **Place** icon as shown in Figure 5.

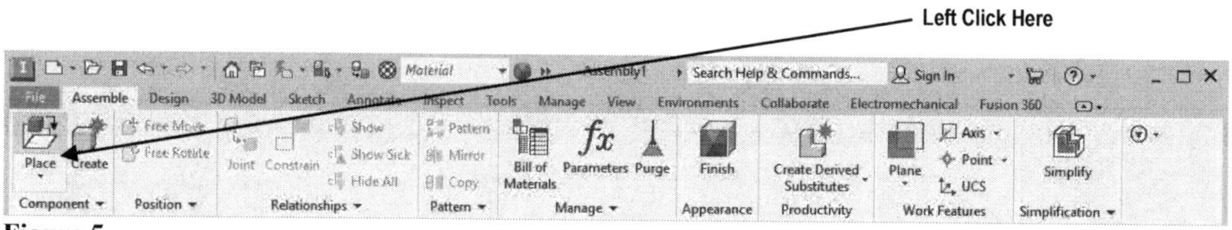

Figure 5

7. Locate the **Part1.(ipt)** file and left click on **Open** as shown in Figure 6.

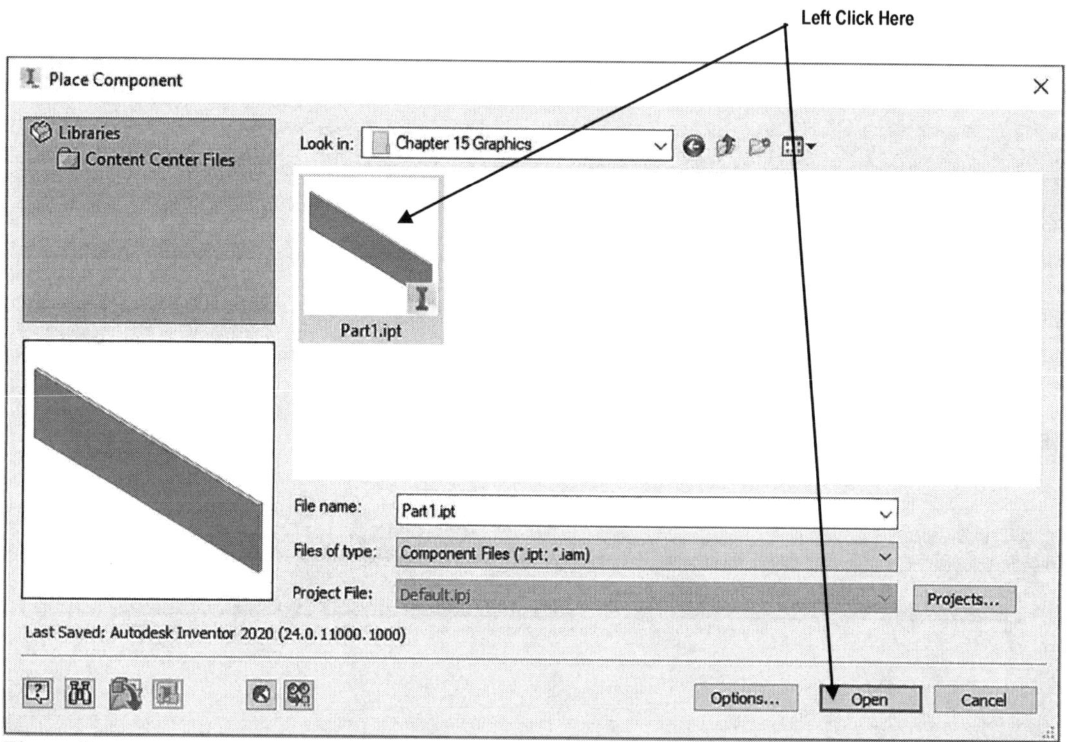

Figure 6

8. The part will be attached to the cursor. Place four (4) parts into the Assemble area. Your screen should look similar to Figure 7.

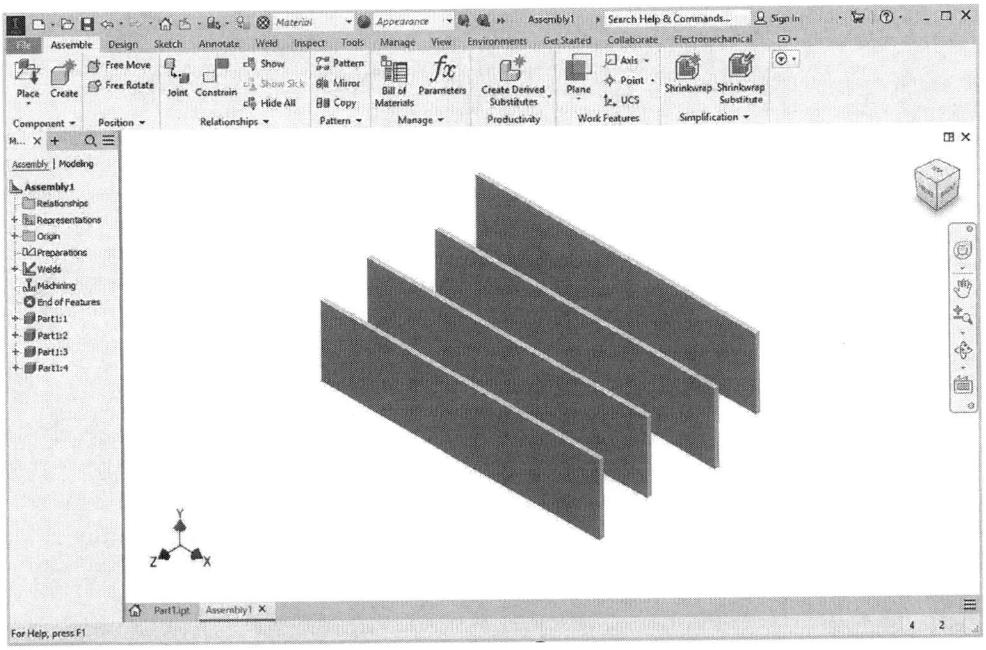

Figure 7

9. Move the cursor to the upper left portion of the screen and left click on the **Constrain** icon as shown in Figure 8.

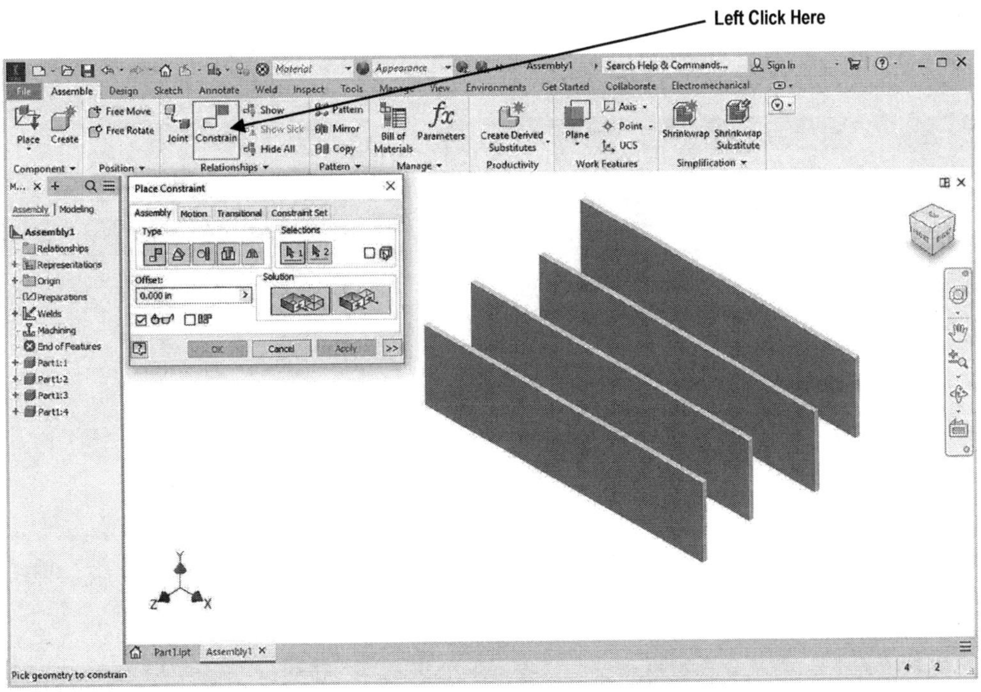

Figure 8

10. Using the Constrain tool, create two (2) T shaped parts as shown in Figure 9. (Hint: You will need to constrain the parts in the X, Y and Z directions while using a Distance offset of -0.50 inches to constrain the center rib.) Your screen should look similar to Figure 9.

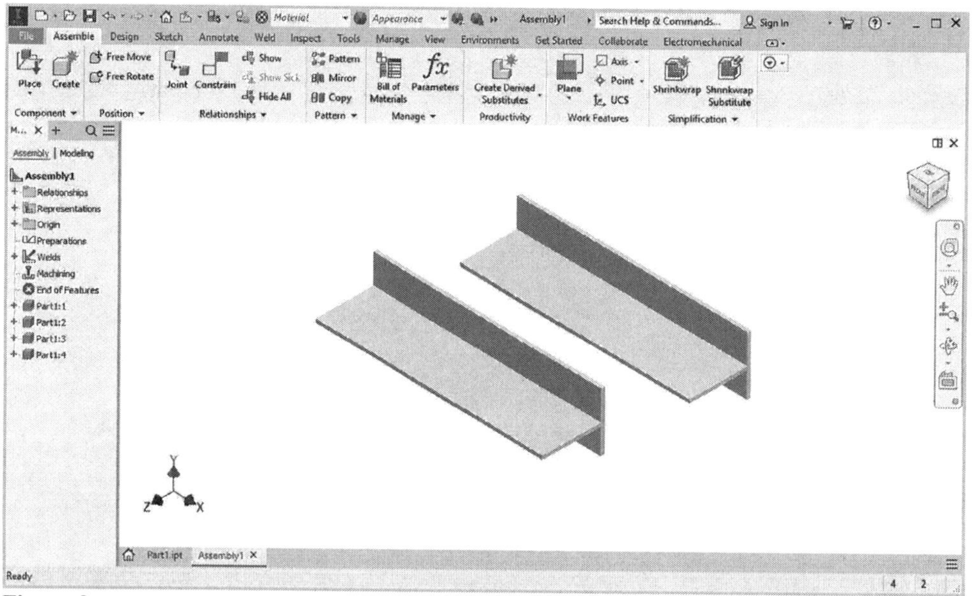

Figure 9

Learn to create a Weldment

11. Move the cursor to the upper left portion of the screen and left click on the **Weld** tab as shown in Figure 10.

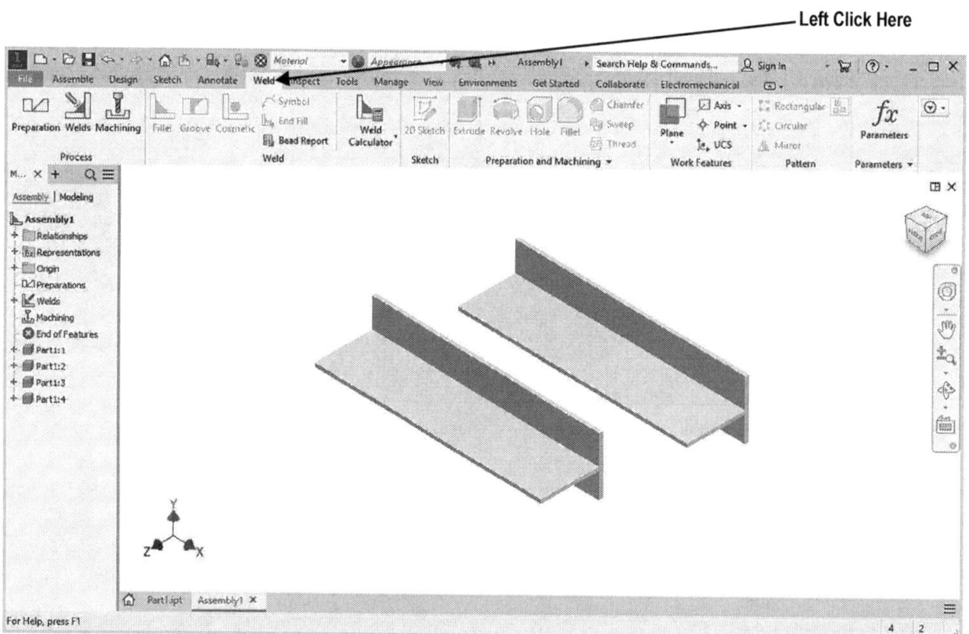

Figure 10

12. Move the cursor to the upper left portion of the screen and left click on the **Welds** icon as shown in Figure 11.

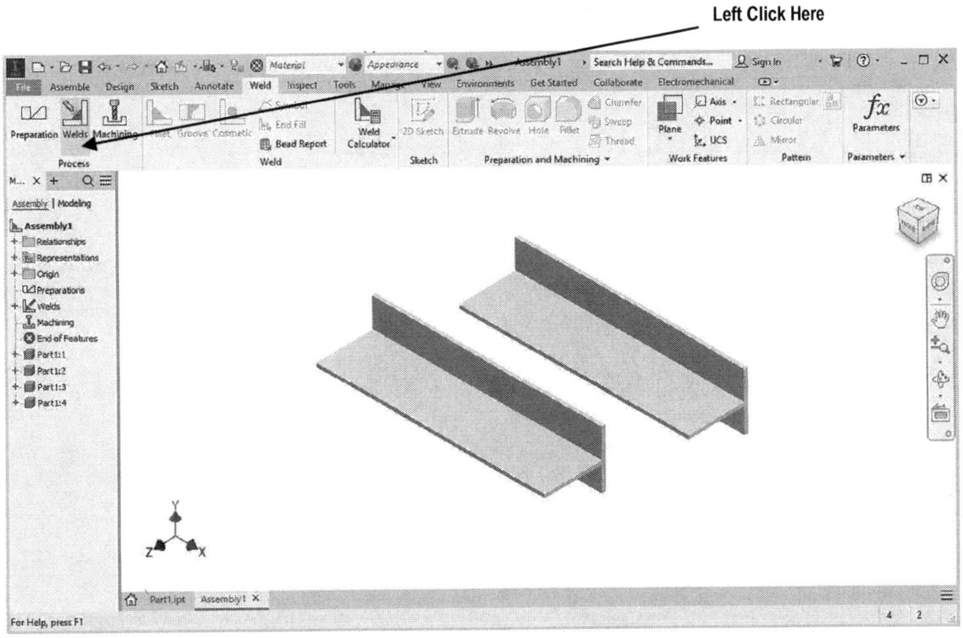

Figure 11

13. Left click on the **Fillet** icon as shown in Figure 12. We will start by creating a Flat Weldment.

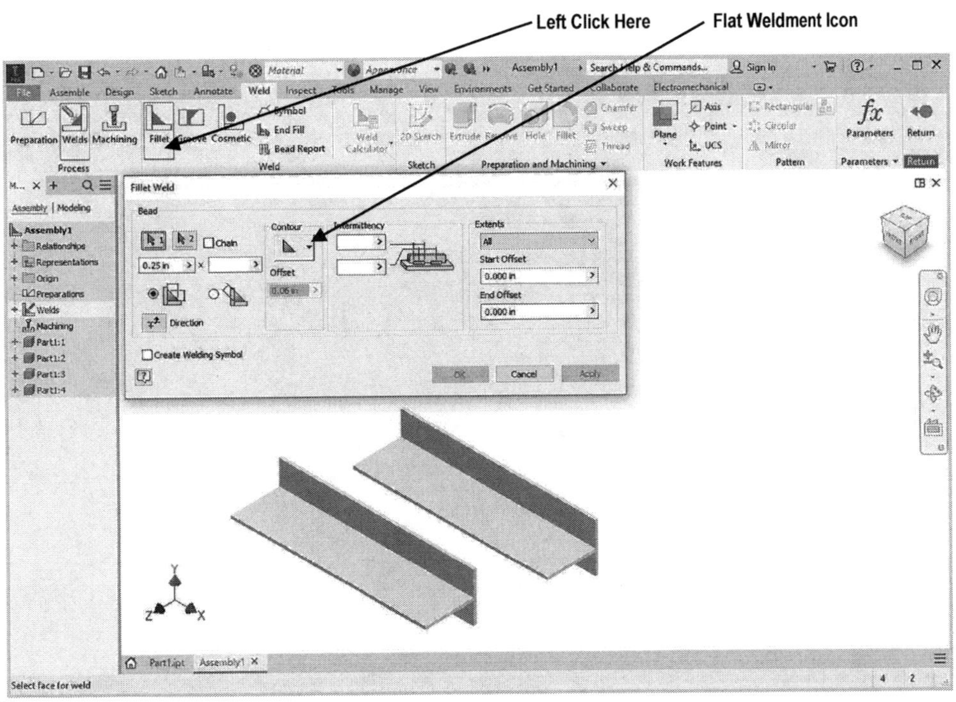

Figure 12

14. Left click on the **Selected Face 1** icon as shown in Figure 13.

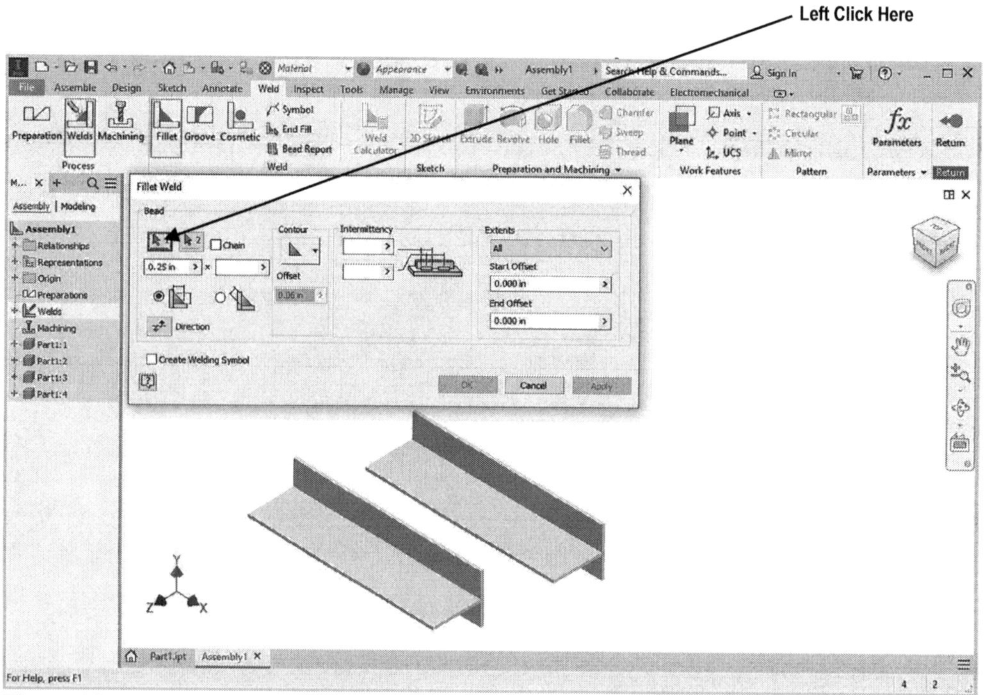

Figure 13

15. Left click on the horizontal Face as shown in Figure 14.

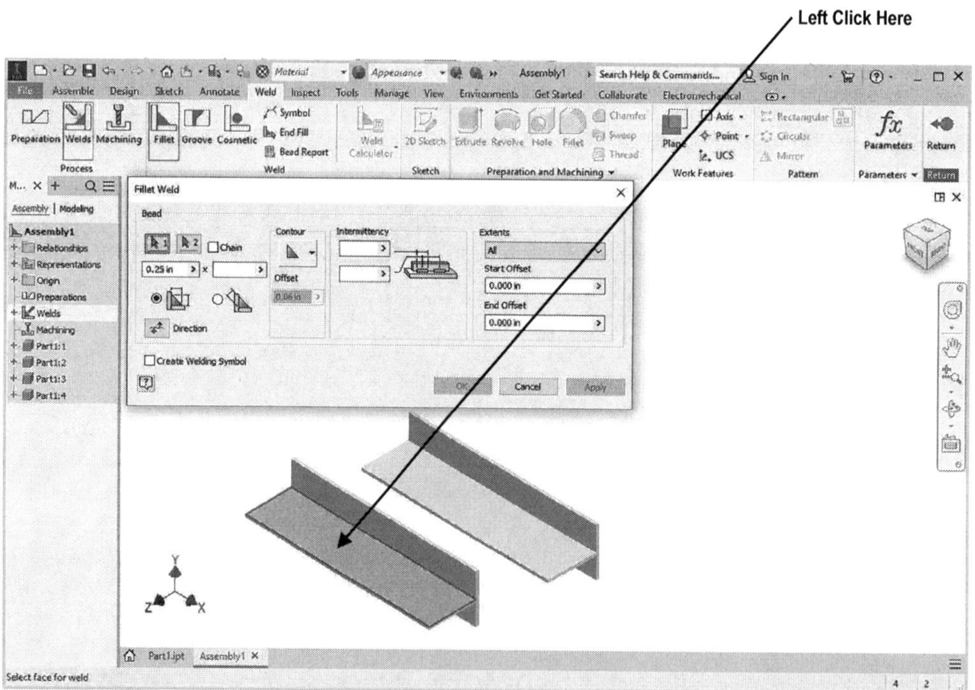

Figure 14

16. Left click on the **Selected Face 2** icon as shown in Figure 15.

Left Click Here

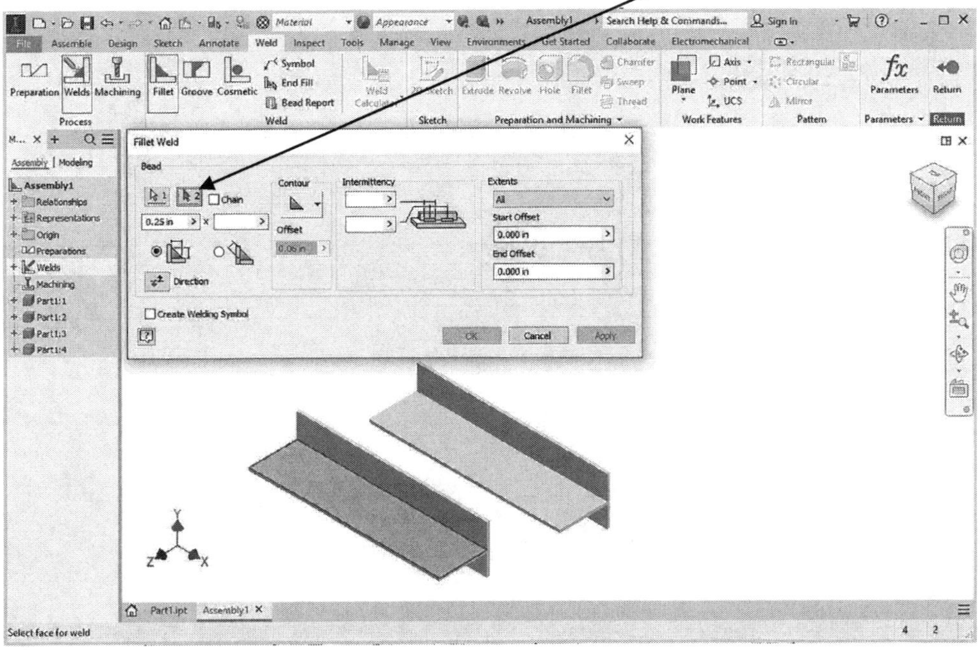

Figure 15

17. Left click on the vertical Face as shown in Figure 16.

Left Click Here

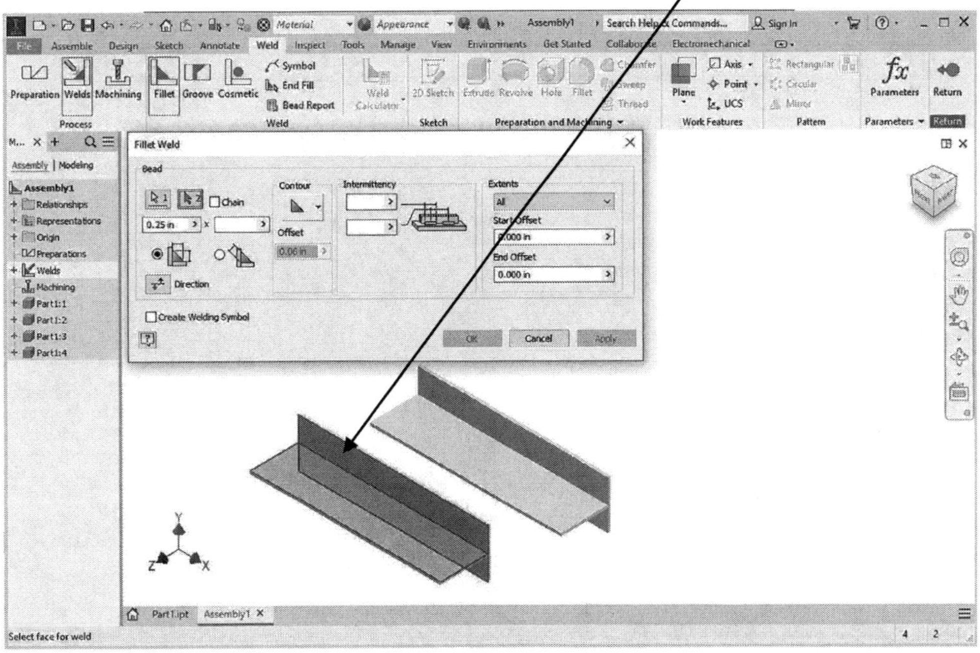

Figure 16

18. Enter **.125** for the Bead width. Inventor will provide a preview of the Weldment. Left click on **OK** as shown in Figure 17.

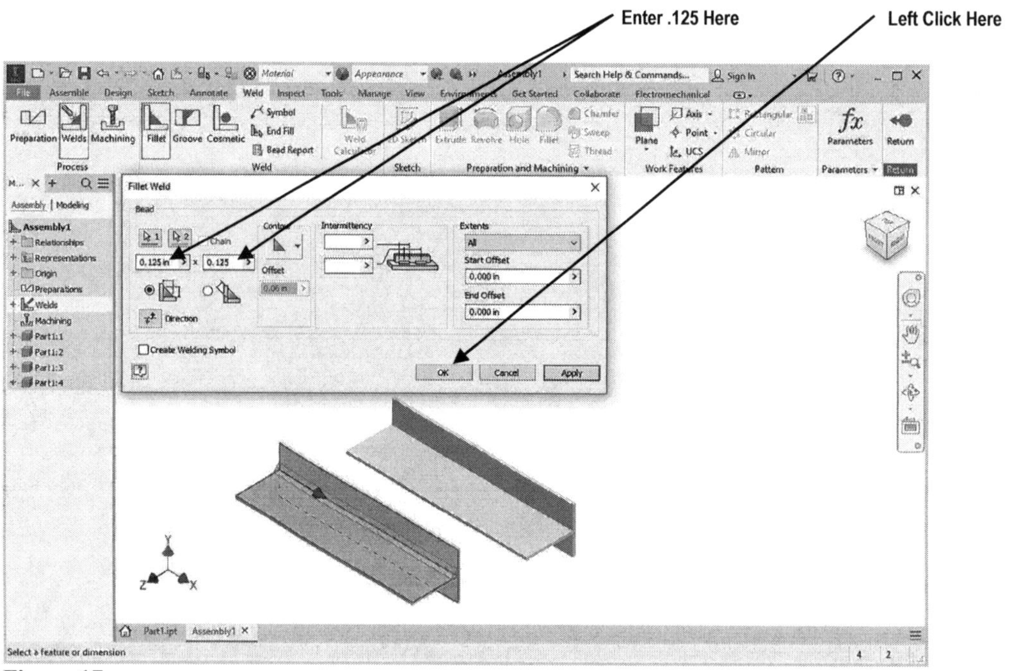

Figure 17

19. Your screen should look similar to Figure 18. You may have to zoom in to see the actual bead depending on your screen resolution.

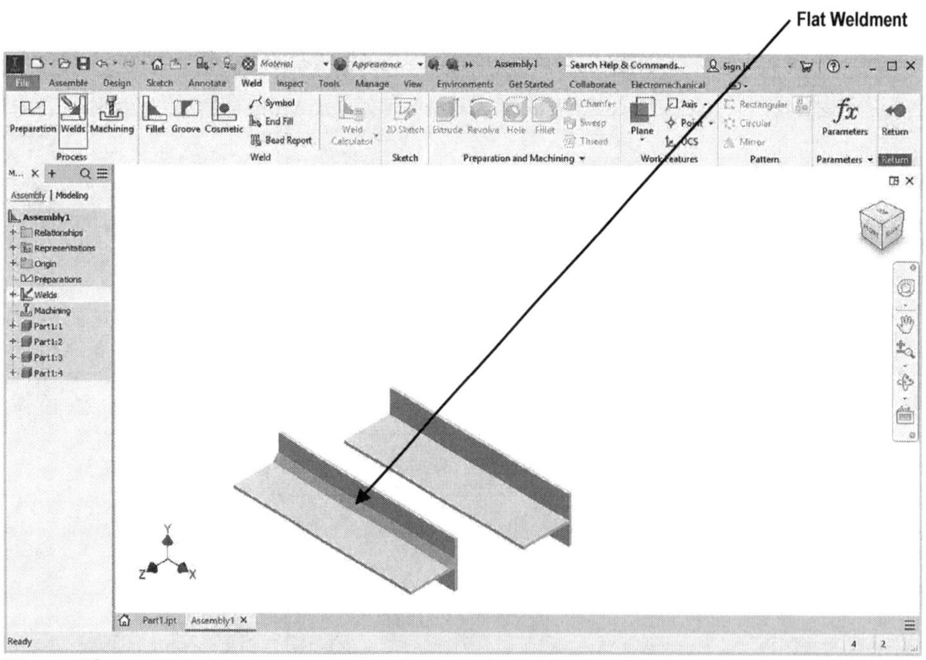

Figure 18

Learn to create a Convex Weldment

20. Now we will create a Convex Weldment. Left click on the **Fillet** icon. Left click on the **Selected Face 1** icon. Left click on the horizontal Face as shown in Figure 19.

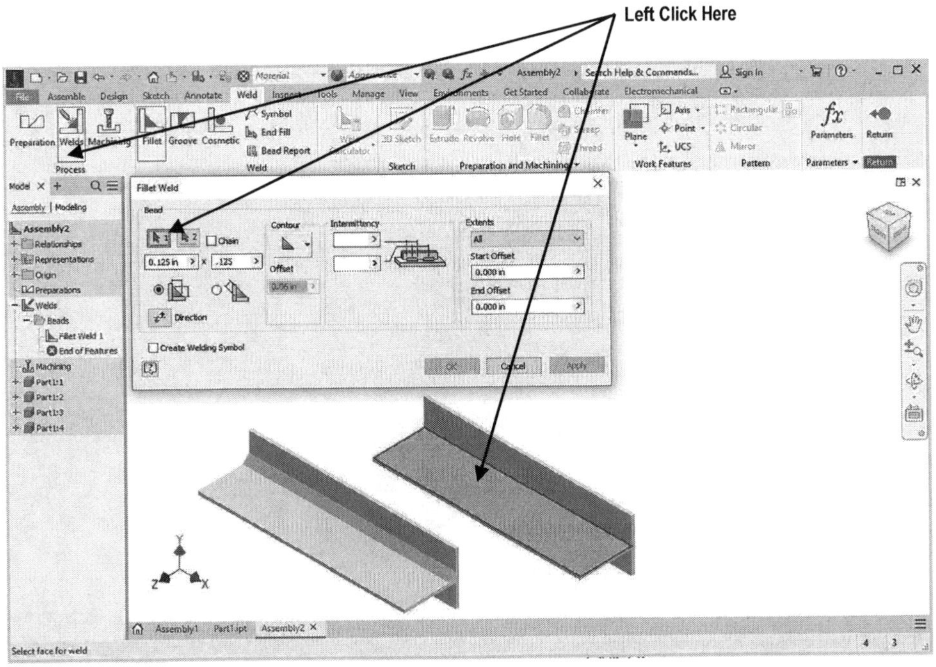

Figure 19

21. Left click on the **Selected Face 2** icon. Left click on the vertical Face as shown in Figure 20.

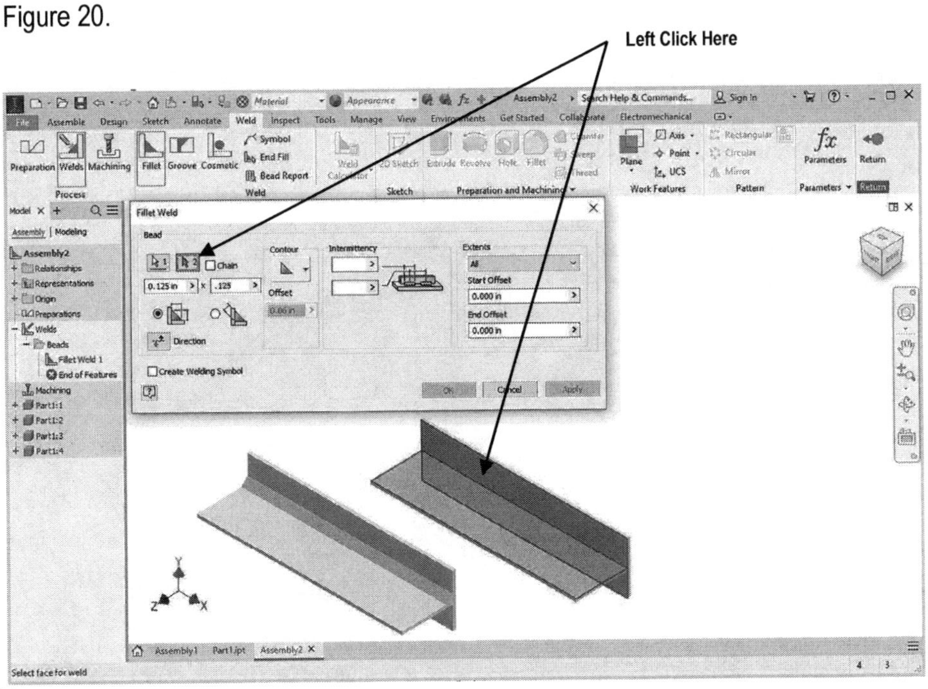

Figure 20

22. Left click on the **Convex** icon. Left click on **OK** as shown in Figure 21.

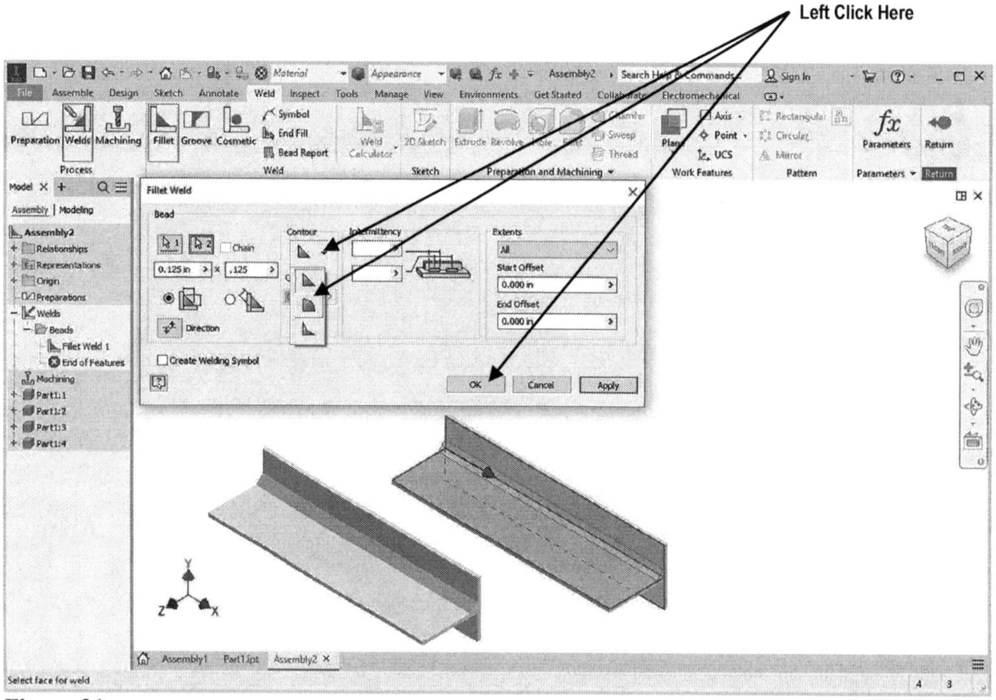

Figure 21

23. Your screen should look similar to what is shown in Figure 22.

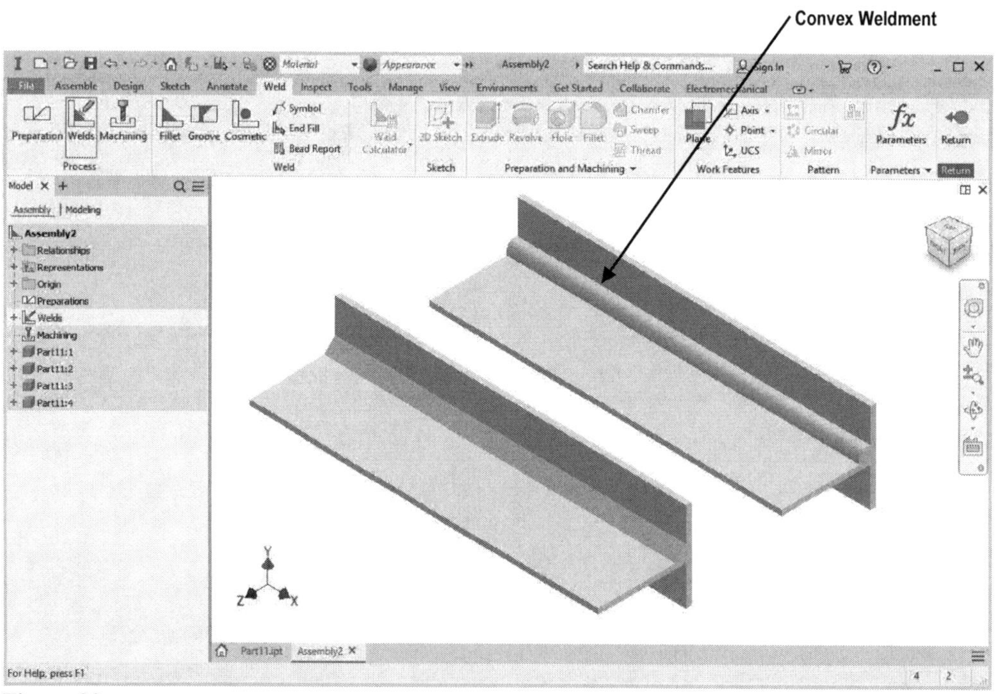

Figure 22

24. Use the Free Orbit tool to rotate the parts around (upside down) as shown in Figure 23.

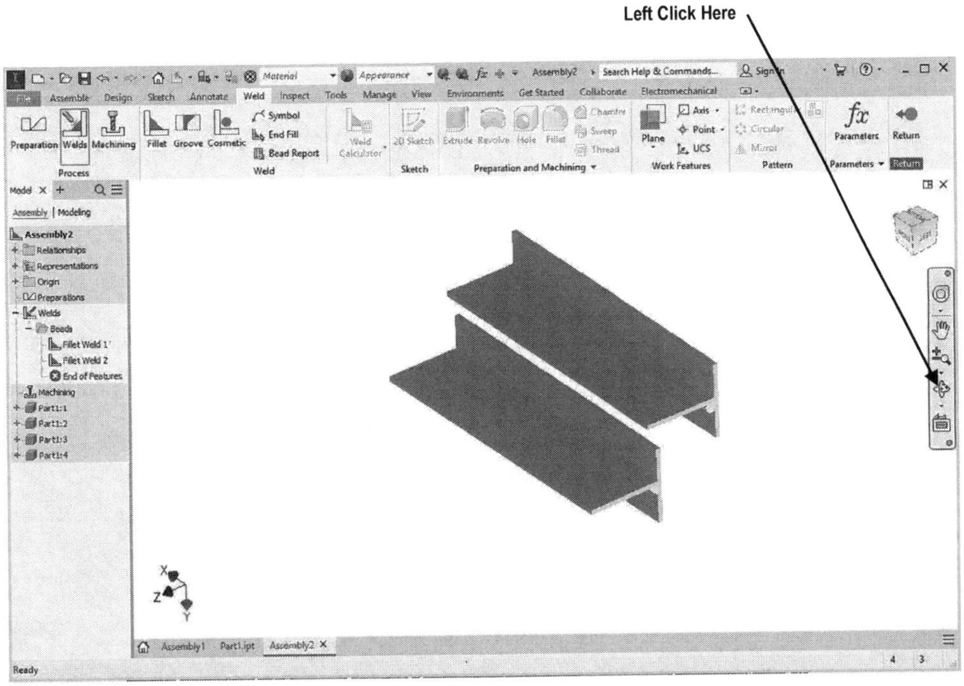

Figure 23

Learn to create a Concave Weldment

25. Now we will create a Concave Weldment. Left click on the **Weld** tab. Left click on the **Fillet** icon as shown in Figure 24.

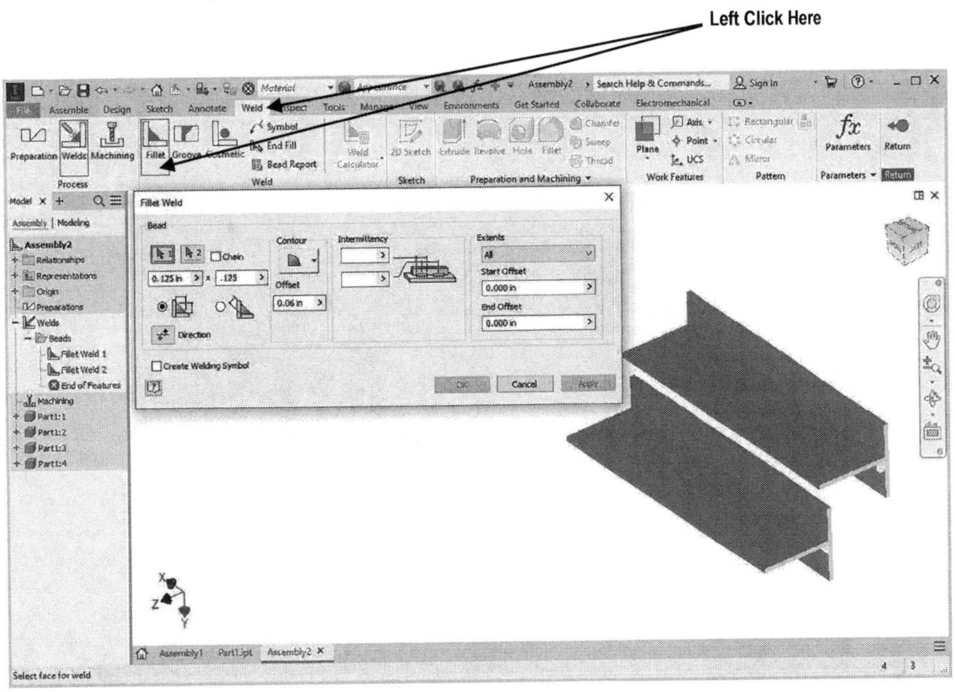

Figure 24

26. Left click on the **Selected Face 1** icon. Left click on the horizontal Face as shown in Figure 25.

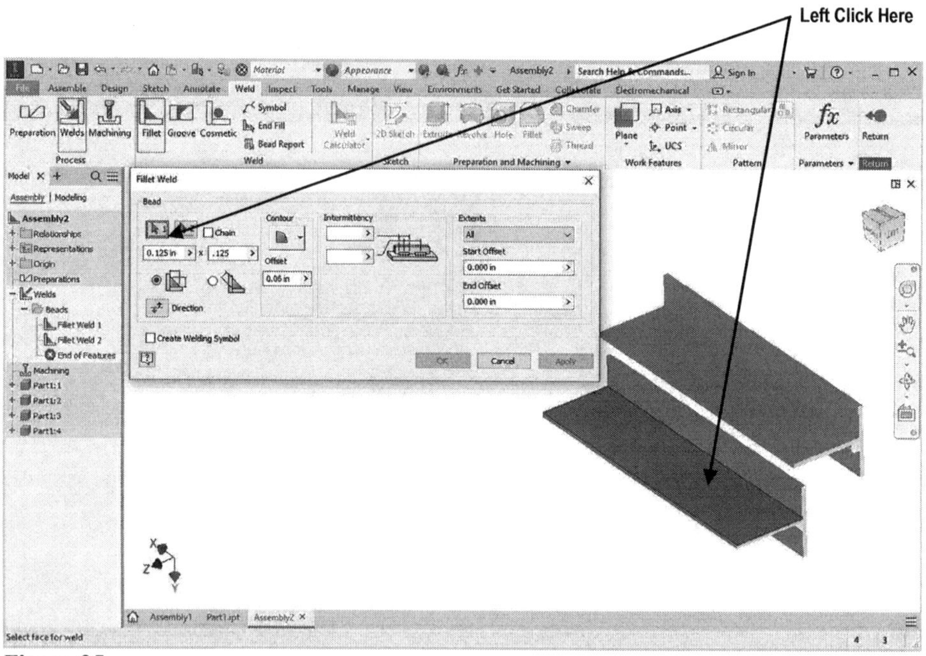

Figure 25

27. Left click on the **Selected Face 2** icon. Left click on the vertical Face as shown in Figure 26.

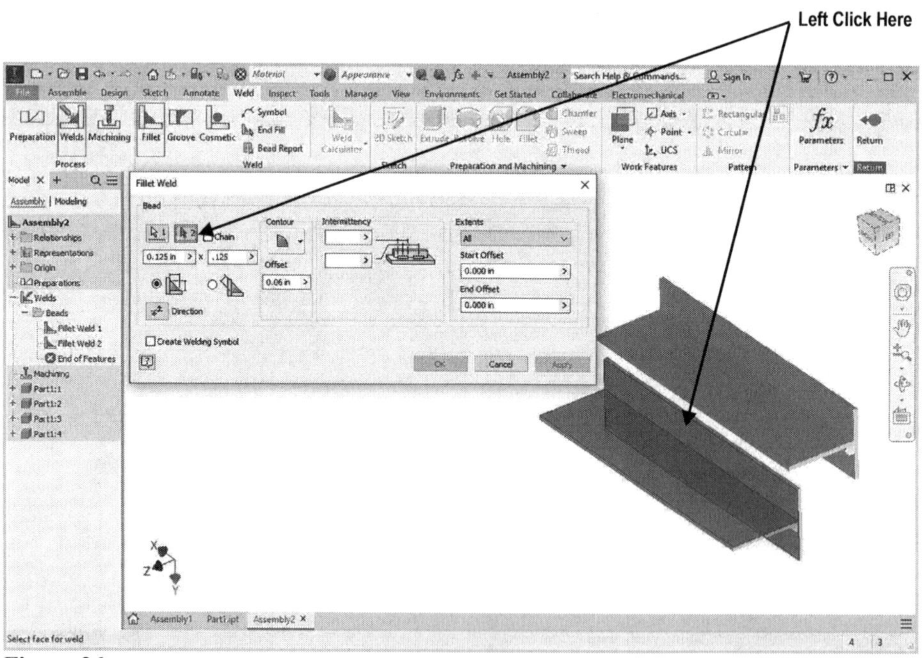

Figure 26

28. Enter **.25** for the Bead width. Left click on the **Concave** icon as shown in Figure 27.

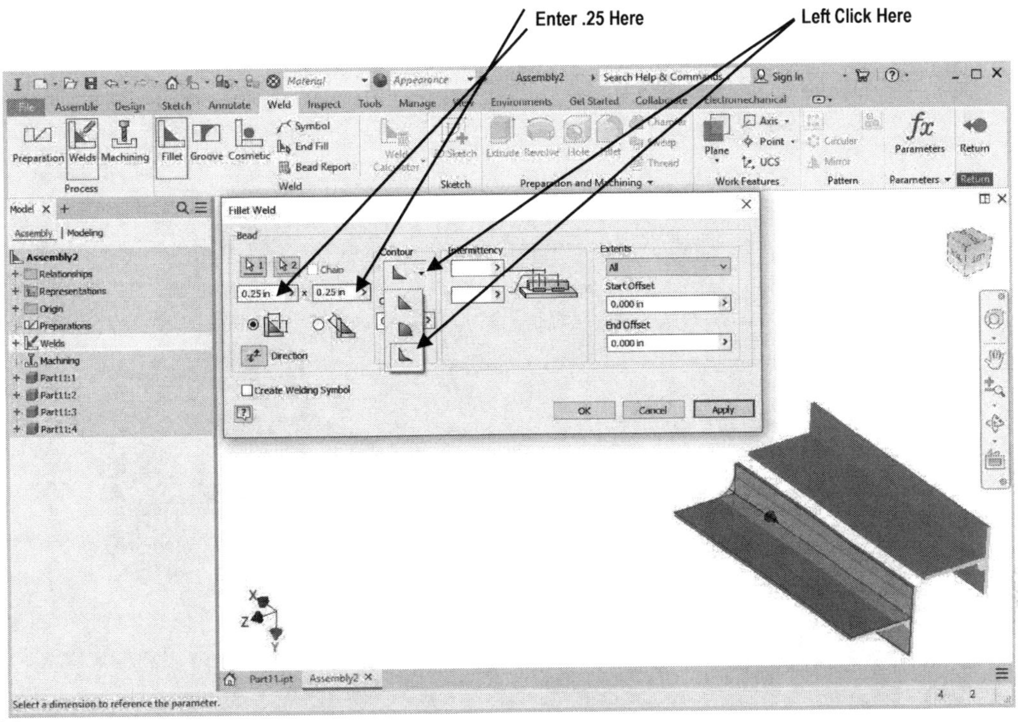

Figure 27

29. Inventor will provide a preview of the Weldment. Left click on **OK** as shown in Figure 28.

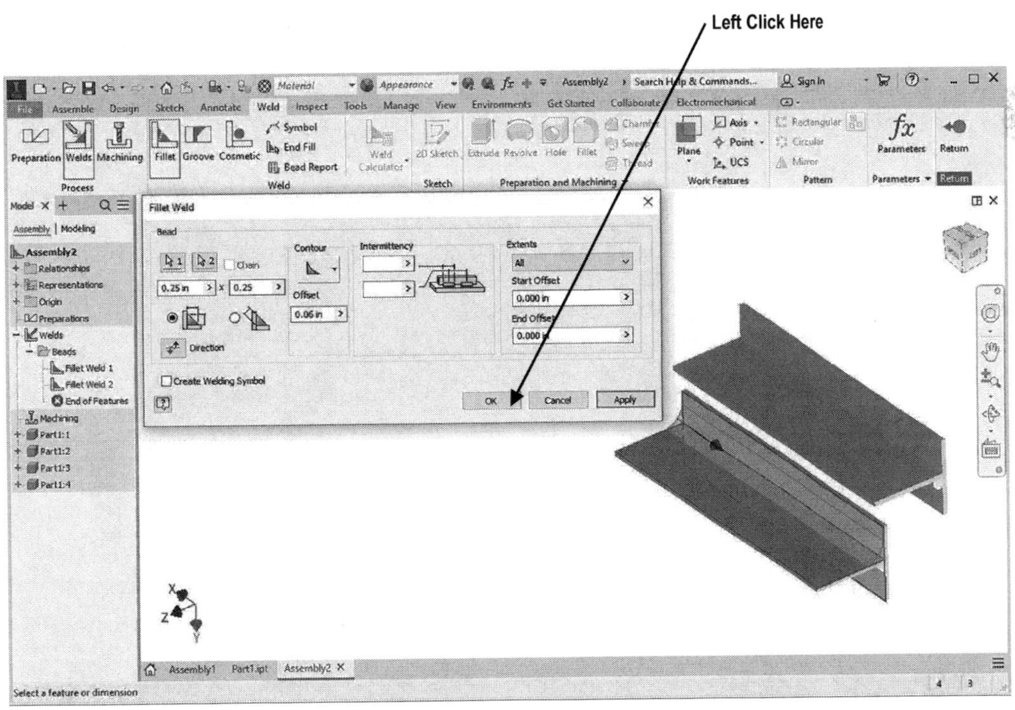

Figure 28

30. Your screen should look similar to what is shown in Figure 29.

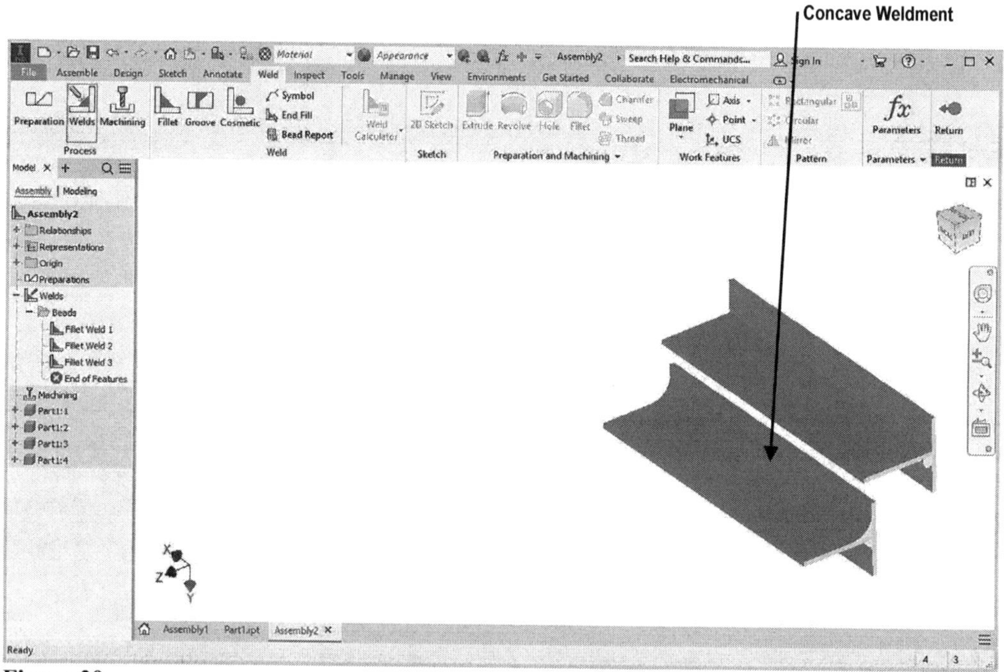

Figure 29

Learn to create a Cosmetic Weldment

31. Now we will create a Cosmetic Weldment. Left click on the **Cosmetic** icon. The Cosmetic Weld dialog box will appear as shown in Figure 30.

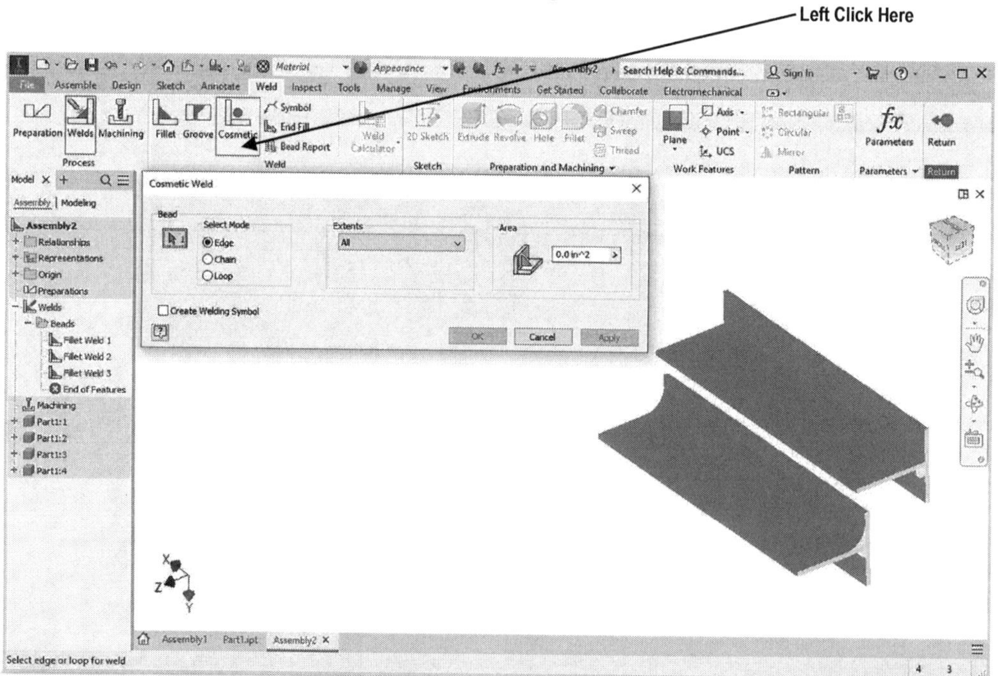

Figure 30

32. Left click on the T part edge (intersection) as shown in Figure 31.

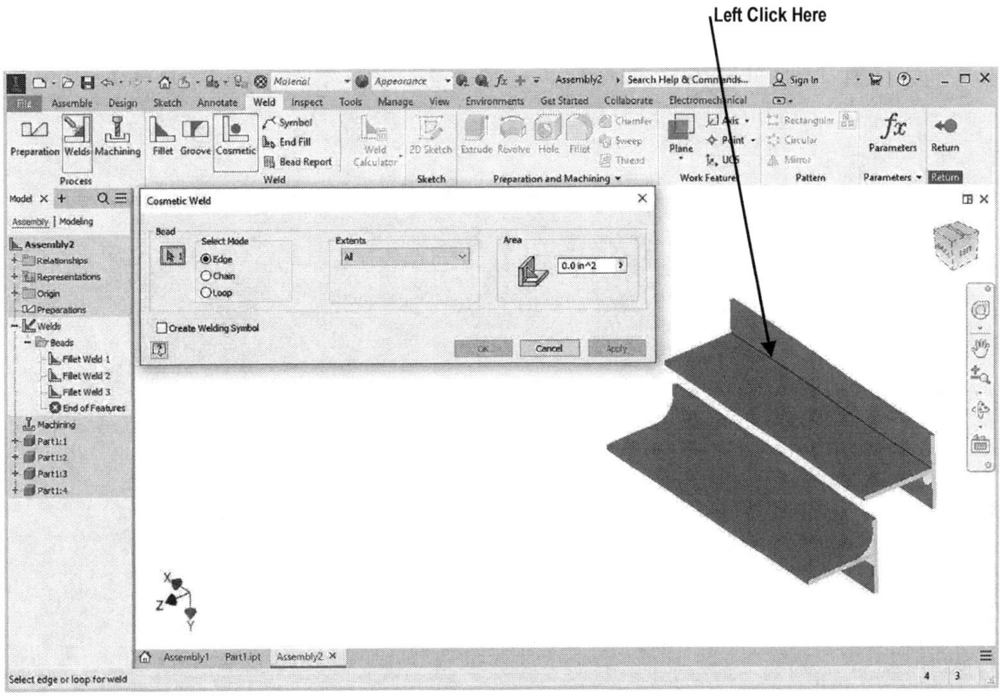

Figure 31

33. Left click on **OK** as shown in Figure 32.

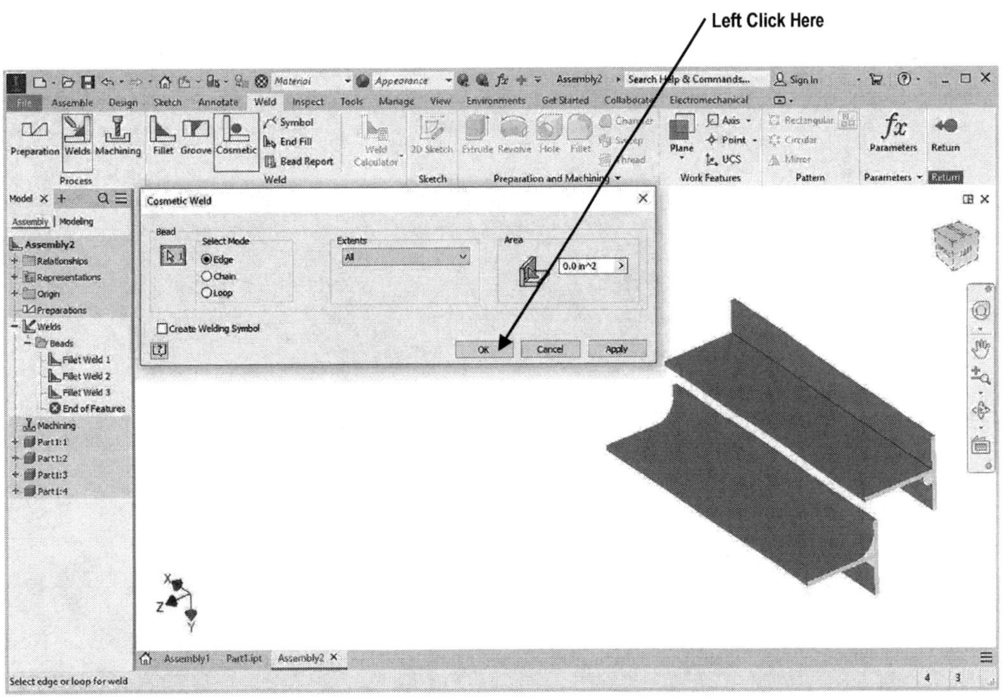

Figure 32

34. Left Click on the **Return** icon as shown in Figure 33.

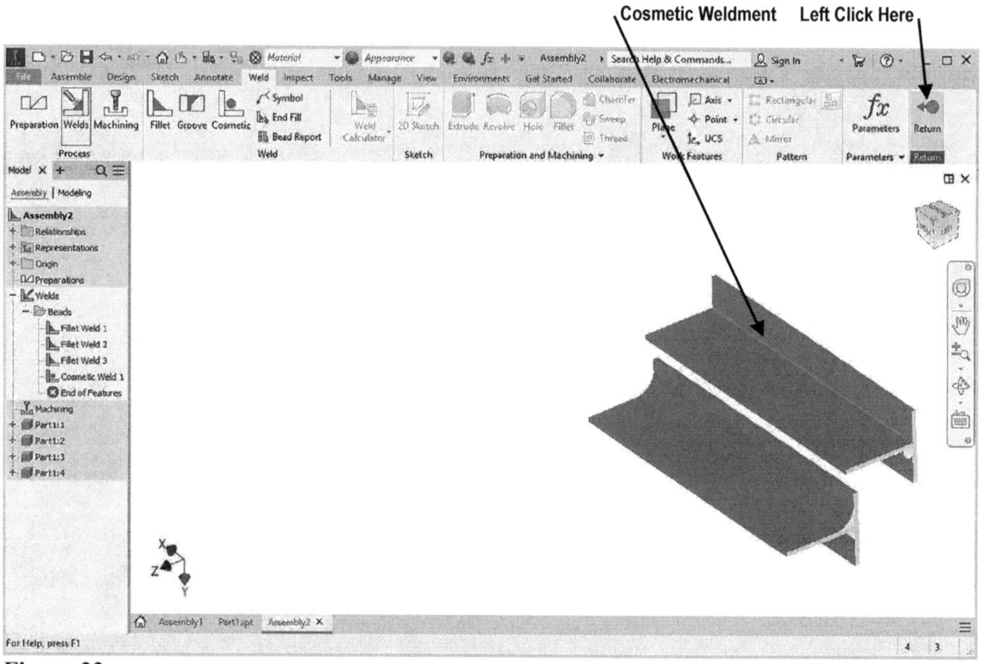

Figure 33

Learn to use the Weld Calculator

35. Move the cursor to the upper middle portion of the screen and left click on the **Weld Calculator** icon. A drop-down menu will appear. Left click **Fillet Weld Calculator (Plane)**.

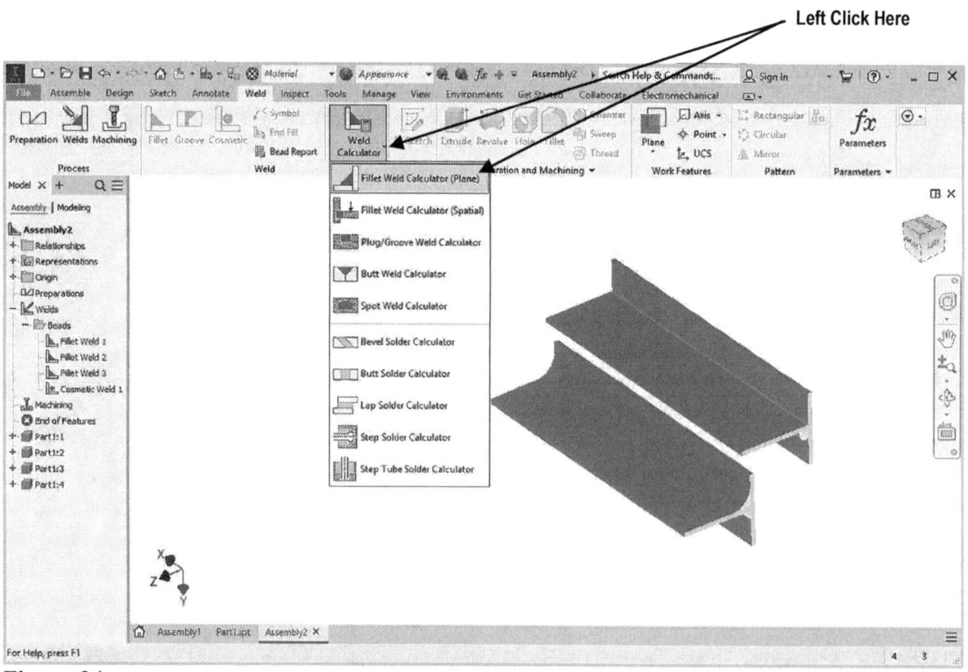

Figure 34

36. The Fillet Weld (Connection Plane Load) Calculator will appear. Left click on **Calculate** as shown in Figure 35.

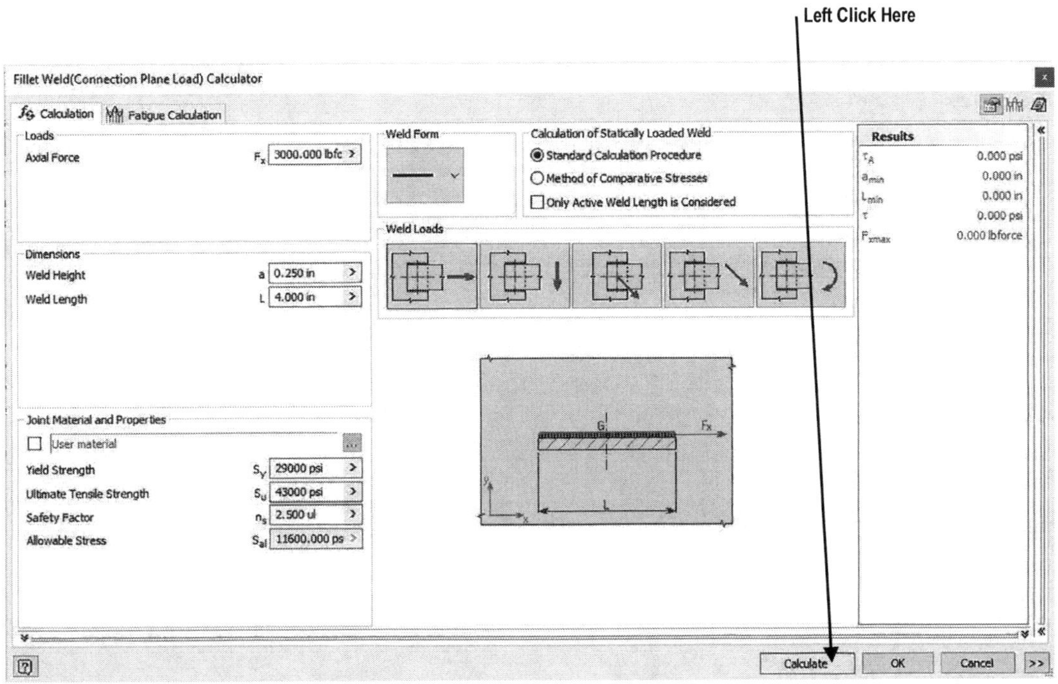

Figure 35

37. Information about the weld will appear under the Results heading as shown in Figure 36.

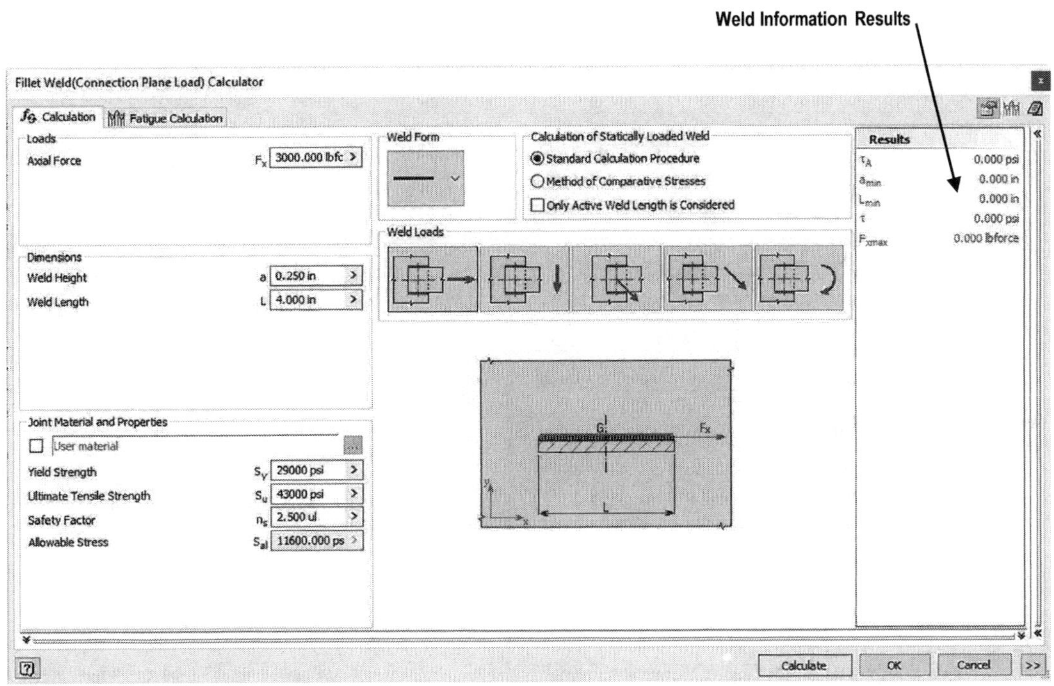

Figure 36

38. Left click on **OK**. The File Naming dialog box will appear. Left click on **OK** as shown in Figure 37. This will cause the dialog box to close.

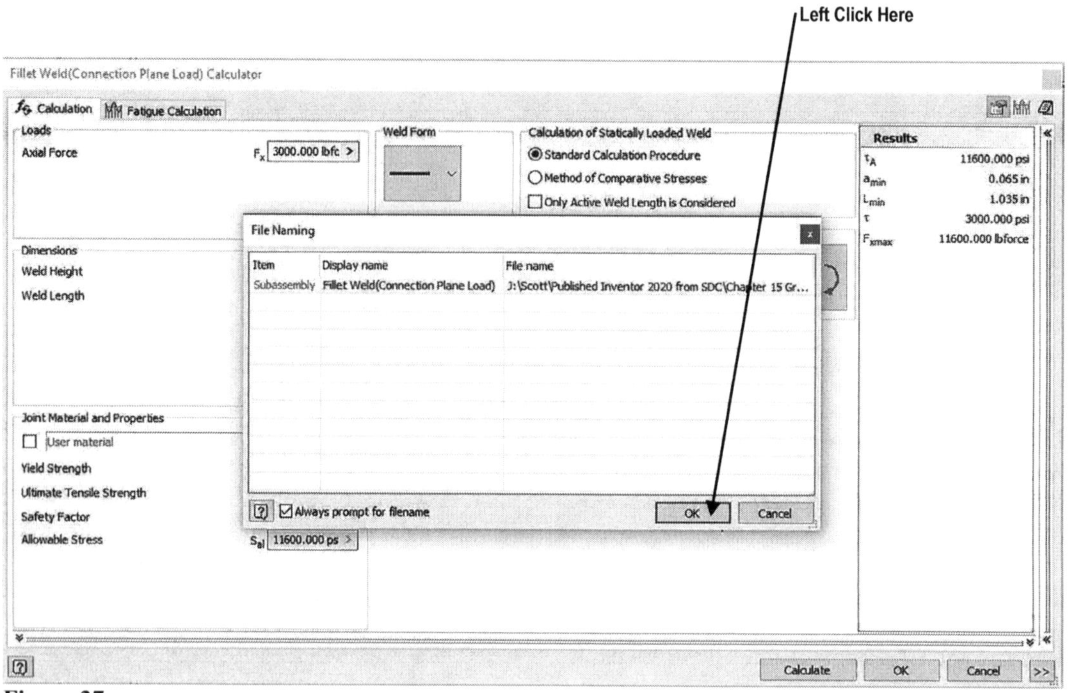

Figure 37

Learn to edit existing Weldments

39. If the need arises to edit an existing weldment, changes can be made in the history tree. Move the cursor to the middle left portion of the screen where the history tree is located. Left click on the plus sign to the left of Welds as shown in Figure 38.

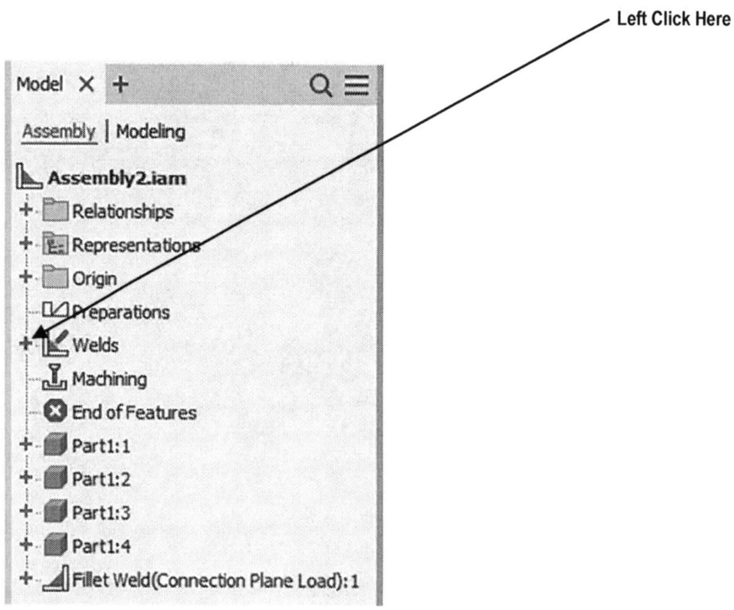

Figure 38

40. This will cause the Beads folder to appear. Left click on the plus sign to the left of Beads as shown in Figure 39.

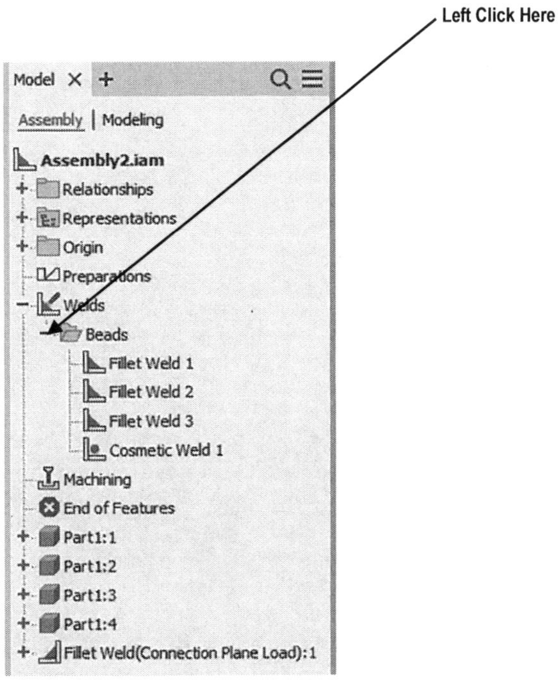

Figure 39

41. This will cause each of the Welds to appear. Move the cursor over Fillet Weld 1 and right click once. A pop-up menu will appear. Left click on **Edit Feature**.

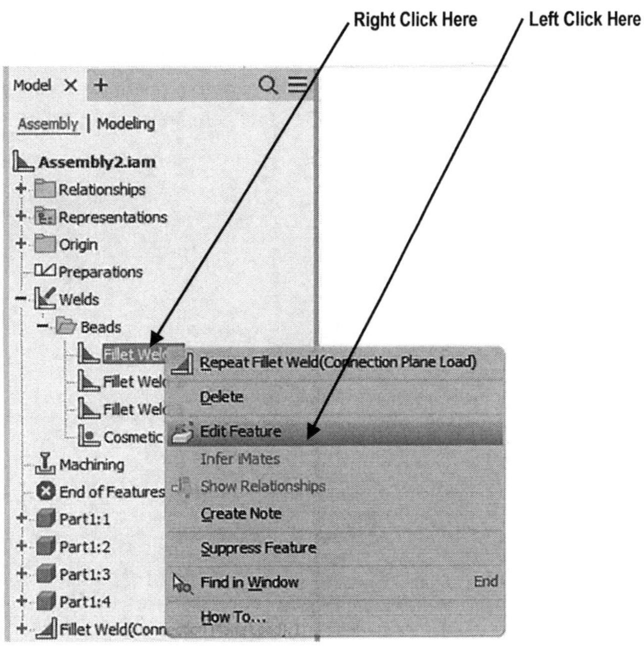

Figure 40

42. This will cause the Fillet Weld: Fillet Weld 1 dialog box to appear. Edits can be made at this point. Once any edits have been made, left click on **OK** as shown in Figure 41.

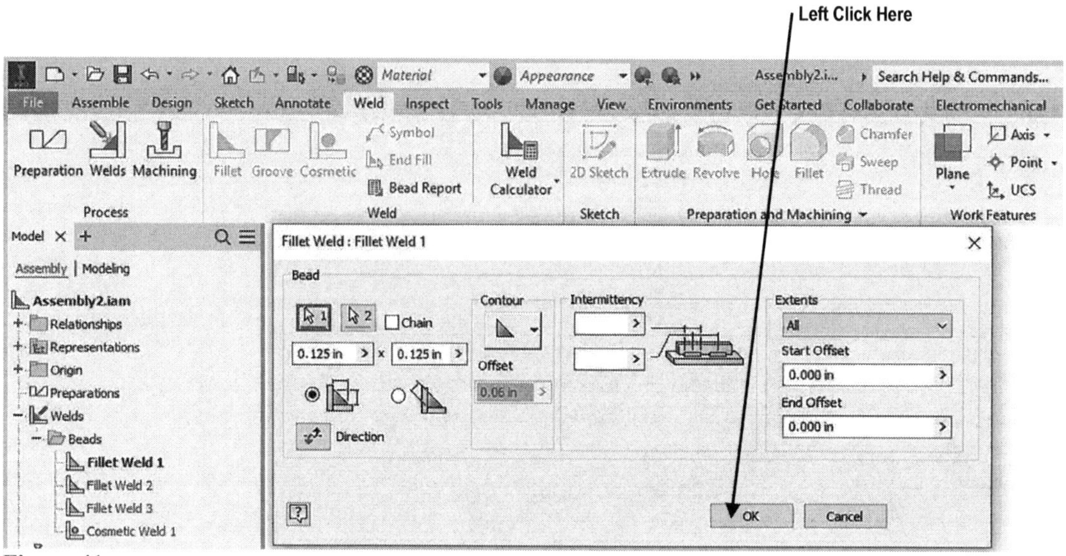

Figure 41

43. Move the cursor to the history tree over **Cosmetic Weld 1** and right click once. A pop-up menu will appear. Left click on **Delete**.

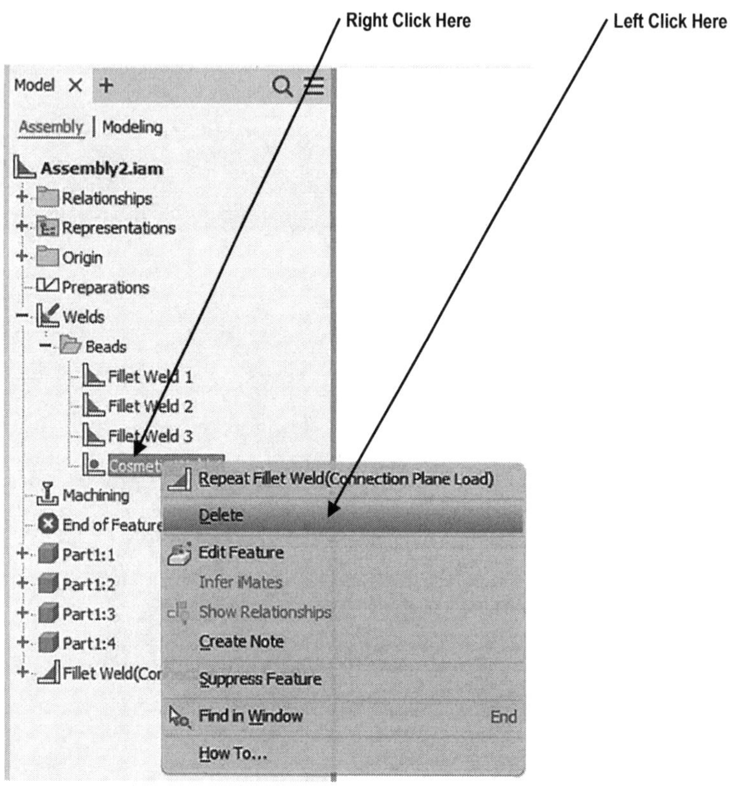

Figure 42

44. Move the cursor to the upper left portion of the screen and left click on the **Welds** icon as shown in Figure 43.

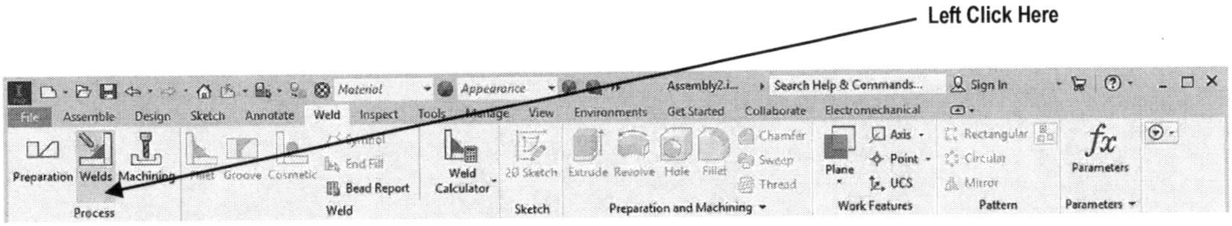

Figure 43

45. Left click on the **Fillet** icon. The Fillet Weld Dialog box will appear. Left click on **Selected Face 1.** Left click on the horizontal face of the part. Left click on **Selected Face 2**. Left click on the vertical face of the part as shown in Figure 44.

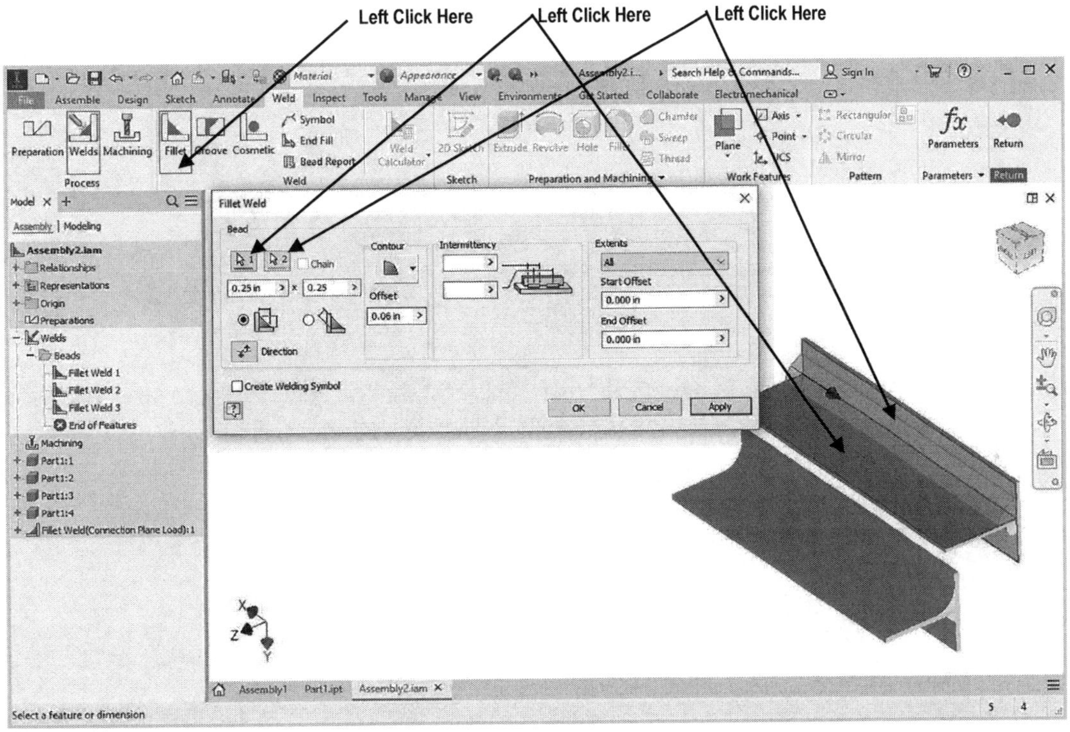

Figure 44

46. Left click on the **Concave** icon. Enter **0.5** and **1** under "Intermittency". The first value is the length of each individual weldment. The second value is the center to center distance between each individual weldment. Inventor will provide a preview of the intermittent weldment as shown in Figure 45.

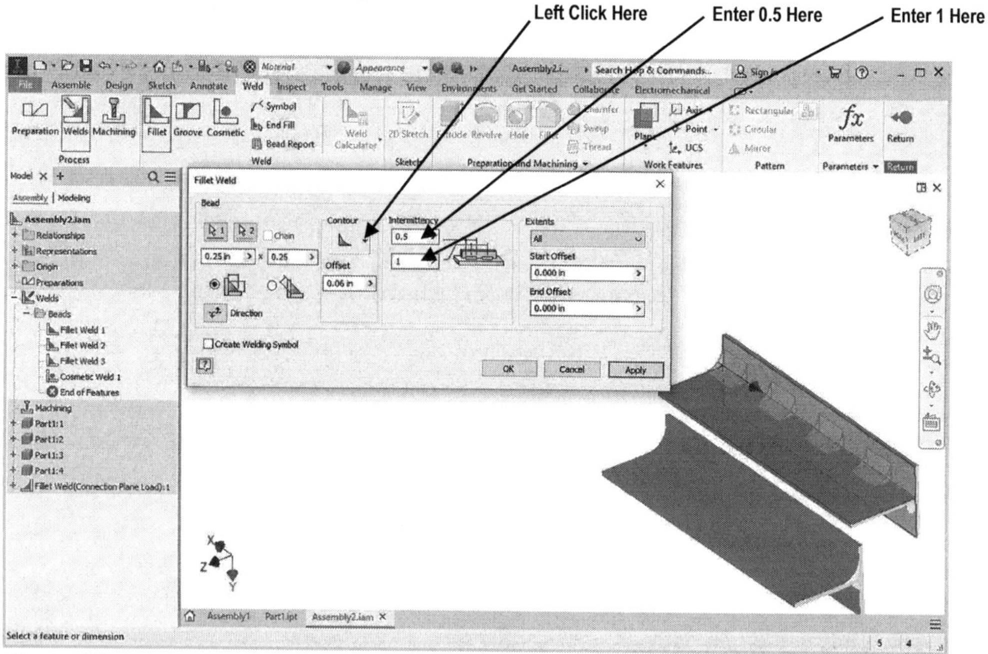

Figure 45

47. Left click on **OK**. Your screen should look similar to what is shown in Figure 46. (Welds are highlighted for illustrative purposes only.) Left click on **Return**.

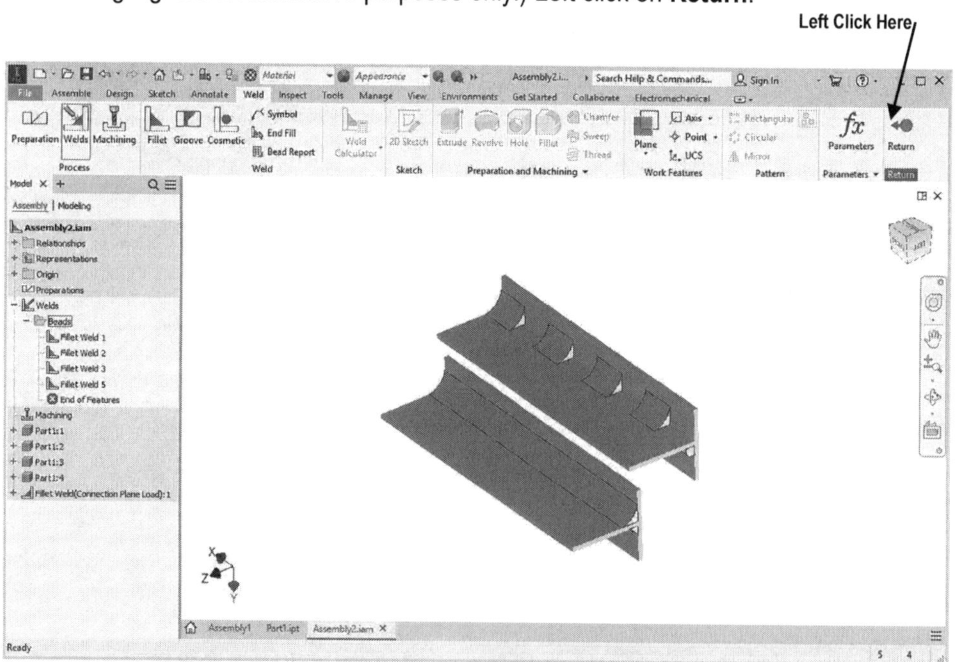

Figure 46

CHAPTER 16

Introduction to the Content Center

Objectives:

1. Learn to import a Hex Bolt
2. Learn to modify a Hex Bolt

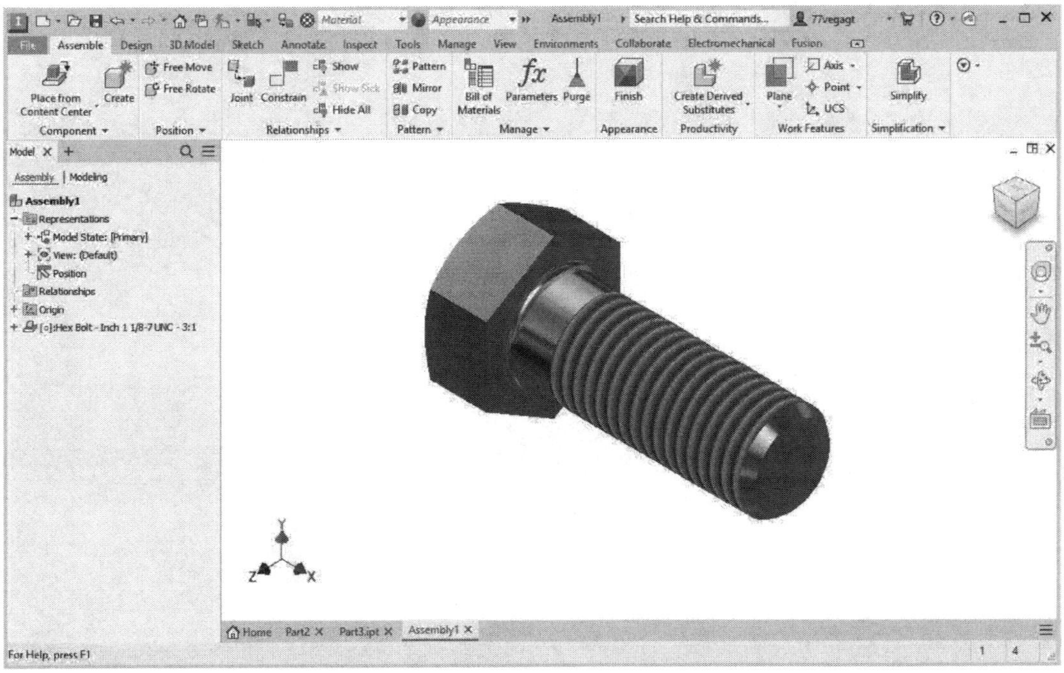

Chapter 16 includes instruction on how to import parts from the Content Center and from McMaster-Carr.

Learn to Import/Place a Hex Bolt

1. Start Inventor by referring to "Chapter 1 Getting Started."

2. Open the Assembly Panel as discussed in Chapter 7. Left click on the Assembly Tab. Left click on the arrow under Place as shown in Figure 1.

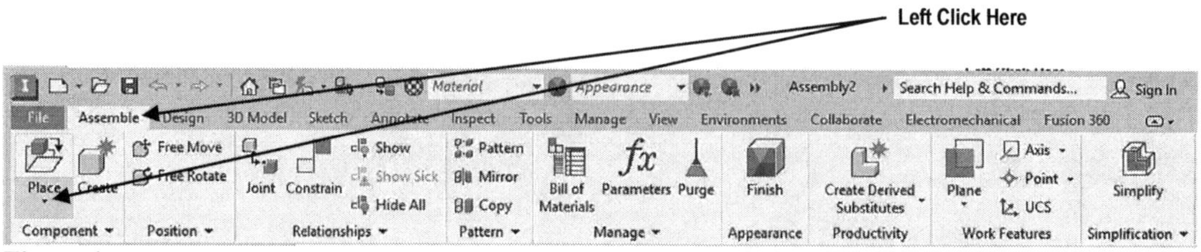

Figure 1

3. A drop-down menu will appear. Left click on **Place from Content Center** as shown in Figure 2.

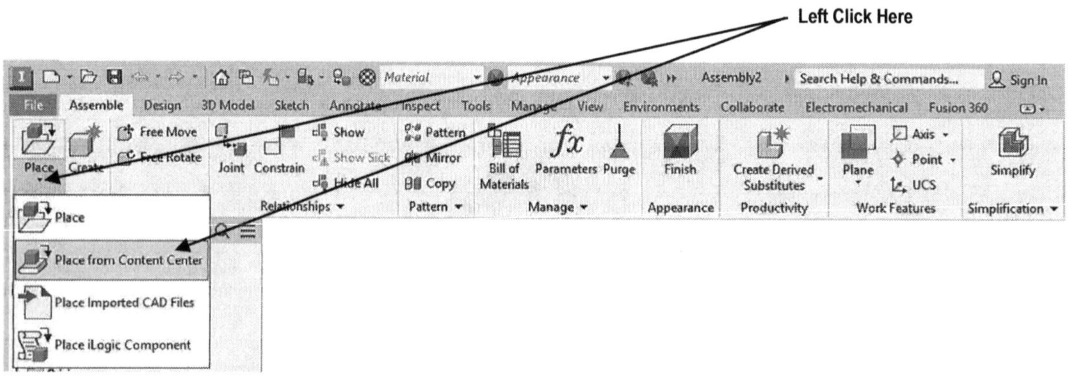

Figure 2

4. The **Place from Content Center** dialog box will appear. Left click on the star (Favorites). as shown in Figure 3.

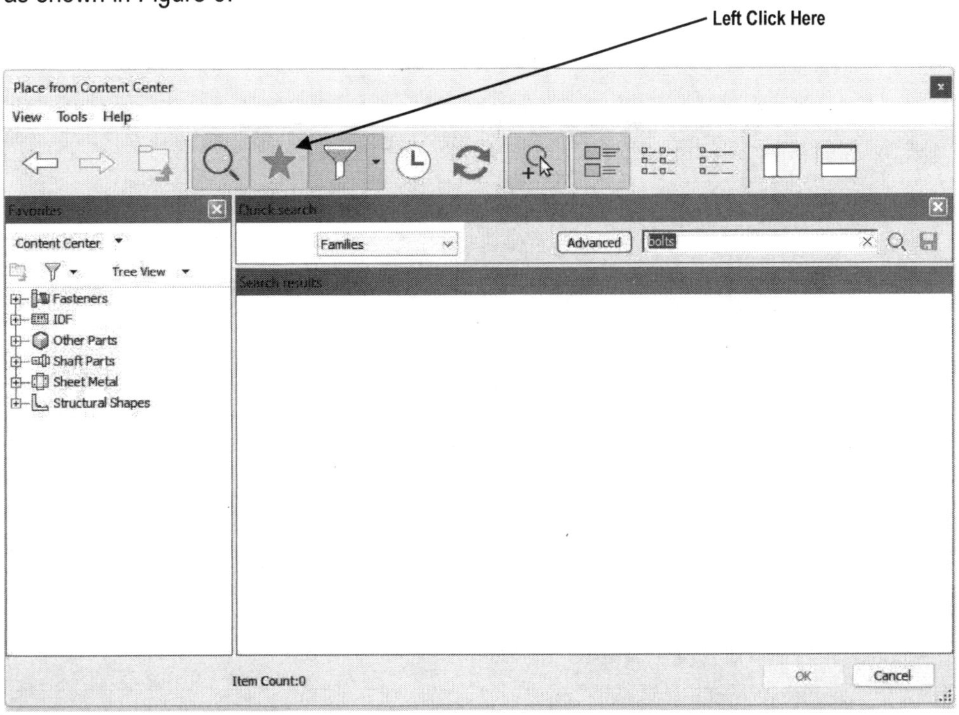

Figure 3

5. Left click on the plus sign to the left of Fasteners. This will cause items in the Browser to expand as shown in Figure 4.

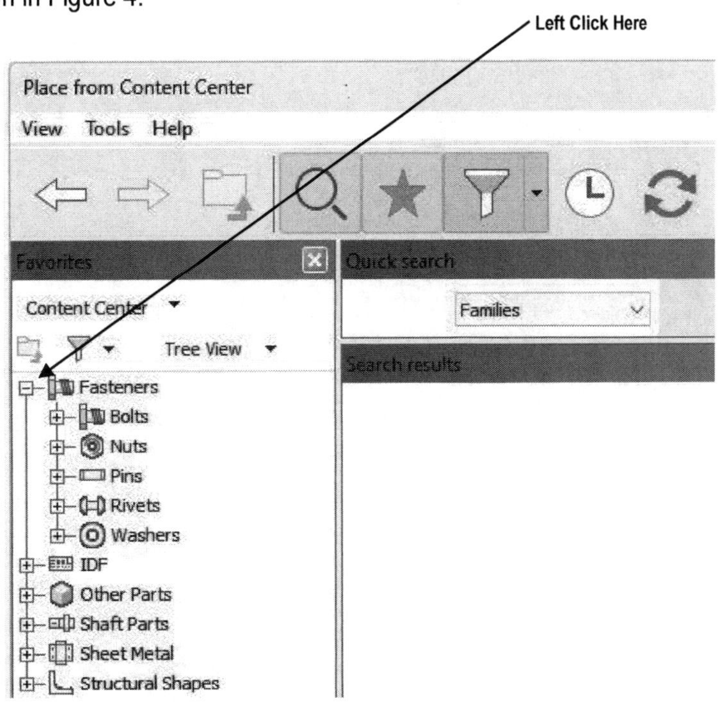

Figure 4

6. Left click on the plus sign to the left of Bolts. This will cause the Browser to expand as shown in Figure 5.

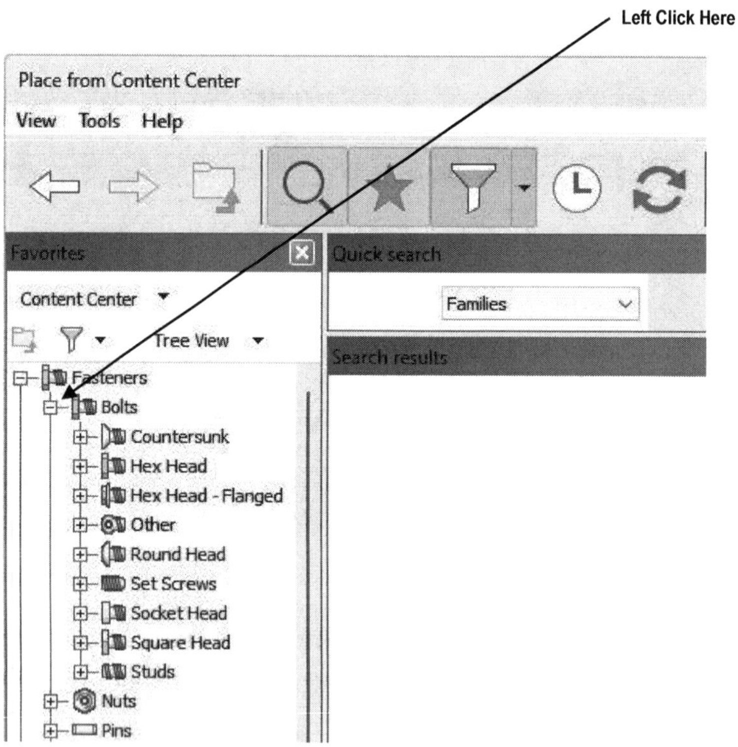

Figure 5

7. Left click on **Hex Head** in the Browser. Left click on **Heavy Head Hex Bolt-Inch**. Left click on **OK** as shown in Figure 6.

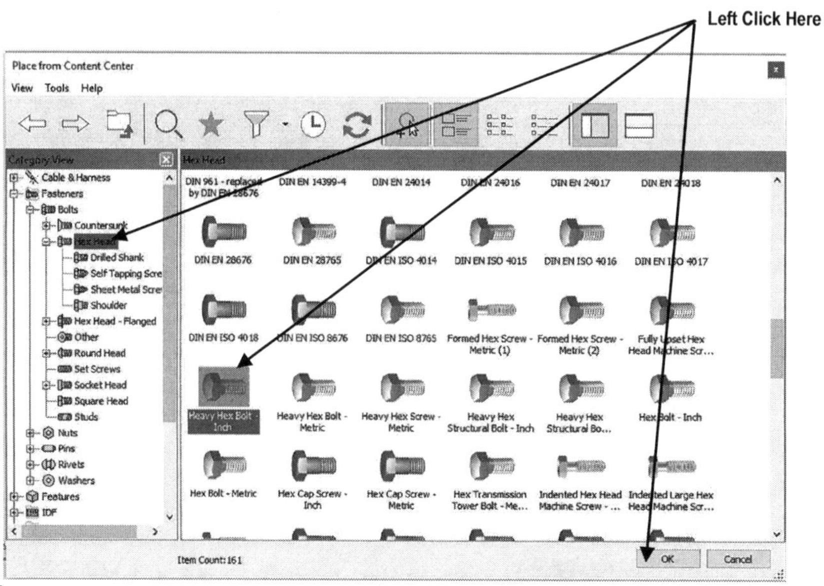

Figure 6

8. The Heavy Hex Bolt – Inch dialog box will appear as shown in Figure 7.

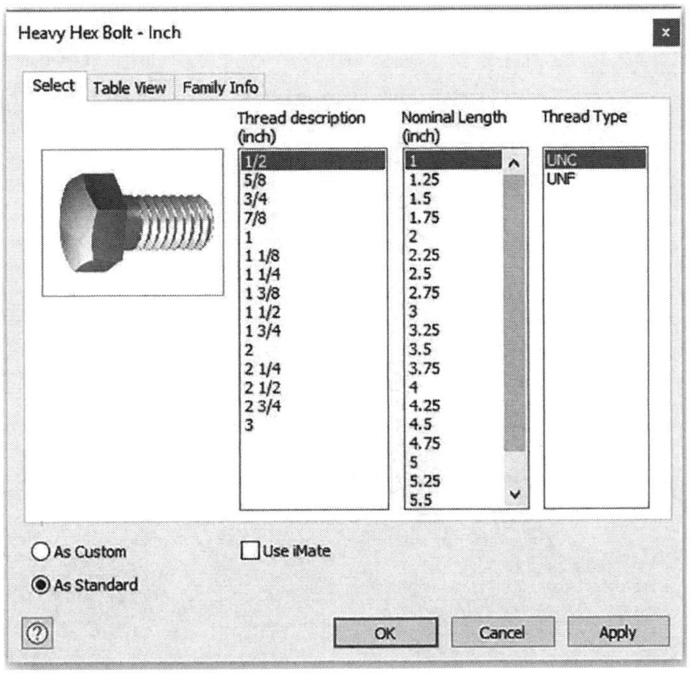

Figure 7

9. Left click on **1 1/8** for the Thread description (inch). Left click on **3** for the Nominal Length. Left click on **UNC** for the Thread Type and left click on **OK** as shown in Figure 8.

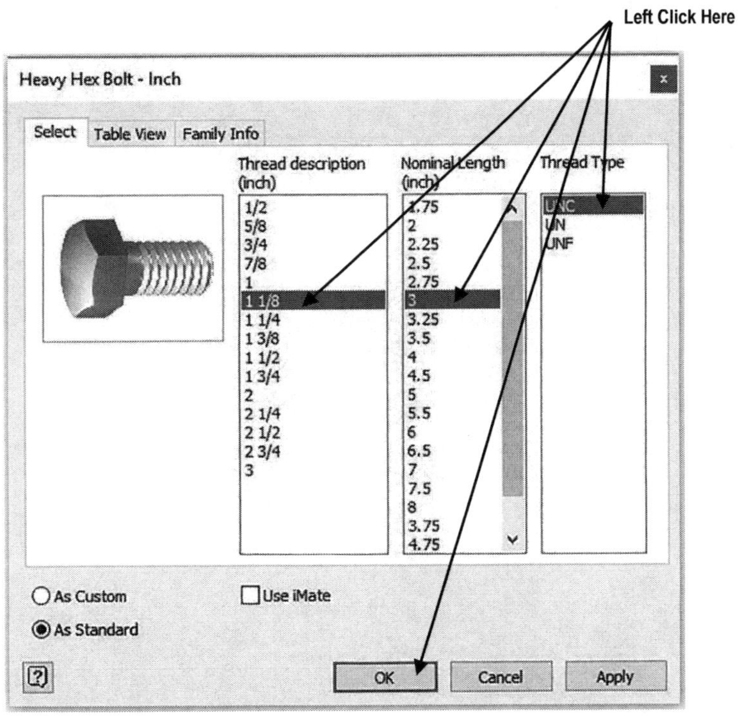

Figure 8

10. A bolt that is 1 inch in diameter and 3 inches in length will appear attached to the cursor as shown in Figure 9.

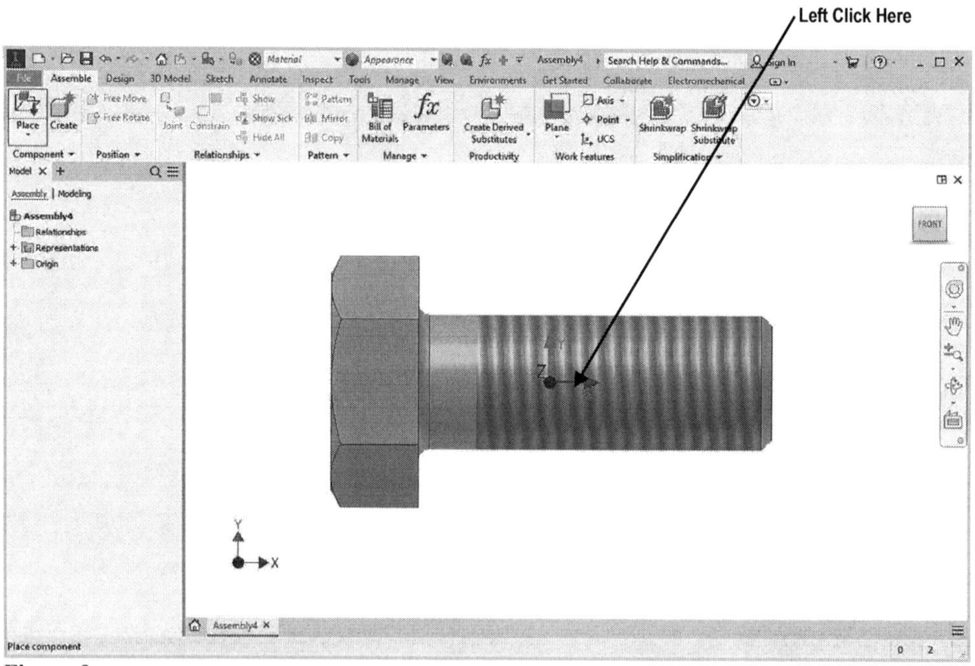

Figure 9

11. Left click once. If an additional bolt is attached to the cursor, press Esc once. Inventor will place the bolt as shown in Figure 10.

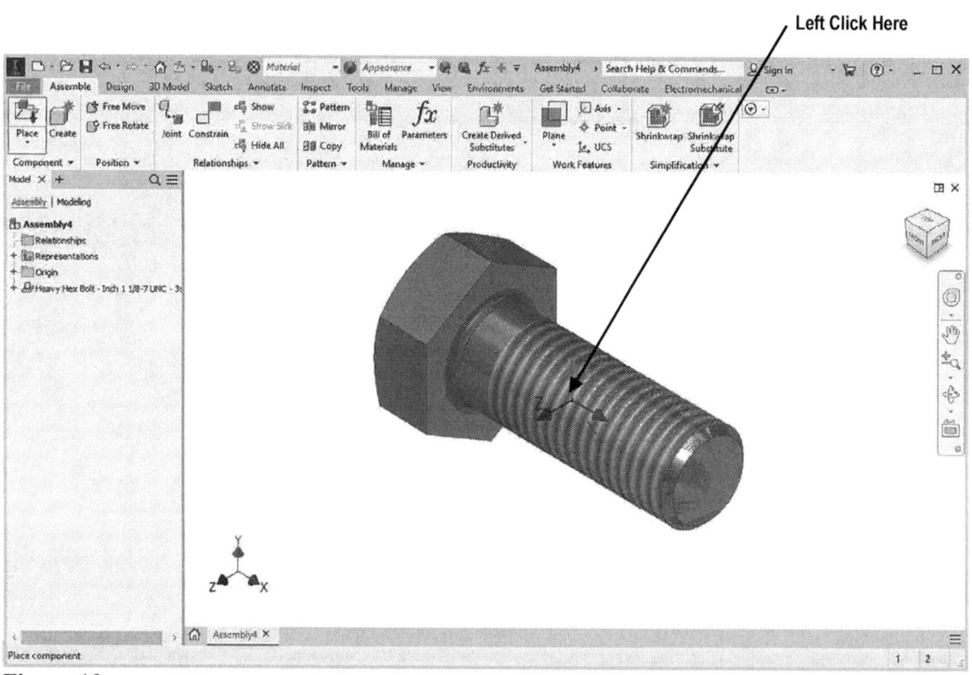

Figure 10

12. The Imported/Placed Hex bolt appears in the Browser at the left. If you were creating an Assembly, you would save the part where you have saved other parts of an Assembly. Your screen should look similar to Figure 11.

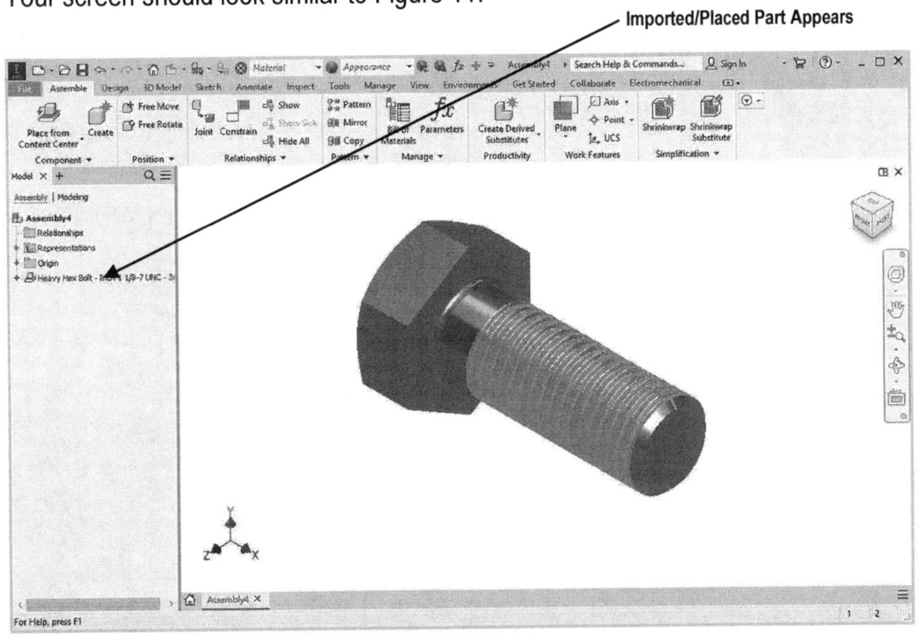

Figure 11

Learn to edit a previously Imported/Placed Hex Bolt

13. If for some reason the size of the bolt needs to be changed, move the cursor to the Browser and right click on **Heavy Hex Bolt – Inch 1-8 UNC – 3:1**. A pop-up menu will appear. Left click on **Change Size** as shown in Figure 12.

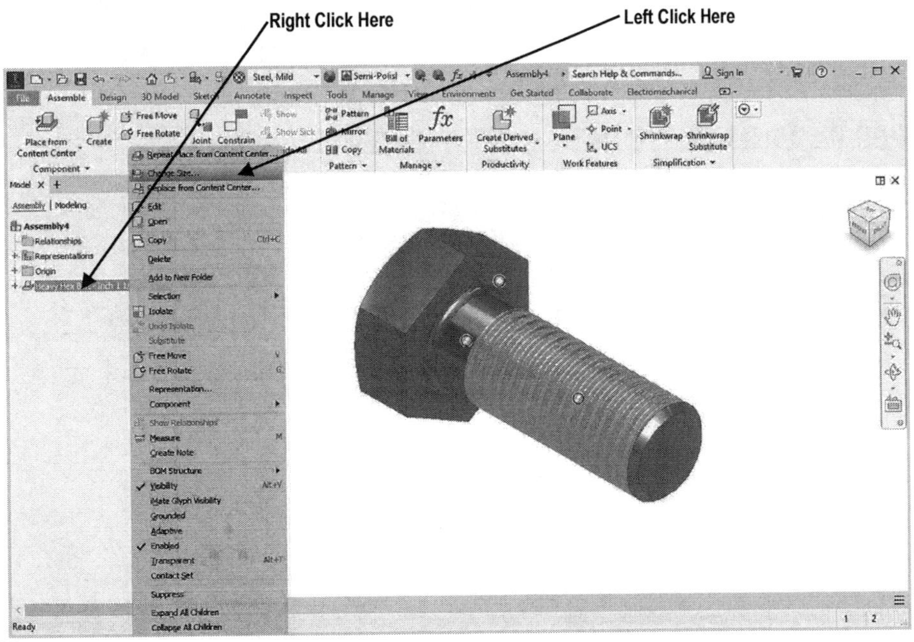

Figure 12

14. The Heavy Hex Bolt – Inch dialog box will re-appear as shown in Figure 13. Changes to the existing Heavy Hex Bolt can be made here.

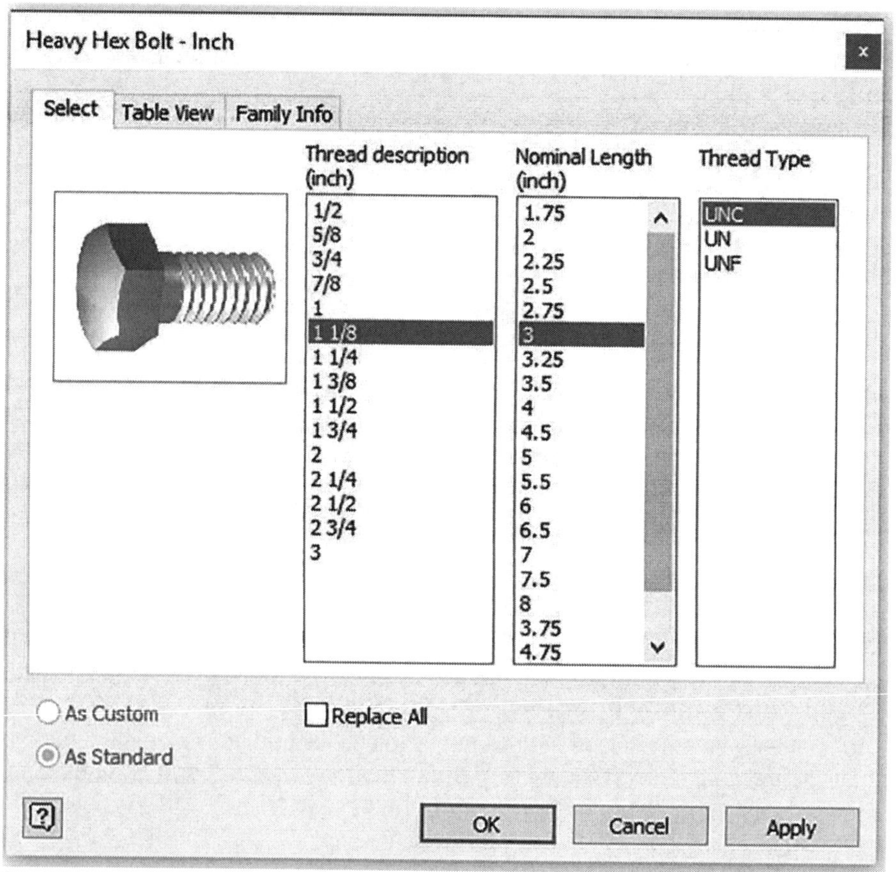

Figure 13

Learning to import standardized parts from the internet

15. Open an internet browser and go to www.mcmaster.com. The McMaster-Carr website will appear. McMaster-Carr produces numerous varieties of standardized parts available in large quantities. There are other standardized part supply houses as well.

16. Your screen should look similar to what is shown in Figure 14.

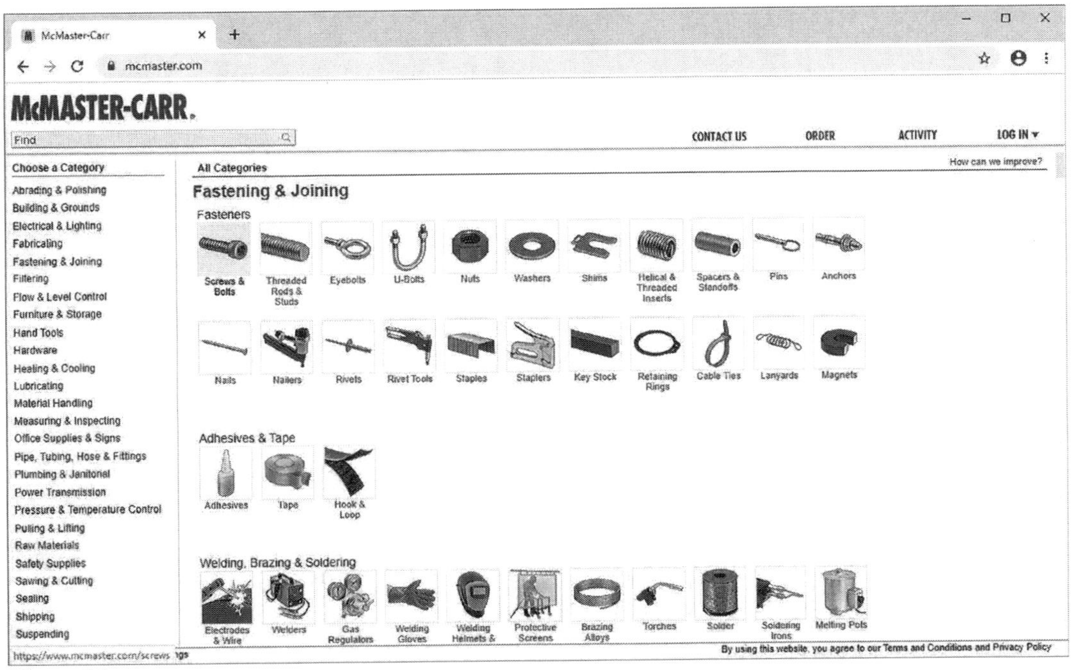

Figure 14

17. Move your cursor to the upper left portion of the screen and left click on **Screws and Fasteners** as shown in Figure 15.

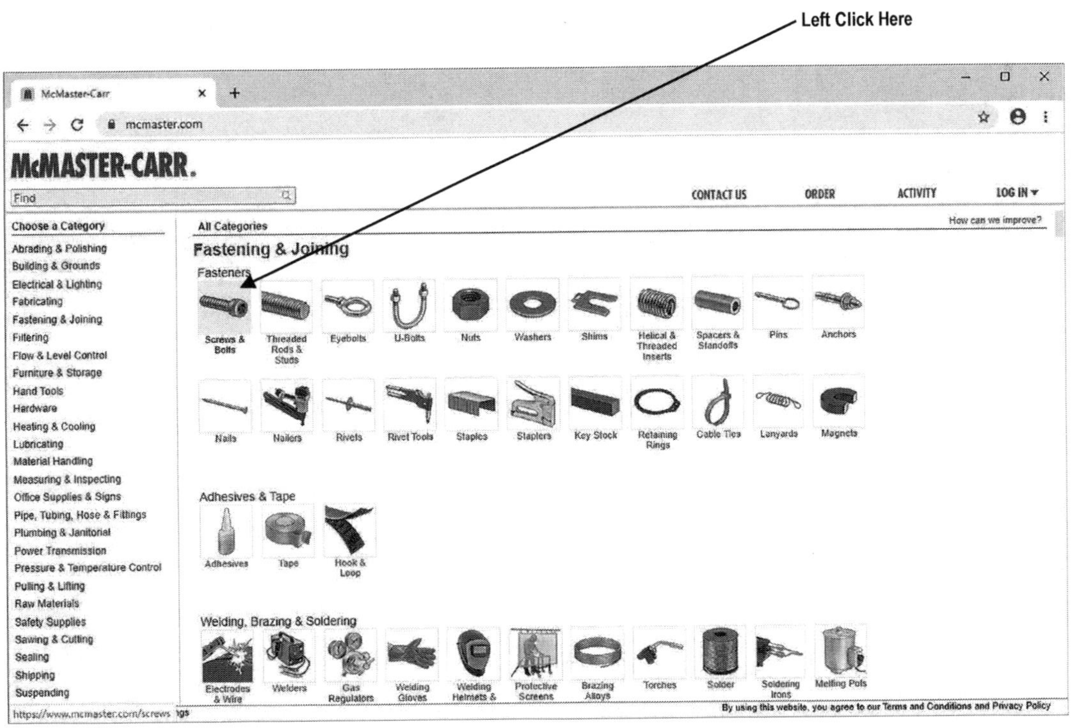

Figure 15

18. Your screen should look similar to what is shown in Figure 16.

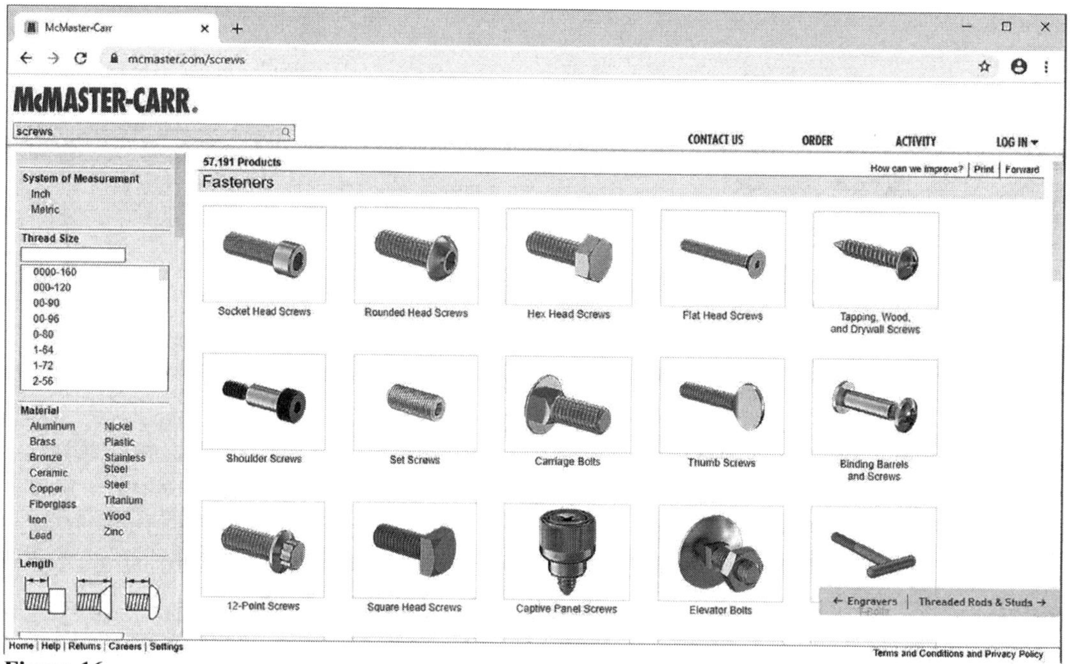

Figure 16

19. Left click on **Hex Head Screws** as shown in Figure 17.

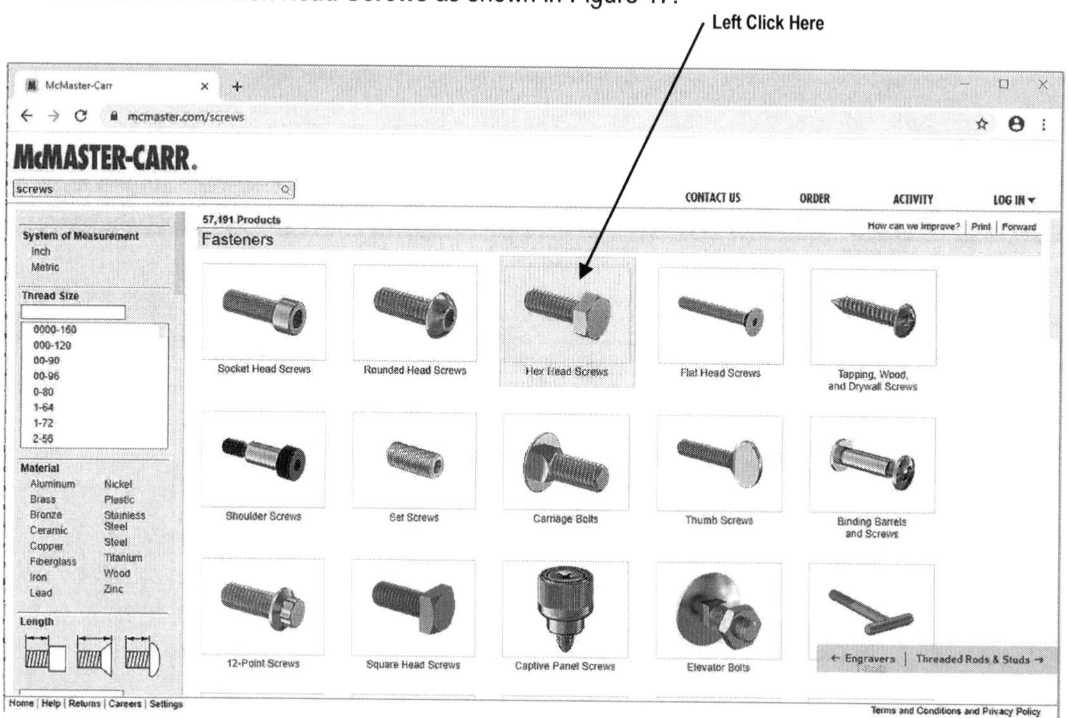

Figure 17

20. Your screen should look similar to what is shown in Figure 18.

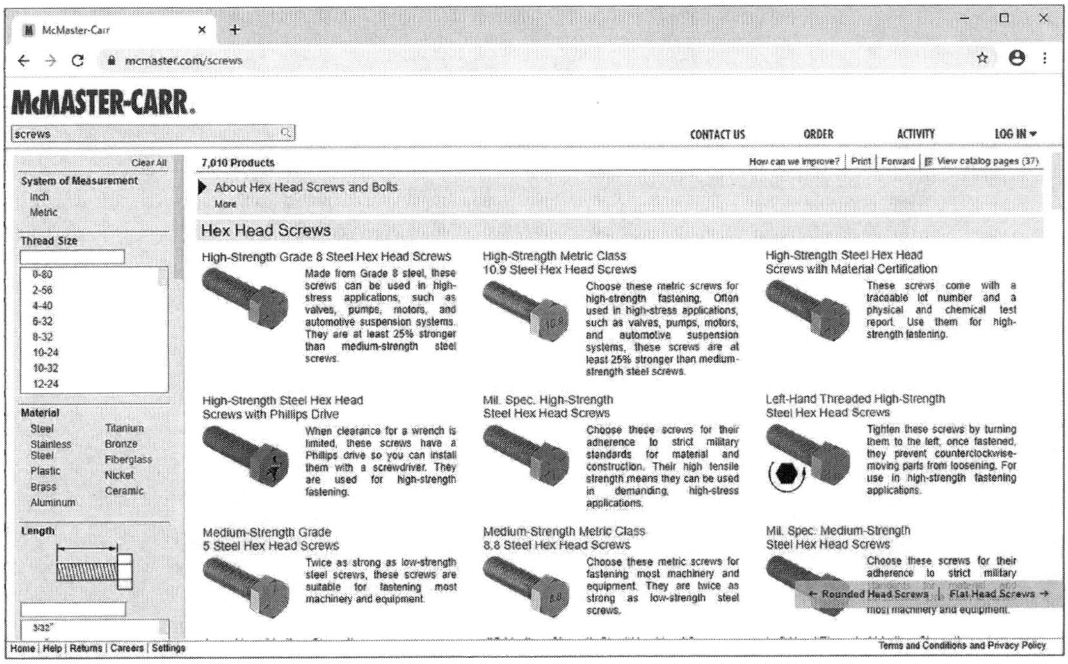

Figure 18

21. Left click on **High Strength Grade 8 Steel Hex Head Screws** as shown in Figure 19.

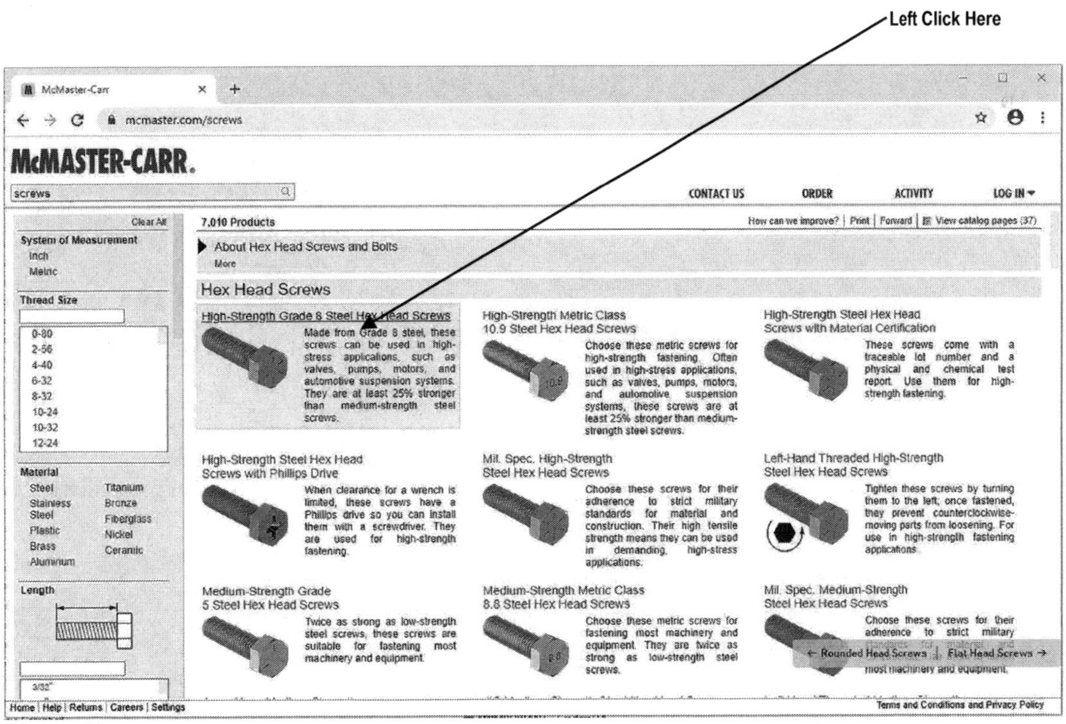

Figure 19

22. McMaster-Carr will begin loading the types of hex head screws that are available. Your screen should look similar to what is shown in Figure 20.

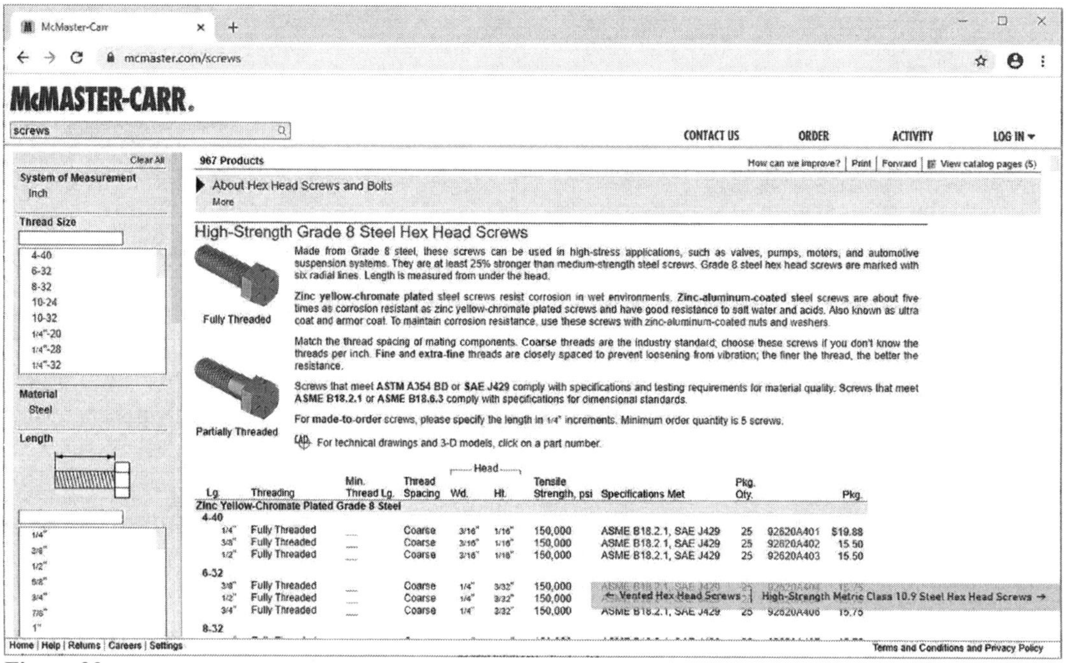

Figure 20

23. Scroll down to 5/16-18 - 2" Fully Threaded as shown in Figure 21.

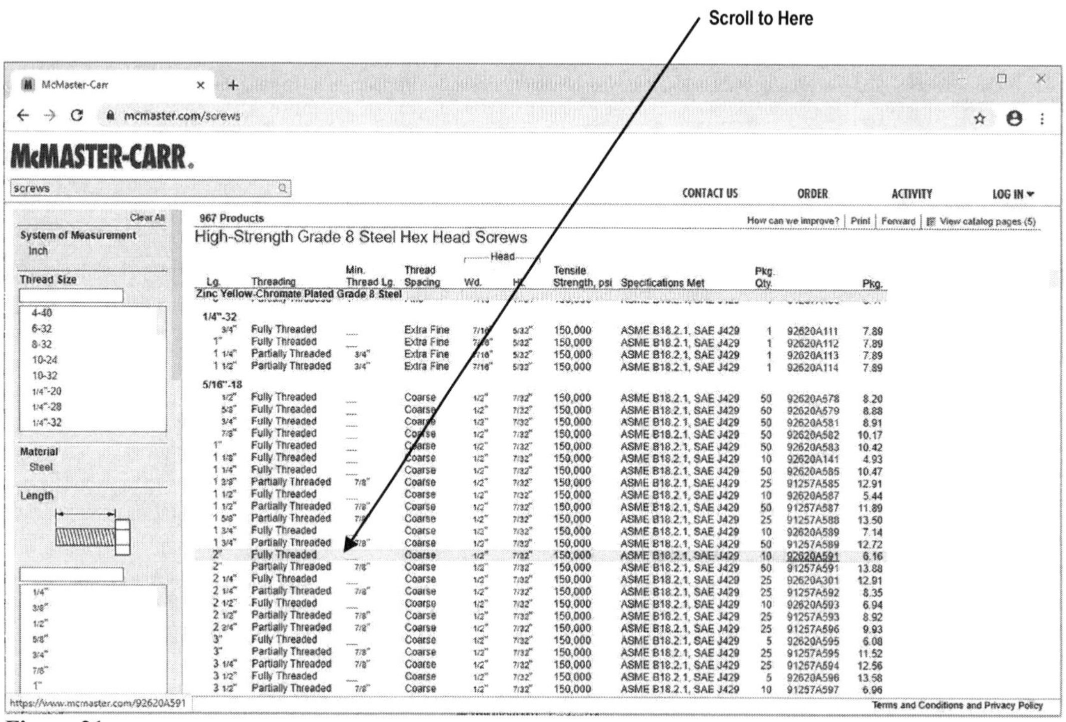

Figure 21

24. Move the cursor to the middle right portion of the screen and left click on the corresponding part number. A pop-up menu will appear as shown in Figure 22.

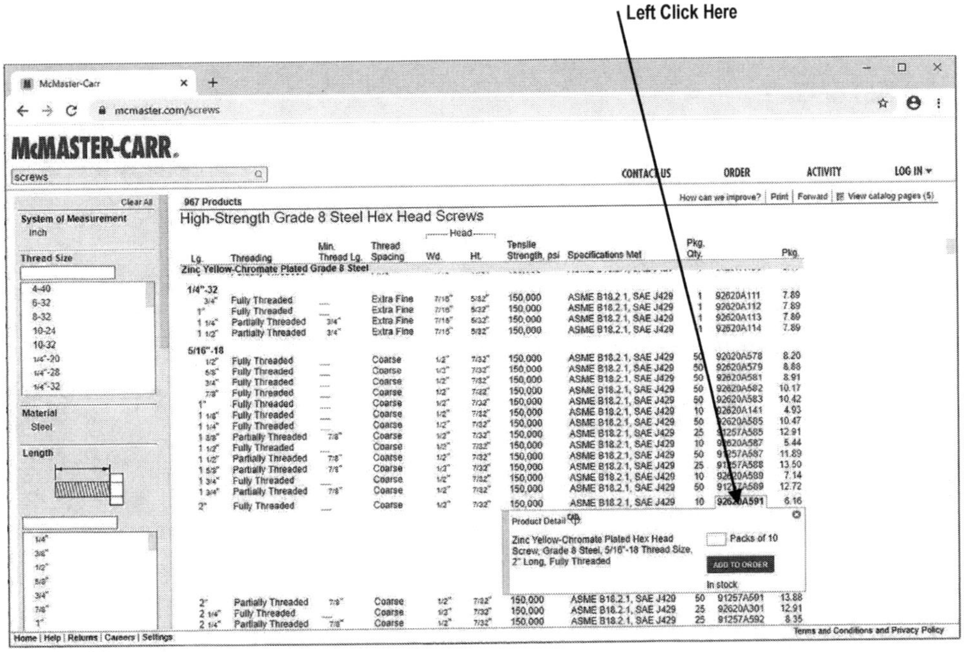

Figure 22

25. Move the cursor over the link "Product Detail". Notice the CAD symbol to the right of Product Detail. The CAD symbol indicates that there is a downloadable CAD file for this part. Left click on the **Product Detail** link as shown in Figure 23.

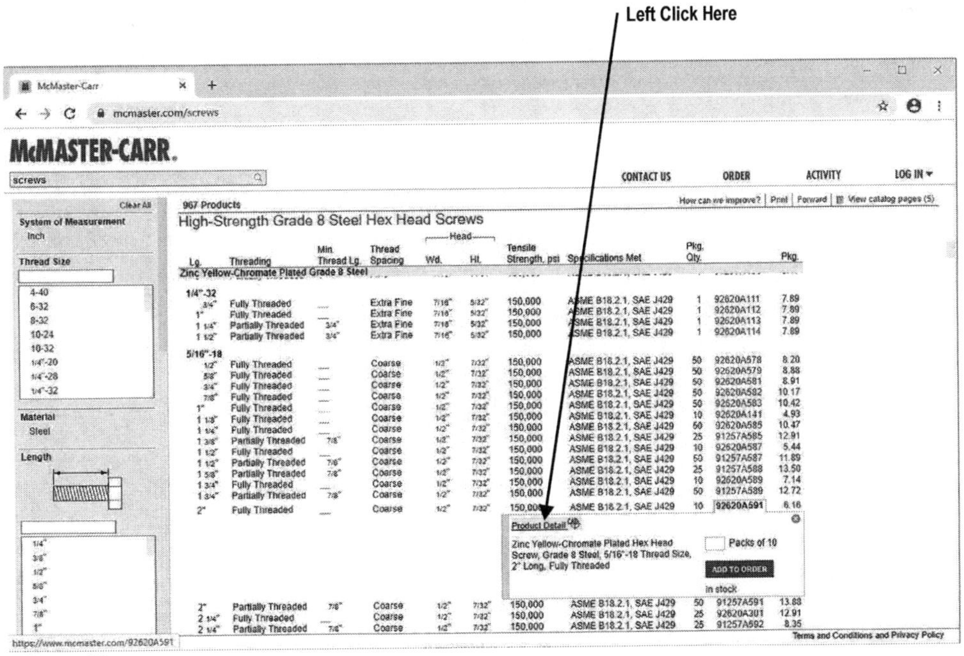

Figure 23

26. McMaster-Carr will provide a detailed webpage that includes the selected part's specifications as shown in Figure 24.

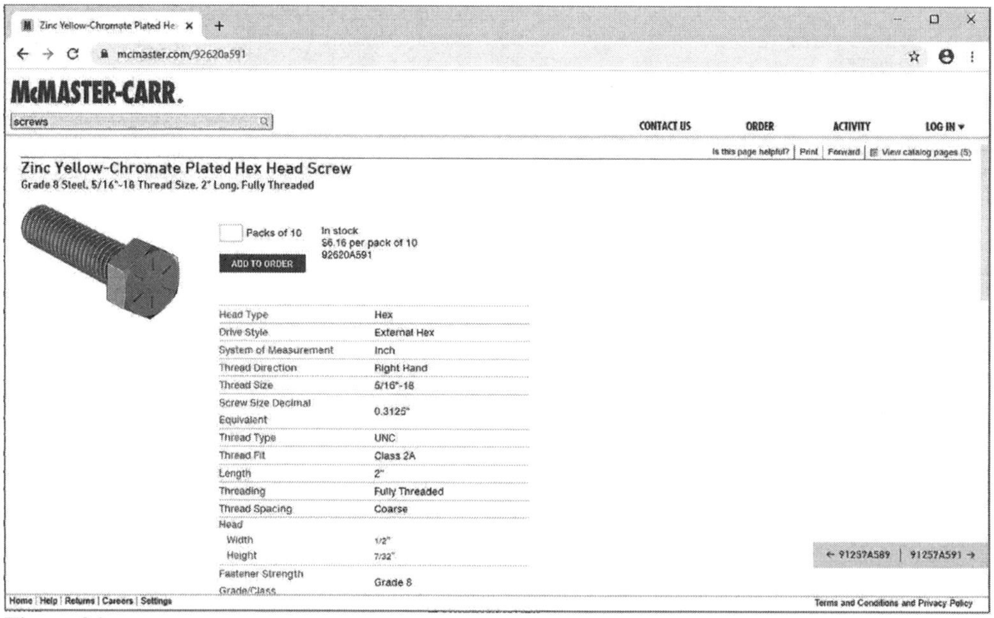

Figure 24

27. Scroll down to the bottom of the page. A detailed drawing of the part will appear. To the right of the drawing a drop-down box with the text 3-D SolidWorks will appear as shown in Figure 25.

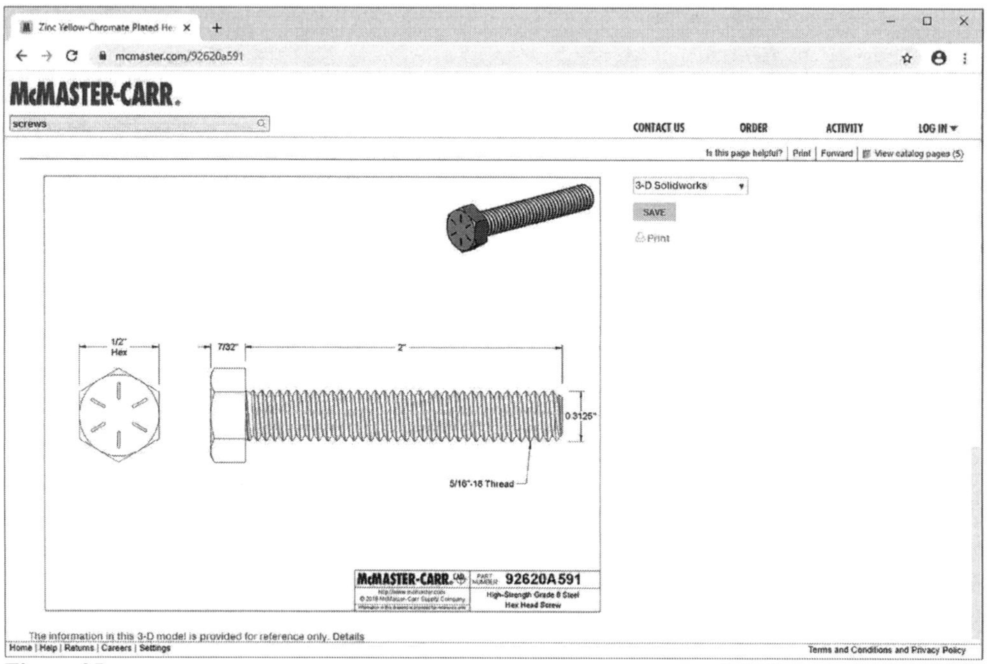

Figure 25

28. Drop the arrow down to the right of 3-D SolidWorks. Left click on **3-D IGES**. Left click on **Save** as shown in Figure 26.

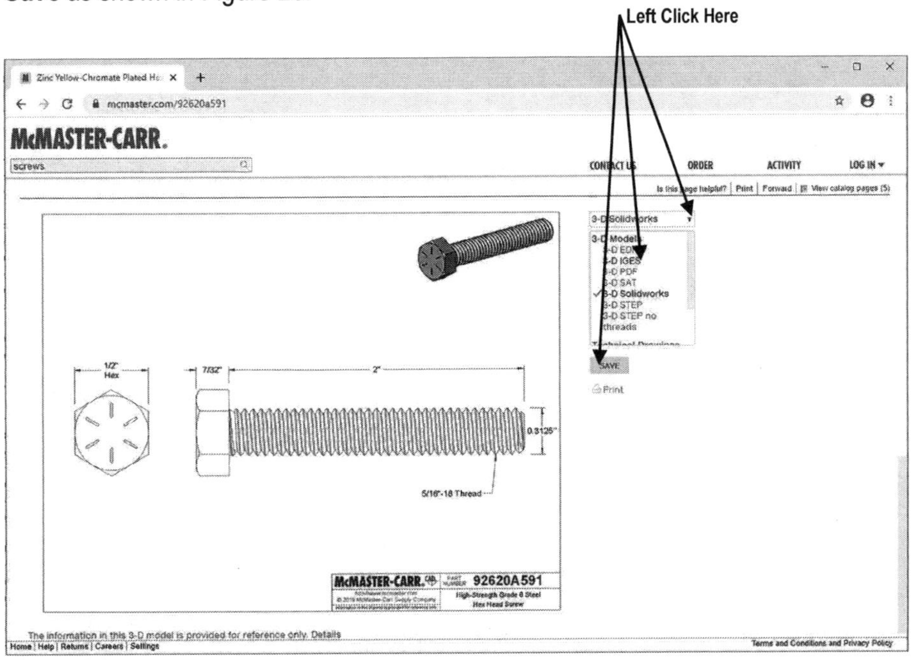

Figure 26

29. McMaster-Carr will place the 3-D IGES file in the Downloads folder of the browser you are using. Now go to Inventor and left click on the Open folder. This will cause the Open dialog box to appear. Scroll down and left click on the **Downloads** folder as shown in Figure 27.

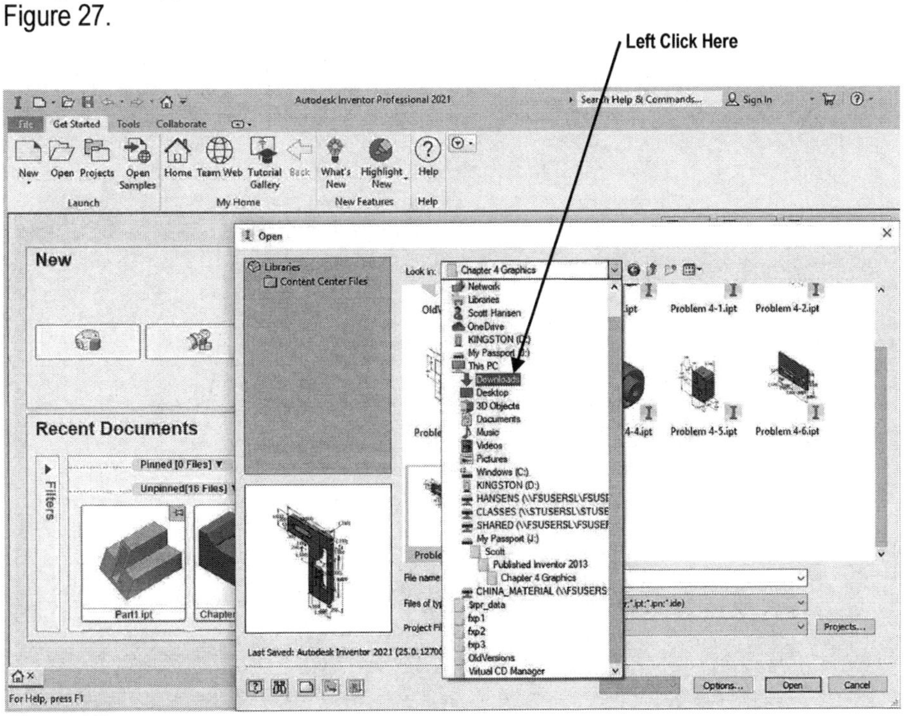

Figure 27

30. The Downloads folder will appear empty as shown in Figure 28.

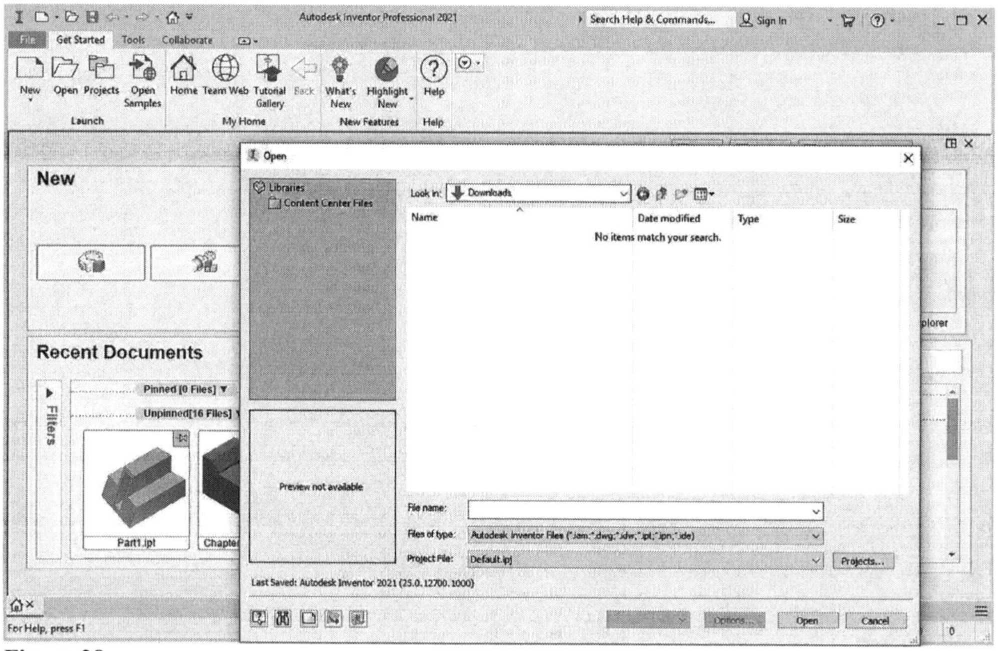

Figure 28

31. Move the cursor to the lower right portion of the screen and left click on the drop-down arrow to the right of **Files of type**. All the different file types that Inventor will read will appear. Scroll down and left click on **All Files** as shown in Figure 29.

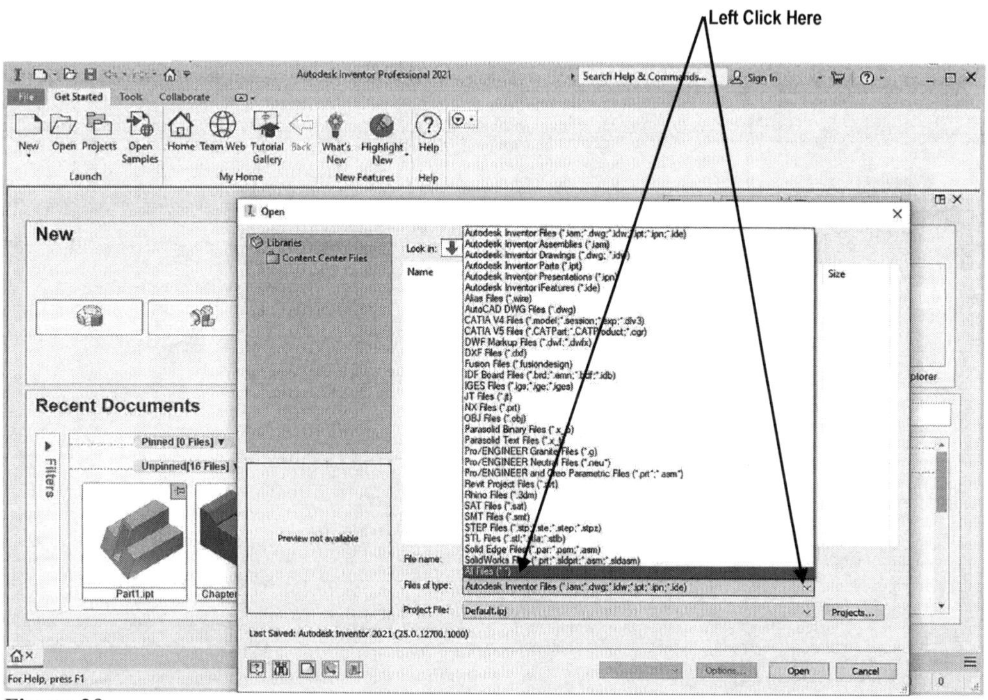

Figure 29

32. The downloaded file from McMaster-Carr will appear as shown in Figure 30.

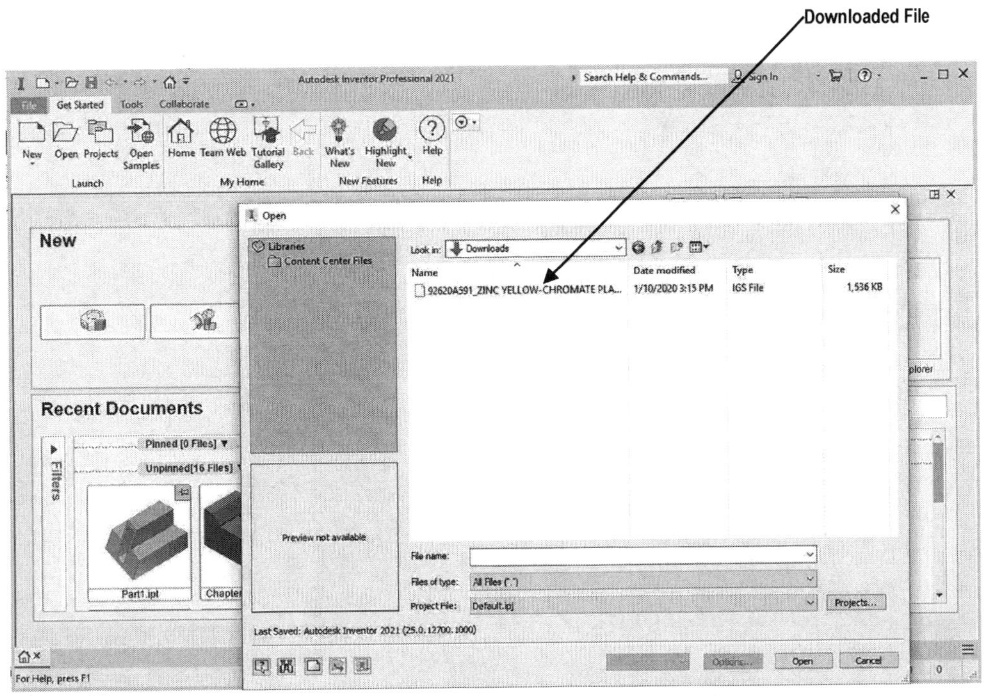

Figure 30

33. Left click on the downloaded McMaster-Carr file. Left click on **Open** as shown in Figure 31.

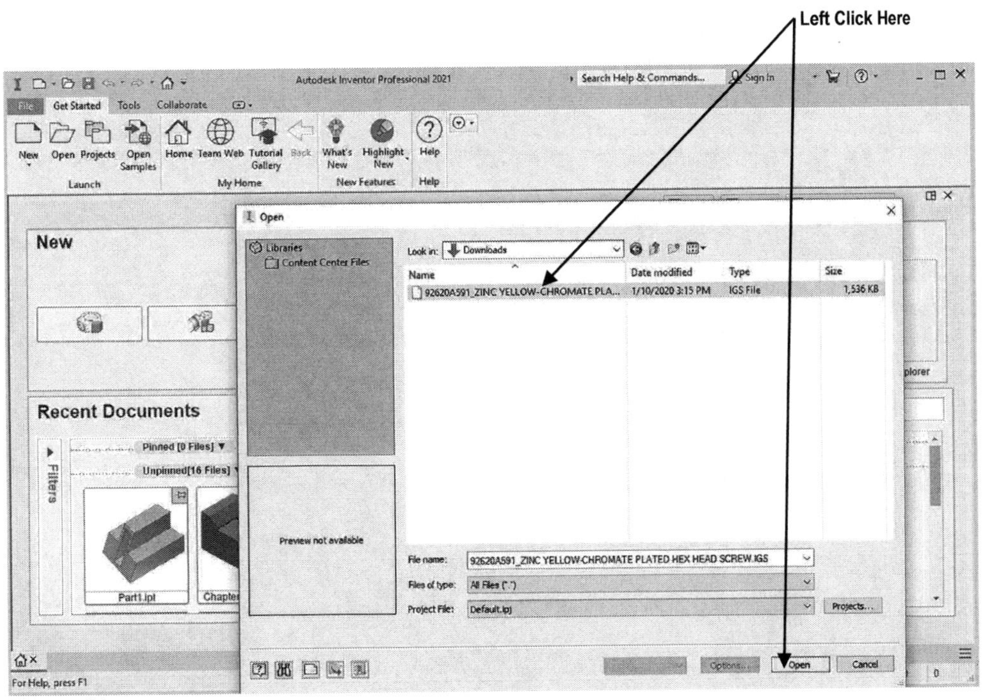

Figure 31

34. The Import dialog box will appear. Left click on **OK** as shown in Figure 32.

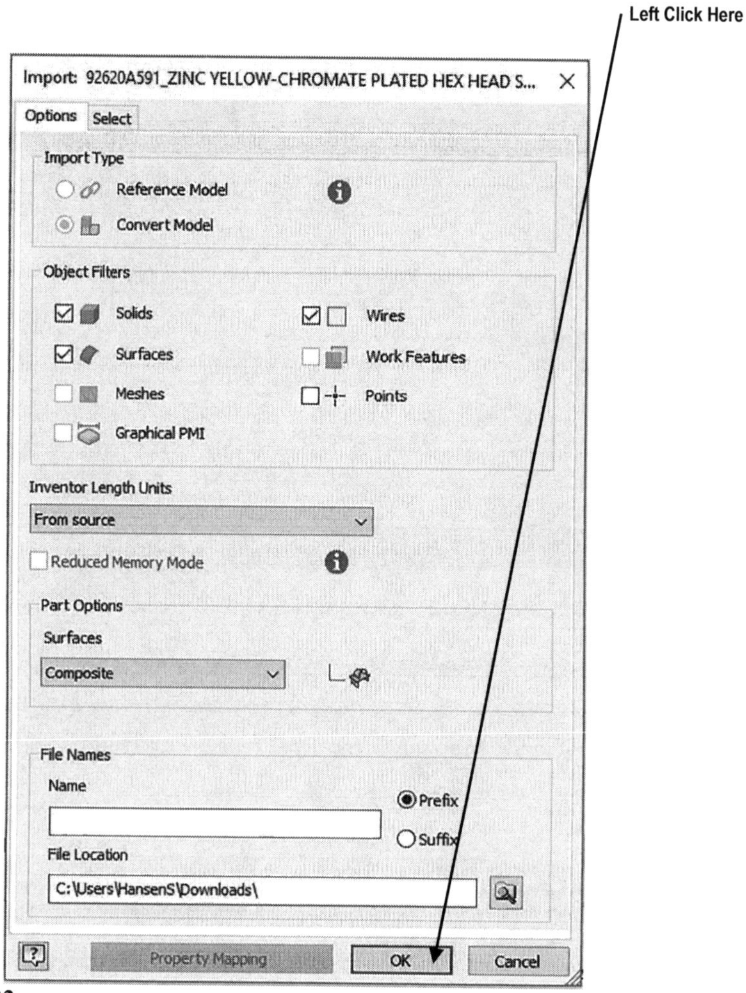

Figure 32

35. Inventor will provide a preview of the imported part. It will appear Translucent. Move the cursor to the middle left portion of the Browser and right click on **Composite1**. A pop-up menu will appear. Left click on **Translucent** as shown in Figure 33.

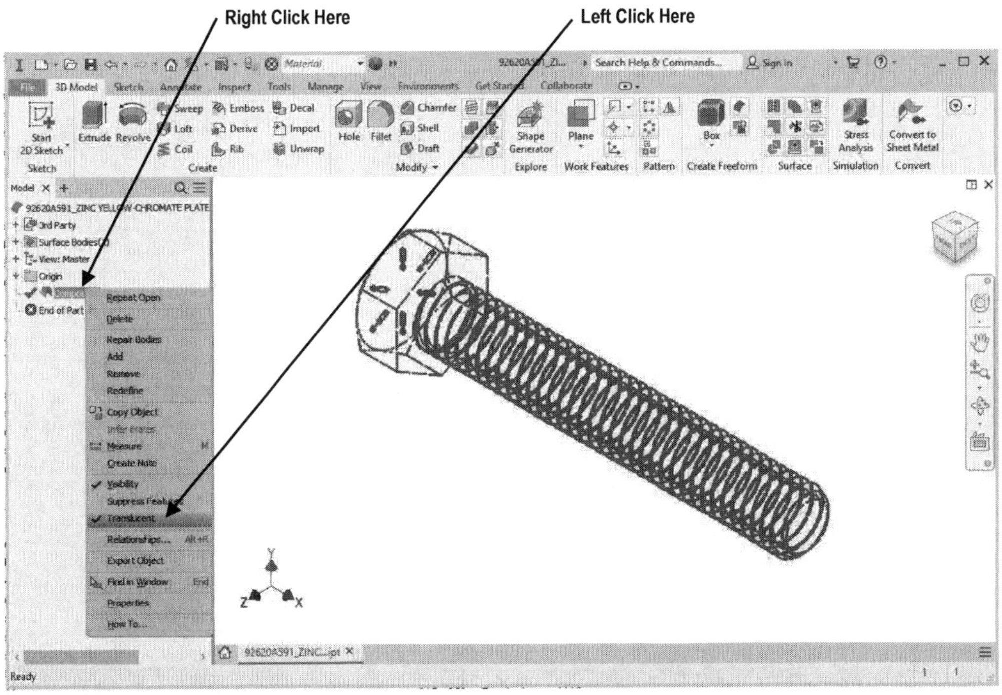

Figure 33

36. The part will appear as a normal 3D Solid as shown in Figure 34.

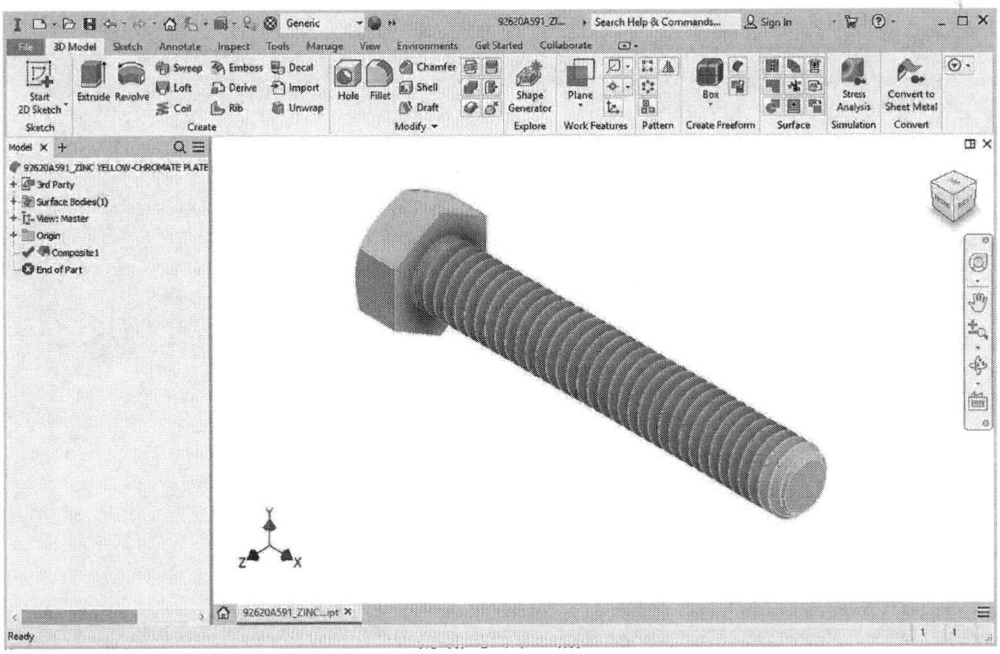

Figure 34

37. Save the imported part where other parts are saved. If you were creating an assembly of several part files you would "Place" the imported part in the Assembly the same way you would place parts you created.

CHAPTER 17

Introduction to iLogic Components

Objectives:

1. Learn to Place iLogic Components
2. Learn to modify iLogic Components

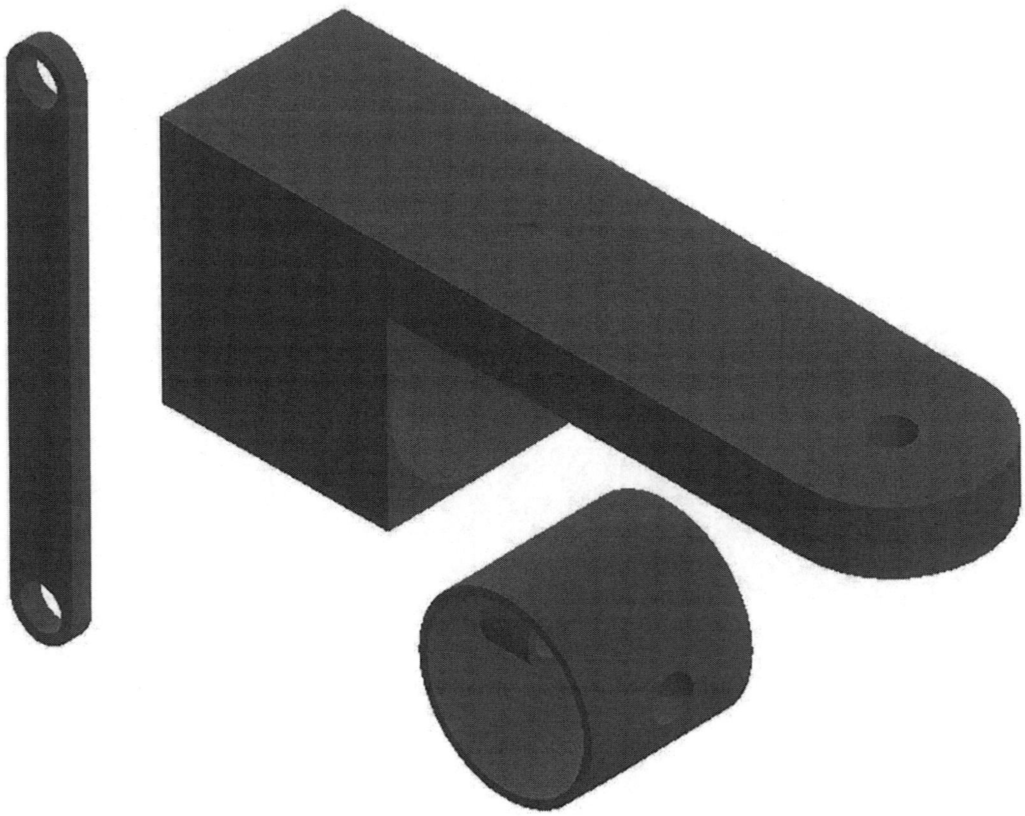

Chapter 17 includes instruction on how to edit the parts shown.

1. Start Inventor by referring to "Chapter 1 Getting Started."

2. Start a new Assembly as shown in Figure 1.

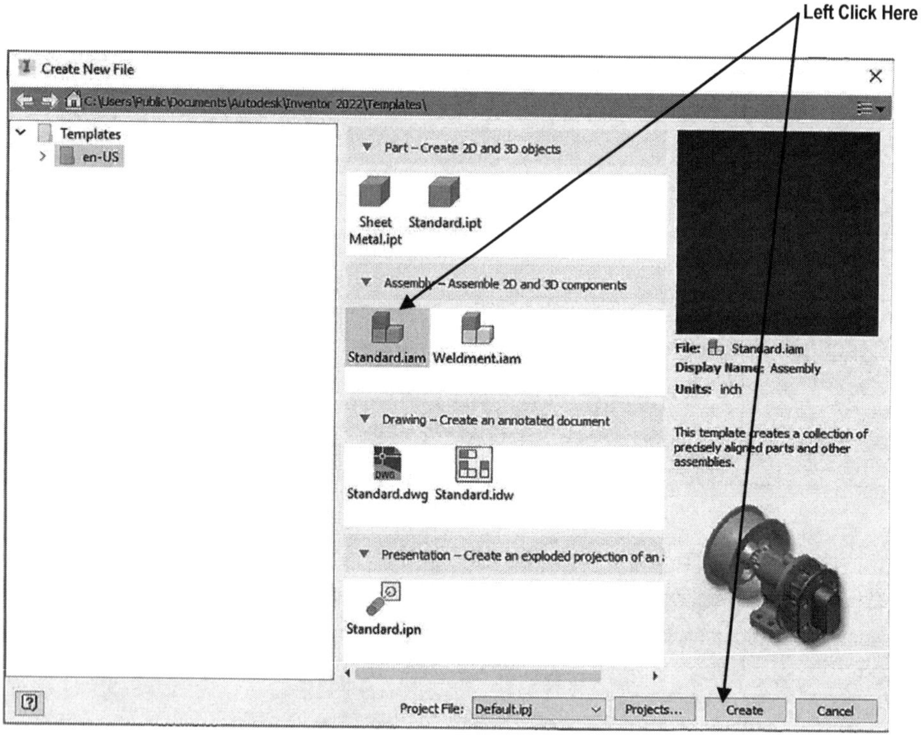

Figure 1

3. Save the Assembly as iAssembly1 before starting. Now move the cursor to the upper left portion of the screen and left click on the arrow under Place. A drop-down menu will appear. Left click on **Place iLogic Component** as shown in Figure 2.

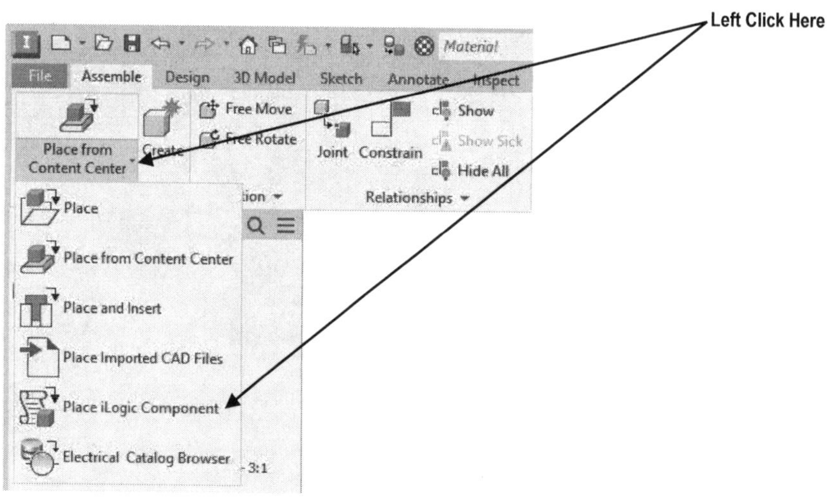

Figure 2

4. The Place iLogic Component dialog box will appear as shown in Figure 3.

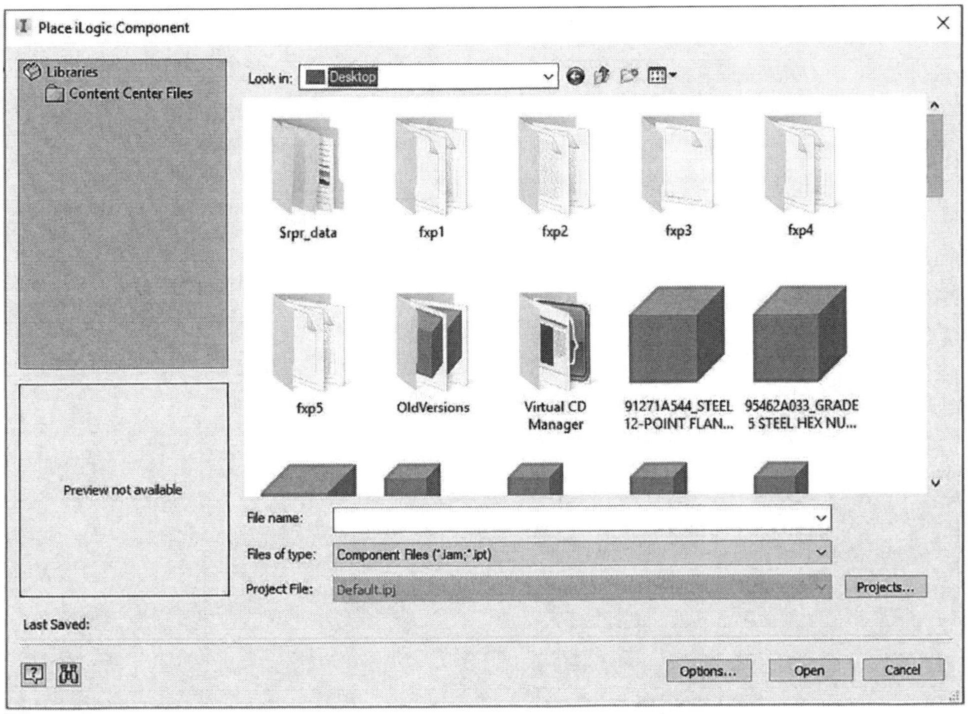

Figure 3

5. Locate the piston assembly parts that were created in Chapter 6 as shown in Figure 4.

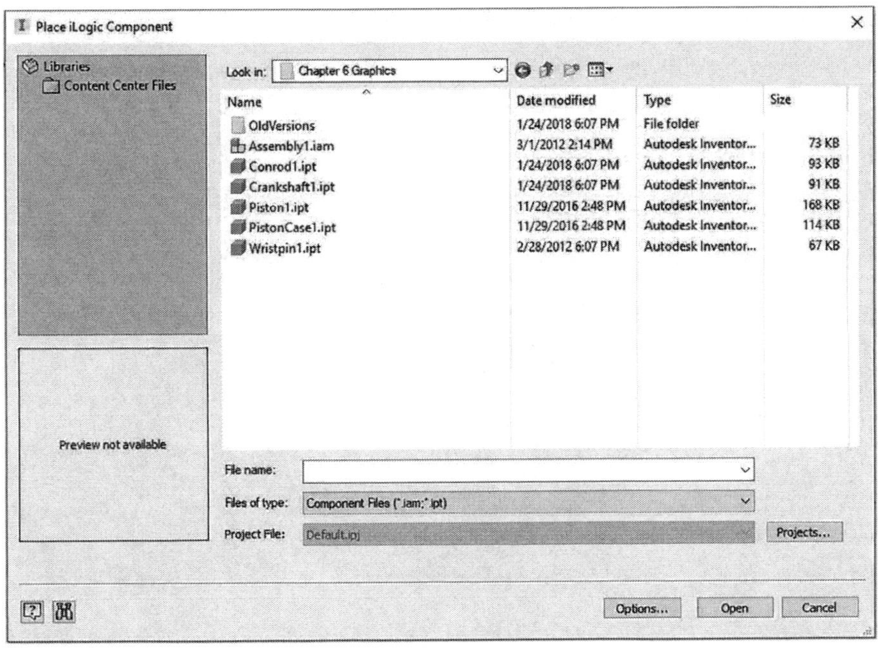

Figure 4

6. Left click on **PistonCase1.** Left click on **Open** as shown in Figure 5.

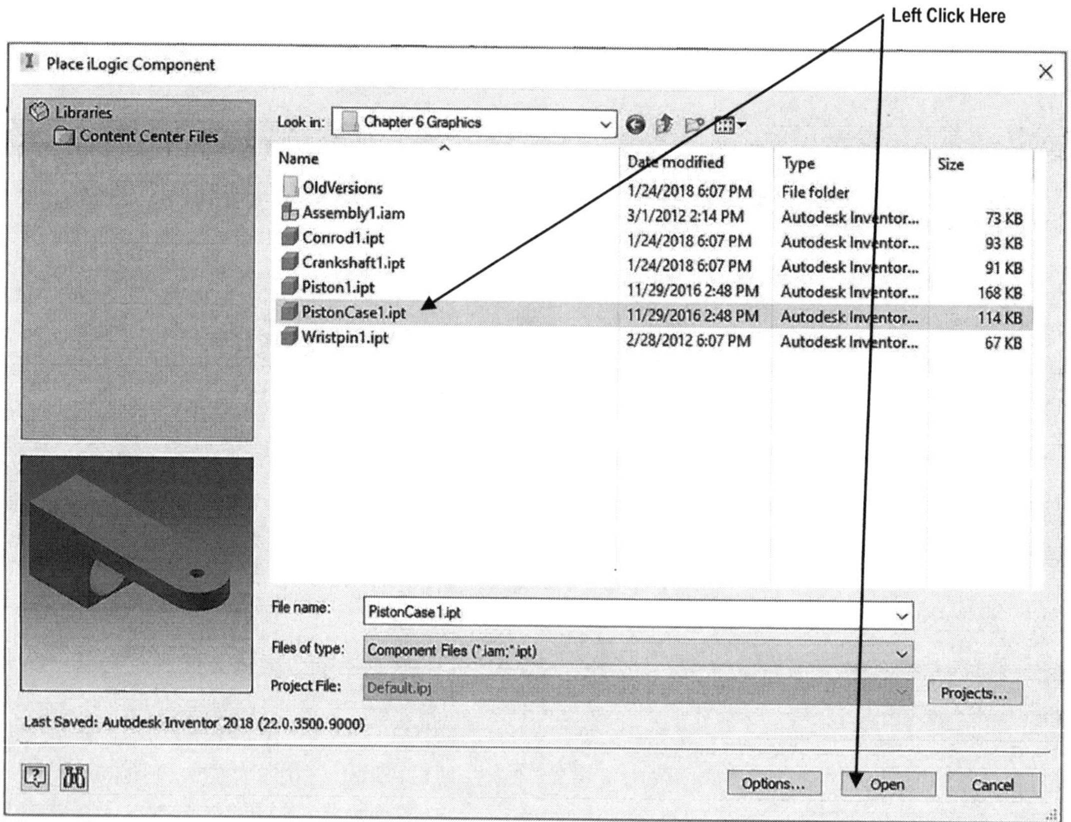

Figure 5

7. The Place iLogic Component dialog box will appear as shown in Figure 6.

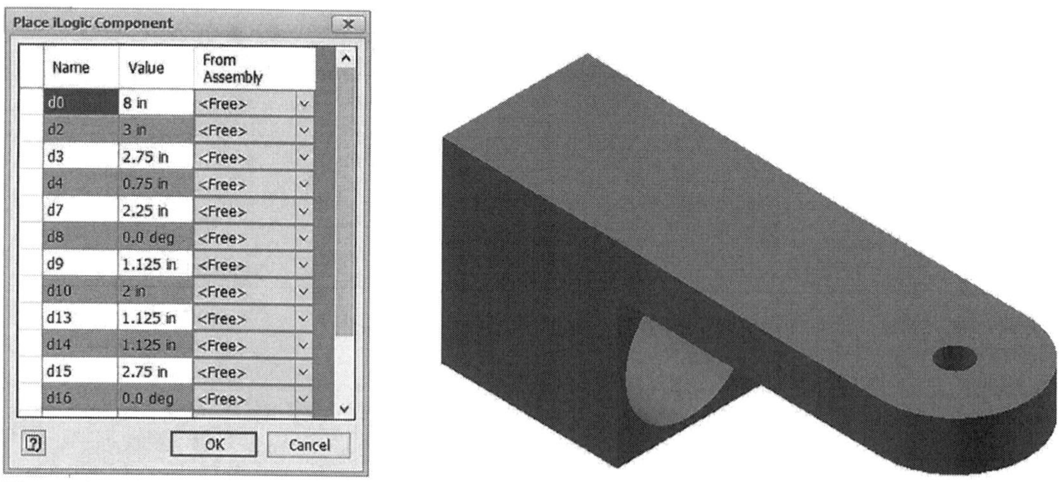

Figure 6

8. The Place iLogic Component dialog box contains “Values” in the center column as shown in Figure 7. These values are the Sketch dimensions that can be edited to change the part dimensions.

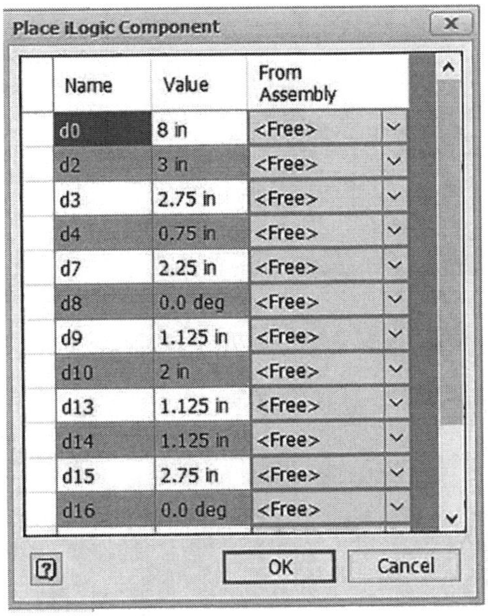

Figure 7

Learn to Edit iLogic Component Values

9. Left click on the **8 in** Value as shown in Figure 8. It may or may not be d0. This Value is the length of the piston case. Change the Value from 8 inches to 9 inches and press **Enter** on the keyboard. This will cause the length of the piston case to increase from 8 inches to 9 inches.

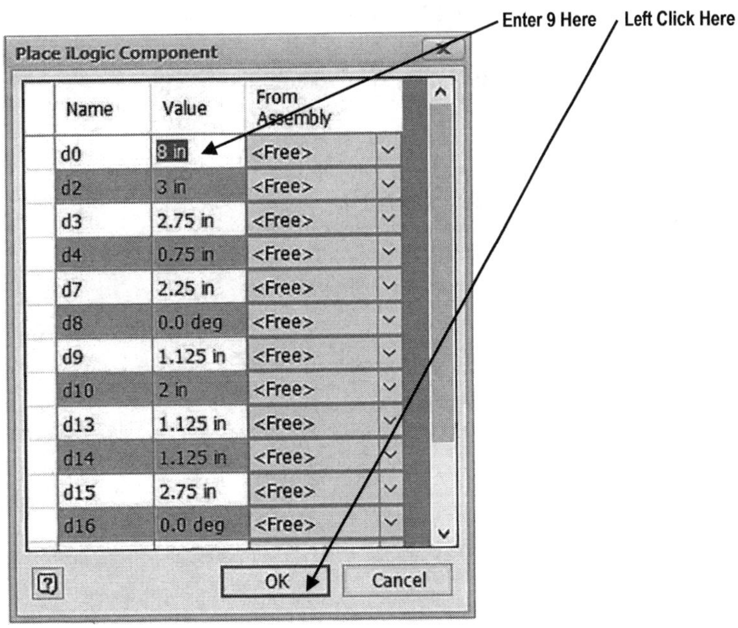

Figure 8

10. Move the cursor down to the 2.0 in value in the Value column. It may or may not be d10. Once the value is located, left click once. Change the value from 2 in to **2.125** in as shown in Figure 9. Press **Enter** on the keyboard. This will cause the diameter of the bore to increase from 2 inches to 2.125 inches.

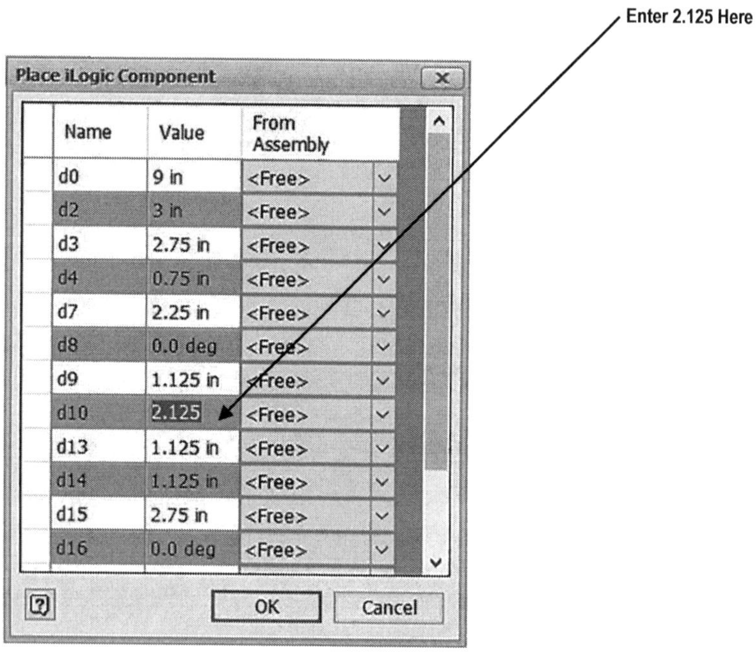

Figure 9

11. Inventor has increased the length of the piston case from 8 inches to 9 inches and has also increased the diameter of the cylinder bore from 2 inches to 2.125 inches. Left click on **OK** as shown in Figure 10. The piston case will be attached to the cursor. Place the piston case into the Assembly as described in Chapter 7.

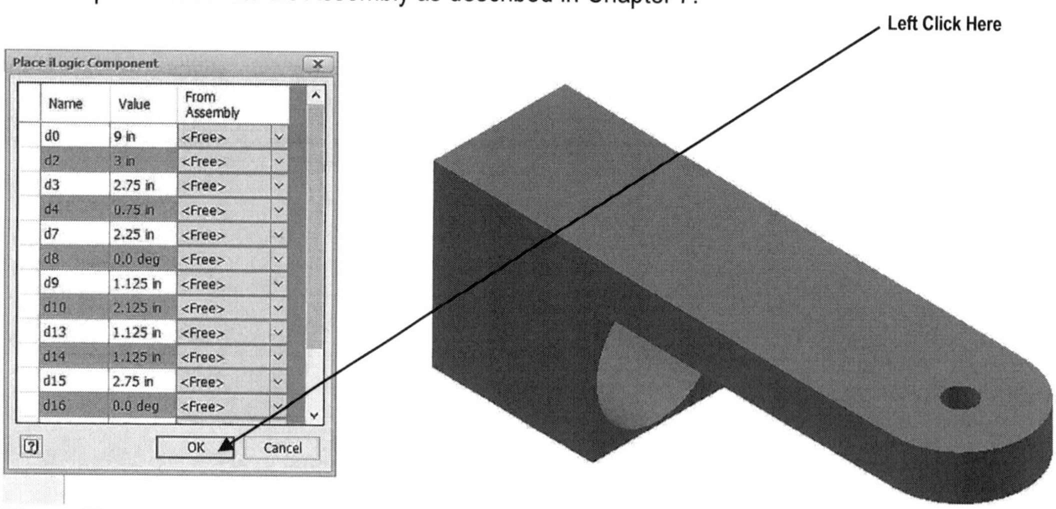

Figure 10

Learn to save an iLogic Component

12. Save the Assembly before proceeding. You will notice that Inventor has created a new part with a similar file name (a 01 or 02, etc. will be added to the original file name) illustrating that the part is an edited version of the original part as shown in Figure 11.

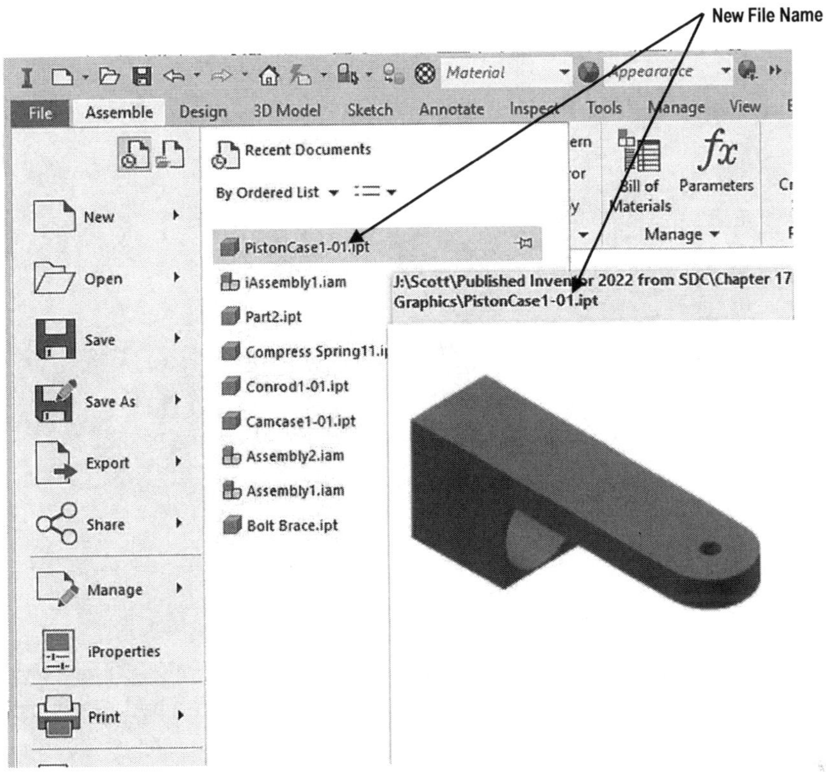

Figure 11

13. Use the iLogic Component steps described previously to "Place" the Piston in the Assembly. Your screen should look similar to what is shown in Figure 12.

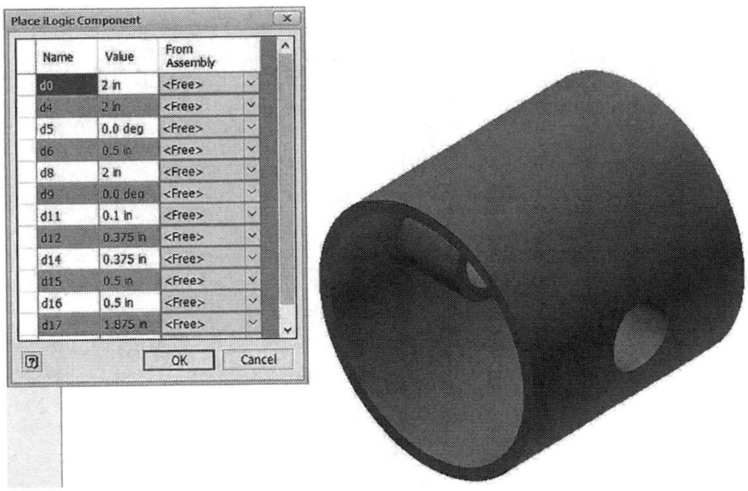

Figure 12

14. Move the cursor to the first 2.00 in value listed in the table. It may or may not be d0. Once you have located the first 2.00 in value, highlight the text and left click once. Change the value from 2 in to **2.125** in as shown in Figure 13. Press **Enter** on the keyboard.

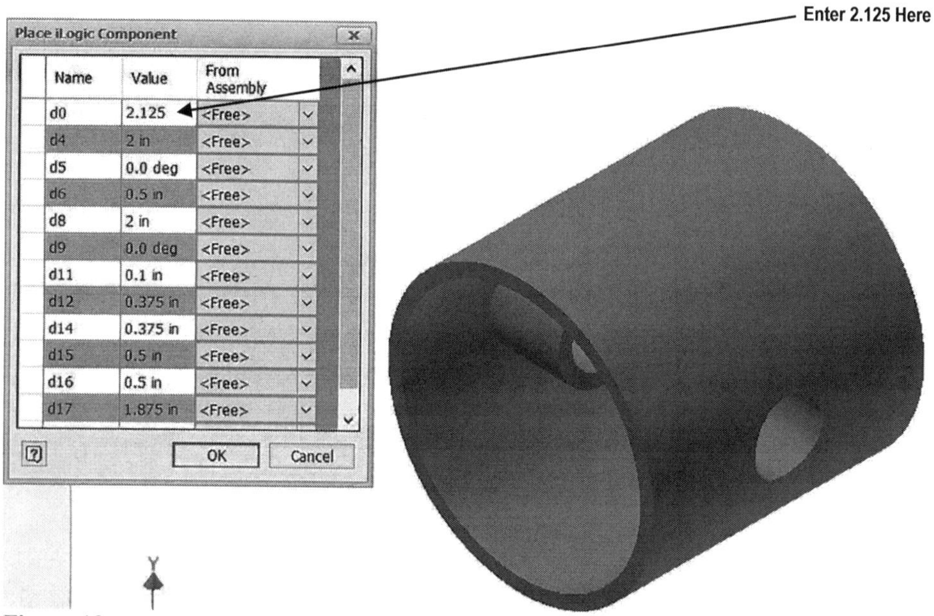

Figure 13

Inventor will increase the diameter of the piston from 2.00 inches to 2.125 inches. <u>Editing the part may cause errors that will have to be addressed by editing other values</u> as shown in Figure 14.

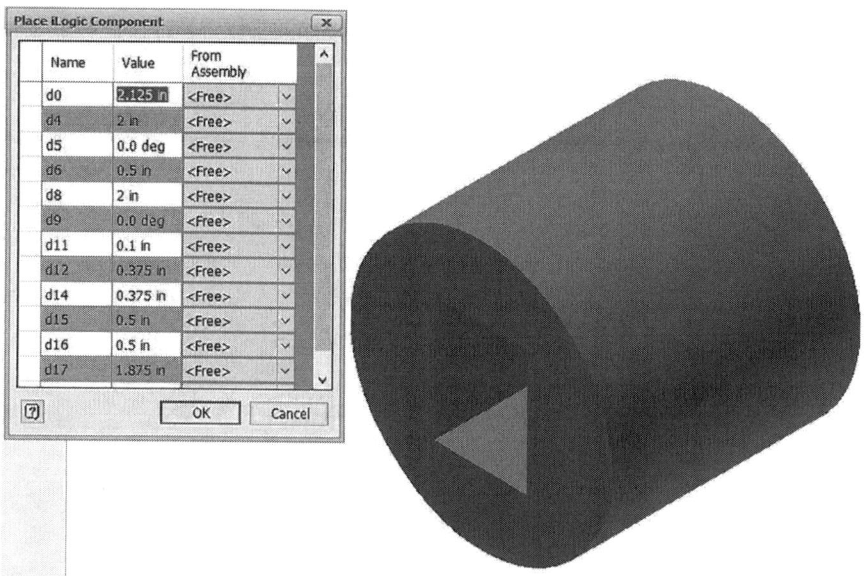

Figure 14

15. Move the cursor to the second 2.00 in value listed in the table. It may or may not be d4. Once you have located the second 2.00 in value, highlight the text and left click once. Change the value from 2 in to **2.125** in as shown in Figure 15. Press **Enter** on the keyboard. Place the piston into the Assembly as described in Chapter 7.

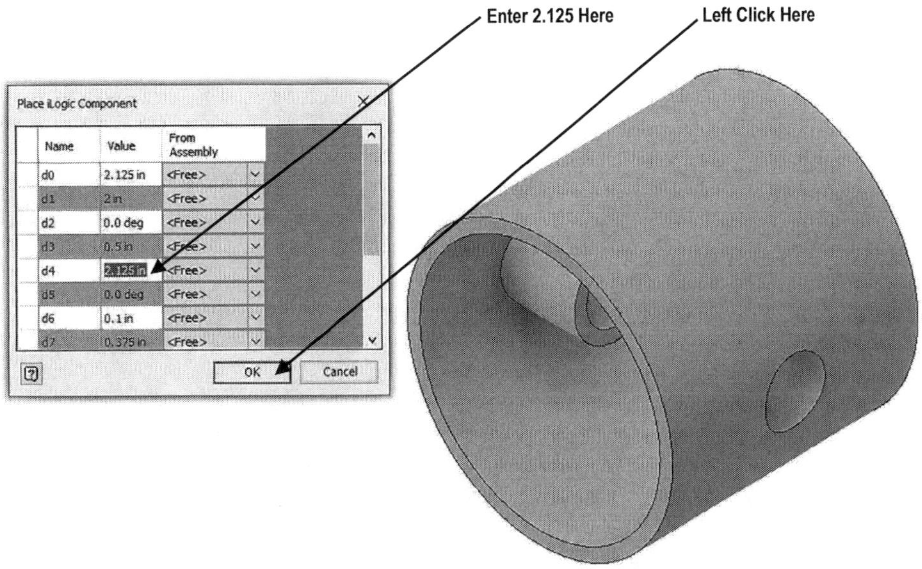

Figure 15

16. Use the iLogic Component steps described previously to "Place" the conrod in the Assembly. Your screen should look similar to what is shown in Figure 16.

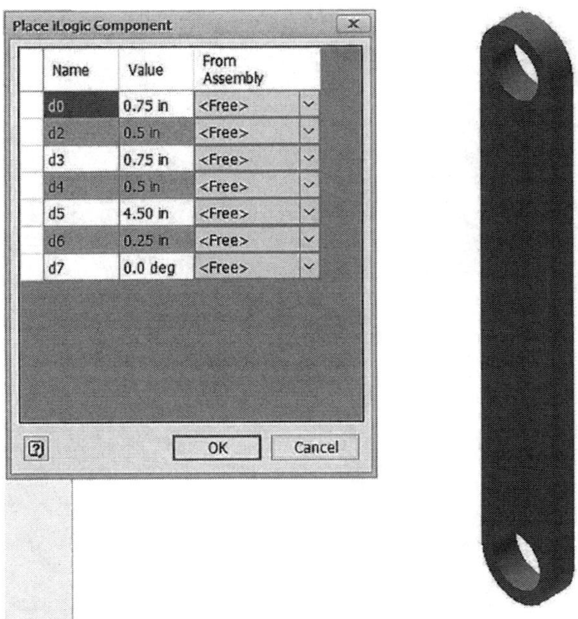

Figure 16

17. Move the cursor to the 4.75 in value listed in the table. It may or may not be d5. Once you have located the 4.75 in value, highlight the text and left click once. Change the value from 4.75 in to **5.5** in as shown in Figure 17. Press **Enter** on the keyboard.

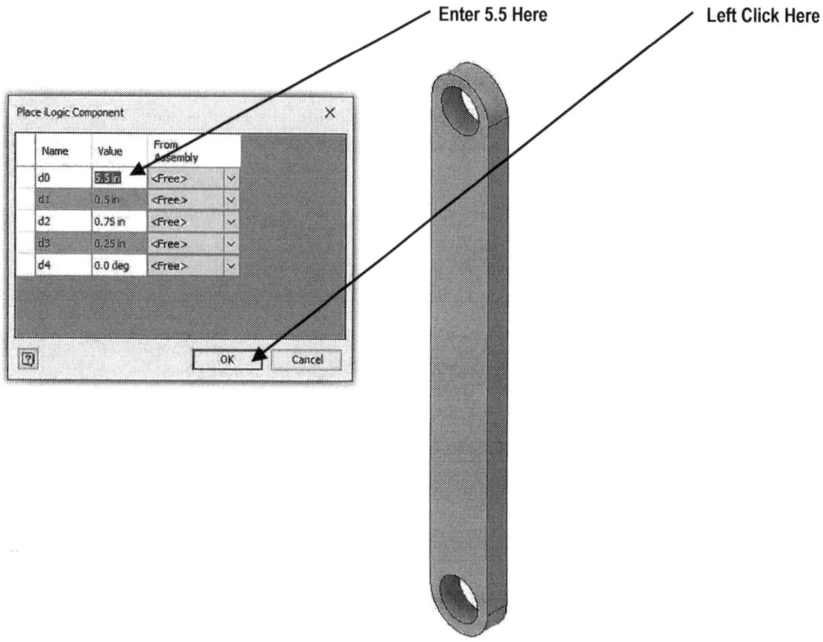

Figure 17

18. Your screen should look similar to Figure 18. Finish "Placing" the wristpin and crankshaft into the Assembly and assemble the parts using the directions from Chapter 7.

Figure 18

CHAPTER 18

Introduction to Spur Gear Design using the Design Accelerator

Objectives:

1. Learn to create a gear set
2. Learn to import a gear set into an Assembly
3. Learn to modify a gear set in an Assembly
4. Learn to animate a gear set in an Assembly

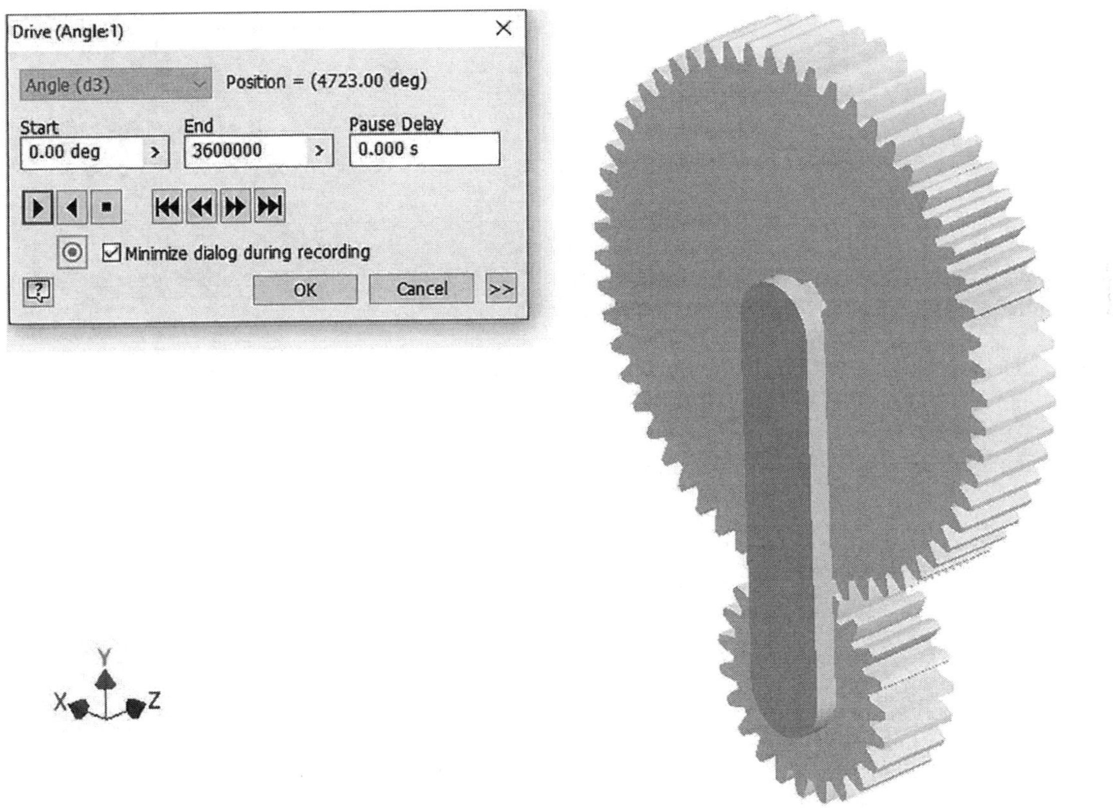

Chapter 18 includes instruction on how to create the parts shown.

1. Start Inventor by referring to "Chapter 1 Getting Started."

2. Start a new Assembly as shown in Figure 1.

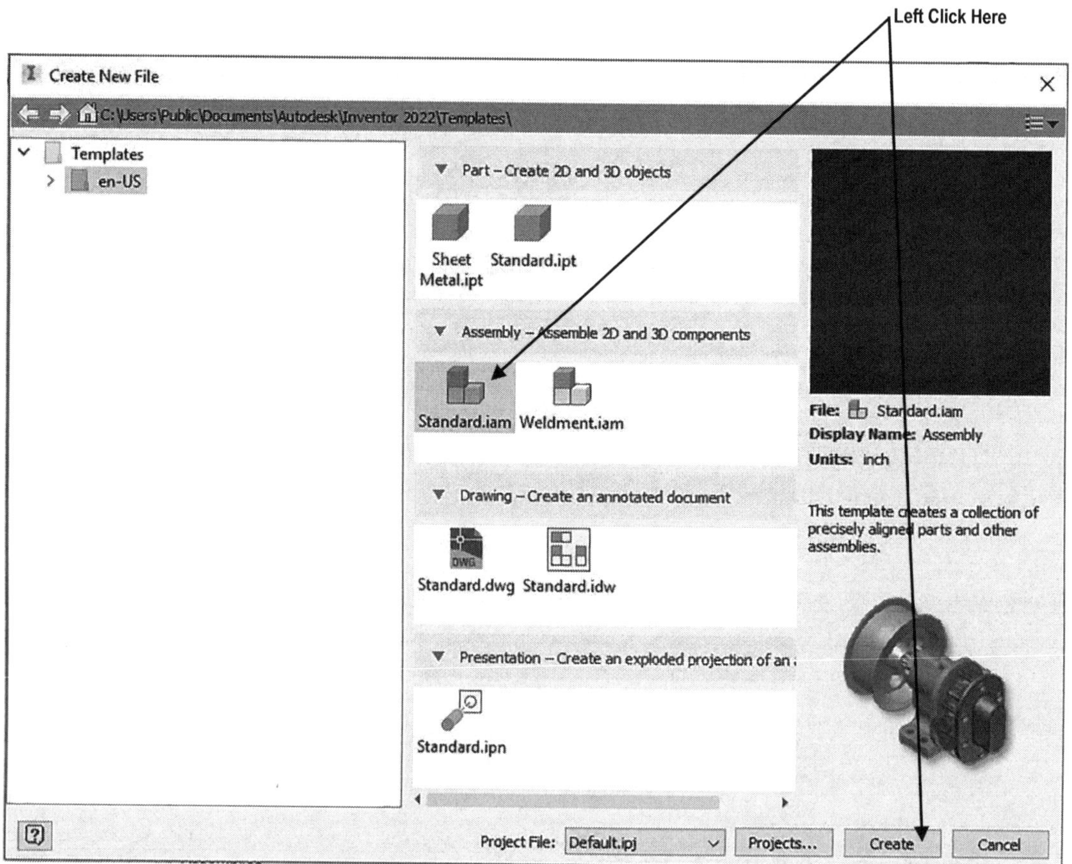

Figure 1

3. Save the Assembly before starting even though there are no Parts in the Assembly. Now move the cursor to the upper left portion of the screen and left click on the Design tab as shown in Figure 2.

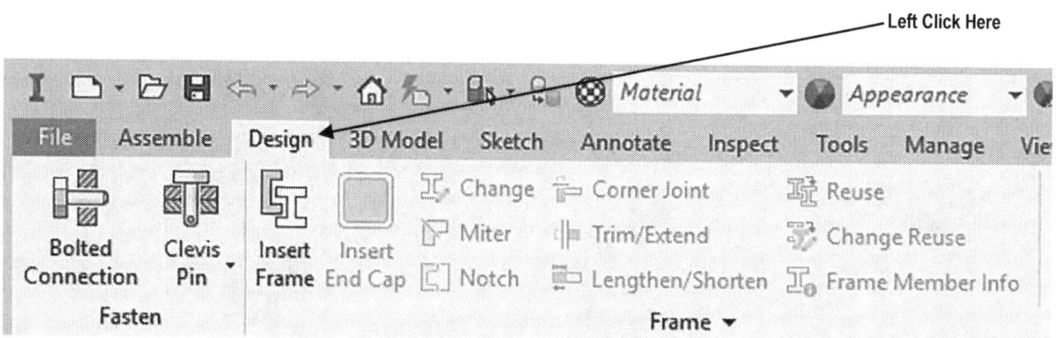

Figure 2

Learn to Create a Spur Gear Set Using the Spur Gears Component Generator

4. Move the cursor to the upper middle portion of the screen and left click on the **Spur Gear** icon as shown in Figure 3.

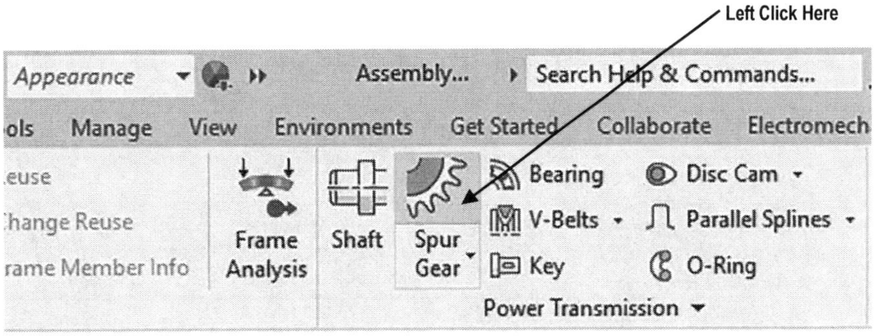

Figure 3

5. The Spur Gears Component Generator dialog box will appear as shown in Figure 4.

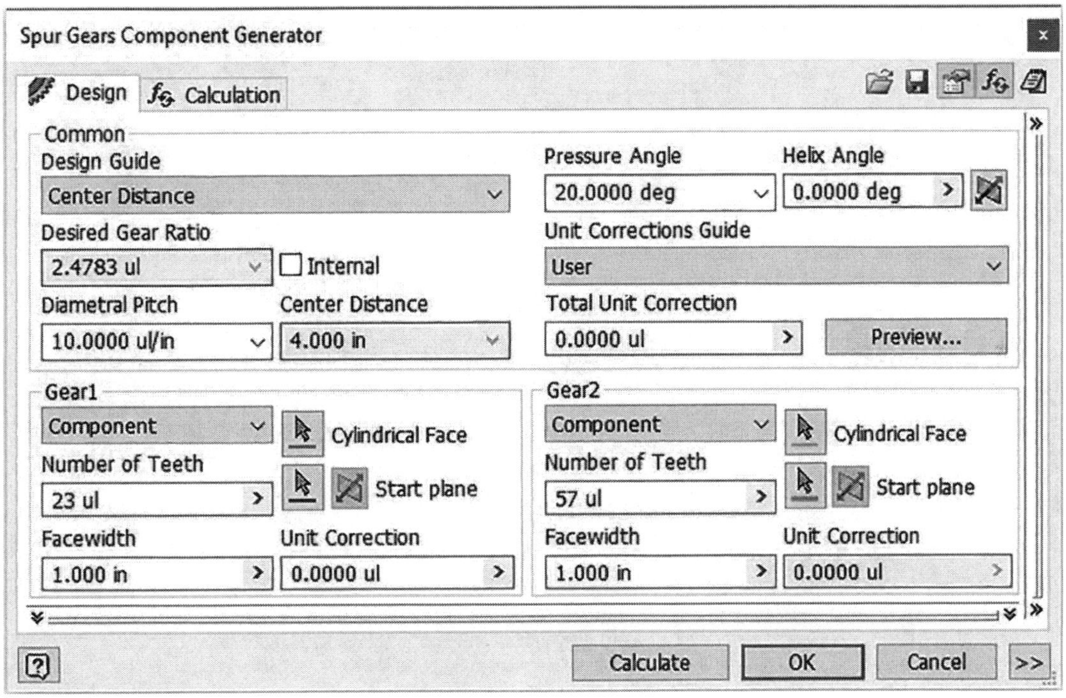

Figure 4

6. The Spur Gears set will become a sub assembly. The default values will create a gear set with 23 teeth on the 1st gear and 57 teeth on the 2nd gear. This results in a ratio of 2.4783:1 meaning the small gear will make 2.4783 revolutions each time the large gear makes only 1 revolution. One way to find the ratio of a gear set is to divide the number of teeth on the large gear by the number of teeth on the small gear. We will use the default values to create a gear set. Left click on **Calculate.** Left click on **OK** as shown in Figure 5.

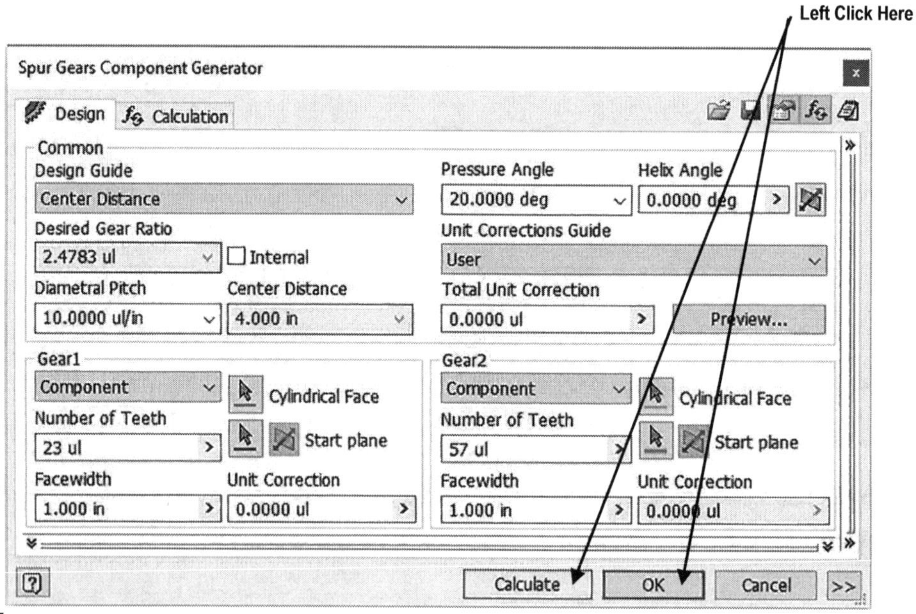

Figure 5

7. The File Naming dialog will appear. Left click on **OK** as shown in Figure 6.

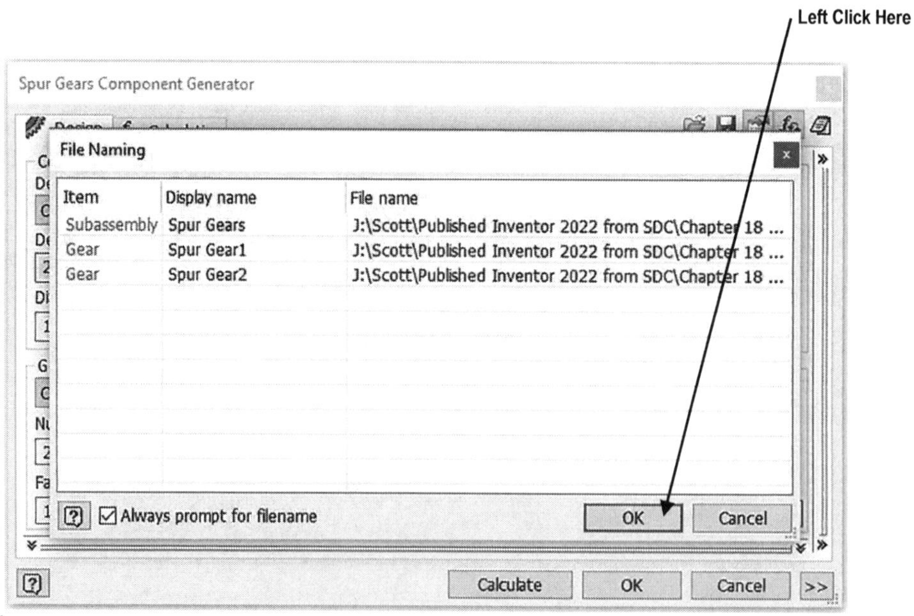

Figure 6

8. The gear set will be attached to the cursor. Left click placing the gear set as shown in Figure 7. You may have to Zoom out.

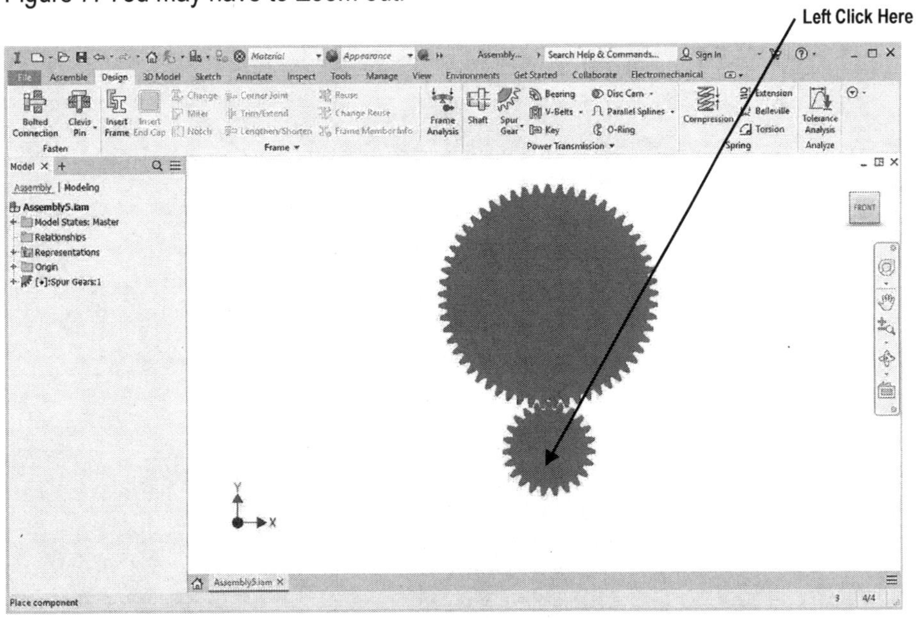

Figure 7

Learn to Edit Spur Gears

9. We need to create small center holes in each of the gears similar to what we did in Chapter 13 Introduction to the Design Accelerator. Move the cursor to the center of the large gear and double left click once. You will notice that the gear has become highlighted. Once the gear has become highlighted, right click once. Pop-up menu will appear. Left click on **Edit** as shown in Figure 8.

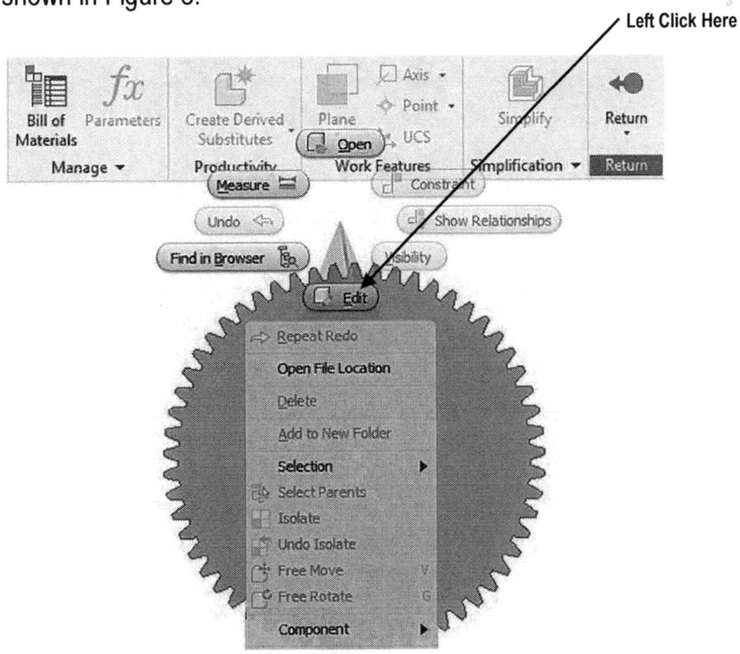

Figure 8

10. Right click again and then left click on **New Sketch** as shown in Figure 9.

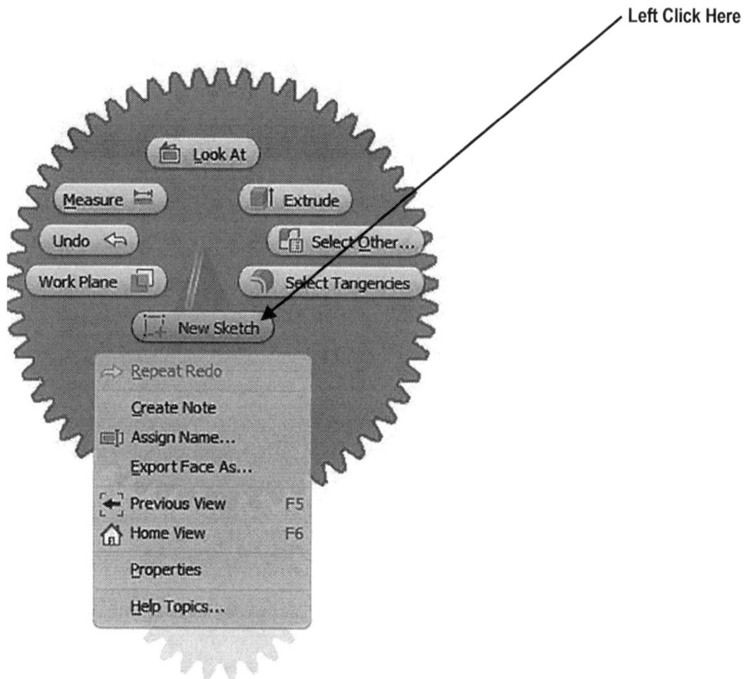

Figure 9

11. Move the cursor to the center of the large gear and complete the sketch as shown in Figure 10. Once the sketch is complete, Extrude Cut the sketch all the way through to create a hole and slot.

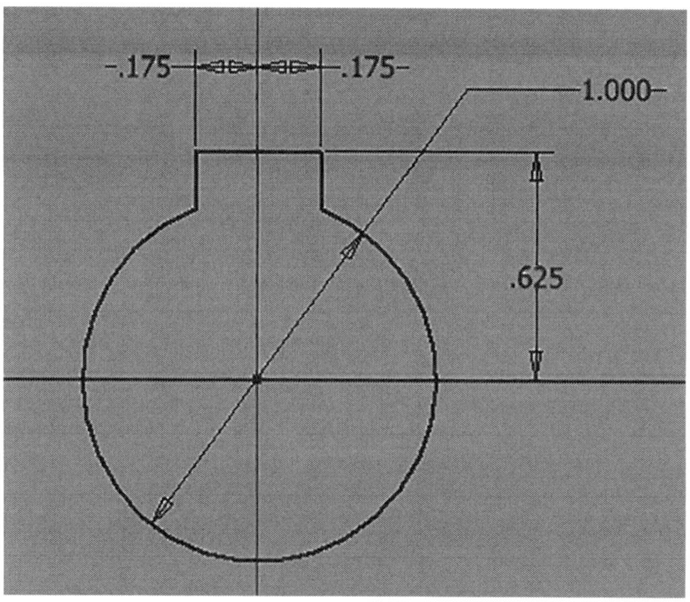

Figure 10

12. Repeat these same steps to create a hole (excluding the slot) in the small gear. When complete, your screen should look similar to what is shown in Figure 11.

Figure 11

13. Move the cursor to the upper right portion of the screen and left click on **Return** twice (if needed) as shown in Figure 12.

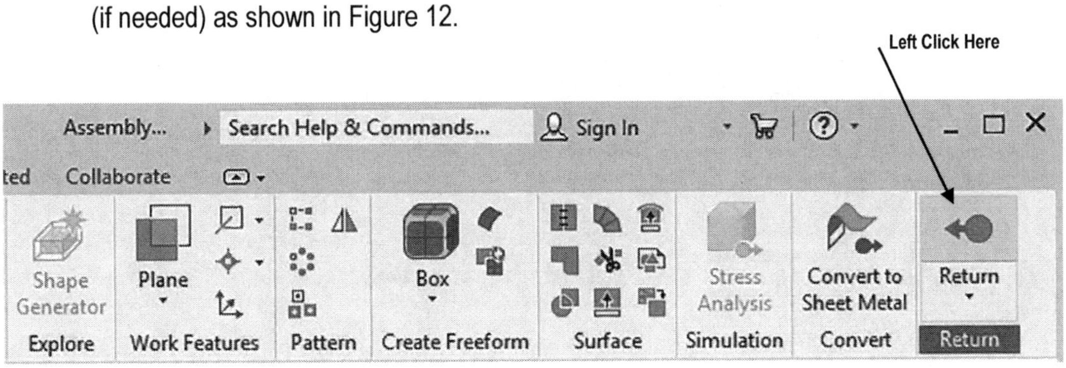

Figure 12

Learn to Perform Edits Using the Design Accelerator

14. We will now make a mount for the gear set to sit on. The center to center distance between the gears is crucial. To find this distance, we will need to open the Spur Gears Component Generator dialog box. To do this, move the cursor to the Browser located at the far left portion of the screen. Right click on **Spur Gear:1**. A pop-up menu will appear. Left click on **Edit using Design Accelerator** as shown in Figure 13.

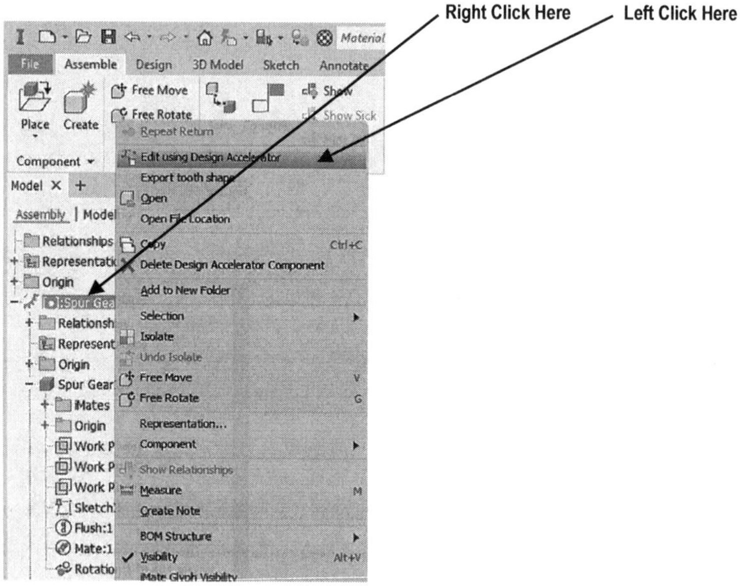

Figure 13

Learn to Identify the Center to Center Distance of a Spur Gear Set

15. The Spur Gears Component Generator dialog box will appear. The Center to Center distance between the gears is displayed as shown in Figure 14. The Center to Center Distance is crucial on any gear set. The Center to Center distance is 4.000 inches. This information will be used in the creation of a mount for the gear set.

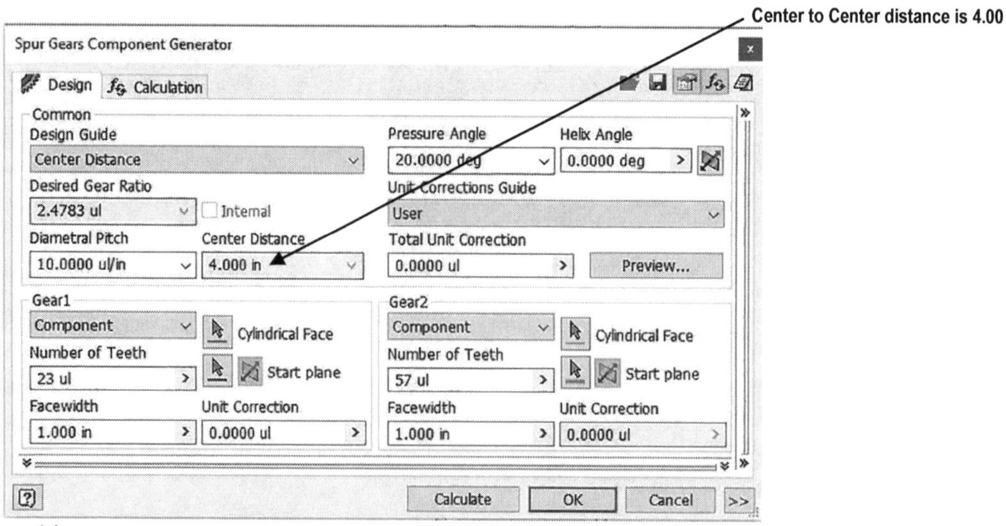

Figure 14

16. Complete the mount for the gear set as shown in Figure 15. Save the part in the Assembly that contains the gear set.

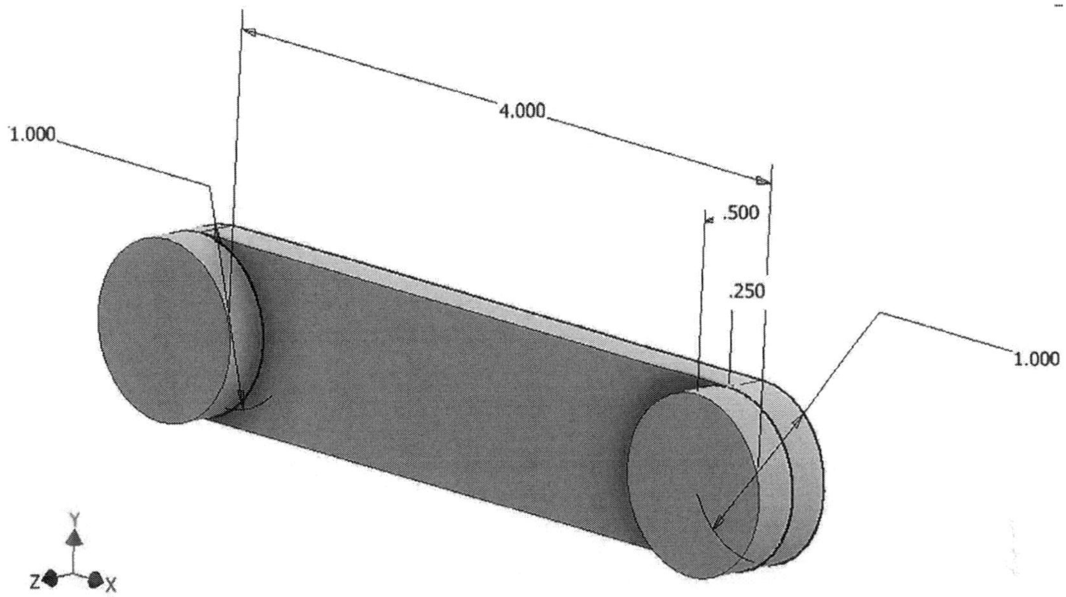

Figure 15

17. Use the Place Component steps described previously to "Place" the mount for the gear set into the Assembly. Your screen should look similar to Figure 16.

Figure 16

18. Using the Constrain function, constrain the centers of the gear set mount to the holes in the gears. Your screen should look similar to Figure 17.

Figure 17

19. Using the Constrain function, constrain the gear set mount flush with the side of the gears as shown in Figure 18.

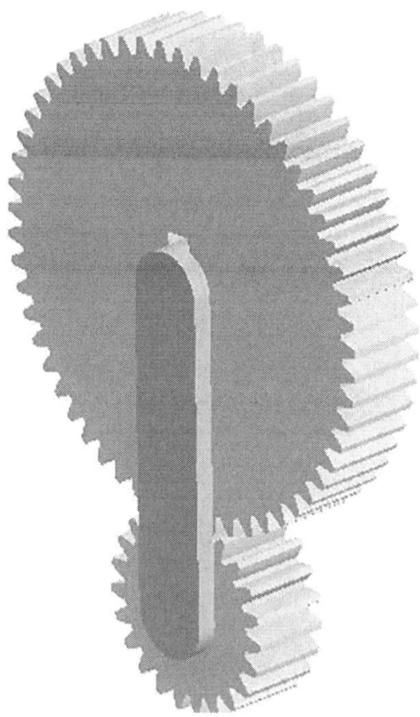

Figure 18

Learn to Animate a Spur Gear Set

20. The Spur Gear set is a sub-assembly. Because of this it will act as a single ridged part. Before the gear set can be animated, it will need to be made "Flexible". To do this, move the cursor to the Browser and right click on **Spur Gears:1**. A pop-up menu will appear. Left click on **Flexible** as shown in Figure 19. This will allow the gears to rotate.

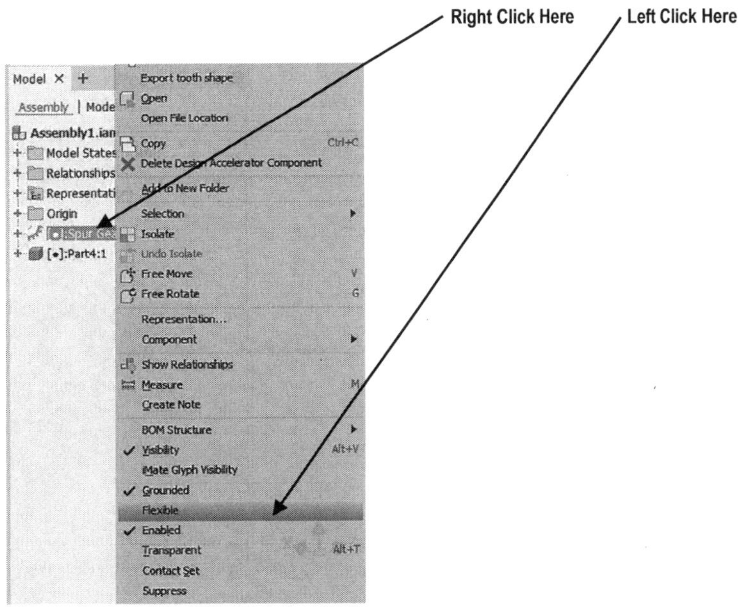

Figure 19

21. Create an Angle Constraint as previously described in Chapter 7 between the key slot in the large gear and the side of the gear set mount. Left click **OK** as shown in Figure 20.

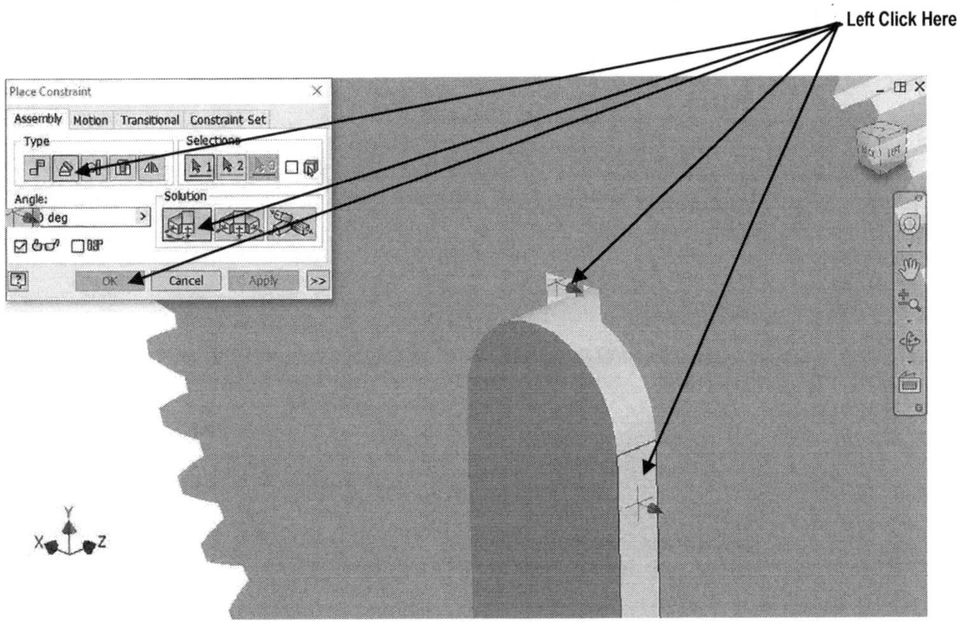

Figure 20

22. Animate the gear set using the steps previously described in Chapter 7. When complete, your screen should look similar to what is shown in Figure 21. The gears will rotate at the proper speed/ratio.

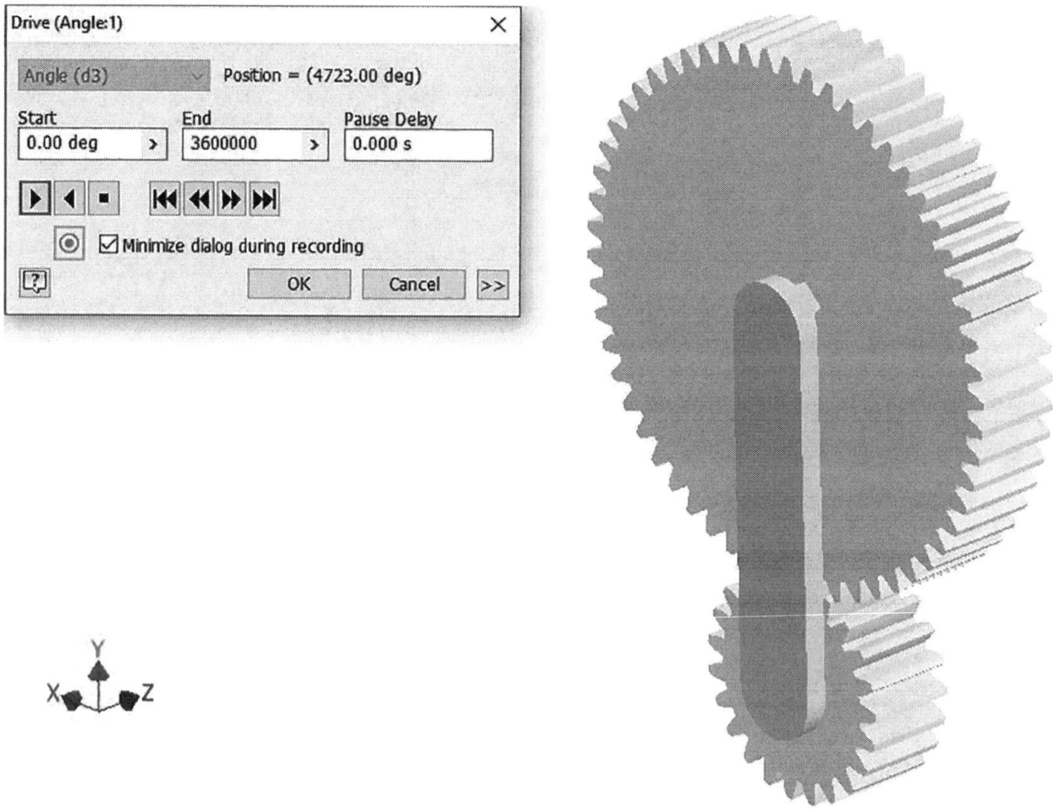

Figure 21

CHAPTER 19

Introduction to Shaft Design using the Design Accelerator

Objectives:

1. Learn to create a shaft
2. Learn to add multiple Sections to a shaft

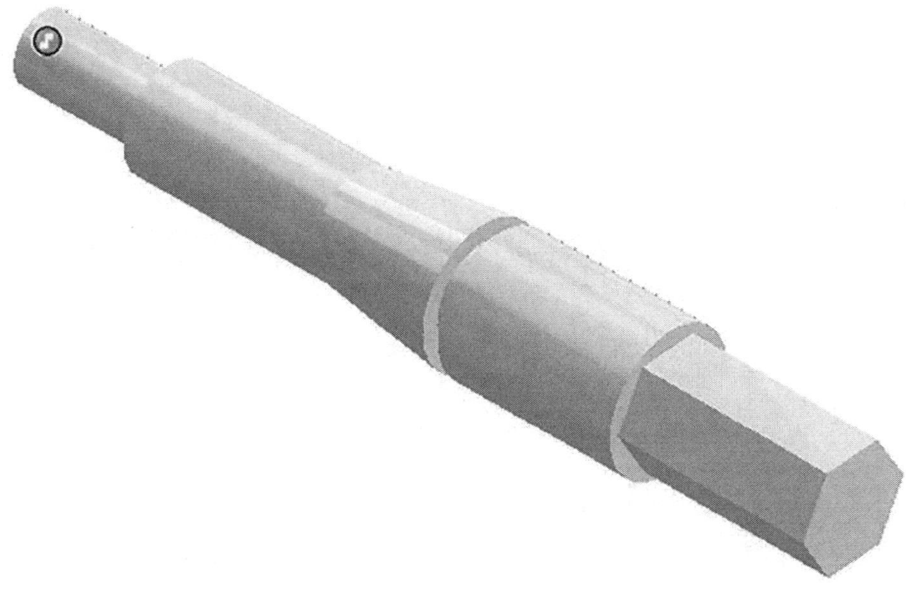

Chapter 19 includes instruction on how to create the part shown.

1. Start Inventor by referring to "Chapter 1 Getting Started."

2. Start a new Assembly as shown in Figure 1.

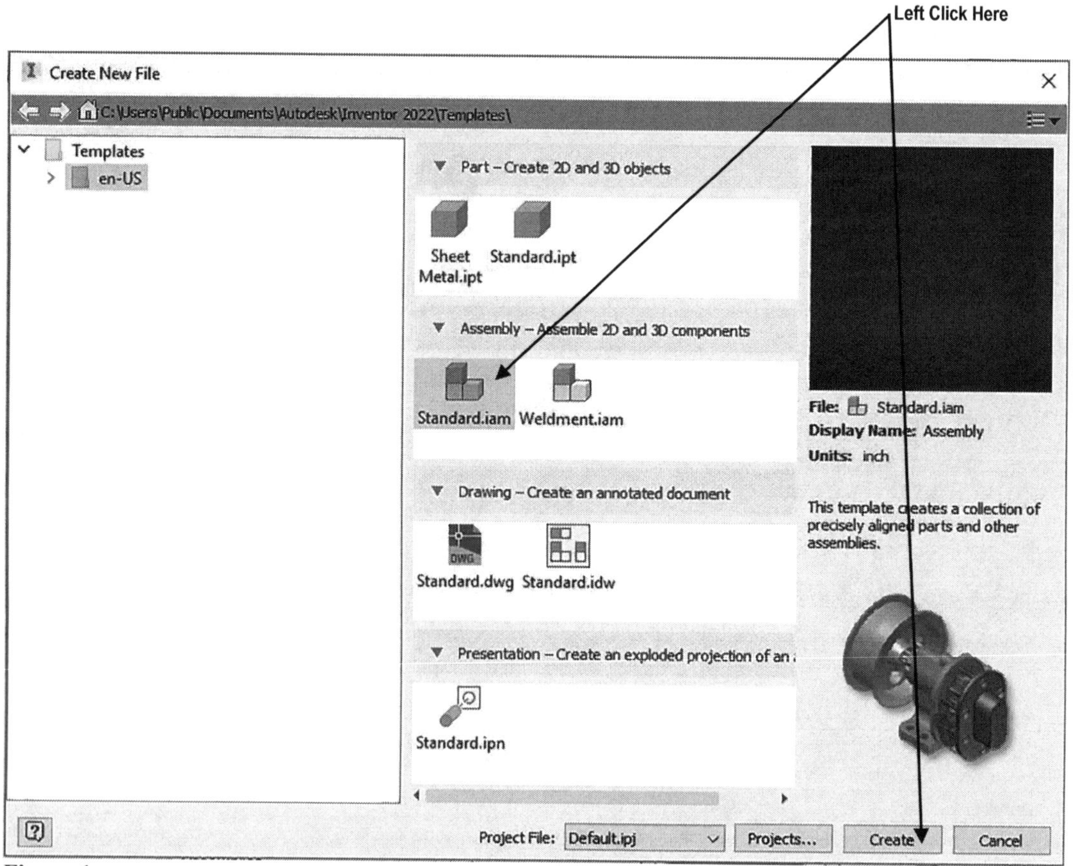

Figure 1

3. Save the Assembly before starting. Now move the cursor to the upper left portion of the screen and left click on the Design tab as shown in Figure 2.

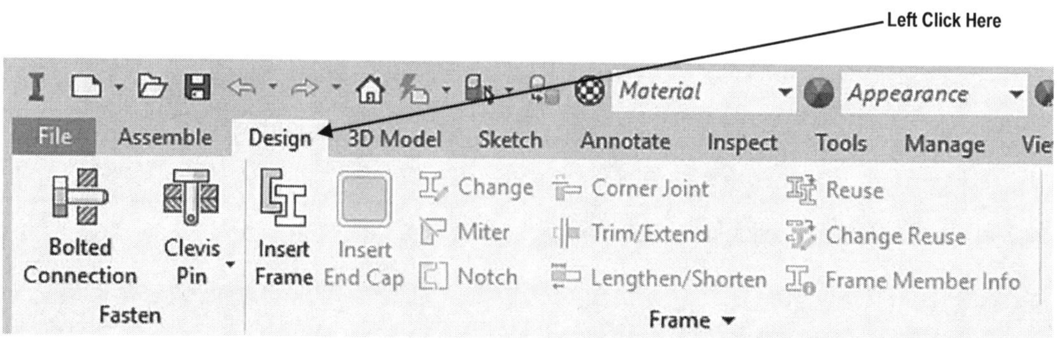

Figure 2

Learn to Use the Shaft Component Generator

4. Move the cursor to the upper middle portion of the screen and left click on the **Shaft** icon as shown in Figure 3.

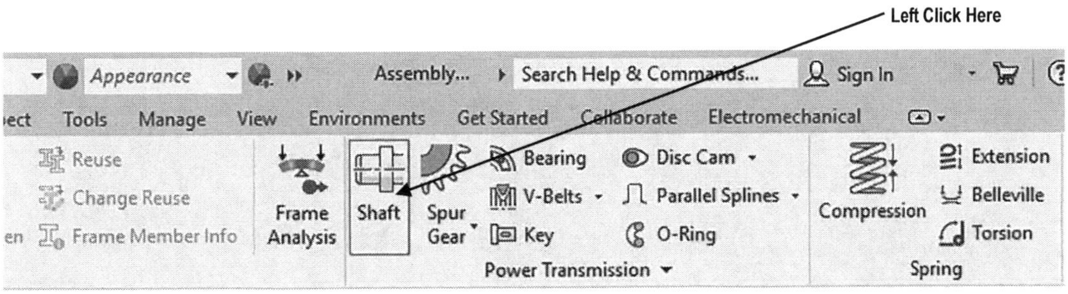

Figure 3

5. The Shaft Component Generator dialog box will appear as shown in Figure 4.

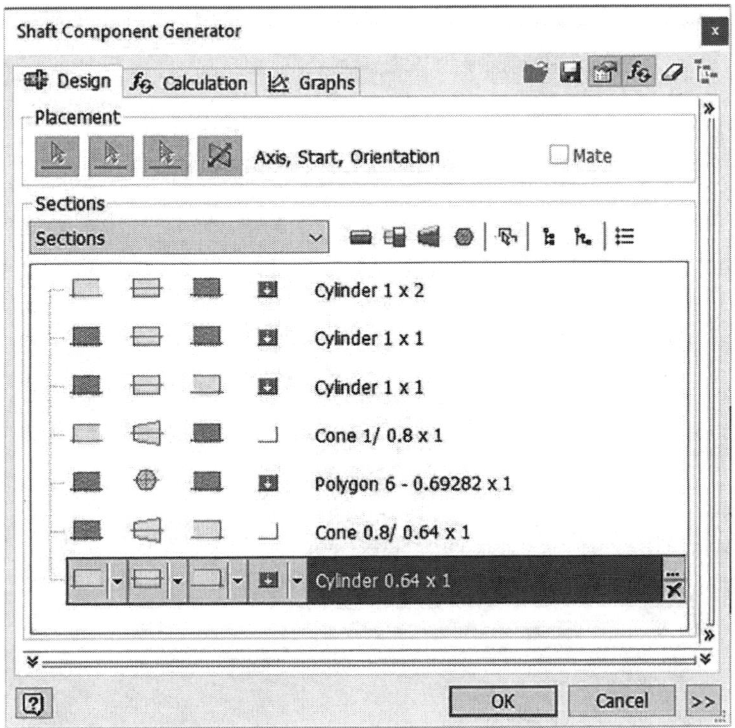

Figure 4

Learn to Add new Shaft Sections

6. A list of Sections will appear as the default. Left click on the red "X" and delete all Sections but one, as shown in Figure 5. By default, Inventor will not let you delete the last Section in the list.

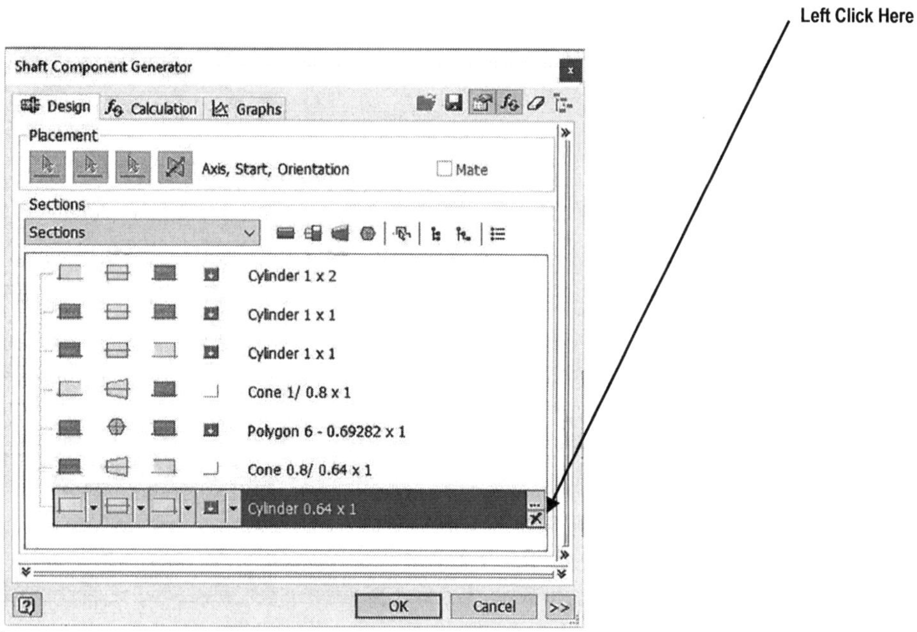

Figure 5

7. One Section will appear. This Section will be attached to the cursor. If the remaining Section is not a Cylinder (such as a Cone or Polygon) left click on the drop-down arrow and select **Cylinder** as shown in Figure 6.

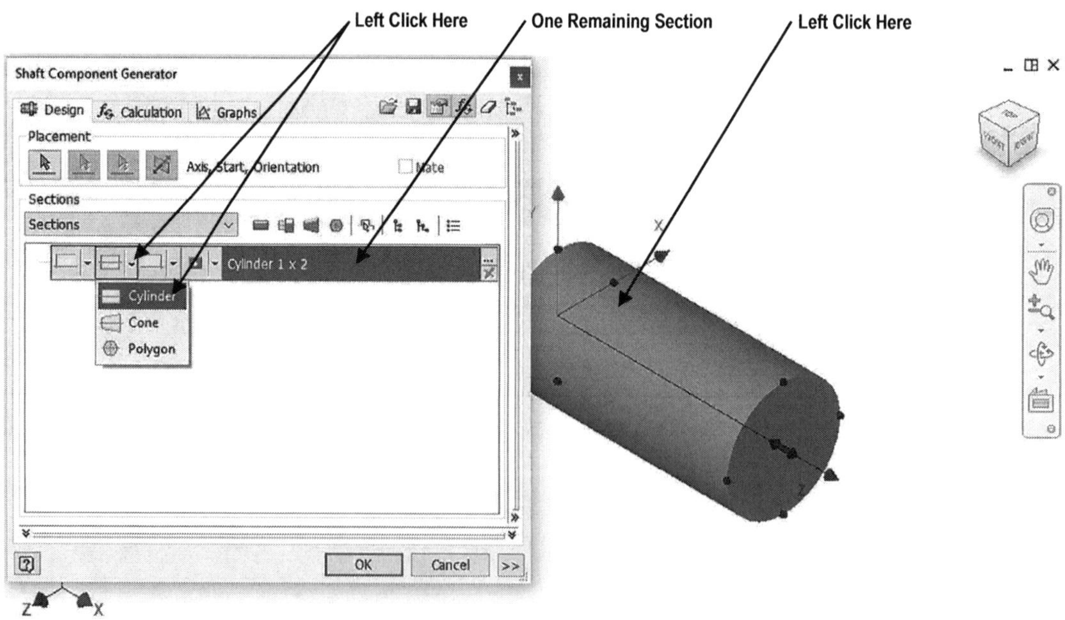

Figure 6

8. Left click on the Insert Cylinder icon. Inventor will place an additional Section of the shaft which will be a cylinder as shown in Figure 7. You may have to Zoom out.

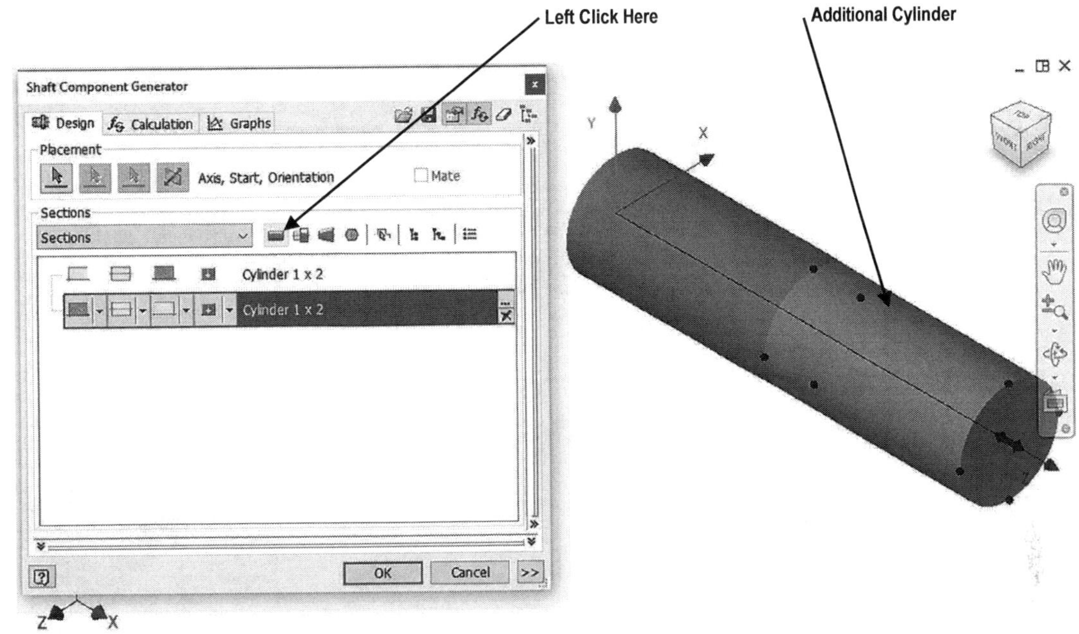

Figure 7

9. Move the cursor to the highlighted section of the newly added cylinder and double left click. The Cylinder dialog box will appear as shown in Figure 8.

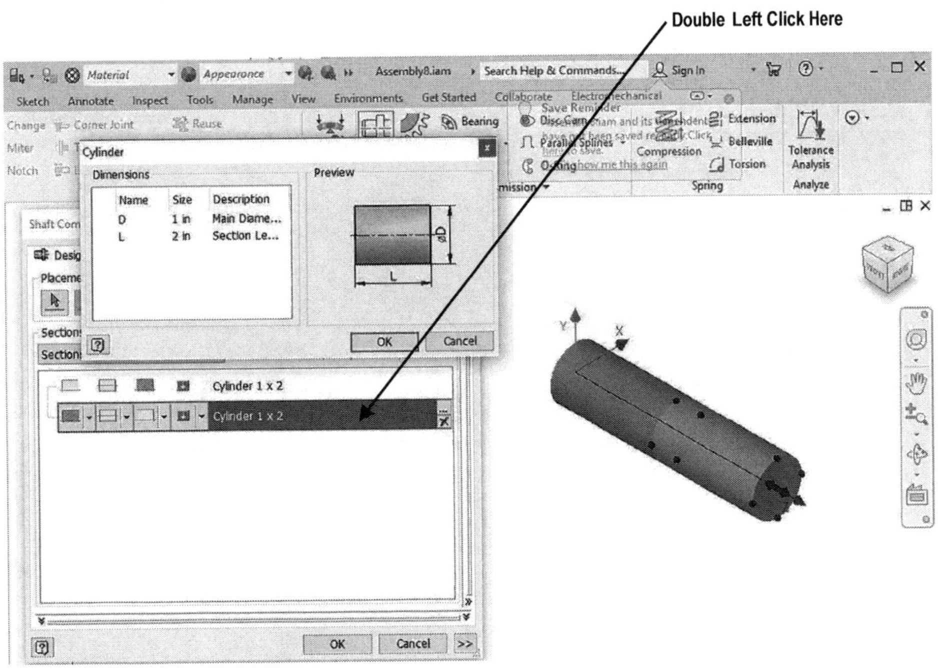

Figure 8

10. Enter **1.5** for the Main Diameter (D) and **3** for the Section Length (L). Left click on **OK** as shown in Figure 9.

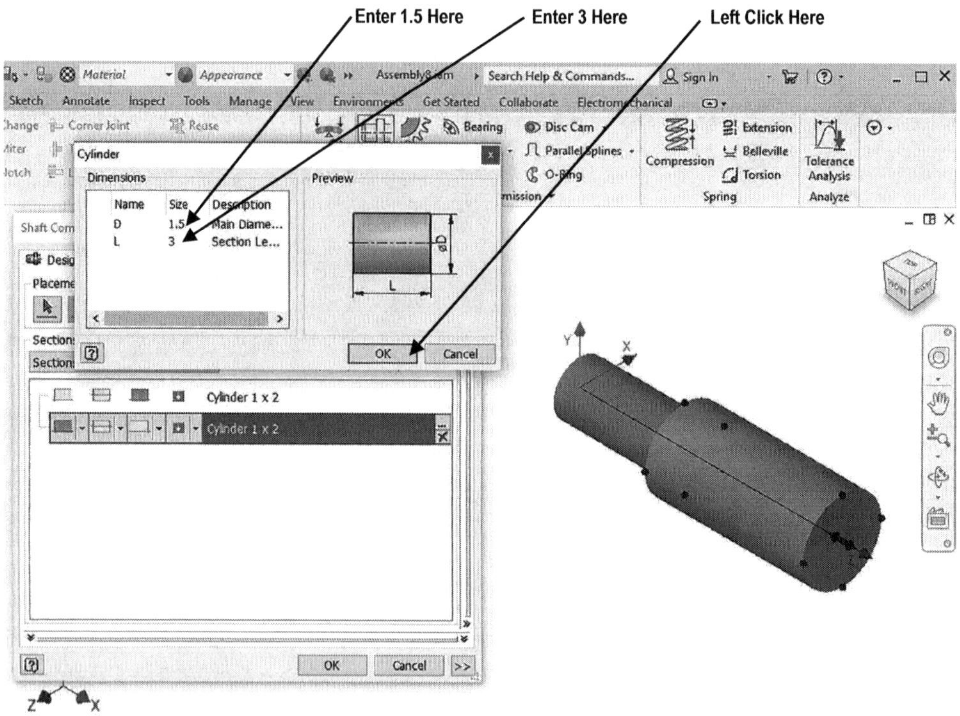

Figure 9

11. Left click on the **Insert Cone** icon as shown in Figure 10.

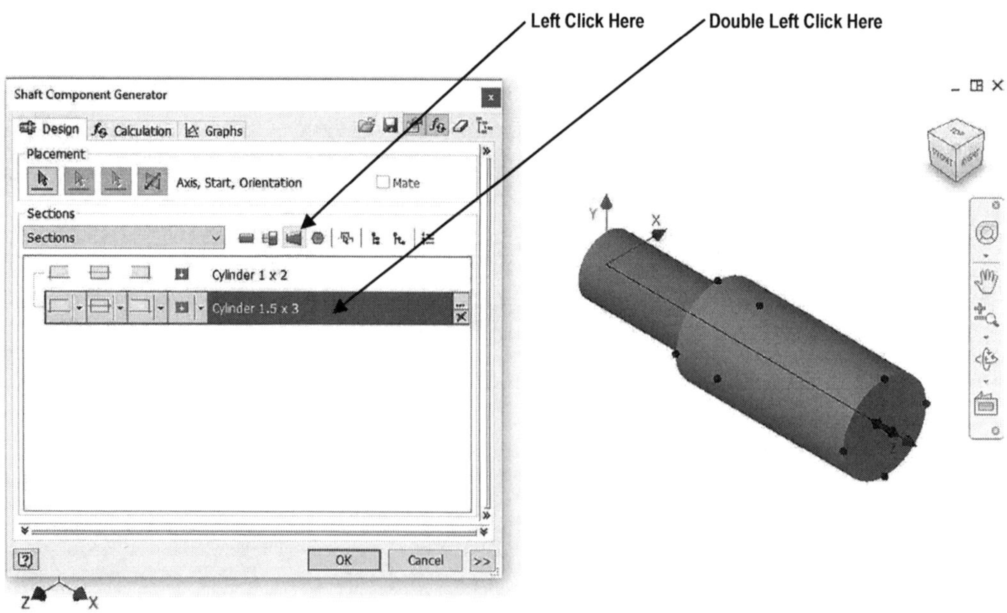

Figure 10

12. Enter **2** for Section Diameter (D) and **2** for Section Length (L). Left click **OK** as shown in Figure 11.

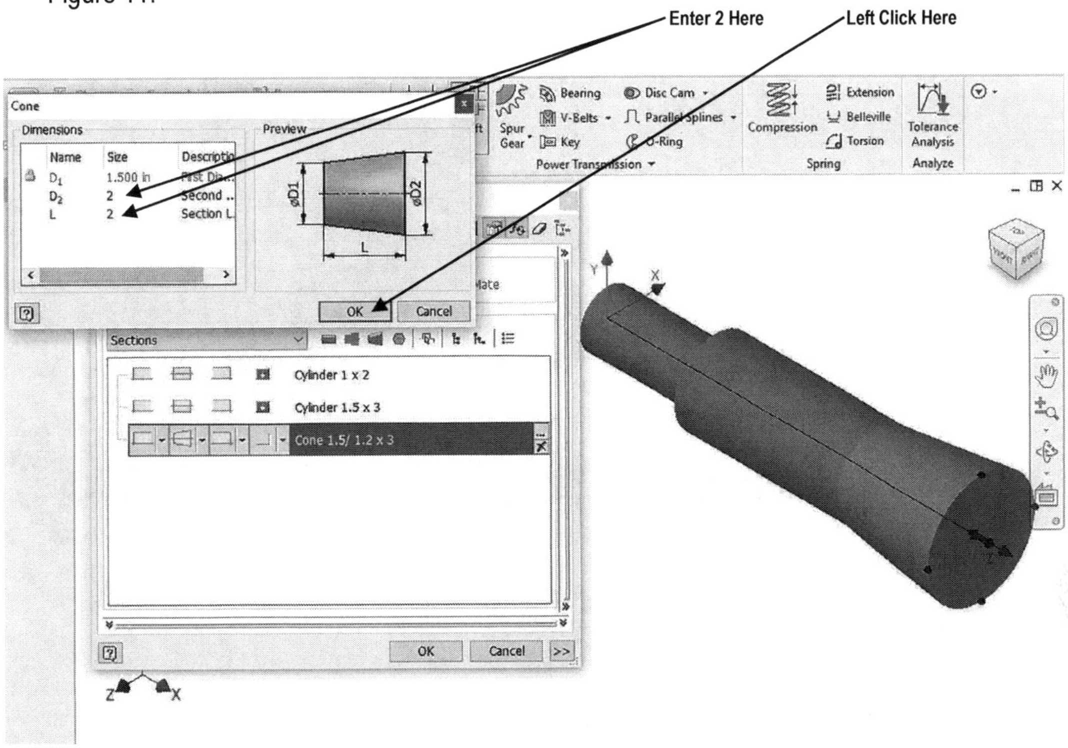

Figure 11

13. Left click on the Insert Cylinder icon. Double left click as shown in Figure 12.

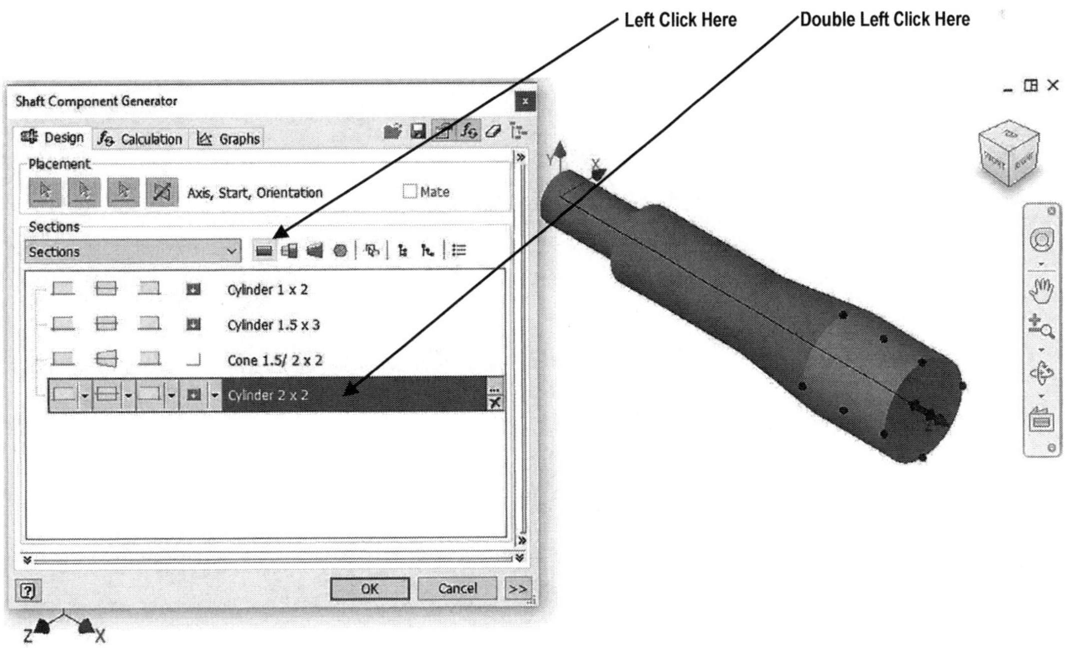

Figure 12

14. Enter **2** for Main Diameter (D) and **3** for Section Length (L). Left click on **OK** as shown in Figure 13.

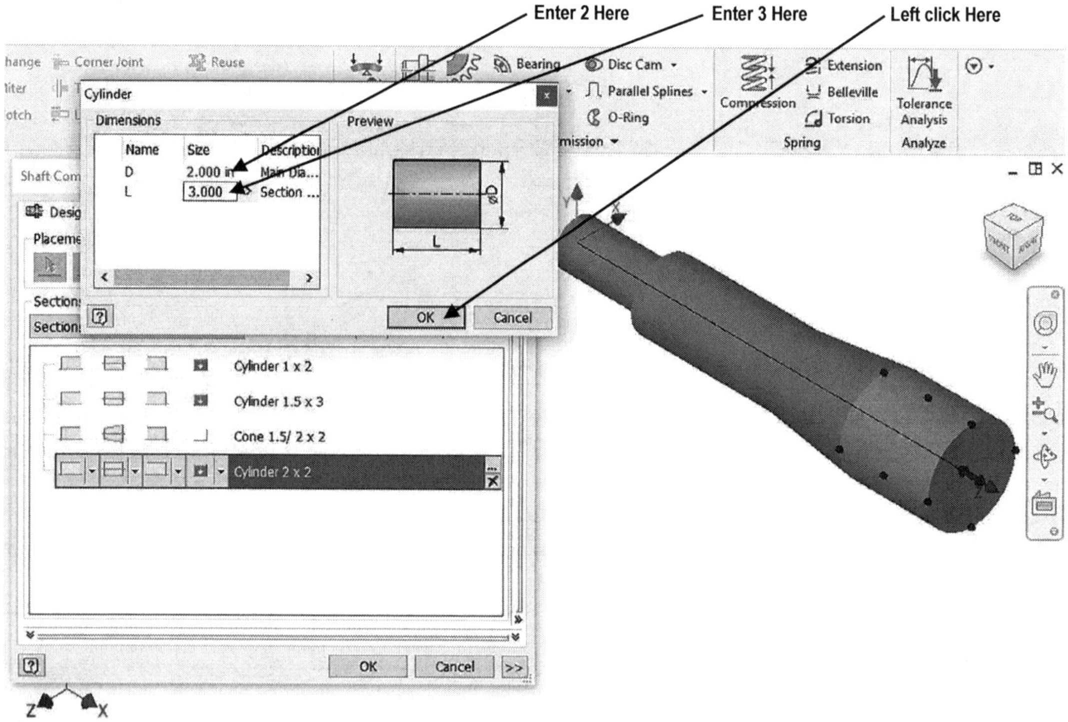

Figure 13

Learn to Unlock Dimensions

15. Double left click on the highlighted area for the Cone. The Cone dialog box will appear. Left click on the small locks to unlock the dimensions as shown in Figure 14.

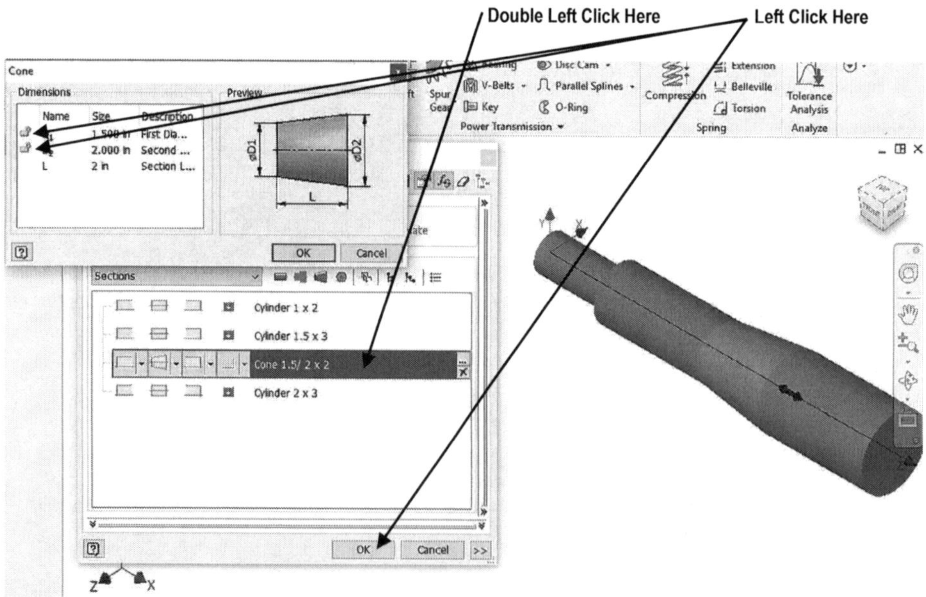

Figure 14

Learn to Create a Split Section

16. Left click on the highlighted area of the Cylinder. Left click on the Split Selected Section icon as shown in Figure 15.

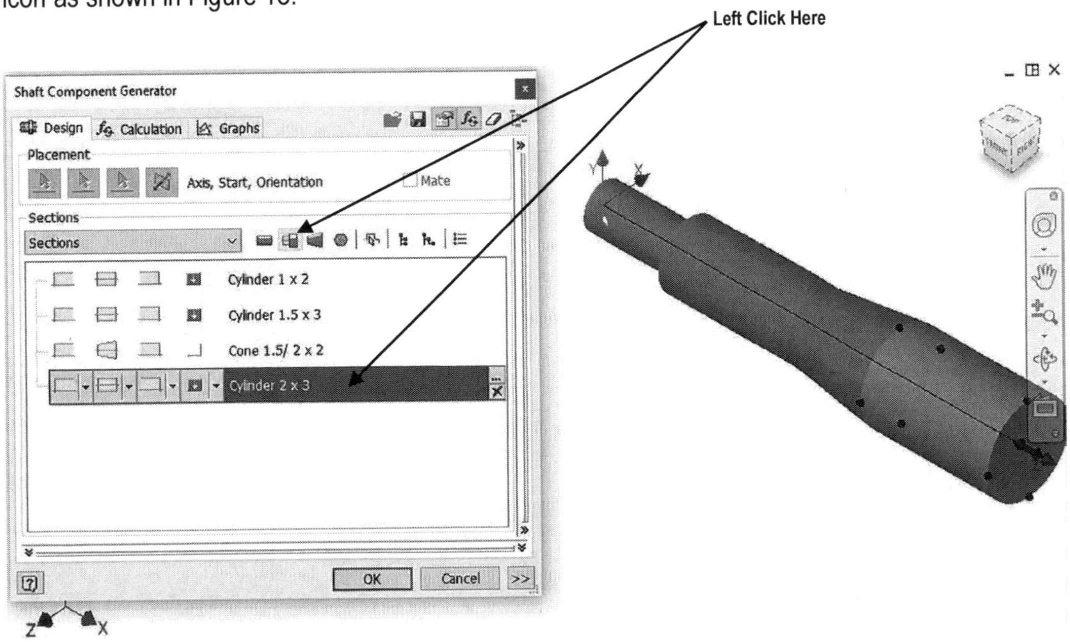

Figure 15

17. The Cylinder dialog box will appear. Enter **1.5** inches for Main Diameter (D) and **.25** inches for Section Length (L). Left click on **OK** as shown in Figure 16.

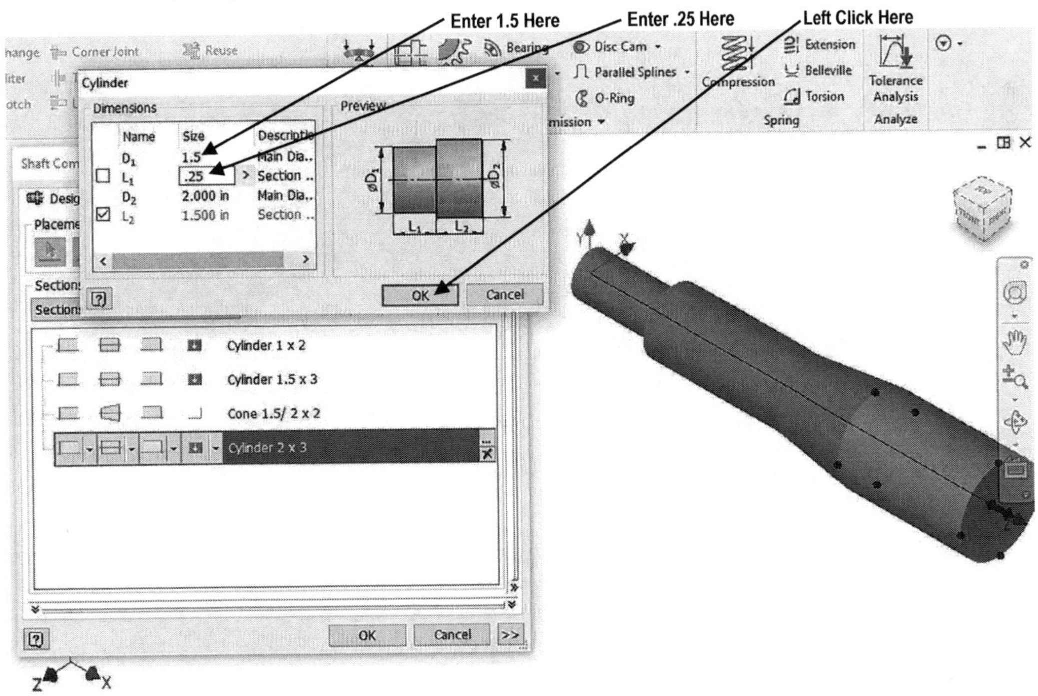

Figure 16

18. Left click on the Insert Polygon icon. Double left click in the highlighted area of the Polygon as shown in Figure 17.

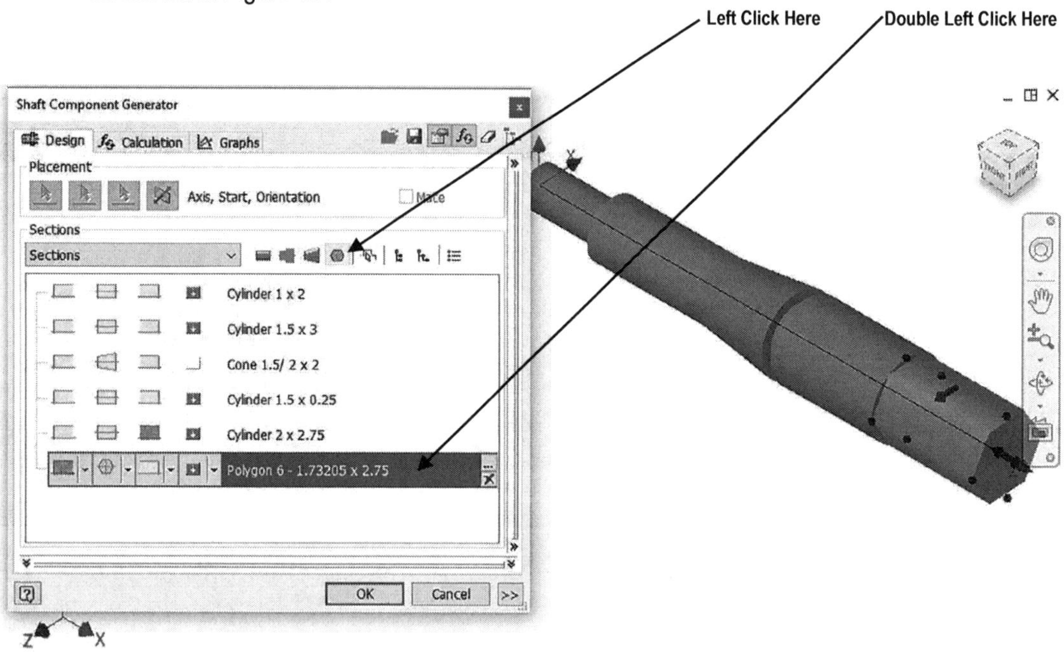

Figure 17

19. The Polygon dialog box will appear. Enter **1.5** for Diameter Inscribed (D) in and **3** for Section Length (L). Left click on **OK** as shown in Figure 18.

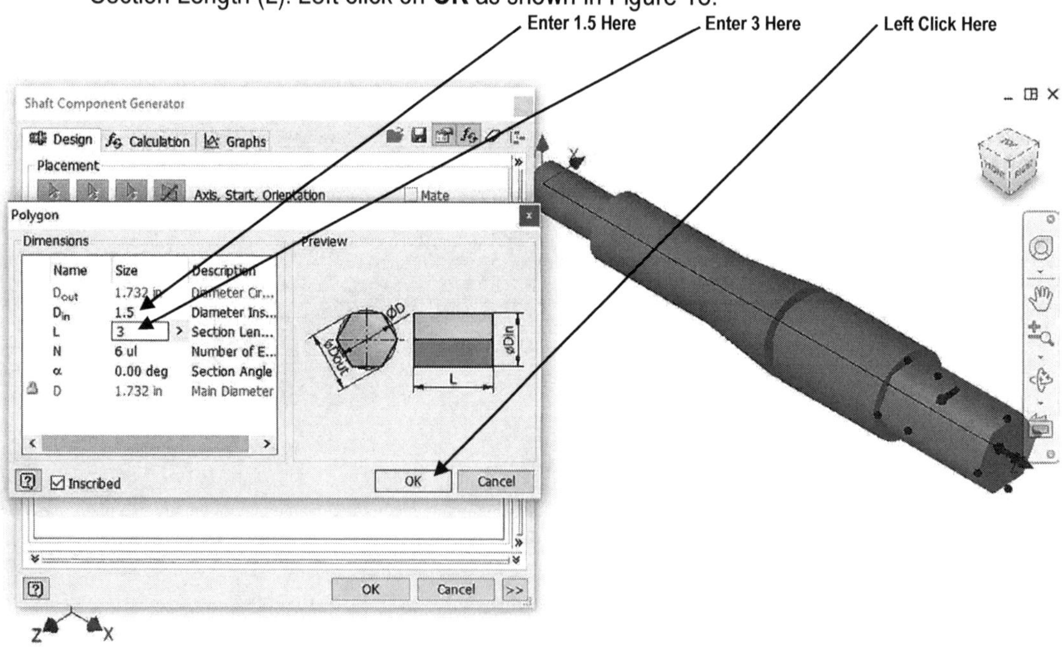

Figure 18

20. The shaft is now complete. Left click on **OK** as shown in Figure 19.

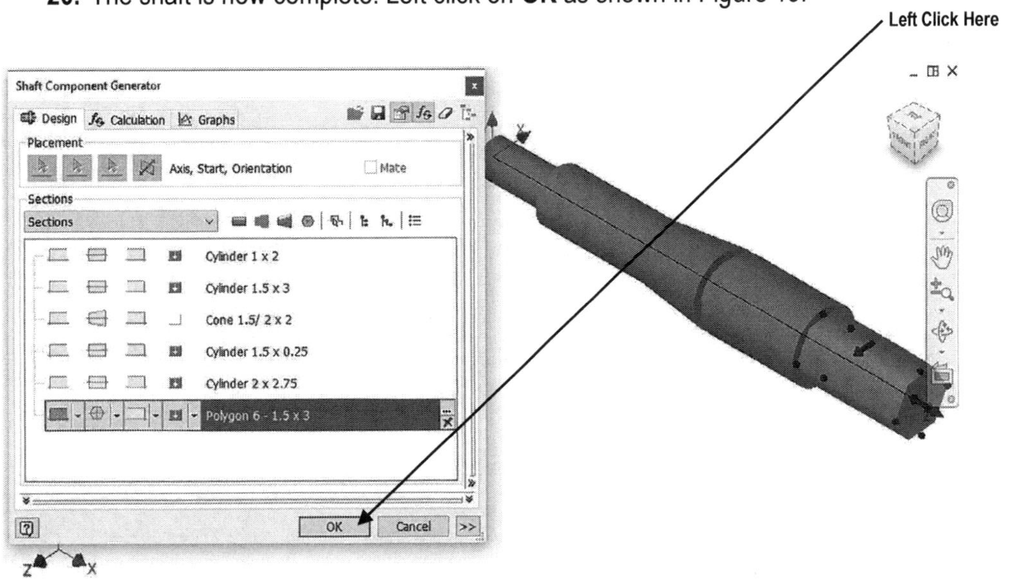

Figure 19

21. Your screen should look similar to what is shown in Figure 20.

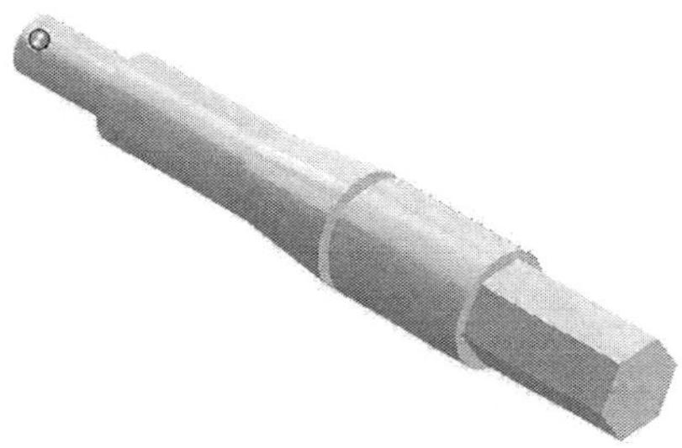

Figure 20

22. To edit any portion of the Shaft, right click on that particular portion and left click on **Edit using Design Accelerator** as shown in Figure 21.

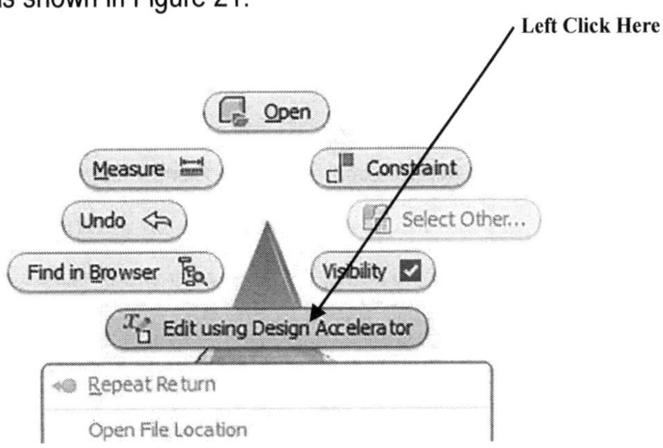

Figure 21

CHAPTER 20

Introduction to Bearing Design using the Design Accelerator

Objectives:

1. Learn to create a bearing

Chapter 20 includes instruction on how to create the part shown.

1. Start Inventor by referring to "Chapter 1 Getting Started."

2. Start a new Assembly as shown in Figure 1.

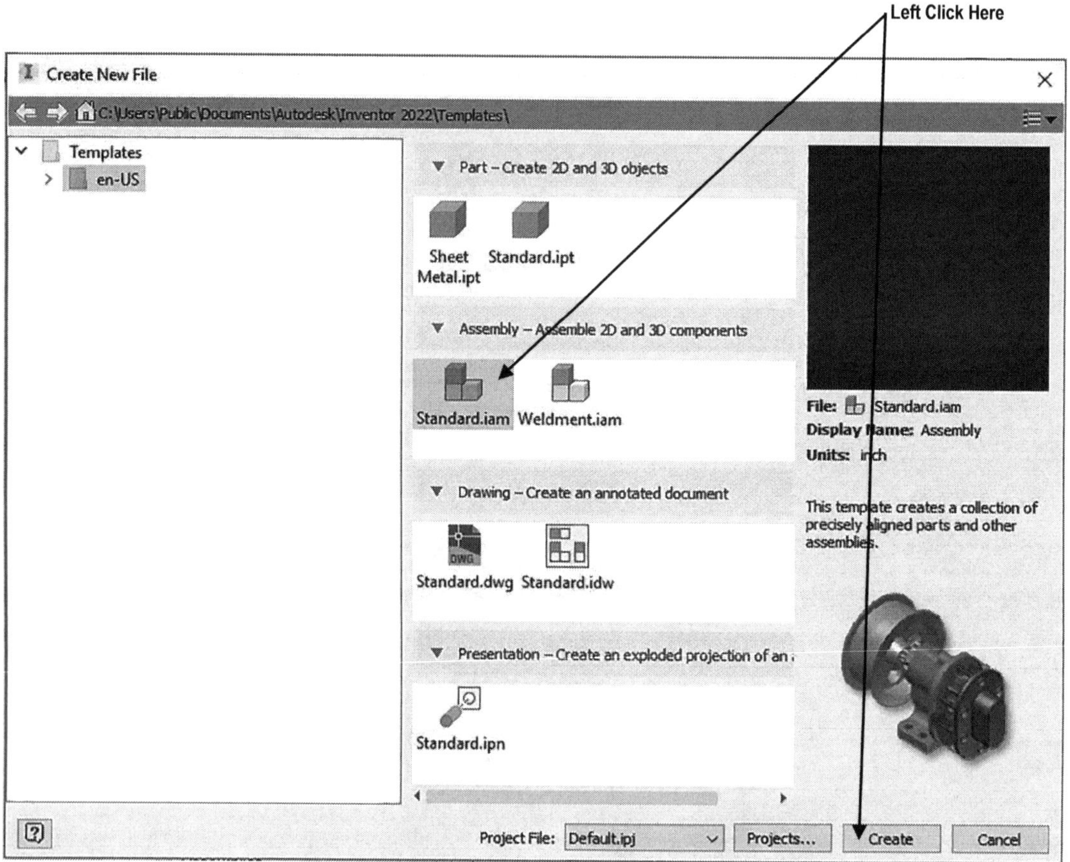

Figure 1

3. Save the Assembly before starting. Now move the cursor to the upper left portion of the screen and left click on the **Design** tab as shown in Figure 2.

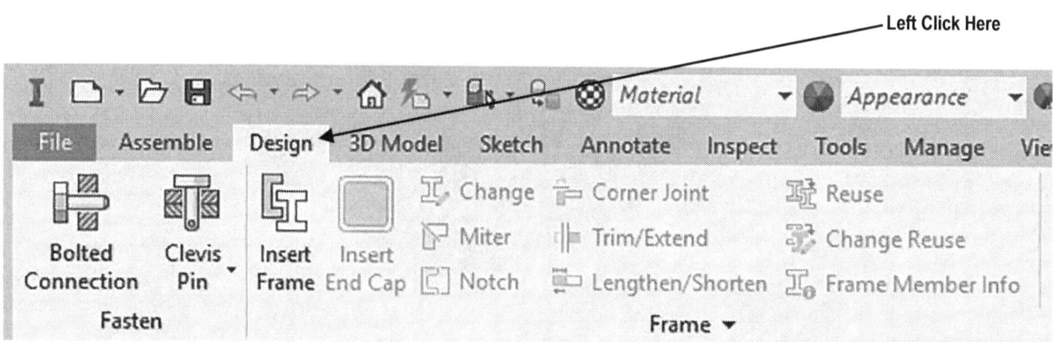

Figure 2

4. Move the cursor to the upper middle portion of the screen and left click on the **Bearing** icon as shown in Figure 3.

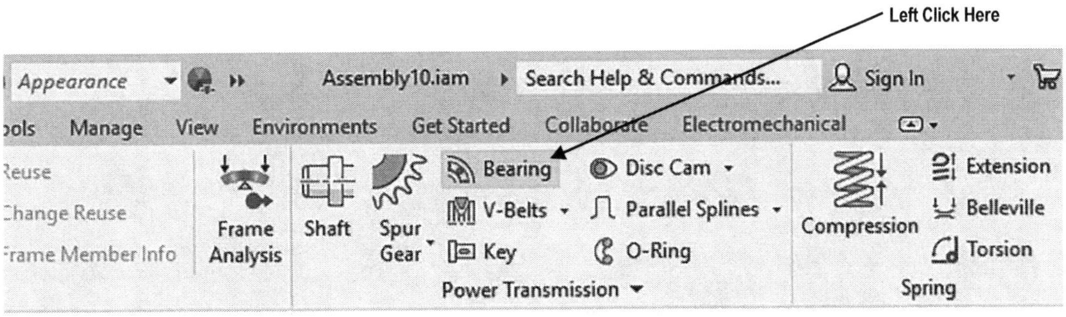

Figure 3

5. The Bearing Generator dialog box will appear as shown in Figure 4.

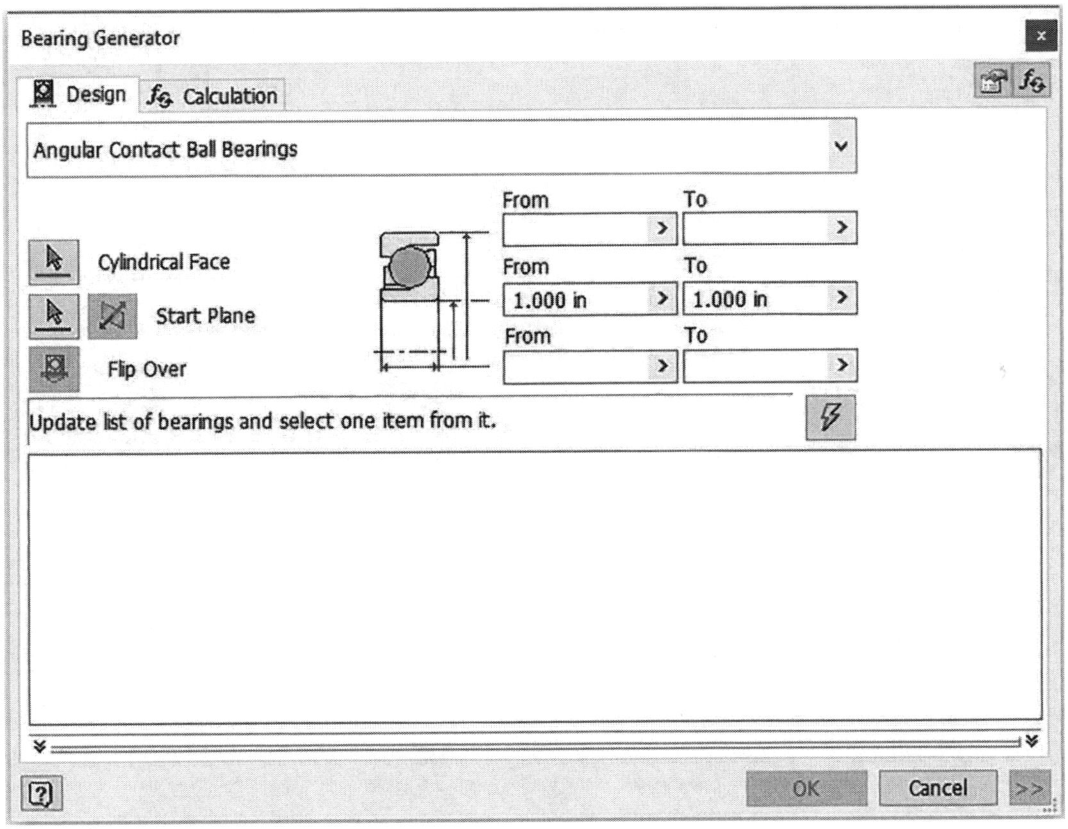

Figure 4

Learn to Enter Values in the Bearing Generator Dialog Box

6. The first set of values is the outside bearing diameter. The second set of values is the inside bearing diameter. The third set of values is the bearing width. Enter the following values as shown in Figure 5.

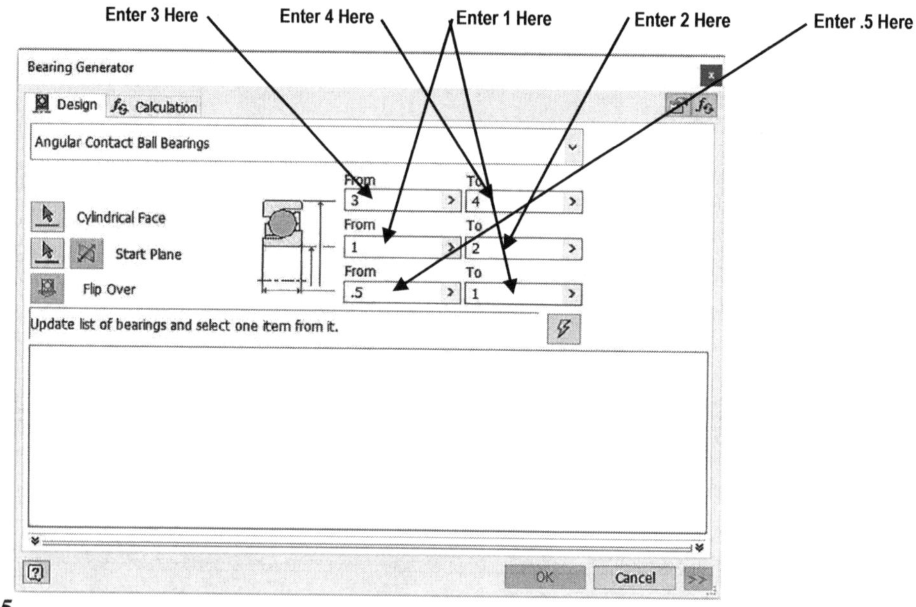

Figure 5

Learn to Populate the Bearing Generator Dialog Box

7. Left click on the Update icon (lightning bolt). Inventor will populate the Bearing Generator dialog box with any bearings it finds that fit the parameters that were entered above as shown in Figure 6.

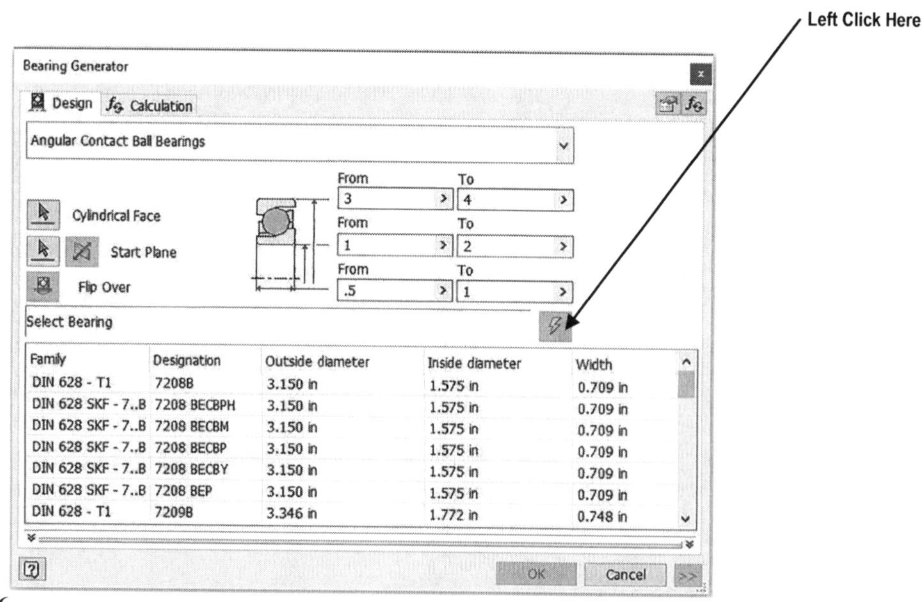

Figure 6

8. Left click on the first bearing in the list. Left click on **OK** as shown in Figure 7.

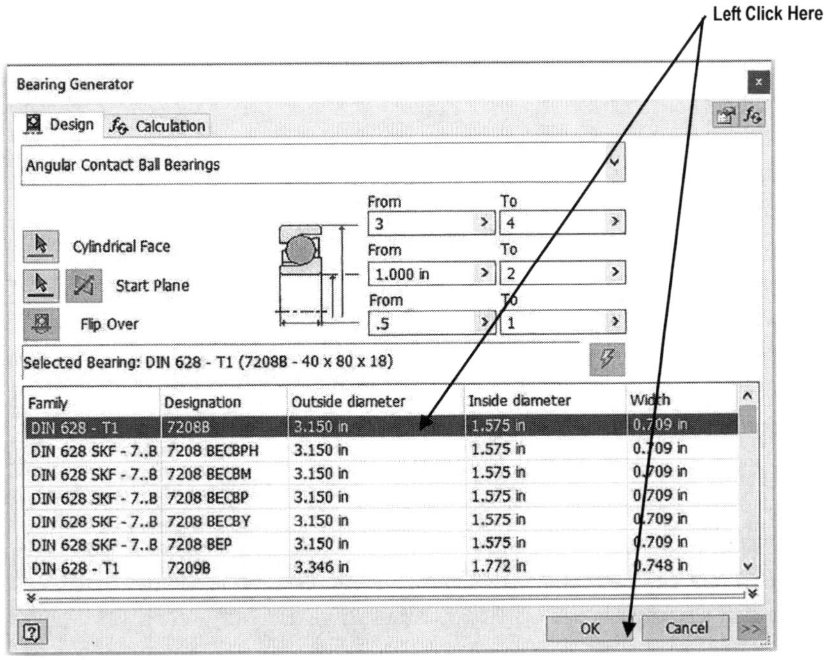

Figure 7

9. The bearing will be a Subassembly. The File Naming dialog box will appear. Left click on the file. Left click on the 3 dots icon as shown in Figure 8. The Save As dialog box will appear (not shown). Save the file where it can be easily retrieved later. Left click on **OK**.

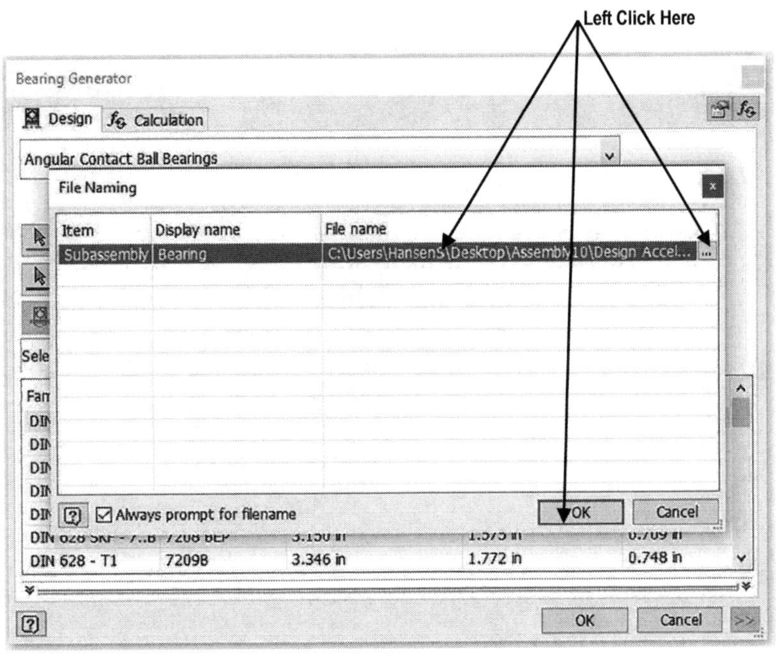

Figure 8

Learn to Place a Bearing in the Assembly Panel

10. The bearing will be attached to the cursor; left click to place the bearing as shown in Figure 9. The bearing will not be Grounded. Right click on the bearing and left click on Grounded as previously described in Chapter 7.

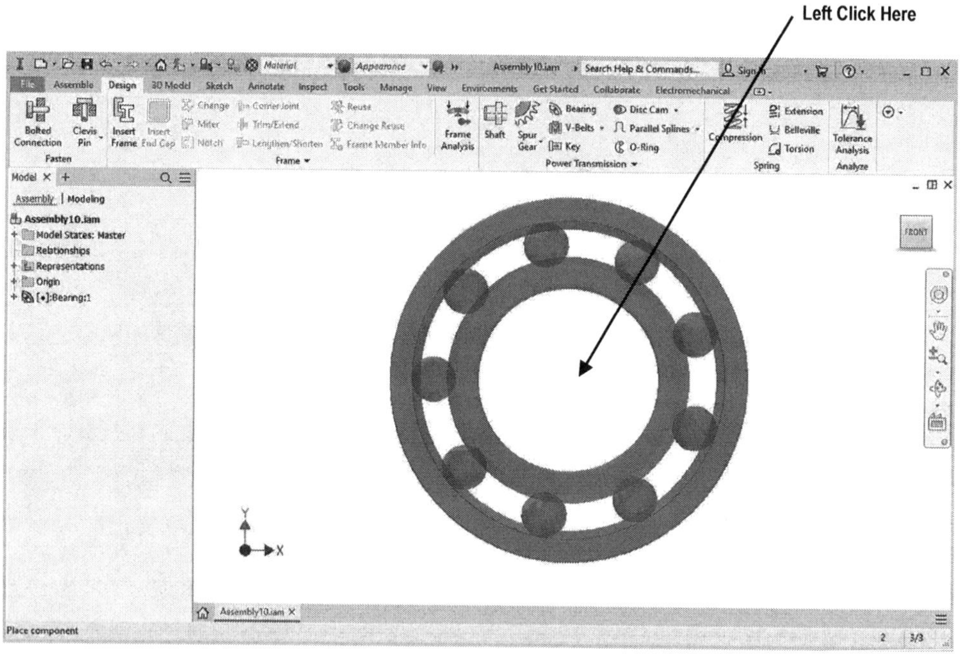

Figure 9

11. Change the view to the **Home View** as shown in Figure 10.

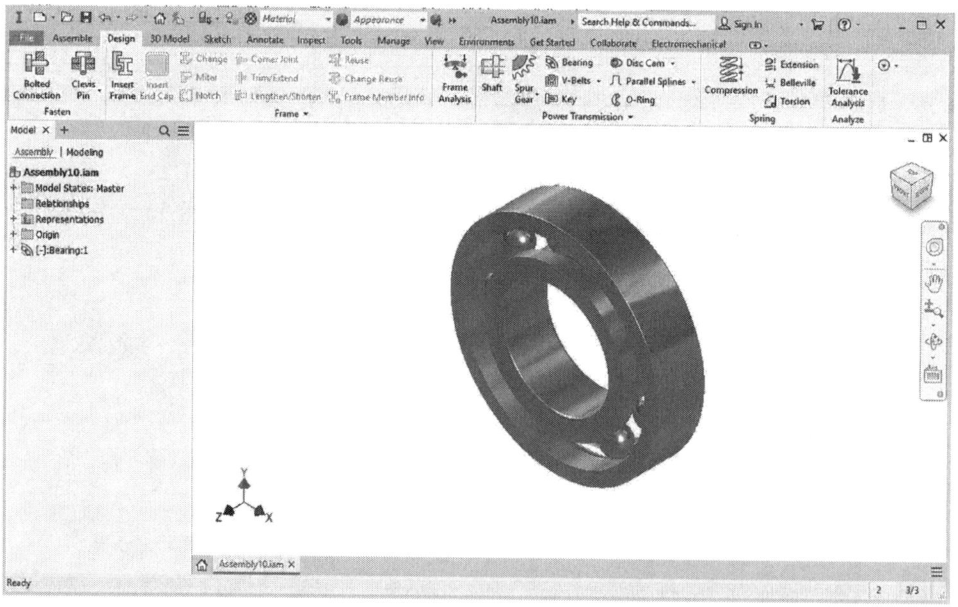

Figure 10

CHAPTER 21

Advanced Sheet Metal Design Procedures

Objectives:

1. Learn to create Sheet Metal strip, Punch Sheet and Contour Roll

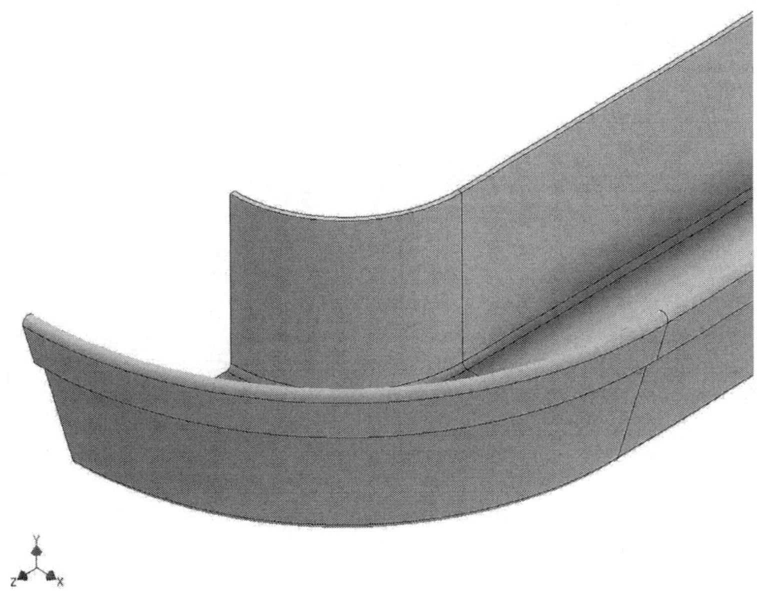

Chapter 21 includes instruction on how to create the parts shown.

1. Start Inventor by referring to "Chapter 1 Getting Started."

2. Start a new **Sheet Metal** part. Left click on **Create** as shown in Figure 1.

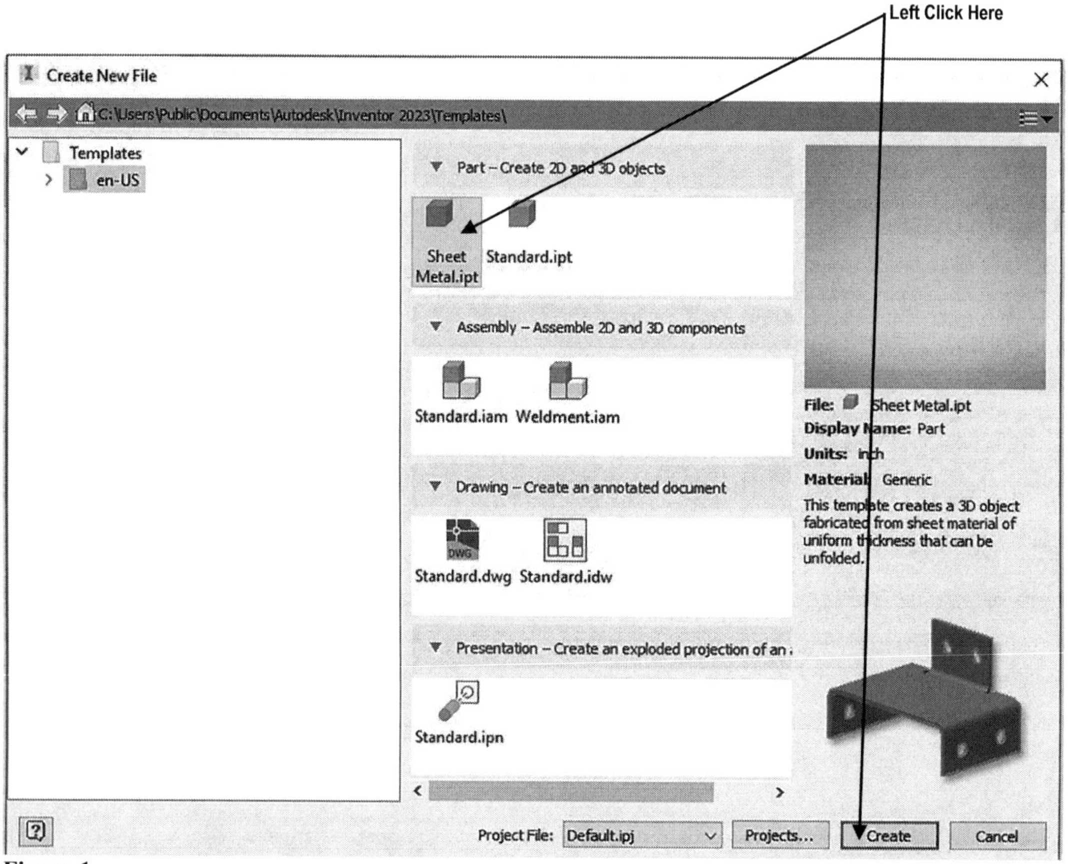

Figure 1

3. Left click on the **Sheet Metal** tab. Left click on **Start 2D Sketch** as shown in Figure 2.

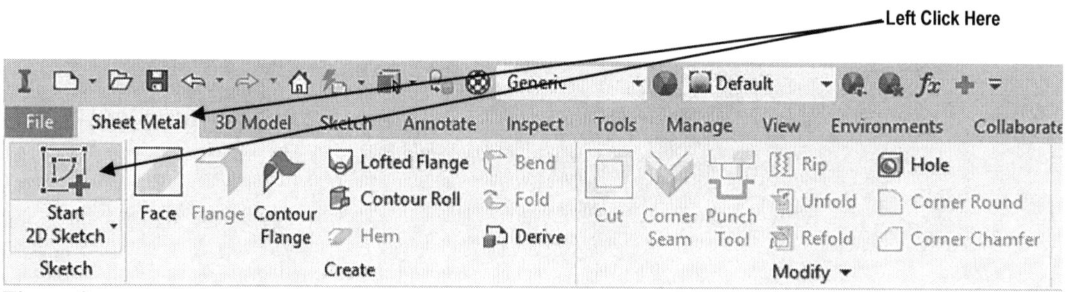

Figure 2

4. Use the Rectangle command to complete the sketch as shown in Figure 3.

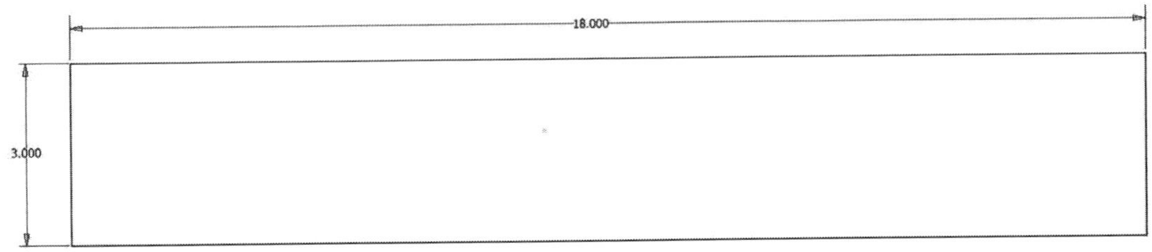

Figure 3

5. Exit the Sketch Panel. Left click on the **Face** icon. The Face dialog box will appear. Left click **OK** as shown in Figure 4.

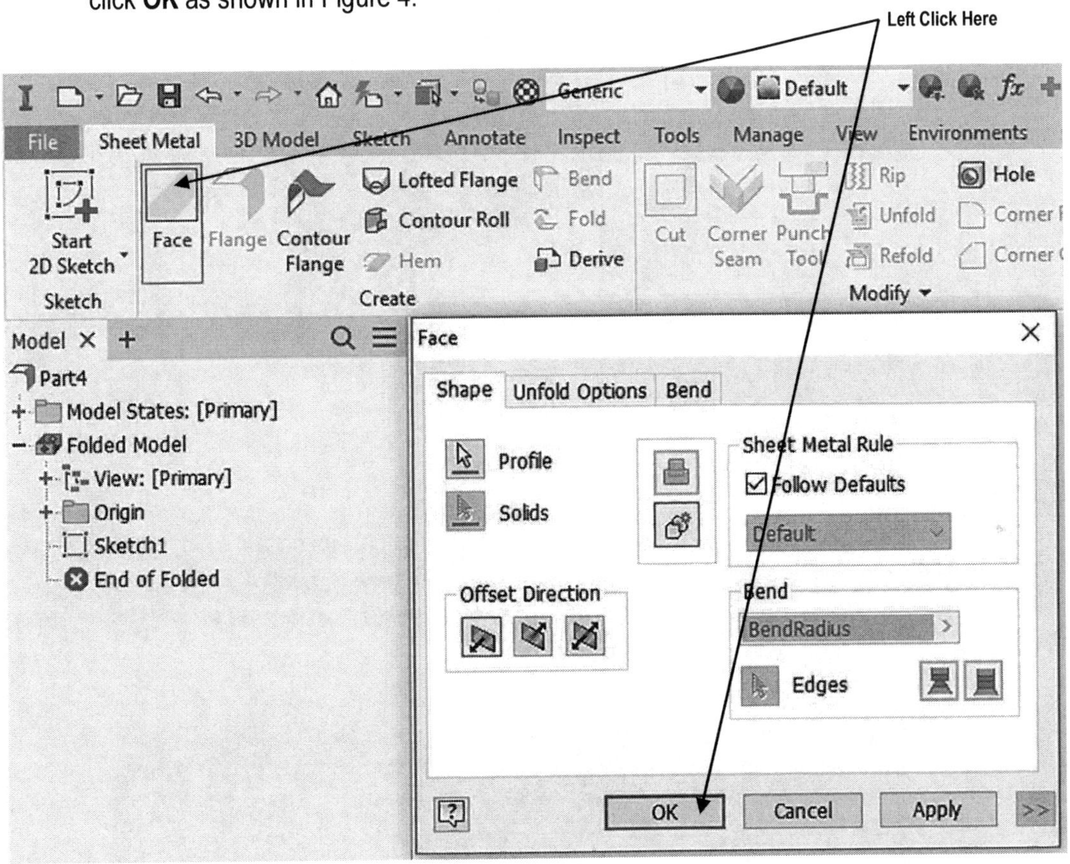

Figure 4

Learn to Create a New Sketch on an Existing Face

6. Create a **New Sketch** on the front face as shown in Figure 5.

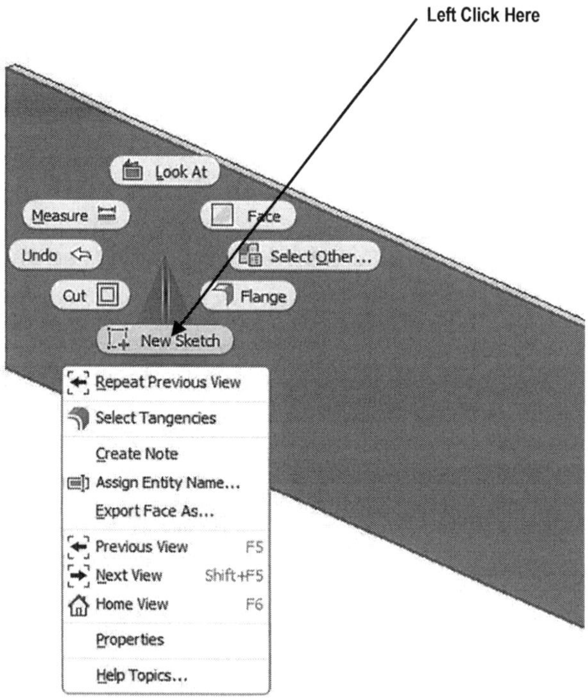

Figure 5

Learn to Create a Fold

7. Draw a line from top to bottom on the left portion of the part as shown in Figure 6. Be sure that the endpoints of the line snap to the top and bottom of the part.

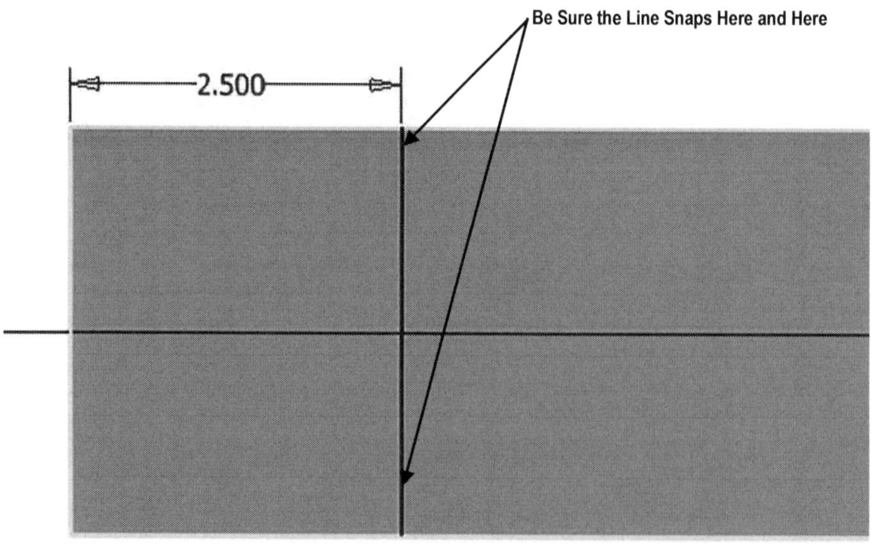

Figure 6

8. Exit the Sketch Panel. Left click on the **Sheet Metal** tab. Left click on the **Fold** icon. Left click on **Home View** to change the view to Isometric. The Fold dialog box will appear. Left click on the Bend Line icon as shown in Figure 7.

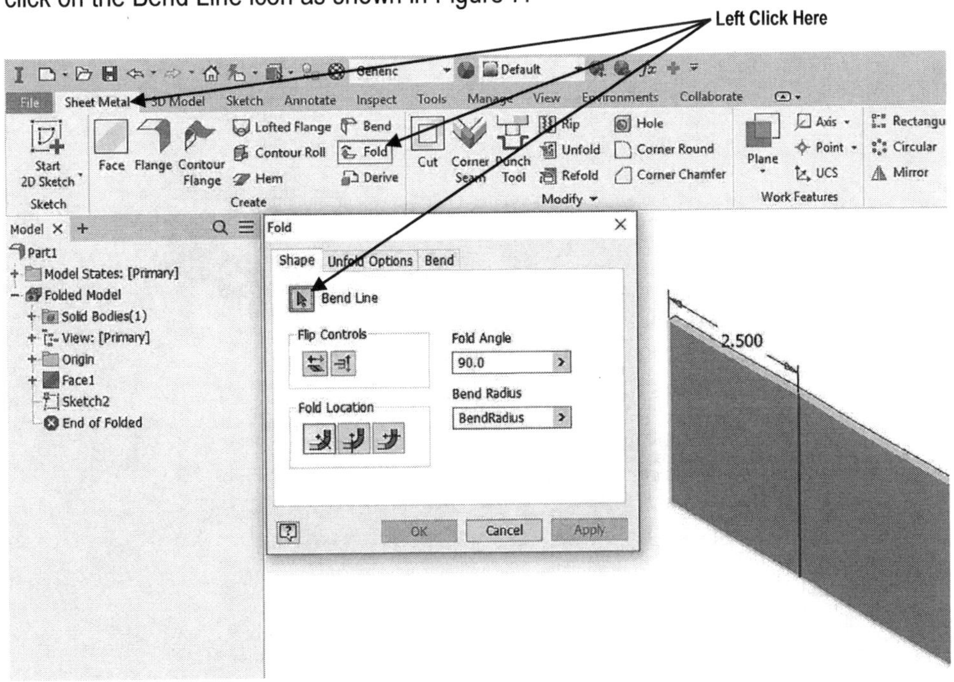

Figure 7

9. Left click on the line that was drawn in the Sketch Panel. The arrows indicate the direction and location of the bend. Left click on **OK** as shown in Figure 8.

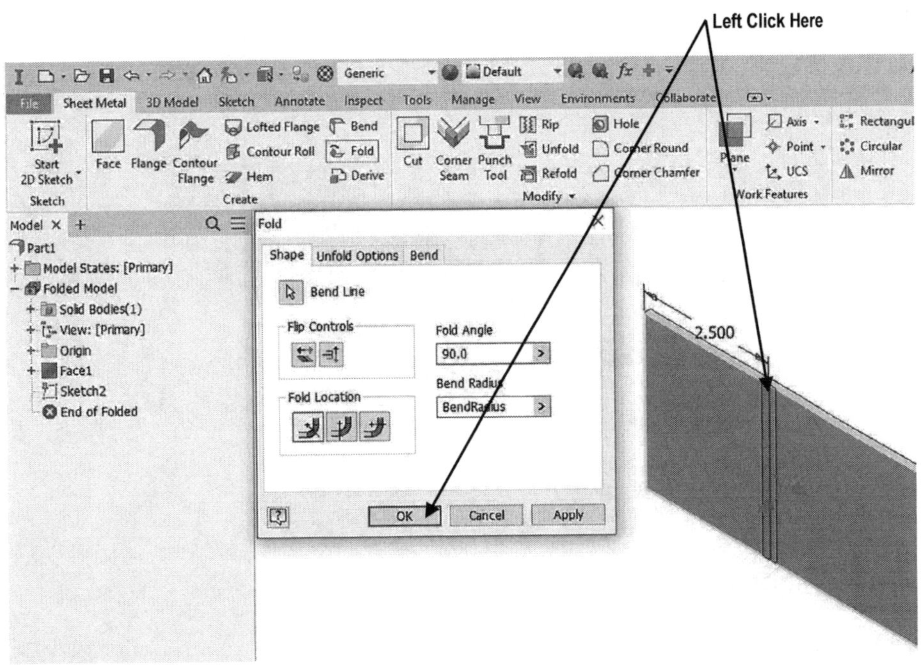

Figure 8

10. Inventor will put a 90 degree bend in the part. Your screen should look similar to what is shown in Figure 9.

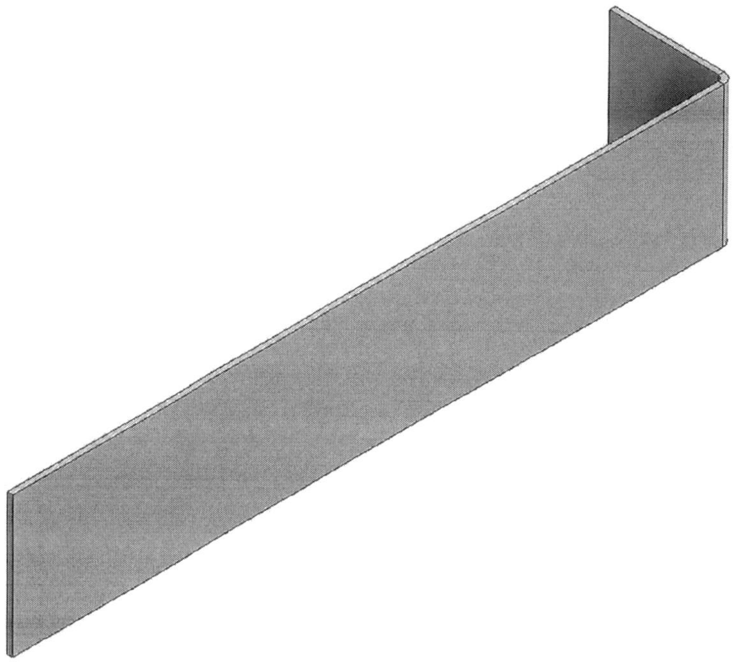

Figure 9

11. Begin a **New Sketch** as shown in Figure 10.

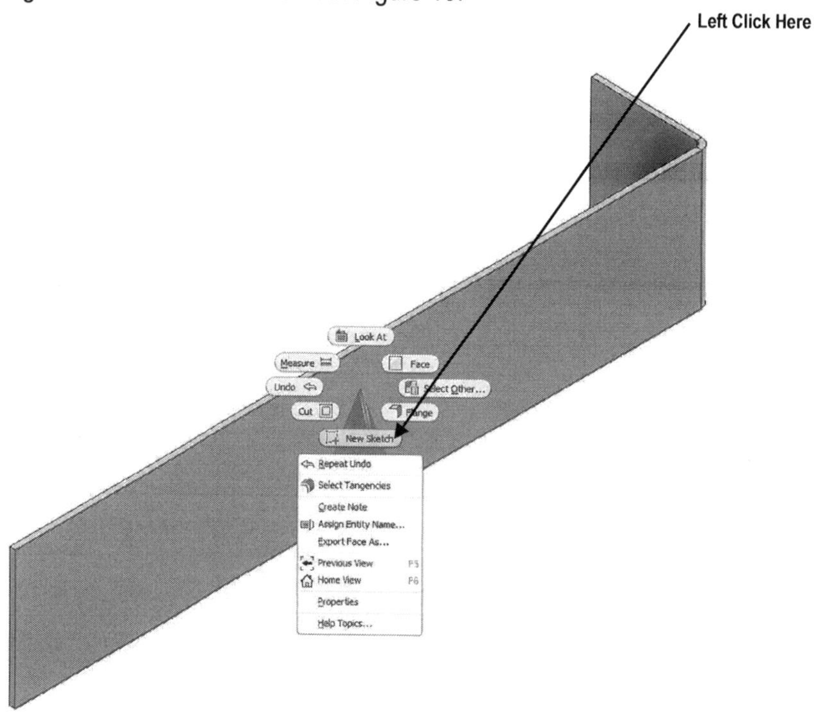

Figure 10

12. Complete the sketch as shown in Figure 11.

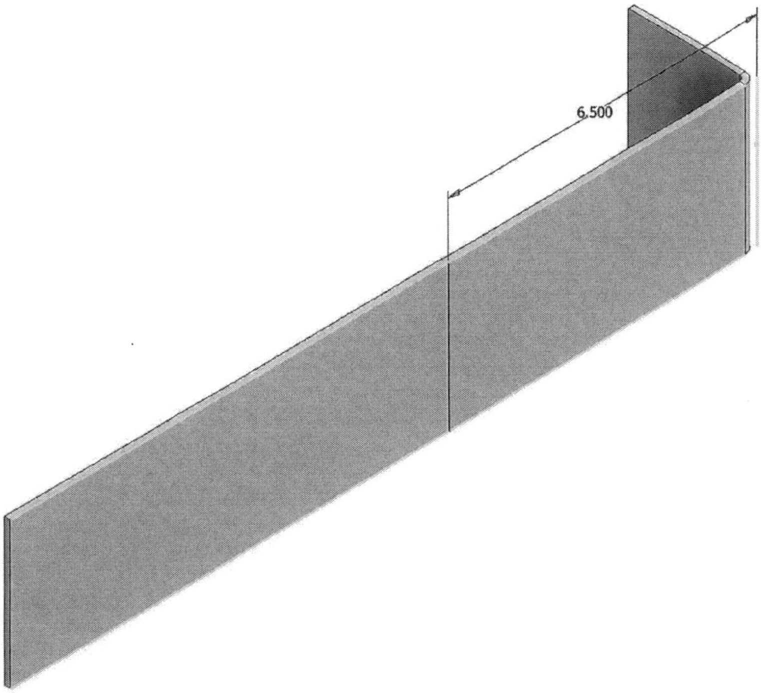

Figure 11

13. Exit the Sketch Panel. Left click on the **Sheet Metal** tab. Left click on the **Fold** icon. Left click on **Home View** to change the view to Isometric. The Fold dialog box will appear. Left click on the Bend Line icon as shown in Figure 12.

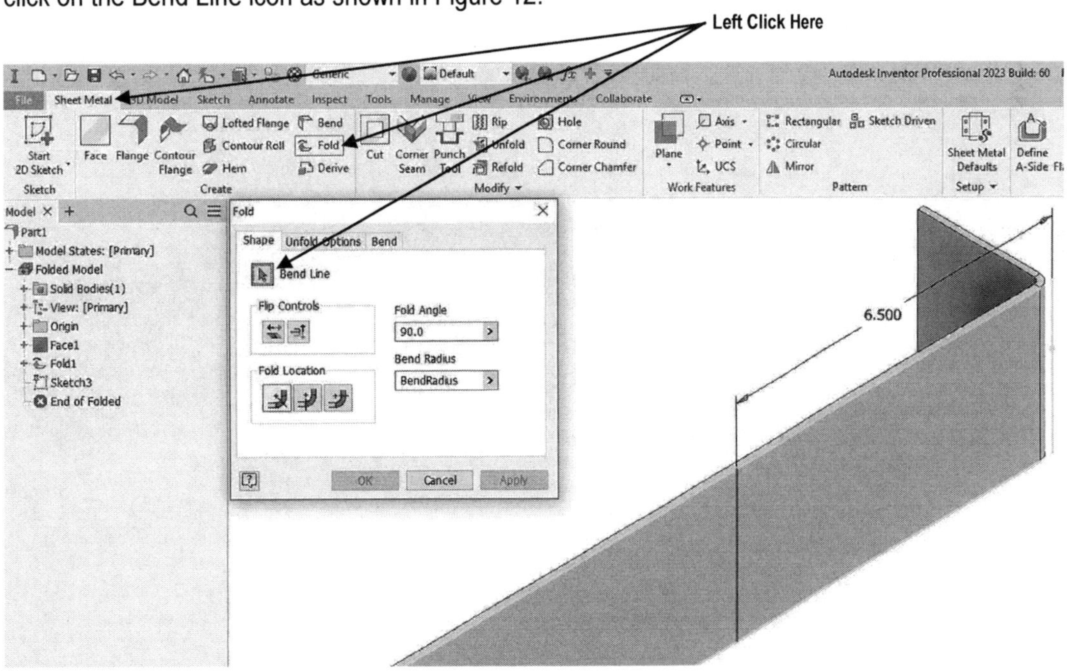

Figure 12

14. Left click on the line that was drawn in the Sketch Panel. The arrows indicate the direction and location of the bend. Left click on **OK** as shown in Figure 13.

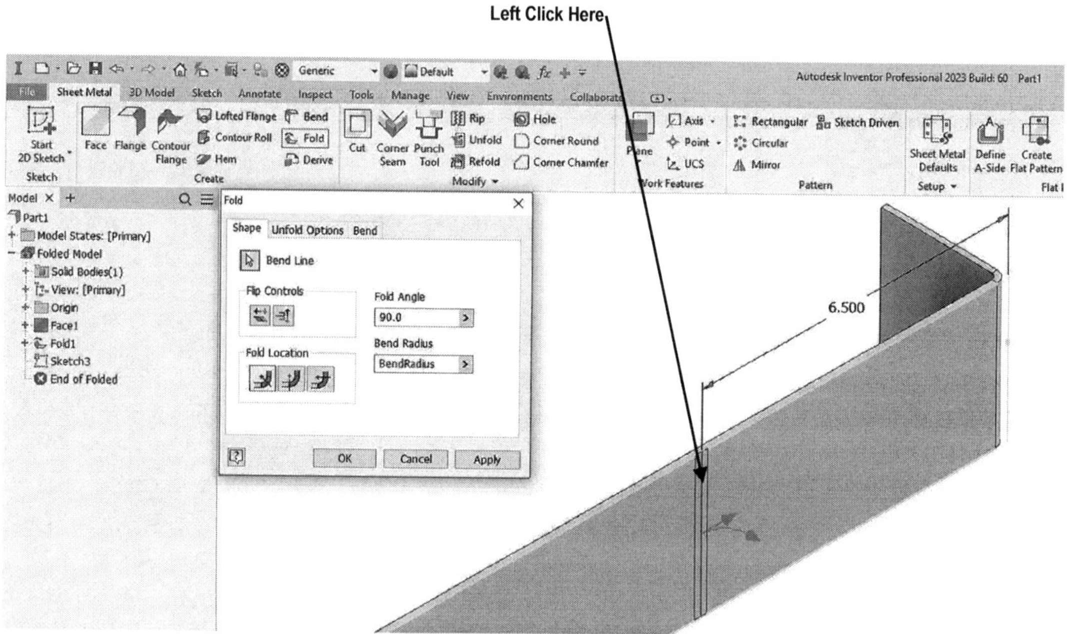

Figure 13

15. Inventor will put a 90 degree bend in the part. Your screen should look similar to what is shown in Figure 14.

Figure 14

Learn to Create a Hem

16. Left click on the **Hem** icon. The Hem dialog box will appear. Left click on the edge as shown in Figure 15.

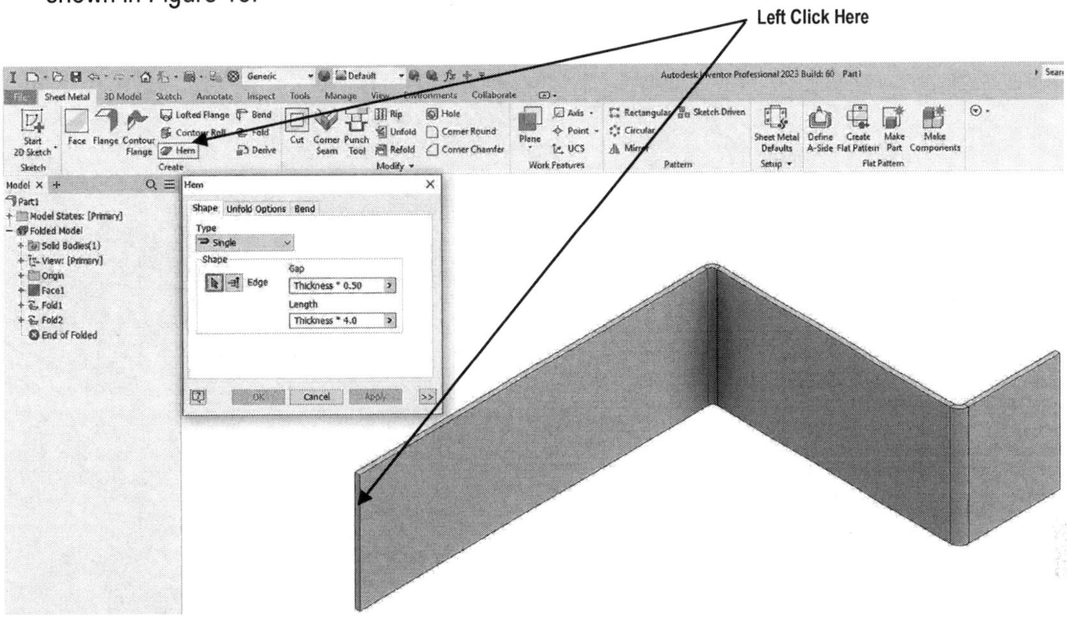

Figure 15

17. Enter **.250** for the Gap Thickness and **10.0** for the Length Thickness. A preview of the Hem will appear as shown in Figure 16.

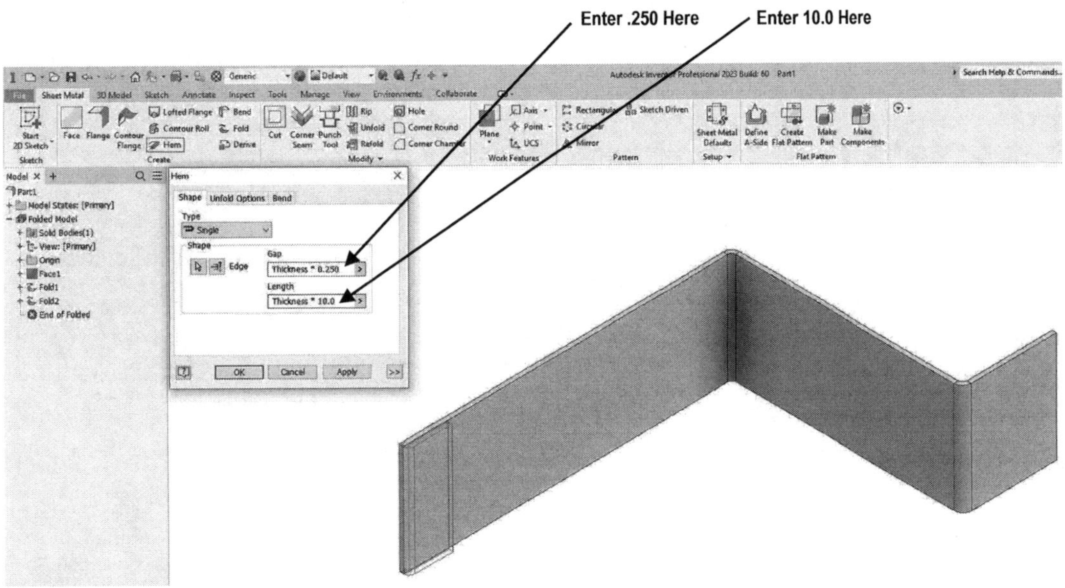

Figure 16

18. Left click on **OK**. Your screen should look similar to what is shown in Figure 17.

Figure 17

Learn to Create a Punch Sheet

19. Start a new **Sheet Metal** part. Let click on **Create** as shown in Figure 18.

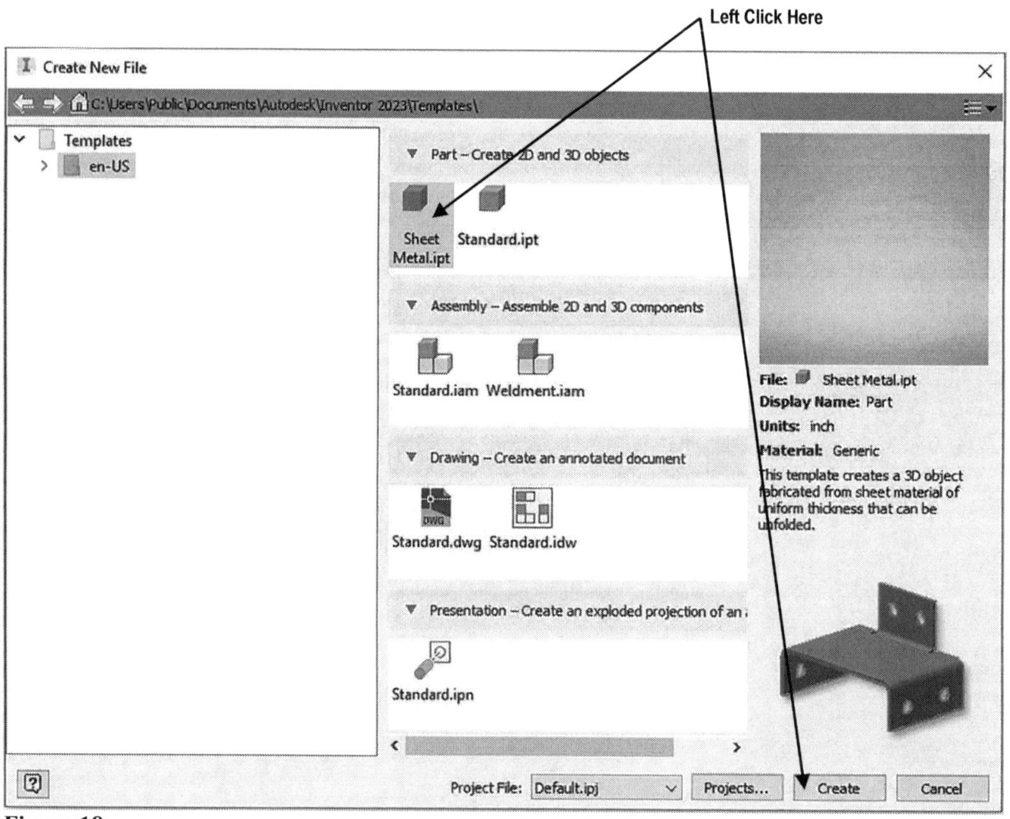

Figure 18

20. Left click on the **Sheet Metal** tab. Left click on **Start 2D Sketch** as shown in Figure 19.

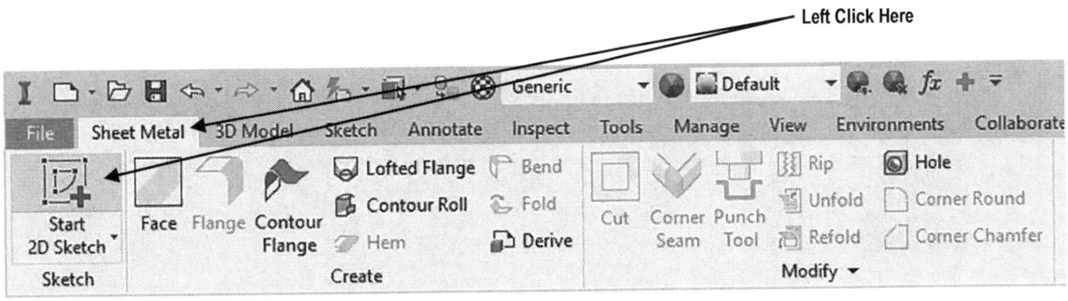

Figure 19

21. Use the Rectangle command to complete the sketch as shown in Figure 20.

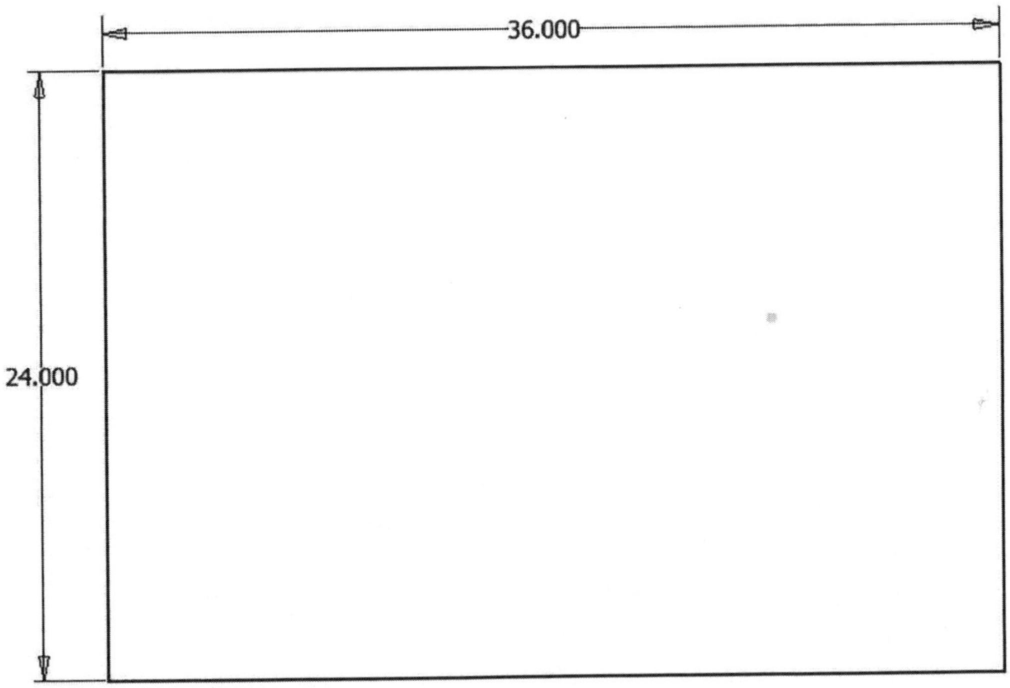

Figure 20

22. Exit the Sketch Panel. Left click on the **Sheet Metal** tab. Left click on the **Face** icon. The Face dialog box will appear. Left click **OK** as shown in Figure 21.

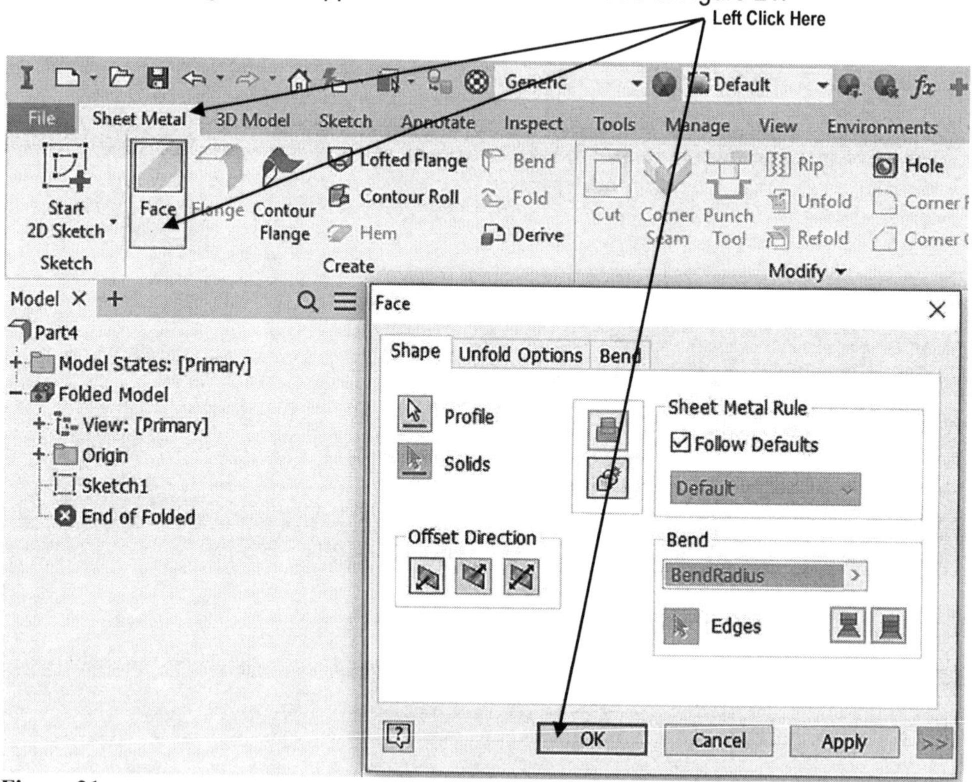

Figure 21

23. Begin a **New Sketch** on the newly created Face as shown in Figure 22.

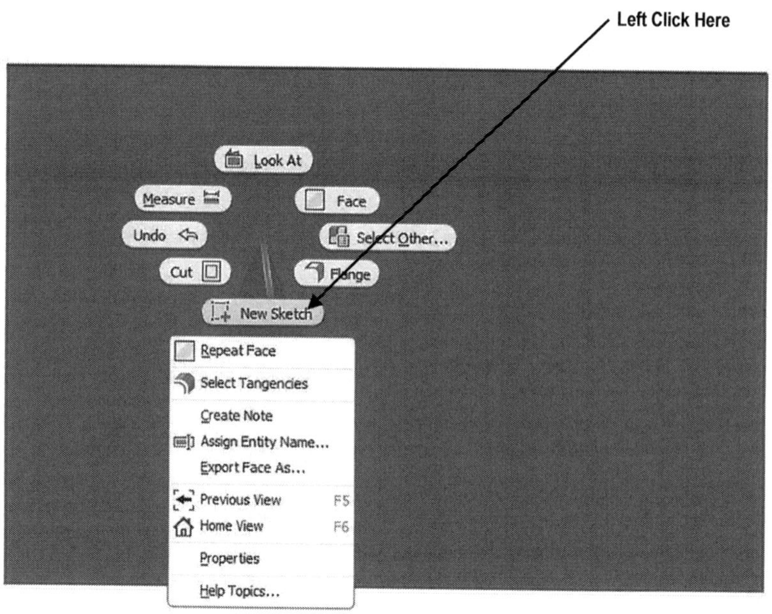

Figure 22

24. Use the **Point** command to place a single point on the sketch 3 inches from each edge of the part as shown in Figure 23.

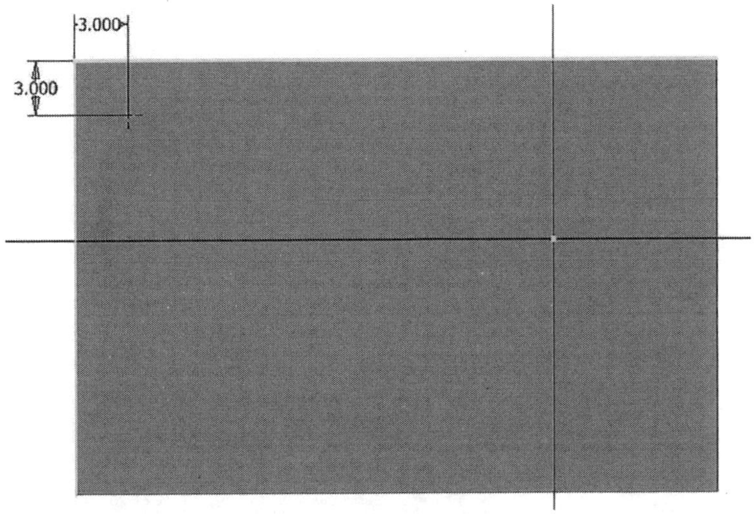

Figure 23

25. Use the **Rectangle Pattern** command in the Sketch Panel (refer to pages 9-9 if needed) to place points. You may have to use the Project Geometry tool (right click on the edge of the part then left click on Project Geometry) to project the X and Y edges of the part as shown in Figure 24.

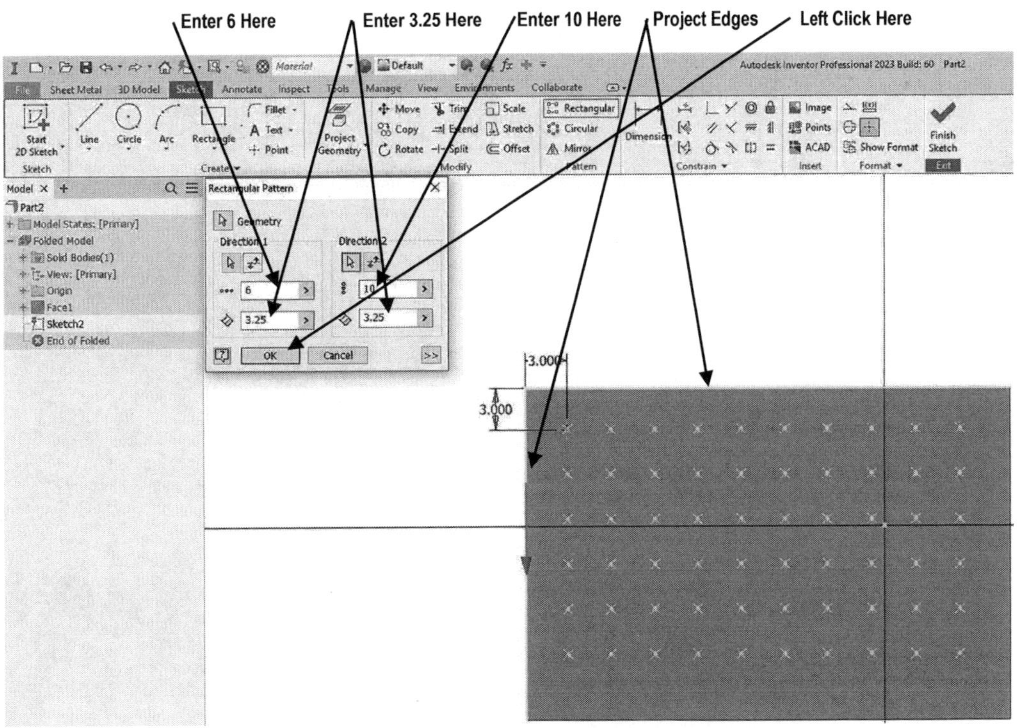

Figure 24

26. Your screen should look similar to what is shown in Figure 25.

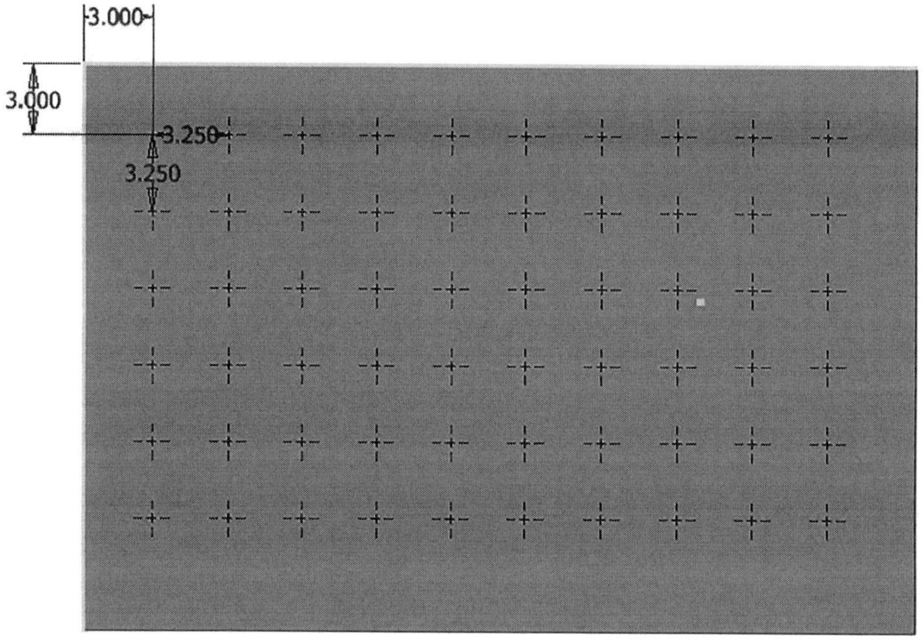

Figure 25

27. Exit the Sketch Panel. Left click on the **Sheet Metal** tab. Left click on the **Punch Tool** icon as shown in Figure 26.

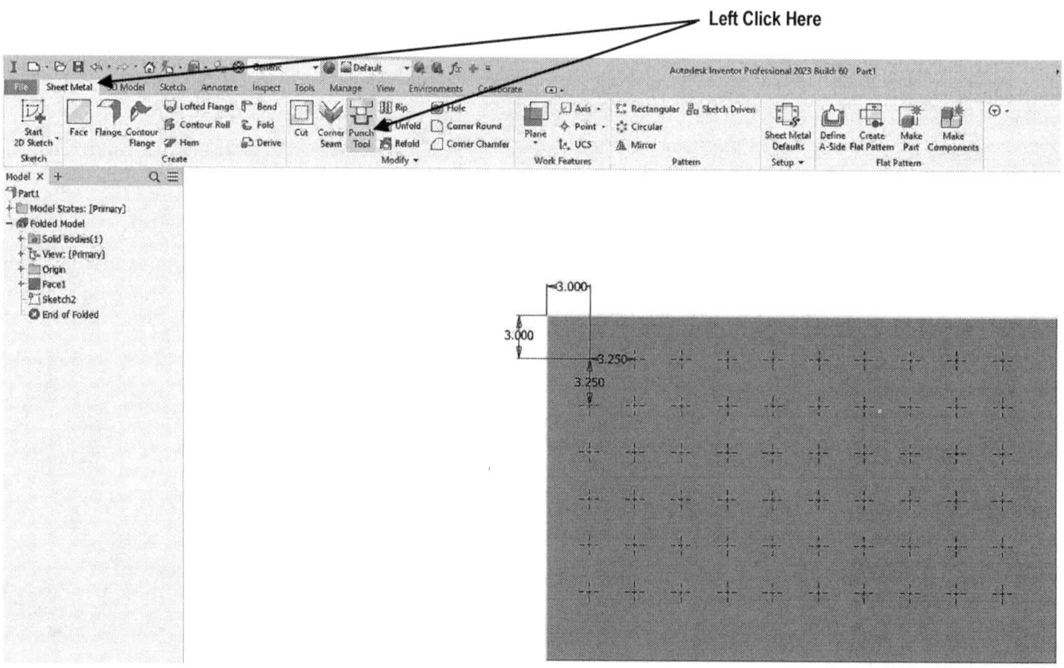

Figure 26

28. The PunchTool dialog box will appear as shown in Figure 27.

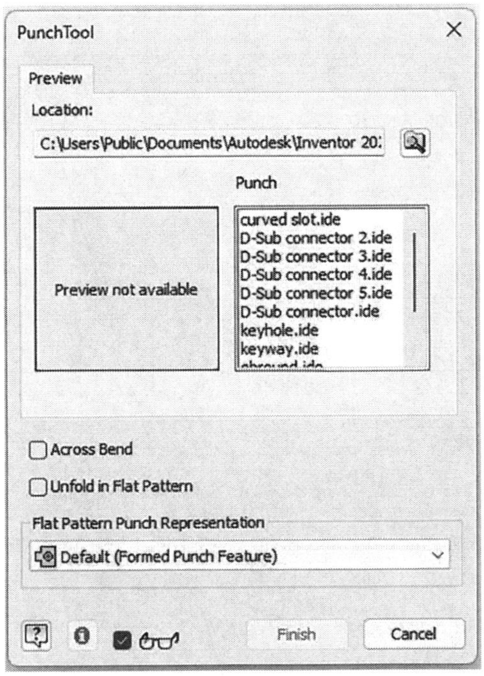

Figure 27

29. Left click on **D-Sub connector 4.ide**. A preview of the file will appear as shown in Figure 28.

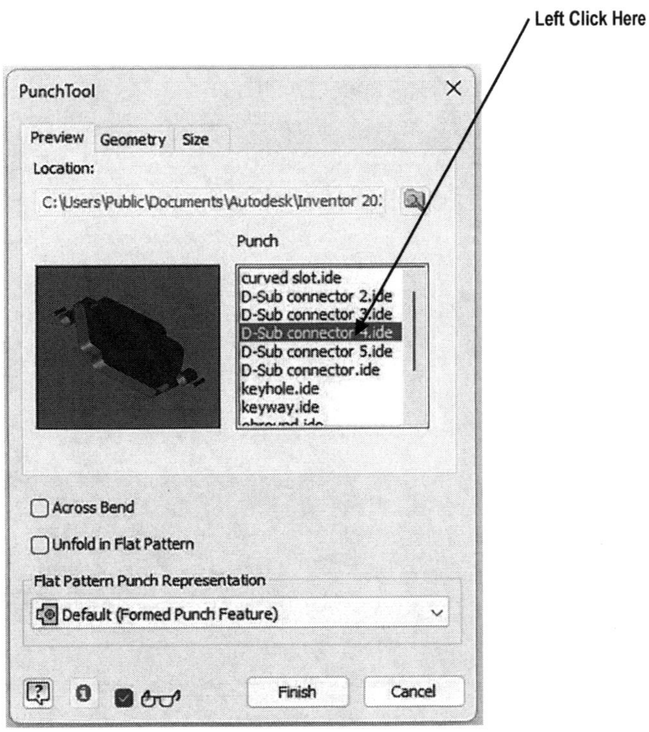

Figure 28

30. Left click on **Finish** as shown in Figure 29.

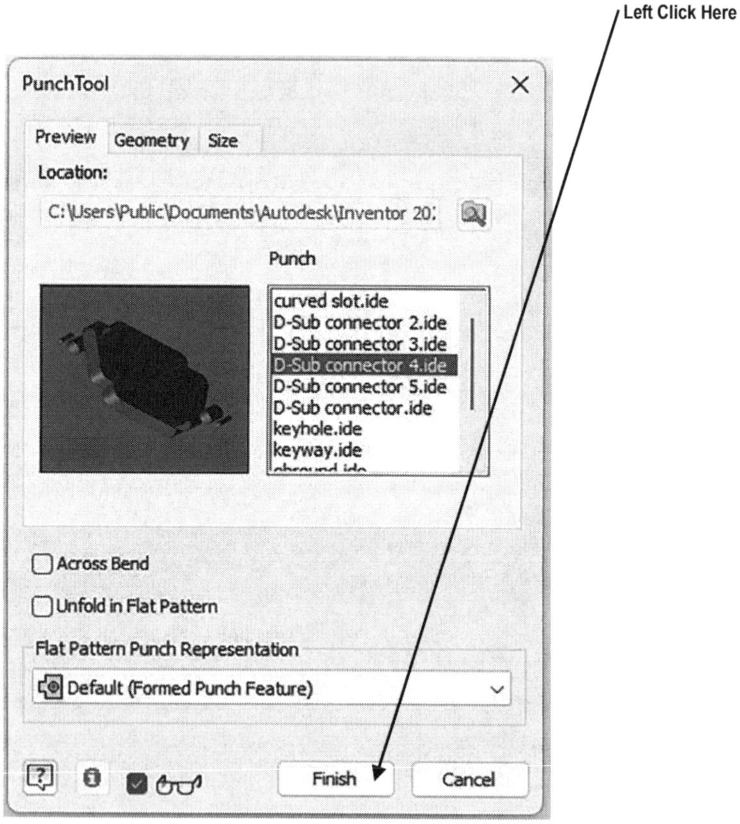

Figure 29

31. The PunchTool dialog box will appear with a preview as shown in Figure 30.

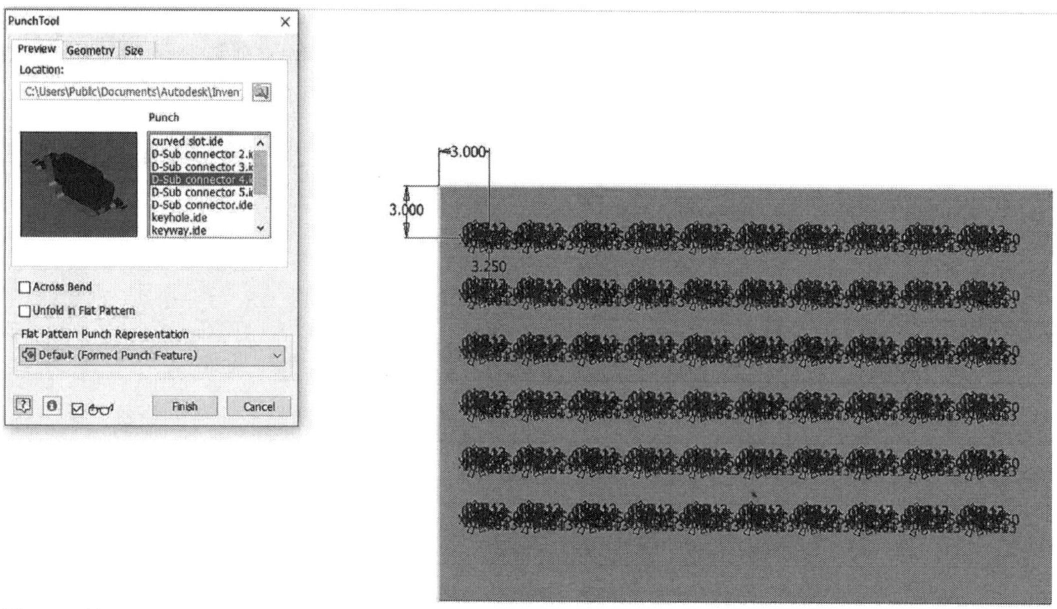

Figure 30

32. Left click on **Finish** as shown in Figure 31.

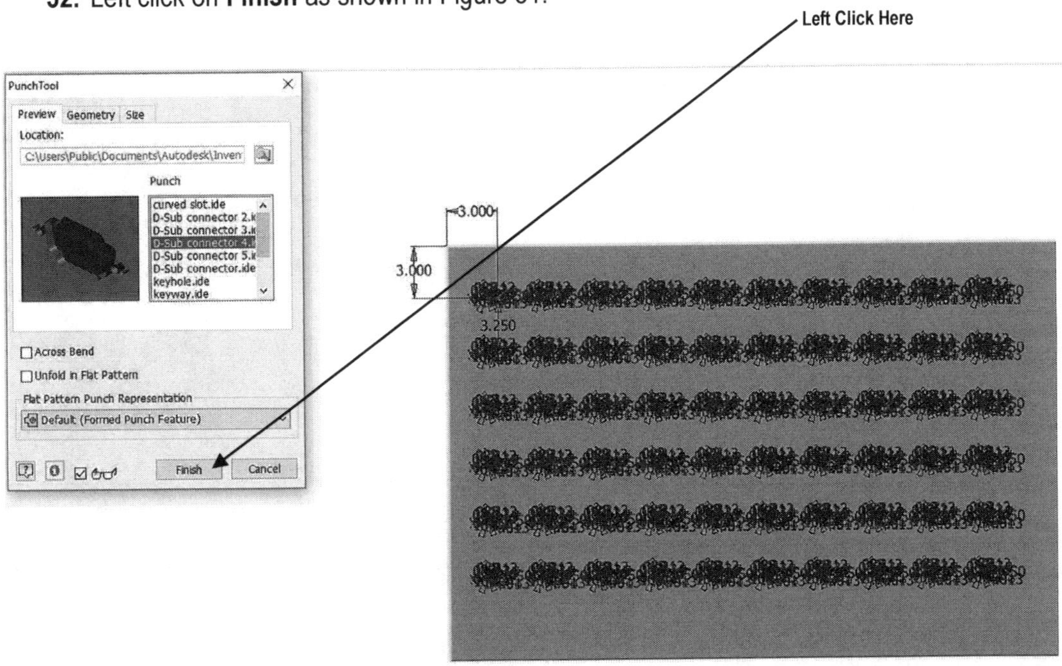

Figure 31

33. Your screen should look similar to Figure 32.

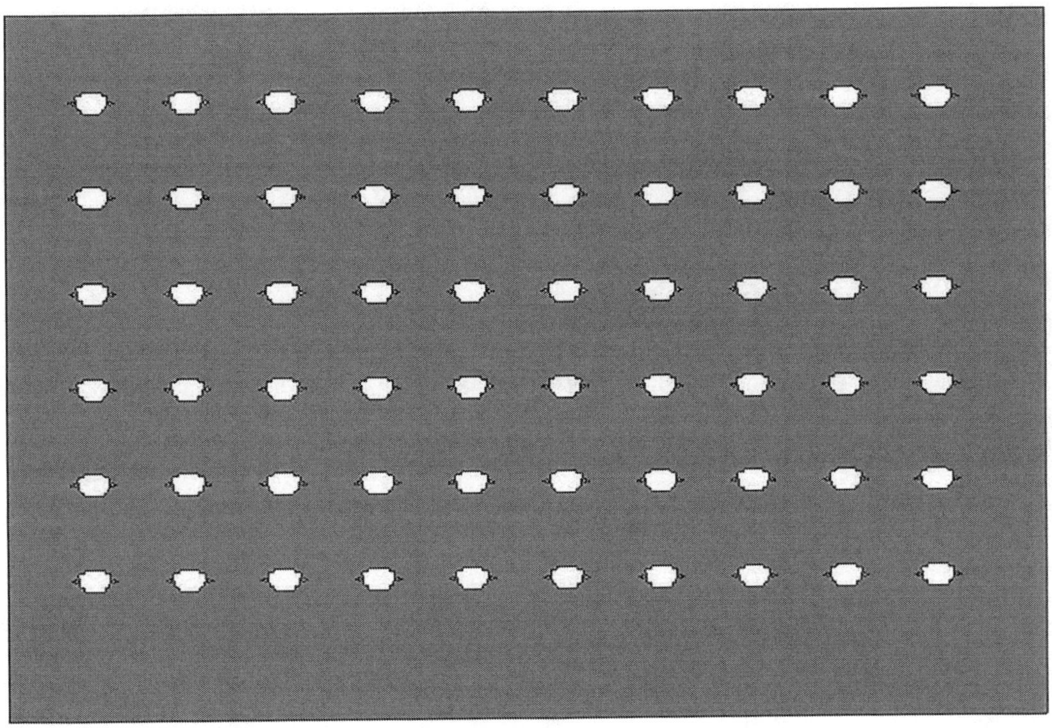

Figure 32

34. Zoom in close to examine the punched holes as shown in Figure 33.

Figure 33

Learn to Edit a Punch Tool

35. To make any necessary edits to the hole sizes and locations, move the cursor to the part tree and right click on **iFeature 16:1.** A pop-up menu will appear. Left click on **Edit Feature** as shown in Figure 34.

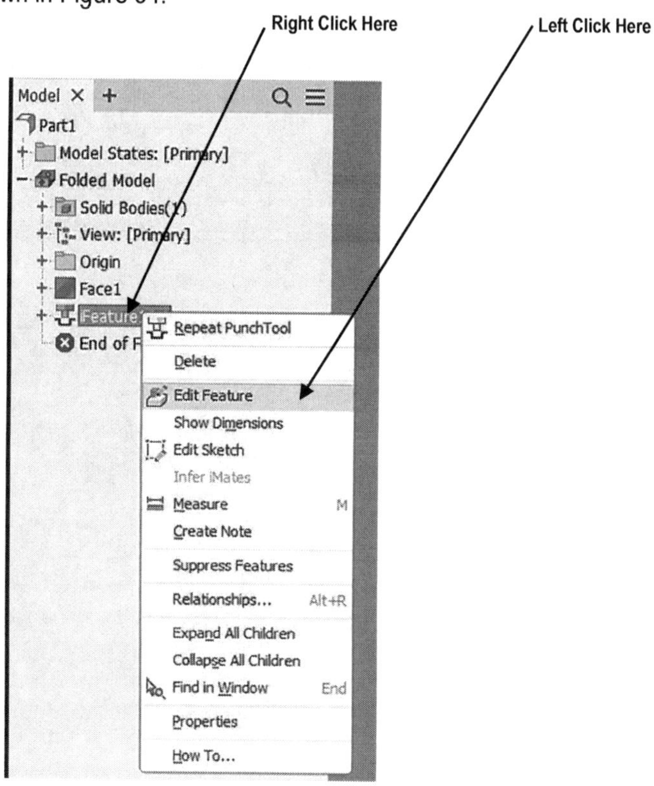

Figure 34

36. The PunchTool dialog box will appear along with Dimensions as shown in Figure 35.

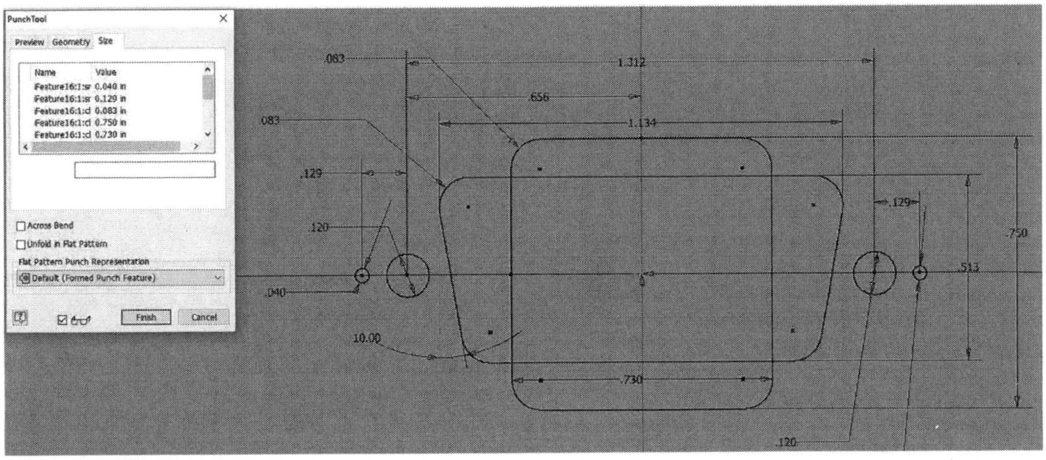

Figure 35

37. Scroll down to the .120 in the Value column. Left click highlighting the text as shown in Figure 36.

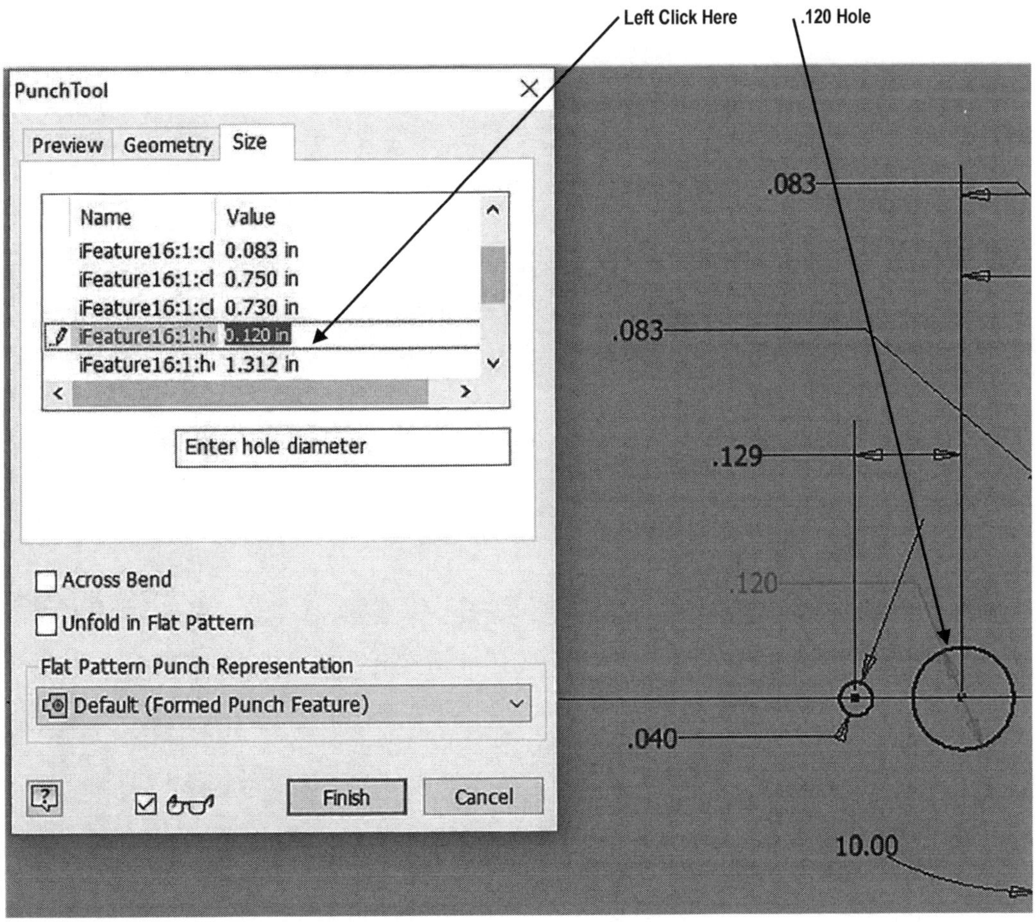

Figure 36

38. Enter **0.140**. Left click on **Finish** as shown in Figure 37.

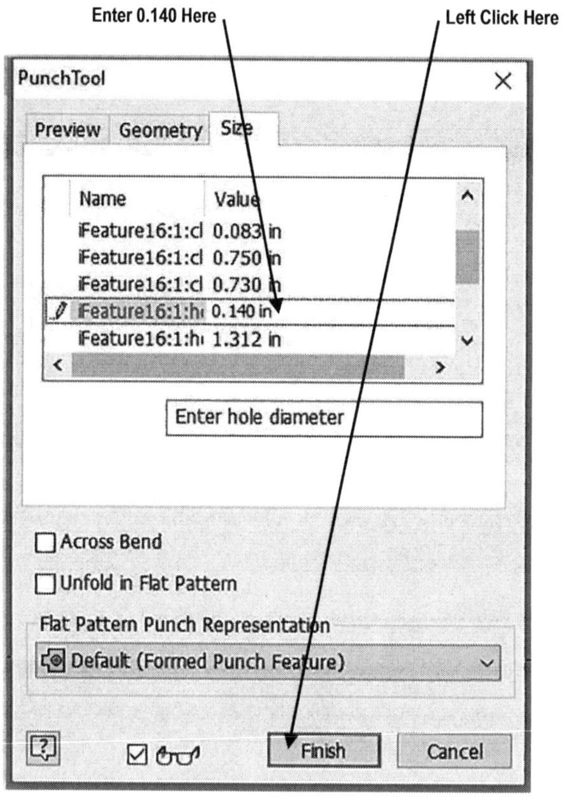

Figure 37

39. Inventor will edit the dimension and exit out of the Edit Feature command automatically. Your screen should look similar to what is shown in Figure 38.

Figure 38

40. To confirm that Inventor actually updated the hole size, move the cursor to the part tree and right click on **iFeature 16:1.** A pop-up menu will appear. Left click on **Edit Feature** as shown in Figure 39.

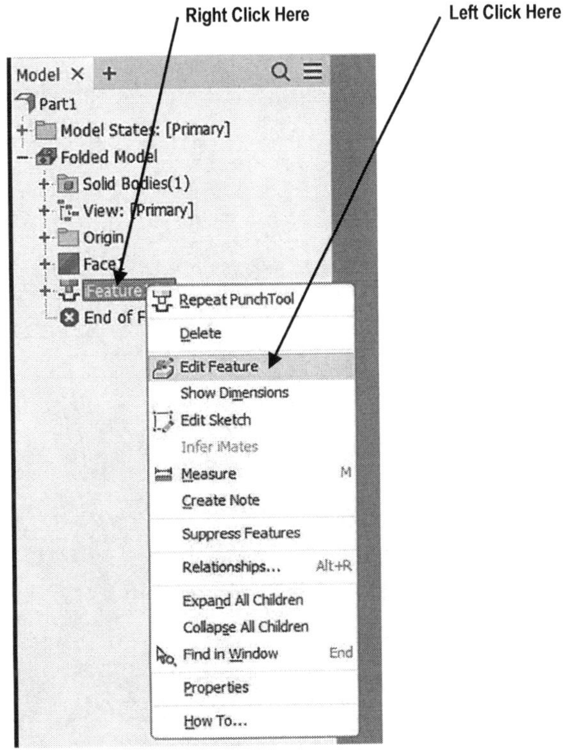

Figure 39

41. The PunchTool dialog box will appear. You will notice that Inventor changed the hole size from 0.120 to 0.140 for both holes on the Sketch as shown in Figure 40.

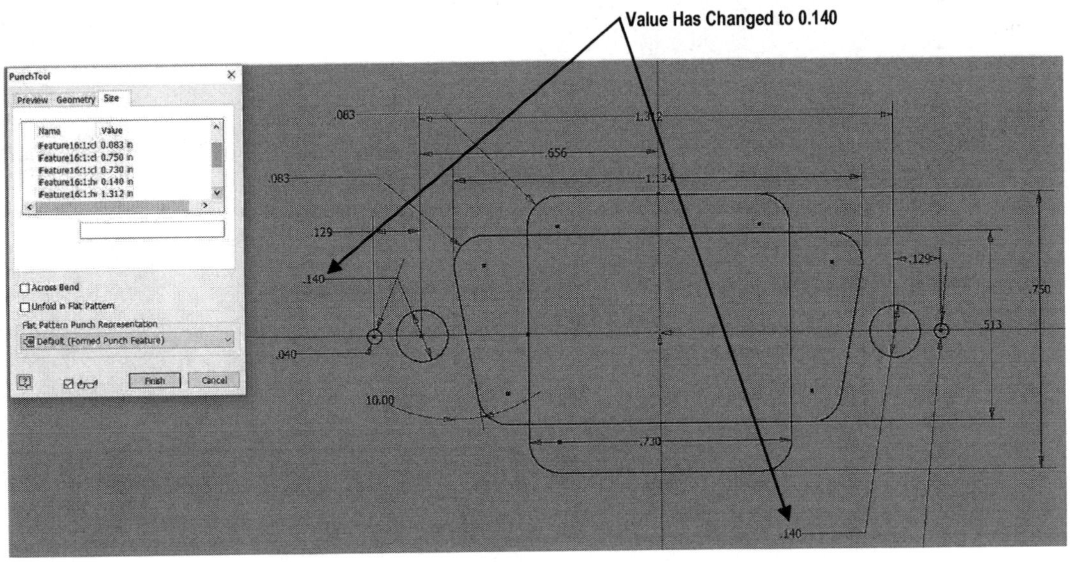

Figure 40

42. Left click on **Finish** as shown in Figure 41.

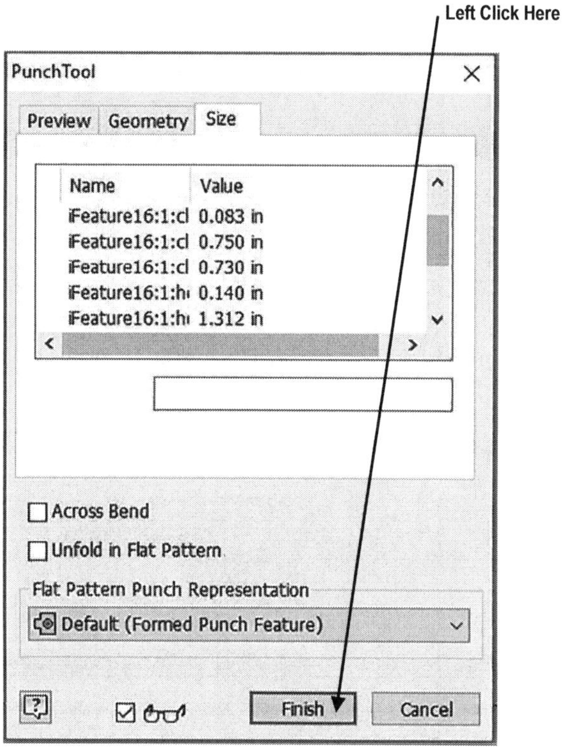

Figure 41

43. Your screen should look similar to Figure 42.

Figure 42

44. Start a new **Sheet Metal** part. Left click on **Create** as shown in Figure 43.

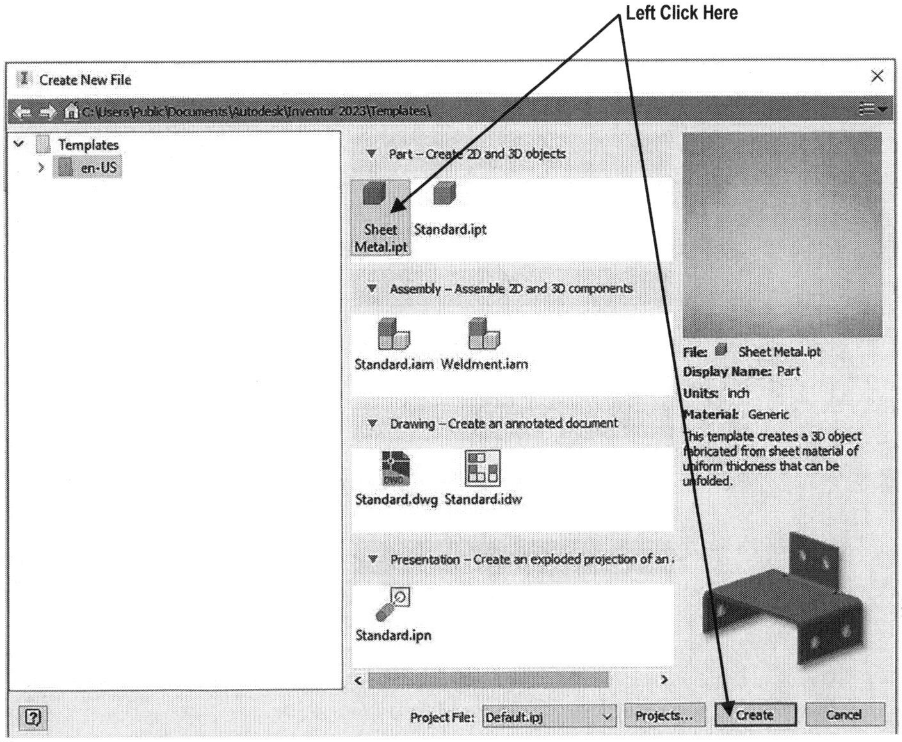

Figure 43

Learn to Create a Contour Flange

45. Complete the following Sketch as shown in Figure 44.

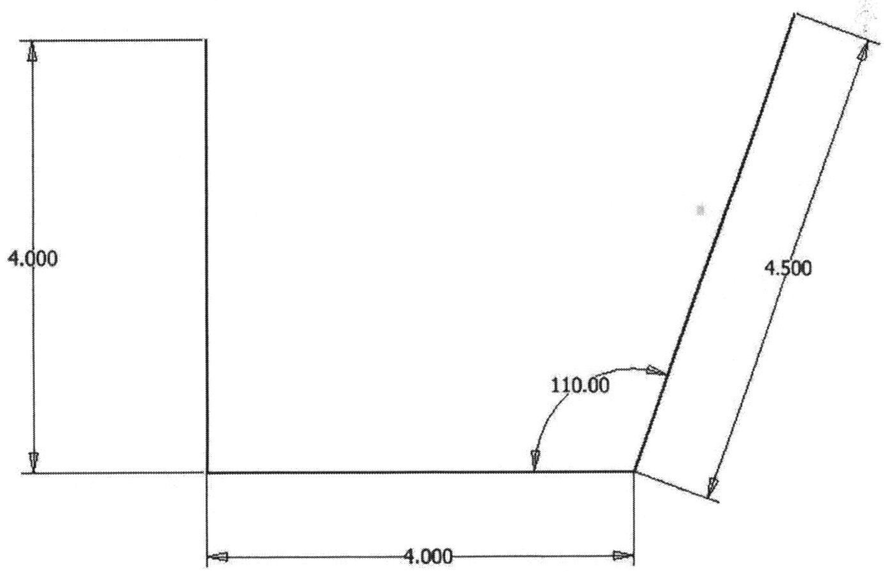

Figure 44

46. Exit the Sketch Panel. Left click on the **Contour Flange** icon. The Contour Flange dialog box will appear as shown in Figure 45.

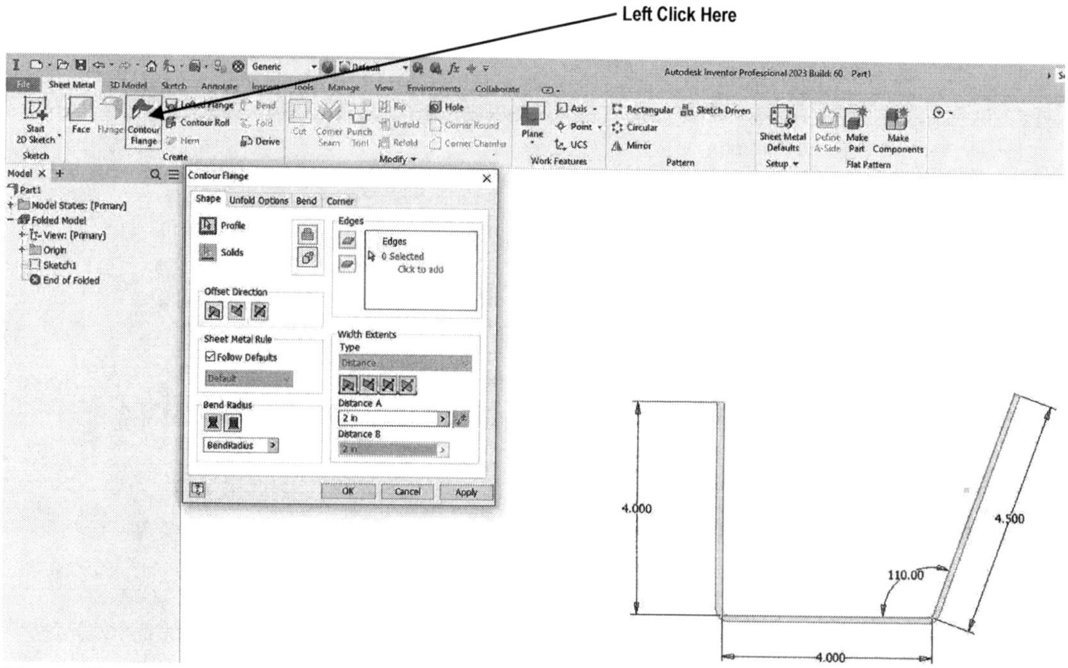

Figure 45

47. Enter **60** for Distance A. Left click on **OK** as shown in Figure 46.

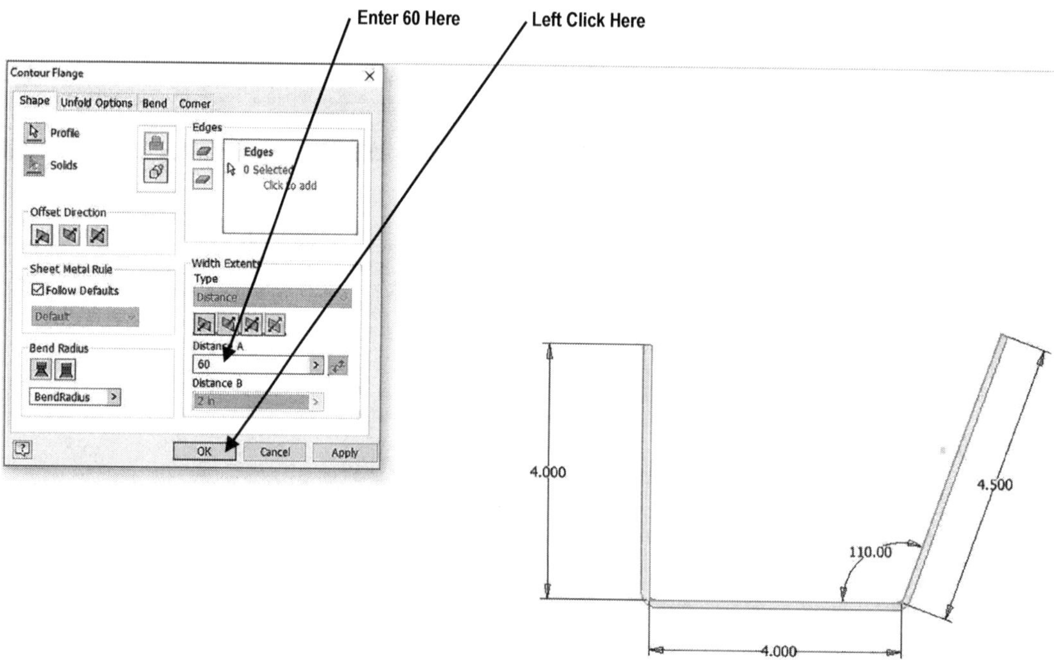

Figure 46

48. Right click anywhere around the part. A pop-menu will appear. Left click on **Home View** as shown in Figure 47.

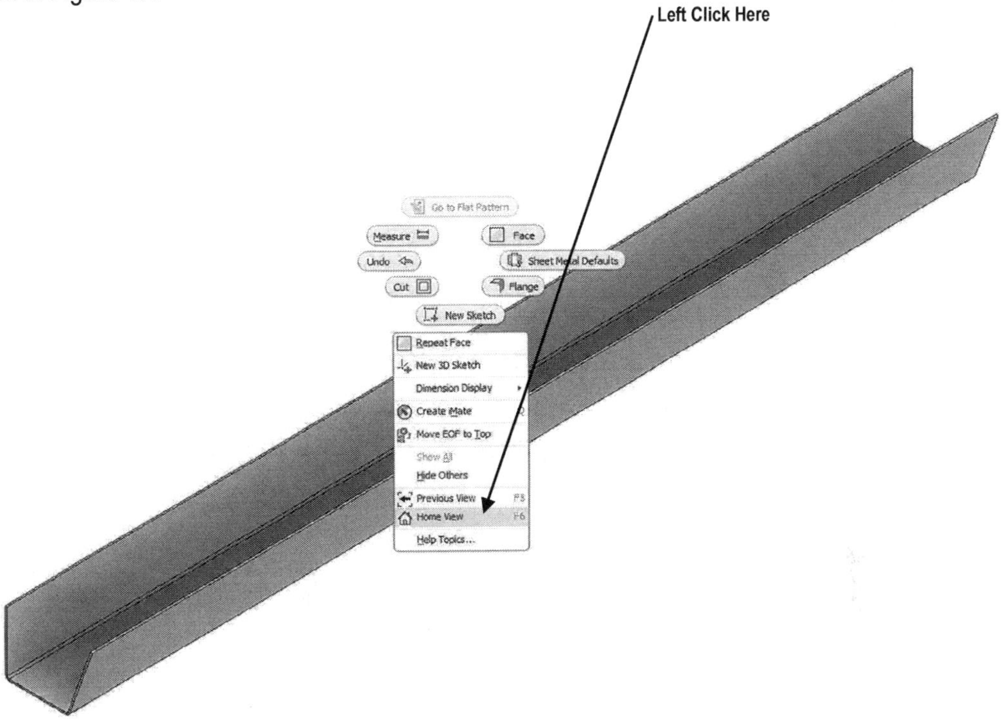

Figure 47

49. Your screen should look similar to what is shown in Figure 48.

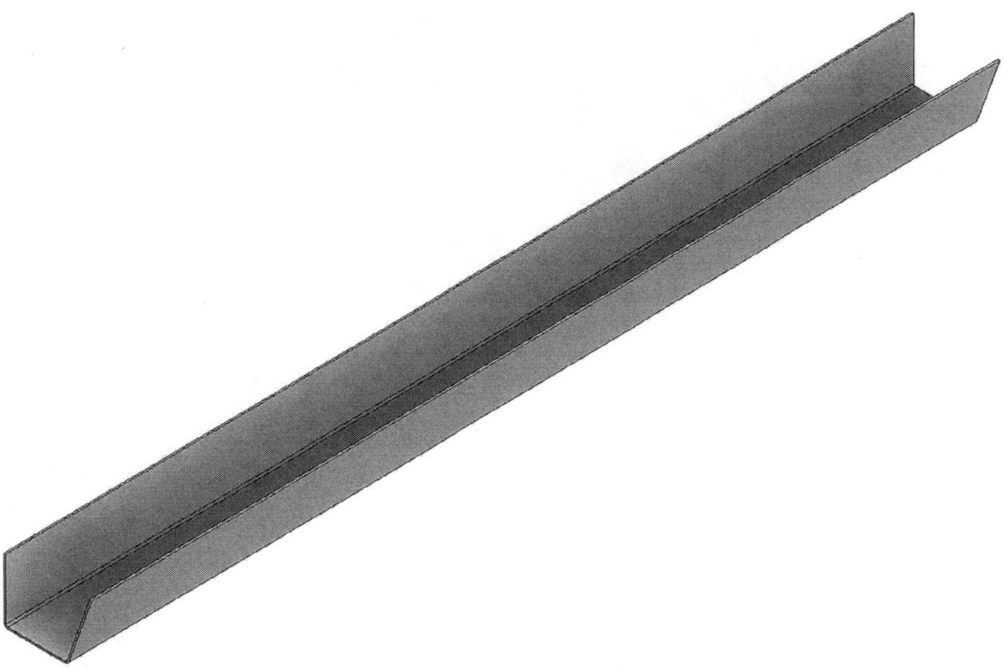

Figure 48

50. Left click on the **Hem** icon. The Hem dialog box will appear as shown in Figure 49.

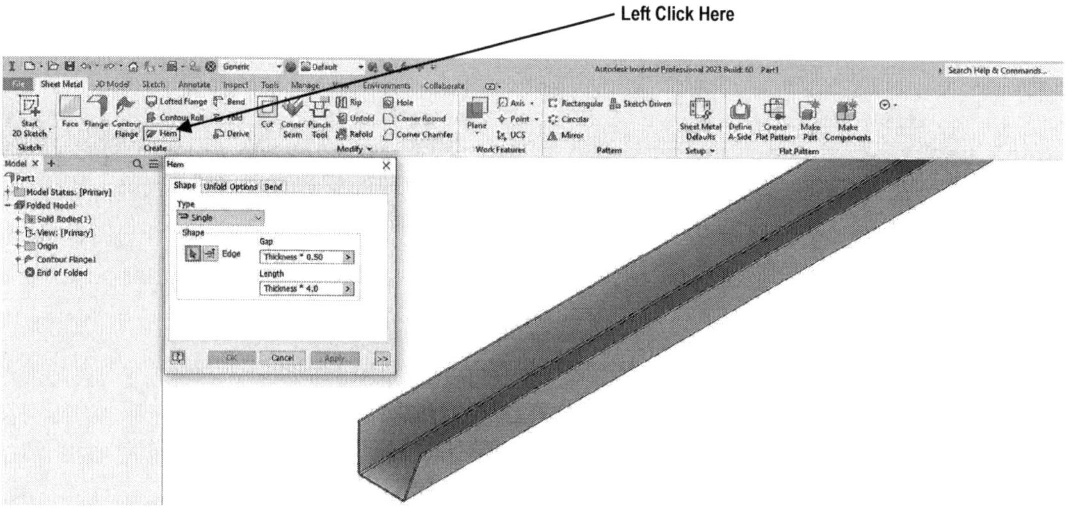

Figure 49

51. Left click on the outside edge shown. Enter **10.0** for the Length. A preview of the Hem will appear as shown in Figure 50.

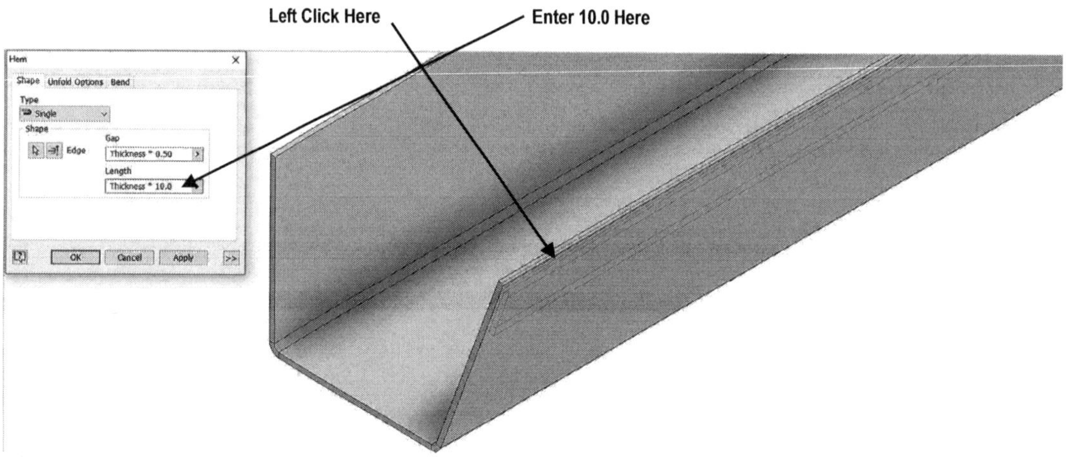

Figure 50

52. Left click on **OK** as shown in Figure 51.

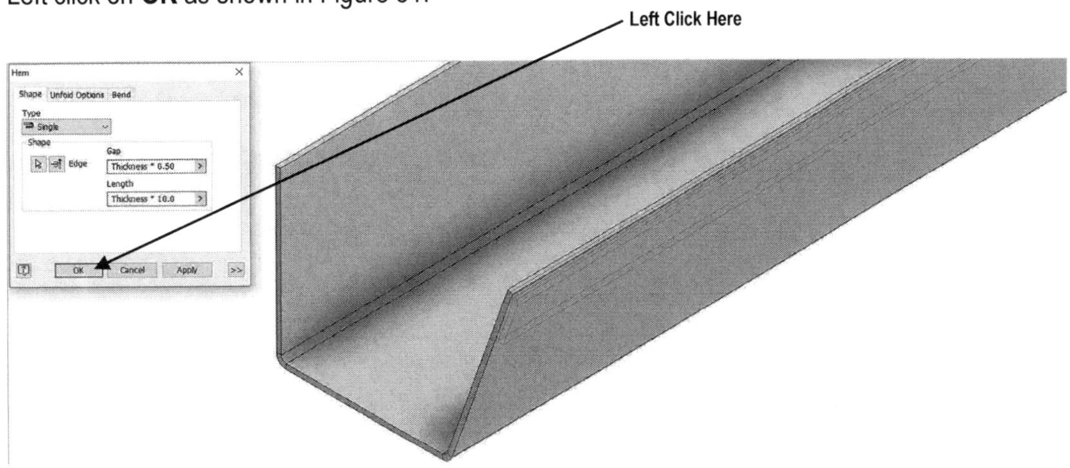

Figure 51

53. Your screen should look similar to what is shown in Figure 52.

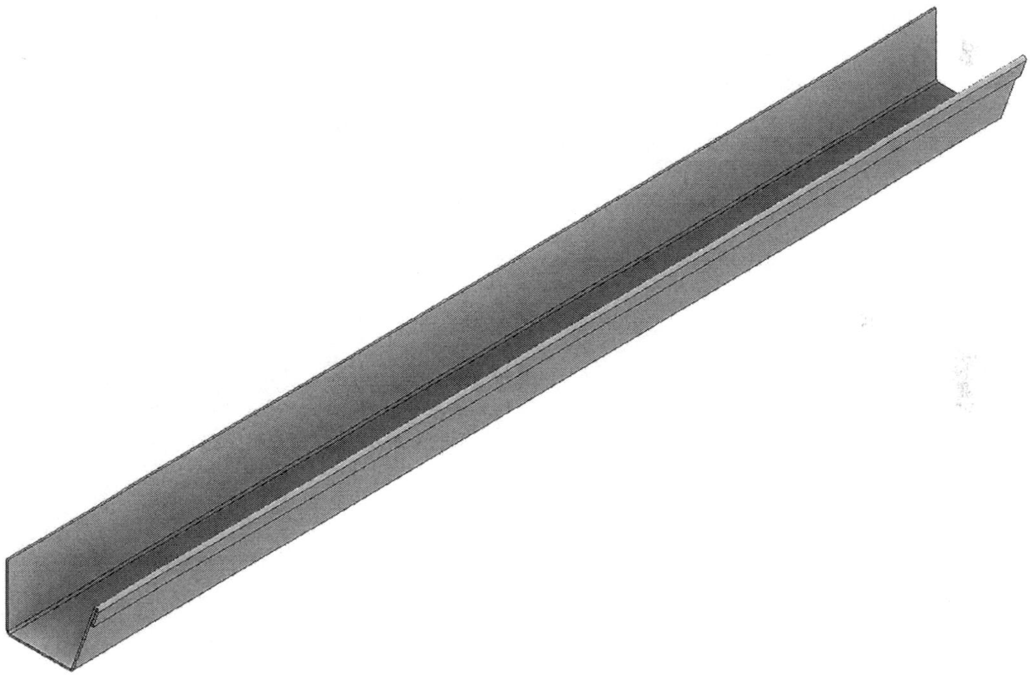

Figure 52

Learn to Create a Contour Roll

54. Zoom in close to the edge of the part and begin a **New Sketch** as shown in Figure 53.

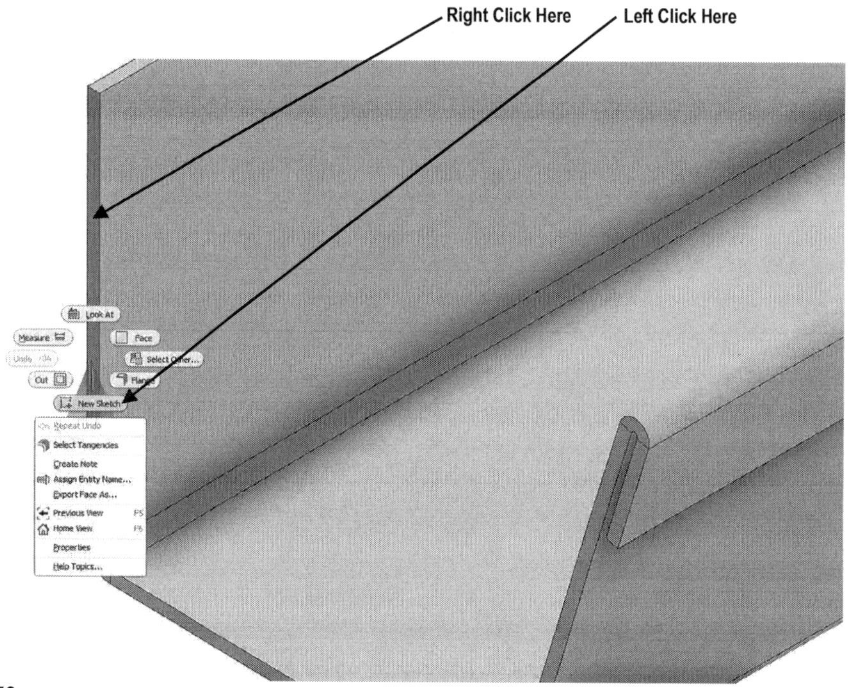

Figure 53

55. Inventor will rotate the part as shown in Figure 54.

Figure 54

56. Left click on the **Project Geometry** icon. Left click on the outside edges of the part causing them to become highlighted. Don't forget to select the small half circle inside the Hem as shown in Figure 55.

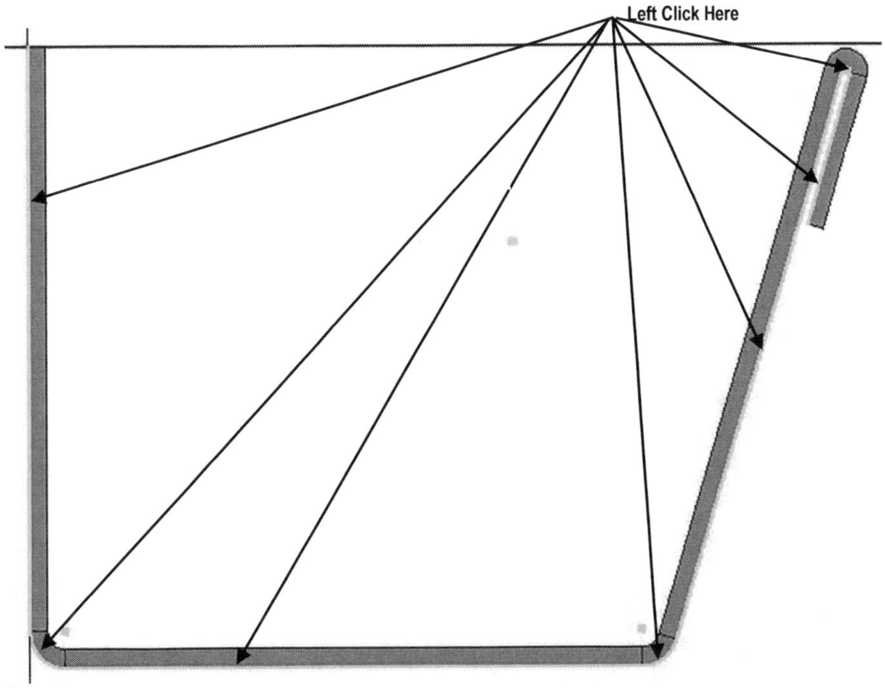

Figure 55

57. Draw a vertical line 3 inches to the left outside edge of the part as shown in Figure 56.

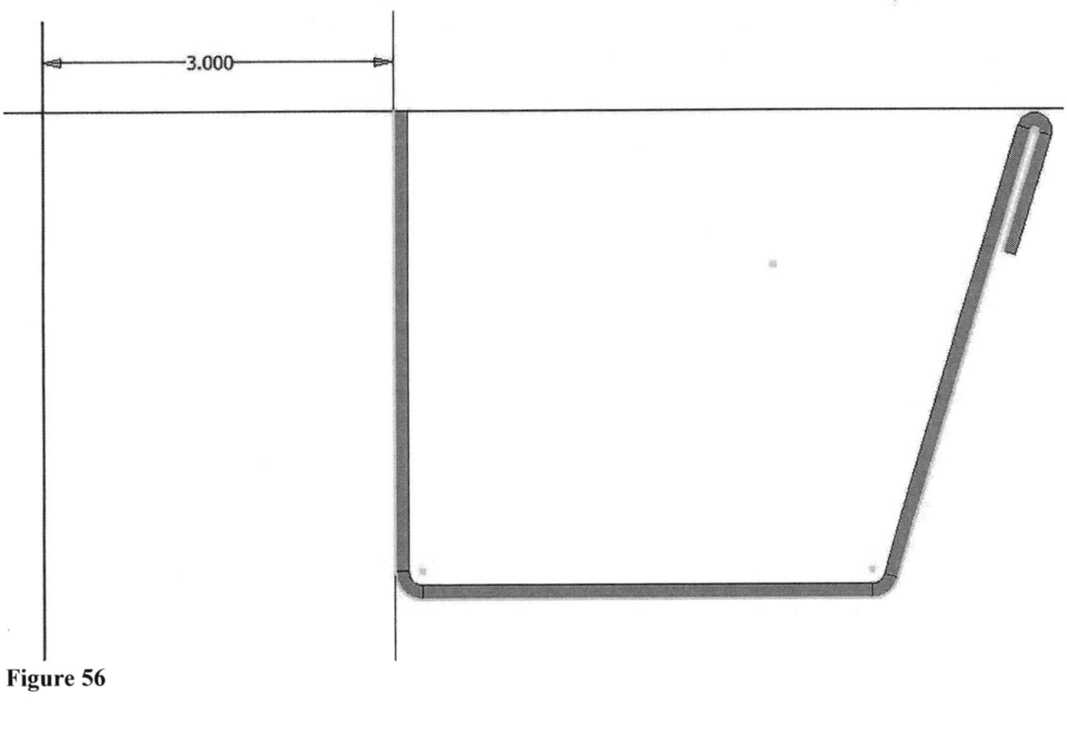

Figure 56

58. Exit out of the Sketch Panel. Inventor will turn the view Isometric as shown in Figure 57.

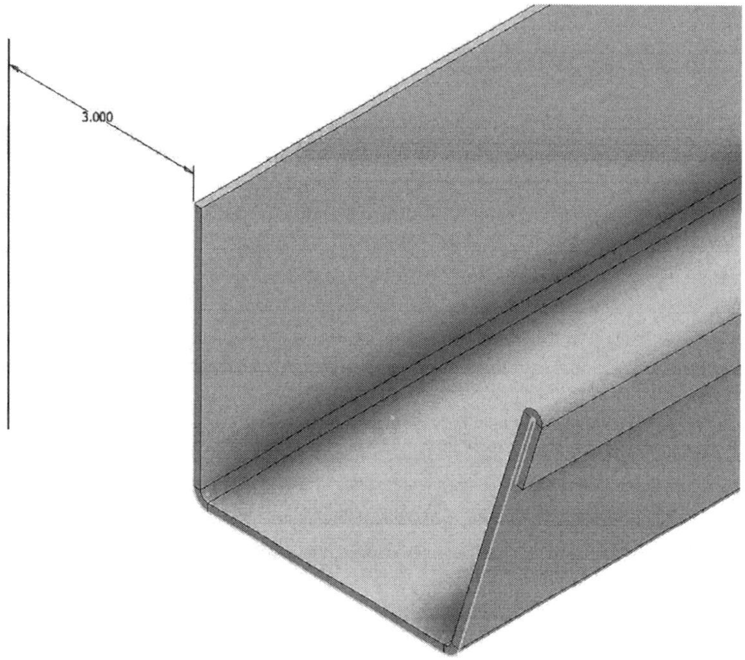

Figure 57

59. Left click on the **Contour Roll** icon. The Contour Roll dialog box will appear as shown in Figure 58.

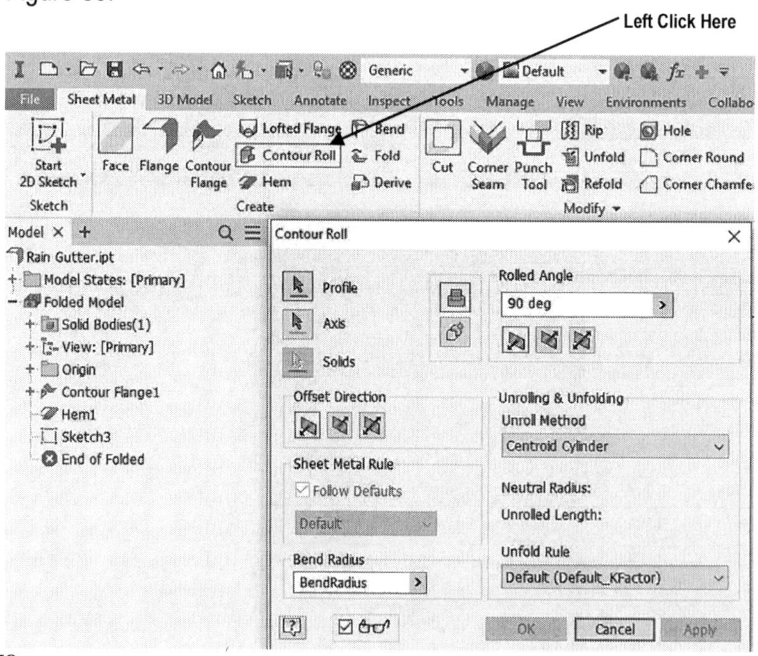

Figure 58

60. The Contour Roll dialog box will appear as shown. Left click on the **Profile** icon as shown in Figure 59.

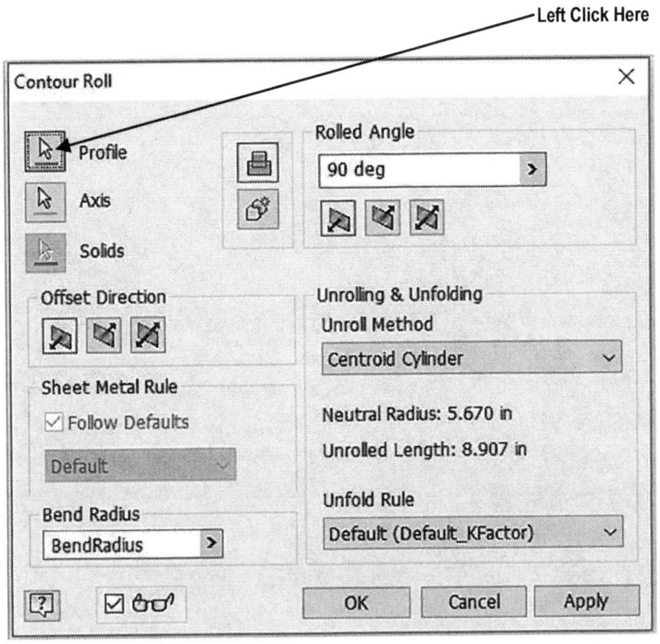

Figure 59

61. Left click on any line. All of the lines will become highlighted as shown in Figure 60.

Figure 60

62. Left click on the **Axis** icon as shown in Figure 61.

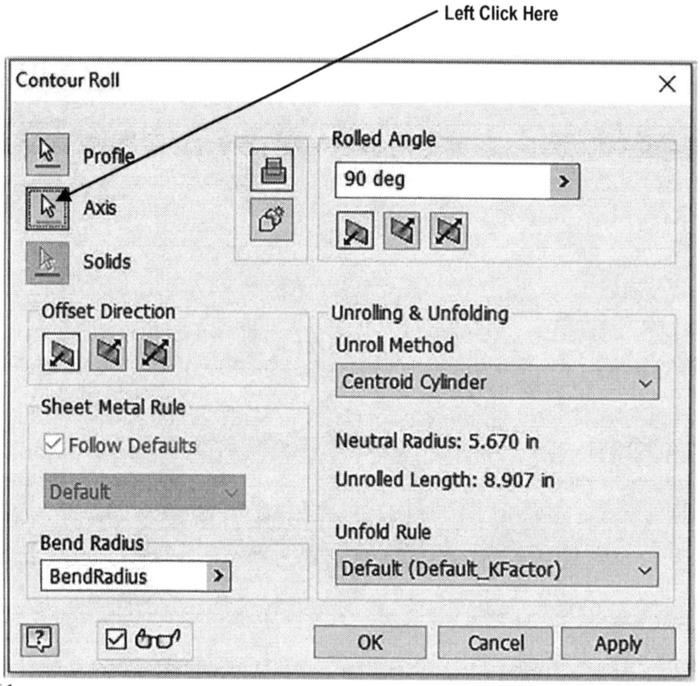

Figure 61

63. Left click on the axis. A preview of the Contour Roll will appear. Left Click on **OK** as shown in Figure 62.

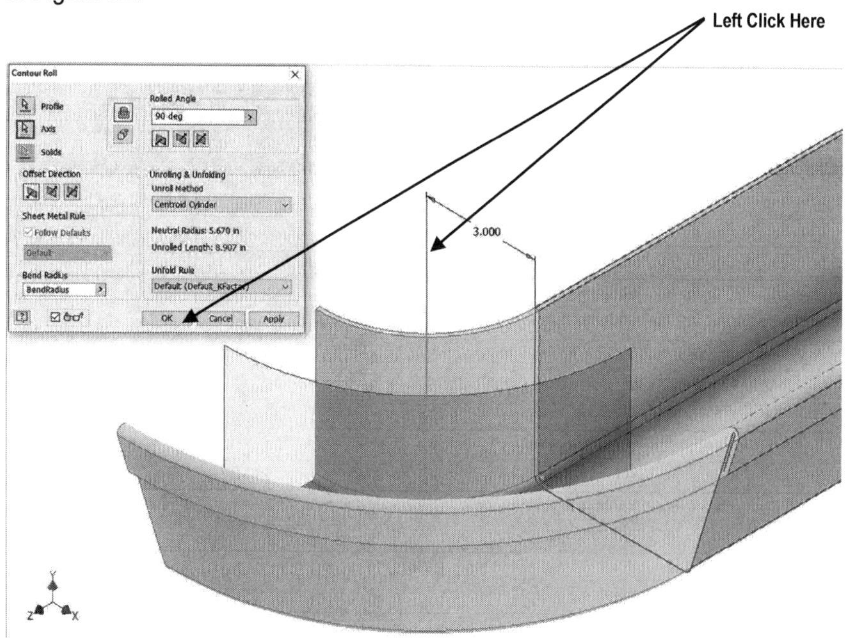

Figure 62

64. Your screen should look similar to what is shown in Figure 63.

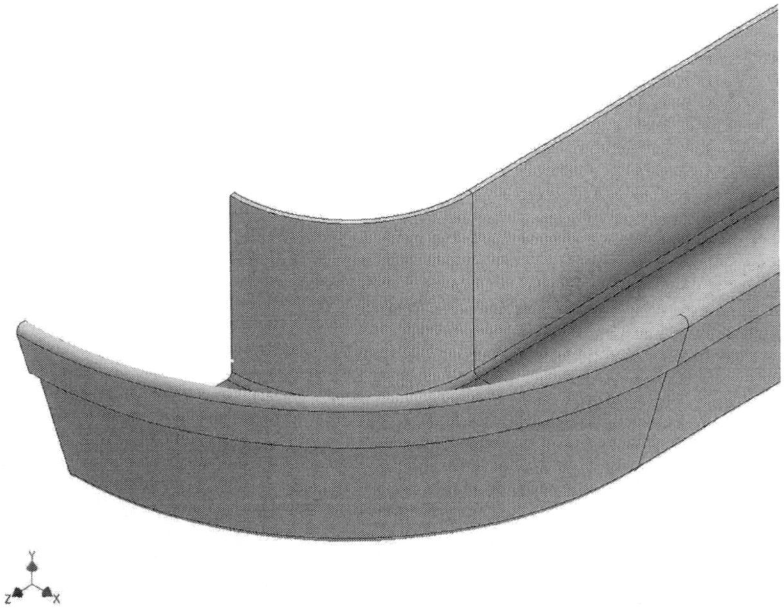

Figure 63

65. Repeat the same steps to create what is shown in Figure 64 using a 12 inch radius.

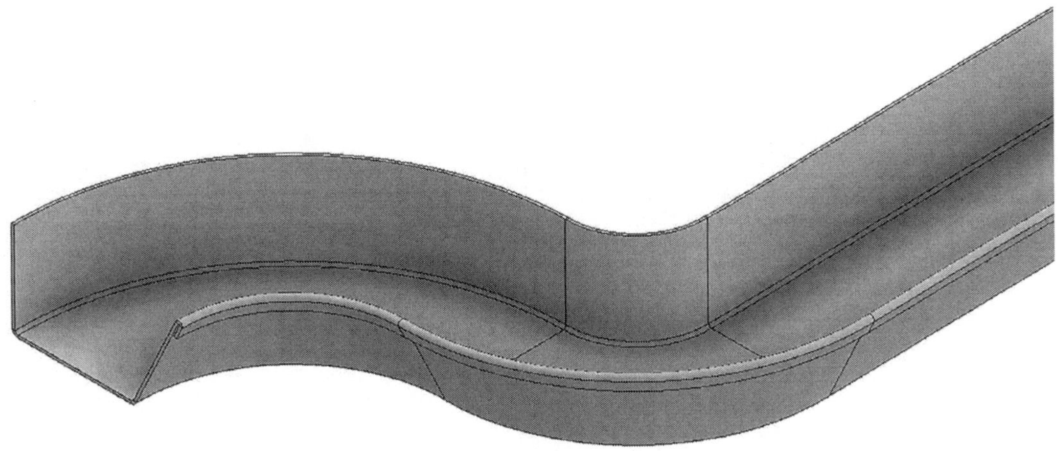

Figure 64

Index